A COMPANION TO

*T*WENTIETH-CENTURY POETRY

EDITED BY **NEIL ROBERTS**

 **Blackwell**
Publishing

© 2001, 2003 by Blackwell Publishing Ltd
except for editorial material and organization © 2001, 2003 by Neil Roberts and
Chapter 37 © 2001, 2003 by A. David Moody

350 Main Street, Malden, MA 02148-5018, USA
108 Cowley Road, Oxford OX4 1JF, UK
550 Swanston Street, Carlton South, Melbourne, Victoria 3053, Australia
Kurfürstendamm 57, 10707 Berlin, Germany

First published 2001
First published in paperback 2003 by Blackwell Publishing Ltd

Library of Congress Cataloging-in-Publication Data

Roberts, Neil, 1946–
A companion to twentieth-century poetry / edited by Neil Roberts.
p.   cm. – (Blackwell companions to literature and culture ; 9)
Includes bibliographical references and index.
ISBN 0-631-21529-8 (alk. paper) – ISBN 1-4051-1361-8 (pbk : alk. paper)
1. English poetry – 20th century – History and criticism.   2. American peotry – 20th
century – History and criticism.   3. English peotry – 20th century – Handbooks, manuals,
etc.   4. American poetry – 20th century – Handbooks, manuals, etc.   I. Title.   II. Series.
PR601 .R5 2001   821'.9109 – dc21   00-051914

A catalogue record for this title is available from the British Library.

Set in 11 on 13 pt Garamond 3
by SNP Best-set Typesetter Ltd., Hong Kong
Printed and bound in the United Kingdom
by T. J. International Ltd, Padstow, Cornwall

For further information on
Blackwell Publishing, visit our website:
http://www.blackwellpublishing.com

A Companion to Twentieth-Century Poetry

Blackwell Companions to Literature and Culture

This series offers comprehensive, newly written surveys of key periods and movements and certain major authors, in English literary culture and history. Extensive volumes provide new perspectives and positions on contexts and on canonical and post-canonical texts, orientating the beginning student in new fields of study and providing the experienced undergraduate and new graduate with current and new directions, as pioneered and developed by leading scholars in the field.

Contents

PART IV *Readings*

Acknowledgements

Although the original plan for this book was drawn up by myself, I have benefited enormously from the suggestions of individuals too numerous to name, but mostly of my contributors, whose influence on the book, in many cases, has extended far beyond their named contributions. I am indebted to many of them for the final shape of the book, and often for suggesting other contributors. Above all I want to thank Hugh Witemeyer for the conversations in New Mexico, at the very beginning of the project, which helped enormously to start it off. I am also grateful to Peter Derlien for generously giving me his time to help to accomplish the daunting task of proofreading.

The editor and publishers wish to thank the following, who have kindly given permission for the use of copyright material.

W. H. Auden, 'Watershed', 'Venus Will Now Say a Few Words', 'The Letter' from *Collected Poems*. Copyright c W. H. Auden 1934 & 1962. Published by Faber and Faber Ltd. Reproduced by permission of Faber and Faber, Curtis Brown Inc. and Random House Inc.

Frank Chipisula, 'Manifesto on Ars Poetica' from *The Heinemann Book of African Poetry*, 1990. Edited by Maja-Pearce. Reproduced by permission of Heinemann Educational.

Robert Creeley, 'Something' from *The Collected Poems of Robert Creeley 1945–1975*, University of California Press. Reproduced by permission.

Louis MacNeice, 'In Lieu' and 'Soap Suds' from *Collected Poems*, 1979, ed. E. R. Dodds. Published by Faber and Faber Ltd. Reproduced by permission of David Higham Associates.

Charles Olson, *The Maximus Poems*, ed and trans. George Butterick, copyright c 1983 the Regents of the University of California, reprinted by permission of the University of California Press.

Ezra Pound, 'In a Station of the Metro' and 'Papyrus' from *Selected Poems*. Reproduced by permission of Faber and Faber Ltd.

Jonathan Williams, 'The Hermit Cackleberry Brown' from *An Ear in Bartram's Tree*, published as a New Directions paperback, reprinted by permission of Jonathan Williams.

Every effort has been made to trace all copyright holders, but if any have been inadvertently overlooked the publishers will be pleased to make the necessary arrangement at the earliest opportunity.

Notes on Contributors

Neil Roberts is Professor of English Literature and former Head of the School of English at the University of Sheffield. He is the author of *George Eliot: Her Beliefs and Her Art* (1975), *Ted Hughes: A Critical Study* (with Terry Gifford, 1981), *The Lover, the Dreamer and the World: The Poetry of Peter Redgrove* (1994), *Meredith and the Novel* (1997) and *Narrative and Voice in Postwar Poetry* (1999), as well as numerous essays on contemporary poetry. He is currently working on a study of D. H. Lawrence, travel and cultural difference.

Tim Armstrong is Reader in Modern English and American Literature at Royal Holloway College, University of London. His recent publications include *Modernism, Technology and the Body: A Cultural Study* (1998) and *Haunted Hardy: Poetry, History, Memory* (2000).

Rand Brandes is Writer-in-Residence and Martin Luther Stevens Professor of English at Lenoir-Rhyne College in Hickory, North Carolina. Specializing in Modern and Contemporary British and Irish poetry, he has published articles on W. B. Yeats, Ted Hughes, Seamus Heaney, Ciaran Carson, Medbh McGuckian and D. H. Lawrence. He has recently completed *A Poet's Album*, a bibliography of the primary works of Seamus Heaney, including uncollected poetry and prose.

Peter Brooker is Professor of Modern Literature and Culture at University College, Northampton. Among other publications, he is editor of *Modernism/Postmodernism* (1992) and author of *New York Fictions: Modernity, Postmodernism, the New Modern* (1996) and *Cultural Theory: A Glossary* (1999). A volume of essays, *Modernity and Metropolis*, is forthcoming.

Terence Brown is Professor of Anglo-Irish Literature at Trinity College, Dublin. He is the author of *The Life of W. B. Yeats: A Critical Biography* (1999), *Ireland's Literature: Selected Essays* (1988), *The Whole Protestant Community: The Making of a Historical Myth* (1985) and *Ireland: A Social and Cultural History 1922–79*, and editor of *Celticism* (1981).

Stephen Burt is Assistant Professor of English at Macalester College in St Paul, Minnesota and is completing a study on Randall Jarrell. He reviews new poetry frequently for several journals in Britain and America, and his longer essays and articles include work on Jarrell, Paul Muldoon and John Donne. His book of poems, *Popular Music*, appeared in 1999.

Alex Calder is Senior Lecturer in the English Department of the University of Auckland. He recently co-edited *Voyages and Beaches: Pacific Encounters, 1769–1840*, and has published many essays on American, New Zealand and Pacific literature.

Matthew Campbell is Senior Lecturer in English Literature at the University of Sheffield. He is the author of *Rhythm and Will in Victorian Poetry* (1999) and co-editor of *Beyond the Pleasure Dome: Writing and Addiction from the Romantics* (1994) and *Memory and Memorials, 1798–1914: Literary and Cultural Perspectives* (2000). He is currently working on *Irish Poetry in the Union, 1801–1921* and editing the *Cambridge Companion to Irish Poetry, 1939–1999*. He is editor of the *Tennyson Research Bulletin*.

Victor L. Chang is Senior Lecturer, Department of Literatures in English, University of the West Indies, Mona, Kingston, Jamaica. He is the Chairman of the West Indian Association for Commonwealth Language and Literature Studies, the editor of *Pathways: A Journal of Creative Writing*, and the co-editor of *The Journal of West Indian Literature*.

Lucy Collins is Lecturer in English at St Martin's College, Carlisle. She has published on twentieth-century Irish poetry, especially contemporary women poets. She has an additional research interest in American poetry of the 1950s and 1960s.

William W. Cook is Israel Evans Professor of Oratory and Belles Lettres and Professor of African and African American Studies at Dartmouth College, where he is also Chair of the English Department. He is the author of *Hudson Hornet and Other Poems* (1989) and *Spiritual and Other Poems* (1999). He has also published 'The Black Arts Poets' in *The Columbia History of American Poetry* (1993) and *Members and Lames: The Theater of August Wilson* (2000).

Reed Way Dasenbrock is Professor of English and Dean of the College of Arts and Sciences at the University of New Mexico. He has written *The Literary Vorticism of Ezra Pound and Wyndham Lewis* (1985), *Imitating the Italians* (1991) and *Truth and Consequences: Intentions, Conventions and the New Thematics* (2001), and edited five books, including Wyndham Lewis's *The Art of Being Ruled* and *The Revenge for Love*.

Alex Davis lectures in the Department of English, University College, Cork. He is the author of *A Broken Line: Denis Devlin and Irish Poetic Modernism* (2000), and co-editor of two collections of essays: *Modernism and Ireland: The Poetry of the 1930s* (1995) and *Locations of Modernism: Region and Nation in British and American Modernist Poetry* (2000). He is currently editing Denis Devlin's uncollected and unpublished poems.

Vinay Dharwadker is currently Associate Professor of English at the University of Oklahoma. He has published *Sunday at the Lodi Gardens* (1994), a book of poems, and has co-edited *The Oxford Anthology of Modern Indian Poetry* (1995). He is an editor of *The Collected Poems of A. K. Ramanujan* (1995) and the general editor of *The Collected Essays of A. K. Ramanujan* (1999). He has contributed essays to *The New Princeton Encyclopedia of Poetry and Poetics* (1993), *New*

National and Post-Colonial Literatures (1996) and *Post-Colonial Translation* (1999), among other publications. His new and forthcoming projects include *Cosmopolitan Geographies* (2000), *The Columbia Book of South Asian Poetry* and *English in India, 1580–2000: The Migration of a Language, the Formation of a Literature.*

Joanne Feit Diehl is Professor of English at the University of California, Davis. She is the author of three books on women poets: *Dickinson and the Romantic Imagination* (1981), *Women Poets and the American Sublime* (1990) and *Marianne Moore and Elizabeth Bishop: The Psychodynamics of Creativity* (1993). Her current interests include psychoanalysis and the visual arts, contemporary theory, and literature and medicine.

Livio Dobrez is Italian by birth and came to Australia as a postwar refugee. Educated at Adelaide University, he is currently Reader in English at the Australian National University, having for a time held the chair at Bond, Australia's first private university. He teaches courses in European and Australian literature, theory and film, usually combining interests in the literary with philosophy and art history. He has a special interest in Aboriginal writing and art. Many published articles include the entry on Australian poetry for the *New Princeton Encyclopaedia of Poetry and Poetics.* He has edited the Australian volume XI of *Review of National Literatures* (1982) and *Identifying Australia in Postmodern Times* (1994). He has also written *The Existential and its Exits: Literary and Philosophical Perspectives on the work of Beckett, Ionesco, Genet and Pinter* (1986) and *Parnassus Mad Ward: Michael Dransfield and the New Australian Poetry* (1990).

David Ellis has written widely on D. H. Lawrence and is the author of *Dying Game* (1998), the third volume of the Cambridge biography. He is Professor Emeritus of English Literature at the University of Kent at Canterbury and the designate director of the Centre for the Study of Comedy which is being established there.

Jonathan Ellis teaches English and Film at Hull University. He has published articles on Elizabeth Bishop, Amy Clampitt and Jeanette Winterson and is currently completing a critical study of Bishop's work.

Roger Gilbert is Professor of English at Cornell University, where he teaches courses in American poetry. He is the author of *Walks in the World: Representation and Experience in Modern American Poetry* (1991), and co-editor of *The Walker's Literary Companion* (2000). His articles and essays on contemporary poetry and popular culture have appeared in *Contemporary Literature, Epoch, Michigan Quarterly Review, Partisan Review, Southwest Review, Salmagundi* and other journals.

David Goldie is Lecturer at Strathclyde University. He is the author of *A Critical Difference: T. S. Eliot and John Middleton Murry in English Literary Criticism 1919–1928* (1998).

John Haffenden is Professor and Head of Department of English Literature at the University of Sheffield. His publications include *The Life of John Berryman, W. H. Auden: The Critical Heritage, Viewpoints: Poets in Conversation, Novelists in Interview* and *Berryman's Shakespeare.* He has edited several collections by William Empson, including *The Complete Poems of William*

Empson, and is working on a critical biography of Empson. He is a Fellow of the Royal Society of Literature and has been a British Academy Research Reader.

David Herd is Lecturer in English and American Literature at the University of Kent at Canterbury. He is the author of *John Ashbery and American Poetry* (2000).

Philip Hobsbaum is Professor Emeritus of the University of Glasgow. He is the author of four collections of poems and seven books of criticism, including *A Theory of Communication* (1970) and *Tradition and Experiment in English Poetry* (1979). He has been the chairman of Writers' Groups in London (1955–9), Belfast (1963–6) and Glasgow (1966–75). He is currently researching into Wallace Stevens and his background.

Douglas Houston was born in Cardiff in 1947 and educated at the University of Hull, where he obtained a Ph.D. in English and achieved recognition as one of the Hull poets. His collections of poetry are *With the Offal Eaters* (1986), *The Hunters in the Snow* (1994) and *The Welsh Book of the Dead* (1999). He works as a literary researcher and editorial consultant and lives outside Aberystwyth.

Jacob Korg is Emeritus Professor of English at the University of Washington in Seattle. He has taught at the City College of New York and the University of Maryland and has been Visiting Professor at National Taiwan University. He writes on Victorian and modern literature, and his publications include *Language in Modern Literature* (1979) and *Ritual and Experiment in Modern Poetry* (1995).

Edward Larrissy is Professor of English Literature at the University of Leeds. He is the author of *William Blake* (1985), *Reading Twentieth-Century Poetry: The Language of Gender and Objects* (1990) and *Yeats the Poet: The Measures of Difference* (1994). He is the editor of *The Oxford Authors: Yeats* (1997) and a book of essays by various hands, *Romanticism and Postmodernism* (1999).

Jennifer Lewin is a graduate student in the English Department at Yale, where she is completing a dissertation on dreams in early modern literature and philosophy. She has also published reviews and presented papers on contemporary American poetry.

Peter McDonald is Christopher Tower Student and Tutor in Poetry in English at Christ Church, Oxford. He has written widely on poetry, and has published two books of criticism: *Louis MacNeice: The Poet in his Contexts* (1991) and *Mistaken Identities: Poetry and Northern Ireland* (1997), as well as an edition (co-edited with Alan Heuser) of *Louis MacNeice: Selected Plays* (1993). He is an editor of the journal *Notes and Queries*. He has published two volumes of poems, *Biting the Wax* (1989) and *Adam's Dream* (1996). A third volume of poetry, and *Sound Intentions: Rhyme, Repetition and Nineteenth Century Poetry*, are forthcoming.

Stephen Matterson is Senior Lecturer in English and a Fellow of Trinity College, University of Dublin. He has published widely on poetry and American literature, including *Berryman and Lowell: The Art of Losing* (1988) and *Studying Poetry*, with Darryl Jones (2000).

Cynthia Messenger is Director of the Writing, Rhetoric, and Critical Analysis Program at Innis College, University of Toronto. Her academic speciality is Canadian poetry. She has published on Canadian literature in various journals, including *Canadian Literature* and *Essays on Canadian Writing*.

A. David Moody is an Emeritus Professor of English and American Literature at the University of York. He has published over a dozen essays on the poetry of Ezra Pound, and is currently working on a critical biography of Pound. He is the author of *Virginia Woolf* (1963), *Thomas Stearns Eliot: Poet* (1979, 1994) and *Tracing T. S. Eliot's Spirit* (1996), and he edited the *Cambridge Companion to T. S. Eliot* (1994).

Sean O'Brien has published four books of poems. *Ghost Train* (1995) won the Forward prize. His new collection, *Downriver*, is due in 2001. He is the author of *The Deregulated Muse: Essays on Contemporary British and Irish Poetry* and editor of the anthology *The Firebox: Poetry in Britain and Ireland after 1945*, and of the magazine *The Devil*. His political verse drama *Laughter When We're Dead* was staged in 2000, and he is writing a music theatre work, *Downriver*, with the jazz composer Keith Morris. He lives in Newcastle upon Tyne and teaches writing at Sheffield Hallam University.

Bernard O'Donoghue is Fellow in English of Wadham College, Oxford. He is the author of several volumes of poetry: *Razorblades and Pencils* (1984), *Poaching Rights* (1987), *The Absent Signifier* (1999), *The Weakness* (1991), *Gunpowder* (1995) and *Here nor There* (1999), as well as *Seamus Heaney and the Language of Poetry* (1994). He is also editor of the *Selected Poems of Thomas Hoccleve* (1982) and *The Courtly Love Tradition* (1982).

John Osborne is Lecturer in American Studies at the University of Hull. In the period 1985–95 he edited the magazine *Bête Noire* ('a landmark in the geography of literary non-conformism', *Times Literary Supplement*) and ran what the *Guardian* described as 'the premier poetry reading series in the English-speaking world'. Thereafter he co-founded the annual Hull literature festival and the Philip Larkin Society. He has published approximately a hundred essays and reviews in books and journals in the United Kingdom, the United States and Poland, and is currently writing a critical monograph on the poetry of Philip Larkin.

Kwadwo Osei-Nyame teaches African Literature at the School of Oriental and African Studies, University of London. His interests include the politics of gender, nationalism and national identity in literature. He has published in *Research in African Literatures*, *Kunapipi*, *Journal of Commonwealth Literature*, *Current Writing*, *Ariel*, *Journal of African Cultural Studies* and *Commonwealth: Essays and Studies*.

Simon Perril is Lecturer in English at University College, Northampton, where he teaches modern poetry. He has written on Iain Sinclair, Barbara Guest and Leslie Scalapino among others, and has published poetry with Reality Street Editions. He is currently bringing to completion a book-length study of contemporary Anglo-American avant-garde poetry.

Jahan Ramazani is Professor of English at the University of Virginia, where he teaches twentieth-century poetry and postcolonial literatures. He is the author of *Yeats and the Poetry of*

Death (1990) and *Poetry of Mourning: The Modern Elegy from Hardy to Heaney* (1994), which was a finalist for the National Book Critics Circle Award. His *PMLA* article on Derek Walcott's *Omeros*, drawn from his book-in-progress on postcolonial poetry, won the William Riley Parker Prize of the MLA (1997). With degrees from Virginia, Oxford and Yale, he has held a Rhodes Scholarship and an NEH Fellowship.

Stephen Regan is Lecturer in Modern Poetry at Royal Holloway College, University of London. He has written extensively on twentieth-century poetry, especially the work of Philip Larkin. His publications include *Philip Larkin* (1992) and the *New Casebook* on Larkin (1997). He is also editor of *The Eagleton Reader* (1998) and founding editor of *The Year's Work in Critical and Cultural Theory*. He is currently editing an anthology of Irish writing for Oxford University Press.

Jeffrey Skoblow, Professor of English at Southern Illinois University Edwardsville, is the author of *Paradise Dislocated: Morris, Politics and Art* and *Dooble Tongue: Scots, Burns, Contradiction*, as well as articles on Scottish and other writers.

Lisa M. Steinman is Kenan Professor of English and Humanities at Reed College in Portland, Oregon. She is also the author of three volumes of poetry, *A Book of Other Days, All that Comes to Light* and *Lost Poems*, as well as numerous articles and two books about poetry: *Made in America: Science, Technology, and American Modernist Poetics* (1987) and *Masters of Repetition: Poetry, Culture, and Work* (1998).

Terry Sturm is Professor of English at the University of Auckland. He edited the *Oxford History of New Zealand Literature in English* (1991, 1998), contributing the section on popular fiction, and was New Zealand editor of *The Routledge Encyclopaedia of Post-colonial Literatures in English* (1994). He has also published widely on Australian literature, including the drama section of *The Oxford History of Australian Literature* (1981).

Sue Vice is Reader in English Literature at the University of Sheffield. Her publications include *Malcolm Lowry Eighty Years On* (1989, ed.), *Beyond the Pleasure Dome: Literature and Addiction from the Romantics* (1994, co-ed.), *Psychoanalytic Criticism: A Reader* (1996, ed.), *Introducing Bakhtin* (1997) and *Holocaust Fiction* (2000).

Elizabeth Wilson is a member of the Department of English at the University of Auckland. Tenured in 1991, she lectures in Twentieth Century Studies, Modernism, Theory, Poetics, Contemporary Poetry. She is herself a poet.

Hugh Witemeyer is Professor of English at the University of New Mexico, where he teaches modern British and American literature. He is the author of *The Poetry of Ezra Pound* (1969) and *George Eliot and the Visual Arts* (1979). He is the editor or co-editor of *William Carlos Williams and James Laughlin: Selected Letters* (1989), *Ezra Pound and Senator Bronson Cutting: A Political Correspondence* (1995), *Pound/Williams: Selected Letters of Ezra Pound and William Carlos Williams* (1996), *The Future of Modernism* (1997) and *William Carlos Williams and Charles Tomlinson: A Transatlantic Connection* (1999).

Bruce Woodcock is Senior Lecturer in English at Hull University. He has published three books: *Male Mythologies: John Fowles and Masculinity* (1984), *Combative Styles: Romantic Prose and Ideology* (1995, with John Coates) and *Peter Carey* (1996), and he has written essays and articles on contemporary poets including Tony Harrison, Thom Gunn and Sean O'Brien, and on Caribbean literature. His most recent book is *The Selected Poems of William Blake* (2000). He is currently researching for a book on post-colonial cultural translations.

Introduction

Neil Roberts

The subject of this volume, twentieth-century poetry in English, is vast, hetero-geneous and paradoxical. To say that it attempts to represent the poetry of a hundred years and more than twenty countries is to suggest only one dimension of the difficulty of the project. The phrase 'in English' is no mere neutral description, but signifies a complex, violent and still bitterly felt political and cultural history: some contributors question the division between poetry in English and other languages, and rightly transgress it; for others the historical role of the English language in shaping the culture and consciousness of poets is itself the main theme. This subject exists because of the successive historical phenomena of British imperialism and American cultural, economic and political dominance. The volume begins with the transatlantic connection in modernism and ends with contemporary postcolonial poetry. The trajectory of the century – of the English language and its poetry – is from a predominantly bipolar axis to an increas-ingly decentred heterogeneity. The country in which the English language originated had already ceded the leading role to America in the modernist era, and by the end of the century its current poetic production has little influence on the rest of the Anglophone world. If poetry from England still manages to hold up its head in this volume it is partly because of the still powerful influence of the country's cultural past, and partly no doubt due to the nationality of the editor.

'English' exerts an undeniable if not always welcome influence on all the poets discussed in this book. However, it must also be stressed that poetry, unlike the novel, is genuinely universal; it is not an Anglophone, nor a European cultural invention. It can draw on a potentially inexhaustible multiplicity of roots, and however marginal or irrelevant it may seem to have become in some parts of the English-speaking world, no one has ever spoken of the 'death of poetry' as some spoke (perhaps prematurely) not long ago about the death of the novel. Even Theodor Adorno did not quite go that far.

The terms 'modernism' and 'postcolonial' remind us that this is a century in which poetry has not only been written and discussed, but the writing and discussion have been exceptionally closely related. To a large extent the writers of poetry have defined the terms in which the criticism of poetry has been conducted. It is a century in which poetry has been overwhelmingly self-conscious and self-reflexive. Taking their lead from writers and visual artists on the European continent, above all France, the men and women in the English-speaking world who wrote the poetry that later came to be labelled 'modernist' gathered together in explicit movements, wrote manifestos and largely created the cultural environment in which their work was received. Writers such as T. S. Eliot and Ezra Pound had an influence hugely disproportionate to their number, or to the sales of their books. As the century progressed this tendency persisted, though the groups became more disparate. Hence the importance of poetic movements in the organization of this book. Some groups of poets, such as the Black Mountain and Language poets, formed conscious alliances and articulated shared principles. Other movements, such as Confessionalism and the so-called 'Movement' itself, were named by others, but the poets profited from the labels, which gave their utterances a more than individual authority, even if they often distanced themselves from the labels.

Throughout the twentieth century poetry has had an immensely important and uncomfortable relationship with the academy. William Carlos Williams condemned Eliot for handing poetry to the academics, and there are many poets who have at different times abused university departments of English and accepted salaried posts from them. Especially in America, to be a professional poet almost necessarily means teaching writing in a university, and in the latter part of the century, especially in postcolonial studies and the influence of poststructuralism on writers such as the Language poets, the discourse of writers and the discourse of academics have merged.

However, if one image, and perhaps the most numerically accurate, of the poet is the unheroic one of a man or woman in a classroom, there are other images no less real, if less numerous, of poets dying on battlefields in Flanders, Spain or Biafra, poets enduring hardship and poverty for their art, poets in prison for their political convictions, poets in Ginsberg's phrase 'destroyed by madness'. And they may of course be the same people: Wole Soyinka is not the only one to have seen the inside of both a classroom and a prison cell.

One has to admit, though, that the heroic image of a Wilfred Owen, a Ken Saro-Wiwa or a Soyinka fails to conceal the fact that poetry's relation to the main tendencies of twentieth-century history and culture has largely been one of disapproving marginality. Inheriting an already slightly tarnished Arnoldian conception of culture as a value to be set against the dominant civilization, the 'modernists' (at least the Anglophone poets who set the agenda of literary modernism) were – despite the label later attached to them – notoriously, like Pound's Mauberley, 'out of key with [their] time'. As the reading public grew in size, the proportion of it that was interested in poetry shrank dramatically. As the century wore on, many poets must have harboured an alter ego like Tony Harrison's skinhead who mocks, 'It's not poetry we want in this class war'.

Looking back from the beginning of the twenty-first century, then, I find myself forming contradictory impressions. Poetry in the English language is practised on every continent: there is more of it, and it is more various, than at any time before. At the same time, at least in those countries most responsible for the spread of the language, its cultural importance seems questionable. This apparent paradox is perhaps explained by a first-world perspective. The universality of poetry, on which I have already remarked, assures that it will continue to be written and received in some form. However, the elitist modern conception of poetry (a description that I don't intend abusively – it produced the greatest poetry of the century) which still influences the practice, social role and reception of the art, will surely not survive. The global erosion of the centre–periphery structure, most dramatically witnessed by the fact that the most celebrated living Anglophone poet, Derek Walcott, comes from a tiny Caribbean island, may be reflected within societies and nations. There is evidence of this in some of the chapters on contemporary poetry, and on national poetries.

The critical discussion of poetry, like that of all art, entails dizzying shifts of perspective. It cannot be understood without awareness of an immense historical context, yet it can be dependent for its power on a single word resonating in the mind of a reader. This necessitates a corresponding range of discourses, from William W. Cook's statistical account of the movement of African Americans in the first half of the century, to John Osborne's close reading of the syntax, rhythm and line-endings of a single poem by Robert Creeley. The tasks addressed by the contributors vary enormously, from the history of the poetry of a whole continent to the elucidation of an individual volume. It is this latter aspect of the book, the 'Readings' section, which is likely to provoke most debate, since any gesture towards canon formation (or reinforcement) is intensely controversial. The texts chosen are best considered as a selection of the most influential, widely discussed and characteristic poetry of the period; the concentration on specific volumes a recognition that even the most canonical poetry is born of a particular historical moment.

These essays were being written as all of us were making the adjustment to thinking of the twentieth century as a period of the past, as the possibilities for what twentieth-century poetry in English might be were finally exhausted and determinate. At the same time, this past is of course not sealed off from us, and our understanding of the century is inseparable from our feeling for the present and the contemporary. Hence the volume ends with consideration of the poetry still being written, that may form the starting point, if such things are still produced, of a Companion to Twenty-first Century Poetry. In those essays above all the authors are committed to the first-hand response and judgement that characterizes all worthwhile criticism. Several of the contributors are themselves publishing poets, and in one case at least, that of Sean O'Brien, it is certain that his own work would have featured if the chapter had been written by someone else.

In the twentieth century more people spoke English than in the whole of previous history, and more people wrote poetry than in the whole of previous history. I think this book registers something of the crowded life of the extraordinary century, even as it struggles to bring it under some kind of control.

PART I
Topics and Debates

1

Modernism and the Transatlantic Connection

Hugh Witemeyer

In September 1908 the young American poet, John Gould Fletcher (1886–1950), left Harvard University for Europe. In his autobiography, *Life Is My Song* (1937), Fletcher explains the reasons for his pilgrimage:

> I had come abroad to try to acquire an education, to learn something concerning the aesthetic, moral, and spiritual values by which man was made worthy of the world he lived in, and which had created man's highest civilizations. . . . Were there values in Europe, were there values anywhere in the world, which were living and functioning vitally in sufficient strength, to enable me to build up anything from my own American background, to make anything more of myself than a complete failure of adjustment to the standards of my country and my people? I had come to Europe, at all events, to find out. And I knew from the outset that my exile would be neither a short nor an easy one. (Fletcher, 1937, p. 34)

Fletcher here articulates some of the motives that impelled idealistic poets of his generation into self-exile: a profound alienation from contemporary America, an uncertain sense of identity, a yearning for permanent aesthetic and spiritual values, and a readiness to search for such values in the great centres of European civilization. In London Fletcher found, if not the grail of his quest, at least a congenial company of like-minded seekers. By 1910 he had joined the Guild Socialist movement, and by 1914 he was engaged in the poetic revolution known as Imagism.

Fletcher's progress exemplifies the interaction of European and American energies that gave rise to modernist poetry in English during the early decades of the twentieth century. The innovative, experimental verse that helped to shape the sensibility of several succeeding generations grew out of a restless, dynamic nexus of international contacts. With these transatlantic connections in mind, scholars sometimes characterize the revolution in the arts of the period as 'International Modernism' (Kenner, 1988, pp. 3–4).

International modernism arose in a world of improved communications, commerce and travel. Transoceanic telegraphy, wireless radio and superior shipping dramatically accelerated the transmission of words, documents and people. Travel between Europe and North America came within the reach of groups who could not previously afford it. Appropriately enough, two influential patrons of modernist writing – Winifred Ellerman and Nancy Cunard – were heiresses of wealthy shipping magnates. The 'global village' of Marshall McLuhan was not yet in sight, but a transatlantic community had swum into ken.

This link between culture and technology involved a historical irony, for the proponents of a cosmopolitan cultural vision tended to be critics of industrialism and rampant capitalism. When Matthew Arnold advocated an international standard of culture in his influential treatise *Culture and Anarchy* (1867–8), he wrote in opposition to a provincial philistinism that he associated with bourgeois profit-seeking. In turn-of-the-century America, young writers to whom Arnold's analysis appealed deplored the triumph of this materialism even as they benefited from the prosperity, leisure and mobility that it provided. They were the first generation of Americans who could afford to take Arnold's prescriptions to heart as educational imperatives.

To observers on both sides of the Atlantic, the pursuit of material wealth seemed to dominate the last quarter of the nineteenth century. The novelist and short-story writer, Sherwood Anderson (1876–1941), described the years in which he grew up as

> the most materialistic age in the history of the world, when wars would be fought without patriotism, when men would forget God and only pay attention to moral stand-ards, when the will to power would replace the will to serve and beauty would be well-nigh forgotten in the terrible headlong rush of mankind toward the acquisition of possessions. (Anderson, 1997, p. 57)

These developments had only begun to affect the rural community of which Anderson wrote in *Winesburg, Ohio* (1919), but their effects are full-blown in F. Scott Fitzgerald's *The Great Gatsby* (1925). Here the ethos of the so-called Gilded Age is personified by the degenerate mining millionaire, Dan Cody, from whom Jay Gatsby absorbs his meretricious version of the American Dream.

The coarsening of the moral and aesthetic fibre of America in the late nineteenth century impelled some artists and writers to pull up stakes, and others to dig in. One group expatriated themselves, choosing self-exile in a European society whose upper-middle class, at least until 1914, was more securely established and more receptive to the arts than was its American equivalent. The other group of artists and writers stayed at home, choosing to combat Babbittry on its native ground. (The protagonist of Sinclair Lewis's satirical novel, *Babbitt*, published in 1922, became a byword for the self-righteous and hypocritical boosterism that flourished in many American small towns.)

Although the indigenists sometimes criticized the expatriates as turncoats and cowards, the division between them was more apparent than real. Both groups were fighting the same cultural battle, and both were fundamentally internationalist. They travelled and published on both sides of the Atlantic, and they collaborated closely with European artists who were combating similar trends in their countries. Only an international alliance of artists could mount an effective resistance against the transnational forces that seemed to threaten the life of the spirit.

In what follows, we will chart some of the transatlantic connections among modernist poets by focusing upon major centres of creative activity. We will look first at the European centres, especially London and Paris, where American expatriates such as John Gould Fletcher congregated with kindred spirits in an endeavour to renew Old World ideals. Then we will examine the American centres, especially New York and Chicago, where the indigenists collaborated with European expatriates who shared their vision of New World possibilities.

Like John Gould Fletcher, many American expatriates who came abroad before the Great War of 1914–18 found a congenial home in London. No other literary community in the English-speaking world offered such advantages to ambitious young writers: a wealth of literary publishers and periodicals, a receptive and liberal audience devoted to spiritual pursuits, a venerable and prestigious literary tradition, and an established poetic discourse acknowledged by writers, publishers and readers alike. Moreover, these advantages were no less available to aspirants from the British colonies and former colonies than to home-country hopefuls. Among the important modern poets who began their careers in Edwardian and Georgian London are Ezra Pound, T. S. Eliot, 'H. D.' (Hilda Doolittle) and Robert Frost.

The career of Ezra Pound (1885–1972) illustrates the opportunities that London offered to new arrivals. Pound reached the capital in December 1908 and stepped almost immediately into an extensive literary network. He soon met William Butler Yeats, whom he considered the greatest living poet, and Ford Madox Ford, who published Pound in the *English Review* and tutored him in the aesthetics of modern French fiction. Pound also attended meetings of an informal poets' club convened by T. E. Hulme and F. S. Flint, whose discussions often centred upon the role of images in poetic communication.

Into these cosmopolitan circles, Pound was generously accepted. He soon had a regular publisher, Elkin Mathews, who brought out five volumes of the young American's work between December 1908 and May 1913. Pound regularly contributed poetry and prose to the *New Age*, a Guild Socialist weekly edited by A. R. Orage. He lectured on early medieval European literature at the Regent Street Polytechnic, and J. M. Dent published the lectures as *The Spirit of Romance* (1910). He was introduced to Olivia Shakespear, a novelist and an intimate friend of Yeats; and five years later, in 1914, he married Mrs Shakespear's daughter, Dorothy. 'Am by way of falling into the croud [*sic*] that does things here', Pound told William Carlos Williams. 'London, deah old lundon is the place for poesy' (Pound and Williams,

1996, p. 13). In 1913, Pound even arranged for Williams's second book of poems, *The Tempers*, to be published by Elkin Mathews in London.

Like Pound, Robert Frost (1874–1963) found London to be the place for poesy. Unable to obtain a publisher for his work in the United States, Frost brought his family to England in 1912. There, he befriended Edward Thomas, Lascelles Abercrombie, and others among the Georgian school of poets. David Nutt and Co. agreed to publish Frost's first two books of poetry, *A Boy's Will* (1913) and *North of Boston* (1914). The favourable reviews of his work on both sides of the Atlantic whetted the interest of American publishers. When he returned to the United States in 1915, Frost was taken up by Henry Holt and Company of New York, who remained his principal publisher for the rest of his long and successful career. Although Frost never intended his transatlantic exile to be permanent, his trip across the ocean was indispensable to his launching as a poet.

Meanwhile, Pound was forming a cosmopolitan alliance with other young poets who lived in London. The Imagists, as they called themselves, included Pound's old Philadelphia friend, Hilda Doolittle (1888–1961), who was just beginning her European expatriation under the pen-name of 'H. D.' The English poets and translators, F. S. Flint and Richard Aldington, threw in with the Americans, and Aldington consolidated the bonds even further by marrying H. D.

The principal outlets for the writing that emerged from the movement were no less transatlantic than its personnel. Poems and manifestos appeared in London (in the *Egoist* and the *New Age*), New York (in *Others*) and Chicago (in *Poetry*, of which Pound became Foreign Editor). The heroic age of the international little magazine was getting under way, and a heady mixture of work by British, Irish and American authors might be found in almost any issue of the liveliest periodicals.

The new movement also had a Continental flavour. *Imagisme*, as it was sometimes styled, aped the cultural politics of the French and Italian avant-garde schools such as Post-Impressionism, Cubism and Futurism. Outrageous proclamations, interviews and readings attracted media attention and shocked bourgeois sensibilities. Furthermore, the Imagist advocacy of free verse had a French dimension because turn-of-the-century French poets had taken up and developed the legacy of Walt Whitman as an alternative to the hegemony of fixed forms in their tradition. When Pound and Flint promoted a poetry of 'the musical phrase', they were thinking less of Whitman than of the *vers libre* and other metrical experiments of Parisian poets such as Remy de Gourmont, Jules Romains, Charles Vildrac, Emile Verhaeren and others (see Pound, 1954, p. 3, and Pound, 1913). The free-verse tradition in modern English-language poetry originated in America with Whitman, but one branch of it returned to its home only after a detour through Paris and London. Such a journey is thoroughly characteristic of modernism's transatlantic circulations.

Imagism is probably the most important single movement in English-language poetry of the twentieth century. Hardly any prominent poet of Pound's generation and the next two after it went untouched by Imagist theory and practice. The aesthetic of Imagism might nowadays be called minimalist. It emphasized a romantic return to origins, a simplification of needless complexities, a zealous, Puritanical stripping-away of the excrescences that had attached themselves to the art of poetry like barnacles to a clean hull. Among the luxuries to be relinquished were traditional metre and rhyme, artificial poetic diction, superfluous verbiage, explicit philosophizing and editorializing, rhetoric, and transitional filler. The poem was to be made as economical and functional as possible, and its chief *raison d'être* was to present images unmediated by authorial commentary (see Coffman, 1951; Schneidau, 1969; Gage, 1983).

Classic examples of Imagism in action include Pound's 'In a Station of the Metro', H. D.'s 'Oread' and William Carlos Williams's 'The Red Wheelbarrow'. More compact even than these exercises in condensation is a poem by Pound entitled 'Papyrus'. Here Pound purports to translate a Greek lyric accidentally and only partially preserved on a recycled manuscript. In how few words can the essence of a Sappho love-poem be conveyed?

> Spring . . . . . .
> Too long . . . . . .
> Gongula . . . . . .
> (Pound, 1990, p. 115)

In theme and form, the poem enacts a drama of presence and absence. The presence of spring whets Sappho's appetite for the absent Gongula. The presence of three line-beginnings whets our appetite for an absent text. By honing language's presence to an absolute minimum, the Imagist poem sharpens our intuition of its expressive gaps and omissions (see Kenner, 1971, pp. 54–64). An Image, Pound explained, 'presents an intellectual and emotional complex in an instant of time' (Pound, 1954, p. 4).

The London Imagists soon attracted imitators. Of these the most important was Amy Lowell of Boston, whose entrepreneurial energies, if not her poetic talent, rivalled those of Pound. Lowell visited London and won several of Pound's colleagues to her banner, including Aldington and Fletcher. Lowell edited three anthologies entitled *Some Imagist Poets*, which appeared in 1915, 1916 and 1917.

Muttering darkly against 'Amygism', Pound immediately co-founded a new school known as 'Vorticism'. This movement differed from Imagism by incorporating the sister arts. Thus, the Vorticists included experimental painters (Wyndham Lewis, William Roberts, David Bomberg, Edward Wadsworth) and sculptors (Jacob Epstein, Henri Gaudier-Brzeska) as well as writers (Pound, Lewis, T. S. Eliot). As with Imagism, the personnel of the movement was distinctly international. Bomberg, Roberts and Wadsworth were British; Epstein, Pound and Eliot, American; and Gaudier-Brzeska, French. Characteristically, Lewis carried the idea to an extreme, by being born on a yacht off the coast of Nova Scotia to a British mother and an American father of French-Canadian ancestry.

Vorticist polemics championed the principles of abstract formalism and celebrated the dynamic nature of creative processes and products (a 'vortex' is a swirl of creative energy within an artist's psyche, within his work, or within his milieu). The style of Vorticist visual art and experimental writing ranged from stylized representation to outright non-representation or abstraction. In their typographically audacious journal, *BLAST*, the Vorticists pushed avant-garde cheekiness to levels previously unknown in English publications (see Wees, 1972).

Although T. S. Eliot (1888–1965) is no longer remembered primarily as a Vorticist, he made his literary debut as a member of the London avant-garde. 'Preludes' and 'Rhapsody on a Windy Night' were published in the second number of *BLAST* (1915), and *Prufrock and Other Observations* (1917) appeared under the imprint of The Egoist, Ltd. Eliot came to England in the early autumn of 1914. He was soon introduced to Pound, who immediately conscripted him into the modernist movement. Eliot 'is the only American I know of who has made what I can call adequate preparation for writing', Pound told Harriet Monroe, the editor of *Poetry*, shortly before he sent her the manuscript of 'The Love Song of J. Alfred Prufrock'. 'He has actually trained himself *and* modernized himself *on his own*' (Pound, 1950, p. 40).

So taken with the London scene was Eliot that he abandoned his plans for an American academic career, married an Englishwoman, and turned himself into an English man of letters. Eventually, he became a British subject, proclaimed his allegiance to the Crown, and embraced the Church of England. So transatlantic did he become that today both British and American students of literature claim him as a national author.

In their expatriations, Eliot and Pound were inspired by the example of the great American novelist and short-story writer, Henry James (1843–1916). James spent much of his life in Europe and died a British subject. In his fiction he often explored what he called the 'international theme': the clash of European and American values, the allure and the terror of culture shock, and the challenges to personal identity of prolonged residence abroad. Eliot addresses these Jamesian issues in many of the poems that he published between 1915 and 1922. Indeed, 'Portrait of a Lady' (1915) explicitly acknowledges Eliot's indebtedness by taking its title from one of James's best-known novels.

In developing the international theme, Eliot seems especially concerned with the perils of cosmopolitanism. His poems often satirize the deracination and demoralization of characters who have lived too long abroad: for example, the hollow men of 'Mélange adultère de tout' and 'A Cooking Egg'; the shadowy drifters mentioned by Gerontion in his monologue; and the sinister conspirators in 'Sweeney among the Nightingales'. In a Ruskinian meditation on the decline of Venice entitled 'Burbank with a Baedeker: Bleistein with a Cigar' (1919), Eliot sketches the debilitating effects of modern commercial and sexual tourism upon both the inhabitants of and the visitors to the city:

> Burbank crossed a little bridge
>   Descending at a small hotel;
> Princess Volupine arrived,
>   They were together, and he fell.

Although Eliot's early essays seem to further Matthew Arnold's project of extending intellectual sweetness and light through cosmopolitanism, his early poetry explores the darker side of a purely selfish and materialistic internationalism.

Eliot's Sweeney, who may have been modelled upon a boxer the poet saw in Boston, reminds us that an Irish-American connection was no less crucial to the development of modernism than was the Anglo-American connection. In William Butler Yeats (1865–1939), Ireland produced perhaps the greatest English-language poet of the twentieth century; and in James Joyce (1882–1941), perhaps the greatest novelist. The careers of both Yeats and Joyce were shaped, in part, by their transatlantic alliances, not least by their friendships with Ezra Pound.

Initially, Yeats was the master and Pound the apprentice. Pound may have heard the Irish poet read his work at the University of Pennsylvania in 1903. The young American soon began to write in a Yeatsian manner and to read his own work with an Irish intonation. Esteeming Yeats as the greatest living poet, Pound secured an introduction to him in 1909. Pound shared his mentor's interest in the occult, and regularly attended the weekly meetings that Yeats convened when he was resident in London.

Soon, however, the influence became reciprocal. Between 1913 and 1916, Pound spent several winter months each year with Yeats at Stone Cottage in Sussex. There, he helped Yeats with business and correspondence, and acted as his interlocutor in a wide-ranging dialogue on mysticism, medieval and Renaissance courtly poetry, the relationship of verse and music, and the conversational modes of such writers as François Villon and Walter Savage Landor. Yeats had already begun to incorporate colloquial elements into his own poetic style, and Pound encouraged him in this process of self-refashioning. The young American 'helps me to get back to the definite and the concrete away from modern abstractions', Yeats told Lady Gregory. 'To talk over a poem with him is like getting you to put a sentence into dialect. All becomes clear and natural' (Longenbach, 1988, p. 19). Pound saw to it that poems in Yeats's modern style were published in American little magazines. When *Responsibilities*, the volume which announced Yeats's mature mode, appeared in 1914, Pound saluted it with a strong review in *Poetry* (Pound, 1954, pp. 378–81).

Pound also had an impact upon the style of Yeats's later plays. During their winters at Stone Cottage, Pound was completing unfinished translations of classic Chinese poems and Japanese Noh plays that he had received in 1913 from the widow of the eminent American historian of Oriental art, Ernest Fenollosa. When Yeats read the plays, he found their conventions highly congenial. He set about creating a poetic drama that employed stylized declamation and movement, masks, and personifications of gods and spirits. He employed these techniques to dramatize Irish myths and legends for sophisticated, aristocratic audiences. In this genre, too, the twentieth-century transformation of Yeats's style owed much to transatlantic influences.

James Joyce had a less personal, but no less momentous, relationship with Pound than did Yeats. Joyce left Ireland for Trieste several years before Pound arrived in London, and the two men did not meet until 1920. However, Pound took an active interest in Joyce's career from the time he first learned of Joyce's difficulties in finding a publisher for *Dubliners*. He included a poem by Joyce in the anthology *Des Imagistes* (1914), and he arranged for *A Portrait of the Artist as Young Man* to be serialized by the *Egoist* and published in book form under the Egoist imprint in 1916. Pound also steered the editor of the *Egoist*, Harriet Shaw Weaver, in Joyce's direction, so that she became one of the Irish writer's most helpful patrons.

Pound was likewise instrumental in the publication of Joyce's modernist master-piece, *Ulysses*. As Joyce finished the episodes of his new novel, he sent them to Pound in London, who forwarded them to the *Little Review* in New York. There, beginning in 1918, they were serialized, at least until the New York Society for the Prevention of Vice persuaded a court that the 'Nausicaa' episode is obscene. Eventually, *Ulysses* was published in its entirety by Sylvia Beach, an American expatriate who operated an English-language bookstore in Paris. The novel appeared in the same year as Eliot's *The Waste Land* (1922). Both Eliot and Pound reviewed Joyce's book enthusiastically, and the structure of *Ulysses*, which Eliot described as the 'mythical method' of paralleling ancient narrative with modern events, helped the two poets to shape their respective modernist masterpieces, *The Waste Land* and *The Cantos* (Eliot, 1975, p. 178).

Around 1920, the European 'vortex' of modernism began to shift from London to Paris. In that year, Pound published *Hugh Selwyn Mauberley* as his poetic farewell to London. In 1921 he moved to Paris, convinced that the French capital was now the more vital creative centre. Joyce came to Paris from Zurich in 1920. Many others soon followed. Paris was alluring because of its moral and racial tolerance and because of the favourable rate of exchange between the French franc and the dollar or pound. After the passage of Prohibition in 1919–20, Paris also became known as a place where Americans could drink with impunity. F. Scott Fitzgerald, Ernest Hemingway and the so-called 'lost generation' began to frequent the cafés and boulevards that lined the Seine. The doyenne of the foreign artistic community, Gertrude Stein, who had lived in Paris since 1902, observed the newcomers with an amused and critical detachment.

When William Carlos Williams visited Paris in 1924, he relished the contacts he made there. He met or re-met French artists (Constantin Brancusi, Fernand Léger, Jean Cocteau, Louis Aragon, Philippe Soupault), British and Irish writers (Joyce, Ford Madox Ford, Mina Loy and Clive Bell), and American expatriates (Pound, Hemingway, H. D., Robert McAlmon, George Antheil, Man Ray). An international group of monied patrons supported modern art in Paris: they included Natalie Barney, Peggy Guggenheim, Nancy Cunard, Winifred Ellerman, Sylvia Beach, Samuel Putnam, Harold Loeb and William Bird. Bird operated the Three Mountains Press, which published Williams's *Spring and All* (1923), Pound's *A Draft of XVI. Cantos* (1925) and Hemingway's *In Our Time* (1924). Cunard started the Hours Press, which brought out Pound's *A Draft of XXX Cantos* (1930). New magazines sprang up, not only in Paris (*transition*, the *Transatlantic Review*, *Bifur*) but also in Milan (*This Quarter*) and Berlin (*Broom*). Williams found it difficult to stay in touch with everything that was going on.

Not all of the literary action centred in Paris, however. Pound's *Mauberley* notwith-standing, London was far from moribund. John Rodker, whose Ovid Press published Pound's sequence, also brought out T. S. Eliot's *Ara Vos Prec* (1920) and the first British edition of *Ulysses* (1922). Virginia and Leonard Woolf started the Hogarth Press, which published Eliot's *Poems* (1919) and the first British edition of *The Waste Land*, as well as the first English translation of the complete works of Sigmund Freud. Eliot maintained close relations with the Bloomsbury group, and founded an influential new journal called the *Criterion*, which ran from 1922 to 1939.

The Waste Land, first published in 1922, is the landmark poem of the transatlantic modernist movement. International in both content and provenance, it stunned readers with its disjunctive style, its wide-ranging allusions, and its polyphonic use of languages (English, Latin, French, Italian, Provencal, German, Sanskrit).

> London Bridge is falling down falling down falling down
> *Poi s'ascose nel foco che gli affina*
> *Quando fiam uti chelidon* – O swallow swallow
> *Le Prince d'Aquitaine à la tour abolie*
> These fragments I have shored against my ruins.

Eliot seemed to assume an audience conversant with all the tongues that filled the world after the destruction of the Tower of Babel.

No less cosmopolitan were the circumstances of the poem's composition and pub-lication. Eliot began *The Waste Land* in England during a period of nervous break-down, and continued it in Lausanne, Switzerland, during his convalescence. Returning from Switzerland, he delivered fifty-seven typescript pages of disconnected poetic fragments to Pound in Paris. Pound condensed and shaped the manuscript into the nineteen-page version that we know today. In October 1922 *The Waste Land* was pub-lished in London by the *Criterion*; in the following month, it appeared in New York in the pages of the *Dial*. The poem was then issued in book form by Boni and Liv-eright of New York and the Hogarth Press of London. The transatlantic migrations of the poem continued when the typescript was sold to a New York collector named John Quinn. Long thought to be lost, the original version was rediscovered among Quinn's papers in the New York Public Library in 1968 and published in a facsim-ile edition in 1971 (see Eliot, 1971). The poem created an instant furor on both sides of the Atlantic; William Carlos Williams later compared its impact upon New York to that of an atomic bomb (Williams, 1951, p. 174).

The role of New York in the provenance of *The Waste Land* reminds us that London and Paris were not the only vortices of the modernist movement. New York and Chicago were major centres as well. American writers who stayed at home read Arnold, Ruskin and William Morris, but they also followed a nativist tradition that had its nineteenth-century roots in the work of Ralph Waldo Emerson, Henry David Thoreau and Walt Whitman. In the ideology of this Romantic Transcendentalism, America is a 'New World' with a unique historical opportunity to create an ideal society, to devise an order that surpasses the failed and weary feudalism of Europe. This new order will be cosmopolitan in the true, global sense of the term; its culture will be transpacific as well as transatlantic, incorporating indigenous and Oriental as well as European elements. The mission of the American artist, then, is to document the experience and the vision of the New World: to embody its new way of seeing in the visual arts, and to represent its new forms of speech and action in literature. William Carlos Williams summarized his life's work as a pursuit of 'the American idiom' (Mariani, 1981, pp. 758–9).

For all of its declarations of independence, however, New York modernism preserved its transatlantic links with Europe. The Armory Show of 1913 gave many artists and writers their first glimpse of post-Impressionist painting. The bold experimentation of the Fauvists, Cubists and Futurists heartened their American counterparts to break with nineteenth-century conventions. E. E. Cummings tried his hand at avant-garde painting as well as poetry. William Carlos Williams learned to look at nature with the eyes of a non-representational painter, as in the opening lines of 'Spring Strains' (1916):

> In a tissue-thin monotone of blue-grey buds
> crowded erect with desire against
> the sky –
> > tense blue-grey twigs
> slenderly anchoring them down, drawing
> them in –
>
> > two blue-grey birds chasing
> a third struggle in circles, angles,
> swift convergings to a point that bursts
> instantly!

Williams, Wallace Stevens and Marianne Moore gravitated to Alfred Kreymborg and his little magazine, *Others*. Soon, New Yorkers could choose among other little magazines published in their city: the *Little Review*, the *Dial*, *Contact*, *Hound and Horn*, *Blues* and *Pagany*. Adventurous publishers and editors such as Horace Liveright, Alfred A. Knopf, Pascal Covici, Macaulay and Co., J. Ronald Lane Latimer, Thomas Seltzer, Caresse and Harry Crosby, Scofield Thayer, and Maxwell Perkins were willing to take financial risks on unconventional manuscripts. Enlightened patrons such as John Quinn supported new trends in the arts, and perceptive critics such as Kenneth Burke, Gorham Munson and Edmund Wilson mediated experimental poetry to interested but puzzled readers.

The receptive cultural milieu of New York in the 1920s also prompted groundbreaking work by Afro-American writers. An audience whose interest in innovative poetry had been stimulated by well-publicized debates over the merits of free verse, *The Waste Land* and the typography of Cummings was undaunted by the challenging verse of the Harlem Renaissance poets. Countee Cullen and Claude McKay expressed radical sentiments in traditional poetic forms, whereas Jean Toomer and Langston Hughes adopted more experimental techniques. The versatile Hughes employed free verse, *dramatis personae* and disjunctive poetic sequences in a body of work distinguished by its variety and inventiveness. In addition to drawing upon Afro-American folk culture, Harlem Renaissance writers made use of mainstream poetic traditions. They readily adapted Whitman's democratic voice and vision to an assertive poetry of pan-African pride. They drew inspiration as well from the Irish Celtic Renaissance, a movement which, like theirs, affirmed the identity and heritage of a colonized people (see Bornstein, 1996).

Walt Whitman was also a source of inspiration for the Chicago modernists. When Harriet Monroe and Alice Corbin Henderson founded *Poetry: A Magazine of Verse* in 1912, they took their motto from Whitman's 'Notes Left Over': 'To have great poets there must be great audiences too'. Originally, Monroe and Henderson intended *Poetry* to be a democratic organ of the American Midwestern heartland. They favored Illinois poets such as Carl Sandburg, Edgar Lee Masters, Vachel Lindsay, and Canadian disciples of Whitman such as Bliss Carman. *Poetry* also took up Robert Frost as the epitome of New England regionalism.

Yet the focus of the magazine was not exclusively nativist. With Pound as Foreign Editor from 1912 to 1917, *Poetry* carried work by Yeats, Eliot and the Imagists alongside that of the Midwesterners. This eclectic mixture of new writing by indigenist, expatriate and foreign poets made *Poetry* arguably the most significant of all the modernist little magazines.

The cohabitation of indigenists and expatriates in the pages of the little magazines was not always amicable. In 1918–19 a quarrel broke out between them, triggered by English critic Edgar Jepson's attack upon 'The Western School' of American poets (see Pound and Williams, 1996, pp. 5, 36–45). Jepson accused Lindsay, Masters and Frost of verbal posturing and poor workmanship; he cited the work of Eliot as the best that contemporary American poetry had to offer. In his Prologue to *Kora in Hell* (1919), William Carlos Williams responded to Jepson, contending that Eliot and the other expatriate poets were too Europeanized to be representative of American verse.

Despite such tensions, the two groups co-operated more than they squabbled. The indigenists were not simply provincial xenophobes, although their rhetoric could sound that way. Williams travelled and published in Europe even as he quarrelled with Pound and proclaimed his detestation of Eliot. Wallace Stevens, although he never visited Europe, drew much of his inspiration from books on French culture and art. And Hart Crane (1899–1933), a Midwestern poet who achieved literary success in New York, tried to reconcile the influences of Whitman and Eliot in his long poem, *The Bridge* (1930). Both predecessors can be heard, for example, in the closing stanzas of Crane's 'Harbor Dawn' section:

> The window goes blond slowly. Frostily clears.
> From Cyclopean towers across Manhattan waters

> – Two – three bright window-eyes aglitter, disk
> The sun, released – aloft with cold gulls hither.
>
> The fog leans one last moment on the sill.
> Under the mistletoe of dreams, a star –
> As though to join us at some distant hill –
> Turns in the waking west and goes to sleep.
> (Crane, 1966, p. 56)

If the first stanza recalls Whitman's descriptions of Manhattan and its harbour, the second echoes 'The Love Song of J. Alfred Prufrock' in its animation of the fog. *The Bridge* celebrates America, but does so in the international modernist style as Crane understood it: allusive, elliptical and densely metaphoric.

The transatlantic bridge soon became a two-way street. Between the wars, the lure of America drew many Europeans who dreamed of starting afresh in a land of limitless opportunity. Thus, the English poets Iris Barry and Mina Loy migrated to New York, where both made successful careers. Ford Madox Ford married an American painter and spent time during the last decade of his life in New York, Tennessee and Michigan. A. R. Orage, the editor of the *New Age*, likewise married an American and lived in New York from 1922 to 1932; there, he studied and disseminated the teachings of G. I. Gurdjieff. Aldous Huxley moved to California in 1937 and made his home in Hollywood until his death in 1963. Thomas Mann and Bertolt Brecht came to California as refugees from Nazi Germany. And in 1939, W. H. Auden and Christopher Isherwood took up more or less permanent residence in the United States.

Of all the literary exiles who came to the land of promise from Britain between the wars, perhaps the most important was D. H. Lawrence (1885–1930). Embittered by the treatment they had met with during the Great War, Lawrence and his wife Frieda left England in 1919, never to return except for brief visits (see Delany, 1978). They lived in Sicily, Ceylon and Australia before arriving in California in September 1922. At the invitation of a wealthy patron, Mabel Dodge Luhan, the Lawrences travelled directly to Taos, New Mexico. There they stayed on three separate occasions between 1922 and 1925; they also undertook two extended trips into Old Mexico.

The idea of the New World as a utopian alternative to Europe had long appealed to Lawrence. He dreamed of founding an ideal colony in Florida, to be called 'Rananim'. Since the suppression of *The Rainbow* by English authorities in 1915, his principal publisher was Thomas Seltzer of New York. Lawrence was also a keen student of American literature. His fascinating series of essays on American authors and works was published in 1924 under the title *Studies in Classic American Literature*. As a poet of social and psychological liberation, he had long modelled his style upon the free verse of Walt Whitman.

The mountainside ranches above Taos proved to be congenial to Lawrence's work. Mexican and New Mexican settings appear frequently in the writings of his last decade (see Sagar, 1995), and a group of poems composed at Taos became part of the collection published in 1923 as *Birds, Beasts, and Flowers*. In the following passage from 'The Red Wolf' the autumnal landscape of New Mexico inspires a characteristically Lawrentian redefinition of religion:

> Now that the sun has gone, and the aspen leaves
> And the cotton-wood leaves are fallen, as good as fallen,
> And the ponies are in corral,
> And it's night,
> Why, more has gone than all these;
> And something has come.
> A red wolf stands on the shadow's dark red rim.
>
> Day has gone to dust on the sage-grey desert
> Like a white Christus fallen to dust from a cross;
> To dust, to ash, on the twilit floor of the desert.
> And a black crucifix like a dead tree spreading wings;
> Maybe a black eagle with its wings out
> Left lonely in the night
> In a sort of worship.

In this description, dark gods emerge from the stark, wild earth after nightfall. A Dionysian–chthonic reality displaces or inverts the Apollonian–Christian order of the daylight hours. The passage illustrates the process by which Lawrence's evolving ideas about Western religions were shaped by his experience of the landscapes and pre-Columbian cultures of Mexico and the American Southwest. It is no exaggeration to say that Lawrence's variety of modernism owes as much to the idea and reality of America as T. S. Eliot's does to the idea and reality of England.

Such influence is characteristic of the dynamic interaction of cross-cultural energies that sustained the modernist movement in English-language poetry. As materialism numbed and war convulsed the world, transatlantic modernism struggled to affirm the human spirit and the value of art. In an era of contending visions of global order, the cosmopolitanism of the modernists did not prevail. But it remains as a standing challenge to our shrinking world of standardized markets and commercialized tourism.

BIBLIOGRAPHY

Anderson, Sherwood (1977). *Winesburg, Ohio.* Oxford: Oxford University Press.

Bornstein, George (1996). 'Afro-Celtic Connections: From Frederick Douglass to *The Commitments.*' In Tracy Mishkin (ed.), *Literary Influence and African American Writers.* New York: Garland.

Coffman, Stanley (1951). *Imagism: A Chapter in the History of Modern Poetry.* Norman: University of Oklahoma Press.

Crane, Hart (1966). *The Complete Poems and Selected Letters and Prose of Hart Crane,* ed. Brom Weber. New York: Liveright.

Delany, Paul (1978). *D. H. Lawrence's Nightmare.* New York: Basic Books.

Eliot, T. S. (1963). *Collected Poems 1909–1962.* London: Faber and Faber.

Eliot, T. S. (1971). *The Waste Land: A Facsimile and Transcript of the Original Drafts including the Annotations of Ezra Pound*, ed. Valerie Eliot. London: Faber and Faber.

Eliot, T. S. (1975). '*Ulysses*, Order, and Myth.' In Frank Kermode (ed.), *Selected Prose of T. S. Eliot*, pp. 175–8. London: Faber and Faber.

Fletcher, John Gould (1937). *Life Is My Song: The Autobiography of John Gould Fletcher.* New York: Farrar and Rinehart.

Gage, John (1983). *In the Arresting Eye: The Rhetoric of Imagism.* Baton Rouge: Louisiana State University Press.

Kenner, Hugh (1971). *The Pound Era.* Berkeley: University of California Press.

Kenner, Hugh (1988). *A Sinking Island: The Modern English Writers.* London: Barrie and Jenkins.

Lawrence, D. H. (1986). *Poems*, ed. Keith Sagar. Harmondsworth: Penguin.

Longenbach, James (1988). *Stone Cottage: Pound, Yeats, and Modernism.* New York: Oxford University Press.

Mariani, Paul (1981). *William Carlos Williams: A New World Naked.* New York: McGraw-Hill.

Pound, Ezra (1913). 'The Approach to Paris . . . I–VII.' *New Age*, 13, 551–2, 577–9, 607–9, 631–3, 662–4, 694–6, 726–8. Rpt. (1991)

Ezra Pound's Poetry and Prose: Contributions to Periodicals, Vol. 1, ed. Lea Baechler, A. Walton Litz and James Longenbach. New York: Garland.

Pound, Ezra (1950). *Selected Letters of Ezra Pound, 1904–1941*, ed. D. D. Paige. New York: Harcourt Brace Jovanovitch.

Pound, Ezra (1954). *Literary Essays*, ed. T. S. Eliot. London: Faber and Faber.

Pound, Ezra (1990). *Personae: The Shorter Poems of Ezra Pound*, ed. Lea Baechler and A. Walton Litz. New York: New Directions.

Pound, Ezra and William Carlos Williams (1996). *Pound/Williams: Selected Letters of Ezra Pound and William Carlos Williams*, ed. Hugh Witemeyer. New York: New Directions.

Sagar, Keith (ed.) (1995). *D. H. Lawrence and New Mexico.* Paris: Karl Orend.

Schneidau, Herbert (1969). *Ezra Pound: The Image and the Real.* Baton Rouge: Louisiana State University Press.

Wees, William (1972). *Vorticism and the English Avant-Garde.* Toronto: University of Toronto Press.

Williams, William Carlos (1951). *The Autobiography of William Carlos Williams.* New York: Random House.

Williams, William Carlos (1986). *The Collected Poems of William Carlos Williams: Vol. I, 1909–1939*, ed. A. Walton Litz and Christopher MacGowan. New York: New Directions.

2

Modernist Poetry and its Precursors

Peter Brooker and Simon Perril

Writing in *The New Age* in 1911, Allen Upward claimed that 'It is a sign of the times that so many of us should be busy in studying the signs of the times' (Upward, 1911, p. 297). A lifetime and more later the newness which captivated Upward's contemporaries is a thing of the past, though it is by name 'modern' and 'modernist' still. One of the paradoxical signs of our own times is that we are 'after' the modern and view from this perspective. But in a sense modernism has never synchronized with its times. It has always been a retrospective formation, both in its internal history, as Stan Smith (1994) has shown, and in its later construction as an orthodoxy valued by criticism. The modernist movement can only be understood then as this discursive and cultural construction; a combined aesthetic and idea of civilization in the making rather than a point of undisputed identity. If follows that there was no queue of precursors leading up one by one to the modernist moment. Certainly, its history includes a number of acknowledged influences and can be read quite feasibly, at a distance anyway, as a narrative of before and after. There was a time in the 1920s when the first move – 'to break the iamb' as Pound had put it – had been made, when a new poetry, modern in its materials and idiom, had been decisively introduced. But then this seems more true if Eliot rather than Pound or some others is the example. And if Eliot is taken to be the exemplary modernist we might remember William Carlos Williams's reaction to *The Waste Land* – 'a catastrophe to our letters' which 'gave the poem back to the academics' (Williams, 1951, p. 146). One man's modernism was one culture's preferred modernism and another modernist's or other culture's retrograde traditionalism. There is therefore no avoiding the now common understanding of 'modernism' as entailing a network of 'modernisms'; less a united revolution or homogeneous orthodoxy than a heterodox weave of anticipations, traces, tensions and contested positions. In this sense modernism is a script, written over, revised and above all 'edited': in the re-making of tradition as in the composition of individual poems and in the promotion, publication and reception of poets, poems and lines of verse – a process involving obstruction and suppression as much as a coming into print and into view.

Most of the discussion below concerns T. S. Eliot and Ezra Pound, primarily because of their immersion in this process and their pivotal role as conduits and instigators in the making of modern verse. It is not our intention in this way to endorse the Anglo-American modernist canon (which has anyway never received both poets equally). Our concern is rather to return these poets to the transitional and symbiotic histories of verse and modernity. The effect of such an examination, introductory though it is, is rather to undermine than shore up their monumentalism, to unravel rather than fix the text of modernism and to disperse rather than determine any supposed point of origin.

Tradition and Modernity

Allen Upward's observation above recalls Thomas Carlyle's essay 'Signs of the Times' which appeared as 'early' as 1829. Nor is this a simple echo. Isobel Armstrong suggests how Carlyle's work diagnoses a new historical situation of increasing alienation that parallels Marx's account of the division of labour under capitalism. Carlyle describes an emerging modern industrial society where a new distribution of wealth was, he said, 'strangely altering the old relations' (Armstrong, 1993, p. 4). For Armstrong this is closely related to Victorian poetry's sense of itself as 'modern' (she cites the resurgence of the term in Arnold's 'modern' element in literature and Meredith's 'modern' love). The result was a self-conscious and historicizing sense by which 'Victorian modernism sees itself as new but it does not, like twentieth-century modernism, conceive itself in terms of a radical break with the past' (Armstrong, 1993, p. 3).

As we have suggested, twentieth-century 'modernism' as a category emerged as a belated description of a sometimes violently heterogeneous and unstable set of initiatives. Any distinction, furthermore, between an earlier and later modernism in the terms Armstrong chooses, proves unconvincing. While there were European modernisms (notably futurism) which did indeed cultivate a radical break with the past, the Anglo-American variety was haunted by its relationship to tradition. Ezra Pound's rallying cry of 'make it new' precisely emphasizes the possibilities for reconstruction and 'translation' rather than the destructive joys of Dada or the Italian futurist Marinetti's glorification of modern technology and war. Pound came to London in 1908, he said, to learn 'how Yeats did it' (Paige, 1971, p. 296) and there joined an Edwardian literary world in many ways living off the fading inheritance of the Pre-Raphaelites and Rhymers Club of the 1890s. In the words applied to the persona 'Hugh Selwyn Mauberley' at the point of Pound's departure for Paris in 1920, he was himself in these early years 'out of date': an American specialist in European Romance literatures who stepped out in literary London more as the eccentric bohemian and latter-day troubadour than the radicalizing modernist. He was in his own person, that is to say, a rather awkward translation across cultures whose practice of 'creative trans-lation' and imitation of earlier literatures helped in the event to create a modernist idiom with all the estrangement this implied. The often scandalized response of Pound's contemporaries to his work showed how inflammatory this assault upon ideas of authorship, originality, scholarship and tradition could be. The protests mounted as Pound worked upon forms and figures in an expanded tradition (in 'translations' of the Anglo-Saxon 'Seafarer', of Cavalcanti, Propertius and early Chinese poets). Still 'out of key' he became within a dozen years too up to date for postwar English literary taste.

Criticism has been happy to couple Pound and Eliot together as canonic mod-ernists. Certainly Eliot shared Pound's sense of the modern poet's relation to a revised, living tradition and to the place within it of, for example, Dante, and, among late nineteenth-century French poets, Laforgue, Corbière and Gautier. Beyond this the tra-ditions (in the plural, as we should think of them) which these modernists brought into being ran off in different directions.

This complex relation between Anglo-American modernism and its precursors – as well as its contemporaries – in which different sides wrestled over notions of a received or rebuilt tradition, is suggestive at the same time of a broader, equally complex relationship to modernity. A difference between Pound and Eliot shows itself here too, for whereas the 'out of date' Pound had to make himself new, Eliot, as Pound himself reported on seeing Eliot's poem 'The Love Song of J. Alfred Prufrock' in 1914, had seem-ingly 'modernized himself' at a stroke (Paige, 1971, p. 40). Eliot was 'modernist' earlier and more transparently than others. And behind this there lay Eliot's keener sense of modern poetry's relation to the modern world. The need to innovate and experiment with new forms and techniques was motivated, Eliot concluded in his 1921 essay on 'The Metaphysical Poets', by the evident complexity of the modern world:

> We can only say that it appears likely that poets in our civilization, as it exists at present, must be *difficult*. . . . The poet must become more and more comprehensive, more allu-sive, more indirect, in order to force, to dislocate if necessary, language into his meaning. (Eliot, 1951, p. 289)

At first sight this would seem to suggest a relation of cause and effect, a synchronic-ity at least, between a complex age and the complex art it requires. However, the modern poets' 'language' and 'meaning' (Pound's as much as Eliot's own) was deployed in a rebarbative relation to modern civilization. Anglo-American modernism came in fact to regard modernity with, at best, suspicion – and at worst with contempt for the cultural decline it had instigated. Its experimentalism was therefore a 'revolu-tionary' means to a literally 'reactionary' end; a paradoxical project in which the open-ness to new forms and the openness of a reconfigured tradition were governed by a reaction to social and economic changes it deplored. In Pound's case these tensions broke the surface in manifest gaps across his practice and propaganda; in his fondness, on the one hand, for an archaic idiom and his felt need, on the other, for a contemporary reference and relevance. Without some reconciliation between these impulses the critique of modernity in the name of a preferred minority civilization modelled on the best of the past could not take hold.

This tension showed itself in the attack and clarity of Pound's prose arguments and the intertextual weave of his early poetry, spoken through the 'personae' of, among others, Dante, Bertran de Born, Villon, Yeats, Robert Browning, Swinburne and the Pre-Raphaelites. The most important response to the latter was Ford Madox Ford's famous roll on the floor in side-splitting agony at the tortuous 'errors of contemporary style' in Pound's *Canzoni* in 1911. This roll, said Pound, saved him 'at least two years' and sent him 'back to my own proper effort, namely, toward using the living tongue' (Pound, 1973, pp. 431, 432). Pound's immersion within poetic history, as this begins to tell us, was more complex than a simple case of what Harold Bloom has called anxiety of influence. He needed to revise and renovate the past rather than overcome it, while weaning himself at the same time from the 'stilted language' of a contemporary 'arthritic milieu' (ibid., p. 431). After *Canzoni* Pound began to find a solution in the more straightforward translations of Cavalcanti in 1912 and in the significantly titled series 'Contemporania' (in *Poetry*, April, 1913), a series including his most successful Imagist poem, 'In a Station of the Metro'.

Anglo-American modernism's intended critique of modernity can be contrasted with the more common hostility towards art as an institution in European modernism and the consequent attempt within European avant-garde movements to dissolve the boundaries between art and life. The issues here are complex and diffuse. The examples of Charles Baudelaire – surely the most commonly cited figure in accounts of modernism's originating moment – and of the later French Symbolist poets, Stephane Mallarmé and Paul Valéry, can nevertheless help identify two key strands in the relation between a modernist aesthetic and modern life. T. S. Eliot's reflections on the Symbolist poets, and on Baudelaire and Mallarmé's acknowledged American precursor, Edgar Allan Poe, are also instructive.

Baudelaire's seminal essay 'The Painter of Modern Life' (1859–60) defines a split modernity; one half comprised of 'the transient, the fleeting, the contingent', the other of 'the eternal and the immovable' (Kolocotroni, Goldman and Taxidou, 1998, p. 107). This key description echoes through the Anglo-Modernist attempt to pull the materials of modern life – reverberating with the manifold traces of the past and of other cultures – into some new transcendent order and coherence. Eliot discovered in Baudelaire 'a precedent for the poetical possibilities . . . of the more sordid aspects of the modern metropolis' (Eliot, 1965, p. 126) and consistently acknowledged his importance, along with the English poets James Thomson and John Davidson, in establishing a contemporary urban idiom. In his 1930 essay on Baudelaire, he detected something else, however; something 'permanent' which made Baudelaire more than 'the voice of his time'; an 'essentially Christian' attitude, said Eliot, which realized 'the real problem of good and evil . . . that what really matters is Sin and Redemption' (Eliot, 1951, pp. 421, 427). In this capacity Baudelaire served less as a precursor of 'modernist' poetry than as an ideological precedent for Eliot's own emerging project, apparent from *The Waste Land* onwards, to return the sordid new modern world to the faith it had lost. Thus a 'Christian modernism', if anti-modern ideology and modernist aesthetic could hold together, would evoke a redemptive order (the eternal and immutable) to shore up and reshape the chaotic fragments (the fleeting, the contingent) of modernity.

Clearly Eliot reads his own modern age and compulsions back into Baudelaire. A similar re-reading in Eliot's 'From Poe to Valéry' (1948) acknowledged while it distanced itself from the influence of Poe upon Baudelaire, Mallarmé and Valéry and the doctrine of 'pure poetry'. Both Baudelaire and Mallarmé had avidly consumed the aestheticist doctrine announced in Poe's 'The Poetic Principle'. Here, setting his face against the 'heresy of *The Didactic*' and the rising tide of American materialism, Poe had championed the 'poem *per se* – this poem which is a poem and nothing more – this poem written solely for the poem's sake' (Poe, 1986, pp. 503, 504). Art would appear here to remove itself from life. However, as developed both in the 'l'art pour l'art' movement in France and in the equivalent Aestheticist movement associated with Walter Pater and the Nineties in England this apparent retreat into the self-sufficient autonomy of art voiced its own protest against the moralizing and utilitarian values of capitalist modernity.

Eliot's 'From Poe to Valéry' will have none of this. He finds in Poe an 'irresponsibility towards the meaning of words' and an arrested, uncoordinated emotional sensibility (Eliot, 1965, pp. 32, 34). He therefore tracks this Symbolist and aestheticist lineage in order to determine its limits. The idea of the '*poète maudit*, the poet as outcast of society' which Baudelaire found in Poe 'corresponds to a particular social situation', Eliot concludes, while the doctrine of 'la poésie pure' developed in Mallarmé and Valéry 'has gone as far as it can go' (ibid., pp. 37, 41). As always, the tradition is refashioned for particular ends, belonging more to a present-day project than to a self-evident heritage. If Eliot here closes off one route, however, his earlier essay discerns another: a 'Christian' Baudelaire, who at that essay's close, Eliot can set alongside the doctrine of discipline and original sin in the 'classicist' T. E. Hulme.

Eliot had praised Hulme's 'classical, reactionary and revolutionary' stand against 'suburban democracy' in the *Criterion* in the mid-twenties (Ackroyd, 1984, p. 143) and at such points the reactionary conservative inflection given to this modernism is most explicit. It was accompanied, however, by a further, and until recently, less recognized gendered aspect. Though tortuously suppressed in Eliot this was openly displayed in Hulme's masculinist cult of violence and to different degrees in Hulme's sometime rivals, Wyndham Lewis – ever the cultural pugilist – and Pound, in his more swaggering and opinionated moods.

Geoff Ward speculates that this peculiarly macho posturing of the 'Men of 1914' had its source in the trial of Oscar Wilde in 1895. Before the trial, he argues, 'the posturings of the Decadents were tolerable eccentricities, fodder for the cartoonists of *Punch*'. After it, 'the artist was exiled to the social periphery: this was the queer birth of the English *avant-garde*, the artist as cryptic, deviant, misunderstood, comparable to the criminal and the anarchist' (Ward, 1993, p. 123). The effect, says Ward, was a two-fold anxiety: the first 'that writing poems could be thought effete in a sexual-ized sense; the second . . . the related fear that to write poems is not to be at *work*, in the usual male provinces' (ibid., p. 122).

Both Eliot and Pound had to negotiate this compound anxiety on their entry into English literary culture. They did so through a selective reading of the poetry of the French and English 1880s and 1890s and by producing themselves as profes-sional poets. Eliot, as we have seen, attempted to reject the aestheticist languor and hermeticism of these immediate precursors while appropriating their sophisti-cated ironies, urban subject matter and contemporary idiom. The ambience of ennui and neurosis characteristic of the *fin de siècle* lingered nonetheless in his 'Preludes' and in 'Prufrock'. In Pound the ambivalence was more marked. While socially he played the dandy and bohemian and while his poetry was enough to make Ford Madox Ford choke on its precious locutions, his public career as an American in London was from the start propelled by a pedagogic intent and campaigning drive. His 'The Serious Artist' (1913) opened as a latter-day *Defence of Poetry* and this was a role Pound never relinquished, as later titles such as 'How To Read', *ABC of Reading* and *Guide to Kulchur* testify. Pound always had a syllabus to hand, listing Homer, Catullus, Dante, Cavalcanti and Arnaut Daniel, Villon, Flaubert, Corbière and Théophile Gautier, Fenollosa and the Chinese poets Lui Ch'e and Li Po as a bare minimum. And to these 'how to' letters and handbooks for apprentice poets he was to add primers on economic democracy and Confucian ethics as his sense of 'civilization' broadened and the case for the artist's importance to the public realm appeared more desperate.

Here too, however, Pound's commitment to *'The Didactic'* which Poe had opposed, found a further, surprising, echo – in the cultural mission of the Victorian sages: Arnold, Ruskin and Morris. As Mary Ellis Gibson reports, Pound's cultural mission

> was deeply rooted in nineteenth-century thought and in the Victorian response to indus-trial capitalism. It was crucial for William Morris and before him Ruskin. Indeed the combination of canonical, pedagogic, and social concerns in Ruskin's later essays pre-figures Pound's urgent efforts to propagate a canon. (Gibson, 1995, p. 11)

Thus while it was 'new' and moved 'forward' out of aestheticism, Eliot and Pound's renovative project took them 'backwards' to an anthology of 'pre-texts', among them a Victorian discourse of social concern which reappeared, edited and in 'translation', in the heteroscript of Anglo-American modernism.

Victorian into Modern: Interiority and Impersonality

The Victorians, however, provided technical solutions as well as a social and ideolog-ical precedent for the later modernists. Robert Browning's penchant in his use of the dramatic monologue for 'grotesque' non-poetic diction and eccentric metres mimetic of what Walter Bagehot termed a *'mind in difficulties'* (Faas, 1986, p. 21) were an example to Eliot and especially the early Pound.

Above all, the dramatic monologue is distinguished by the 'objective' position of the poet (the term was Browning's own), set apart from the speaker who unravels his/her own emotional life to a silent listener – in effect the reader, who is therefore drawn into the poem as doctor/analyst in a psychological case history. The 'impersonality' of detached scientific observation and the analogous language of precise observation so prized by Eliot, Hulme, Pound and the Imagists was therefore already installed within Victorian poetics. Browning's 'My Last Duchess' and 'Porphyria's Lover', as well as Tennyson's 'Maud' and 'St Simeon Stylites', testify to Victorian poetry's 'modern' fascination with extreme states of mind: evidence for Arthur Symons in 1886 of 'this intensely subjective and analytic nineteenth century, with its . . . ceaseless restless introspection' (Faas, 1986, p. 25), though he might as well have been discussing the ambience of the early T. S. Eliot.

Pound's reassessment of his poetry in the wake of Ford's historic roll began in the volume *Ripostes* (1912) to bear some modernized fruit, in places gravitating towards what in 'The Serious Artist' he termed 'the cult of ugliness' and the 'surgery' of satire (Pound, 1960, p. 45). Many examples fed into this change of mind and manner: Villon, Baudelaire, Corbière, Beardsley (ibid., p. 45); the French and English philosopher critics, Remy de Gourmont and Allen Upward, as well as Anglo-Saxon and Latin models in the poems of *Ripostes* themselves. Meanwhile the tradition of English verse was narrowing for Pound to little more than Browning, who by the late 1920s he saw as the lone English example after Landor of 'serious experimentation' (ibid., p. 33). Ford had insisted on the use of spoken rhythms and the standards of good prose in verse. The dramatic monologue undoubtedly assisted Pound in this aim, presenting a form capable of registering the ironies playing across spoken tone and overt statement. To this was soon added the lesson of the American Sinologist Ernest Fenollosa on the dynamics of the ideogram and the more technical lessons, learned from Mallarmé's 'Un Coup de Dés' (1897), on the importance of the spacing of the line, and from Théophile Gautier on the sculptured 'hardness' of verse form (Pound, 1960, pp. 285–6). In *Ripostes* (1912), *Cathay* (1915) and *Lustra* (1916) Pound was applying the knowledge of spoken forms, spacing, syntax and composition taken from this diverse but radically selective tradition. His watchwords were 'precision' and 'energy', but above all he was seeking a modernized form for modern content. The accomplished result, arguably, was *Hugh Selwyn Mauberley* (1920). But these were the years also of the early draft Cantos. In the original Canto 1 (as published in *Poetry*, June 1917) Pound staged a dialogue with Browning on exactly this question. Was Browning's youthful long poem *Sordello* (1840) a model for the modern epic? The Canto opened:

> Hang it all, there can be but one *Sordello*!
> But say I want to, say I take your whole bag of tricks,

> Let in your quirks and tweeks, and say the thing's an art-form,
> Your *Sordello*, and that the modern world
> Needs such a rag-bag to stuff all its thought in

For Canto II, as finally published, Pound cut this version's long colloquy to three opening lines. Browning, Pound's last Victorian, was edited out as he was absorbed into the more assured phrasing and heightened formal speech of Pound's modernism in the *Cantos*. The dialogue with the literary past, and the question Pound put to it at this point concerning modern epic form (a question Joyce and Eliot were also asking), would continue, however, to govern this project.

The intense subjectivity and introspection Arthur Symons detected in the nineteenth century also proved a continuing, if contradictory, feature in modernism. Its expression was influenced, like many ideas of the new century, by the French philosopher Henri Bergson. Bergson's formulation of experience as a continual flux importantly blurred the demarcation between the internal and the external realms, while his concept of 'duration' unstitched the conventionally separate categories of past, present and future. Eliot attended Bergson's lectures in Paris, and at Harvard worked on the thesis later published as *Knowledge and Experience in the Philosophy of F. H. Bradley* (1964). Bradley too was concerned with the relativity of experience, though when Eliot came to provide footnotes to *The Waste Land* he disclosed a darker side to this preoccupation with interiority. His note to line 411 of the poem makes characteristic reference to Dante's *Inferno*. However, the hellish mental condition of imprisonment – 'We think of the key, each in his prison / Thinking of the key, each confirms a prison' as the poem goes on – is further glossed by a quotation on the innate privacy of external sensations from Bradley's *Appearance and Reality*. In the contextual ambience of *The Waste Land*, with its dramatic clatter of voices, Bradley's relativism suggests confinement and disconnection: 'my experience falls within my own circle, a circle closed on the outside' (Eliot, 1974, p. 86). His conclusion that 'the whole world for each is peculiar and private to that soul' taps into the failure of communication and affection that pervades the poem; its nadir voiced in the blank confession: 'I can connect / Nothing with nothing.'

Bergson and Bradley aside, there is a further precursor to the treatment of inner and outer sensations with whom the recognized modernist poets were in a restless dialogue. Walter Pater's *The Renaissance* (1873) is a key document in any discussion of the breaks and continuities across the text of Victorian and modernist poetics. Pater's aestheticist doctrine is apparent from his 'Preface' where, anticipating some of the terms already of Eliot and Pound's 'impersonality', he posits a distanced contemplation which takes science as its model. The 'aesthetic critic', he writes, fulfils his function when he has 'disengaged' a 'special impression of beauty' and noted its virtue 'as a chemist notes some natural element' (Pater, 1986, p. xxx).

However, it was the 'Conclusion' to *The Renaissance* (in fact written five years before the rest of the volume) which proved profoundly influential. Pater's own anxiety over the impact of its discourse on 'sensation' upon impressionable young men (as, for example, upon Oscar Wilde's character Lord Henry Wotton in *The Picture of Dorian Gray*) led him to withdraw the 'Conclusion' from the second edition. It opens with an epigraph from Heraclitus upon the instability of things and seeks then to reconcile 'the splendour of our experience' with its 'awful brevity' (Pater, 1986, p. 152). Pater's answer was to cram the limited 'interval' between birth and death full of experience: 'For our one chance lies in expanding that interval, in getting as many pulsations as possible into the given time' (ibid.). We can detect here the germ of Joyce's notion of 'epiphany' and of Pound's early doctrine of the 'luminous detail' (Pound, 1973, p. 23), even of his definition of the image as presenting 'an intellectual and emotional complex in an instant of time' (Pound, 1960, p. 4). Once more, however, if Pound was at first attracted to the Nineties and an English aestheticism inspired by Pater, he was soon to distinguish his own emphasis on hardness and precision from the associative Symbolism he found in Yeats, and from Pater's 'impressionism'. Thus, in 1918, he could find 'beautiful bits' in Yeats's book of Noh plays, 'But it's all too damn soft. Like Pater . . . not good enough' (Paige, 1971, p. 137).

Such was the fluidity of ideas across these transitional decades, however, that traces persisted nonetheless. In one astonishing example, Pater anticipates the imagery of self-imprisonment Eliot employs, by way of Bradley, in *The Waste Land*. 'Experience', Pater writes,

> already reduced to a group of impressions, is ringed round for each one of us by that thick wall of personality through which no real voice has ever pierced on its way to us. . . . Every one of those impressions is the impression of the individual in his isolation, each mind keeping as a solitary prisoner its own dream of a world. (Pater, 1986, p. 151)

Eliot's early poetry is full of instances of neurotic isolation, blending the dramatic monologue's concern with the objectification of introspection and the *ennui* of the *fin de siècle* that Pater's work, however inadvertently, fostered. We find this combination in 'The Love Song of J. Alfred Prufrock', where the persona's *ennui* echoes the urban background whose 'Streets . . . follow like a tedious argument' (Eliot, 1974, p. 13). As in the dramatic monologue all the 'evidence' the reader is given has been filtered through the externalized consciousness of the speaker. This method came therefore to assist Eliot in the adaptation of Symbolist doctrine to his own 'poetics of impersonality'. The major statement of this theory was Eliot's 'Tradition and the Individual Talent' (1919). Aided by the scientific analogy of the poet as a 'catalyst', Eliot trounced the subjectivist and 'inexact' conventions of Romanticism. For all its confidence, however, the strict separation the essay makes between the poem and the life of sensations (between 'the mind which creates' and 'the man who suffers') risked an aestheticism Eliot otherwise eschewed. The problem was how to register the inner life of emotions in an 'impersonal' poetry. The solution Eliot discovered, in the essay 'Hamlet' published in the same year, was the notion of the 'objective correlative':

in other words, a set of objects, a situation, a chain of events which shall be the formula of that particular emotion; such that when the external facts, which must terminate in sensory experience, are given, the emotion is immediately evoked. (Eliot 1951, p. 145)

What is most interesting in Eliot's account, however, is that this formulation of an equivalence between emotion and object was occasioned by an example of its perceived failure. Eliot's essay, that is to say, concerns the *deficiency* of Shakespeare's play, since 'Hamlet (the man) is dominated by an emotion which is inexpressible, because it is in *excess* of the facts as they appear' (ibid.). This unresolved tension between control and excess appears elsewhere in Eliot (notably, in his view of Joyce's 'mythic method' in *Ulysses* as 'ordering . . . the futility and anarchy' of contemporary history; Kolocontroni, Goldman and Taxidou, 1998, p. 373) and underlies the exhausted struggle of male protagonists in the poems. Most frequently this emotion is that of disgust. Its general object might be the 'futility and anarchy' of modernity, but its focus is alarmingly often on women. This is most graphically the case in the poem 'Hysteria' which Rainer Emig reads, without apology 'in Freudian terms as a prototypical description of castration anxiety' (Emig, 1995, p. 71). Prufrock's disgust is emphasized by the exclamation mark that accompanies his realization that the statuesque beauty of female 'white and bare' arms is actually '(. . . in the lamplight, downed with light brown hair!)' (Eliot, 1974, p. 15); an emotion 'in excess of the facts' which is contained as soon as uttered by the closed parenthesis. Prufrock is 'not Prince Hamlet' but it is Hamlet, in Eliot's reading, who comes to serve as the extreme case of this type, bewildered by an 'excess' emotion for his mother, Queen Gertrude.

Decadent into Modern: The Poet in Society

The problem of 'excess' and of its related feminization derived, once more, from the cultivated artifice of the decadent 1890s. An example of modernist poetry's unsettled dialogue with this mode and idiom appeared in Ezra Pound's 'The Garden' from the collection *Lustra* (1916). The poem enacts the complex reactions of a male observer to the figure of a middle-class, even aristocratic, woman enclosed by the railings of Kensington Gardens, beyond which lurk 'the filthy, sturdy, unkillable infants of the very poor' (Pound, 1952, p. 93). As if to associate the poem with the tones of Decadence, the woman's boredom is described as 'exquisite and excessive'. As she is framed by the railings, so the poem is framed by an epigraph from Albert Samain's 1893 collection of poems *Au Jardin de L'Infante*. And in invoking this context it replays an archetypal scene in the emergence of modernism. Peter Nicholls traces this to Baudelaire's poem 'To a Red-haired Beggar Girl' ('A Une Mendiante Rousse'), a seemingly innocuous but founding instance of modernism's defensive tactics of irony and distance. Beneath the surface sense of identification between poet and beggar girl as sharing a parallel social fate, Nicholls senses a problematic inequality:

> For while the poet claims to abolish the distance between himself and the girl, he actually replaces it with another which is primarily aesthetic. . . . It is as if there are two voices at work in the poem: one which sympathizes with the girl and expresses admiration for her 'natural' charms, and another which simply takes her as an occasion for a poem. This second, more devious voice will force upon the reader the unsentimental and cruelly ironic recognition that in fact she is nothing without the artifice of his poem to commemorate her. They may be poor, but the gap between them is not one which the poet wishes to cross. (Nicholls, 1995, p. 2)

Pound's 'The Garden' is similarly entwined in a duplicitous poetics of voyeurism. Fifty years on, however, Baudelaire's heroic dandyism has undergone some changes. Baudelaire's poem is addressed, even in its title '*A Une Mendiante Rousse*' (our italics) to its subject. Pound's poem, written under the stricter ethos of modernist impersonality, is titled by location. In fact, it is the very poetics of impersonality that make it curiously a poem *about* location: where do we locate the speaking voice, and its sympathies, in the poem? Where is it positioned: within or outside the scene described? The garden itself, and its frustrated occupant, are enclosed by railings. It is tempting to read the situation as dramatizing Anglo-American modernist poetry's own ambiguous reading of tradition – most particularly of the immediate Victorian period and its Decadent close. Thus the garden surrounded by railings is a modernist counterpart to the Tennysonian castle surrounded by a moat; the figure inside a modern sister to the 'high-born maidens' of Tennyson's 'The Lady of Shalott', 'Mariana' and *Maud*. The poem seems itself to allude to such a lineage, for 'In her is the end of breeding' (Pound, 1952, p. 93): a description which productively oversignifies by presenting the woman ('the end') as both high point and last inheritor – 'dying piece-meal / of a sort of emotional anaemia'. Pound's irony is directed at the decadent cult of refinement and excess (and to an extent at his earlier self), the woman standing in for the aestheticist withdrawal from modern city life into the 'ivory tower' (the 'Garden') of art.

Thus the poem emerges as a commentary on poetry's autonomy and its relation to the modern world and on Pound's own involvement in these debates. The railings separate while they protect the woman from the ravages of modernity embodied by the 'infants of the very poor'. Despite their condition, these children are the opposite of the puny and enfeebled '*chétif*' Baudelaire identified with: they are 'sturdy' and 'unkillable' in contrast to their anaemic class superior. 'Unkillable' is characteristic of Pound's introduction of a jarringly non-poetic diction at key moments in his poems. The previous line has broken the pattern of starting each line with a strong stress, and playfully apes a Tennysonian sonorous balladry 'And round about there is a rabble'. The question for Pound, however, was what the contemporary poet's idiom and position should be compared with these earlier examples. Nicholls suggests Baudelaire's beggar girl, though 'sexy' and appealing, prompts the poet to create the ironic distance which is the foundation of this particular aesthetic. In submitting his desire to the discipline of irony, the poet thus achieves a contrasting *dis*embodiment (he is absent from his words and the text says the opposite of what it seems to say). (Nicholls, 1995, p. 3)

Pound's poem seems to represent this situation in reverse. Baudelaire's modernism lies in the construction of ironic distance out of overt desire. It contrasts with the social romanticism of Hugo, and draws upon the poet's vocation as 'outsider' and dandy. Pound may have dabbled with this last but he resisted the role of outsider, even though social attitudes had further marginalized the artist in the wake of the Wilde trial. His mission (like Eliot's) was to reclaim art's social function from the position of distance and superiority which it guaranteed. Such were the tensions of the modernist poetics of impersonality. It is this virtually impossible position that contributes to the speaker's ambivalence in 'The Garden'. The poem evades the question of which side of the fence ('the railing') the poet is on. Nicholls claims that Baudelaire submits his desire to the discipline of irony. In 'The Garden' Pound's irony submits to desire, or a knowingness about the dynamics of desire. The closing lines slowly dissolve the speaker's separateness in the simplicity of spoken syntax:

> She would like some one to speak to her,
> And is almost afraid that I
>   will commit that indiscretion.

Pound's garden has changed from the protective retreat of tradition to an enclosure emblematic of class stratification, the codes of caste and sexual encounter which the woman (as read by the observing male poet) wants but does not want to transgress. The final line-break is characteristically revealing. Its movement in from the left-hand margin enacts the weakening of detachment under the pressures of (male) desire, formally committing the indiscretion that social formality has rendered taboo. Its opening word 'will' indicates the likelihood that the desiring, indiscreet male poet will transgress social and poetic convention to approach the woman. Of course, by rendering the encounter this way, Pound both reaffirms the stereotype of the 'femme fatale' and conforms to the very decadence the poem means to reject. The woman's supposed 'fear' of indiscretion is a displacement of the impersonal poet's own anxieties: positioned outside the very world he would approach – seduce even – but which regularly rebuffs his advances.

The Doctrine of the Image, the Metropolis and Gender

The most commonly recognized moment of modernist poetry's arrival was the publication of three poems by 'H. D. Imagiste' (so named by Pound) in *Poetry* in January 1913. The key Imagist principles of economy, direct treatment and the use of musical or spoken rhythms were set out in a combined statement by F. S. Flint and Pound in the March number of that year, and the first collection *Des Imagistes*, edited by Pound and retaining his Frenchified label, followed in spring 1914. The dates seem definite enough, but like modernism as a whole Imagism proved a retrospective construction which in different accounts credited T. E. Hulme, Pound himself or H. D. as founding or exemplary figures. The term had first appeared in print in Pound's introduction to 'The Complete Poetical Works of T. E. Hulme', presented as a product of 'the "School of Images"' of 1909 in an appendix to Pound's *Ripostes* (1912), but its acknowledged models, in further evidence of the discovery cum invention of precursors, were Sappho, Catullus and Villon, certain contemporary French poets, and also for Pound, Dante, Cavalcanti, Lui Ch'e and Li Po (Rihaku) (Pound, 1960, pp. 7, 11, 27; 1970, pp. 82–3).

In these terms it made sense for Pound to praise H. D.'s classicism as the defining aspect of its modernism: 'It's straight talk, straight as the Greek!' he exclaimed to Harriet Monroe (Paige, 1971, p. 11). Pound's Hellenism was not necessarily H. D.'s however. Talk of 'straight talk', of the sculptural 'hardness' and 'crystalline' clarity of the Image confirmed the masculinist discourse of Pound's modernism. As Rachel Blau du Plessis (1986) has argued, H. D.'s Imagism had its roots in Sappho. Her poetry therefore reclaimed a female precursor whose work significantly survived only in fragments and whose erotic writing and associations with the island of Lesbos make her a force in undermining the cultural silence concerning female sexuality and lesbianism. For critics such as du Plessis – concerned at a later moment in literary and cultural history to reclaim H. D. herself – she is the premier Imagist and belongs at the centre of modernist poetry.

This gendered construction of events combined with more general socio-historical conditions to produce Imagist verse. As a social grouping, the Imagists were based in London, with outlets in the United States and occasional forays to Paris, and London as a burgeoning metropolis was experiencing 'the intensification of emotional life' which the sociologist Georg Simmel had attributed to 'the swift and continuous shift of external and internal stimuli' in the city. The telescoping of images, sharp differences 'grasped at a single glance' and 'violent stimuli' were consuming new amounts of energy, Simmel argued, as 'with every crossing of the street, with the tempo and multiplicity of economic, occupational and social life', the city was transforming 'the sensory foundations of mental life' (Kolocotroni, Goldman and Taxidou, 1998, p. 52).

One can see how such conditions fed into Pound's formulations of the Image and the Vortex (he spoke of 'new masses of unexplored facts and facts pouring into the vortex of London'; Pound, 1970, p. 117). His most famous Imagist poem, 'In a Station of the Metro' (importing Japanese Haiku into this complex), for example, seeks to capture precisely one such 'single glance' when a series of beautiful faces ascends from the Paris Metro. However, Simmel's reflections on the effects of the rush of stimuli in the metropolis present a further strand in the network of ideas contributing to modernism's cult of impersonality. The 'metropolitan type' reacts to this climate of overstimulation, says Simmel, by adopting a 'blasé outlook'. This 'psychic mood' entails 'an indifference toward the distinction between things' equivalent to the 'colourless and indifferent quality' of a money economy and comes in social relations to imply 'a slight aversion, a mutual strangeness and repulsion' (Kolocotroni, Goldman and Taxidou, 1998, p. 55). There are echoes here of Walter Benjamin's interest in the figure of the *flâneur* (and thus, once more, of Baudelaire and Poe) and of the related perception Benjamin discovers in Simmel of the heightened visuality of modern culture, including a markedly 'greater emphasis on the use of the eyes' in interpersonal relationships (Benjamin, 1973, p. 193).

Some of these threads are pulled together in Andrew Thacker's (1993) account, 'Imagist Travels in Modernist Space'. Thacker draws on Simmel and Benjamin, as well as on recent work in cultural geography, to consider 'early twentieth-century visual relations as experienced on transport' in relation to a set of Imagist poems concerned directly with the experience of the Underground system (ibid., p. 224). Thacker reminds us that 'In considering space we must also consider theories of the gaze, and of the gendered nature of the spatial relations of looking' (ibid., p. 225). He refers in this connection to what he calls 'the great *flâneur* debate' and the interventions especially of feminist critics on the issue of 'the availability or unavailability of city space for women from the nineteenth century onwards' (ibid., pp. 227–8). Elizabeth Wilson's argument is especially suggestive in relation to our discussion of Pound's 'The Garden' above. She sees the *flâneur* as 'actually a fiction':

> an embodiment of the special blend of excitement, tedium and horror aroused by many in the new metropolis, and the disintegrative effect of this on the masculine identity. . . . He is a . . . shifting projection of angst rather than a solid embodiment of male bourgeois power. (Thacker, 1993, p.228)

As Thacker comments, 'The "male gaze" of the *flâneur* is an anxious response to the presence, rather than the absence, of women in the modern city' (ibid.). Ultimately, this gaze represents the instability of the masculine in the new sexual, social and spatial relations of the modern metropolis. Pound's 'The Garden' registers exactly these sexual, social and urban spatial relations, even as it negotiates the influence of the decadent 1890s. The woman is 'objectified' much as Richard Aldington, sometime Imagist and in these years H. D.'s husband, had described in an article 'Modern Poetry and the Imagists' in *The Egoist* in 1914: 'we present that woman, we make an "image" of her' (Thacker, 1993, p. 238). Such a depiction and such a poem would possess 'hardness, as of cut stone', with 'No slop, no sentimentality'; Woman and Image alike might be 'nicely carved marble' (ibid., p. 238).

What did this reification which so evidently replicates the 'impersonality' of the new metropolis mean not only for the observed woman in the London street or park but for the woman Imagist poet? H. D.'s poem 'Helen' written just under a decade after Aldington's article seems to engage directly with such issues. The Helen of its title is the classical 'femme fatale' whose famed beauty has long been presented as the cause of the Trojan war. And yet the poem elects not to give a voice to Helen to speak a counter-history. Instead it takes the temperature of the nation's hatred for this woman who 'All Greece hates', 'all Greece reviles' (H. D. 1984, p. 154). The final stanza completes a macabre transformation: the mounting whiteness of Helen's skin signalling 'her death as a woman and her birth as a statue, a symbol of beauty' (Friedman, 1987, p. 235). Only as such a symbol of safe and lifeless beauty ('nicely carved marble') can Greece love Helen. What Friedman describes as a 'hate filled gaze' turns Helen to stone – even while the poem's sexualized rhyme of 'maid' and 'laid' undermines the final stanza's opening assertion that 'Greece sees, unmoved'. As in Pound's 'The Garden', and in the broader modernist aesthetic and metropolitan mentality it encodes, detachment emerges as a thinly disguised cocktail of desire, fear and disdain.

And yet, however modern, at base such a cocktail serves up the persistent Victorian image of woman: one part virgin or angel, one part whore or monster. Nicholls speculates that 'If the feminine seems a suitable surrogate for social relations in general it is because the illusion of some absolute otherness is required to protect the poet's self from the full recognition of identity with other people' (Nicholls, 1995, p. 4). He asks whether 'this grounding of the aesthetic in an objectification of the other' can be thought to 'constitute *the* recurring problem of the later modernisms?' (ibid., p. 4). The present survey of the intertextual, gendered and social relations marking the emergence of a dominant Anglo-American modernist poetic goes some way to confirm precisely how problematic this objectification of the other was. Partly, we have to conclude, because the attempt to make 'hard', 'exact' and scientific was an attempt to distance the other – effeminate decadence, impressionist sensation, softness, immaturity, 'excess' – which was so patently a formative part of the modernist self.

BIBLIOGRAPHY

Ackroyd, Peter (1984). *T. S. Eliot*. London: Hamish Hamilton.

Armstrong, Isobel (1993). *Victorian Poetry: Poetry, Poetics and Politics*. London: Routledge.

Benjamin, Walter (1973). *Illuminations*. Ed. Hannah Arendt. London: Fontana.

Du Plessis, Rachel Blau (1986). *H. D. The Career of That Struggle*. Brighton: Harvester.

Eliot, T. S. (1951). *Selected Essays*. London: Faber.

Eliot. T. S. (1965). *To Criticise the Critic*. London: Faber.

Eliot, T. S. (1974). *Collected Poems 1909–1962*. London: Faber.

Emig, Rainer (1995). *Modernism in Poetry: Motivations, Structures and Limits*. London: Longman.

Faas, Ekbert (1986). *Retreat into the Mind: Victorian Poetry and the Rise of Psychiatry*. Princeton, NJ: Princeton University Press.

Friedman, Susan Stanford (1987). *Psyche Reborn: The Emergence of H. D.* Bloomington: Indiana University Press.

Gibson, Mary Ellis (1995). *Epic Reinvented: Ezra Pound and the Victorians*. Ithaca, NY: Cornell University Press.

H. D. (1984). *Collected Poems*. Ed. Louis L. Martz. Manchester: Carcanet.

Kolocotroni, Vasiliki, Jane Goldman and Olga Taxidou (eds) (1998). *Modernism: An Anthology of Sources and Documents*. Edinburgh: Edinburgh University Press.

Nicholls, Peter (1995). *Modernisms: A Literary Guide*. London: Macmillan.

Paige, D. D. (ed.) (1971). *Selected Letters of Ezra Pound 1907–1941*. New York: New Directions.

Pater, Walter (1986). *The Renaissance: Studies in Art and Poetry*. Oxford: Oxford University Press.

Poe, Edgar Allan (1986) *The Fall of the House of Usher and Other Writings*. London: Penguin.

Pound, Ezra (1952). *Collected Shorter Poems*. London: Faber.

Pound, Ezra (1960). *Literary Essays of Ezra Pound*. London: Faber.

Pound, Ezra (1970). *A Memoir of Gaudier-Brzeska*. New York: New Directions.

Pound, Ezra (1973). *Selected Prose*. Edited with an introduction by William Cookson. London: Faber.

Smith, Stan (1994). *The Origins of Modernism: Eliot, Pound, Yeats and the Rhetorics of Renewal*. Hemel Hempstead: Harvester Wheatsheaf.

Thacker, Andrew (1993). 'Imagist travels in modernist space.' *Textual Practice*, 7: 2, 224–46.

Upward, Allen (1911). *The New Age* 8: 13, 297, 26 Jan.

Ward, Geoff (1993). *Statutes of Liberty: The New York School of Poets*. Houndmills: Macmillan.

Williams, William Carlos (1951). *The Autobiography of William Carlos Williams*. New York: Random House.

3

The Non-modernist Modern

David Goldie

F. R. Leavis began his epoch-defining book, *New Bearings in English Poetry* (1932), with the confident assertion that 'poetry matters little to the modern world'. Even allowing for Leavis's deliberate provocativeness and the subtlety of his subsequent argument this would seem, on the face of it, a little overstated. For Leavis was writing at a time in which poetry was experiencing a popularity that it will probably never exceed. The reasons for this popularity can be traced back to the First World War and to the needs of an educated, literate population, exposed to a print (though not yet a broadcast) mass media, for a language adequate to the unprecedented experiences of modern war. The sheer bulk of the outpourings of verse that appeared in newspapers, popular songs, and in the memorial volumes of the work of soldier poets, on commemorative cards and war memorials, that was spoken and sung in remembrance ceremonials, testifies to a widespread belief in the ritual and consolatory powers of poetry. To read the elegies of soldier poets like Edmund Blunden and Robert Graves for dead comrades, or the poems in Vera Brittain's *Testament of Youth* (1933), or those collected by Catherine Reilly in *Scars Upon My Heart: Women's Poetry and Verse of the First World War* (1981), is to experience and be moved not just by the poetry itself but by a recognition that poetry is the most appropriate and direct medium for the articulation of deep human feeling.

Virginia Woolf had her narrator in *To the Lighthouse* (1925) remark that, 'the war, people said, had revived their interest in poetry', and this can be seen in the sales of poetry books in the years after the war. Samuel Hynes has estimated that during the war some 3,000 volumes of poetry were published by 2,225 poets (Hynes, 1990, p. 29). Between the wars the first two Georgian anthologies would sell 34,000 copies, a figure topped by John Masefield's *Collected Poems* (1923) which would reportedly go on to sell some 200,000 copies (Ross, 1967, p. 128). But even these sales were put into the shade by Rupert Brooke, whose work had, in Britain alone, sold by 1923 some 300,000 volumes (Hassall, 1964, p. 528). Anthologies, too, continued to be popular: wartime anthologies like those of the Georgians and the Imagists, and the

Sitwells' *Wheels*, were followed after the war by J. C. Squire's two volumes of *Selections from Modern Poets* and Frank Sidgwick's *Poems of Today*, prompting Robert Graves and Laura Riding to issue a blast against the trend in their pamphlet *Against Anthologies* in 1928.

What Leavis was signalling, then, was not that there weren't enough people reading and writing poetry, but rather that there weren't enough people reading and writing the right kind of poetry. The existence of a large number of people for whom poetry mattered didn't in itself matter to Leavis because his project was an academic one in which quality was to be carefully isolated from quantity. The modernism (though he didn't use the word) that Leavis was asserting, and which the academy would broadly accept, was a literature that tended to articulate the experience of modernity not of the mass who were formed by it and who moved freely within it, but the singular individual who worked in despite of, and often in direct contradiction to that mass. For Leavis, it was not enough for modern poetry simply to move people, or otherwise engage a primarily emotional response; poetry must rather bring into play what he called the 'cerebral muscles' and integrate emotion with an undissociated play of poetic wit and intelligence. Leavis's thinking here can be seen retrospectively to form part of an identifiable modernist project, coming as it does out of T. S. Eliot's essays in *The Sacred Wood* (1920) and anticipating what Wallace Stevens in his poem 'Of Modern Poetry' (1942) would call 'the poem of the act of mind'. The experimental freedom licensed by this conception of modern poetry has, incontrovertibly, led to some of the finest poetry of the twentieth century. But it is not to criticize the project of modernism, or Leavis's impassioned advocacy of several of its practitioners, to notice what it left out; to see that it closed some doors as it opened others and that its strictures would lead to a critical neglect of poets and types of poetry that had a very good claim to think themselves modern.

The writers that will be discussed here were, for the most part, born at around the same time as the modernists – from the late 1870s to the early 1890s – and as a generation they shared with them, often very closely, a common diagnosis of contemporary poetry's ills. They perhaps showed more tolerance towards Housman, Hardy and Bridges, but otherwise shared with the modernists a recognition that English poetry had, in the late-Victorian and Edwardian years, turned into a rather overgrown and lush cul-de-sac. The Poet Laureate during their formative years was the dire Alfred Austin, arguably the least competent holder of that much maligned post. His poem 'Why England is Conservative' sums up in its title much that younger poets found disagreeable in his work and in the work of established poets like Henry Newbolt, Alfred Noyes, Stephen Phillips and William Watson, who seemed content to make poetry a conservative celebration of Imperial values. Here, for example, is William Watson praising an American poet for the directness and purity of his style:

> And so, though all the fops of style misuse
> Our great brave language – tricking out with beads
> This noble vesture that no frippery needs –

Help still to save, while Time around him strews
Old shards of empire, and much dust of creeds,
The honour and the glory of the muse.
('To an American Poet', 1907)

Most poets coming of age in the first two decades of the twentieth century would agree on the redundancy of his kind of verse, with its wearying generalizations about empires and creeds and honour and glory, its periphrases, its free use of personification and obvious metaphors, and its chronic ignorance of the ironies it generates in making such a baroque production out of a hymn to plainness.

For modernism, there were two complementary ways out of this: to strip poetry of what Richard Aldington called 'the cult of the decorated adjective', restoring to it a cadence and a vocabulary better suited to a direct presentation of its objects; and to re-examine the tradition creatively in an attempt to uncover poetic roots older and stronger than Victorian Romanticism onto which a modern poetry might be grafted. The first tendency is most clear in Imagism, in Pound's desire for a poetry that is 'austere, direct, free from emotional slither' and in T. E. Hulme's call for 'a period of dry, hard, classical verse'. The second is apparent in the researches of Eliot and Pound into, among others, Dante, the Metaphysicals, the Troubadours, and Eastern poetry that prompted Stephen Spender to categorize them as 'revolutionary traditionalists' (Spender, 1965, p. 222). The result of these complementary emphases, worked into forms that experiment boldly with rhyme, rhythm and the juxtaposition of images, is a poetry that offers a calculated challenge to the assumptions of Romanticism, and which is characterized by irony, precision, allusiveness and self-reflexiveness. These are the qualities that modernist writing foregrounds and which for Leavis are the markers of intelligence and modernity. But an examination of the work of a selection of non-modernist writers from this period suggests two things: that there are types of worthwhile modern poetry for which these qualities are only marginally appropriate; and that the qualities of irony, precision, allusiveness and reflexiveness which the modernists foreground can be found operating as subtly (if not always in the same combinations) in the work of their less celebrated peers.

John Masefield, to take the first example, is a poet who tends to be viewed as more of a relic of Edwardianism than a poetic modernizer. It may seem strange, then, that in the early years of the twentieth century Masefield (born the year before Wallace Stevens) was considered a disturbing radical for his advocacy of a new poetic realism. The editors of *The English Review*, the first publishers of his highly popular narrative poem *The Everlasting Mercy* (1911), declared themselves 'terrified' of the poem and saw in its 'oaths and curses, language to shock every drawing-room and literary *salon*'. Lord Alfred Douglas described it as 'nine-tenths sheer filth' and a terrible example of 'wicked licentiousness' (Spark, 1992, pp. 4–5). In view of the poem's rather mild evocations of rural debauchery and its ultimate affirmation of evangelical Christianity, this criticism might be seen as an example of that prim English insularity that was, contemporaneously, being so outraged by Nietzsche, Ibsen and almost anything

French. But to accept this wholly is to overlook the very real innovations that
Masefield was attempting in presenting unconventional poetic subjects in a realistic
manner. Without challenging metrical or rhyming forms, he was trying to produce
a dramatically charged narrative poetry which relied for the most part on what might
pass for real speech. His particular skill was in being able to accommodate this speech
in what was for the most part a regular verse scheme. An early section of the poem,
in which the protagonist, Saul Kane, confronts another poacher in a territorial dispute,
shows how far Masefield was prepared to push his experiment:

> He tells me 'Get to hell from there.
> This field is mine,' he says, 'by right;
> If you poach here, there'll be a fight.
> Out now,' he says, 'and leave your wire;
> It's mine.'
>   'It ain't.'
>   'You put.'
>   'You liar.'
> 'You closhy put.'
>   'You bloody liar.'
> 'This is my field.'
>   'This is my wire.'
> 'I'm ruler here.'
>   'You ain't.'
>   'I am.'
> 'I'll fight you for it.'
>   'Right, by damn.'

This verse, with its direct speech and frequent caesuras, might easily be re-transcribed
from its octosyllables into prose with little loss. It employs a metrical regularity, but
is successful at least as much for its dramatic and narrative qualities – a combination
that allows Masefield to discipline his poetry with the precision of novelistic reportage.
His experiments here can certainly be said to stand up well against Eliot's similar
attempts to incorporate direct speech into a poem like *The Waste Land* and in his
attempts to domesticate blank verse in his later plays.

One of the earliest strictures of modernism was that its poetry should work hard
to emulate the precision of prose: Ford Madox Ford famously called for a poetry that
'should be at least as well-written as prose', an axiom taken to heart by Ezra Pound
who prescribed, in addition, 'no book words, no periphrases, no inversions' (Jones,
1972, p. 141). At his best, Masefield came close to this, in putting popular poetry
back in touch with vernacular speech and applying a novelistic observation and structure to his narrative verse. The resulting directness can be seen in a stanza from the
long sea poem *Dauber* (1913):

> They stood there by the rail while the swift ship
> Tore on out of the tropics, straining her sheets,

> Whitening her trackway to a milky strip,
> Dim with green bubbles and twisted water-meets,
> Her clacking tackle tugged at pins and cleats,
> Her great sails bellied stiff, her great masts leaned:
> They watched how the seas struck and burst and greened.

This has all the exhilaration that one might hope for in narrative verse, and it is technically accomplished. Masefield adopts the rhyme-royal stanza of Chaucer's *Troilus and Criseyde* (later taken up by Auden in *Letter to Lord Byron*) and without giving up on its music still writes a poetry that carries the best qualities of descriptive prose. There is little of Watson's redundancy here, as even the most apparently poetic elements like the 'milky strip' offers, in conjunction with the descriptions of bubbles and turbulent water-meets, a precise and detailed description of the complex wake created by a ship under way. Similarly, Masefield observes closely the actual processes of sailing, the fact that masts lean under sail and that the sails themselves belly out stiffly rather than softly, and thus reinvigorates from observation what might otherwise be tired poetic metaphor.

Masefield would never be able to match Eliot's fine discrimination and psychological complexity, nor would he ever have anything like Stevens's exquisiteness. But, by way of compensation, poems like *Dauber* and *Reynard the Fox* (1919) have a capacity to grip and exhilarate the reader, to offer a persuasive account of physical action and thrill that is almost entirely absent in modernism. And where modernism tends to assert in form and content a deracinated individualism at odds with its social and political contexts, Masefield's poetry maintains a tolerant Chaucerian awareness of and integration in those contexts, making itself in its accessibility and its openness ultimately answerable to them. He was, as many commentators have noted, an uneven poet, writing too much and proving too susceptible to the importunate rhyme. But at its best his poetry offers a realism in subject matter and colloquialism in diction that, in its vitality and concern with social value, suggests that he is less conservative, and much more modern, than he is often portrayed.

This combination of social conscience and a realist technique was one that similarly concerned Rupert Brooke and the Georgians. Like many of the other contributors to the *Georgian Poetry* anthologies, Brooke was encouraged by the popular success of Masefield's realism, and by the continuing example of the poetry of Housman and Hardy, to attempt to put a little grit into the oyster of English poetry. The result was sometimes challenging and bold, in sonnets like 'Lust' or 'A Channel Passage', which combined a graphic descriptive style with an updated metaphysical playfulness reminiscent of Donne:

> The damned ship lurched and slithered. Quiet and quick
> My cold gorge rose; the long sea rolled; I knew
> I must think hard of something or be sick;
> And could think hard of only one thing – *you*

You, you alone could hold my fancy ever!
And with you memories come, sharp pain and dole.
Now there's a choice — heartache or tortured liver!
A sea-sick body, or a you-sick soul!
Do I forget you? Retchings twist and tie me,
Old meat, good meals, brown gobbets, up I throw.
Do I remember? Acrid return and slimy,
The sobs and slobber of a last year's woe.
And still the sick ship rolls. 'Tis hard, I tell ye,
To choose 'twixt love and nausea, heart and belly.

It could be argued that there are elements of an undergraduate prankishness here in the clever heartlessness of the piece. The realism might perhaps be little more than a shock tactic. But to view it in a more positive light, there might also be said to be a very modern self-consciousness in, for example, the deliberate incongruity of the juxtaposition of the poeticisms of 'woe' and 'sobs' with the more mundane 'slimy' and 'slobber' within a single short sentence. Equally, the final couplet which in another context might be viewed as simply bad, can perhaps rather be seen to be knowingly self-reflexive — playing with an acknowledged sense of its own weakness that can be compared to the earlier forced rhymes of *Don Juan* or to the later playful and thoroughly modern sophistication of Cole Porter or Lorenz Hart.

The use of an intelligent irony is a typical, though sometimes unrecognized characteristic of Brooke's verse. Those readers, for example, who celebrate the patriotic rusticism of 'The Old Vicarage, Grantchester' tend to forget that Brooke's original title for the poem was the much more equivocal 'The Sentimental Exile'. While this kind of irony is not a modernist quality as such, it is worth noting how much it contributes to the perceived modernism of a writer like Eliot. Eliot is frequently praised for reintroducing a quality of metaphysical intelligence, characteristic of Donne, in which wit and sensuality are playfully combined. But it is worth noting the extent to which Brooke pre-empted Eliot, both in his taking of Donne as a source and in recognizing the techniques by which a writer like Webster created a personal style. Brooke's 1916 work *John Webster and the Elizabethan Drama* showed the extent to which he appreciated 'the heaping-up of images and phrases', the agglutination of 'external fragments', by which Webster constructed a synthetic creative persona 'encrusted with a thousand orts and chips and fragments from the world around' (Lehmann, 1981, p. 74). Brooke had obviously come some way to grasping the principles of bricolage and montage that would serve Eliot and Pound so well. In choosing not to employ them, then, he made, we must believe, a conscious choice. He was not ignorant of modernism, but made an informed decision as to the suitable vehicle for his modern, ironic English voice. This is worth noting, if only because there are times when the modernist Eliot, exercising his ironic or dramatic faculties, sounds rather like the Georgian Brooke. Brooke's 'Heaven' and the poem Eliot adapted from Gautier, 'The Hippopotamus', might, for example, be seen to share a similar sensibility. Both poems use an anthropomorphized animal to guy organized Christianity, both enjoy wittily rhyming off incongruous pairs of words – Brooke's 'good' and 'mud' and Eliot's 'mud' and 'blood' – and both take a delight in introducing awkward, unpoetic words and grotesque images into their mock-solemn measures: Brooke's 'squamous, omnipotent, and kind' fish God feeding on 'paradisal grubs'; Eliot's hippo, who 'Betrays inflexions harsh and odd' as it rejoices 'at being one with God'.

Like Eliot, Brooke employs a sophisticated irony and a levity, derived in part from Metaphysical poetry, that offers an implicit challenge to Edwardian poetic convention. But where Eliot exhibits an outsider's willingness to think outside that box, to offer a radical alternative to meliorative Edwardian poetry, Brooke shows a characteristically Georgian reticence about taking his challenge too far. This is most obvious in the formal qualities of Georgian verse, and in particular its unwillingness to deviate far from accepted metrical and rhyming forms in its lyric poetry and from blank verse in its dramatic poetry. This is not, of course, in itself necessarily a bad thing, and there are some notably bold and successful experiments within conventional forms – in, for example, Walter de la Mare's presentation of chaotic direct speech in 'The Feckless Dinner Party' or the way in which in 'The Dove' he creates the effect of 'the languageless note of a dove' through the use of repeated long vowel sounds – but the principal impression that Georgianism tends to leave is that its acceptance of the formal straitjacket is a token of its acceptance of a larger poetic decorousness. The one Georgian contributor who can perhaps be absolved of this is D. H. Lawrence, but the way his indecorous *vers libre* sticks out as an exception only reinforces the general impression. For all that Brooke and Wilfrid Wilson Gibson might try to incorporate a political edge and a unsettling realism into their poetry, qualities that Gordon Bottomley and Lascelles Abercrombie extended into the occasional brutality of Georgian verse dramas like 'King Lear's Wife' and 'The End of the World', their writing as a group never seems to suggest that it is anything other than the work of 'advanced' but thoroughly decent chaps – of what John Middleton Murry called 'a fundamental right-mindedness' (Rogers, 1977, p. 233). What Kenneth Hopkins said of Walter de la Mare might be taken as a more general truth about Georgianism: that here are poets 'working within a conventional tradition whose genius is not for flamboyant disregard for the rules, but for triumphant conformity with them' (Hopkins, 1957, p. 31).

Abercrombie had, in the opening work of the first Georgian anthology, 'The Sale of St Thomas', had his St Thomas condemned and sold into slavery for the weakness not of fearfulness, but prudence: 'prudence is the deadly sin' he is told as he is taken into servitude. But it is prudence that too often mars Georgianism. What Abercrombie called the Georgians' 'determination to undertake new duties in the old style' (Rogers, 1977, p. 62), meant that they were, too often, lacking the ambition to attempt radical experiment, and thereby challenge an aesthetic of poetry, a sense of its beauty and music, that they still shared with Victorian Romanticism. Compare, for example, the prudence and tact of de la Mare's 'Miss Loo' or Gibson's 'Geraniums' with the probing boldness of Eliot's 'Portrait of a Lady' and 'Preludes': poems that deal with the ostensibly similar subjects of a young speaker-poet's relationship with an older woman and with the urban poor respectively. In these instances the Georgian poetic voice seems sentimental and evasive, introducing us to speakers who are less complex and less credible because they seem complacently free of the barbs of self-consciousness on which the speakers of Eliot's poems continually snag themselves. The Georgian speakers appear to be forced by the forms they employ into a polite reticence about their subjects that leaves those subjects both distanced and idealized, whereas Eliot's less decorous freedom with line-length and rhyme seems to allow his speaker to engage in a more trenchant examination, both of his subjects and his own motives in attempting to aestheticize them. De la Mare's Miss Loo remains obscure because the poet, perhaps out of tender respect, refuses to scrutinize her:

> And I am sitting, dull and shy,
> And she with gaze of vacancy,
> And large hands folded on the tray,
> Musing the afternoon away;
> Her satin bosom heaving slow
> With sighs that softly ebb and flow,
> And plain face in such dismay,
> It seems unkind to look her way.

Eliot spares his lady and his speaker no such delicacy. Both are brought to a complex and vivid life by the animating emotion of the speaker's self-mistrust. The scrutiny under which he puts his own mixed motives in cultivating this older, genteel woman is applied in an equally unsparing way to her own harmless self-dramatizations:

> Now that lilacs are in bloom
> She has a bowl of lilacs in her room
> And twists one in her finger while she talks.
> 'Ah, my friend, you do not know, you do not know
> What life is, you who hold it in your hands';
> (Slowly twisting the lilac stalks)
> 'You let it flow from you, you let it flow,
> And youth is cruel, and has no more remorse
> And smiles at situations which it cannot see.'
> I smile, of course,
> And go on drinking tea.

This is the kind of flexing of cerebral muscles of which Leavis approved: the construction of psychological depth through the employment of an ironic, experimentally inclined poetic intelligence; the example of an intelligence wedded to a poetic sensibility that can devour all kinds of experience, and not just those susceptible to what the modernist would see as the orotund heartiness of the Edwardians or the empirical timidity of the Georgians. But while there might be general agreement with Leavis in this particular instance, there are other writers who bypassed Georgian limitations in other ways and proved able to create a viable modern, but not necessarily modernist, poetry: among these are Robert Frost, Edward Thomas, Wilfred Owen, Isaac Rosenberg and Edna St Vincent Millay.

Frost (like Pound) came close to being included in one of the Georgian anthologies. In the case of Frost it's perhaps easier to see why this might be, for his work shares with Georgianism a preoccupation with rural life and ordinary speech. The Georgians, as we have seen, strained hard to create an effect of everyday speech within the patterns of rhyme and metre that they seemed contented to accept. Rather like their elder contemporary, Masefield, they had difficulty in avoiding occasional poeticisms of diction and form, which tended to give their countryside a slightly inauthentic air, making it seem a kind of slightly soiled weekender's pastoral. Frost's poetry avoided this: partly because he had experience as a working farmer, partly because the American tradition from which he sprang tended to make fewer assumptions about nature's beneficence than the English tradition, but more especially because he had consciously developed a technique which enabled a direct and forceful diction. This technique began in his belief that it was the sentence that ought to be taken as the basic measure of poetry. 'The living part of a poem', he wrote, 'is the intonation entangled somehow in the syntax idiom and meaning of a sentence' (Thompson, 1965, p. 107). It is this basic unit of the sentence, couched in the rhythm of normal speech that Frost called the 'sound of sense' and then stretched over the frame of a basic iambic verse, that gives Frost's poetry its characteristic sense of discursive range and freedom. It is not quite the freedom of *vers libre* – which Frost would later compare to playing tennis with the net down – but is rather a play that comes from the tension between the rhythm of the sentence and the metre of the poetic line. It is, as Frost put it, the getting of 'cadences by skillfully breaking the sounds of sense with all their irregularity of accent across the regular beat of the metre' (ibid., p. 80). The uses to which this can be put might be seen in lines from 'Birches':

> He always kept his poise
> To the top branches, climbing carefully
> With the same pains you use to fill a cup
> Up to the brim, and even above the brim.
> Then he flung outward, feet first, with a swish,
> Kicking his way down through the air to the ground.
> So was I once myself a swinger of birches.
> And so I dream of going back to be.

This is fascinating for its playful assonance and inventive central metaphor alone, but if we look at the verse form we can see the way the idiomatic syntax complements the blank verse. In the fourth line here, the additional syllable ('above' rather than a monosyllable like 'past') reinforces the idea of a brimming over, and in the next line the use of two spondees (two spread feet) to mimic the attitude of the boy jumping are flashes of crafted wit. Frost might easily have rendered the next two lines more regularly, too, but imagine what would be lost by having the sixth line read 'Kicking his way through the air to the ground' or the line after read 'So was I once a swinger of birches.' In the first instance, the additional word 'down' alters the cadence of the line and gives the effect of making the jump appear longer, and hints at that momentary illusion of suspension in space during a fall. It also reminds us, in the assonance of 'down' and 'ground', of the paradoxical relationship on which the poem insists between the tip of the tree and the earth down to which it will grow after it is bent by the jump. Similarly, in the following line the apparently idiomatic tautology of 'I once myself' alters the cadence of the line to create a swinging between sibilants in a triple metre that gives a new vigour to the image of a boy swinging on the birches.

It is this cadence that perhaps makes Frost's work seem less pat than the poetry of the Georgians, and therefore a more apt medium for the colloquial and meditative voice. The result is a poetry that artfully manages at once to be both formally sophisticated and apparently unliterary. The sophistication can be found in both the form and the content, for when he wants to be Frost can be as allusive as Eliot or Pound. However, when he alludes, say, to Dante's *selva* or *stella* in his New England woods and stars, or when he is recreating Virgilian eclogues in the contemporary Yankee pastoral of *North of Boston*, he is careful to ensure that these sources are fully digested: they are not employed to draw attention to the brittle self-consciousness of a cultured speaker but are rather the means by which a rich, textured voice is given to a persisting modern culture embedded in its natural environment.

This quality of voice is one that Frost shares with the writer whom he helped encourage into poetry, Edward Thomas. Thomas followed the example of Frost's freedom with blank verse, writing a poetry that seems to be governed more by the cadence of its phrasing, its hesitations and qualifications, than the measured march of iambic feet. But where Frost's speakers, troubled though they sometimes are, tend ultimately to be reconciled with the folk or cultural wisdom they articulate, Thomas's speakers characteristically express a more equivocal relationship between the individual and his rural and cultural context. A flavour of this can be found in the final two stanzas of 'Old Man', in which the speaker describes the effect on him of the herb commonly called by that name:

> As for myself,
> Where first I met the bitter scent is lost.
> I, too, often shrivel the grey shreds,
> Sniff them and think again and sniff again and try
> Once more to think what it is I am remembering,
> Always in vain. I cannot like the scent,
> Yet I would rather give up others more sweet,
> With no meaning, than this bitter one.
>
> I have mislaid the key. I sniff the spray
> And think of nothing; I see and hear nothing;

> Yet seem, too, to be listening, lying in wait
> For what I should, yet never can, remember:
> No garden appears, no path, no hoar-green bush
> Of Lad's-love, or Old Man, no child beside,
> Neither father nor mother, nor any playmate;
> Only an avenue, dark, nameless, without end.

As well as seeing the freedom with the iambic line here, it is worth noting the tacit repudiation of Wordsworthian romanticism. Wordsworth, one thinks, would never express in this way the loss of the childhood key to the sensation engendered by the Old Man (the first two lines of the second stanza might rather, perhaps, be mistaken for the Eliot of *The Waste Land*). More especially, though, where Thomas parts with Wordsworth, and perhaps comes much closer to Eliot, is in the sense his poetry gives of what Andrew Motion has called 'a mind actually engaged in the act of thinking, rather than offering its concluded thoughts' (Motion, 1980, p. 82). Whereas a Wordsworthian poetry – and within this can be included much of Georgianism – gains a consistency and a satisfying unity from its sense of the tranquil recollection of emotion, Thomas's poetry looks edgy and equivocal because of what would appear to be this unresolved tension between its phrasing and its poetic form, and its emphasis on the processes of thought rather than its final forms. It is this sense of irresolution, this lack of formal and thematic closure and the ability to turn romantic and conventional poetic tropes reflexively back upon themselves, that makes Thomas's poetry seem so subtly disturbing and so modern.

This is perhaps similar to the kind of corrupted romanticism that can be found in Wilfred Owen's poetry. In 'Strange Meeting' Owen reworks a romantic situation and diction (in this case the models are Canto V of Shelley's 'The Revolt of Islam' and the beginning of Keats's 'Hyperion') in order to create (using the terms he employed in his unpublished prefatory statement) a poetry of pity but not consolation. Owen makes a qualified refusal of several of the consolations of romanticism – most notably trust in the natural – and signals this formally in his corresponding refusal of the satisfaction of full, rounded rhymes. The half-rhymes he employs chime, but they chime uneasily, throwing a discord into the formal Georgian harmony. In 'Strange Meeting' this is especially pertinent, as the half-rhymes reinforce the uneasy symmetry of the relationship between the speaker and the dead enemy with whom he shares a dialogue: the man he has killed as the other but whom he now begins to identify obscurely as a brother:

> 'Strange friend,' I said, 'here is no cause to mourn.'
> 'None,' said the other, 'save the undone years,
> The hopelessness. Whatever hope is yours,
> Was my life also; I went hunting wild
> After the wildest beauty in the world,
> Which lies not calm in eyes, or braided hair,
> But mocks the steady running of the hour,

And if it grieves, grieves richlier than here.
For by my glee might many men have laughed,
And of my weeping something had been left,
Which must die now. I mean the truth untold,
The pity of war, the pity war distilled.

The sense that Owen's work gives of a poetic form bending, but not breaking, in order to accommodate a discomforting modernity is one that is shared by two other interesting modern poets who have evaded the modernist categorization. The work of the first, Isaac Rosenberg, exhibits in its experiments with free verse in a poem like 'Louse Hunting' or with the sprung rhythm of the variably stressed lines of 'Dead Man's Dump' another way in which the directness is achieved for which the Georgians strove and from which their formal tentativeness held them back. A stanza from 'Dead Man's Dump' shows the freedom in diction that this allows:

A man's brains splattered on
A stretcher-bearer's face:
His shook shoulders slipped their load,
But when they bent to look again
The drowning soul was sunk too deep
For human tenderness.

While this might in itself be calculated to shock, Rosenberg's poetry like Owen's does more than simply assert an attitude or an anger about the absurdity of war — something that is characteristic of the more limited Sassoon. Rather, these two poets balance in an even, discursive tone a compassionate romantic lyricism against a horror that is overt and realistically portrayed, and in so doing present a complex human solidarity of which the fragmenting solipsism of modernism characteristically despairs.

This way of reinvigorating romantic modes by applying a complex irony is subtly different from most Georgianism. It is not merely to put modern wine into antique bottles, but is rather a way of modernizing romantic impulses and forms while at the same time acknowledging the difficulty of doing this in the present: adding a crucial element of formal self-consciousness to the Georgian mix. It is analogous to the ironic reworking of conventional forms through which Edna St Vincent Millay expressed a forceful and original modernity. Millay's occasional ventures into *vers libre* allowed her a great freedom with metaphor, as when in 'Spring' she tells us 'April / Comes like an idiot, babbling and strewing flowers'. Her most consistent achievement, though, is in her reworking of the sonnet. This doesn't so much involve formal innovation as a play against the conventional expectations created by the form. What Millay particularly excels at is stripping away the conventional language of romance to reveal the pragmatic sexual opportunism and the occasional desperation that underlie it. This is not in itself new, as the sonnet has always entertained an element of this self-consciousness about the uses to which it puts its artifice. What is particularly modern is that the underlying cynicism comes from the traditional object of the sonnet, the woman. In particular, we see in Millay's speakers a kind of precursor of the strong modern female of cinematic screwball comedy: by turns shrewd and tender, but well able to play and beat the men at their own game. This character can be seen in sonnets like 'I, being born a woman and distressed', or 'I shall forget you presently', in which she puts a characteristically modern spin on the *carpe diem* theme:

> I shall forget you presently, my dear,
> So make the most of this, your little day,
> Your little month, your little half a year,
> Ere I forget, or die, or move away,
> And we are done forever; by and by
> I shall forget you, as I said, but now,
> If you entreat me with your loveliest lie
> I will protest you with my favourite vow.

This is typical in the way that it contrasts the traditional hyperbole of the theme with a deflating colloquialism – 'your little half a year', 'my favourite vow'. Millay can be allusive too, but her allusions are often wittily revaluative in ways that can make more orthodox modernism seem ponderous. In the short poem 'Daphne', for example, she turns the conventional relationship between Daphne and Apollo on its head, making Daphne a modern woman fully in control of her predicament. Daphne opens the poem by querulously demanding of Apollo (and perhaps the reader) 'Why do you follow me?' when, as she points out, 'Any moment I can be / Nothing but a laurel-tree'. However, if her chastened god is content to continue in his folly, she shows willing to lead him in it: 'Yet if over hill and hollow / Still it is your will to follow, / I am off; – to heel, Apollo!' The revaluative irreverence is especially remarkable if it is compared to the use Eliot makes of another tale from Ovid, the rape of Philomela, in *The Waste Land* or the use to which Yeats puts the Leda myth in 'Leda and the Swan'. These two poets are content to repeat and unreflexively exploit an aggressive male fantasy, while Millay spiritedly makes it new with a recognizably modern attitude.

Leavis was undoubtedly right to suggest that modernist poets like Eliot and Pound offered a remedy for the debilitations of Edwardian poetry. But it is to take too narrow a view of the period of modernism to see the modernist experiment as the only cure. The poets discussed here tended to prefer evolution to revolution, but that is not to say they were less radical or somehow less true to modernity. In conceiving of Poetry as a single discipline desperately in need of modernizing, Leavis was willingly pursuing a modernist polemic. It was the means by which Eliot and Pound, as much in their prose as their poetry, effected an astonishingly swift change in the cultural reception of poetry. But for all its power in the shaping of poetic taste and academic opinion, this singular idea of Poetry should perhaps itself be revalued. We might then be better able to appreciate the range of practices, the poetries rather than the Poetry, in which early twentieth-century writers sought to explore the conditions of their modern world.

Bibliography

Brodsky, Joseph, Seamus Heaney and Derek Walcott (1997). *Homage to Robert Frost*. London: Faber & Faber.

Hassall, Christopher (1964). *Rupert Brooke: A Biography*. London: Faber & Faber.

Hobsbaum, Philip (1979). *Tradition and Experiment in English Poetry*. London: Macmillan.

Hopkins, Kenneth (1957). *Walter de la Mare*. London: Longmans, Green.

Hynes, Samuel (1990). *A War Imagined: The First World War and English Culture*. London: Bodley Head.

Jones, Peter (ed.) (1972). *Imagist Poetry*. Harmondsworth: Penguin.

Leavis, F. R. (1972). *New Bearings in English Poetry*. Harmondsworth: Penguin.

Lehmann, John (1981). *Rupert Brooke: His Life and Legend*. London: Quartet.

Lucas, John (1986). *Modern English Poetry: From Hardy to Hughes*. London: Batsford.

Martin, Graham and P. N. Furbank (eds) (1975). *Twentieth Century Poetry: Critical Essays and Documents*. Milton Keynes: Open University Press.

Motion, Andrew (1980). *The Poetry of Edward Thomas*. London: Routledge & Kegan Paul.

Parker, Rennie (1999). *The Georgian Poets: Abercrombie, Brooke, Drinkwater, Gibson and Thomas*. Plymouth: Northcote House.

Pritchard, William H. (1984). *Frost: A Literary Life Reconsidered*. Oxford: Oxford University Press.

Reeves, James (ed.) (1962). *Georgian Poetry*. Harmondsworth: Penguin.

Rogers, Timothy (ed.) (1977). *Georgian Poetry 1911–1922: The Critical Heritage*. London: Routledge & Kegan Paul.

Ross, Robert H. (1967). *The Georgian Revolt: The Rise and Fall of a Poetic Ideal 1910–22*. London: Faber & Faber.

Sisson, C. H. (1981). *English Poetry 1900–1950*. Manchester: Carcanet.

Smith, Constance Babington (1978). *John Masefield: A Life*. Oxford: Oxford University Press.

Smith, Stan (1986). *Edward Thomas*. London: Faber & Faber.

Spark, Muriel (1992). *John Masefield*. London: Pimlico.

Spender, Stephen (1965). *The Struggle of the Modern*. Berkeley: University of California Press.

Stead, C. K. (1975). *The New Poetic: Yeats to Eliot*. London: Hutchinson.

Thomas, R. George (1985). *Edward Thomas: A Portrait*. Oxford: Clarendon Press.

Thompson, Lawrance (ed.) (1965). *Selected Letters of Robert Frost*. London: Jonathan Cape.

Williams, John (1987). *Twentieth-Century British Poetry: A Critical Introduction*. London: Edward Arnold.

Woolf, Virginia (1992). *To the Lighthouse*. Harmondsworth: Penguin.

4

Poetry and Politics

Reed Way Dasenbrock

In this essay I have taken on a potentially infinite task. Today most critics and theorists hold that the connection between poetry and politics is not limited just to situations in which poets become politically involved in an explicit way, but instead all cultural expression is related to the social and political context – whether implicitly or explicitly – in which it is produced. In this expansive definition all poetry is political in one way or another, since even the choice to eschew explicit political involvement or references constitutes a form of political action (or perhaps more precisely inaction). To write an essay on the relation between poetry and politics in the twentieth century would in this view require discussing all poetry written in the century and virtually everything of political significance which occurred in the twentieth century. This is of course a tall order indeed.

Let me set your mind at ease immediately: such an expansive discussion – whatever its merits or demerits – is obviously impossible within the limits set for me here. In any case, the gesture of making everything political effaces a crucial distinction, perhaps not between the political and the non-political (since that depends on a notion of the aesthetic critiqued by those who hold this more expansive notion), but at the very least between the intentionally political and the intentionally non-political. In other words, some poets have aspired to write political poetry, have aspired to make a difference in the politics of their place and time. Clearly, these poets have not worked with a theory that all poetry was political, and they believed that the poetry they rejected or at least chose for the moment not to write wasn't political in the sense that the poetry they wished to write was. This distinction – whatever we might think of its ultimate validity – is an important one to understand and recognize if we wish to understand the poetry which follows from this distinction. However, this does not create a Maginot Line between poets of a political persuasion and poets of a non-political persuasion, since the same poet can in the course of his or her career adopt different stances towards this issue. For instance, William Butler Yeats expressed the argument for the ultimate irrelevance of politics with wonderful succinctness in the opening lines of his 1937 poem, 'Politics':

> How can I, that girl standing there,
> My attention fix
> On Roman or on Russian
> Or on Spanish politics?

Yet Yeats is the central example of a twentieth-century poet whose life and work were caught up in political events from the very beginning. If politics didn't fix his attention when he wrote this poem, it did fix his attention elsewhere in many of his most important poems.

In this essay I plan to cover a few of the more significant moments in twentieth-century poetry in English in which the history of poetry and the history of society have intersected in this narrower sense and in which poets sought to have an effect on political events. Percy Bysshe Shelley, in a quotation which in some senses anticipates the contemporary view, stated famously that 'poets are the unacknowledged legislators of the world'. By this, he meant something close to Ezra Pound's equally epigrammatic dictum, 'poets are the antennae of the race', that poets are somehow ahead of society in anticipating new modes of perception, new social arrangements, and ultimately new political arrangements. These views are crystallized in the metaphor of the avant-garde, that artists somehow are like soldiers in advance of the mass of the army, a metaphor which has become so familiar to us that we largely forget that it is a metaphor borrowed from the unfamiliar world of military tactics and theory.

But Shelley's phrase begs an important question, which is whether the unacknowledged character of poets' legislative status is inevitable or something to be overcome. Would poetry or society be better off if poets were widely acknowledged as carriers of a special vision, as legislators of a peculiar because unrepresentative variety? There are two different questions here, I would judge: one whether it would be good for poetry to have a more explicit acknowledgement of its influence on society and the second whether it would be good for society to recognize this influence.

One of the central aesthetic principles and themes of the Irish Renaissance is captured in Oscar Wilde's maxim, 'life imitates art'. A broad spectrum of nineteenth-century thinking, from English liberalism to Marxism, felt rather decidedly that the opposite was true, that art should realistically reflect the society around it, that to use the Marxian terms the cultural superstructures should (and do) reflect the economic base. Marx believed that the 'mode of production in material life determines the social, political and intellectual life processes in general. It is not the consciousness of men that determines their being, but, on the contrary, their social being that determines their consciousness' (preface to *A Contribution to the Critique of Political Economy*, 1859). If you agree with Marx that our social condition determines our being, not vice versa, then art and the imagination take on a distinctly secondary importance in society, since it leaves only a passive role – simply the task of recording – for art, for culture and for the imagination. But this view doesn't make very much sense of Irish history, which for good or for ill is full of attempts by men to determine their social being by their consciousness, to reshape the world according to their dreams about it.

Yeats was fond of quoting Berkeley's response to Locke, 'We Irish think otherwise'. Just as Berkeley reversed the earlier English empiricism of Locke, so the modern Irish writers wrought a comparable reversal of English economism, rejecting the notion that art is to be valued primarily as an imitation of life. It is not just that Irish history is full of people who did believe otherwise and acted on their beliefs; it is also that reflecting on the way life imitates art is a central theme in modern Irish literature. This can be seen in any number of ways: in the calculated verbal extravagance of Irish drama from Wilde and Shaw through Synge and O'Casey, in the extended flights of fancy of James Stephens, Flann O'Brien and many others, and throughout the work of James Joyce, especially *Ulysses*. But of all the Irish it is Yeats who meditated most profoundly on the complex relationship of art and life, not just in the poems on which we will concentrate but also in his drama, most clearly in *The King's Threshold*:

> I said the poets hung
> Images of the life that was in Eden
> About the child-bed of the world, that it,
> Looking upon those images, might bear
> Triumphant children.
> (*Collected Plays* 111–12)

This passage announces a central – perhaps *the* central – theme of Yeats's final poems. According to 'The Statues', it was the forms of Phidias the sculptor – not the Greek galleys – that 'put down / All Asiatic vague immensities, / And not the banks of oars that swam upon / The many-headed foam at Salamis'.

Elsewhere, in 'The Long-Legged Fly' and more memorably in 'Under Ben Bulben', we learn that the purpose of Michelangelo's Adam on the Sistine Chapel ceiling is to

> disturb globe-trotting Madam
> Till her bowels are in heat,
> Proof that there's a purpose set
> Before the secret working mind:
> Profane perfection of mankind.

One of the things to be realized here is just how far we are (and Yeats has come) from Yeats's favourite phrase from Villiers de l'Isle Adam's play *Axel's Castle*, 'As for living, our servants will do that for us'. Rather than any sense of art being removed from life, as in the aestheticism of Yeats's early career, art is to be valued precisely for its power to form life. Moreover, life, in this view, gains a good deal from this imitation of art, at least of the right kind of art:

> Poet and sculptor, do the work,
> Nor let the modish painter shirk
> What his great forefathers did,
> Bring the soul of man to God,
> Make him fill the cradles right.
>
> Measurement began our might:
> Forms a stark Egyptian thought,
> Forms that gentler Phidias wrought.

Here, in 'Under Ben Bulben', Yeats takes the prevailing metaphor about life imitating art and takes it quite literally: look at good art and you'll have better looking babies.

This is typical of Yeats at his most extravagant, in that he pushes a good point to its totally illogical but wonderfully memorable extreme. But we don't have to accept his extreme position to take his point: what do we see art for? If we see it but do not let it influence us, it is sterile and we aren't really seeing it. Art exists for its use, for the effect it will have on life. Yeats here is also commenting on how he wants his art to be taken:

> Irish poets, learn your trade,
> Sing whatever is well made, . . .
> Cast your minds on other days
> That we in coming days may be
> Still the indomitable Irishry.

Life imitates art, so it should imitate the best art it can find: implicitly here, Yeats's own poetry. The message here is essentially not to take Yeats's words as aesthetic objects to be valued for their isolated beauty, but rather to take them as forms to be imitated, as forms to form the future around.

For Yeats, all of this seemingly abstract aesthetic speculation has a direct relationship to politics. For if life should imitate art, then political life should as well or even especially. Moreover, it is largely by way of reflecting about the connection between art and politics, specifically between his art and Irish politics, that Yeats develops the themes we have just been exploring. These reflections come late in Yeats's life, in poems such as 'The Man and the Echo' and 'The Statues'. The key line from 'The Man and the Echo' is of course the famous one, 'Did that play of mine send out / Certain men the English shot?' That play is *Cathleen Ni Houlihan*, Yeats's 1902 play that with Maud Gonne in the title role was a powerful and influential piece of nationalist propaganda, and the certain men the English shot are of course the Easter 1916 rebels, Padraic Pearse and others. So Yeats is asking if – or is he obliquely telling us that –

the 1916 rebels were so moved by Yeats's art, specifically by the portrayal of revolutionary heroism in *Cathleen Ni Houlihan*, that they went out and imitated that art in life. Elsewhere, in 'The Statues', he refers to the same complex of events less egocentrically and probably more acceptably: 'When Pearse summoned Cuchulain to his side, / What stalked through the Post Office?' Pearse was himself a poet, of course, though hardly one of Yeats's calibre, and he and some of the other 1916 rebels made a virtual cult of Cuchulain, inspired in their revolutionary dreams by Cuchulain's energy and warlike nature. Here was a Celt who did not always go forth to battle and fall; here was a figure to be imitated by anyone wishing a resurgent Ireland. But here is also another example of life imitating art: what Pearse knew of Cuchulain came from the *Táin* and, more immediately, through Yeats's plays and the translations of Lady Gregory and others.

Yeats's question in 'The Statues' is both perfectly serious and quite precise: what stalked through the Post Office to help the 1916 rebels in their doomed stand in the Dublin PO? Yeats does not ask, 'did something stalk?', for he is perfectly sure that something did. Cuchulain was a real presence for Pearse, real in the sense that Pearse accomplished more in imitation of the story of Cuchulain than he ever could have on his own without the story to guide his actions. Life did imitate art here, and it seems to be Yeats's contention that life was the better for it. This moment is one Yeats wants to celebrate and pass on to us. This passage appears in the same poem as the claim that Phidias was more important than the galleys at Salamis, and the connection Yeats is drawing should be crystal clear: Pearse summoning Cuchulain to his side is juxtaposed with and clearly to be compared to this seminal event in Western civilization. The 1916 rebellion, I take it, is comparable to the defeat of the Persians at Salamis, the birth of a nation through the defeat of an Empire. But the implicit parallel also suggests that as Phidias's work in defining the ideal forms of Greek civilization was more important than Salamis, so too Yeats's work in defining the forms of the Irish Renaissance was more important than the Easter Rebellion.

The Irish Revolution and the cultural revival which preceded it constituted the first important moment in the twentieth century in which poetry and politics are in significant relation and in which the work of a great poet responds to and actively shapes important political events. For after one cuts through some of the self-absorption in Yeats's poems, one does have to concede that in crucial respects Yeats was right. No material, economic or political facts about the relation between the British Empire and Ireland made the success of the Irish Revolution probable or even conceivable. The political struggle of 1916 to 1923 which won Ireland independence was unthinkable without the cultural revival which came before. In this respect, these poets were legislators of this particular world, nor were they entirely unacknowledged: when one walks into the Dublin Post Office today, there is a statue of Cuchulain. Life imitated art, and now on a smaller scale life is imitating art about how life imitated art.

This story – in which a group of cultural nationalists recover folk-cultural traditions, repudiate metropolitan norms of the Empire in which they live, produce nationalistically inspired work and help create a sense of national identity which helps create a nation-state – is not unique. The map of Europe carved at Versailles, Woodrow Wilson's Europe, was full of new countries made up of nations who had had a linguistic and cultural but no political existence for centuries, if not forever. As the Russian, Austro-Hungarian and Ottoman Empires collapsed, nations became nation-states and Poland, Finland, Latvia, Estonia et al. re-emerged or emerged for the first time from the ashes. There are many comparisons to be drawn between the Irish Literary Revival and developments in these countries in the late nineteenth and early twentieth centuries, though of course in other countries other forms of artistic expression such as music or painting took the pride of place assigned to literature in Ireland. Yet Ireland is unique in one crucial respect: the other states created in Europe after 1918 had viable national languages to return to. Despite some fascinating counter-examples (Kafka and Rilke above all), for the most part the importance of the former imperial languages quickly receded, and the rich cultural life of these new nations took place in their native languages, newly restored to a governmental as well as cultural role.

The English, always more efficient in these matters than anyone else (in a way which renders the generally more favourable impression of British Imperialism all the more incomprehensible), had virtually eradicated Irish as a spoken language in Ireland. This meant that the Irish literature which created the Irish Renaissance was written in English and Irish was not – despite great efforts which continue today – restored as the actual functional national language. This has had crucial if unforeseen consequences for all of literature in English: even if the Irish of the Literary Revival considered themselves primarily writing to an Irish audience, they weren't read exclusively or even primarily by themselves. They wrote in the emerging world language of English, by now the official language of countries located on every inhabited continent, spread around the globe in the first instance by the very Imperial power they opposed in their work. There are long-term consequences here we will consider at the end of this essay, but the short-term consequence was that the Irish literature of the early twentieth century – as the most powerful and influential body of writing in English – became central to the movement we now know as modernism.

One reason why this matters is that Anglo-American modernism is the second key moment in the literary history of the twentieth century when poetry and politics intersect fatefully. But this is an intersection which is considerably more troubling than the link between the Irish Literary Revival and the Irish Revolution. At once one of the best-known and yet least understood facts about modernist literature in English is that many of the major modernist writers displayed considerable sympathy – even support – for fascism. Just to review the major cases: Yeats, well after the period of the Irish Revolution, supported the closest thing Ireland ever had to a fascist movement, O'Duffy's Blue Shirts, and though Yeats, too, died before the war, in 1939, some of his final poems and prose works seem to welcome a Nazi victory and in their support of eugenics are unpleasantly close to Nazi thought in some crucial respects. D. H. Lawrence's poetry, fiction and essays after the war are consistently antidemocratic, and although his explicit references to fascism are negative, many commentators have followed Bertrand Russell in accusing him of fascist leanings. T. S. Eliot moved from the received anti-semitism of his early poetry to an endorsement of Charles Maurras' Action Française in the 1920s, before adopting the Christian traditionalism in the 1930s that led to the powerful evocations of the British experience of the Second World War in *Four Quartets*. Wyndham Lewis wrote a book in praise of Hitler in 1930, *Hitler*, and though he backed away from that position as the 1930s went on, he contributed to the *British Union Quarterly* as late as 1937, and Auden's description of him in this period as a 'lonely old volcano of the right' seems apt enough. But Lewis, like Eliot, chose the Allied side firmly enough once war was declared. It was left to Ezra Pound to carry the modernist flirtation with fascism to its logical extreme: Pound, by far the most fervent supporter of fascism of all these writers before the war, broadcast from Rome Radio throughout the war until the fall of Rome to the Allies, continued propaganda work in favour of the Axis until his capture in 1945, and spent the next thirteen years in an insane asylum as the only alternative to being tried and possibly executed for treason.

Pound obviously poses the question of the relation between fascism and modernism most sharply, but given the larger context just sketched, the relation seems to be a real one not just because of Pound. However, it should also be understood that there is nothing in the least necessary about this connection between modernism and fascism, for James Joyce – as central to any definition of modern Irish literature as Yeats and to modernism as Ezra Pound – had impeccable anti-fascist credentials and composed in *Ulysses* the most prescient analysis in literature in English of how anti-semitism and nationalism could lead to something like the Holocaust. However, this is not to argue for a disconnection between the Irish cultural revival and the intersection of modernism with fascism. The two most significant moments where poetry and politics intersected themselves intersect in significant ways.

Modernist writers became distinctly more interested in politics after the First World War, as should occasion little surprise, since it seemed only a matter of self-interest to analyse the causes of the war and see what could prevent its reoccurrence. The response of writers to the actual war is outside the scope of this essay, given the 'Poetry and War' essay also included in this volume (chapter 5), but suffice it to say that most modernists who survived the war were left convinced that substantial changes in the structure of European society were desirable, probably essential. In *Kangaroo* Lawrence wrote of the war-atmosphere in England, 'No man who has really consciously lived through this can believe again absolutely in democracy'.

Inspired by the Irish example which showed that poets could have an effect on society, modernist writers sought to align themselves with forces of social change which left an important place for art and the artist. The Marxist tradition – as we have already seen – left no such place, and although modernist art flourished in the early period of the Russian Revolution, few modernists in English-speaking countries were convinced (or remained convinced for more than a moment) that the Soviet example was one to follow. Thus, when modernist writers turned to politics, they looked therefore to a political theory and movement that shared their rejection of economism. They were therefore by and large hostile to the values and beliefs of orthodox liberalism as well as to Marxism. The only political movement with any viability in their youth before the First World War that assigned anything like the place to art and ideology they did was the political tradition of anarcho-syndicalism, in particular the work of the heterodox French socialist Georges Sorel. Sorel broke sharply with orthodox (what we now call 'vulgar') Marxism over the base–superstructure model and the secondary role for culture that this model entailed. For Sorel, ideas were not simply determined by the base but had a vital effect on it. People in their actions were powerfully directed and motivated by the ideas they had about what would happen, by the myths – to use Sorel's phrase – that they held to be true. Ideas literally made things happen, and the figures who best showed how ideas influence events were the inventor and the artist. Sorel nicely turned Marxism on its head when he suggested that the Marxist notion of the inevitability of the revolution was just such a Sorelian myth, not an objective truth but a construct designed to direct future action, though – as Sorel suggested – it wasn't a very good myth since it was likely to induce passivity in the proletariat: if the revolution was inevitable, why fight for it?

Syndicalism as an organized movement flourished before the war, primarily in France and Italy, not in English-speaking countries, although Guild Socialism was a variant of anti-statist socialism in Britain with links to syndicalism. What happened to the syndicalists after the war? Syndicalism remained an important element of the anti-Marxist left, but after the success of the Russian Revolution in 1917, the anti-Marxist left sharply diminished in importance compared to the Marxist tradition. Many syndicalists – following some swerves of Sorel himself just before the war – switched from the left to the right of the political spectrum and became fascists as fascism became a coherent political force first in Italy and then in other countries in the 1920s and 1930s. Benito Mussolini himself is, of course, the most famous example of this: he was the editor of *Avanti!* and a leading if somewhat heterodox Italian socialist before the war, but he discovered the power of both nationalism and violence during the war and became the founder of fascism. But he is far from the only such figure, and Sorel's influence was felt at both ends of the political spectrum in the postwar years. It must be said that the precise relationship between syndicalism and fascism remains controversial. On the one hand, it has been argued that Sorel's stress on violence and on action is a close prefiguration of fascism and that much of the irrationality of fascism can be traced back to Sorel. Clearly, Mussolini and other leading Italian fascist ideologues liked to trace their intellectual ancestry back to Sorel and even to claim that fascism was the true heir of nineteenth-century socialism. But it has also been argued that these claims were largely intellectual camouflage, that fascist practice owed little or nothing to syndicalism, that syndicalism was only window-dressing to make the regime appeal to a broader spectrum of Italian society and world opinion.

But the precise relation of Sorel's ideas to fascist practice is less important for our purposes than the fact that the politics of Anglo-American modernism – as difficult to summarize as it is – is best summarized as a kind of Sorelian politics, which like Sorel's own influence retained leftist affinities but after 1918 was largely of the right. James Joyce and Wyndham Lewis – both off to one side here, given our focus on poetry – are Sorelian in their politics, in Joyce's case influenced by the Italian syndicalism of his youth, in Lewis's case more directly by Sorel himself and by T. E. Hulme. If I may oversimplify a little in the interests of space, I regard Joyce as a classic Sorelian of the left, Lewis as close to Sorel himself in oscillating between the left and the right, while Ezra Pound is the classic type of the Sorelian intellectual who began on the left but moved most emphatically to the right. Pound's initial political socialization was as a contributor to the Guild Socialist periodical *The New Age*, and any reader of *The New Age*, let alone a regular contributor, would have been introduced to the full anti-statist left's critique of Marxism, Fabianism and economistic leftism. T. E. Hulme was of course a central figure in this group as well, and he was an ardent Sorelian, translating Sorel's *Reflections on Violence* into English. (Through Hulme, Sorel had a strong influence on T. S. Eliot, who listed *Reflections on Violence* and Hulme's own collection of essays, *Speculations*, as two of the six exemplifications of the neo-classicism he advocated in *Criterion* in 1924.) As *The New Age* shifted to the right after the First World War, so did Pound, first to the theories of Social Credit (discovered by Pound in *The New Age*) and other theories of monetary reform, and then after his move to Italy in 1924, increasingly to Italian fascism.

Throughout his support of Italian fascism, moreover, the themes of Pound's economics remained deeply syndicalist, in his preference for the industrialist or active capitalist over the banker or passive capitalist, in his fascination with inventions and with technical progress and in his stress on the need for action. Although Pound was enthralled by the personality of Mussolini, and this was a major factor in his support of Italian fascism, his closest political affinities in Italian politics were with forms of 'left fascism' at some remove from the official politics of the regime, such as those advocated by his friend and former syndicalist Odon Por. However, it was comparatively easy to imagine Italian fascism (Nazi Germany offers a stark contrast here) as Sorelian in one respect at least, in the key roles in fascism played by artists and intellectuals. The novelist Gabriele D'Annunzio has been called the 'John the Baptist' of fascism, the philosopher Giovanni Gentile served as the Minister of Education, and the founder of futurism and Pound's friend F. T. Marinetti was a key supporter of the regime. Fascism, in short, was aligned with forces of artistic modernity in a way no other political regime in the 1930s was. Pound, at least, returned the compliment, coming close to losing his life and certainly wrecking it by his fanatical and life-long support of Il Duce.

If Yeats is unquestionably the greatest and most influential Irish poet of the twentieth century and Pound is arguably the greatest and unquestionably the most influential American poet of the twentieth century, then one can certainly draw the conclusion that some of the century's most important poetry stands in close relation to the politics of its time. Yet the conclusions one might want to draw from these two important examples would be very different. Surely, if poets are the unacknowledged legislators of the world and the antennae of the race, the generally optimistic view one might draw from this relation in the case of Yeats and Irish politics does not survive the example of Pound and fascism. Some antennae point in the wrong direction, and some legislators are better off unacknowledged.

It is at least fortunate that Pound was substantially unacknowledged, and no one has claimed or can claim for Pound the kind of generative role *vis-à-vis* fascism (in Italy or in the English-speaking world) which Yeats had in Ireland. Life emphatically did not imitate the art of Ezra Pound. This was not for lack of trying, but the circle around Mussolini had grave reservations about Pound's sanity even while giving him the forum of Rome Radio, and though he had a few followers in the United States, he had essentially no influence on the events he sought so desperately to influence. There are two conclusions to draw from this, and both would certainly be correct. First, the kind of role Yeats played in Ireland is much easier to play in a small, emerging country than on a world stage. Second, it was *Cathleen Ni-Houlihan*, not *A Vision* or 'The Statues', which had the effect on Irish society Yeats sought, at least at moments in his career. Aesthetically complex art of the kind produced in modernism is much less likely to influence political events than works written in simpler, more popular modes. Although I would argue that Pound's *Cantos* is a deeply fascist poem, it was also too complex to have significant influence as it was being written, an altogether unintended but desirable consequence of Pound's commitment to modernist aesthetics.

The English reader of this essay will have noted the almost complete absence of English poets in my discussion so far. But England's turn now comes, in the work of the first generation of poets after modernism, the 'Auden generation', who constitute the third and in an important sense the last moment in which a central movement in the literary history of the twentieth century intersects with a central movement in political history. The Auden generation (or even the 'Auden gang' in some accounts) – W. H. Auden, C. Day Lewis, Stephen Spender, Louis MacNeice, with the novelist Christopher Isherwood as a crucial component – was born between 1904 and 1909. This means that they came to maturity after the war but were deeply marked by it; they also came to maturity after the flowering of modernism but were also deeply marked by it. I think it is fair to say that they understood and absorbed only one of the differences between Yeats and Pound which accounted for the differences in the effectualness of the two poets. The poets in the 1930s understood that if they were to have any influence on political events, they needed to work with aesthetic models which were less complex than the High Modernism of Eliot and Pound, even though Eliot was a crucial mentor for the group. However, they failed to develop anything like Yeats's productive relationship to the forces of nationalism, as Auden implicitly acknowledged in his elegy, 'In Memory of W. B. Yeats', when he wrote 'mad Ireland hurt you into poetry'. Clearly situated on the left and part of the Marxist left, the Auden group were not in a position where nationalism and a revolutionary politics were compatible. Ever since 1917, Marxism was synonymous with a sympathetic attitude towards the Soviet Union, the only living example of a socialist state, and in the crucial years of 1936 to 1939, it was even more closely identified with a sympathetic attitude towards the Spanish Republic. This constitutes a crucial break with the internationalism of pre-1914 socialism, but these particular commitments to specific nation-states incumbent on any Marxist between the two world wars were not compatible with English or British cultural or political nationalism. In other words, there were countries you were supposed to care about, but they didn't include your own. The widespread sardonic commentary on Auden and Isherwood's emigration to the United States at the onset of the Second World War represented these particular chickens coming home to roost, and the fact that the Christopher Isherwood figure of *Goodbye to Berlin* is transformed into an American in the musical adaptation *Cabaret* without this feeling like a significant change makes this point in another way. It was George Orwell who showed how one could amalgamate leftist politics with cultural nationalism in the 1930s, even if this alliance didn't survive 1945, and not surprisingly his alliances among the left were with the syndicalist tradition.

It is the orientation towards Marxism, however, which most sharply differentiates the Auden generation from their modernist predecessors. The question of how genuine their commitment to the Communist Party ever was has been the subject of considerable debate in the subsequent years, and certainly one is not to imagine that these young men had a thorough command of Marxist political thinking. But to use some of the jargon of the time, they were clearly identified as 'pink' if not deep 'red', and this commitment strengthened until the Spanish Civil War and Auden's catastrophic and disillusioning experiences there. I can't say, however, that their work represented any solution to the problems posed by the dominant economism of Marxism. Not well read enough in the socialist tradition to have discovered some of the alternatives to the base–superstructure reflection model proposed in the 1920s by such thinkers as Antonio Gramsci or Hendrik de Man, they did not successfully imagine a productive role for a Marxist poetry in the absence of a role for poetry in Marxism. Auden – clearly the most significant poet of the group – came to regard his politically engaged work of the 1930s as a profound aesthetic embarrassment, and he did his level best to excise that work from his canon. 'September 1, 1939' describes the 1930s as 'a low dishonest decade', and Auden came to see much of his own work written in the 1930s as contained in that description. The contrast between Yeats's willingness to dwell on his own earlier work at the end of his life with a complex mixture of fondness and detachment, and Auden's excision of 'September 1, 1939', 'Spain 1937' and other of his most influential poems of the period from his *Collected Shorter Poems*, is instructive. Although it is certainly to Auden's credit that he came to view phrases like 'The conscious acceptance of guilt in the necessary murder' from 'Spain 1937' with distaste, even revulsion, it is probably not to his credit that he wrote such lines in the first place. There are turns in all writers' careers, but the turn of the Auden generation away from politics was a recognition that their political poetry failed as poetry and also failed as politics. Yeats could dwell with some satisfaction on his success, but to the degree that Auden's political poetry succeeded in having an effect on its time, this was not a source of comfort for Auden after the war.

There are certainly critics who are more sympathetic to the Popular Front aesthetics of the 1930s than I am, and they would certainly see more enduring value in the poetry of the 1930s than I can see. However, it is certainly fair to say that the work of the 'Auden gang' of the 1930s hasn't fared particularly well in the literary 'stock market' of the last generation, although I leave it up to you whether to judge that decline to be a fair estimation of a movement which hasn't translated well or an evaluation ripe to be overturned and challenged. Nonetheless, the work of this group of poets did have an enormous effect on the life and society of its times, shaping perhaps not a whole nation but certainly decisively influential for a whole generation's investment in the anti-fascist struggles of the 1930s. But as the overture of Spain gave way to the much larger conflict of 1939 to 1945, neither Auden – newly denizened in the United States – nor his contemporaries successfully responded to the war in their poetry. It was that cosmopolitan High Modernist transformed into a pillar of the English establishment, T. S. Eliot, who in *Four Quartets* composed the enduring poetic English response to the event of the war.

After 1945, I cannot claim that any of the major poets in Anglo-American culture have written poetry which has substantively engaged with the major political events of their time. Robert Lowell opposed the war in Vietnam and was widely known for that opposition, but it was not in or through his poetry that he opposed the war. Despite the theoretical perspective I began by sketching which denies that one can separate poetry from the political, it must be said that the poets writing at the same time as these theorists have certainly thought they could and have not for the most part sought to engage directly in their work with political events.

The exception is Ireland, but it isn't just Ireland. In 1900, English was spoken all over the world, but it was spoken in just two political entities, the British Empire and the United States. English is spoken even more widely today, but the British Empire has gone the way of the Austro-Hungarian, the Russian and the Turkish, so that the territory which formerly constituted the Empire is now something upwards of forty distinct nations. The sun may have set on the British Empire, but the proud boast can be recast: the sun never sets on countries where they speak and write English as a result of the British Empire. A few of these are the former Dominions, with a population comprised mostly of European immigrants, but the vast majority are former colonies, with a population mostly made up of the people who were there before the British arrived and started to issue imperatives to them in English. These countries are therefore more like Yeats's Ireland than they are like Auden's England: although most of them retain indigenous languages like the former colonies of Austria, Russia and Turkey, nonetheless given English's role as a world language, most have kept an official place for English as well. These nations have rivalled the Irish in using the English language more brilliantly in literature than the English or the Americans, and the 'post-colonial' literature which has emerged – represented by such writers as Chinua Achebe, Wole Soyinka, Nuruddin Farah, R. K. Narayan, Salman

Rushdie, V. S. Naipaul, Derek Walcott, just to name a few – constitutes the significant literature in English of our time and of the past half-century. Writing literally *in medias res*, I cannot cull out of this complex literature, made up of writers born on and resident in every continent, with many different languages, religions and cultures, a literary history composed of organized groups with anything like the cohesiveness of the Irish Literary Revival or the Auden generation. However, it is among these writers that we find the writers significantly engaged with the politics of their place and time. The novel has been the dominant genre of post-colonial literature, not poetry, but Seamus Heaney in Northern Ireland, Wole Soyinka in Nigeria, Kamau Brathwaite in the Caribbean – to name a prominent few – have composed bodies of poetry which intersect profoundly with the political trajectories of their society. Of the movements of work discussed in this essay, it has been the Irish of the Literary Revival who have had the most profound influence on these writers, since they find themselves in situations not unlike the Irish one of the first quarter of the twentieth century. However, Wole Soyinka writing in *A Shuttle in the Crypt* about his imprisonment for questioning the military junta in Nigeria and the Biafran War takes us into dimensions of the human experience not found previously in poetry in English. This is where poetry and politics continue to intersect most profoundly, often because most tragically: stay tuned in the twenty-first century for what happens next.

BIBLIOGRAPHY

Auden, W. H. (1966), *Collected Shorter Poems: 1927–1957*. London: Faber & Faber.

Casillo, Robert (1988), *The Genealogy of Demons: Anti-Semitism, Fascism, and the Myths of Ezra Pound*. Evanston: Northwestern University Press.

Chace, William (1973), *The Political Identities of Ezra Pound and T. S. Eliot*. Stanford: Stanford University Press.

Cullingford, Elizabeth (1981), *Yeats, Ireland and Fascism*. New York: NYU Press.

De Man, Henry (1929), *The Psychology of Socialism*. Trans. Eden & Cedar Paul. London: Allen & Unwin.

Eliot, T. S. (1971), *The Complete Poems and Plays: 1909–1950*. New York: Harcourt, Brace & World.

Howarth, Herbert (1958), *The Irish Writers, 1880–1940: Literature under Parnell's Star*. London: Rockliff.

Hulme, T. E. (1924), *Speculations: Essays on Humanism and the Philosophy of Art*. Herbert Read (ed.). London: Routledge & Kegan Paul.

Lawrence, D. H. (1964). *Kangaroo*. New York: Viking.

Lewis, Wyndham (1989), *The Art of Being Ruled*. Reed Way Dasenbrock (ed.). Santa Rosa: Black Sparrow Press.

Pound, Ezra (1975), *The Cantos*. London: Faber & Faber.

Sorel, Georges (1950), *Reflections on Violence*. Trans. T. E. Hulme & J. Roth. Glencoe: Free Press.

Soyinka, Wole (1972), *A Shuttle in the Crypt*. New York: Hill and Wang.

Yeats, William Butler (1972), *Collected Plays*. London: Macmillan.

Yeats, William Butler (1953), *The Collected Poems*. London: Macmillan.

5

Poetry and War

Matthew Campbell

Before he published his translation of Virgil's *Aeneid* in 1952, Cecil Day Lewis saw
out the 1930s with a version of the *Georgics*. It was published in 1940, in the early
days of the Second World War, a poem of retreat written in a besieged Britain. In the
'Dedicatory Stanzas' (to Stephen Spender) which preface his version, Day Lewis confronts Shelley's declaration of the part that the poet plays in history and asks the question of one of his own most famous lyrics, 'where are the war poets?'

> it gives us the hump
> To think that we're the unacknowledged rump
> Of a long parliament of legislators.
>
> Where are the war poets? The fools inquire.
> We were the prophets of a changeable morning
> Who hoped for much but saw the clouds forewarning:
> We were at war, while they still played with fire
> And rigged the market for the ruin of man:
> Spain was a death to us, Munich a mourning.
> No wonder then if, like the pelican,
> We have turned inward for our iron ration,
> Tapping the vein and sole reserve of passion,
> Drawing from poetry's capital what we can.

Day Lewis, like many Irish and English writers of the 1930s, ended that decade with
little hope for the legislative influence of the Shelleyan poet and turned deliberately
'inward'. The global market is now pursuing takeover and merger by violent means,
so, 'Drawing from poetry's capital what we can', poets must tune the martial resonance of political poetry down to aesthetic questions of adequacy and appropriateness
in the midst of a historical trauma which is 'No subject for immortal verse'. Failing
in this, poets can find themselves taking sides and then defending 'the bad against
the worse' ('Where are the War Poets?' 1940).

A poet such as Day Lewis feels that he can no longer allow himself to sing, in Dryden's version of Virgil, of 'arms and the man': in 1952, his version of the *Aeneid* opens as flatly as he can manage: 'I tell about war and the hero . . .'. For many, most notably Theodor Adorno, the horrors of the twentieth century leave little room for lyric, let alone the martial concerns of epic. Yet throughout the century, poets continually worried over poetry's response – in terms of genre as much as subject matter – to the horrors of twentieth-century history. The poetry from Britain and Ireland which was written about the wars in which those countries engaged – imperial and civil wars as well as the world wars – is a poetry which no longer feels that it can sing in celebration of arms and the man, but rather must turn to Wilfred Owen's theme, the 'pity of war' or its absurdity.

There was much heroic verse written during the century as there was verse which invoked the mythic: David Jones's *In Parenthesis* (1937) writes his experience of the Great War through classical and Arthurian legend. There was also verse written in praise of revolutionary struggles for freedom, in Spain, Ireland, Russia, Latin America or Africa. But for all the twentieth-century soldier-poets, there were many who, though they viewed war from a distance, felt its effects no less. Even a poet who wrote for Empire, Rudyard Kipling, found that the unfolding of the century would turn the martial camaraderie and the heroism of the White Man's Burden to the elegiac note which the loss of his son in the First World War taught him. In his excellent anthology, *The Oxford Book of War Poetry*, Jon Stallworthy includes thirty-four of Kipling's epitaphs of the Great War. They are written from the 'Home Front', but memorialize with sympathy and horror experiences of war which cast any previous urge for epic into the delicate and powerless responses of epitaph:

> A SON
> My son was killed while laughing at some jest. I would I knew
> What it was, and it might serve me in a time when jests are few.
> THE COWARD
> I could not look on Death, which being known,
> Men led me to him, blindfold and alone.
> SHOCK
> My name, my speech, my self I had forgot.
> My wife and children came – I knew them not.
> I died. My mother followed. At her call
> And on her bosom I remembered all.

Bereavement, the unheroic, psychic distress, the forgetting in this life matched only by the irony of knowledge in immortality: all of these responses could be felt at the heart of the establishment as well as by the Shelleyan radical poet. The tone is often closer to overwhelming irony than debilitating horror, yet from both – irony and horror – come a set of aesthetic issues which face the war poem, of response, representation, adequacy and eventual failure.

Objecting to 'Jean Baudrillard's notorious analysis of the Gulf War as a series of rhetorical performances unattached to any material reality', Simon Featherstone says that poems written *at* war 'seem to insist on the closeness of writing to often appalling personal experience' (Featherstone, 1995, p. 3). Writing and experience are as one, the writing often simultaneous with experience. Yet in his classic study *The Great War and Modern Memory*, Paul Fussell (1975) writes about the long periods of doing nothing in a 'Literary War', in which soldiers filled much time reading and writing. Fussell takes nearly a page to list the reading and literary correspondence of 1917 to 1918 undertaken by Herbert Read in the trenches, a list which ranges from Plato and Cervantes to Marx and H. G. Wells. Hospitals, too, became sites of writing, in which writing became a convalescent occupation, putting in the time. The literary collaboration of the two most-celebrated of Great War poets, Siegfried Sassoon and Wilfred Owen, was cemented in a psychiatric hospital in Scotland, well away from the experiences which had put them there.

Given such a long time to fill not thinking about impending death or mutilation, the war poet must attend to a problem of style similar to that which also confronts the historian. Paul Fussell summarizes the questions of rhetoric and style which faced Kipling, writing one of his 'most decent and honourable works', *The Irish Guards in the Great War*:

> ... how are actual events deformed by the application to them of metaphor, rhetorical comparison, prose rhythm, assonance, alliteration, allusion, and sentence structures and connectives implying clear causality? Is there any way of compromising between the reader's expectations that written history ought to be interesting and meaningful and the cruel fact that much of what happens — all of what happens? — is inherently without 'meaning'? (Fussell, 1975, pp. 171–2)

We could adapt these questions to ask them of poetry written about war. Kipling's subject is war, and a war which killed many in the Irish Guards along with his son. But finding an appropriate language, according to Fussell, would mean finding 'the clinical — or even obscene — language' which 'would force itself up from below. . . . It was a matter of leaving, finally, the nineteenth century behind'. Fussell finds that Kipling's history fails this test, but the author of the *Barrack-Room Ballads*, written in the last years of the reign of Queen Victoria, knew about language from below. 'A SON' shows this: 'My son was killed while laughing at some jest. I would I knew / What it was, and it might serve me in a time when jests are few.' There is only one word of more than one syllable in the epitaph, and it is the last terrible action of the son, 'laughing'. The couplet rhymes, but the monosyllables, the two long, nearly unmetrical lines, and the late and early caesurae, recreate in the speech of this war poem the flat experience of the final numb facing of a long bereaved future in 'a time when jests are few'.

For all its economy as it faces its terrible subject matter, the artistic achievement of 'A SON' is rhetorical: it suggests the correct tone for marking both grief and the terrible irony of the manner of the laughing son's death. At the same time, while it may accede to Fussell's 'cruel fact that much of what happens . . . is inherently without meaning', the 'happening' of the response recreated in the poem has in itself created meaning. This meaning is not consolation or in any way redemptive of the ironies of a violent death; rather it is a pointing up of the irony and, in the epitaph form, a memorial to the unforgettable. Fussell's 'much of what happens', inevitably drawn at first to horror but ultimately to irony, suggests a famous elegy of W. H. Auden, written while Europe was contemplating another world war in 1939 and 1940:

> For poetry makes nothing happen: it survives
> In the valley of its making where executives
> Would never want to tamper, flows on south
> From ranches of isolation and the busy griefs,
> Raw towns that we believe and die in; it survives,
> A way of happening, a mouth.
> ('In Memory of W. B. Yeats')

Auden's riposte to the political efforts of Yeats may have come from the same disillusion which prompted Day Lewis's repudiation of the Shelleyan poetic role, faced with Europe's return to war. Certainly, his grudging 'way of happening, a mouth', in which poetry is a conduit, a medium, rather than an effective historical agent in its own right, places poetry well away from the scenes of politics or war.

Yeats himself had acted as observer and elegist on the subject of war, no matter how he too had indulged in the hubris of wondering if his poetry had exercised effective political agency. In 1939, reviewing his career, he had asked himself the question, 'Did that play of mine send out / Certain men the English shot?' ('Man and the Echo' – the reference is to *Cathleen ni Houlihan*, 1900, and the execution of the leaders of the Easter Rising in Ireland in 1916). But it is in 'Lapis Lazuli', viewing a Europe suffering under new wars of annexation and aerial bombing, as well as the obliteration of ancient cities, that Yeats attempts to find a poetry which both faces the destruction of culture and attempts to find an aesthetic response.

> On their own feet they came, or on shipboard,
> Camel-back, horse-back, ass-back, mule-back,
> Old civilisations put to the sword.
> Then they and their wisdom went to rack:
> No handiwork of Callimachus,
> Who handled marble as if it were bronze,
> Made draperies that seemed to rise
> When sea-wind swept the corner, stands;
> His long lamp-chimney shaped like the stem
> Of a slender palm, stood but a day;
> All things fall and are built again,

> And those that build them again are gay.
> ('Lapis Lazuli')

This poem was written in 1938 while the Spanish Civil War was underway, and views the refugees and emigrants swarming from previously settled societies with some ambivalence. In Yeats's authoritarian worldview, traumatic historical change may not entirely be a bad thing. And there is an aesthetic rather than political embrace of the rebuilding of societies as a necessary, comic, resolution. Yeats will not allow that the wiping out of cities and civilizations is merely an aestheticized act of history: irony remains, in that the classical form of the architect Callimachus stands but a day in these circumstances. But it is perhaps a chilling act of artistic ambition that he attempts to push tragic circumstances out to the comic resolution where the rebuilders, whether or not they also be the destroyers, are 'gay'.

It is Yeats who mounted the strongest arguments against the very possibility of war poetry in the twentieth century. If 'joy' is a mark of great art, then poets who 'felt bound . . . to plead the suffering of their men' were not included in Yeats's *Oxford Book of Modern Verse*, because 'passive suffering is not a theme for poetry'. Consequently, twentieth-century war poetry loses the mythic or heroic along with the loss of joy from the tragic:

> In all great tragedies, tragedy is a joy to the man who dies; in Greece the tragic chorus danced. When man has withdrawn into the quicksilver at the back of the mirror no great event becomes luminous in his mind; it is no longer possible to write *The Persians*, *Agincourt*, *Chevy Chase*: some blunderer has driven his car on to the wrong side of the road – that is all.
>
> If war is necessary, or necessary in our time and place, it is best to forget its suffering as we do the discomfort of fever, remembering our comfort at midnight when our temperature fell, or as we forget the worst moments of more painful disease. (Introduction to *The Oxford Book of Modern Verse*, 1936)

Yeats makes only a small move from war as motor accident to the forgetting of historical necessity, since it is no more significant than a bout of 'flu. But the shock of Yeats's call for such forgetting does ask important questions about the representation of a suffering which may, in Fussell's words respecting Kipling, have no meaning at all. Even Yeats, in his elegy for his friend Lady Gregory's son, killed in the Great War, knows that tragic joy is not an easily achieved consolation for bereavement after violent death. His poem fails to achieve the heroic at its end, tactfully granting the overpowering fact of death.

> I had thought, seeing how bitter is that wind
> That shakes the shutter, to have brought to mind
> All those that manhood tried, or childhood loved
> Or boyish intellect approved,
> With some appropriate commentary on each;

Until imagination brought
A fitter welcome; but a thought
Of that late death took all my heart for speech.
('In Memory of Major Robert Gregory', 1918)

'Appropriate commentary' is not appropriate in these circumstances. Yet such appropriateness is a major aesthetic preoccupation of those British poets of the Great War who were excluded from Yeats's anthology. The question is not only what commentary can be made facing the subject, but also whether the conventions of previous martial literary genres – epic, heroic, tragic – are appropriate to convey the apparent meaninglessness of an experience newly emptied not only of its epic, heroic and tragic significance, but, frequently, politics and history as well. The new twentieth-century genre which Yeats dismisses, that of the war poem, emerged from these poets. This new genre shares much with the elegy, particularly as the Romantic conception of that literary form often founders on the ineffable, moments like that of Yeats above, where the heart is taken for speech. The genre of elegy performs, in therapeutic terms, the 'work of mourning', a work in which the conclusion of the poem ought to coincide with consolation: Yeats's conclusion above seeks consolation through the very act of writing its 'appropriate commentary', which promises to provide a kind of therapy, while still facing the absolute sense of loss. The losses of bereavement can be daily occurrences for those at war, but the related problem for the early twentieth-century war poet, the accompanying loss of meaning (patriotism or a cause along with mental stability or even sanity), mounts powerful opposition to the generic expectations of a form which ostensibly performs this 'work of mourning' – reintegration of the bereaved personality through the consolations of elegy.

Take these two poems written from within the hell of war, 'The Rear Guard', by Siegfried Sassoon and 'Strange Meeting' by Wilfred Owen. Both Sassoon and Owen enlisted to fight and were decorated for bravery. The Sassoon poem was written ten days after arriving in hospital, supposedly suffering from shell-shock, a diagnosis, according to Sassoon, which was repudiated by the quality of his poem. It tells of an officer groping by torchlight through the tunnels of the Hindenburg Line, and is filled full of the detritus of an experience which presents itself to the soldier in terms of overpowering smell and the discarded objects of war, alternately vivid and obscure according to the beam of the torch: 'Tins, boxes, bottles, shapes too vague to know'. The packed stresses at the beginning of this line, followed by the regularizing iambic beat show Sassoon's sense of great formal control over his verse, even as it suggests those horrors which are held just outside perception. (The prosody of its list also suggests a Miltonic hell: 'Rocks, Caves, Lakes, Fens, Bogs, Dens, and shades of death / A Universe of death', *Paradise Lost*, II, 621–2.) The poem as a whole is enclosed by three rhymes, the first three and the last three of its twenty-five lines rhyming with each other in reverse. So the poem's opening line, ending with 'step by step' is supposedly completed by the last line's account of a therapeutic coming through, 'Unload-ing hell behind him step by step'. Both experience and memory of the experi-ence have literally and metaphorically been unloaded by the very writing of the poem, a poem resolutely shifted by its ill author into the third person.

Yet at the centre of 'The Rear Guard' is an encounter which may not be so easily unloaded by the consolations of this elegiac pattern. The officer trips and seeing 'some one' he assumes to be asleep, asks for directions. Hearing no response he then makes an order followed by a sudden moment of frustrated savagery:

> 'Get up and guide me through this stinking place.'
> Savage, he kicked a soft unanswering heap,
> And flashed his beam across the livid face
> Terribly glaring up, whose eyes yet wore
> Agony dying hard ten days before;
> And fists of fingers clutched a blackening wound.

A pause now follows in the text and narrative of the poem, before the officer is supposedly led out of this hell. But it is the absence of appropriate commentary after this experience of beating a ten-days-dead body that resounds most strongly through the poem. We have been presented with a number of objects an army has left behind and one of them is a human body. The officer's eye is led from the unannounced 'livid face / Terribly glaring up', across the body into the eyes and finally to the 'blacken-ing wound', in a sort of numb assessment of information. This is then forced, by a necessary act of repression in the text, to lie without commentary behind the staggering man seeking the light above hell. There is no effort to find meaning here, just to seek escape.

Sassoon's lyric is formally quite enclosed between its rhyming first and last lines, and plays with triple rhymes throughout. Such a technique, and the encounter with the dead in the underworld, suggests Dante. Wilfrid Owen's 'Strange Meeting' is also a Dantesque dream of conversation with the dead, and is no less remarkable for its attempt to find a prosodic form for the experience. In Owen's case this is achieved by sustaining pararhyming couplets throughout the poem. If the Sassoon poem was a deliberate attempt to enclose the experience in poetic form – and therefore to leave it behind – Owen's poem refuses the consolations that the aesthetic completion of full rhyme might bring. The poem was written only a few months before its author's death and was, of course, not prepared for publication by the poet: but it ends with a lacuna, the truncated 'Let us sleep now . . .', which suggests that such experience cannot be allowed to complete itself.

It is in these terms that 'Strange Meeting' suggests a development from the sig-nificant achievement of Sassoon's poem. It looks to immortality as it thinks of the life after death of the war poet; but it also looks to the irony that after such experience wars will continue, and that writing poetry about war, or from war – this very poem – will have minimal effect on the future. The dead man whom the poet meets in his dream reveals himself at the end as the enemy he killed yesterday. Yet he too is a poet, a poet who mourns that poetry has proved supremely ineffective in this war. In his way, the dead enemy is the poet Owen used to be:

> Whatever hope is yours,
> Was my life also; I went hunting wild
> After the wildest beauty in the world,
> Which lies not calm in eyes, or braided hair,
> But mocks the steady running of the hour,
> And if it grieves, grieves richlier than here.

Yeats had excluded Owen from his *Oxford Book of Modern Verse* because his poetry told only of suffering and pity, and did not achieve tragic or comic resolutions. Here Owen gives us a late nineteenth-century Yeatsian poet, but also one who might suggest his Romantic masters, Shelley and Keats. The lyric poet chases after the 'wildest beauty', careless of mortality and time given the generic opportunity of the luxury of elegy where he can grieve 'richlier than here'. That is lost forever to Owen and his vision, and is added to by the irony of his own imagined death, where what he could have said, 'The pity of war, the pity war distilled', is now denied to the world due to that death. Owen views history – the progress of nations and capital – inevitably girding up to repeat this experience. Yet he resolutely refuses a historical gloss, or to allow any Clausewitzean consolations of political objectives resolving themselves through war.

All that is left is the ineffective Keatsian poet cleaning up after the massacre:

> Then, when much blood had clogged their chariot-wheels,
> I would go up and wash them from sweet wells,
> Even with truths which lie too deep for taint.
> I would have poured my spirit without stint
> But not through wounds; not on the cess of war.
> Foreheads of men have bled where no wounds were.

Two previous texts haunt the poet's task here. The first is from Homer, and the description of the chariot wheels of the unquenchably bloodthirsty Achilles at the end of Book XX of the *Iliad*, where, in Pope's translation, 'The spiky wheels through heaps of carnage tore; / And thick the groaning axles dropp'd with gore'. The other is from Keats's 'Ode to a Nightingale', where the poet had asked to die while the bird was 'pouring forth thy soul abroad / In such an ecstasy!' Here Owen's poet thinks of what he could have done with poetry after war, pouring his spirit through poetry and achieving the psychic cleansing of this experience. The dead poet's speech reaches back to epic for some possible analogy for this cleansing. Yet it concludes such argument as it presents with a riddling last line: 'Foreheads of men have bled where no wounds were'. Through the closing insistence of the last three stressed syllables here, and the uncertain rocking of their internal rhyme ('where nó woúnds wére') Owen may be suggesting that lyric pain can be expressed without war, or that those who follow the poets can insist that we sustain poetic pain. But he may also be alluding to the sacrifice of Christ on the cross, sweating redemptive blood.

'Strange Meeting' is a dream of conversation with a dead lyric poet, or possibly even dead lyric itself. After numerous twentieth-century wars, the death of poetry has long been proclaimed by those who found, along with Owen and Auden, that the poet's cultural cleansing through pouring out his lyric spirit will make nothing happen. Like Day Lewis and Kipling, much of this effect was felt by those who were not soldiers themselves, but who felt the long memories of war suffered by their parents and grandparents resonate throughout the century. British culture has memories of significant victory to look back on when thinking about war, but epic triumphalism has not generally been the tone in which poets have written. Writing about family experiences in the Great War, personal experience of the Blitz, or facing the fact of the Holocaust, poets who choose to write on public subjects, like Ted Hughes or Geoffrey Hill, filter them through the difficult questions of appropriateness and genre that the war poets raise.

When the troubles broke out again in Ireland in the 1970s, poets turned again to the genre of war poetry in order to find form for writing not only about contemporary horrors but also the responsibilities, political as well as artistic, of the poet. Seamus Heaney returns to elegy through Dante, talking, like Sassoon or Owen, with the ghosts of the dead. These include the seeming 'enigma' presented by an Irish nationalist First World War poet, Francis Ledwidge ('You were not keyed or pitched like these true-blue ones / Though all of you consort now underground'). But the more recent dead in 'The Strand at Lough Beg' and the explicitly Dantesque *Station Island* sequence, exist uncomfortably between the British war poem and conventional elegy. Not that comfort would be provided by solving the generic problem, dependent on irony as it is. These are the ghosts of the violent dead which face Heaney:

> I turn because the sweeping of your feet
> Has stopped behind me, to find you on your knees
> With blood and roadside muck in your hair and eyes,
> Then kneel in front of you in brimming grass
> And gather up cold handfuls of the dew
> To wash you, cousin.
> ('The Strand at Lough Beg', 1978)

The cleansing of the elegiac poet amounts here to no more than the laying out of a body in a ritual – religious and aesthetic – which approximates burial rites. The action of the poet is of course, as the Irish poet Eavan Boland says, 'always too late' (Boland, 1990).

In *Station Island* another murdered ghost has 'an athlete's cleanliness', but produces only an apology for inadequacy from the poet:

> 'Forgive the way I have lived indifferent –
> forgive my timid circumspect involvement,'
>
> I surprised myself by saying. 'Forgive
> my eye,' he said, 'all that's above my head.'
> And then a stun of pain seemed to go through him
>
> and he trembled like a heatwave and faded.
> (*Station Island*, VII, 1984)

Heaney's plea for forgiveness is in its way an Audenesque show of bad faith, to be rejected peremptorily by its recipient. The ghost here was the 'perfect, clean, unthinkable victim', but becomes eventually one more in a series of the wasted male youth of the century killed in wars which they had no part in starting, and little sense of how to prevent: 'all that's above my head'.

The prophecy of Owen's dead enemy carries on through the century, like wounds which refuse to heal. In Michael Longley's elegy 'Wounds' (1972), his father, wounded in the First World War, carries not only vivid memories, but also the lead traces which would flare up and kill him fifty years later: the wound is unhealable by time or poem. The father is buried as other wounds erupt into more than irritation, and a long unhealed history results in explosions, assassinations and the unaccommodated ironies of the war poem. In such contemporary wars there is not even the difference of language to separate combatants. At the end of 'Wounds' a killer turns to the wife of the man he has killed in front of her, addressing her in the intimacy of the vernacular: 'I think "Sorry Missus" was what he said'.

This sense of the impossibility of closure, or of creating a form which will do the work of the epitaph or the elegy, and thus enable an adequate representation of the experience of war, either at the front or among the bereaved at home, remains at one and the same time a liberation and challenge to poetry. As I have said, the irrelevance of the poet and his poem to these events is marked by many poets and commentators, as Paul Muldoon (1998b) asks: 'How does one find an adequate reprise to the latest reprisal, a strophe equal to the latest catastrophe?' But also the necessity of response is there as a powerful compulsion. It is odd then that as one of the most influential of late twentieth-century poets writing in English, Muldoon returned to the old interchange of pastoral and epic which had attracted Cecil Day Lewis to Virgil, and had in its turn led Virgil himself to withdraw from the poem of empire and war. Muldoon's *Hay* (1998) performs what Seamus Heaney in *The Spirit Level* and Michael Longley in *Gorse Fires* also did during the 1990s, and attempts to rewrite classical versions of aftermath. Heaney recasts Aeschylus ('Mycenae Lookout') and Longley gives a grim version of the blood-bath at

Ithaca wrought by Odysseus after he finally returned from war ('The Butchers'). In Muldoon's rewriting of the sack of Troy, the end of war is poised ambivalently between a final catastrophic blood-letting and the deliverance of the poet and hero, escaping from the massacre into a new world:

> 'The beauty of it,' ventured Publius Vergilius Maro,
> 'is that your father and the other skinnymalinks
> may yet end up a pair of jackaroos
> in the canefields north of Brisbane.' We heard the tink
>
> of blade on bone, the Greeks alalaes
> as they slashed and burned, saw Aeneas daddle-dade
> his father Anchises, and his son, Iulus,
> to a hidey-hole on the slopes of Mount Ida.
>
> 'The beauty of it is that I delivered them from harm;
> it was I who had Aeneas steal
> back to look for Creusa, I who had her spirit rub
>
> like a flame through his flame-burnished arms,
> I who might have let him find his own way through the streel
> Of smoke, among the cheerless dead, the dying's chirrups.'
> (Paul Muldoon, *The Bangle (Slight Return)*)

BIBLIOGRAPHY

Auden, W. H. (1991). *Collected Poems*, ed. Edward Mandelson, London: Faber.

Bevan, David (ed.) (1990). *Literature and War*, Amsterdam: Rodopi.

Boland, Eavan (1990). *Outside History*, Manchester: Carcanet.

Boland, Eavan (1995). *Collected Poems*, Manchester: Carcanet.

Day Lewis, Cecil (1940, 1952). *The Eclogues, Georgics and Aeneid of Virgil*, Oxford: Oxford University Press.

Day Lewis, Cecil (1992). *Collected Poems*, London: Faber.

Desmond, Graham (1984). *The Truth of War: Owen, Blunden, Rosenburg*, Manchester: Carcanet.

Featherstone, Simon (1995). *War Poetry: An Introductory Reader*, London: Routledge.

Fussell, Paul (1975). *The Great War and Modern Memory*, Oxford: Oxford University Press.

Heaney, Seamus (1998). *Opened Ground: Poems 1966–1996*, London: Faber.

Jones, David (1937). *In Parenthesis*, London: Faber.

Lane, Arthur (1972). *An Adequate Response: The War Poetry of Wilfred Owen and Siegfried Sassoon*, Detroit: Wayne State University Press.

Ledwidge, Francis (1992). *Selected Poems*, Dublin: New Island.

Lehman, John (1981). *The English Poets of the First World War*, London: Thames and Hudson.

Longley, Michael (1998). *Selected Poems*, London: Cape.

Muldoon, Paul (1998a). *Hay*, London: Faber.

Muldoon, Paul (1998b). 'Getting Round: Notes Towards an Ars Poetica', *Essays in Criticism*, 48: 2.

Owen, Wilfrid (1985). *Poems*, ed. Jon Stallworthy, London: Chatto.

Parfitt, G. (1990). *English Poetry of the First World War*, Brighton: Harvester.

Piette, Adam (1995). *Imagination at War: British Fiction and Poetry, 1939–1945*, London: Macmillan.

Pope, Alexander (1967). *The Twickenham Edition of the Poems of Alexander Pope, Vols 7 & 8: The Iliad of Homer*, ed. Maynard Mack, London: Methuen.

Silkin, Jon (1972). *Out of Battle: The Poetry of the Great War*, Oxford: Oxford University Press.

Smith, Stan (1982). *Inviolable Voice: History and Twentieth-century Poetry*, Dublin: Gill and Macmillan.

Stallworthy, Jon (1984). *The Oxford Book of War Poetry*, Oxford: Oxford University Press.

Thomas, Edward (1981). *A Language Not to be Betrayed: Selected Prose of Edward Thomas*, ed. Edna Longley, Manchester: Carcanet.

Yeats, William Butler (1936). *The Oxford Book of Modern Verse, 1892–1935*, Oxford: Clarendon Press.

Yeats, William Butler (1940). *Collected Poems*, London: Macmillan.

6

Poetry and Science

Tim Armstrong

The editors of the 1984 Penguin anthology *Poems of Science*, John Heath-Stubbs and Phillips Salman, note that almost all major poets in English, 'from Chaucer onwards, have, in some way, been concerned with the science of their day' (Heath-Stubbs and Salman, 1984, p. 34). However, they add that in the twentieth century 'the picture is rather different', suggesting that since the Victorians poetry and science have moved apart. For all that it has a partial truth, this is a claim that must be contested. Certainly the practice represented by verse translations of Lucretius or such didactic poems as Erasmus Darwin's *The Botanic Garden* have few modern equivalents. It is also true that with an increasingly technological science on the one hand, and with poetry increasingly seeking an alienated stance, on the other, the distance between cultural spheres has widened (a distance most famously represented by the 'two cultures' debate which erupted between F. R. Leavis and C. P. Snow in 1962). Other factors exacerbate this cultural divide: the corporatization and militarization of science; disciplinary separations in education; recent 'cultural' readings of science which have produced a defensive empiricism within the scientific community.

Nevertheless, twentieth-century poetry, at least, displays if anything a more complex involved relationship with science than that of almost any other period. The main explanation for this lies in the fact that scientific development and technological change have been central to notions of modernity. And if poetry has become an increasingly marginal and arcane activity, no longer granted the cultural centrality it had in the nineteenth century, it has for that very reason sought cultural authority and justification for its experimental stance through recourse to scientific metaphor. Poetry has incorporated science, then; but it has also continued to make Arnoldian claims that it offers a way of seeing the world with more fidelity to human experience than science, and the ability to bind knowledge into the human subject where science disperses and objectifies. These two aims – to incorporate the findings of science and to offer a critique of it – offer a partial contradiction, representing an ambivalence which is itself one of the keynotes of modernity.

To consider the conjunction of poetry and science involves raising a number of questions about what is at issue in that linkage: the field includes poems *about* science, its theories, historical development, and its leading figures, obviously; but more important are the relations between the conceptualization of poetry and science as fields, including their respective claims to cultural power, the impact of scientific models of communication on poetry, and the use of science-based metaphors. In what follows, a number of these topics will be considered within the framework of a chronological survey.

Modernist Responses to Science and Technology

The nineteenth century saw rapid advances in science which increasingly seemed to displace 'man' from the centre of the universe. Darwinian science suggested vast timescales in which recorded history was a pin-prick; the social sciences traced histories of languages and peoples; psychology depicted humans as driven by powerful and hidden forces; medicine and psychophysics represented the human body as a highly fallible apparatus. Most importantly, physics postulated new forces beyond the scale of the human, abandoning the mechanistic world of Newtonian physics for a new universe of invisible forces and energies: of electromagnetism ('Hertzian waves', 1888; X-rays, 1895), unstable matter (radium, 1898); of atoms conceived as vortices in the 'ether' rather than as stable entities.

At the same time, a tradition of critique of science's truth-claims developed. Critiques could be offered from within science itself: for a radical empiricist like Ernst Mach, scientific ideas are heuristic fictions which tell us as much about the organization and limits of our perception as about the 'real' world. Henri Poincaré – an inspiration to many modernists – argued that science simply offered ways of describing the world rather than absolute 'truth', seemingly closer to poetry than to mathematics. Perhaps the most influential attack on science was the Idealist F. H. Bradley's *Appearance and Reality* (1883). Bradley argued that the 'real' is better represented by the complex imagination of the poet rather than by the bloodless and abstract relations of the scientist, who creates the pretence that atoms and electromagnetic forces are the reality of the world. T. S. Eliot, who was to study Bradley as a research student, shared his understanding of the multiple world of the senses as well as his sense of the fracture between poetry and science (though in a typical reverse appropriation of science, Eliot was famously to declare that the best analogue for poetic creation was the action of a catalyst in chemistry, a substance which enabled other things to combine while remaining intact itself). Bradley's work fuelled the debate on whether science was a thin reduction of natural process (as Henri Bergson and T. E. Hulme contended) or in fact the best means of representing process and relatedness (Ernest Fenollosa: 'Poetry agrees with science and not with logic. . . . The more concretely and vividly we express the interactions of things the better for poetry') (cited in Bell, 1981, p. 101).

In fact, it was because the world posited by science, particularly after Einstein, was becoming so abstract and hypothetical that it came to seem like a kind of poetry. Using multi-dimensional geometries, statistical analyses of particles, positing matter with the properties of radiation, relativistic measurements, physics produced, as Wallace Stevens commented, 'a world in which there are no facts', in which science could be reclaimed for poetry. As Lisa Steinman puts it, in its indeterminacy 'the new physics seemed to heal the gap between the subjective and objective worlds' (Steinman, 1987, p. 65). We should perhaps stress the 'seemed' here, and the fact that modernist poets often gleaned their science second- or third-hand – from Arthur Eddington's *The Nature of the Physical World* (1928) and James Jeans's *The Mysterious Universe* (1930); from writings by Bertrand Russell and C. E. M. Joad. Perhaps the most influential exposition of scientific modernity was the philosopher Alfred North Whitehead's *Science and the Modern World* (1925), which with its discussions of quantum physics and its rejection of nineteenth-century materialism, was read by Stevens, Hart Crane and others as justifying a poetry of process, reflecting a chaotic new world.

As we will see, the poet who is central to the dissemination of scientific ideas within Anglophone modernism is Ezra Pound, who signed some of his essays 'Helmholtz' and who employed throughout his career a vocabulary derived from science, engineering and medicine: 'energy', 'precision', 'economy', 'diagnosis', 'antisepsis'. Pound's scientism served two broad purposes: to buttress the cultural authority of the critic; and to provide metaphors which might explain or energize a new style. In *Quantum Poetics* Daniel Albright argues that Pound, Yeats and Eliot were all inspired by particle physics in seeking the most elementary 'unit' of poetic utterance: the symbol, the image as dynamic monads. Mina Loy, in her poem 'Gertrude Stein' (*c.* 1924), describes her in a similar way as a 'Curie / of the laboratory / of vocabulary' who extracts 'a radium of the word' – countering Pound's linkage of scientific aesthetics to an anti-feminine stance.

Science was also, of course, linked to the huge technological changes of the new century, particularly in the USA. When Henry Adams sought a metaphor for the new era, he chose the giant Dynamo at the Paris Exposition in 1900, and for many modernist poets – for Yeats, Lawrence and others – the world of technological modernism was the enemy of the imagination. But another prominent strand of modernism, influenced by Italian futurism, celebrated the machine age. Gorham B. Munson, founder of the literary magazine *Succession*, declared in 1922 'a negative attitude towards modern life' and particularly 'Machinery' should be replaced by a more 'positive equilibrium'. William Carlos Williams's 'Classic Scene' celebrates an industrial landscape in which sits 'A power-house / in the shape of / a red brick chair / 90 feet high', a commanding American presence itself symbolic, like Adams's Dynamo, of modernity. Yet Williams also recognized the horror of technology disarticulated, or as *Paterson* III puts it 'Dürer's *Melancholy*, the gears / lying disrelated to the mathematics of the / machine / Useless'. His attitude is, then, complex and even dialectical: the disarticulations of a motor car, for example, might even be a kind of creative process (as the car crash is in *The Great American Novel*). Others distinguished between different uses of science and technology: Hart Crane in the 'Cape Hatteras' section of *The Bridge*, for example, juxtaposes 'the looming stacks of the gigantic power house' and 'Power's script, – wound, bobbin-bound, refined' with the aspiration towards 'marathons new-set between the stars' represented by the Wright brothers. Crane insisted that poetry must 'absorb the machine', but he shared a general suspicion of what machine-age culture meant in practice.

Finally, it is important to note that relations between science and poetry are complex and mobile. Attitudes to Einstein act as a kind of indicator of these fluctuating and highly charged links. Hardy's 'Drinking Song' (1928) sees him as the culmination of the process of stripping away human illusion that began with Copernicus: 'And now comes Einstein with a notion – . . . / That there's no time, no space, no motion, / Nor rathe nor late, / Nor square nor straight, / But just a sort of bending-ocean'). Archibald MacLeish's 'Einstein' (1929) sees him as a solitary Prometheus, wrestling with the secrets of the universe. Marianne Moore's 'The Student' (1932) sees him as the embodiment of scientific open-mindedness. But for Pound, Lewis and others the relativistic universe was repellently fluid, offering the very opposite to the precision and classicism they sought (compare Lewis's fulminations against the 'slick' and 'streamlined'). Indeed, Lewis's 1934 description of Einstein as the 'race-mate' of Spinoza and Bergson anticipates the 'German Science' of the Nazis.

Technologies of Communication

In more material ways, new technologies shifted poetic styles. The typewriter completed the move towards the poem as a design on the page begun by Mallarmé in *Un Coup de dés*, making way for the ludic typographies of e e cummings and A. R. Ammons's *Tape for the Turn of the Year* (1965), written on adding-machine tape. In the new technologies of reproduction, Friedrich Kittler has argued, language is disconnected from subjectivity, becomes a pure system, describable in the manner that the linguist Ferdinand de Saussure was developing in the early years of the century. At the very least, the technological (re)production of language exacerbated the split between what Charles Olson was to call 'discrimination (logos)' and 'shout (tongue)' (Olson, 1989, p. 155). Such de-natured language might even be occult, as in the babble of voices at the seance table which seems to inform *The Waste Land*, or the automatic writing techniques used or referred to by the Surrealists, Stein, Williams and others. Modernist typographers also revolutionized design; Bob Brown imagined new machines for reading and printed poems in microscopic typefaces.

More importantly, science and technology provided new metaphors for poetic communication: telegraphy, telephony, radio and even television all suggested the possibilities of a swifter and less mediated transmission of ideas; as did the related pseudoscience of spiritualism (always important in modernism as a way of reclaiming science for the human). The Italian Futurists as well as Pound and other anglophone modernists (under the influence of Fenollosa on the Chinese written character) promoted the fantasy of an unmediated language, whether mathematical or pictographic, shorn of ambiguity and interpretive uncertainty, transmitted directly to the reader. The modernist poets were all fascinated by wave-forms as a model for the transfer of energies. In 'Psychology and Troubadours' (1912), later published in *The Spirit of Romance*, Pound had declared that 'Man is – the sensitive part of him – a mechanism . . . rather like an electric appliance, switches, wires, etc.' (Pound, 1952, p. 92). F. T. Marinetti's idea of the 'wireless imagination' is taken up in Pound's enthusiasm for radio broadcasts as a direct mode of communication, and in Wyndham Lewis's enthusiasm for radio work. In *Canto* 38 Pound depicts Marconi meeting (and in some sense supplanting) the pope.

A second outcome of the technologizing of writing is a stress on the 'efficiency' of the poem – as if it were the object of the scientific management or streamlined design. In Pound's various Imagist and Vorticist manifestos, he repeatedly insisted that the poet's approach should be that of the engineer or surgeon, using no word which does not contribute to the effect, stripping out the 'subjective' element, the 'waste'. This was a programme Pound shared with contemporaries: with Marianne Moore, whose poems not only celebrate scientists and American efficiency, but themselves seem like carefully engineered and precisely observed experiments (many of them stamped out on a syllabic grid like industrial products). As Lisa Steinman shows, Moore refuses an opposition of science and poetry, stressing instead the pragmatics of thinking, and holding in tension her idealized version of America's modernity with its commercial reality (Steinman, 1987, pp. 113–32). William Carlos Williams, trained in the new specialized and rationalist Flexnerian medicine, like Pound and Moore stressed the clinical eye of the poet and the efficiency of the poem, a programme exemplified by his stripped-down language and emphasis on the edge, the cut. In his introduction to *The Wedge* (1944) Williams was still insisting that 'A poem is a small (or large) machine made of words'; a machine which, in a characteristic dovetailing of the organic and the mechanical, must be 'pruned to a perfect economy'.

Modernist aesthetics found a ready response in literary criticism in the period between the wars, which also sought to ground its authority in notions of scientific objectivity and exactitude. The New Criticism, claiming that it had succeeded in isolating the poem as the unit of analysis, aspired to a scientific objectivity. I. A. Richards – famous for his experiments with unlabelled poems and undergraduate readers – begins the *Principles of Literary Criticism* (1924) with the claim that 'A book is a machine to think with'. Here and in *The Meaning of Meaning* (co-authored with Ogden) Richards is obsessed with the physiology of literary response in a way which has its origins in the physiological aesthetics of the nineteenth century. Yet in *Science and Poetry* (1926) Richards also stresses that the two are opposed, like Matthew Arnold giving poetry a central role in balancing experience. The poetic career of Laura Riding represents one end-point of this rationalism: just as Richards turned to the certainties of communication in positing a 'Basic English', Riding abandoned poetry in the late 1930s, escaping what Jerome McGann calls the 'Kantian ghetto' –

the 'lying word' of metaphor – for the ideal of exact definitions which was to culminate in the dictionary of rationalized concepts prepared with her husband Schuyler B. Jackson.

Darwinism and Vitalism

The Darwinian world-view initiates two different currents in modern literature. One tends towards the analysis of the world as system and incipient order. The biologist Louis Agassiz's doctrine of 'correspondences', espoused by Emerson, finds echoes throughout the twentieth century: not only in Pound's use of his work, but in comments like Moore's declaration that Williams's strength is 'the ability to see resemblances in things which are dissimilar' (Moore, 1986, p. 56). To be sure, for the strict Darwinist the world is a place of disorder, of random variations – and the best example here is Thomas Hardy. As a Victorian novelist Hardy read Spencer and Comte and moved in scientific circles in London; as a largely twentieth-century poet he kept abreast of scientific thinking. Hardy's Darwinism refuses even the comforts of 'organic memory' (the idea that memory may be inherited biologically, taken up by Lawrence and others), and depicts a world dominated by chance, a universe in which human beings are, like the rest of creation, struggling to adapt. He meditates on the determination of the self by its genetic inheritance in 'Heredity', 'The Pedigree' and other poems. Hardy describes a universe which seems (as the Second Law of Thermodynamics stated) to be running down, radiating its energies outwards.

Robert Frost's Darwinism is gentler than Hardy's in its stress on the flow of existence (the metaphors of the stream and the forking path recur in his poetry) rather than the painful anomaly of human consciousness. It is apparent not only in such overtly Darwinian poems as 'Accidentally on Purpose', 'Design' and the late satire 'Etherializing', but also in poems like 'The Most of It', in which the poet confronts the blank unresponsiveness of the natural world, an unresponsiveness which pauses between the mythic and the merely natural. Frost's aesthetic flourishes on the particular; in an interview he insisted that 'Life has lost none of its mystery and romance', despite science's incursions into the unknown, adding 'The more we know the less we know' (cited in Faggen, 1997, p. 39).

Later examples of Darwinian thinking can be seen in Charles Olson's geological planes and layerings, exploring the effect of the encounter with the new landscape on the making of Americans and tracing continental origins back to Gondwanaland (though subsuming this narrative to the mythical figure of Maximus), and using the American geographer Carl Sauer and the biologist Edgar Anderson. The nineteenth-century life sciences continue to foster an observational poetics. Writing of her favourite naturalists in the 1950s, Lorine Niedecker lists 'Audubon, Gilbert White, Agassiz, Crèvecoeur', adding 'I will look into Humboldt'. Niedecker's late sequence of five poems entitled 'Darwin' explores the Victorian naturalist's

apprehension of a world of disorder and cataclysm, resolved in the 'Paradise Puzzle'
of the Galapagos Islands into his 'carcass- / conclusions':

> the universe
>   not built by brute force
>   but designed by laws
> The details left
>
> to the working of chance
>   'Let each man hope
>   and believe
> what he can'

This sounds like a programme for Niedecker's own tentative poetics in the Thoreau-
vian ramble of 'Wintergreen Ridge' (1968) and other poems of landscape, botany and
geology: the future and the landscape are open, even within the constraints of scientific understanding; the fragilities of human time are defended. Similar explorations
of landscape can be found in such poems as A. R. Ammons's 'Corson's Inlet' (1965),
with its description of the ebb and flow of life, 'pulsations of order / in the bellies of
minnows', corresponding in turn to the poet's own 'eddies of meaning . . . running /
like a stream through the geography of my work'. A more radical example is Lyn
Hejinian's *The Cell* (1992), which cannot be directly related to biology, but which
exists in close relation to ideas of growth, ageing, randomness, even selection:

> There is a sentence and
>   therefore a sensation, an incorporation
> The body, but it cannot
>   hold
> Blueness holds the sky and
>   the sea is bound
> Discontinuity without certainty of end
> This is society, not science
> Where are your polarities, your
>   transitions
> Only gerunds, during a seduction,
>   it being a selection

In a way which is never fully explicit, this is an aleatory poetry which in its terms
and arguably in its method could not exist without modern science; without field
theory and the critique of Newtonian physics (and if Hejinian seems to recall Tyndall's
famous demonstrations of the scattering of light to create the blueness of the sky, that
too was a demonstration of the 'poetry' of science).

If the first inheritance of Darwinian science is thus in notions of disorder and order
in the natural world, the second consequence of evolutionary thinking as promulgated

by Spencer, Lamarck and others (and as reinforced by Nietzsche) is Vitalism: the idea that a unique (often sexual) energy impels all life. The result is a stress on the individual's need, as Bruce Clarke puts it, to 'clear out the dead wood of instrumental thought and fill itself with nature's "rhythmic urge" towards higher forms' (Clarke, 1996, p. 159). A vitalist egoism underpins accounts of creativity in the work of Pound (influenced by the French essayist Remy de Gourmont), Lawrence, Stein, Mina Loy and other modernists. For these writers, creation is sexual; for the male writers, a result of masculine sexuality acting on the 'passive' and 'conservative' world of social life. Williams shared this vitalist stress on sexual energy, developed from Dora Marsden's version of the ideas of the sexologist Otto Weininger. *Spring and All* (1923) includes 'Sometimes I speak of imagination as a force, an electricity or a medium, a place. It is immaterial which: for whether it is the condition of a place or a dynamization its effect is the same: to free the world of fact from the impositions of "art" . . . and to liberate the man to act in whatever direction his disposition leads.' 'The true procreative process', Williams wrote, 'is at the back of all genius.' In such accounts of creativity – which find postwar echoes in any number of poets – the body becomes fundamental to writing, and bodily interventions (like W. B. Yeats's Steinach Operation, designed to rejuvenate the failing poet) might have effects on poetry. Charles Olson, who was in many ways Pound's most significant inheritor as an appropriator of science, insisted in a 1962 essay that 'the soul is proprioceptive', that 'total experience' goes as deep as the cell (Olson, 1989, p. 183).

Field Theory: Energy as Organization

The modernist interest in the new physics, described above in terms of communication, also had implications for poetic design for Pound and his followers. 'The rose in the steel dust' – the pattern produced by electromagnetic forces Pound described in 'Psychology and Troubadours' and other essays – seemed to embody the mysterious flow of energies towards a design he saw in primitive art; and to provide a model for the image as a 'radiant node or cluster'; and slightly later for the 'vortex' which was both a historical confluence of forces and an aesthetic design like that of the *Cantos*. Pound derived the term 'vortex' from a reading of the pre-Socratics as well as from modern sciences (specifically, as Ian Bell shows, Helmholtz's work on the vortex in hydrodynamics, developed by Kelvin for use in describing the twisting of atoms in the 'ether') (Bell, 1981, p. 163). What the term allowed was an idea of design as dictated by the energies of the materials involved, producing the poem as a field of activity in which elements exist in dynamic and organic relation to each other (here, as so often, rather vaguely specified ideas flow together: the vitalism described above could produce similar conclusions).

The semiotician C. S. Peirce is one point of reference here. Not only does he, as Gillian Beer points out (Beer, 1996, p. 297), argue against determinism in 'The Doctrine of Necessity Examined' (1892), but for later writers like Muriel Rukeyser he serves as a foundational thinker in relation to the notion of an interpretive field in which poet, poem and reader all interact. Rukeyser began by exploring such subjects as aviation and industrial technology in *Theory of Flight* (1935), the volume with which she won the Yale Younger Poets prize. Rukeyser attacked industrial America in *The Book of the Dead*, her account of silicosis in West Virginia, but continued to incorporate the language of science into her poetry and later served as an adviser to the Exploratorium, the pioneering San Francisco museum. In 1942 she published a study of the American theoretical physicist and mathematician Willard Gibbs, often described as the founder of thermodynamics. Gibbs provided a 'language of process . . . language of the kind of life that is not a point-to-point movement, but a real flow in which everything is seen as deeply related to everything else'. In *The Life of Poetry* (1949) she expounds this poetics of connection, bringing in biology, the cutting of film, the study of sound-waves; asserting that the poet, scientist and mathematician seek 'a system of relations', and that the exchange of energies is central to both poetry and science.

In the work of other poets this becomes a fully elaborated theory of poetry. William Carlos Williams considered that Einsteinian physics had opened the way to a new conception of poetic form, as well as of space-time. In 'The Poem as a Field of Action' (1948) he formalizes the theoretical foundation of what becomes, in Charles Olson and his followers, 'composition by field' – a conceptualization of poetry as an array of forces, as a discursive space with its own internal relations between elements. Like Williams, Olson saw modern science's non-Euclidian space (which he studied via such texts as Whitehead's *Process and Reality*, 1929) as justifying his procedures, suggesting that the real may in fact be a matter of *form*: a dynamic arrangement of forces or pathways (method is 'the science of the path', he writes in *Letters for Origin*) (Olson, 1989, p. 106). His 1957 essay 'Equal, That Is, to the Real Itself' spells out the implication of this view of poetry in terms of what he calls a 'Riemannian' metrical field in which textual space bends around reality (Olson, 1997, p. 125).

One result of field theory is a heightened sense of intertextual relations. From Pound onwards, poets have produced texts in which are suspended the words of others, leaving the reader to see a dynamic relationship between the fragments so dispersed: Pound's multiple sources in the *Cantos*, bound together within the vortex of history; Williams's letters and other found texts in *Paterson* and Olson's records of early and later Gloucester in *Maximus*, associated by location; the scattered texts of Melville and Mangan in Susan Howe's 'Melville's Marginalia'. As Olson's annotator George Butterick comments, such widespread borrowing raises 'fundamental questions as to . . . the limits of originality in art' (Butterick, 1978, p. xi).

Other Postwar Poetry

In the postwar world, one keynote of earlier responses to science and technology, the use of these fields to lend cultural authority to literary experimentation, becomes harder to sustain. The Second World War saw science's claims to detachment compromised (eugenics was discredited by Nazi policies; nuclear physics enabled the horror of Hiroshima). In the USA, the war left the legacy of what Eisenhower in his 1961 valedictory address dubbed the 'military–industrial complex', spawning napalm and the neutron bomb as well as moon landings. Within the counterculture of the 1950s and 1960s, science could offer little that seemed attractive, beyond an engagement with the death drive. Gregory Corso's 'Bomb' (1960), with its exuberant mock paean, is a representative example of the nuclear sublime:

> BOOM ye skies and BOOM ye suns
> BOOM BOOM ye moons   ye stars BOOM
> nights ye BOOM   ye days ye BOOM

The troubled, promethean status of technology (explored in English poet Tony Harrison's recent film–poem on the declining coal industry, *Prometheus*, 1998) means that it inspires few direct celebrations. Moreover the confessional bent of American poetry, in particular, and later its turn towards identity politics and recovered histories, means that meditation on science has easily seemed mandarin (and, too often, masculine).

Nevertheless, science remains a field of knowledge which challenges the poet whose ambitions include all twentieth-century knowledge, and which continues to provide resources for an avant-garde. As in modernism, one way of reappropriating science is through the occult. An example is the American poet James Merrill, who in 1953 began to spin out sequences from the Ouija board. In *Mirabell's Books of Number* (1978), his spirit-overseers suddenly demand, in 1975–6, 'POEMS OF SCIENCE' adding 'WE SPEAK FROM WITHIN THE ATOM'. Although the poet dislikes this demand he sets to work reading a 'biophysichemical / Textbook' and produces a mathematically arranged poem, taking in histories of science and technology offered by his interlocutors, antimatter 'batwing angels'. The first fruits of this effort are like a parody of science poetry:

> Proton and Neutron
> Under a plane tree by the stream repeat
> Their eclogue, orbited by twinkling flocks.
> And on the dimmest shores of consciousness
> Polypeptides – in primeval thrall
> To what new moon I wonder – rise and fall.

The poet eventually does better, but what he learns remains notably occult: that the batwing angels create black holes and pure mind; that they fell away from the GOD BIOLOGY who is the positive force within the atom (creating sunlight, from which life comes); and that since Fermi split the atom humankind is in similar danger. The human sector of Creation is governed by spirits who create the leaders of humankind and pursue other experiments, including slipping the first human soul 'INTO AN APE FETUS'. In Merrill's text science appears as a demand. Science and poetry are drawn together as fields of imaginative activity; the Fall is retold as nuclear physics. Numerology and gnostic stories of light jostle with meditations on photosynthesis, DNA and nuclear physics. But Merrill's plunge into science reserves a role to creative imagination: if the spirits insist that their science governs history, the bat-spirit Mirabell changes into a peacock, schooled in humanity and love by Merrill, his partner David Jackson and their favourite spirits Maria and Wystan (Auden).

If Merrill – like the English poet Peter Redgrove, who also explores the occult – works within a humanist tradition which seeks accommodation with science, later poets have been as interested in science as a linguistic field, and as providing accounts of the control and dispersal of information. In particular, recent mathematical studies of the concepts of noise and chaos (and philosophical elaborations of those concepts by Michel Serres and others) have allowed the reconceptualization of literary obscurity. Where the early twentieth century saw a world of disorder and chaos which the poet might order in a leap of imagination (an evolutionary extension which Olson was still celebrating when he described his hero Maximus as a principle of 'selectivity'), chaos theory provides an explanation for patterns which emerge spontaneously from complex and highly random dynamic systems. If such systems are highly sensitive to initial conditions (as in the famous 'butterfly's wing' effect), they nevertheless do produce order.

It is arguably recent British rather than American poets who respond most interestingly to such ideas. Examples of contemporary British poets working with science are the Scottish poet Edwin Morgan and the English poet Allen Fisher (though others including J. H. Prynne, Thomas A. Clarke and Gilbert Adair could as equally be picked out). Morgan works in a more ludic and eclectic mode, taking in geology and paleography ('The Archaeopteryx's Song'), physics, cybernetics, language processing, communication technologies and computing (*Emergent Poems*, 1967). 'Pleasures of a Technological University' imagines a curriculum written across the Arts/Science divide; *Star Gate: Science Fiction Poems* (1979) borrows the conventions of science fiction to imagine new particles, new forms of life which in fact are new forms of poetry. 'From the Video Box' (1986) amusingly borrows a television format to comment on technologies of reproduction ('There is something wrong with Channel 49', he reports having found his set bleeding). For Morgan, science is an area to be raided, recycled, recombined; a set of procedures, languages, topics which the poet can use productively rather than seeing technology as in opposition to culture.

Fisher – who worked as the manager of a lead factory – is more systematically and materially interested in science's construction of the world; he reads modern science in a Lucretian sense as offering a key to the flux of existence, to connections and interactions which in its abstraction it has never fully humanized. He is also attentive to the way in which technology threatens the human subject. In his earlier work he experimented with techniques of 'randomizing', processing existing texts to loosen meaning and focus attention on procedure (in contrast to Morgan whose 'randomized' texts are always artfully constructed); his later work explores optics, fractals, gravitation, biology, genetics, technology, carefully sorting among these fields (and detailing his sources in booklists at the end of each volume). To some extent he inherits the field theory of earlier writers. In *Place*, XXXV he writes

> we are part of an interaction
> ununified
> electromagnetic and gravitational
>
> fields contradict
> birds sensitive to axis not polarity
> fish
> thru sea water see
> through a moving conductor
> flowing
> past the lines of force
> thru the magnetics
> setting up a perpendicular current
> a direction
> of flow and field
> contradicting reason

Brixton Fractals (1985) use the fact that fractals are used in image processing to 'estimate a vector of survival from seriously incomplete or hidden data'. Elsewhere Fisher also employs catastrophe theory and 'phase change'. The result is an aesthetic of fragmentation and disorder which neither seeks an implied higher order which might organize the text, nor simply remains dispersed. Instead the idea of the fractal allows Fisher to imply a set of correspondences, of patterns that emerge and re-emerge in different forms. For example, 'Hubble' (in *Dispossession and Cure*, 1994) is subtitled 'In celebration of the confirmation that the universe is expanding', but also includes biological references:

> Lambda DASH and FIX clone your DNA
> into superior vectors surrounded by
> Not I sites that facilitate easy excision
> of inserts and rapid gene mapping

Another area in which science has impinged on poetry is in information technologies. Given the fascination with the processing of words in L = A = N = G = U = A = G = E poetry, it is unsurprising that computer programs have been used to generate or alter texts: for example the American poet Jackson Mac Low's poem 'Giant Philosophical Otters' uses a program called TRAVESTY to mix an earlier poem by the author and Wittgenstein's *Philosophical Investigations*. This tradition has its origins in the interface between literature, science and mathematics represented in earlier avant-gardes by Raymond Roussel's self-generating texts, Gertrude Stein's work in the Harvard psychology laboratories at the turn of the century, Duchamp's 'playful physics', and John Cage's language experiments.

Finally, technologies have profoundly influenced the material production of poetry. If early in the century a gap opened between the luxury of the hand-press and mass-market publishing, in the period after the Second World War the possibility of roneoed, cyclostyled or photocopied work expanded small-press publication. The advent of the CD-Rom and internet has also begun to offer new possibilities; not only cheaper and targeted delivery of poetry but also ongoing innovations in the use of multimedia, hypermedia and design.

BIBLIOGRAPHY

Albright, D. (1997). *Quantum Poetics: Yeats, Pound, Eliot and the Science of Modernism*. Cambridge: Cambridge University Press.

Armstrong, T. (1998). *Modernism, Technology and the Body: A Cultural Study*. Cambridge: Cambridge University Press.

Beer, G. (1996). *Open Fields: Science in Cultural Encounter*. Oxford: Clarendon Press.

Bell, I. F. A. (1981). *Critic as Scientist: The Modernist Poetics of Ezra Pound*. New York: Methuen.

Butterick, G. F. (1978). *A Guide to the Maximus Poems of Charles Olson*. Berkeley: University of California Press.

Clarke, B. (1996). *Dora Marsden and Early Modernism: Gender, Individualism and Science*. Ann Arbor: University of Michigan Press.

Faggen, R. (1997). *Robert Frost and the Challenge of Darwin*. Ann Arbor: University of Michigan Press.

Hamilton, R. (1982). *Science and Psychodrama: The Poetry of Edwin Morgan and David Black*. Frome, Somerset: Bran's Head Books.

Hayles, N. K. (1984). *The Cosmic Web: Scientific Field Models and Literary Strategies in the Twentieth Century*. Ithaca, NY: Cornell University Press.

Heath-Stubbs, J. and P. Salman, eds. (1984). *Poems of Science*. Harmondsworth: Penguin.

Kenner, H. (1987). *The Mechanic Muse*. New York: Oxford University Press.

Kittler, F. A. (1990). *Discourse Networks 1800/1900*. Trans. Michael Metteer. Stanford, CA: Stanford University Press. (Original work published 1985.)

McGann, J. (1993). *Black Riders: The Visible Language of Modernism*. Princeton, NJ: Princeton University Press.

Moore, M. (1986). *The Complete Prose of Marianne Moore*. Ed. P. C. Willis. New York: Viking Penguin.

Olson, C. (1997). *Collected Prose*. Ed. D. Allen and B. Friedlander, intro. R. Creeley. Berkeley: University of California Press.

Olson, C. (1989). *Letters for Origin 1950–1956*. Ed. A. Glover. Foreword J. Tytell. New York: Paragon House. (Originally published 1969.)

Otis, L. (1994). *Organic Memory: History and the Body in the Late Nineteenth and Early Twentieth Centuries*. Lincoln: University of Nebraska Press.

Pound, E. (1952). *The Spirit of Romance*. Revised edn. London: Peter Owen.

Rabinbach, A. (1990). *The Human Motor: Energy, Fatigue, and the Origins of Modernity*. New York: Basic Books.

Ross, D., ed. (1994). *Modernist Impulses in the Human Sciences 1870–1930*. Baltimore, MD: Johns Hopkins University Press.

Scholnick, R., ed. (1992). *American Literature and Science*. Lexington: University Press of Kentucky.

Serres, M. (1995). *Genesis*. Trans. Geneviève James and James Nielson. Ann Arbor: University of Michigan Press. (Original work published 1982.)

Steinman, L. M. (1987). *Made in America: Science, Technology and the American Modernist Poets*. New Haven, CT: Yale University Press.

Tichi, C. (1987). *Shifting Gears: Technology, Literature and Culture in Modernist America*. Chapel Hill: University of North Carolina Press.

Tiffany, D. (1995). *Radio Corpse: Imagism and the Cryptaesthetic of Ezra Pound*. Cambridge, MA: Harvard University Press.

Walker, N. W. and M. F. Walker (1989). *The Twain Meet: The Physical Sciences and Poetry*. New York: Peter Lang.

7
Poetry and Literary Theory
Joanne Feit Diehl

Despite many poets' explicit aversion to literary theory, poetry and theory have been closely entwined throughout the twentieth century. Indeed, from the era of the New Criticism to the current experimentation of the Language Poets, poetry has reflected and responded to theoretical premises, sometimes to embrace and at other times to challenge theory's presuppositions. In this essay, I assert that poetry has a distinctive relationship to theoretical issues because poetry, by its very nature, foregrounds structural elements and the deployment of language. Poetry I suggest is *proprioceptive*: discreet, idiosyncratic choices of language cast a self-reflexive light onto the underlying theoretical assumptions that inform the poem's writing. Thus, poetry might be regarded as a staging, a theatricalization of whatever premises govern that poem's specific, imaginary construction. Historically, poetry has been on the cusp of controversy as its shifting forms experiment with issues of expressivity, language usage, and the poetic 'self'.

Given the richness and complexity of the relationship between poetry and theory throughout the century, I present here a description of that relationship which focuses upon three facets of this historical interplay: the controversy surrounding the applicability of psychoanalytic methods to literary works, the effect of deconstruction on contemporary poetics, and the theoretical issues that inform contemporary poetry. My emphasis on these three historical moments does not, however, mean to suggest that other theoretical movements were not of crucial importance both to the reader and writer of poetry over the course of the past century. The rise of the New Criticism, the significance of reader-response theory, the underlying premises of Marxist practice – all deserve a forum for discussion. Yet I remain convinced that a more thorough exploration of how a few schools of thought affect the writing of poetry will better illustrate the ways in which the creative imagination is influenced by and itself transforms ideology.

Crucial to recent developments in poetry and literary theory is the controversy surrounding the self – whether a poem accurately represents the voice of a singular, unified authorial imagination or whether the poem comes from a 'subject position' and denies its author the status of an identifiable, writerly self. As Terry Eagleton, writing of the Russian formalists, recalls, 'Pushkin's *Eugene Onegin*, Osip Brik once airily remarked, would have been written even if Pushkin had not lived' (Eagleton, 1996, p. 3). While poets have struggled with the contested nature of the self, psychoanalytic criticism, in contrast to deconstruction, has shored up the authorial subject and argued that the expressive voice of a poem finds its source in a singular imagination. What the contemporary psychoanalyst, Jessica Benjamin, remarks *vis-à-vis* the deconstructive position of the self can equally be applied to the literary field:

> Psychoanalysis has to retain some notion of the subject as a self, a historical being that preserves its history in the unconscious, whatever scepticism we allow about reaching the truth of that history. Even if the self is not unitary but has multiple positions and voices, psychoanalysis must be able to conceive of the person's singularity, his or her aesthetic or unique idiom (Bollas, *Being A Character*, 1992). Even if the subject's positions are 'constructed, psychoanalysis must imagine someone who does or does not own them' (Rivera, 'Linking the Psychological and the Social: Feminism, Poststructuralism and Multiple Personality,' *Dissociation* 2, no. 1, 1989). And precisely because psychoanalysis claims that something else that is not-I (not ego but *It*) speaks, that the self is split and unconsciousness is unknown, It must also be considered to belong to the self. And this idea of an otherness within, an unconscious, unavoidably both transforms and preserves (*Aufhebung*) the idea of a transhistorical, essential self: not a Cartesian ego, not even all ego, but still a being separately embodied, and in that sense an individual psyche. (Benjamin, 1998, p. 13)

The current controversy between the psychoanalytic understanding of the self and the postmodernist concept of the discontinuous and elided 'subject' is, moreover, just the latest forum for the ongoing debate about the nature of the authorial subject and its relation to poetic voice. We are descendants of a Wordsworthian past, and Wordsworth's definition of the subject of his poems, 'emotion recollected in tranquillity', affects his Romantic and post-Romantic heirs, predicated as it is upon a unified, continuous, historically constitutive self that draws upon the memories of a knowable and present identity. This sense of an abiding identity of mind is intimately related to the Romantic and post-Romantic notion of poetry's mission, its special grace. Writing in 1998, Robert Pinsky, the United States Poet Laureate, expressed his view of the distinguishing quality of poetry:

> Poetry is a vocal, which is to say a bodily, art. The medium of poetry is a human body: the column of air inside the chest, shaped into signifying sounds in the larynx and the mouth. In this sense, poetry is just as physical or bodily an art as dancing.
>
> Moreover, there is a special intimacy to poetry because, in this area of the art, the medium is not an expert's body, as when one goes to the ballet: in poetry, the medium is the audience's body. (Pinsky, 1999, p. 8)

This intermingling of poet and reader in which the reader assumes the role of corporeal vessel expressing the poet's voice is predicated upon the Wordsworthian ideal. Interestingly, T. S. Eliot, who elsewhere advocates the displacement of emotion upon the object world and enforces thereby an illusory distance between poet and poem, draws upon a similar constellation of Wordsworthian feelings. In 'The Music of Poetry' Eliot writes that poetry 'remains, all the same, one person talking to another; and this is just as true if you sing it, for singing is another way of talking. The immediacy of poetry to conversation is not a matter on which we can lay down exact laws. Every revolution in poetry is apt to be, and sometimes to announce itself to be, a return to common speech. That is the revolution which Wordsworth announced in his prefaces, and he was right' (Eliot, 1957, p. 23). Strikingly, Louise Glück and Adrienne Rich, two poets who could not be more different, share this aesthetics of intimacy and bodily speech. In her extraordinary sequence 'Marathon', Glück draws upon the myth of Cupid and Psyche to inscribe the corporeal as Eros marks the body, transforming it into a sign that testifies to desire:

> 3. The Encounter
> You came to the side of the bed
> and sat staring at me.
> Then you kissed me – I felt
> hot wax on my forehead.
> I wanted it to leave a mark:
> that's how I knew I loved you.
> Because I wanted to be burned, stamped,
> to have something in the end –
> I drew the gown over my head;
> a red flush covered my face and shoulders.
> It will run its course, the course of fire,
> setting a cold coin on the forehead, between the eyes.
> You lay beside me; your hand moved over my face
> as though you had felt it also –
> you must have known, then, how I wanted you.
> We will always know that, you and I.
> The proof will be my body.

Of the relation between poet and reader, Glück comments, 'When you read anything worth remembering, you liberate a human voice; you release into the world again a companion spirit. I read poems to hear that voice. And I write to speak to those I have heard' (Glück, 1995, p. 128). So important is the voice for Rich that numerous poems ventriloquize as they inhabit other women of power. Rich reclaims silenced women of history by capturing the powerful cadences of her own imagination. Thus, she both identifies herself with courageous women from the past and provides access to their autonomous selves. Repeatedly Rich has argued for a 'common language', a Wordsworthian, Romantic notion, but here applied to the desire for a demotic and female-identified speech. Conversation is her model for poetic communication. In a similar vein, Glück states, 'I wanted a poetry that said, "Come here, let me whisper in your ear." Clandestine' (Glück in private conversation with the author).

As powerful as Rich and Glück are, however, they exemplify only one hitherto dominant ideological position, that of the late Romantic, expressive poet. If literary theory has exercised a major influence upon poetic tradition, it is in the area of autho- rial subjectivity, the very tenet of primary importance for the Wordsworthian poet. Here, following the lead of Roland Barthes and Jacques Derrida, theorists have pos- tulated the disappearance of a unified subjectivity – the author vanishes. Philosoph- ically, what these thinkers challenge is the concept of a single, transhistorical consciousness that can be identified as a unified self. As Ron Silliman has remarked of the LANGUAGE poets, who have embraced the absence of a coherent selfhood, 'Our work denies the centrality of the individual artist. . . . The self as the central and final term of creative practice is being challenged and exploded in our writing' (Silliman et al., 1988, p. 264; quoted by Perloff, 1999). Along with this dispersal of subjectivity has come a sweeping experimentalism as the linearity and conventionally normative patterns of poetic discourse are uprooted, replaced by a radical poetics that abjures linear reasoning along with an overt subjectivity. Interestingly, however, many of the most experimental poets advocate the importance of the voice, the performa- tive aspects of poetic production. Poetry readings, poetry 'slams', open-mike events – all privilege the poet as performer. Of course, the performative aspects of oral pre- sentation emphasize spontaneity and the illusion that one is creating one's self in the moment, qualities contrary to the notion of a unified self-coherence.

Diametrically opposed to the postmodernist condemnation of the traditional poetic self, psychoanalytic theorists predicate their work on the very presence postmodernists would deny. Perhaps the most noteworthy and notorious of these theorists is Harold Bloom, whose theory of poetic influence is nothing if not, to use Jacques Lacan's phrase, 'The Language of The Self'. Yet the self Bloom invokes is not simply the bio- graphical author but what he calls 'the poet within the poet'. Reaching back to Freud, particularly to his theory of the Oedipus Complex, Bloom posits an agon (a struggle or war) between the would-be young poet and his most powerful precursors. The young poet *misreads* his formidable progenitor and responds to that reading by swerv- ing from his interpretation to create his own version of a poem. This process of mis- reading, swerving and reconstituting the imaginative field is laced with oedipal anxiety. As Bloom states, 'Battle between strong equals, father and son as mighty opposites, Laius and Oedipus at the crossroads; only this is my subject here' (Bloom, 1973, p. 11). Indeed, Bloom conceives of this agon as defining the Western poetic tradition from the Renaissance to the contemporary:

> Poetic Influence – when it involves two strong, authentic poets – always proceeds by a misreading of the prior poet, an act of creative correction that is actually and neces- sarily a misinterpretation. The history of fruitful poetic influence, which is to say the main tradition of Western poetry since the Renaissance, is a history of anxiety and

self-saving caricature, of distortion, of perverse, wilful revisionism without which modern poetry as such could not exist. (Ibid., p. 30)

Although Bloom insists that the authorial self he describes is the 'poet *as poet*', the psychodynamics of poetic influence that he elaborates is based upon a psychology of the creative self. As Bloom asserts, 'Poems are written by men, [*sic*] and not by anonymous Splendors' (ibid., p. 43). For Bloom, the individuality of the poet is synonymous with the authenticity of the poem:

> Yet a poet's stance, his Word, his imaginative identity, his whole being *must* be unique to him, and remain unique or he will perish, as a poet, if ever even he has managed his re-birth into poetic incarnation. (Ibid., p. 71)

What Bloom offers is not simply a psychological portrait of 'influence' but a 'practical criticism'. In line with this stated ambition, Bloom designates six phases in the life of the 'poet as poet' which provide a guide to reading. According to Bloom, the stages – Clinamen, Tessera, Kenosis, Daemonization, Askesis and Apophrades – constitute a rubric through which to understand the process by which the 'strong' poet comes to write. 'Clinamen' the first term, is a swerve, or a poetic 'misprision', by which the poet creates a space for 'himself' by misreading the powerful precursor's work:

> Let us give up the failed enterprise of seeking to 'understand' any single poem as an entity in itself. Let us pursue instead the quest of learning to read any poem as its poet's deliberate misinterpretation, as a poet, of a precursor poem or of poetry in general. Know each poem by its clinamen and you will 'know' that poem in a way that will not purchase knowledge by the loss of the poem's power. (Ibid., p. 43)

For Bloom, 'the true history of modern poetry would be the accurate recording of these revisionary swerves', a process by which the younger poet misreads his precursor and swerves away from what he misperceives.

Once he has misperceived the poem and in that act created an opening for himself, the poet establishes both a link to and a 'correction' of the poetic father's poem: 'In the *tessera*, the later poet provides what his imagination tells him would complete the otherwise "truncated" precursor poem and poet, a "completion" that is as much misprision as a revisionary swerve is' (ibid., p. 66). What the young poet accomplishes is the requisite need for his own intervention. In Bloom's words, 'the *tessera* represents any later poet's attempt to persuade himself (and us) that the precursor's Word would be worn out if not redeemed as a newly fulfilled and enlarged Word of the ephebe' (ibid., p. 67).

Coming to the precursor's poem belatedly, the 'ephebe' (the younger poet) performs a '*kenosis*' or '"emptying", at once an "undoing" and an "isolating" movement of the imagination' (ibid., p. 87). Bloom is now ready to posit a 'pragmatic formula': '"Where the precursor was, there the ephebe shall be, but by the discontinuous mode of emptying the precursor of *his* divinity, while appearing to empty himself of his own." However plangent or even despairing the poem of *kenosis*, the ephebe takes care to fall soft, while the precursor falls hard' (ibid., p. 91).

Asserting that 'every poem is a misinterpretation of a parent poem' and that 'criticism is the art of knowing the hidden roads that go from poem to poem', Bloom reiterates the intrapoetic nature of the theory he presents (see ibid., pp. 94, 96). In order to acquire the authority of poetic power, the poet engaged in this intrapoetic struggle seeks access to the Sublime by claiming it for his precursor. '*Daemonization* attempts to expand the precursor's power to a principle larger than his own, but pragmatically makes the son more of a daemon and the precursor more of a man.' Ironically, '*daemonization* . . . is a self-crippling act, intended to purchase knowledge by a playing at the loss of power, but more frequently resulting in a true loss of the powers of making' (ibid., p. 109).

Not yet assured that he has gained primacy over his precursor, the younger poet performs an apparently ironic manoeuvre, which Bloom calls *askesis*, 'a self-curtailment which seeks transformation at the expense of narrowing the creative circumference of precursor and ephebe alike'. 'The final product of the process of poetic *askesis*', Bloom continues, 'is the formation of an imaginative equivalent of the superego, a fully developed *poetic will*, harsher than conscience, and so the Urizen in each strong poet, his maturely internalized aggressiveness' (ibid., p. 119).

For his description of the final phase of the imagination's agon, Bloom invokes the ancient calendrical term *apophrades*, 'the dismal or unlucky days upon which the dead return to inhabit their former houses'. The 'strongest' poets 'achieve a style that captures and oddly retains priority over their precursors, so that the tyranny of time almost is overturned, and one can believe, for startled moments, that they are being *imitated by their ancestors*' (ibid., p. 141). Although 'the mighty dead return', they do so 'in our colours, and speaking in our voices, at least in part, at least in moments, moments that testify to our persistence, and not their own' (ibid., p. 141). The final imaginative gestures of the strongest poets are at once 'cunning' and uncanny, for these poets create the literalistically absurd phenomenon of themselves seeming to have generated their predecessors' language.

As should by now be eminently clear, Bloom's theory of influence presupposes that the war between precursor and ephebe poet is modelled after an Oedipal scenario which places the male writer at the centre of the drama of influence. Thus, for all its revisionist authority, this theory remains untouched by a major theoretical move of the last decades of the twentieth century, the emphasis on feminist criticism and the re-emergence of the centrality of women poets. As both poet and feminist theorist, Adrienne Rich has been a major force in encouraging women poets and readers to consider the consequences of an alternative female-authored tradition that speaks from a gendered subjectivity.

For Rich, the political and poetic projects are one. Describing the importance of a feminist, revisionary poetics, Rich remarks, 'Re-vision – the act of looking back, of seeing with fresh eyes, of entering an old text from a new critical direction – is for women more than a chapter in cultural history: it is an act of survival. Until we can understand the assumptions in which we are drenched we cannot know ourselves' (Rich, 1995, p. 35). Rich identifies a 'radical critique of literature' as more than a new understanding of the literary past; she advocates such a critique because it enables women to break free of the conventions of patriarchy. And yet Rich's poetry insists upon bodily presence, an eroticized, corporeal self that speaks of its desires in ways that we can strongly identify as deriving from the Romantic bodily self. In 'Twenty-One Love Poems' Rich captures the nuances of lesbian desire in a revisionist echo of the magisterial poems of the dominant tradition of male corporeal longing. In the 'Floating Poem, Unnumbered', Rich writes,

> Whatever happens with us, your body
> will haunt mine – tender, delicate
> your lovemaking, like the half-curled frond
> of the fiddlehead fern in forests
> just washed by *sun*. Your traveled generous thighs
> between which my whole face has come and come –
> the innocence and wisdom of the place my tongue has found there –
> the live, insatiate dance of your nipples in my mouth –
> your touch on me, firm, protective, searching
> me out, your strong tongue and slender fingers
> reaching where I had been waiting years for you
> in my rose-wet cave – whatever happens, this is.

This lyric with its explicit description of homoerotic love-making is at once a radical testimony to lesbian desire and a profoundly revisionist return to the poem of the impassioned 'self'. Elsewhere in Rich the poetic persona plays what I earlier termed a 'ventriloquized' role. One of the functions of speaking through and for a marginalized historical woman is to enter her subjectivity to release her hitherto silenced voice. Again *immanence* is of foremost importance as the poem conveys presence to what has long been denied. In a poem which takes as its subject the ambiguities associated with creativity, Rich speaks from the imagined consciousness of the chemist and physicist, Marie Curie:

> Power
>
> . . . . . .
>
> Today I was reading about Marie Curie:
> she must have known she suffered from radiation sickness
> her body bombarded for years by the element
> she had purified
>
> . . . . . .

> She died a famous woman denying
> her wounds
> denying
> her wounds came from the same source as her power
> 1974

While ostensibly 'Power' expresses Curie's ambivalence towards acknowledging the self-destructive aspects of her quest to understand radioactivity, the poem closes with a more generalized characterization of the dangerous origins of power for the woman of imagination. This vatic close exemplifies the highly ambitious claims Rich makes in her poems as it speaks to the essentially conservative poetics that inform her politically and sexually radical project. Deeply influential, Rich combines theoretical boldness and a revisionist poetics to recuperate the imaginative legacy of women.

Rather than subscribe, as Rich does, to the centrality of a continuous, expressive representation of self, other contemporary poets respond to postmodern theories by decentring the self/subject. Marjorie Perloff, the foremost critic of LANGUAGE poetry, quotes from a group manifesto written by six poets associated with this movement. In 'Aesthetic Tendency and the Politics of Poetry' (1988), Ron Silliman, Carla Harryman, Lyn Hejinian, Steve Benson, Bob Perelman and Barrett Watten state that 'our work denies the centrality of the individual artist. . . . The self as the central and final term of creative practice is being challenged and exploded in our writing' (quoted by Marjorie Perloff in 'Language Poetry and the Lyric Subject', *Critical Inquiry*, 25: 3, spring 1999). Not only does this school of poets variously reconceptualize notions of selfhood in light of postmodernist theories of subjectivity; they call into question the representational function of language and thereby the nature of reality itself. Without a certainty that language refers to an authoritative, knowable reality outside the poem and experienced by the poet, the traditional relationship between a poem and the 'real' world is undermined. Instead, as Perloff notes, 'language constructs the "reality" perceived' (Perloff, 1996, p. 432). Freed from the burdens of an illusory referentiality and a unitary subjectivity, LANGUAGE poets experiment with lineation and aleatory (chance) linguistic phenomena. Interestingly, the overthrow of a traditionalist poetics, while, on the one hand, rejecting the notion of the singularity of the author, on the other hand, sets the stage for a reassertion of poetic presence through performance. In *Close Listening: Poetry and the Performed Word* Charles Bernstein (a LANGUAGE poet and theorist) comments on the contribution performance makes to a poem:

> The poetry reading extends the patterning of poetry into another dimension, adding another semantic layer to the poem's multiformity. The effect is to create a space of authorial resistance to textual authority. For while writing is normally – if reductively and counterproductively – viewed as stabilizing and fixing oral poetic traditions, authorial poetry readings are best understood as destabilizing, by making more fluid and pluriform, an aural (post-written) poetic practice. And here the double sense of reading is acutely relevant. For in realizing, by supplementing, the semantic

possibilities of the poem in a reading, the poet encourages readers to perform the poem on their own, a performance that is allowed greater latitude depending on how reading-centred the poem is – that is, how much the poem allows for the active participation of the reader (in both senses) in the constitution of the poem's meaning. (Bernstein, 1998, p. 10)

The improvisatory element in oral presentation is accompanied by linguistic experimentation, a process 'by which the instrumental function of language is diminished and the objective character of words foregrounded . . . language poetry regards its defamiliarizing strategies as a critique of the social basis of meaning, i.e. the degree to which signs are contextualized by use' (Rothenberg and Joris, 1998, p. 663). Thus, for the LANGUAGE poets, defamiliarization is a way not only to redefine the function of language and its relation to representation, but also a technique that offers a social commentary, that challenges the traditional notion of the unitary, expressive, poetic 'I'. Instead, LANGUAGE poetry proffers a socially contextualized, multiple site of meaning that invites the participation of the listener/reader.

Undecidability and the problematic aspects of the very act of representation come to the fore in much LANGUAGE poetry. Here, from his volume *First Figure*, is Michael Palmer's version of creating a poem by means of the epistemological uncertainties that might block expression:

The name is felt without letters how can this be. The cat then the ghost of the cat continually reappearing. A reading of an evening. Here the first figure, here the false figure of speech playing with a ring. Here once more the coffee and moth, damp bread in hunks, habits of afterwards and opposite. There are no steps leading to this. Not ours not theirs. A city of domes soon to be torn down. A sad monkey-house or the five random letters for the fingers of the hand. The story you've been looking for may well lie there. She steps from the shower and reaches for a towel. The story may well lie there in a cloud. Everyone knows these things by heart. Everyone tells these things from the heart.

The word is all that is displaced. This illness I stole from my father. A love of figures, tidiness, fear of error. There are the new remains. She shifted her position almost imperceptibly. He was reluctant to agree at first. They might have it otherwise, simpler perhaps, deducting shadow. The field itself is yellow, with the usual points of reference. Then evening with its blue coat, perfume jars, obstacles, machines held onto. It was quite a short pleasure. The police know all about it.

The status of referentiality is called into question even as fragmented images from the 'Real' appear. Without the tissue of explanation to make these images cohere, the reader is called upon to 'make sense', which in this context means to bring her/his syntax of meaning to the poem, to make it cohere. A shifting point of view is complicitous in conveying a sense of mystery (rather than authorial mastery). The reader, therefore, is drawn in, implicated in the construction of the poem as a vehicle for meaning.

While the LANGUAGE poets respond most immediately to postmodernist theories, other contemporary poets continue to engage longstanding philosophical questions through the poetic medium itself. Among the most distinguished of these poets is Jorie Graham, who incorporates philosophical discourse into poems that are acutely responsive to human feeling. Without sacrificing her subjectivity, Graham calls into question the very categories she invokes. In *Materialism* she interpellates passages from Sir Francis Bacon, Wittgenstein, Walter Benjamin, Brecht and Benjamin Whorf (as well as Dante, Audubon, McGuffey's *New Fifth Reader*, Whitman and Jonathan Edwards). The philosophical texts shadow the volume's neighbouring poems; emphasizing Graham's metaphysical and ontological interests. Most provocative in this regard are five poems with the same title, 'Notes on the Reality of Self', which simultaneously posit an immanent consciousness along with an acute sensibility and a sceptical, agnostic voice that self-reflexively questions the categories of space and time that the poem has invoked. The simultaneity of these two voices creates a deep inwardness that does not sacrifice sensory pleasures to philosophical investigations:

> . . . How the invisible
> roils. I see it from here and then
> I see it from here. Is there a new way of looking –
> valences and little hooks – inevitabilities, proba-
> bilities? It flaps and slaps. Is this body the one
> I know as me? How private these words? And these?

The speaker not only questions her physical presence; she calls into question the status of the very language she is putting into currency. Time is a central issue throughout the volume, and here Graham conveys a sense of the uncanny as the speaker asks both her 'self' and the reader to assess the 'privacy' of the words in the poem. In the final 'And these?' the speaker holds up for question the very words that articulate her uncertainty. This is one of a number of occasions in *Materialism* when Graham asserts the immanent power of her language in much the way that Whitman does. Indeed, Graham quotes just such a Whitmanian moment when Whitman's speaker alludes to a secret shared with the reader but never explicitly articulated:

> We understand, then, do we not?
> What I promis'd without mentioning it, have you not accepted?
> What the study could not teach – what the preaching could not accomplish, is
>   accomplish'd, is it not?
> What the push of reading could not start, is started by me personally, is it not?
> (Whitman, 'Crossing Brooklyn Ferry', Graham, 1998, p. 108)

Whitman uses this linguistic ploy to insist upon his own authority; in Graham's work, however, the questions are open; they address the reader not through coercion but in a more egalitarian way as they posit a philosophical compact with the reader. Surely, Jorie Graham's work exemplifies the powerful, always unsettled amalgam of theory and poetry. She repeatedly returns to a broad spectrum of contemplative thinkers to complicate and enrich her poems, thus exemplifying the force theoretical speculation has for contemporary poets.

Casting our glances back over the twentieth century, we can see the enormous impact theory has had for poets, and the range of that influence. The subjects I discuss here exemplify the intensity of the theory–poetry connection. While, for some poets, theory has a largely descriptive usefulness, for others such as Jorie Graham, theory inhabits a poem, giving it a self-reflexive function that acts in uncanny, surprising ways. Certainly, the impact theory has had on the LANGUAGE poets is great. And in whatever guise, theory and poetry have conducted a powerful dialogue that has transformed the reading and the writing of poetry in this century. If a poem is a the-atricalization of the writer's world, then theory is a part of it, urging the poet to re-examine the premises of her work, to engage with questions of origin, voice and referentiality. Theory invites the poet to examine her assumptions, to question the very nature of her craft. Theory does not simply serve a descriptive or tutelary role; instead, in various ways it enters and may even transform the poem. In some of the strongest work produced at the turn of the millennium, poetry actively engages theory to create work that, while rich in its allusiveness, is wholly new.

BIBLIOGRAPHY

Altieri, Charles (1979). *Enlarging the Temple: New Directions in American Poetry During the 1960s.* Lewisburg, Bucknell University Press.

Altieri, Charles (1984). *Self and Sensibility in Contemporary American Poetry.* Cambridge: Cambridge University Press.

Bedient, Calvin (1974). *Eight Contemporary Poets.* London: Oxford University Press.

Benjamin, Jessica (1998). *Like Subjects, Love Objects.* New Haven, CT and London: Yale University Press.

Bernstein, Charles (1998). *Close Listening.* New York: Oxford University Press.

Bloom, Harold (1973). *The Anxiety of Influence.* New York: Oxford University Press.

Bove, Paul A. (ed.) (1995). *Early Postmodernism: Foundational Essays.* Durham, NC and London: Duke University Press.

Breslin, James (1983). *From Modern to Contemporary: American Poetry, 1945–1965.* Chicago and London: University of Chicago Press.

Corcoran, Neil (1993). *English Poetry Since 1940.* London and New York: Longman.

Day, Gary and Brian Docherty (1995). *British Poetry, 1900–1950: Aspects of Tradition.* New York: St Martin's Press.

Eagleton, Terry (1996). *Literary Theory: An Introduction,* 2nd edn. Minneapolis: University of Minnesota Press.

Easthope, Anthony (1983). *Poetry as Discourse.* London and New York: Methuen.

Eliot, T. S. (1957). *On Poetry and Poets.* New York: Farrar, Straus and Cudahy.

Elliott, Emory (ed.) (1988). *Columbia Literary History of the United States.* New York: Columbia University Press.

Gioia, Dana (1992). *Can Poetry Matter?: Essays on Poetry and American Culture.* Saint Paul, MN: Graywolf Press.

Glück, Louise (1995). *Proofs and Theories.* New York: Ecco.

Graham, Jorie (1998). *Materialism.* New York: Ecco.

Hassan, Ihab (1987). *The Postmodern Turn: Essays in Postmodern Theory and Culture.* Ohio: Ohio State University Press.

Lyotard, Jean-François (1984). *The Postmodern Condition: A Report on Knowledge.* Minneapolis: University of Minnesota Press.

O'Sullivan, Maggie (1996). *Out of Everywhere: Linguistically Innovative Poetry by Women in North America and the UK*. London: Reality Street Editions.

Perkins, David (1987). *A History of Modern Poetry: Modernism and After*. Cambridge, MA: Belknap Press of Harvard University Press.

Perloff, Marjorie (1996). *Wittgenstein's Ladder: Poetic Language and the Strangeness of the Ordinary*. Chicago: University of Chicago Press.

Perloff, Marjorie (1999). 'Language Poetry and the Lyric Subject: Ron Silliman's Albany, Susan Howe's Buffalo.' *Critical Inquiry*, 25: 3, spring.

Pinsky, Robert (1976). *The Situation of Poetry: Contemporary Poetry and Its Traditions*. Princeton, NJ: Princeton University Press.

Pinsky, Robert (1999): *The Sounds of Poetry: A Brief Guide*. New York: Farrar, Straus & Giroux.

Rich, Adrienne (1995). *On Lies, Secrets and Silence*. New York: Norton.

Rothenberg, Jerome and Pierre Joris (1998). *Poems for the Millennium*, Vol. 2. Berkeley and Los Angeles: University of California Press.

Selden, Raman and Peter Widdowson (1993). *A Reader's Guide to Contemporary Literary Theory*, 3rd edn. Lexington: University Press of Kentucky.

Silliman, Ron, et al. (1988). 'Aesthetic Tendency and the Politics of Poetry: A Manifesto.' *Social Text*, 19–20, fall.

Vendler, Helen (1980). *Part of Nature, Part of Us: Modern American Poets*: Cambridge, MA and London: Harvard University Press.

Von Hallberg, Robert (1985). *American Poetry and Culture: 1945–1980*. Cambridge, MA: Harvard University Press.

8

Poetry and Gender

Edward Larrissy

I

One still encounters the complaint that the word 'gender', as used in literary theory, is a misnomer for 'sex'. This complaint is based on the traditional usage whereby 'gender' is a grammatical term, referring to the inflections of nouns and adjectives in certain languages – German and French, for example. While sex is certainly a topic that raises its head in literary discussions of gender, the latter word is used precisely because it implies, with its overtones of grammar, a social or conventional organization or structuring of sexuality. One reason why the topic of gender has been so productive of theory and controversy is that it has naturally become intertwined with many of the theories of human society and signification produced in this century. Yet all theories of gender, even those which see our perceptions of sexuality as socially determined, refer to sexual difference – to the binary categorization of male and female, or (and they are not the same thing) masculine and feminine. However, this does not mean that all the theories to which we shall refer see a stable binary categorization as truthful or illuminating. But it is always a topic of debate, even when rejected in favour of more subtle representations of gender difference. The importance of this point may be gauged by the readiness with which theories of gender employ the word 'difference', or seek illumination from theories where 'difference' is a central concept. A crude but instructive way into the topic of poetry and gender would therefore point out that it demonstrates the relevance of gender difference, however conceived, to the study of poetry. Thus, it would entertain the possibility that, whether for social or biological reasons, or both, men and women write about different things or in different ways. To put it another way, gender difference, as it influences writing, may be studied under the headings of content and form, always bearing in mind the ultimate artificiality of this division, to which I shall give provisional credence in what follows.

The persistence of the great binary is also evident in the way one can categorize types of theory in relation to it. Thus, much of the most vital work on gender and literature has been more or less overtly feminist, and has been chiefly preoccupied with describing or theorizing women's (or 'feminine') writing. In the process, theories about men's (or 'masculine') writing have been generated; and more recently there has been a relatively autonomous growth of interest in this question. In seeking illumination for the study of poetry, then, I shall first examine salient points in the voluminous tradition of theorizing which orients itself chiefly in relation to women's writing, or the feminine, and then go on to look more briefly at work on 'masculine' writing.

II

An obvious way in which the content of women's writing might be expected to differ from that of men's would be by virtue of the experiences it records. Men's and women's biological experiences are different. Historically the differences have been emphasized and supplemented by marked differences in upbringing, education and pursuits. It is understandable that Jan Montefiore, in her lucid book on *Feminism and Poetry*, should use the phrase 'Poetry and Women's Experience' as a subtitle for her introductory chapter (Montefiore, 1987, pp. 1–25). To the extent that the point is still valid in the second half of the twentieth century, it might be worth considering poems such as Sylvia Plath's 'Morning Song' or 'Cut' as examples of a domestic women's poetry. But the statement of domestic location or occupation is hardly interesting in itself. Most readers would claim that there is far more to Plath's rendering of female experience than this: that she manages to convey with absorbing complexity the experience of a woman interacting with her environment while at the same time undergoing a period of intense suffering. This would be true of the poems mentioned, and the point could be amplified by a reading of some of Plath's more sexually explicit poems – 'Poppies in July', for instance, in which the speaker refers to the flowers as 'little hell flames', as 'wrinkly and clear red like the skin of a mouth', and as 'little bloody skirts'. Here, as Montefiore (1987, p. 17) observes, the speaker luridly evokes the power and danger of sexuality through associations of whorishness, lipstick, menstruation and deflowering. The poem ends with the speaker's wish that she could distil the opiates of the poppies, and thus find tranquillity without their frightening redness ('But colorless. Colorless.'). This, as much as anything, makes it seem natural to regard the poem as a representation of female experience. But equally important, as Montefiore points out, is the traditional association of women's sexuality with flowers. Women's writing is bound to operate in relation to traditions which have been predominantly shaped by men, and this complicates any account of women's poetry which privileges the idea of experience.

Nevertheless, the very consciousness of this fact may enhance women's writing, a point made by Marianne Dekoven in relation to a much-anthologized poem by H. D.

(Hilda Doolittle), a co-founder with Ezra Pound of Imagism. 'Sea Rose', like 'Poppies in July', makes use of the traditional flower imagery, this time in the time-honoured form of the rose, emblem of feminine beauty. But the opening lines of the poem contain what Dekoven calls 'a jarring invocation' (Dekoven, 1999, p. 189):

> Rose, harsh rose,
> marred and with stint of petals,
> meagre flower, thin,
> sparse of leaf

Dekoven comments on the way in which the vocabulary employed here contradicts 'the opulence, the concupiscent lushness, of conventional images of the rose' (ibid, p. 190). She places this observation in the context of a discussion which demonstrates the innovativeness of modernist writing, especially modernist writing by women, in subverting gender stereotypes. 'Sea Rose' is a very good example, since it is so fully at one with the Imagist injunctions about brevity, concision and rhythmic accuracy. Indeed, its language could be seen as referring to these ideals, and thus, by its mingling of topics, as suggesting a new, modern female sexuality.

'Experience' is a broad term, of course. It can suggest the relative amorphousness of unreflective response; but it can also point to the direction taken by a life, or given to it. Autobiographical writing, in the widest sense, is an obvious example of the shaping of experience; and so is any writing that seems to be offering a view about the emergence of identity. For many women critics and writers it is important to keep in mind the way in which writing can offer a means of reflecting on female identity. Montefiore (1987, p. 18) gives the example of a poem by Alison Fell, 'Girl's Gifts', which offers a glimpse of a girl's relationships with older women, and by implication of the importance of these relationships to the forming of a woman's identity. Equally relevant would be a poem such as Denise Levertov's 'Hypocrite Women', which reflects on the weaknesses to which mature women may be vulnerable. Considerations such as these predominate in the mode of criticism to which Elaine Showalter, in her essay 'Towards a feminist poetics', has given the name 'gynocritics': that is to say, criticism which focuses on women's writing and on the value it has for the writer (Showalter, 1979, p. 25).

Toril Moi has analysed the inconsistency, imprecision and confusion to which an emphasis on experience, such as is to be found in Showalter's essay, may be prone: the text tends to be ignored, becoming merely a transparent medium for experience; theory is overtly rejected as 'male', but ends up being reintroduced in a haphazard fashion (including via the work of male theorists) (Moi, 1985, pp. 76–7). But, as Moi concludes, 'what "knowledge" is ever uninformed by theoretical assumptions'? A major part of the constitution of feminist criticism over the past thirty years or so has been strongly theoretical, not least in the shape of that body of work which can be encapsulated in the phrase 'French feminism'. Furthermore, theory assumes that experience cannot even be relied upon to understand itself. A major topic addressed by theory is ideology: that is to say, the socially dominant forms of thought which may be providing an unconscious shape and structure to what seems like the freedom of experience. Feminist theory addresses this topic; and French theory, in particular, may have a special interest for the student of poetry, since it lays a strong emphasis on types of language use which could be called poetic.

For the Marxist–Feminist Literature Collective (1978), whose work was accomplished in the 1970s, but whose influence is still discernible, the study of the gender ideology of texts must work in tandem with the broad social critique and analysis offered by Marxism. In particular, they draw insight from the work of the French Marxist literary critic Pierre Macherey, a follower of Louis Althusser. The traditional Marxist view is that the dominant forms of thought in any society reflect the interests of the dominant social class. These interests will take their specific shape from the dominant mode of economic production in that society. This means that the way any society thinks about itself and the world will, to a significant degree, be independent of individual will and will thus be unconscious. Fredric Jameson uses the phrase *The Political Unconscious* as the title of one of his books, and he is indebted for his detailed analysis to Macherey, who employs the image of a broken and distorting mirror to convey the selective blindness of ideology. There are two overlapping ways in which this conception is of use to socialist–feminist criticism of the kind practised by the members of the Collective: first, in providing the conceptualization of the general ideology of a society; and second, in suggesting that attitudes to gender are shaped in like manner by selective blindness. My own book on modern poetry, *Reading Twentieth Century Poetry: The Language of Gender and Objects*, though not of a notably feminist cast, emerges from the same kind of theoretical ambience, in that it attempts to add some of the insights of Marxism to certain observations about gender. It argues that the concentration of the appearance of objects in much twentieth-century poetry, from Pound to Heaney, can be seen in terms of the Marxist concept of alienation, but it supplements the point by adding that this concentration is also seen by many male poets as an arena for self-conscious virtuosity, and even as a sign of masculine virtue (Larrissy, 1990).

There is another obvious way in which the notion of ideology is relevant to the question of gender, and that is because of its use in the phrase 'patriarchal ideology'. This may sound like a dogma. Yet, by its very nature, it cannot merely be an external body of imposed thought. For a dominant ideology infects those whom it oppresses. Much feminist poetry has been concerned not just with an attack on the presumptions of patriarchy, but with 'consciousness-raising' for women. This concern may overlap with the emphasis on women's experience; but it may also give evidence of an awareness of the complex problems involved in the attempt to assert the value of women's experience. Claire Buck notes, for instance, that Denise Riley's poem 'A note on sex and "the reclaiming of language"' explicitly addresses 'the dangers of assuming any kind of authenticity about women's experience or about a utopian ideal that postulates an essential femininity undistorted by patriarchal impositions' (Buck, 1996, p. 95).

III

But many feel that patriarchal ideology cannot convincingly be explained solely in terms of capitalism or any other particular socio-economic formation. The search for the roots of sexual oppression has seemed to necessitate a profound engagement with psychological theories. Among these, it is the work of Freud which has been most conducive, albeit quite indirectly, to radical thinking. In Britain, Juliet Mitchell made a plea for the serious consideration of Freud in her *Psychoanalysis and Feminism* (1974) on the basis of the rigour of his analysis, however unpalatable it might superficially appear. But she herself acknowledges the importance of Jacques Lacan in fostering a sympathetic reappraisal of Freud's work. The attraction of Lacan for theorists of gender, including feminists, can be epitomized in the crucial reorientation involved in his special use of the term 'phallus' instead of the Freudian 'penis'. This modification is intended to convey that the valuing of the penis represents a social consensus rather than a biological imperative. Nevertheless, this is a notoriously question-begging ruse; and feminist theorists in France have been happy to develop it in ways that make the consensus seem not at all normative or natural. At the same time they have developed another facet of Lacan's psycho-analytic thought: namely, his insistence on the linguistic basis of unconscious mental formations.

Lacan's use of the term 'phallus', and for that matter his concentration on language, is inseparable from his account of the central feature of the Freudian narrative, the Oedipus complex. Freud deduced that the first object of desire, for both boy and girl child, was the mother. In the Oedipal stage both children must consciously renounce this desire in deference to the prior claim of the father, a claim asserted and maintained by his possession of the penis desired by the mother. The boy must defer satisfaction of his desire until maturity permits him to be the father in another relationship; the girl must accept that, by virtue of her lack of the penis, her role will be to take the mother's place at maturity. These different paths taken by boy and girl child are both motivated by the sense of a figurative castration relative to the father. As we have seen, Lacan's development of this idea involved his use of the term 'phallus', to emphasize that the valuing of the penis was a social convention. But this symbolic status of the phallus is entirely bound up with the child's entry into the symbolic structures of language and culture, which occurs at the same moment as the Oedipal stage – which could indeed be seen as an aspect of the Oedipal stage. For Lacan, the phallus is the crucial signifier of difference, and in apprehending this, the child apprehends also the character of linguistic symbolism – which relies on substitution and deferral of meaning – and of the symbolic order of society, in which the role of the father is fundamental. This complex of ideas Lacan sometimes refers to as the Symbolic, or the Symbolic Order. It is to be contrasted with what he terms the Imaginary: the pre-Oedipal state in which the child enjoys an illusion of unity and plenitude which derives from its undisturbed relationship with the mother. The transition from Imaginary to Symbolic is also the moment when the unconscious is precipitated, for the child now has to repress its desire for the mother. Lacan's emphasis on linguistic phenomena in the unconscious registers the fact that the primal repression which inaugurates the unconscious is the same phenomenon as entry into the Symbolic.

IV

For the French feminist Hélène Cixous, Lacan's concept of the phallus is a prime example of pervasive patriarchal phallocentrism, which is founded in 'patriarchal binary thought'. She gives examples of the typical binaries which overlap with and support the binary of masculine and feminine:

> Activity/passivity
> Sun/Moon
> Culture/Nature
> Day/Night
> (Sellers, 1994, p. 37)

The list goes on to include terms which hint at Cixous' analysis:

> Head/Heart
> Intelligible/Palpable
> Logos/Pathos
> (Ibid., p. 37)

The second term, associated with the feminine, is inferior in relation to the first. The first is privileged in a 'hierarchy' (ibid., p. 38) which finds stability in this structure. To this stability Cixous opposes the insecurity of *difference*, which is heterogeneous and does not organize itself around stable structures. In this she reveals her indebtedness to Jacques Derrida's critique of logocentrism and to his concept of *différance*. Derrida's thesis is that the illusions of logocentrism are founded on the notion that discourse can organize itself securely around certain privileged terms which are identified with the truth, and can thereby give an accurate and unified representation of the truth. But Derrida insists that the character of language is bound up with difference, multiplicity and deferral of meaning. This means that logocentric discourse, when analysed, is found not to achieve its goal, and indeed is forced to depend on the use of the supposedly inferior or subordinate term. The demonstration of this effect (and not destruction or pulling apart) is what is meant by *deconstruction*. Derrida believes that the attributes of language which can be summed up in his coinage *différance* are revealed by writing (*écriture*). For this reason, *écriture* is his model of language – as opposed to *voice*. Adherence to the idea of voice can lead, and has routinely led in Western culture, to the buttressing of logocentrism, with its illusions of unified meaning and intention.

Cixous' indebtedness to Derrida is particularly obvious in her adoption of the term *écriture féminine* ('feminine writing'), which allows itself the freedom of the play of difference. Yet one should not think of this as *female* writing, even though the French adjective is ambiguous: Cixous is ostensibly referring to a particular orientation which historically has been easier for women to adopt, but which in principle is also available to men. In support of this idea, she asserts that she believes in bisexuality. This is not a bisexuality which would merely reinstall the binary, nor the representation of a unified being, but what she calls '*other bisexuality*' (Sellers, 1994, p. 41): the presence of both sexes in different ways in each individual. Nevertheless, Cixous can sometimes sound as if she has returned to a familiar kind of mysticism and mystique of the female. Such is the claim of Toril Moi, who concludes that Cixous' 'vision of female writing is . . . firmly located within the closure of the Lacanian Imaginary: a space in which difference has been abolished' (Moi, 1985, p. 117). This unexpected conclusion can hardly be quite what Cixous had intended, however; and it remains the case that the idea of *écriture féminine* is seen as a fertile and suggestive contribution to feminist theory. However, its potential relevance to the theory of poetic language is arguably capable of being treated alongside the arguments of other French feminists. So it will be convenient, before examining this possibility, to consider the work of Luce Irigaray and Julia Kristeva.

Irigaray, more than Cixous, reacts in quite detailed and specific ways against Lacan. But this is partly because the development of her thought was so profoundly shaped by his. She criticizes his conservatism in a section of her 'Psychoanalytic Theory: Another Look' (Irigaray, 1985, pp. 60–7). But her training as a psychoanalyst means that she has much to contribute to the discussion of psychoanalysis in general; and her intellectual ambition has issued in wide-ranging philosophical debate.

Irigaray's most influential work, *Spéculum de l'autre femme* (1974; tr. 1985, *Speculum of the Other Woman*) refers to the mirror used by doctors for internal examination of women, but also comments on the way Lacan had used the image of the mirror to represent a stage in the development of the child's self-consciousness: a child whom he assumed to be male. The mirror image also refers to the mimetic logic of representation, which she equates with an ideology of monolithic identity, and which she implies has dominated Western culture from Plato onwards. Her term for this ideology is 'the logic of the Same'. It is easy to see how notions of *différance* might be invoked as applied to this logic, and indeed Irigaray, like Cixous, displays the influence of Derrida. The best-known image by means of which she seeks to convey the nature of feminine difference is that in which she offers an alternative image to that of the phallus: the lips of the vagina. This image implies that women's sexuality is 'always at least double' – at least; and indeed predominantly plural: for *'woman has sex organs more or less everywhere'* (Irigaray, 1985, p. 28). This plurality runs deep: woman is 'other in herself', and not least in 'her language, in which "she" sets off in all directions leaving "him" unable to discern the coherence of any meaning. Hers are contradictory words, somewhat mad from the standpoint of reason, inaudible for whoever listens to them with ready-made grids, with a fully-elaborated code in hand' (ibid., p. 29). As in the case of Cixous, feminine language sounds like certain Romantic and post-Romantic definitions of poetic language.

Julia Kristeva has made poetic language the subject of an important work, *La Révolution du langage poétique* (1974; tr. 1984, *Revolution in Poetic Language*). Its broad linguistic basis is an analysis of what she calls the *'signifying process'* (Kristeva, 1986, p. 91), in the study of which she discerns two trends: one, the *semiotic* and the other the *symbolic*. She believes these trends do indeed correspond to two interacting aspects of signification. The *semiotic* is a preliminary ordering of the pre-Oedipal drives, which are gathered in what she terms the *chora* (the Greek for a womb), a term used by Plato in the *Timaeus* for a formless receptacle of all things. For Kristeva, the semiotic chora is 'an essentially mobile and extremely provisional articulation' (Kristeva, 1986, p. 93). Her definition of the *symbolic* follows closely Lacan's description of entry into the Symbolic Order: once this has occurred, the *semiotic* will be subject to repression, and will make itself felt only as a pressure on symbolic language: in rhythmic play, in redundancy, contradiction, nonsense, discontinuity and gaps. Poetic language has been a practice where this marginalized aspect of language in general has been allowed limited license. But the symbolist poets Lautréamont and Mallarmé are studied by her in *Revolution in Poetic Language* as exponents of a 'signifying practice' which gives unprecedented expression to 'the semiotic disposition'. Neither of these poets is a woman; and for Kristeva, while 'the feminine is defined as marginal under patriarchy' (Moi, 1985, p. 166), it is, partly for this very reason, only a patriarchal construct, a way of conceiving the marginal. In fact, Kristeva believes that a subversively marginal position of avant-gardism is patently as open to male as to female writers, even though, as John Lechte points out, the 'unnameable, heterogeneous element is called "feminine" in Kristeva's writings of the mid seventies' (Lechte, 1990, p. 201).

V

The writings of the French feminists might lend themselves to the claim that there were 'feminine' and 'masculine' poetic forms and uses of poetic language, although, as we have seen, it would require considerable qualification to make use of Kristeva in this way. Jan Montefiore has sketched the outlines of an Irigarayan analysis of poetry, and consistent with the work of Irigaray herself, has suggested that there are actual differences between men's and women's poetry. Referring to love poems by Edna St

Vincent Millay and Christina Rossetti, she notes that 'whereas the [male] Imaginary poem enacts a fantasy of plenitude, of an Other who creates and grants one's own identity, these women poets begin with the premise that love is, for whatever reason, not fully returned, and satisfaction is not granted even in fantasy' (Montefiore, 1987, p. 136). This finding is congruent (though not to be equated) with an undoubted tendency among critics both of Romantic and twentieth-century poetry to see women's poetry as less egotistical than that of men, and for women writers and critics to look to a *tradition* of women's writing, marked by differences such as these. Yet it might be that differences of this kind, which are not necessarily a matter of language only, are historically determined, and do not require Irigaray's theories to explain them. Montefiore focuses on 'ambiguity' and 'contradiction' (ibid., p. 158), which are well-worn terms in the analysis of poetic language. But it emerges that poetic language is not really the object of Montefiore's analysis. For instance, in discussing Adrienne Rich's sequence, 'Twenty-One Love Poems', Montefiore notes the references to 'the paradoxes of language encountered by the lovers, notably the distance between experience and its articulation, the difficulty of speech and the need for an honest response' (ibid., p. 165). But this is a matter of language as subject matter in the poem. Montefiore does not claim (it would certainly be an implausible claim) that Rich's use of poetic language is remotely avant-garde or subversive. Furthermore, addressing the content of the poems, Montefiore concedes that 'I am not clear that these problems, as presented in the poems, are really specific to women' (ibid., p. 166). But this is not to surrender the struggle: the strength of women's poetry, for Montefiore, must lie in 'oppositional engagement' in the 'struggle to transform inherited meanings' (ibid., p. 179). In so far as this is a matter of language and form, feminist criticism may seek to demonstrate that this struggle makes itself felt in the language and texture of avant-garde poetry such as that of Gertrude Stein or H. D.; or that the adventurous use of language by more recent poets, such as Sylvia Plath, Veronica Forrest-Thomson or Medbh McGuckian, provides instances of feminine writing. But many critics and readers agree with Montefiore that feminine writing, according to any meaningful definition, is always a relative condition, the product of a transformative struggle with inherited forms. Montefiore herself offers the relevant example of a type of innovation which, though formal, is not linguistic: Stevie Smith, she claims, transforms well-known fables and fairy-tales in an ironic fashion which amounts to a characteristically feminine social critique (ibid., pp. 45–6). Marianne Dekoven makes a different but related point, which now enjoys wide acceptance, about formal innovation in the twentieth century: that if we define 'the salient formal features of Modernism' we find 'that women writers were just as instrumental in developing these forms as the great male writers' (Dekoven, 1999, p. 175). This recognition was one of the motivations behind the compiling of a widely disseminated anthology, Bonnie Kime Scott's *The Gender of Modernism* (Scott, 1990). Another motivation, however, was the recognition of the importance for modernism of ideas about gender, both at the thematic and the formal level, in the works of male as well as female writers.

VI

If there is anything specific to women's writing, it seems natural to ask whether or not there is a specifically male (or masculine) type of poetry. The claims made about twentieth-century male poets have tended to link their anti-Romanticism with their misogyny. Thus, Dekoven cites Pound's vorticist manifesto as 'characteristic of Modernism's self-imagination as a mode of masculine domination' and puts it in the context of modernist advocacy of 'firm, hard, dry, terse, classical masculinity, over against the messy, soft, vague, flowery, effusive, adjectival femininity of the late Victorians' (Dekoven, 1999, p. 176). She explains this rhetoric largely in terms of 'fear of women's new power' at the turn of the century (ibid., p. 174), although in my own book, I suggest that it is still very much at work in the latter half of the twentieth century (Larrissy, 1990). Nor, of course, is the rhetoric merely a foundation for criticism. It is present in a profound way within the poetry: a complex but readily apprehended example can, I think, be found in William Carlos Williams's 'For Elsie' (Larrissy, 1990, pp. 81–4). Dekoven adds a useful qualification, however, when she notes that 'masculinist misogyny . . . was almost universally accompanied by its dialectical twin: a fascination and strong identification with the empowered feminine' (Dekoven, 1999, p. 174). Whatever about the 'almost universally', this is certainly the case with a number of important modernist poets. Dekoven herself cites Yeats as a rather obvious example of such ambivalence. Gloria C. Kline in her *The Last Courtly Lover: Yeats and the Idea of Woman* (Kline, 1983) had pointed to the mixture of exaltation and subjugation involved in Yeats's attitude. Readers and critics had always been more or less aware of the importance to Yeats of the traditional female personification of Ireland; and Maud Ellmann (1986) and C. L. Innes (1993, pp. 93–108) offered valuable insights into the extent to which the boundaries between masculine and feminine could become eroded in his work. Elizabeth Cullingford (1993) showed how perceptions such as these could be understood in relation to Yeats's place in history; and in my own book on Yeats I seek to demonstrate that his ambivalent understanding of woman is interwoven with everything that is essential to his artistic thought and practice, and with the changes they undergo (Larrissy, 1994). Thus his doctrine of the Mask (to take but one example) is indebted to his sense of women's self-presentation, but is also something the male poet may learn from as a way of gaining power over women. This specific ambivalence is woven into his occult theories and into his sense of what is the appropriate poetic style and tone: the commanding rhetoric of many of his middle and later poems, for instance, is something he thinks of as masculine. Furthermore, he is capable of writing in the spirit of a number of different positions in the spectrum suggested by this ambivalence, ranging from complete identification with woman to overt misogyny. Nor is the misogyny itself simply to be rejected as unpalatable. Yeats was not the kind of poet who shied away from confronting the part played in life by hatred; and he was inclined to think that there was a fundamental antipathy between the sexes which was inextricably interwoven with fundamental attraction: 'Love is like the lion's tooth' ('Crazy Jane Grown Old Looks at the Dancers').

A broadly comparable ambivalence is to be found in Eliot. Readers have always commented on lines about 'female smells in shuttered rooms', about the presentation of Grishkin or the woman in 'Hysteria', and Tony Pinkney (1984) has documented the pervasiveness of misogynist overtones in Eliot as a central piece of evidence in a psychoanalytic study. Maud Ellmann has connected fear of woman with the fear of what undermines and 'confuse[s] . . . the sense', and has demonstrated the connection of such fears with the development of Eliot's fragmentary and suggestive poetic, which deliberately embodies the contagion even as it expresses the anxiety (Ellmann, 1987, pp. 106–7). In this regard, the general tendency of Eliot criticism is comparable to that of Yeats criticism: namely, to emphasize the extent to which gender images become an opportunity for experimental identification and projection, and thus encourage innovative poetry. Similar conclusions have been drawn about Heaney (Haffenden, 1987; Larrissy, 1990, pp. 148–58) and about another 'misogynist', Larkin (Clark, 1994, pp. 220–57). It does seem that, whether the subject be men's or women's poetry, critics are achieving a broad measure of agreement around the notion that gender identifications provide an opportunity for a profound exploration of the human. They can do this because they are a matter of culturally determined roles and dispositions, rather than of biology. Indeed, recent theorizing, notably the work of Judith Butler (1990), has tended to move on decisively from the argument about sex and to promote the concept of gender as performance. This would appear to be a notion with considerable potential for critics and readers of poetry.

BIBLIOGRAPHY

Buck, Claire (1996). 'Poetry and the Women's Movement in Postwar Britain.' In James Acheson and Romana Huk (eds), *Contemporary British Poetry: Essays in Theory and Criticism* (pp. 81–111). Albany: State University of New York Press.

Butler, Judith (1990). *Gender Trouble*. New York: Routledge.

Clark, S. H. (1994). *Sordid Images: The Poetry of Masculine Desire*. London: Routledge.

Cullingford, Elizabeth (1993). *Gender and History in Yeats's Love Poetry*. Cambridge: Cambridge University Press.

Dekoven, Marianne (1999). 'Modernism and Gender.' In Michael Levenson (ed.), *The Cambridge Companion to Modernism* (pp. 174–93). Cambridge: Cambridge University Press.

Ellmann, Maud (1986). 'Daughters of the Swan.' *m/f*, 11 and 12, 119–62.

Ellmann, Maud (1987). *The Poetics of Impersonality: T. S. Eliot and Ezra Pound*. Brighton: Harvester.

Haffenden, John (1987). 'Seamus Heaney and the Feminine Sensibility.' *The Yearbook of English Studies*, 17, 89–116.

Innes, C. L. (1993). *Woman and Nation in Irish Society, 1880–1935*. Hemel Hempstead: Harvester Wheatsheaf.

Irigaray, Luce (1985). *This Sex which Is Not One*, trans. Catherine Porter. Ithaca, NY: Cornell University Press.

Kline, Gloria (1983). *The Last Courtly Lover: Yeats and the Idea of Woman*. Epping: Bowker.

Kristeva, Julia (1986). *The Kristeva Reader*, ed. Toril Moi. Oxford: Blackwell Publishers.

Larrissy, Edward (1990). *Reading Twentieth Century Poetry: The Language of Gender and Objects*. Oxford: Blackwell Publishers.

Larrissy, Edward (1994). *Yeats the Poet: The Measures of Difference*. Hemel Hempstead: Harvester Wheatsheaf.

Lechte, John (1990). *Julia Kristeva*. London: Routledge.

Marxist–Feminist Literature Collective (1978). 'Women's Writing: *Jane Eyre, Shirley, Villette, Aurora Leigh*', *Ideology and Consciousness*, 1: 3, spring, 27–48.

Moi, Toril (1985). *Sexual/Textual Politics: Feminist Literary Theory*. London: Methuen.

Montefiore, Jan (1987). *Feminism and Poetry: Language, Experience, Identity in Women's Writing*. London: Pandora.

Pinkney, Tony (1984). *Women in the Poetry of T. S. Eliot: A Psychoanalytic Approach*. London and Basingstoke: Macmillan.

Scott, Bonnie Kime (1990). *The Gender of Modernism: A Critical Anthology*. Bloomington: Indiana University Press.

Sellers, Susan (ed.) (1994). *The Hélène Cixous Reader*. London: Routledge.

Showalter, Elaine (1979). 'Towards a Feminist Poetics.' In Mary Jacobus (ed.), *Women Writing and Writing about Women* (pp. 22–41). London: Croom Helm.

9

Interrupted Monologue: Alternative Poets of the Mid-century

Philip Hobsbaum

To begin with a point of theory: appreciation of a given text is bound up with awareness of form. The term is 'awareness' rather than 'consciousness', because one may apprehend certain signals without consciously analysing them. The contention would be that a good deal of misapprehension takes place because readers invoke inappropriate criteria. It is no good, when reading a tragedy by Shakespeare, complaining that nobody 'in real life' talks in blank verse. One should look at what the text is doing rather than seeing what it doesn't do.

What Shakespearian tragedy misses out, with regard to 'naturalism', it gains in stylization – which allows for the foreshortening of plot, short cuts across action, enhancement of character, heightening of speech. Nobody in a downtown bar would remark 'The multitudinous seas incarnadine / Making the green one red'. But Macbeth is not in a downtown bar, nor is he a naturalistic character. He is not defining, but representative; in this case, representative of what happens to a man possessed by evil. Nor is this an ordinary man but a superman, a hero, a being larger than any of us, with larger virtues and larger faults. He will therefore, appropriately, use a wider range of language, with heights we are none of us going to reach, and with self-deflationary commentaries. His diction anticipates the Miltonic sublime, with its Latinate polysyllables – 'multitudinous', 'incarnadine' – and also comprises, in contrast, the bleak Anglo-Saxon simplicity of 'making the green one red'.

What has been said here is a way into reading poetic drama. Poetic drama loses 'naturalism' in favour of poetry.

Especially among contemporary texts, the reader is liable to a good deal of genre confusion. It is historically true that certain writers, now accounted classics, suffered neglect or resistance in their own time. Examples of this that could be propounded include Blake, Wordsworth, Emily (but not Charlotte) Brontë, Melville (but not Hawthorne), Whitman, Browning, Eliot, Lawrence, Joyce: to go no further. One reason for this is that readers approached a given text with expectations that were irrelevant. Dr Johnson said that if you read Richardson's *Clarissa* for the story, you might as well hang yourself. If this is true, what else, other than 'story', does *Clarissa* give us? In that particular instance, one could say 'psychological analysis' – we see more deeply into Clarissa than into any previous fictional character, and this in its time brought about a great access of self-consciousness by providing means of access – the very prose, the nature of the detail.

Similarly, *Moby Dick* is not so much a story about catching whales – perused as such, it has its longueurs – but an allegory of Man assuming the task of God, exacting vengeance, and violating character and distorting circumstance in so doing.

When it comes to twentieth-century writing, a good many texts are misunderstood and rejected because readers approach them with inappropriate expectations. As it happens, and this is the nub of the argument, a crucial genre-confusion may be identified that has led to unnecessary difficulties in reading a whole hantle of contemporary poets.

The decline of poetic drama led to the rise of the dramatic monologue. The effect was for key speeches to detach themselves from dramatic context and, in lieu, to supply that context from hints within their own framework. Thus, we do not need a whole plot concerning an evil duke and his murdered wife. The substance of that story is given in a single speech, the 56 lines of 'My Last Duchess'. A prime effect of the text, however, is not to tell a story but to reveal a character; in this case, a repulsive one.

That is the form of the dramatic monologue: it is ostensibly spoken by a person other than the author himself; it embodies some revelation of character; it feels like drama.

There is, however, a distinction to be made among specimens of the form. Some monologues are spoken in the void, addressed to no one in particular, and therefore should properly be termed soliloquies. The protagonist of Tennyson's 'Ulysses' speaks quite dramatically – there is a sensational recording by the late Sir Lewis Casson – but he is not addressing anyone, unless it be his fellow-mariners, who, however, remain quite inert and play no role in the drama. Whereas in Browning's 'Fra Lippo Lippi' the monk addresses the guard who has captured him, and, in winning him round, records his reaction to events and thus renders him a presence in the poem. That is monologue proper, and suggests the inception of a development, the Interrupted Monologue.

Even though not separately recognized, Interrupted Monologue is a form significant in quantity and quality among twentieth-century poets. Characteristically, there is a dominant voice that narrates or explains the central action. This voice, however, is continually set in perspective, and its sentiments commented upon, by another voice that, though subordinate, breaks in, remarks upon, and, in short, interrupts.

It is possible to read an Interrupted Monologue as lyric, as narrative, as soliloquy; however, in each instance, something of value is lost and the reading is necessarily a simplified one. Just as often, it is possible to read an Interrupted Monologue without being aware of any form at all, in which case it is quite likely that the reader will be puzzled, baffled or repelled.

This is one reason why Peter Redgrove, though certainly esteemed, is not on the whole regarded as a great poet. He writes in various forms, but the Interrupted Monologue is highly characteristic of his work. It is developed from the monologue as evinced in 'Fra Lippo Lippi'; one that involves not only a dominating voice, but also an active interlocutor.

One major poem is 'At the White Monument'. Here the interlocutor is crucial, to get across the appearance of the peculiar character who is telling the story. The story involves the owner of a great house who tries to suppress the great winds that sweep through it by filling it with liquid cement, and succeeds, but only at the expense of inundating his wife and children. The house then explodes into flame and leaves only a calcined sarcophagus, which the ignorant populace take to be a white monument. The story borders on the impossible, but is made all the more effective because of the prosaic personality of the man who listens to it. This man, this interlocutor, has been sent by the local council to evict the narrator from the monument which they believe to be theirs but which the narration shows to be his. The narrator dominates the poem, with, as seen by the interlocutor, his moon-pate, flashing white eyes, waving hands – and, as heard by the interlocutor, preposterous story. That story is the core of the poem, but the other's reactions form a kind of commentary:

> The other snuffed the wholesome green
> Oxygen of the cut grass gladly,
> And wondered why his eyes wouldn't shut, and could he never get
> The smoke out of his nostrils now . . .

– a reference to the bizarre appearance of the narrator, with his semblance of having been scorched in a great fire; which, of course, he has been.

This concept of a prosaic interlocutor listening to an extravagant storyteller is a feature in several of Redgrove's best poems, some of which are couched in a lyrical prose, a kind of extension of free verse. Let us consider 'The Nature of Cold Weather'. An apparently dominant voice, representing the common man, is gradually encroached upon by a voice representing the winter. This voice is indicated by italics. The phrases in roman type represent the few ejaculations that the Common Man, at length stifled under the snow, is able to emit:

> As one slow ache, out in the windy snow,
> Time to observe a few things *as the flesh*
> *Squeezes pain downwards, bleaching skin into my heart,*
> *My innermost things, underground.*
> *Two ponds of blank grey ice with grizzled reeds,*
> *A heaped-up chine with two dark rabbit-holes,*
> *A slash of almost-frozen stream with meeting teeth,*
> *Clashing and tinkling, with brisk beard tugging at its banks,*
> *A col of thumbed snow in billowed rests . . .*

This voice controls the central sections of the poem, but gradually dies away, and the Common Man once more takes over, representing the thaw. The winter appears (in italics) as one last gasp, while the world melts.

> *The breakup of the giant . . .*
> First the houses burn his fingers
> Flushing up brown soil along his arms,
> His whiteness smutches, and the pricking comes intense,
> Freckles and patches, wens and mud-craters
> Where those beautiful declivities shone,
> And, long before, his eyes broke, and he is blind . . .

We do not hear directly from the winter again, not in this poem. There is a reference to his remnants floating down the river in a wonderful transition whereby the voice of the Common Man takes us into spring:

> The sun shines on the green meadows,
> The chines and valleys, tufts and hillocks
> Quilted with daisies and with buttercups,
> Misty with gossamer and pollen,
> And his heels drum in the stream
> As the playing children come . . .

A related example is 'Mr. Waterman'. This also is narrated by what seems to be a common man, but in this case the narrator is a conduit for the actions of a hyperactive pond, anthropomorphized into a humanoid kind of waterfall, capable of entering a house, seducing the mistress thereof, and hypothetically joining up with other sources of water to inundate the universe. This discourse, in roman type, is interrupted by the terse comments of a kindly but uncomprehending psychiatrist, in italics. The poem begins:

> *'Now, we're quite private in here. You can tell me your troubles. The pond, I think you said . . .'*
> 'We never really liked that pond in the garden. At times it was choked with a sort of weed, which, if you pulled one thread, gleefully unravelled until you had an empty basin before you and the whole of the pond in a soaking heap at your side. Then at other times it was as clear as gin . . .'
> *'Very well. Then what happened?'*
> 'Near the pond was a small bell hung on a bracket, which the milkman used to ring as he went out to tell us upstairs in the bedroom that we could go down and make the early-morning tea . . . One morning, very early indeed, it tinged loudly and when I looked out I saw that the empty bottles we had put out the night before were full of bright green pondwater . . .

In 'The Sermon' the interruptions are more dramatic, not to say theatrical. This poem has been performed on television by Michael Hordern and on radio by Donald

Wolfit. The parson preaches a highly inflammatory discourse, involving an extravagantly pantheistic notion of God and an idiosyncratic theory of heaven, that causes
the congregation to turn from questioning to objurgation – their most sustained interruption yet:

Minister: But God cannot die, and by the same token no more can we! Remember
that whatever happens cannot hurt us, because we *are* God – not hurt us
permanently, anyway. Brothers – and I am speaking to God – do not sit
about wailing here for God's second-coming-before-it-is-too-late – he is
already here, and We will be There, each of us a shard of him, a ward of
him, a bright, piercing, secure, razor-sharp splinter of him, and heaven . . .
where no moth nor rust . . . Matthew 6 . . . We are already Here . . . and
More of Me arrives every day!

Congregation: We've had enough. This is blasphemy. You are Antichrist. You are the
Devil. God is not mocked! In his own house too! And I saw a beast rise up
out of the sea, having seven heads and ten horns, and upon his heads the
name of blasphemy . . . (Revelation 13) . . .

A great deal of Redgrove's effect is gained by highly alliterative diction running
through an enormous dynamic range, from a whisper to a roar. Taken as lyric poetry,
it can seem over-stated. Taken as drama, it may be regarded as grotesque. Read,
however, as a separate genre, the details fall into place. There is a high degree of stylization, and the narrative may be interpreted as allegory, but much of the effect arises
from contrast, and that contrast is between the prosaic and the poetic; the matter-of-
fact and the visionary; what usually happens and what, on the borders of conception,
could happen. Much is lost if the reader decides to consider the poem as being spoken
by a single voice.

Without understanding the nature of the interlocutor, the text will seem unanchored,
a projection into fantasy. The interlocutor provides a framework of possible reference.
It is a failure in recognizing this crucial form that has resulted in the underrating of a
number of modern poems. Form sets the pattern of expectation. It helps to determine
the approach to a given text. If the reader is not aware of the form, he or she is liable
to read the text in some manner inappropriate to what is being proffered.

The poet most akin to Redgrove, though this is a matter of analogy rather than
influence, is Francis Berry. Berry is pre-eminently a chronicler of historical incident,
and the foundation of Greenland is the subject of one of his most evocative poems:
'Illnesses and Ghosts at the West Settlement'. The venture is seen largely through
the eyes of Gudrid, daughter-in-law of Eirik the Red, but her plaintive, hesitant
tones are perpetually broken in upon by the masculine entities who inhabit the poem.
They are all ghosts now. The basic structure is a recollection by the spirit of Gudrid
hovering as a ghost above the settlement where she suffered so dreadfully a thousand
years ago – interrupted, from time to time, by gruff interpolations from the
long-dead Eirik the Red:

> *Eirik:*　These Ghosts and these Illnesses in the West Settlement.
> 　　　　Well, what about them, and what about those bodies
> 　　　　– My son's among them – in that row of black boxes?
> 　　　　Brought them back, you have, Christian.
> 　　　　　　　　　　　　　　　O but they'll smell,
> 　　　　Christians bringing illness to Brattahild.
> 　　　　　　　　　　　　　　　　　Get on
> 　　　　With that story and what you did last winter.
> *Gudrid:*　So I reminded him . . . he is dead now,
> 　　　　And so am I, and so is every man, woman and child
> 　　　　Who ever came out to Greenland, its East Settlement, its
> 　　　　　　West Settlement,
> 　　　　Its sixteen fine churches, its farms, its tall-masted men and all that,
> 　　　　So dead and so dead.
> 　　　　　　　　　　　How we all came to be dead
> 　　　　Many learned discuss, but I know
> 　　　　Because I was living there and dead am there now . . .

The interpolations, from Eirik the Red and others, provide a context. There is an alternative version of this poem, published in *The Northern Review*, 1 (1965), but not collected in a volume. It takes the form of a monologue spoken by Gudrid. Other voices are woven in, by way of quotation, but, though this is done cunningly, the overall effect tends too far towards the grotesque. That is because this particular voice, a female voice redolent of pathos, cannot meaningfully accommodate the highly masculine interrogators that occur in the poem as we have it in *Ghosts of Greenland*. It goes to show that the Interrupted Monologue is a recognizable genre, and not just a generic sub-division.

A curious feature of the Interrupted Monologue is its adaptability. This is not a question of subject only but of basic structure. A close friend of Redgrove, the late Martin Bell, has a poem, 'Headmaster: Modern Style'. It is a monologue spoken in disgruntled tones by a junior teacher in a school:

> This leader's lonely, all right! He sees to that.
> Inspectors, governors, parents, boys and staff –
> His human instruments – are all shocked back
> From the stunned area round him, sound of his voice . . .

Yet the voice itself is never directly heard. This prejudiced auditor is not explicitly interrupted; however, in effect, there are interruptions from the headmaster. It is he who is the central character, even though he exists in indirect speech:

> Well, R.A.F. He was in the R.A.F.
> A ground-staff commission in the R.A.F.
> On heat with reminiscence on Battle-of-Britain day.
> Knew how to get what they wanted, anything, any equipment

> They knew their stuff, all right, when they occupied Germany
> With nudges, winks, and Cockney chuckles . . .

That last line quoted is by way of being a stage direction. Keeping the headmaster at a distance by means of indirect speech is a way of preventing him from overwhelming the poem and gaining a factitious sympathy. This involves the narrative in a considerable play of tonal effect, ranging from the mock-heroic to the near-demotic, often in the space of a remarkably few lines. The preponderantly masculine tone of the basic narration permits this, as a more delicate or yielding fabric of utterance would not.

Just as the headmaster may be said to interrupt the narrative of his disgruntled junior teacher, so, in a quite distinct key, does the deputy head:

> Let's turn aside
> As Augustine might turn from a chapter on pride and concupiscence,
> And consider poor Joe, Conk's deputy.
>
> Joe does administration. It does for him. He's done by it . . .

The poem as a whole may be taken as a comic elegy for an authentic villain. It ends with the voice of the junior teacher assuming a rhetorical grandeur, made absurd by the immediate context – which shows a backward class modelling clay into headmaster-dolls – and by the absurd properties involved in this peroration:

> Give him a surplice of toffee-paper and hymn-book leaves.
> Let bottle-tops stinking of yesterday's milk be gathered for his medals.

At the other extreme, Interrupted Monologue may be distinguishable from dialogue only by dint of setting the one voice in measurable superiority to the other. To illustrate the point, it is necessary to go back in time, to an earlier stage of the twentieth century. Edward Thomas, something of a hero to Martin Bell, is best known for his lyrics. His dialogue poems, however, are technically more intricate and carry a considerable weight of experience. Take, for example, one of his lesser-known pieces, 'Wind and Mist'. This is essentially a foreshortened chronicle of one man's life. It is not, however, told as a straight narrative. Two men meet by chance, and greet each other. The conversation proceeds as though by commonplace interchange, the one man complimenting the landscape and so drawing the other into qualifying that enthusiasm and moving on to a greater intensity of language: The first man goes on to remark, 'You had a garden / Of flint and clay, too', and this draws the response:

> True; that was real enough.
> The flint was the one crop that never failed.
> The clay first broke my heart, and then my back;
> And the back heals not . . .

It is this second man who proves to be the main speaker. He proceeds to narrate the birth of a child, and this part of the narrative is interrupted by the polite hope of the interlocutor that mother and baby were spared. In replying to this interpolation, the poem reaches its most sustained passage. However, that continuity is set off and enhanced by the framework of casual encounter, and the resultant question-and-answer technique. After all the interruptions, the verse soars to its climax:

> But flint and clay and childbirth were too real
> For this cloud-castle. I had forgot the wind.
> Pray do not let me get on to the wind.
> You would not understand about the wind.
> It is my subject, and compared with me
> Those who have always lived on the firm ground
> Are quite unreal in this matter of the wind . . .

Given this level of intensity, brought about by alliteration and repetition, no interruption is likely or necessary, and the main speaker's narrative concludes the poem. Yet the narrative is never soliloquy. We are always conscious of the much younger plainsman being confronted by the Old Man of the Mountains, obdurately retentive of his past. Towards the end, his voice seems to fall in pitch, and he comes to a conclusion:

> But one word. I want to admit
> That I would try the house once more, if I could;
> As I should like to try being young again.

This is one of a number of poems in the oeuvre of Edward Thomas that may be loosely associated together as Interrupted Monologue. Analogous works include 'Up in the Wind', 'The Chalk-Pit', 'House and Man', possibly 'As the Team's Head-Brass'. Thomas may have learned from his friend and contemporary, Robert Frost, who uses dialogue very freely in various narrative poems, such as 'Death of the Hired Man', 'The Mountain', 'A Hundred Collars', 'Home Burial' and 'Blueberries'. All of these may be found in Frost's second book, *North of Boston*. The dialogue in these poems, however, is more evenly balanced. One does not, as is the case with Edward Thomas, have the sense of a central voice being interrupted.

The interruptions may be very slight, or almost non-existent, as in 'The Songbook of Sebastian Arurruz' by Geoffrey Hill. This author has a secure place among the poets of the mid-century and, indeed, later. Nevertheless, 'The Songbook' may not have had the kind of attention that it deserves. Certainly, it seems pre-eminent among Geoffrey Hill's works. The poem in question seems less a soliloquy than a monologue, very definitely addressed to some one: the beckoning fair one, the unattainable beloved, the sphinx without a secret. One might suggest that the tone is akin to that of a novel by Graham Greene, *The End of the Affair*, except that, here, no 'end' is foreseeable.

That bitter voice grinds on, and on, and the fact that little response is elicited from the person addressed, accentuates the agony. The married woman with whom the speaker is in love appears by way of implication:

> 'One cannot lose what one has not possessed.'
> So much for that abrasive gem.
> I can lose what I want. I want you . . .
>
>   . . . you might move and speak my name
> As I speak yours . . .
>
> . . . See how each fragment kindles as we turn it . . .
>
>   . . . your hand running over me
> Deft as a lizard, like a sinew of water . . .

Admittedly, this is a borderline case. One could always argue that, since the woman never says anything that is recognizable as communication, the monologue can scarcely be termed 'interrupted'. To such an objection, the reply might be that the monologue is palpably speech, and speech directed at a particular woman, whose very silence and inaccessibility renders the sense of a presence. One would have to concede, nevertheless, that a more identifiable example of this form is 'A Correct Compassion' by James Kirkup.

Geoffrey Hill must have been conscious of this poem, near-contemporary as he was with Kirkup on the staff of Leeds University, and indeed one would not need to be proximate to Kirkup to know 'A Correct Compassion', since it was a show-piece of the 1950s. It describes a kind of heart operation technically known as a mitral stenosis valvulotomy; that is to say, the cutting open of adhesions that have formed between the cusps of a valve. The poem, however, is more than the description of an operation. Were it only that, it could have been more appropriately phrased in prose. The poem refers, beyond the immediate present, to the act of writing poetry and, beyond that, to the creative skills of the masters of particular crafts, which the author interprets in terms of compassion; a correct compassion.

The poem celebrates skill. Its main voice is that of the guest, the onlooker, the man deeming himself without the talent of the surgeon – the surgeon who, in his turn, stands for the master of a craft. The onlooker addresses that master:

> Cleanly, sir, you went to the core of the matter.
> Using the purest kind of wit, a balance of belief and art,
> You with a curious nervous elegance laid bare
> The root of life, and put your finger on its beating heart . . .

That invocation to 'sir', the surgeon, is, so to speak, voiced silently. However, it typifies the utterance as monologue, rather than as soliloquy. There is a controlled ambiguity of utterance. Those opening lines could refer to almost any activity requiring

skill and self-discipline, be it playing Bach on the clavichord, composing a satire –
'the purest kind of wit', 'nervous elegance' – creating a work of visual art – 'a calli-
graphic master', 'the flowing stroke is drawn' – or, indeed, writing this present poem.
The heart operation can be taken as a literal act of skill, for it is detailed enough to
be authentic, or as a sustained metaphor with regard to performance and composition. Further, the voice of the onlooker intensifies to the accents almost of a love poem,
proving there is emotion behind the discipline:

> The heart, black-veined, swells like a fruit about to burst,
>
> But goes on beating, love's poignant image bleeding at the dart
> Of a more grievous passion, as a bird, dreaming of flight, sleeps on
> Within its leafy cage . . .

Up to now, the narrative voice has proceeded, rising in intensity, with no more
than brief interruptions from the surgeon – 'A local anaesthetic in the cardiac nerve'.
However, after this throbbing presentation of life – 'love's poignant image' – the voice
of the surgeon takes over, very much that of the man of action:

> 'I make a purse-string suture here, with a reserve
> Suture, which I must make first, and deeper,
> As a safeguard, should the other burst. In the cardiac nerve
> I inject again a local anaesthetic. Could we have fresh towels to cover
> All these adventitious ones . . . ?'

The voice of the surgeon is itself interrupted, by an otiose circumstance, marring the
discipline of this transaction, and he rebukes the culprit: 'If you have to cough, you
will do it outside this theatre'.

The onlooker in a way is interrupting the surgeon: he doesn't cough, but he is present
as spectator, and not even a medical one. It is the onlooker whose voice embodies the
dominant of the poem, its experiential core. Yet it is the surgeon whose voice takes over,
just after the formal climax of the poem, in tones very much of this world, practical,
pragmatic. Nevertheless, after the outside world resumes with the sound of people
breathing and a car starting up outside, the lyrical tone comes in again, to sum up:

> For this is imagination's other place,
> Where only necessary things are done, with the supreme and grave
> Dexterity that ignores technique; with proper grace
> Informing a correct compassion, that performs its love, and makes it live.

That is the end of the poem. The onlooker has again taken up the narrative, by way
of comment on the operation, in a quiet manner resembling that of the beginning.
Such an interplay of dreamer and man-of-action was a *leitmotiv* in the middle of the

century, when this poem was written, though 'A Correct Compassion' is one of the supreme examples of such interplay, and has lived on long enough to risk being forgotten.

The poets considered here are among the finest of the mid-century. Yet there is a relatively sparse occurrence of at least some of them in the anthologies. This suggests that their names are in process of slipping off the computer. The *Collected Poems* of Martin Bell were published in 1988; those of Francis Berry in 1994; those of James Kirkup in 1996. They did not, however, seem to attract reviews in what might have been thought many of the appropriate journals. No definitive edition of Peter Redgrove has ever been issued. His immense output has certainly attracted an extent of comment, but one would question whether much of that comment is sufficiently discerning. Some commentators seem to regard his work as little more than an explosion of imagery. Even when discussion is more perceptive than that, still one may question whether there is a due recognition of the tough structure underpinning his verbal efflorescence.

What seems to have failed a number of these poets is the approach to reading favoured by contemporary critics. If the critics do not get lost in the proliferation of image chains, then they seem to extrapolate – as though finding a philosophy or a set of political values in a given author's work is going to tell us much of any value concerning his poetry! Every critic has it in his or her power to decide on the approach made to a literary work. Supposing the work not to be utterly obscure, some approaches are bound to be more relevant than others. It is the critic's job to choose the most relevant of them all.

There is no point in catechizing a literary work for one quality if it exhibits another. The fault may lie in an inflexibility of approach on the part of the reader. This is one reason why criticism habitually lags so far behind creative work. The critic bases an approach on past experience, and only with reluctance extends that approach to accommodate demands upon sensibility that are unexpected. Such demands, however, are made by any genuinely distinguished text. The fact that they are seldom met is clearly seen in the relative neglect experienced by such English poets of the mid-century as have been noticed in the present disquisition.

BIBLIOGRAPHY

Peter Redgrove and Penelope Shuttle (1978), *The Wise Wound*. London: Gollancz.

Edward Lucie-Smith and Philip Hobsbaum (eds) (1963), *A Group Anthology*. London: Oxford University Press.

Philip Hobsbaum (1979), *Tradition and Experiment*, ch. 12. London: Macmillan.

Neil Roberts (1994), *The Lover, The Dreamer and the World: The Poetry of Peter Redgrove*. Sheffield: Sheffield Academic Press.

Francis Berry (1958), *Poets' Grammar: Person, Time and Mood in Poetry*. London: Routledge.

G. Wilson Knight (1971), *Neglected Powers: Essays*

on Nineteenth and Twentieth Century Literature, ch. 17. London: Routledge.

Martin Bell (1988), *Complete Poems*, ed. Peter Porter. Newcastle upon Tyne: Bloodaxe.

Martin Bell (1997), *Reverdy Translations*. Reading: Whiteknights Press.

Edward Thomas (1917), *A Literary Pilgrim in England*. London: Methuen; rep. Oxford: Oxford University Press, 1980.

Edna Longley (ed.) (1981), *A Language Not to be Betrayed: Selected Prose of Edward Thomas*. Manchester: Carcanet Press.

Andrew Motion (1980), *The Poetry of Edward Thomas*. London: Routledge.

Geoffrey Hill (1984), *The Lords of Limit: Essays on Literature and Ideas*. London: Andre Deutsch.

Merle E. Brown (1980), *Double Lyric: Divisiveness and Communal Creativity in Recent English Poetry*, chs 1–4. London: Routledge.

Peter Robinson (ed.) (1985), *Geoffrey Hill: Essays on His Work*. Milton Keynes: Open University Press.

James Kirkup (1996), *Omens of Disaster: Collected Shorter Poems, Vol. 1*, Introduction by Philip Hobsbaum. Salzburg and Oxford: University of Salzburg.

James Kirkup (1988), *I, of All People: An Autobiography of Youth*. London: Weidenfeld and Nicolson.

James Hogg (ed.) (1998), *Diversions: A Celebration for James Kirkup on His Eightieth Birthday*. Salzburg and Oxford: University of Salzburg.

PART II
Poetic Movements

10
Imagism
Jacob Korg

The Imagist movement was initiated by a group of English and American poets led by Ezra Pound as a corrective to what they considered to be the verbose, banal and artificial manner of early twentieth-century poetry. Although it was active as a movement only between 1912 and 1917, its emphasis on economy of language and concrete imagery, and its advocacy of free verse, had a lasting influence, and these features became the hallmarks of modern poetry.

The formation of Imagism is recorded as beginning in the autumn of 1912, as Ezra Pound, Hilda Doolittle (an American poet, who became known as 'H. D.') and Richard Aldington, an English poet, met with each other in various London tea-shops and discussed poetry. Hilda Doolittle had been a friend of Pound's in Pennsylvania, and had recently rejoined him in London. Aldington was the son of a lawyer, who had studied at University College, London. Aldington and H. D. read the Greek Anthology together at the British Museum, became lovers and eventually married, and they, together with Pound, formed the nucleus of the first Imagists. On one occasion, as Aldington described it in his memoir, *Life for Life's Sake*:

> H. D. produced some poems which I thought excellent, and she either handed or mailed them to Ezra. Presently each of us received a ukase to attend the Kensington bun-shop. Ezra was so much worked up by these poems of H. D.'s that he removed his pince-nez and informed us that we were Imagists.
>
> Was this the first time I had heard this Pickwickian word? I don't remember.

Hilda Doolittle's recollection of this event, or some other like it, is different, and more famous. When Pound read her poems, he immediately recognized that she had fulfilled the aspirations for the reform of poetry which he had in mind. There is no substitute for H. D.'s account of this scene:

> Meeting with him alone or with others at the Museum tea room. . . . 'But Dryad,' (in the Museum tea room), 'this is poetry.' He slashed with a pencil. 'Cut this out, shorten this

line. 'Hermes of the Ways' is a good title. I'll send this to Harriet Monroe of *Poetry*. Have you a copy? Yes? Then we can send this, or I'll type it when I get back. Will this do?' And he scrawled 'H. D. Imagiste' at the bottom of the page. (*End to Torment*, p. 18)

Pound adopted a French form for the name of his movement in imitation of the modernist movements he had encountered during a recent visit to France. The initials became Hilda Doolittle's permanent *nom de plume*, and while Pound is usually regarded as responsible for them, there is some reason to believe that H. D. herself used them first. When he submitted the poems for publication to Harriet Monroe, the editor of the Chicago magazine, *Poetry*, he reported that H. D. had lived with the 'laconic speech of the Imagistes' 'since childhood', and summarized the Imagist aims by describing them as: 'Objective – no slither; direct – no excessive use of adjectives, no metaphors that won't permit examination. It's straight talk, straight as the Greek!'

The style that Pound admired is illustrated by the first lines of 'Hermes of the Ways':

> The hard sand breaks
> and the grains of it
> are clear as wine.
>
> Far off over the leagues of it,
> the wind,
> playing on the wide shore,
> piles little ridges,
> and the great waves
> break over it.

According to Aldington, the three poems by H. D. which appeared in the January, 1913 number of *Poetry* were the first to be identified as 'Imagiste'. Pound declared that H. D.'s poems were the best examples of Imagist poetry, and she is generally recognized as the definitive Imagist. Writing in 1930, some years after the movement had run its course, Ford Madox Ford said of H. D., that she was 'our gracious Muse, our cynosure and the peak of our achievement'.

Pound's most famous Imagist poem, 'In a Station of the Metro', uses only two lines to illustrate the movement's principles of concentration, imagery and natural language. It was originally published with significant spacing between the phrases, as if to isolate each group of words (and the punctuation) as a separate 'image':

> The apparition   of these faces   in the crowd   :
> Petals   on a wet, black   bough   .

Pound said that he had first written longer poems about a significant experience he had had, but then, after an interval of eighteen months, produced the '*hokku*-like sentence' that stood as the final poem. In his account of the poem's composition, he declared: 'Since the beginning of bad writing, writers have used images *as ornaments*.

The image is itself the speech. The image is the word beyond formulated language' ('Vorticism', *Fortnightly Review*, 1 September 1914).

Imagism made its early way in a bizarre transatlantic fashion. Its initiators, Pound and H. D., were Americans who, unable to secure recognition in America, went to London, where they published Imagist poems and statements in *Poetry*, and volumes of their work in England. They were joined, however, by the English poets Aldington, D. H. Lawrence and F. S. Flint. Flint, a poet who was devoted to the French Symbolists, had attached himself to the Imagists early, knew much about their activities and remained a member of the group throughout its life.

The historians of Imagism agree that Pound was the publicist, rather than the inventor, of Imagist doctrines, but they disagree about the identity of the true founder. The traditional candidate is T. E. Hulme, a philosopher who had spent some time at Cambridge, had published translations of modern French philosophers, and had written a number of significant essays which remained in manuscript until after his death. Flint, in a 'History of Imagism' which appeared in the *Egoist* in May, 1915, recalled that Hulme had belonged to a Poet's Club that met in 1908, and after leaving it, began a second group together with Flint himself. The new group, which first met at the Tour d' Eiffel restaurant in March of 1909, favoured accurate, economical language, tried such experimental poetic ventures as *vers libre* and the Japanese forms *tanka* and *haikai*, and discussed 'the Image'. Pound joined it in April, met with it for about a year, and according to Flint, picked up many of his Imagist ideas there. Pound was also present at various clubs and meetings where Hulme spoke, and seems to have been indebted to him for at least some of the Imagist doctrines.

When Pound reprinted some of Hulme's poems in his 1912 volume, *Ripostes*, he referred to Hulme's group in a prefatory note as a '"School of Images" which may or may not have existed' and intimated that 'the forgotten school of 1909' was a forerunner of his own *Imagistes*. Hulme, whose notebook essays were not published until after his death on the battlefield in 1917, and after the end of the Imagist movement, favoured a hard, objective, geometric style in art, and argued that poetry should adopt a corresponding verbal idiom, avoiding rhetoric and emotion. Poetry, he said, in his essay 'Romanticism and Classicism',

> is a compromise for a language of intuition which would hand over sensations bodily. It always endeavours to arrest you, and to make you continuously see a physical thing, to prevent you gliding through an abstract process. It chooses fresh epithets and fresh metaphors, not so much because they are new, and we are tired of the old, but because the old cease to convey a physical thing and become abstract counters. . . . Images in verse are not mere decoration, but the very essence of an intuitive language. (Hulme, 1994, p. 70)

Anticipations of the Imagist spirit are seen in such jottings from Hulme's notebook as: 'Each word must be an image seen, not a counter'; 'A man cannot write without seeing at the same time a visual signification before his eyes. It is the image which precedes the writing and makes it firm'; and 'A word to me is a board with an image or statue on it' (ibid., pp. 25, 27).

But Pound declared that the figure who had the most influence in moving him towards the principles of Imagism was Ford Madox Ford, then known as Ford Madox Hueffer. Ford, who objected to the stilted, artificial, derivative idiom of most con-temporary verse, maintained that poetry should be 'modern'. In a two-part article called 'Impressions', which appeared in *Poetry* and clearly supported Imagist doctrine, Ford, saying that he had been repelled by the wordiness of the Victorian poets he had read in his youth, delivered a message that recalls the ideas of Wordsworth's 'Preface' to *Lyrical Ballads* more than a century before; he recommended that poets use natural, living language as it was spoken, direct, clear, natural and precise, resembling the language of prose. Pound, who had admired William Butler Yeats's vague, suggestive poetry, gradually came to accept Ford's views, and to reform his own early poetic style, which had been guilty of all the faults Ford mentioned. By 1913 Pound was clearly moving in Ford's direction towards what he called 'diametric opposition' to Yeats. 'I would rather talk about poetry with Ford Madox Hueffer', he wrote, 'than with any man in London.'

When Ford died in 1939, Pound published an obituary article praising him as an important critical voice, and acknowledging the crucial influence he had had on Pound himself. Pound had come to visit Ford in Germany, and had read to him from his last book, *Canzoni*. A famous scene then occurred, as Pound described it:

> And he [Ford] felt the errors of contemporary style to the point of rolling (physically, and if you look at it as a mere superficial snob, ridiculously) on the floor of the tempo-rary quarters in Giessen when my third volume displayed me trapped, fly-papered, gummed and strapped down in a jejune provincial effort to learn, *mehercule*, the stilted language that then passed for 'good English' in the arthritic milieu that held control of the respected British critical circles.

It was Ford's influence that led Pound to regard his early poems as 'stale creampuffs', and to declare that the language of Imagism must be spare, economical and direct.

Many critics believe that Imagism began with H. D., whose early poems were highly original examples of the kind of poetry the reformers were thinking of. She apparently had no theories to prove in writing them, but when Pound sent them to *Poetry*, he presented them as examples of the Imagist style, and said they were '*modern stuff by an American*'. In later years he declared that the Imagist movement had simply been a device to get her poems (and Aldington's) published. 'The name was invented to launch H. D. and Aldington before either had enough stuff for a volume', he wrote in a 1927 letter. But he did add, 'Also to establish a critical demarcation long since knocked to hell'. The account of Imagism that followed H. D.'s poems in the March 1913 number of *Poetry* two months later corresponded with the style she had invented.

When Pound assumed the role of 'foreign correspondent' for *Poetry* in 1912, he took advantage of his position to propagandize his new movement through it. The first Imagist poems emerged in its pages late in 1912 and early 1913 as *Poetry* published contributions by Aldington and H. D. submitted by Pound. Aldington was introduced in the number of November 1912 as 'a young English poet, one of the "Imagistes", a group of ardent Hellenists who are pursuing interesting experiments in *vers libre*'. Pound soon objected vigorously to this misleading description in a letter to Alice Corbin Henderson, the associate editor of *Poetry*. 'Hellenism and *vers libre*', he wrote, 'have nothing to do with it'. He said he was unwilling to define Imagism until it had produced a large body of work, and maintained that the best poetry of the past contained Imagism.

A definition appeared in March 1913, however, when *Poetry* published a first, and classical explanation of the movement's principles in an article titled 'Imagisme' by Flint and Pound, who signed different portions of it. Flint claimed that he had interviewed the 'Imagists' (his informant was probably Pound) and had learned that they had drawn up three rules.

1. Direct treatment of the 'thing', whether objective or subjective.
2. To use absolutely no word that did not contribute to the presentation.
3. As regarding rhythm: to compose in sequence of the musical phrase, not in sequence of a metronome.

The first of the three rules is generally understood to encourage a reliance on concrete imagery presented without rhetoric or comment, although its inclusion of the 'subjective' seems to allow for the expression of feelings. The second, perhaps the most influential of the Imagist doctrines, enjoined a rigorous economy of language. And the third seems directed towards freeing poetry from standard meters and encouraging the use of *vers libre*.

Flint's portion of the article was followed by a statement by Pound called 'A Few Don'ts by an Imagiste', whose didactic style is explained by the fact that it was originally intended to serve as a rejection slip for would-be contributors to *Poetry*. It began with a definition which has become central in Imagist doctrine. 'An Image', Pound wrote, 'is that which presents an intellectual and emotional complex in an instant of time'.

Pound advised his readers not to consider the three rules as 'dogma', but as subjects of thoughtful consideration. His 'Don'ts' added some further explanation, advising against the use of vague and derivative language, and commanding 'Go in fear of abstractions'. In a long passage on poetic rhythm, Pound advised close study of the sound-patterns in foreign verse, and avoidance of monotony, and told the writer of poetry that he must think of the aural part of verse as a musician would.

In the middle of this discussion of poetic sound, Pound interpolated two brief, but important injunctions on a different subject. He wrote, 'Don't be "viewy"', by which he seemed to mean that poetry was not the place for discursive comment. This sentence is followed by another restriction: 'Don't be descriptive'. The painter, he said, can describe a landscape far better than a poet can.

Buried among these crisp stylistic injunctions were a few statements suggesting that Imagism also involved something mystical or arcane. Flint reported that the Imagists had a certain 'Doctrine of the Image' which was not to be made public. And Pound, in his portion of the article, declared grandiosely that the Image 'gives that sense of sudden liberation; that sense of freedom from time limits and space limits; that sense of sudden growth, which we experience in the presence of the greatest works of art. It is better to present one Image in a lifetime than to produce voluminous works'.

In spite of such statements as this, Pound never fully clarified what was meant by Imagism, and freely applied the term to the work of other poets of the past and present. While he classified Yeats as a Symbolist, not an Imagist, he added that he had produced some 'Images', and employed a direct diction, and cited, as an example of the Imagism to be found in his poetry, some lines from 'The Magi';

> Now as at all times I can see in the mind's eye
> In their stiff, painted clothes, the pale unsatisfied ones
> Appear and disappear in the blue depths of the sky
> With all their ancient faces like rain-beaten stones,
> And all their helms of silver hovering side by side . . .

Pound published poems of his own in _Poetry_ in April and November 1913, terming them 'ultra-modern'. These poems do follow Ford's advice to use direct, contemporary language in contrast to the conventionally poetic diction of Pound's last book of verse, _Ripostes_, and they reflect Hulme's preference for short, hard-edged, unrhetorical verse. Most of them employ a conversational, ironic tone that has little do with Imagism, although 'In a Station of the Metro' is included as the last of the group called 'Contemporania'.

1913 was an eventful year in the history of Imagism. That summer, Pound became literary editor of a small London feminist journal, _The New Freewoman_, first issued on 15 June 1913, which he used as a vehicle for his work and for publicizing Imagism in England. This campaign opened with an article titled 'Imagisme' by Rebecca West in the issue of 15 August 1913, which quoted the _Poetry_ article by Flint and Pound, and was followed by a reprinting of Pound's 'Contemporania'. Writing by Pound and his Imagist circle appeared often in the pages of _The New Freewoman_ in its half-year of publication, and Pound continued to act as the magazine's literary editor and to contribute to it when its name was changed to the _Egoist_ at the beginning of 1914, supplying it with many significant contributions from other writers and installing Aldington as assistant editor.

Throughout 1914 and 1915, the _Egoist_ published frequent reviews, comment and poems by Aldington, occasional poems by H. D., and contributions by Pound and others in his group. It gave considerable attention to Imagism, with reviews of the Imagist volumes issued in 1914 and 1915. The May 1915 number was an Imagist issue, with a series of articles on the Imagist poets, most of them written by other

Imagists. For a period in 1916 and 1917, when she served as an assistant editor, a poem by H. D. appeared in nearly every number.

It was in 1913 also that the American poet, Amy Lowell, a wealthy Bostonian, entered the Imagist scene. It is said that when she read the poems by H. D. in the January 1913 number of *Poetry*, she declared, 'Why, I too am an *Imagiste*'. After seeing the Imagist manifesto in the March issue, she decided to join these new poets, and came to London in July with a letter of introduction to Pound from Harriet Monroe. Having been discouraged by the poor reception of her first volume of verse, she submitted her poetry to Pound's corrections, and by the time she returned to America in September, had revised her style to correspond with Imagist doctrines. Pound, for his part, thought she was a likely recruit, and included one of her poems, 'In the Garden', in his Imagist anthology.

The year 1913 was also when the widow of the American art historian and orientalist, Ernest Fenollosa, gave Pound her late husband's notes on his Chinese studies, and Pound entered on his long involvement with Chinese poetry and history. He felt that the precision, concreteness and objectivity of the Chinese poems in Fenollosa's manuscripts corresponded remarkably well with Imagist principles, and they inspired him to write some poems in the Imagist manner. When he published his translations from the Chinese in his 1915 volume, *Cathay*, the poems struck many as excellent examples of Imagism.

Pound's movement achieved a sort of climax in the early part of 1914 when he edited a volume of poems by the Imagists titled *Des Imagistes: An Anthology*, as the fifth number of the monthly journal called *The Glebe*, which was published in New York in March and in London in April. *Des Imagistes* contained groups of poems by Pound, H. D., Aldington and Flint (some of them reprinted from *Poetry*), single poems from a number of others, including Ford, Amy Lowell and Joyce, and a bibliography of books by Imagist poets. Although Pound was to insist on his authority in controlling what could be published as 'Imagiste', he showed little discrimination in editing this volume, for it contained three comic verse productions having little to do with Imagism, and a poem in Greek by Ford.

When Amy Lowell came back to London in the summer of 1914, Pound was already beginning to separate himself from the Imagist group he had founded. At a dinner she gave to celebrate the publication of the Imagist anthology, *Des Imagistes*, she and Pound had a falling-out, and a new Imagist group independent of Pound was started when Miss Lowell invited some of the members of Pound's circle to a second dinner and planned an annual series of Imagist anthologies in which the poets would choose their own poems and have equal representation. Pound, who insisted on maintaining editorial control over any such volume, objected to the plan and refused to participate. This was the beginning of a schism which saw Pound's Imagist collaborators turning to Amy Lowell in a new phase of Imagism.

Pound himself was losing interest in Imagism and the Imagists at this time, and moving to a new group of friends and a new movement. He joined Wyndham Lewis, an artist and writer, and Henri Gaudier-Brzeska, a French sculptor, in the dynamic, confrontational movement called Vorticism. The most significant products of Vorticism were the crisp, angular graphics of Lewis, the sculptures of Gaudier-Brzeska, and two annual issues of a strident magazine named *BLAST*.

Pound, envisioning a literary Vorticism, attempted a few Vorticist poems and formulated Vorticist principles that exhibited some affinities with those of Imagism. The basic aim of this new movement, according to Pound, was the expression of energy through form. He described the Vortex, the defining pattern of the new movement, as a whirling cluster in which ideas came and went. Its origin, as well as the origin of the Image, was perhaps Pound's earlier formulation of the 'luminous detail', a particular which can be seen as a clue to a larger pattern of particulars. But he seems to have felt that the Image, even considered as a 'complex', was too static, and he embraced Vorticism as a programme more suited to an increasingly technical age. Nevertheless, his thinking maintained a continuity with Imagist doctrine. In his contribution to the 1914 *BLAST* he asserted that each art expressed feelings and ideas in its 'primary form', that the primary form of poetry was the Image, and that the Vorticist poet confined himself to this 'primary pigment'. His illustration of this discipline was H. D.'s Imagist poem 'Oread'. In a sort of farewell to his earlier movement, he seemed to link Vorticism with Imagism by writing, in a 1915 *New Age* article called 'As For Imagisme': 'the Image is more than an idea. It is a vortex or cluster of fused ideas and is endowed with energy'.

When Amy Lowell went back to America in September 1914, she took with her the manuscript of a new Imagist anthology to be titled *Some Imagist Poets*. (The shift from French spelling denoted the break with the earlier movement.) Imagism was now to be centred in America and led by Lowell, although the English Imagists continued to be members. Three annual volumes were published in Boston in 1915, 1916 and 1917, each with work by the same six poets: Lowell, H. D., Flint, Aldington, John Gould Fletcher and D. H. Lawrence. Fletcher, a newcomer to the movement, was an American and an intimate of Lowell's who had known Pound in London, and had moderated his own very different style and poetic principles to fit the Imagist mould. Lawrence's poetry was not written to any pattern, but Lowell admired him and welcomed his poems. The first anthology was prefaced by six principles which echoed the 'Imagisme' article in the 1913 *Poetry*, and, since it sold well, made the aims of the movement clear to a new public. Viewing these developments, Pound said in 1916 that he regretted that he had not declared 'the imagist movement *over*'. He ultimately accepted the schism with equanimity, but contemptuously dubbed the work of the new group 'Amygism'.

Some Imagist Poets aroused considerable interest and controversy, and Lowell continued to forward the Imagist cause in America by lecturing on 'the new poetry', and defending *vers libre* or 'cadenced verse'. When the third and last volume appeared in 1917, it was felt that the series had done its work, and organized Imagist activity came to an end. It is likely that H. D.'s volume, *Sea Garden*, with its excellent examples of pure Imagist poetry, which was published in 1916 in both London and Boston, did as much or more to advance Imagist principles as the anthologies did. While the individual Imagists developed in different directions in succeeding years, poems labelled 'Imagist' continued to be published. A collection entitled *Imagist Anthology, 1930: New Poetry by the Imagists* with prefaces by Ford Madox Ford and Glenn Hughes presented the later work of a number of poets who had been affiliated with the movement. In 1963 a volume called *The Imagist Poem*, edited and introduced by William Pratt, reprinted a collection of Imagist and Imagist-inspired poems.

The Imagist ideas were derived from a variety of literatures, including the Greek, Latin, Chinese and Japanese, but their most immediate inspiration was French Symbolism, which had provided an example by breaking with accepted conceptions of poetry, and centring attention on imagery. The Imagists claimed a kind of universality for their principles, for, by declaring that they were 'the essentials of all great poetry, indeed of all great literature', and by claiming such varied authors as Sappho, François Villon and Théophile Gautier as their progenitors, they came close to asserting that all good writing was Imagist, wherever it might be found.

Imagism attracted little attention in England outside of its official publications. But when *Some Imagist Poets* was published in America there was widespread hostile reaction. The poems were criticized as trivial, precious, simplistic, feeble and fragile and *vers libre* met much critical resistance. A review of the 1915 volume by Conrad Aiken in the *New Republic* complained that the poems lacked 'emotional force', presented only 'frail pictures', and offered nothing new or significant. Nevertheless, Lowell continued to promote Imagism in her lectures and to sponsor the two additional annual volumes.

Even when they did not exert direct influence, Imagism's technical innovations may be said to have played a significant part in authorizing what was meant by 'modernism' in twentieth-century poetry, and they were not without effect in the field of the novel as well. Wallace Stevens, in a 1946 essay, 'Rubbings of Reality', on William Carlos Williams, supported Imagist claims by writing: 'Imagism . . . is not something superficial. It obeys an instinct. Moreover imagism is an ancient phase of poetry. It is something permanent'. And in an address delivered in 1953, T. S. Eliot observed that Imagism was 'The *point de repère*, usually and conveniently taken' as 'the starting-point of modern poetry'.

Stevens and Eliot are among the many poets prominent in the decades following the end of the Imagist movement whose styles corresponded in some ways to the Imagist theories. Pound and H. D. continued to produce important works that embodied Imagist techniques, contributing to the Imagist tone of modern poetry. Many of these techniques have been adopted by such poets as William Carlos Williams, e. e. cummings, Archibald MacLeish, Hart Crane and a number of their contemporaries. The same might be said of the modern British poets of the pre-Second World War period: Auden, Empson, MacNeice and others, though the effects are far less clear.

Only a few of the poems by the original Imagists have entered the canon and become fixed parts of Anglo-American literature, but critical interest in the history of Imagism and its theories continues to outlast the movement itself. Among the topics that have been debated in recent years is the question of whether Ford, and his emphasis on natural language, Hulme, with his emphasis on imagery, or H. D., with her exemplary early poems, is to be considered the true originator of the movement. Imagism is widely understood to depend on the 'Image', that is, the precise presentation of an external object or sensory perception that intensifies and concentrates meaning in a non-discursive context. But it has been argued that what Pound had in mind in describing the Image as 'an emotional and intellectual complex' was a revelatory impression that was not primarily pictorial or representational.

The essence of Imagism has been located instead in the rigorous economy of language, employed with anti-rhetorical irony and wit that is illustrated in Pound's 'Contemporania' sequence. The allusions in the 1913 manifesto to a 'secret Doctrine of the Image' not suitable for public expression and to the Image's capacity for giving 'freedom from time limits and space limits' have led to the theory that Pound thought of the Image as a visionary, transcendental insight, not merely a sense-impression.

Some critics have vigorously attacked Imagist theories and their influence. The claim to objectivity has been challenged on the ground that the selection and juxtaposition of imagery is in itself a reflection of the poet's attitudes and has a persuasive effect. There has been some doubt as to whether Imagism could sustain a long poem, and Pound's *Cantos*, with its many brief, discontinuous segments, might be considered an effort to write one. Imagism has been held responsible for the lack of structure in Pound's long poem, and also for the incoherence, ambiguity, eclectic styles and rootlessness of such major modern works as *The Waste Land* by T. S. Eliot and Joyce's *Ulysses*. It has also been termed a revolution without depth, offering only technical correction, and no deep-seated convictions. Whatever one may think of such criticism, it at least attests to the fact that Imagism is widely regarded as an essential beginning to the course modern English and American literature has taken throughout much of the twentieth century.

BIBLIOGRAPHY

Coffman, Stanley K, Jr. (1951). *Imagism: A Chapter for the History of Modern Poetry*. Norman: University of Oklahoma Press.

Fenollosa, Ernest (1936). *The Chinese Written Character as a Medium for Poetry*. San Francisco: City Lights Books.

Gage, John T. (1981). *In the Arresting Eye: The Rhetoric of Imagism*. Baton Rouge: Louisiana State University Press.

Grieve, Thomas F. (1997). *Ezra Pound's Early Poetry and Poetics*. Columbia and London: University of Missouri Press.

Harmer, J. B. (1975). *Victory in Limbo: Imagism 1908–1917*. New York: St Martin's Press.

Hughes, Glenn (1931). *Imagism and the Imagists: A Study in Modern Poetry*. Stanford, CA and London: Stanford University Press and Oxford University Press.

Hulme, T. E. (1994). *The Collected Writings of T. E. Hulme*, ed. Karen Csengeri. Oxford: Clarendon Press.

Jones, Peter (ed.) (1972). *Imagist Poetry*. London: Penguin.

Longenbach, James (1988). *Stone Cottage*. New York and Oxford: Oxford University Press.

Pound, Ezra (1915). 'Affirmations: As for Imagisme', ed. William Cookson, *Selected Prose 1909–1965: Ezra Pound* (pp. 374–7). New York: New Directions.

Pratt, William (ed.) (1963). *The Imagist Poem*. New York: E. P. Dutton.

Pratt, William and Robert Richardson (eds) (1992). *Homage to Imagism*. New York: AMS Press.

Schneidau, Herbert N. (1969). *Ezra Pound: The Image and the Real*. Baton Rouge: Louisiana State University Press.

Witemeyer, Hugh (1969). *The Poetry of Ezra Pound: Forms and Renewals, 1908–1920*. Berkeley and London: University of California Press.

Xie, Ming (1999). *Ezra Pound and the Appropriation of Chinese Poetry: Cathay, Translation and Imagism*. New York and London: Garland Publishing.

11

The New Negro Renaissance

William W. Cook

In 1917 the following were among letters received and published by the *Chicago Defender*.

Mobile, Ala., 4.26.17
Dear Sir Bro:
We want to get away the 15 or 20 of May . . . so please help us as we are in need of your help as we wanted to go to Detroit but if you says no we go where ever you sends us until we can get to Detroit. We expect to do whatever you says. There is nothing here for the colored man but a hard time which these southern crackers gives us. We has not had any work to do in 4 wks. And every thing is high to the colored man so please let me hear from you by return mail. Please do this for your brother.

New Orleans, La, May 2, 1917
Dear Sir:
Please Sir will you kindly tell me what is meant by the Great Northern Drive to take place May the 15th on Tuesday. It is a rumor all over town to be ready for the 15th of May to go in the drive. The Defender first spoke of the drive the 10th of February. My husband is in the north preparing for our family . . . having a large family I could profit by it if it is really true. Do please write me at once and say is there an excursion to leave the south. Nearly the whole of the south is getting ready for the drive or excursion it is termed. Please write at once. We are sick to get out of the solid south.

These were among the hundreds of articles, letters and poems published by the newspaper and they speak to the widespread attention given to the early twentieth-century population shift called the Great Migration, that phenomenon which so shaped the cultural explosion called the Harlem Renaissance. Three observations should be made before discussion of the Great Migration and its effect on the Renaissance. First, the migration occurred over a number of decades – its first wave was the Exoduster movement (1877–90) under the leadership of 'Pap' Singleton. Second, the Harlem Renaissance, principally a 1920s phenomenon, is not to be confused with the New

Negro Movement which developed over the first four decades of the twentieth century (the Harlem Renaissance is one flowering of the New Negro Movement). Third, the arts of the Renaissance represent the entry into modernism of African American artists. Renaissance artists were far from unified, however, in matters of aesthetics, the role of the artist or the attractiveness/desirability of modernism.

What were the dimensions of the Great Migration and its cultural, social and political effects on the United States? In the period 1900–10, 213,000 African Americans were a part of the South–North migration. In the next decade the numbers rose to 572,000. Some 913,000 were counted in the decade 1920–30, 473,000 in 1930–40 and 1,689,000 in the period 1940–50. Another set of census figures demonstrates how swiftly population changes occurred. One decade will suffice to demonstrate such changes by geographical division.

Geographical division	1910	1920
Northeast	+20,310	+213,325
Middle Atlantic	+186,384	+296,664
East North Central	+119,649	+296,111
West North Central	+40,497	+68,222
South Atlantic	−392,827	−455,410
East South Central	−200,876	−405,511
West South Central	+194,658	+127,350
Mountain	+13,229	+20,085
Pacific	+18,976	+13,164

Source: Numbers tabulated from census studies by James G. Maddox, E. E. Liebhafsky, Vivian W. Henderson and Herbert M. Hamlin (1967), *The Advancing South: Manpower Prospects and Problems*.

Note that the South Atlantic and East South Central states are the only ones experiencing losses in African American population and note the substantial gains in the Middle Atlantic, East North Central and West South Central states.

Another set of numbers further demonstrates the nature of the population shifts which fed the New Negro Movement and its aesthetic climax, the Harlem Renaissance. Census data record that Illinois, New York, New Jersey and Pennsylvania received the largest number of migrants. Of urban areas with African American populations over 100,000 at the end of the 1920s, New York City experienced a 114 per cent increase in African American population, Chicago a 113 per cent increase, Detroit a whopping 194 per cent increase, Los Angeles a 150 per cent increase and Philadelphia a 64 per cent increase. The Great Migration, fully understood, is not simply a movement from the South to the North, but also a movement from rural to urban sites. In the period 1900–10 the following southern cities experienced gains in African American populations: Birmingham (215.6 per cent), Fort Worth (212.5 per cent), Jackson (137.3 per cent); African American populations in Atlanta, Charlotte, Dallas, Houston, Richmond and Shreveport grew from 45–99 per cent (Henri, 1976).

The Great Migration was the result of a series of influences constituting both push forces (those conditions which drove African Americans away from the South) and pull forces (those conditions which attracted the migrants to the cities and the North). Among the push forces, one must consider resistance to black ownership of land and to free movement by blacks; growth in membership of the Ku-Klux-Klan (1920 membership was approximately four million); the Mississippi floods of 1912–13 (powerfully recorded in 'Backwater Blues'); the boll weevil epidemic of 1915–16 (note 'Boll Weevil Blues'); Jim Crow; lynching (1920 and 1921 were terrible years); segregated facilities; technological change and the horrors of sharecropping. Among the pull forces were superior housing and living conditions in the North; letters home and letters in papers like the *Chicago Defender*; curtailed European migration and the rise in the power of unions (both of which increased the need for labour); stepped-up war industries and the possibility of land ownership; the enthusiastic stories about the paradise of 'Phillameyork' and other great urban sites; link migration and the dream of starting anew. The new music – blues, gospel and jazz, but particularly blues – drew its themes and a sense of musical alienation from earlier forms, from the push–pull forces of the migration and the effects of those forces on the migrant. One could argue quite comfortably that blues were the true historical record of the migration, since they record not only events during that movement, but also emotional responses to the migration. Other records also exist. Paul Laurence Dunbar in *The Sport of the Gods* (1902) presents a powerful picture of the dream of the city and the corrupting effect of that space on the innocent migrant. J. W. Johnson's *Autobiography of an Ex-Colored Man* (1912) is an excellent repository of the turn-of-the-century cultural scene in Harlem. In more recent times artists like Ishmael Reed in *Mumbo Jumbo* and Toni Morrison in *Jazz* (1992) anchor their narratives in the experience of the Great Migration. These works – even though the earliest to the most recent are divided by almost a century – include paeans to the city and the wonder it represented to the migrant. They also share a conviction that music and dance were central to the individual and group expression of the migrant.

That the Great Migration would be the source of cultural creativity, solidarity but also a sense of alienation should not be surprising, especially if we pay any attention to the analyses of social scientists like Robert E. Park. 'Civilization', wrote Park in *Human Migration and the Marginal Man*, 'is a consequence of contact and connection. The forces which have been decisive in the history of mankind are those which have brought men together in fruitful competition, conflict, and cooperation' (Park, p. 346). Park saw migration as something more than a simple 'change of residence and the breaking of home ties' (ibid., p. 55). He was interested in the particular type of personality which it produced and the way in which migration emancipated the individual:

Energies that were formerly controlled by custom and tradition are released. The individual is free for new adventure. (Ibid., p. 350)

It [migration] had loosened local bonds, destroyed the culture of the tribe and folk, and substituted for the local loyalties the freedom of the cities, for the sacred order of tribal, the rational organization which we call civilization. (Ibid., pp. 352–3)

The newly emancipated becomes in a certain sense a cosmopolitan, a stranger to the world in which he or she was born, 'a world which is now viewed with something of the detachment of a stranger' (ibid., p. 351). Looking at the United States from the vantage point of the 1920s, Park notes that the effects of the migration can be found in the cities to which the migrants came. He describes them as 'vast melting-pots of races and cultures, the metropolitan city' (ibid., p. 352).

The migrant becomes acculturated to and assimilated into the new cultural space, a cultural space made possible by the dynamic effects of cultural clash and combination. Park is very clear, however, that this is not always the case, since both acculturation and assimilation occur at different rates, particularly when groups in contact are of different races or widely different cultures. In such instances the progress towards cultural blending may be slow or resisted altogether; the new migrant, blocked from full participation and too changed to return home, experiences marginality. This marginal person may choose as a mode of spiritual survival to create those institutions which Farah Jasmine Griffin calls 'safe havens', those spaces in which the 'lost' home may be instantiated in the new surroundings. These spaces may be both physical and spiritual; they may be the store-front church or the juke joints. They may be the healing and shaping power of the blues, the vitality of jazz or the release of new forms of energetic dance. They may be that figure labelled 'the ancestor' by Toni Morrison and present in so much of the literature of the first few decades of the twentieth century, a figure who represents both a real and symbolic mother-life of the migrant; connection rather than loss. It is in response to frustrated assimilation and acculturation that Park introduces 'marginal man', Georg Simmel's 'stranger' adapted to fit the realities of urban America and the migration. More recently 'hybridity' might be the term used by scholars like Homi Bhabha to describe such a figure.

As a result of the migrant participating

in the cultural life of the people among whom he lived, there appeared a new type of personality. Namely, a cultural hybrid, or man living and sharing intimately in the cultural life and traditions of two distinct peoples; never quite willing to break, even if he were permitted to do so, with his past and his traditions, and not quite accepted, because of racial prejudice, in the new society. . . . He was a man on the margin of two cultures and two societies which never completely interpenetrated and fused. (Ibid., p. 354)

This marginal man of Park may well represent that victim of 'double consciousness', of whom W. E. B. DuBois spoke in *Souls of Black Folk*. His is the inward war of Cullen's 'Heritage' or, one might say, of the entire *oeuvre* of Countee Cullen. He is a central figure not only in the New Negro Movement but also in the Harlem Renaissance when we view both as cultural phenomena of the Great Migration. The crisis of marginality which Park describes as a temporary experience of all migrants is a relatively permanent condition of the marginal man.

As should be obvious from the above, Park's marginal man is central to my reading of the New Negro Movement and its importance will deepen as we look at representative writers of the period. One other influence should be given equal attention: that of Johann Gottfried Herder. Detailed studies of the influence of Herder's ideas on DuBois are not readily available in the literature on DuBois's *The Souls of Black Folk*, but I would like to argue here that DuBois's masterful creation can and ought to be read as an application of Herderian ideas of culture. Its influence on and its centrality to twentieth-century black thought needs careful examination. Such an examination will also reveal why – other than their shared occupation of the bottom rung of the prestige ladder with the Irish – the New Negroes saw the Irish revival of the early twentieth century as a model of and justification for their own efforts.

Herder flourished in the late eighteenth century and exerted a powerful influence on late nineteenth-century developments in Romanticism. He is also specifically labelled as the father of Slavic nationalism, of the *Sturm und Drang* school of literature and certainly – given his theories of folk art – of a kind of cultural racialism. DuBois studied in Germany (1892–4) when Herderian notions of culture were powerful. This partially explains DuBois's referencing of Johann Christophe von Schiller and other German romantics in *The Souls of Black Folk*, the closing of chapter 1 with 'the Sturm und Drang' and 'dreams of a credulous race-childhood', and the very title of the work, all clear evocations of Herder. As with Park, we need to ask what there might be in Herder's thought that would make it useful in a reading of DuBois and the New Negro Movement. Most useful in Herder's extensive *oeuvre* are those works which deal specifically with history, language and culture; to place a more particular reading on it, those works which deal with the relationship of modern theories of racial and ethnic sensibilities to folk literature, folklore and folk arts. How does Herder link folk culture with nationhood in such a way as to earn the name 'father of Slavic nationalism' and, by association, of a number of cultural and nationalistic movements including the distortion of his ideas by the Nazis? Far too many readers focus on these distortions as if they were the actual work of Herder and not corruptions of his ideas.

Central to Herder's thought is the notion of *volkgeist*. The 'soul of the folk' is produced by the indigenous cultural development of each nation and expressed in its art and literature. In order to make manifest the *volkgeist* of a people one must look to the art and literature produced in the *childhood* of that people: their folk art and literature. It follows, Herder argues, that there are no superior or inferior people; each possesses a *volkgeist* unique to its history and equal to that of all others.

> There is but one and the same species of man throughout the whole of our earth . . . the ape she has divided into as many species and varieties as possible, and extended these as far as she could: but thou, O man, honour thyself; neither the pongo nor the gibbon

is thy brother; the American and the Negro are: these therefore thou shouldst not oppress, or murder, or steal; for they are men, like thee; with the ape thou canst not enter into fraternity. ('Reflections', Herder, 1986)

For humanity has not one form, but many, and these forms find expression in the host of societies and nations that populate the historical scene. . . . Herder in general maintained that every known society, Chinese, Indian, Egyptian, Greek, Roman, and so on, had grown and developed in a distinctive manner and in response to the combination of environmental conditions presented by its particular time and place. (Gardner, 1967, p. 489)

In conformity with the above view, Herder's song collection *Volkslieder 1778–9* was a project initiated to prove that the *volkgeist* of a people retained its distinctiveness despite their migration to other areas. The nation is defined here not as a particular geographical entity, but as an agglomeration of shared cultural traits. Henry E. Krehbiel's 1925 *Afro-American Folksongs* (Krehbiel, 1962), following Herder's method, subjected black folk music to 'scientific observation', analysing scales and rhythm patterns and comparing them with African music. DuBois had made an earlier study of the spirituals in *The Souls of Black Folk* and his use of citations to the spirituals to introduce each section of that work represents a clear Herderian effort and further clarifies for us the aim of his study: to do for the New Negro what Herder and his followers had done for the Slavs and other 'migrant' or stateless people; to parallel their efforts at nation-building and freedom from oppression with similar efforts on the part of Irish struggles against English cultural and political dominance. The central documents of the New Negro Movement make clear the relationship to Herder outlined above.

Given such patterns for reading culture, it should be clear that artists like Hughes, Zora Neale Hurston and Sterling Brown were much closer to the Herderian pattern than were artists like Countee Cullen, William Stanley Braithwaite or George Samuel Schuyler. Hurston's extensive research in folk custom, language and literature, Hughes's devotion to indigenous black music, and Brown's study and mastery of folk poetry and legend distinguish them from those contemporaries who saw assimilation and acculturation as both desirable and possible. Certainly the Herderian group has experienced a longer life with readers. The desire to become part of a 'universal' artistic and cultural community was doomed to failure given the realities of race in the United States. This racism model provides as accurate an explanation of their relative invisibility in the present day as the dominance of themes of tragedy, bathos and loss in the nineteenth-century models they chose. Such themes, prominent in the poetry of Cullen and his cohort, and an outdated nineteenth-century poetic diction, eventually doom them to irrelevance in the search for cultural uniqueness as opposed to universality. No one today seems to be attempting a Cullen revival or a new reading of Georgia Douglas Johnson or the poetry of Alice Dunbar-Nelson. One exception might be Gloria Hull's *Color, Sex and Poetry* (1987), which deals with Johnson, Dunbar-Nelson and Angelina Weld Grimke. They are interesting as figures in literary and women's history rather than the art of poetry. Far more interesting as a subject of revival is Mae Cowdrey who, unlike her closeted sisters, resisted the highly coded pastoral laments and faced in both her life and her poetry the reality of her lesbian life and called on others to join her. 'The Young Voice Cries' may well be one of the first 'outings' in African American literature, for in that poem she calls on her older sister poet Alice Dunbar-Nelson to do her duty and support young lesbian poets. No response to the poem by Dunbar-Nelson is recorded. Cowdrey, in her suits, bow ties and slicked-back hair, died a suicide. Why is she not a part of the record of the Renaissance? Could it be that scholars forgot that the poems in her book (*We Lift Our Voices and Other Poems*, 1936) were all written during the 1920s at the height of the Renaissance? Did they forget that she was published in the established journals of that movement (*Crisis* and *Opportunity*) and that Hughes, Cullen and Braithwaite praised her work? Being published was difficult for a woman in the period; it was almost impossible for an out-of-the-closet lesbian or for an out-of-the-closet gay man. Bruce Nugent, who was quite publicly a gay man, received more attention than did Cowdrey. The result has been that, with a few exceptions (Cowdrey prominent among them), gay and lesbian life of the period was presented either in highly coded and evasive language or completely silenced. The biographical note for Alice Dunbar-Nelson in Maureen Honey's *Shadowed Dreams* (1989) illustrates the latter condition. The editor refers to Dunbar-Nelson's 'unconventional love life, marriage and domestic arrangements' (ibid., p. 227). Ironically, the book is dedicated to the memory of Mae V. Cowdrey. Cowdrey forcefully speaks to such silencing in the poem addressed to Alice Dunbar-Nelson:

> Can you not hear us?
> Or are you deaf
> To our pleadings . . .
> Can you not see us?
> . . . .
> And when we look
> To see the naked loveliness
> Of things
> There is only a barren cliff
> Veiled in ugly mists
> Of dogmas and fear.
> (Lewis, 1995, pp. 238–9)

In the defining document of the New Negro Movement, Alain Locke in his introductory essay 'The New Negro' links the movement to other nationalistic movements based on Herderian ideas:

> It must be admitted that American Negroes have been a race more in name than in fact, or to be exact, more in sentiment than in experience. . . . In Harlem, Negro life is seizing upon its first chances for group expression and self-determination. It is – or promises to be – a race capital. That is why our comparison is taken with those nascent centres of

folk-expression and self-determination which are playing a creative part in the world today. Without pretense to their political significance, Harlem has the same role to play for the New Negro as Dublin has had for the New Ireland or Prague for the New Czecho-slovakia. (Locke, 1997, p. 7)

In his essay in the anthology *Negro Youth Speaks* Locke returns to the same theme and point of comparison. He adds here another flourish. The new art will not be marked by the 'cautious moralism' or 'guarded idealizations' which marked the old art. Like those movements with which it should be compared, it will ruffle feathers and disturb older ways of making art and defining its mission.

> Just as with the Irish Renaissance, there were riots and controversies over Synge's folk plays and other frank realisms of the younger school, so we are having and will have turbulent discussion and dissatisfaction with the stories, plays and poems of the younger Negro group. (Locke, 1997, p. 50)

These views are clearly linked to earlier statements by James Weldon Johnson. Note the following from Johnson's preface to his 1922 *Book of American Negro Poetry*.

> What the colored poet in the United States needs to do is something like what Synge did for the Irish; he needs to find a form that will express the racial spirit by symbols from within rather than by symbols from without, such as the mere mutilation of English spelling and pronunciation. He needs a form that is freer and larger than dialect, but which will still hold the racial flavor; a form expressing the imagery, the idioms, the peculiar turns of thought and the distinctive humor and pathos, too, of the Negro. (Johnson, 1969, pp. 41–2)

Johnson divides the New Negro poets into three groups. The first he calls the Dunbar school, which constituted the dominant group up through the First World War. The dialect, stereotypes, sentimentality and supplicatory character of this school were rejected by the second group, which arose from the experience of the war. This second group focused upon the disillusionment and despair which marked American and British poetry after the Battle of the Somme. Theirs was a poetry 'of protest, rebellion and despair'. The third group, in their avoidance of 'propaganda', in their objectivity and their focus on the art as opposed to the ideology of poetry, clearly positioned themselves in the modernist revolt. For Johnson, 'the pre-eminent figures in this younger group [were] Countee Cullen, who published his first volume, *Color*, in 1925 and Langston Hughes, who published his first volume, *The Weary Blues*, in 1926' (Johnson, 1969, p. 5).

Because Cullen and Hughes are so frequently grouped together as the brightest lights of Renaissance poetry, a reader may be led to reduce both them and the Renaissance to a sameness which neither their work nor their statements on art and the role of the artist will support. A discussion of the two will offer a brief glimpse at the contrasting faces of the Harlem Renaissance.

The first volume of Langston Hughes's autobiography *The Big Sea* begins with the author on the ship the *S. S. Malone* heading for Africa. His actions are interesting in their break with a longstanding tradition in African American letters. Beginning with the 'talking book' trope of Olaudah Equiano's 1792 narrative, we can trace what is almost an obsession with the centrality of books in the construction of African American identity. Note in the opening words of *The Big Sea* the different relationship of Hughes to the books he has with him:

> Melodramatic maybe, it seems to me now. But then it was like throwing a million bricks out of my heart when I threw the books into the water. . . . I leaned over the rail . . . and threw the books as far as I could out into the sea – all the books I had had at Columbia, and all the books I had lately bought to read. (Hughes, 1940, p. 3)

The epigraph to the autobiography is 'Life is a big sea full of many fish. I let down my nets and pull.' The closing words continue the analogy: 'I'm still pulling'. What is quite clear here is his determination, as he answers his calling as artist, that his art will be drawn not from books but from life. He will not force that life to fit any of the readily available moulds. In this regard, Whitman was a vital and important model for Hughes, not because Hughes borrowed a style from him, but because he borrowed an attitude towards poetry. In the opening sections of 'Song of Myself' Whitman models the poet who, keeping 'creeds and schools' in abeyance, permits life to express itself through him. He becomes a vessel for many voices, even those voices that are contradictory. This is essentially the role of the bard who is concerned with 'life, traditions, and ideals of the community' and is 'far removed from the personal, lyric emotionalism connected with the term' in more recent times ('Bard', 1965, p. 65). Hughes pays homage to this model in a poem that signals something far less formal than the usual relationship between younger and older poets. His title is 'Old Walt'.

> Old Walt Whitman
> Went finding and seeking.
> Finding less than sought
> Seeking more than found.
> Every detail minding
> Of the seeking and the finding.
> Pleasuring equally
> In seeking as in finding.
> Each detail minding,
> Old Walt went seeking
> And finding.

Cullen's poems to that poet he named as his predecessor reveal a very different relationship. Note the closing lines of 'To John Keats, Poet. At Spring Time', from *Color*:

'John Keats is dead,' they say, but I
Who hear your full insistent cry
In bud and blossom, leaf and tree,
Know John Keats still writes poetry.
And while my head is earthward bowed
To read new life sprung from your shroud,
Folks seeing me must think it strange
That merely spring could so derange
My mind. They do not know that you
John Keats, keep revel with me, too.

Also in *Color* (Cullen's first book) can be found a second Keats poem: 'For John Keats, Apostle of Beauty'. Images of 'singing lips', 'cold death kissed' and 'Sweet lyric throat' witness again Cullen's determination to place his poetry outside African American discourse.

Unlike Hughes, Cullen seems to see Keats as an object of reverence, a model of perfection which must be imitated if one wishes to become a poet of what Cullen calls 'the sublime'. The poets differ not only in their choice of and attitude towards earlier poets. Hughes does not want to become another Whitman. He finds in Whitman a method rather than a model. The sea in which he fishes will require a poet closer to its own soul, one that will mirror that soul rather than shame it into elevation.

The function of the poet, Cullen argues, has nothing to do with race. Given this view, it is ironic that the poems for which Cullen is still known are those dealing with race. In the 10 February 1921 issue of the *Brooklyn Eagle* Margaret Sperry published an article on Cullen: 'Countee P. Cullen, Negro Boy Poet, Tells His Story'. In the article she quotes freely from her interviews with the poet. One statement demonstrates how clearly Cullen and Hughes, although representative of a substantial portion of the black reading public, disagreed sharply.

If I am going to be a poet at all, I am going to be POET and not NEGRO POET. That is what has hindered the development of artists among us. Their one note has been the concern with their race . . . I shall not write of Negro subjects for the purpose of propaganda. That is not what a poet is concerned with. Of course, when the emotion rising out of the fact that I am a Negro is strong, I express it. But that is another matter.

Whitman, who had written for the *Brooklyn Eagle* in the nineteenth century, would have been shocked. So was Langston Hughes. Hughes was asked in 1926 to reply to George Schuyler's dismissal of a distinct 'Negro' art. Schuyler's essay, 'The Negro Art Hokum', appeared in *Nation*, which journal invited Hughes to reply. 'The Negro Artist and the Racial Mountain' was more than a reply to Schuyler; it was something of an aesthetic declaration of independence for the younger artists of the Renaissance and it marks Hughes's assumption of the position of major poet of that period, a position then held by Cullen. Hughes's opening lines, lines in which he sets up his adversary, clearly call to mind Cullen's words as quoted in the *Brooklyn Eagle*.

One of the most promising of the young Negro poets said to me once, 'I want to be a poet – not a Negro poet,' meaning subconsciously, 'I would like to be a white poet'; meaning behind that, 'I would like to be white.' And I was sorry the young man said that, for no great poet has ever been afraid of being himself. (Hill, 1998, p. 899)

Hughes defines himself and the sources of his art in radically different ways: 'Most of my poems are racial in theme and treatment, derived from the life I know. In many of them I try to grasp and hold some of the meanings and rhythms of jazz' (ibid., p. 901). Here he is very clear that he does not wish to sound like either the romantic, the sentimental or the local colour poet. He is seeking the sound of the 'Negro' people and on finding that sound is determined to use it as the structuring pattern for his poetry:

Jazz to me is one of the inherent expressions of Negro life in America; the eternal tom-tom beating in the Negro soul – the tom-tom of revolt against weariness in a white world, a world of subway trains, and work, work, work; the tom-tom of joy and laughter, and pain swallowed in a smile . . . the blare of Negro jazz bands and the bellowing of Bessie Smith singing Blues penetrate the closed ears of the colored near-intellectuals until they listen and perhaps understand . . . the tom-tom cries and the tom-tom laughs. If colored people are pleased we are glad. If they are not, their displeasure doesn't matter either. We build our temples for tomorrow, strong as we know how, and we stand on top of the mountain, free within ourselves. (Ibid., pp. 901–2)

It is important to note that the future of which Hughes spoke did hear him. In 1971 when Addison Gayle, Jr. published the anthology *The Black Aesthetic*, he intended to do for the Black Arts Movement what Locke in *The New Negro* had done for the earlier cultural arts movement. Hughes's 1926 essay opened the section on poetry. Locke and DuBois were declared by their inclusion to be still relevant to the Black Arts Movement. How ironic that Hughes, reviled like Whitman by the guardians of the genteel, should, again like Whitman, be singled out for such a signal honour by a later period.

Such was not the case during the Renaissance. While Hughes was a rival to Cullen and, later in the decade, the object of more studied attention, he was not considered by many to be Cullen's equal in his art or his taste. Note Arnold Rampersad's summary of comments that greeted the publication of Hughes's best book of poetry, *Fine Clothes to the Jew* (sales of which were very disappointing.)

Under a headline proclaiming Hughes a 'SEWER DWELLER,' William M. Kelley of the *New York Amsterdam News*, who once had sought out his work, denounced *Fine Clothes to the Jew* as 'about 100 pages of trash . . . it reeks of the gutter and sewer'. The regular review of the *Philadelphia Tribune* adamantly refused to publicize it; Eustace Gay confessed that *Fine Clothes to the Jew* 'disgusts me.' In the *Pittsburgh Courier*, historian J. A. Rogers called it 'piffling trash' that left him 'positively sick.' The *Chicago Whip* sneered at the dedication to Van Vechten, 'a literary gutter rat' who perhaps alone 'will revel in the lecherous, lust-reeking characters that Hughes finds time to poeticize about. . . .

These poems are unsanitary, insipid and repulsing [*sic*].' Hughes was the 'poet low-rate of Harlem.' The following week, refining its position, the *Tribune* lamented Langston's 'obsession for the more degenerate elements' of black life; the book was 'a study in the perversions of the Negro.' (Rampersad, 1986, p. 140)

The Cullen–Hughes rivalry points to a sharp division of opinion as to what constituted good poetry during the Renaissance. Cullen's review of Hughes's *The Weary Blues*, while not marked by the vitriol of the above statements, makes very clear the difference in his and Hughes's aesthetic. The review first appeared in *Opportunity* in February 1926. Cullen argues that the jazz poems of the first part of the book were

Interlopers in the company of the truly beautiful poems in other sections of the book. . . . Taken as a group the selections in this book seem one-sided to me. They tend to hurl this poet into the gaping pit that lies before all Negro writers, in the confines of which they become racial artists instead of artists pure and simple. There is too much emphasis here on strictly Negro themes; and this is probably an added reason for my coldness toward the jazz poems.

Fire!! appeared later in the same year as Cullen's review. This ill-fated journal (only one issue was published) was an aesthetic call to arms by 'the younger Negro artists'. *Fire!!* was privately printed, accepted no wealthy white patrons and was edited by the brilliant Wallace Thurman. Hughes, with Bruce Nugent, Gwendolyn Bennett, Aaron Douglas, John Preston Davis and Zora Neale Hurston, constituted the board of editors. Now that copies of that original edition are available it is clear that the editors saw themselves as creating something new. The patrons were not the usual New Negro patrons. Listed were many names not seen before and home addresses in Minneapolis, Harrisburg, Philadelphia and Baltimore. The cover of the magazine features Aaron Douglas's depiction of a sphinx at centre that becomes, as we take in the entire page, the head of a black man. This pan-African image, like the contents of the magazine, signalled something other than a dream of assimilation or universality.

What many of Hughes's most negative critics seem not to note is the way in which he exploits highly intricate Western European prosody, but does so by always reworking such seemingly antithetical approaches in such a way that they seem to fit seamlessly into a black aesthetic. Note the following observations on Hughes's sequence 'Lenox Avenue Mural', a study of the Great Migration.

In 'Lenox Avenue Mural' Langston Hughes turns to one of the oldest literary genres in the European tradition. His poem belongs to that group of works we label ekphrastic, works that are constructed as literary versions of graphic images. Keats' 'Ode on a Grecian Urn,' Ashbery's 'Self Portrait in a Convex Mirror,' Yeats' 'Lapis Lazuli,' and Tolson's 'A gallery of Harlem Portraits' all aspire to the condition of ekphrasis. The latter text, written by an African American poet, deals however with a gallery and with paintings that exist only in the imagination of the poet. In describing such texts, John Hollander coined the term 'notional ekphrasis.' The popularity of notional ekphrasis with African American writers during the early part of this century may be attributed to their conception of an erased past; there are no 'images,' at least none they would wish to acknowledge as representative of their lives, to be found in the galleries of America. Hence the need to imagine that which is absent. (Cook, 1996, p. 40)

In adapting this classical European approach in his poetry, Hughes does not imitate the language or the cultural cues usually found in such work. His theft is so skilful that not a single print of the owner's hand remains. His prize-winning 'The Weary Blues' is not as flat and derivative as Cullen's 'To One Who Said Me Nay'.

To side with Hughes or Cullen during the Renaissance was not only to choose that poet as exemplary of artistic excellence; it was also to adopt a position in relation to the black masses, to white America and to questions of black identity and specialness. That the choices were clear and sharply defined can be witnessed in the awarding of the 1925 *Opportunity* prize in poetry and the *Crisis* prize of the same year. The choices were the perfect model of decisions marked by indecision; warring and conflicted standards. Hughes was awarded first place in the *Opportunity* contest for 'The Weary Blues' and Cullen won second place for 'To One Who Said Me Nay'. Any student of black poetry knows without a doubt which poem survived. In the *Crisis* contest Cullen won first prize and Hughes was awarded third place. This rivalry and the two careers point powerfully to the 'double consciousness' very much alive in the arts of the Renaissance and in the New Negro Movement. Cullen's finest poem, 'Heritage', brilliantly captures the agony of that struggle in spite of his determination not to write 'Negro' poems.

In *The Harlem Renaissance Remembered* the editor Arna Bontemps (1972) attempts to complicate our view of that particular moment in history.

> What made their decade memorable, of course, was not simply an influx of black migrants from the South and West Indies in that post-World War I era. . . . But an upsurge of Negro creativity, such as New York's Harlem was beginning to detect, to produce, and to foster, required more than a single source. It demanded an array of factors, a favorable conjunction.

The above discussion has been an attempt to rethink the movement and to suggest some directions which that reconsideration is and ought to be taking. Warrington Hudlin, who is given the last word in Bontemps's book, argues that the legacy of the Harlem Renaissance is its art, its artists and its ideas (ibid., p. 276). Its activity, though political, could hardly be considered political in contemporary terms, just as some of the cultural products praised so highly in that period may not stand up to contemporary standards of excellence. Hudlin describes the Harlem Renaissance as 'a point in the evolution of Afro-American literature'. As such its achievements should be placed in perspective to compute its significance. 'It opened the door for the black writing of today' (ibid., p. 277). Larry Neal in 'Any Day Now: Black Art and Black Liberation' links the efforts of the Harlem Renaissance to his own Black Arts

Movement struggle. He singles out DuBois, Hughes and musicians for special mention, but Hughes is the strongest link:

> In the history of Black America, the current ideas of the Black Arts Movement can be said to have their roots in the so-called Negro Renaissance of the 1920s. . . . There was the ascendency of the hip, blues-talking, Langston Hughes . . . Hughes best personifies the Black artist who is clearly intent upon developing a style of poetry which springs forcefully and recognizably from a Black life style. (King and Anthony, 1972, p. 151)

Neal is clear on the gift of which he speaks: 'This is the death of the white lie that our ancestors prophesied. This is the death of the double consciousness' (ibid., p. 164). There is still a great deal of work to be done before we will have exhausted the richness left us.

BIBLIOGRAPHY

Adero, Malaika (ed.) (1993). *Up South: Stories, Studies and Letters of This Century's African American Migrations*. New York: New Press.

Anderson, Jervis (1982). *Harlem: The Great Black Way*. London: Orbis Publishing.

'Bard' (1965). *The Princeton Encyclopedia of Poetry and Poetics*. Princeton, NJ: Princeton University Press.

Bontemps, Arna (ed.) (1972). *The Harlem Renaissance Remembered*. New York: Dodd Mead.

Cook, William W. (1996). 'Langston Hughes' '"painting".' In *Touchstones: American Poets on a Favorite Poem*, ed. Robert Pack and Jay Parini. Hanover: University Press of New England.

Cullen, Countee (1925). *Color*. New York: Harper and Brothers.

Early, Gerald (ed.) (1991). *My Soul's High Song: The Collected Writings of Countee Cullen*. New York: Anchor/Doubleday.

Gardner, Patrick (1967). 'Johann Gottfried Herder.' *Encyclopedia of Philosophy, Vol 3*. New York: Macmillan.

Gayle, Addison, Jr. (ed.) (1972). *The Black Aesthetic*. Garden City, NY: Doubleday.

Griffin, Farah Jasmine (1995). *Who Set you Flowin'? The African-American Migration Narrative*. New York: Oxford University Press.

Henri, Florette (1976). *Black Migration: Movement North 1900–1920: The Road From Myth to Man*. New York: Anchor Press.

Herder, Johann Gottfried. 'Essay on the Origin of Language', trans. John H. Moran and Alexander Gode. In *Two Essays on the Origin of Language: Jean-Jacques Rousseau and Johann Gottfried Herder*. Chicago: University of Chicago Press.

Hill, Patricia Liggins (1998). *Call and Response: The Riverside Anthology of the African American Literary Tradition*. Boston: Houghton Mifflin.

Honey, Maureen (1989). *Shadowed Dreams: Women's Poetry of the Harlem Renaissance*. New Brunswick: Rutgers University Press.

Hughes, Langston (1940). *The Big Sea*. New York: Hill and Wang.

Johnson, James Weldon (ed.) (1969). *The Book of American Negro Poetry*. San Diego: Harvest/HBJ.

Kellner, Bruce (ed.) (1984). *The Harlem Renaissance: A Historical Dictionary for the Era*. Westport, CT: Greenwood Press.

King, Woodie and Earl Anthony (eds) (1972). *Black Poets and Prophets: A Bold Uncompromisingly Clear Blueprint for Black American Liberation*. New York: Mentor/NAL.

Krehbiel, Henry Edward (1962). *Afro-American Folk Songs: A Study in Racial and National Music*. New York: Frederick Unger.

Lemann, Nicholas (1992). *The Promised Land: The Great Migration and How It Changed America*. New York: Vintage/Random House.

Lewis, David Levering (ed.) (1995). *The Portable Harlem Renaissance Reader*. New York: Penguin.

Locke, Alain (ed.) (1997). *The New Negro: Voices of the Harlem Renaissance*. New York: Touchstone.

Marks, Carole (1989). *Farewell – We're Good and Gone: The Great Black Migration*. Bloomington: Indiana University Press.

Rampersad, Arnold (1986). *The Life of Langston Hughes, Vol. 1*. New York: Oxford University Press.

Rampersad, Arnold (ed.) (1995). *The Collected Poems of Langston Hughes*. New York: Alfred A. Knopf.

Thurman, Wallace (ed.) (1982). *Fire!!* New York: Thomas H. Wirth.

Wilson, Sondra Kathryn (ed.) (1999). *The Crisis Reader*. New York: Modern Library.

12

Poetry and the New Criticism

Stephen Burt and Jennifer Lewin

'Never have poetry and criticism in English been so close together', Allen Tate wrote in 1955, as they were at the height of the largely American movement now called the New Criticism (Tate, 1968, p. 214). In the late 1920s, after the upheavals of High Modernism, some younger critics who were also poets began to explain the principles which had emerged from their tastes. These principles helped generate new approaches to literature and especially to poetry, concentrating on close verbal analysis; new journals and textbooks arose to propagate them. By the late 1940s a few of the New Critics' students had become major poets themselves, quietly fulfilling certain New Critical goals even as they rejected others.

The term 'New Criticism' (rarely embraced by those it covers) began life as the title of a 1941 book by John Crowe Ransom (J. E. Spingarn's 1911 book of the same name has nothing to do with the movement). Ransom's study examined the critical practices of I. A. Richards, T. S. Eliot and Yvor Winters, with shorter segments on William Empson and on R. P. Blackmur; it then called for an 'ontological critic' who would describe the special nature of poetry and the structures of individual poems. As Cleanth Brooks wrote later, uncareful readers soon 'assumed that Ransom was the primal New Critic and that his former students and friends were the others' (*Community* 1). Writers who invoke the New Critics normally refer to a loosely allied group whose core included Ransom himself, Tate, Brooks and Robert Penn Warren, along with Empson and Blackmur. Winters worked on the group's *de facto* intellectual margins, as in a different way did F. O. Matthiesen; both combined criticism of modern poetry with studies of nineteenth-century American writing. Others sometimes called New Critics proved important to literary theory, but not directly to twentieth-century poetry: these included René Wellek, William Wimsatt, Austin Warren, Monroe Beardsley, and the ambitious left-wing thinker Kenneth Burke. All these thinkers' 'one common element was [their] special concern . . . for the rhetorical structure of the literary text' (*Community* 2). New Critical ways of reading helped to shape the American poets who emerged in the 1940s, among them Robert Lowell, Elizabeth Bishop, John Berryman and Randall Jarrell.

Origins, Axioms, Aims

All the New Critics emerged from milieux in which, as Ransom put it, 'young men speak up and quote Eliot pertinently on nearly any literary occasion' (Ransom, 1941, p. 146). At Tennessee's Vanderbilt University in 1922, Warren and Tate lived together in rooms on whose walls Warren painted scenes from *The Waste Land*; both studied together under Ransom (himself ambivalent about that poem). Starting from the poems of Eliot, Yeats and Pound, New Critics found themselves following leads from Eliot's criticism. These included his 'classical' ideals and his religious thought; his attention to the poetry and drama of the early seventeenth century; his deprecation of the Romantics, especially Shelley; his proposition that good poems constitute 'not a turning loose of emotion but an escape from emotion'; and his insistence that 'poets . . . at present, must be *difficult*' (Eliot, 1975, pp. 43, 65). Against the passive absorptions of popular entertainment, New Critics elevated poetry whose difficulties required (in Tate's words) 'the direct and *active* participation of a reader' (Tate, 1968, p. 163).

I. A. Richards's *Practical Criticism* (1929) showed that subtle poems escaped the comprehension of students at Cambridge University: Richards used his 'experiments' there to argue that university teachers should convey both analytical skills and literary taste. Richards's other early books proposed structural and linguistic analyses of poetry while stating its effects in psychological terms. Like him, Ransom, Brooks and their allies aimed to teach analysis and taste; like him, they tried to make aesthetically oriented, intensive study of literature as academically respectable as extensive bibliographical and linguistic study already was. American New Critics, however, rejected what they saw as Richards's scientific worldview. They sought instead to defend literary experience against perceived threats from the exact sciences, from behaviourist social science, and from the industrial economy.

Brooks's *Modern Poetry and the Tradition* (1939) and *The Well-Wrought Urn* (1947) have become ideal–typical examples of New Criticism. Lauding metaphor, paradox and productive ambiguity, Brooks argued that 'the difference between metaphysical poetry' – pre-eminently that of Donne – 'and other poetry [was] a difference of degree not of kind' (Brooks, 1939, p. 39). Robert Frost, Brooks contended, 'exhibits the structure of symbolist–metaphysical poetry' where simpler, ostensibly modern poets do not (ibid., p. 116). New Critical thinking accepted the Coleridgean doctrine that a successful poem creates a unified aesthetic whole, containing or reconciling conflicting ideas and attitudes. (Brooks called this attribute, perhaps misleadingly, 'irony'; Tate and Empson both preferred 'tension'.) In one key New Critical locution, 'poems are little dramas, exhibiting actions in complete settings' (Ransom, 1938, p. 249). These dramas, however, play themselves out among words or attitudes rather than among characters. In practice New Critics often wanted poems to resemble little *tragedies*: for Brooks, 'The principles of poetic organization, developed to their logical conclusion, carry the poem over into drama, with the characteristics of tragedy – concreteness, dramatic ambiguity, irony, resolution through struggle – as perhaps their highest expression' (Brooks, 1939, p. 218).

In general, New Critical taste in poetry sought, explicitly: 'tension', paradox, polysemy, ambivalence; central symbols; compression and verbal density; seventeenth-century models; Coleridgean unity, and strong closure. As a result, the New Critical climate favoured implicitly: difficulty, seriousness, violence, frequent allusion, complex syntax and Christian symbolism. The best poems written out of New Critical paradigms reject some of these goals to accomplish the rest.

Fugitives, Agrarians and Others

It is a grim irony that people who argued for the independence of literary art from instrumental political ends should now be impeached or dismissed for their own politics; it makes an even harsher irony that people who insisted on fine distinctions now get lumped together as reactionaries. Nevertheless, some American New Critics' Southern affiliations and anti-liberal predispositions entered their literary thought and (more directly) their own poems. At Vanderbilt, Ransom, Tate, Warren and poet Donald Davidson founded a literary group called the Fugitives, and published a journal, *The Fugitive* (1922–5). The same group, expanded, turned to political and cultural writing, reconstituted itself as the Agrarians, and published *I'll Take My Stand* (1930). That volume's 'Twelve Southerners' argued that the South should retain a traditional farm-based society, rather than accept industrial capitalism. Infused by regional loyalties and by a more or less Eliotic conservatism, the poets' agrarianism, Louis Rubin writes, 'was also . . . a campaign for poetry and religion' (in Young, 1976b).

The volume prompted well-publicized debates. After a few years of research in economics, Ransom returned in the mid-1930s to his literary interests, reluctantly supporting the New Deal. Tate retained the rhetoric of what he called his 'Reactionary Essays', co-editing another political volume, *Who Owns America?* (1936). After 1940 only Davidson remained active in Agrarian polemic, eventually defending racial segregation. An older, liberal Warren repudiated his Agrarian writings. Fiercely Marxist in his youth, Jarrell wanted nothing to do with the politics of the teachers he nonetheless admired. Blackmur, a New Englander, never joined the Agrarian clique, nor did the English, and socialist, Empson.

New Critical ideas could be forced into contradiction, and different critics followed different threads. One such contradiction set moral judgement against aesthetic disinterest; a second posed ambiguity and complexity (one value) against formal authority and control (another). These contradictions and their psychosexual freight emerged (as Langdon Hammer has shown) in New Critics' vexed readings of Hart

Crane, whom both Tate and Winters had known well. Crane's allusive and densely figurative language appealed to their tastes and ideals, while his celebratory temperament, his ambitious optimism, and his homosexuality did not. (Winters, Tate and Blackmur wrote ambivalent appreciations of Crane; Jarrell later abandoned an unfinished book on him.)

Recent analysts often maintain that the New Critics sought to establish for literary thinkers a professional authority, one analogous to the religious or traditional authorities which Eliot, Ransom, Tate and Brooks respected. Demands for rigour and complexity helped the New Critics distinguish their modernism from the more populist free verse espoused by Carl Sandburg and others on the left. During the 1930s, New Critical literary models clashed with those of the Popular Front, an argument played out in poems by Wallace Stevens and William Carlos Williams, and in the New York journal *Partisan Review*. The New Criticism's political overtones, and its effects on subsequent academic work, have been frequently described; the story of the New Critics and their successors *as poets* deserves renewed attention.

Ransom, Tate, Warren

Educated at Vanderbilt and Oxford, Ransom (1888–1974) taught at Vanderbilt from 1914 to 1938, with three years off to serve in the First World War. His students at Vanderbilt included Tate, Warren and later Jarrell. Ransom decamped in 1938 to Ohio's Kenyon College, where Jarrell and Lowell not only studied with him but lived in his family's house. Ransom's essays insist that poetry provides us with non-discursive, particular knowledge of the world, one incommensurable with the knowledge the sciences give. A 'poem celebrates the object which is real, individual, and qualitatively infinite'; it thus opposes 'practical interests [which] reduce the living object to a mere utility, and . . . sciences [which] will disintegrate it into . . . abstracts' (Ransom, 1938, p. 348). *The World's Body* (1938) collects his most important literary essays; later prose appeared in *Beating the Bushes* (1972).

'Almost all [the poems Ransom] chose to preserve', his biographer reports 'were written between 1922 and 1925', though frequently revised for later reprintings (Young, 1976a, p. 185). Ransom's poems balance his intellectual drive towards complication and paradox with the appeal of pastoral settings, formal elegance and naively beautiful subjects. Many are deeply informed by Andrew Marvell, whose stanza-forms Ransom adapted along with his attitudes. The people in Ransom's poems struggle to maintain their emotional equilibrium, to remain (in one of Ransom's titles) 'Agitato ma non troppo', 'shaken, but not as a leaf'. In 'Janet Waking' a girl mourns her dead goose; in 'Bells for John Whiteside's Daughter' a cohort of careful adults mourns a dead girl:

> There was such speed in her little body,
> And such lightness in her footfall,

> It is no wonder her brown study
> Astonishes us all.

Other significant poems describe the transience of youthful beauty, rural scenes from the Upper South, love letters, and the lifelong quarrels of difficult lovers, bound to each other by their need to differ: 'he of the wide brows that were used to laurel / And she, the famed for gentleness, must quarrel. / Furious both of them, and scared, and weeping' ('Two in August').

Ransom was perhaps the last talented poet in English to rely heavily on 'courtly' beliefs about family, age and gender. His women and girls and 'scared strange little boys' seek orderly, beautiful or innocent lives, their elegance measured by his chiming stanzas, while a rough masculinity – embodied by Ransom's rough metres – threatens their innocence:

> To Miriam Tazewell the whole world was villain,
> The principle of the beast was low and masculine,
> And not to unstop her own storm and be maudlin,
> For weeks she went untidy, she went sullen.
> ('Miriam Tazewell')

Though 'it would be wrong to suggest that Ransom is egalitarian in his sexual politics' (Mark Jancovitch writes), neither do his poems exalt male privilege: Ransom records instead 'a profound discomfort with the distinctions between masculinity and femininity, intellectuality and sensibility, abstraction and experience' (Jancovitch, 1993, p. 39). The protective distance in Ransom's antiquarian language gives him one way to describe events otherwise too painful, or too sexually charged, to remember. Ransom's 'Judith of Bethulia' addresses not the biblical heroine's resolve, but the male Israelites' unease: the poem relies on the 'tension' between Ransom's elaborate language and the sexual violence in his story.

Such strenuous balancings link Ransom's critical prescriptions to his poetry, as do his seventeenth-century models. Geoffrey Hill writes that 'At his best [Ransom] is himself a metaphysical poet'; 'his formal grace is in a constant state of alertness against "awkwardnesses" which, even so, contrive to irrupt into the manners and measures of the verse' (Hill, 1984, pp. 133, 135). 'Winter Remembered' closes with a sort of metaphysical conceit, but the rueful self-knowledge it figures is just Ransom's own:

> Dear love, these fingers that had known your touch,
> And tied our separate forces first together,
> Were ten poor idiot fingers not worth much,
> Ten frozen parsnips hanging in the weather.

Allen Tate (1899–1979) grew up in Tennessee and taught at colleges there, in North Carolina, at Princeton with Blackmur, and finally in Minnesota. A Catholic convert for much of his writing life, Tate remained more committed than other New

Critics to drawing meta-political and meta-religious consequences from his ideas about literature: 'The Man of Letters in the Modern World' sees a 'battle . . . between the dehumanized society of secularism . . . and the eternal society of the communion of the human spirit' (Tate, 1968, pp. 4–5). Dehumanized by instrumental, or inappropriately scientific, thinking, we recover our full human natures in acts of aesthetic and moral judgement: 'Our powers of discrimination [as readers] . . . wait . . . upon the cultivation of our total human powers, and they represent a special application of those powers to a single medium of experience, poetry' (ibid., p. 63). Tate on occasion tentatively identified the literary symbol with the Christian Incarnation. Besides critical essays and poetry, he published biographies of Confederate leaders, and later one novel, *The Fathers* (1938).

Tate's poetry emphasizes confrontation and challenge, straining against its own compressed forms, and more gravely against the secular, sunny rationalism he despised. Violence can become an end in itself: 'In bulled Europa's morn / We love our land because / All night we raped her – torn, / Blue grass and glad.' The poetry, like the criticism, can express a violent nostalgia for pre-Enlightenment, Christian worldviews: 'O God of our flesh, return us to Your wrath'. Elsewhere, 'New Critical' demands for dramatic enactment and formal composure balance Tate's tones of fury or resentment. 'Ode to the Confederate Dead' (1927) draws on Eliotic methods and metrics, and on the older sub-genre of graveyard poems, to make buried Rebels instruct a disoriented speaker about the omnipresence of death, defeat, sin and guilt:

> Autumn is desolation in the plot
> Of a thousand acres where these memories grow
> From the inexhaustible bodies that are not
> Dead, but feed the grass row after rich row.

The poem sets a proto-Christian awareness of sin against a Stoic ideal of endurance in a world where the only permanence is death, and 'only the leaves / Flying, plunge and expire'. Tate described the Ode in his own 1938 essay 'Narcissus as Narcissus'. Two significant later poems, 'The Swimmers' and 'The Buried Lake' (1953) began as parts of a never-completed *terza rima* autobiography.

Tate at his best found in strict forms and grave demeanours the poetic correlatives for the unfinished tragedy of the American South, and for a sense (a Southern sense, he might have declared) of honour, futility and original sin. 'Aeneas at Washington' (1933) makes its Virgilian hero into a Confederate officer, brooding on his defeat and his subsequent wanderings. Compressed and loaded with extra stresses, the pentameters of the monologue shoulder Aeneas's failures as he views his opponents' triumphalist, sterile capital:

> I stood in the rain, far from home at nightfall
> By the Potomac, the great Dome lit the water,
> The city my blood had built I knew no more

While the screech-owl whistled his new delight
Consecutively dark.

Stuck in the wet mire,
Four thousand leagues from the ninth buried city,
I thought of Troy, what we had built her for.

Born in Guthrie, Kentucky, Robert Penn Warren (1905–89) met Ransom and Tate
at Vanderbilt in the early 1920s; after a Rhodes Scholarship he taught at Louisiana
State University, Minnesota and Yale. Most widely known for his novel *All the King's
Men* (1946), Warren wrote six other novels, fifteen books of poetry, and numerous
essays, plays and college textbooks. In 1986 he became the United States' first official Poet Laureate. Warren's essays (see Warren, 1989) show him attending to how
American poets like Whittier, Melville and Frost respond to political and historical
phenomena like abolitionism and the American Civil War. His more theoretical writings tirelessly argue that good poetry creates vital knowledge about individual selves
in historical and social contexts, imaginatively transforming lived experience into language faithful to its vicissitudes. This perspective lets Warren use traditionally literary–critical vocabulary to address ethical and historical questions: *Democracy and Poetry*
(Warren, 1975) claims that 'rhythm – not mere meter, but all the pulse of movement,
density, and shadings of intensity of feeling – is the most intimate and compelling
factor revealing to us the nature of the "made thing"', while holding onto poetry's
primary obligation: 'only insofar as the work establishes and expresses a self can it
engage us' (ibid., pp. 74, 70).

The selves that emerge in Warren's poems almost invariably come to know what
he appreciated in the work of Ransom: 'the haunting duality in man's experience'
(Warren, 1989, p. 306). Early poems like 'Love's Parable' (1936) confront a fallen
world in formal terms indebted to Ransom and his metaphysical leanings: 'As kingdoms after civil broil, / Long faction-bit and sore unmanned, / Unlaced, unthewed by
lawless toil . . .'. From *Promises* (1957) onward, Warren combined his search to represent moral severity and mortality with an equally ambitious habit of grouping lyrics
into sequences. These sequences mean to represent the mind exploring single incidents in multiple ways; in one such moment in 'Mortmain', an elegy for his father,
Warren imagines the elusive nature of the past: 'The boy, / With imperial calm, crosses
a space, rejoins / the shadow of woods, but pauses, turns, grins once, / And is gone.'

Book-length poems allowed Warren to scrutinize these concerns in a more sustained fashion; in *Brother to Dragons* (1953, revised 1979) we watch Thomas
Jefferson's unfolding response to a bloody chain of events surrounding an episode in
which Lilburne Lewis, Jefferson's nephew, vengefully vivisects a slave. Jefferson discovers a startling, repulsive human nature: 'Listen! the foulness sucks like mire. / The
beast waits' and turns out to be 'our brother, our darling brother'. *Audubon: A Vision*
(1969) permits biblically inflected glimpses at many kinds of violence, from homi-
cide to game-hunting, which lend themselves neither to easy morals nor to understanding ('He slew them, at surprising distances, with his gun. / Over a body held in

his hand, his head was bowed low, / But not in grief'). Such depictions reveal, in John Burt's words, 'the conflict between lyric and narrative, between the stopped time in which meaning reveals itself and the progressing time in which life is to be lived' (Burt, 1988, p. 111). Warren's fixation on poetry as a means of representing poetic struggles themselves can perhaps best be understood through his signature motif, the sunset flight of the hawk:

> His wing
> Scythes down another day, his motion
> Is that of the honed steel-edge, we hear
> The crashless fall of stalks of Time.
> ('Evening Hawk', 1975)

Empson, Winters, Blackmur

The Yorkshire-born Empson (1906–84) 'became a part of [American New Critics'] common orthodoxy but, they feared, a tricky and a subversive part' (Norris, 1978, p. 3). Sent down from postgraduate studies at Cambridge for harbouring a woman in his rooms, Empson spent most of the 1930s and 1940s teaching English in Japan and China, later settling at the University of Sheffield. His broadest influence came through his first book, *Seven Types of Ambiguity* (1930), begun while he was Richards's student: Empson's vigorous 'method of verbal analysis' showed, as he put it, how 'alternate reactions to the same piece of language' contribute to the meaning and force of poems (Empson, 1947, pp. viii, 1). These extend all the way from apparently trivial puns and overtones to double meanings which 'show a fundamental division in the writer's mind' (ibid., p. 192). Apparently an anatomy of ambiguity, the book is in fact a demonstration of how to respond flexibly and brilliantly to the hints and verbal nuances in any poem.

Empson denied poetry its own ontology, 'treat[ing] the poem as a concentrated species of ordinary language' (Norris, 1978, p. 25). Nevertheless, Empson's verbal analyses, tastes and terms made him part of the New Critical project; reviewing *The Well-Wrought Urn*, he wrote, 'I agree so fully with [Brooks's] general position that if I were attacking him I should be attacking myself' (Empson, 1987, p. 282). *Some Versions of Pastoral* (1935) expands Empson's reach to prose, including John Gay and Lewis Carroll. A 1948 summer at Kenyon College saw Empson's reacquaintance with the American New Critics and the start of his most ambitious and most abstract work, *The Structure of Complex Words* (1951). *Milton's God* (1961) and many later articles combine Empson's unmatched – and entertaining – analytic skills with a sometimes strident campaign against Christian belief.

Empson had written almost all his poems by 1940; he became the only important English poet of the 1930s not to be caught up in the orbit of Auden. Instead Empson, more than his peers could, learned from Donne. Dense with arguments and associations, Empson's poems can be spectacularly intelligent, or unintelligible. Extravagant dry wit, extreme condensation, buried allusion, submerged pathos, and fended-off terrors (of death, of isolation) mark the style he forged. His best-known poem, the villanelle 'Missing Dates', ends:

> It is the poems you have lost, the ills
> From missing dates, at which the heart expires.
> Slowly the poison the whole bloodstream fills.
> The waste remains, the waste remains and kills.

Other poems appropriate modern science. 'To an Old Lady' brings in King Lear and the second law of thermodynamics as it instructs its readers to respect its subject (according to Empson, his mother):

> Ripeness is all; her in her cooling planet
> Revere; do not presume to think her wasted.
> Project her no projectile; plan nor man it;
> Gods cool in turn, by the sun long outlasted.

Several of Empson's poems are free translations from Chinese and Japanese. In 'Chinese Ballad' (1951) two dolls of mud, smashed together, then remade, stand both (as in Donne's 'Valediction Forbidding Mourning') for the common substance of separated lovers, and for the tenacity of guerrillas fighting the occupying Japanese.

The New Critics' force in America is occasionally likened to that of F. R. Leavis in Britain, though New Critical pedagogy focused on close textual explications rather than on explicit moral judgements. The American figure most like Leavis was the poet–critic Yvor Winters (1900–68), who insisted that good poems' structures resemble logical arguments and convey ethical truths. Winters therefore held up as models not Donne's school but Ben Jonson's. Winters described modern poetry provocatively in *Primitivism and Decadence* (1937) and *In Defense of Reason* (1947); *Maule's Curse* (1938) applied his methods and standards to nineteenth-century American literature. Winters's poems of the 1920s follow modernist modes, especially those of Williams. His later work adheres to the strictures of his criticism, marked by clarity and adherence to recognized forms and genres: 'On Teaching the Young' declares:

> The young are quick of speech.
> Grown middle-aged, I teach
> Corrosion and distrust,
> Exacting what I must.
>
> A poem is what stands
> When imperceptive hands
> Feeling, have gone astray.
> It is what one should say.

Winters taught for decades at Stanford University in California, producing there, at first, doctrinaire classicist followers; the best of them is J. V. Cunningham (1911–85), a rigorously dry epigrammatist. Winters's greatest influence on poetry came indirectly in the 1960s and 1970s, through his later students and admirers. Donald Davie introduced Winters's *Collected Poems*, while Robert Pinsky and Thom Gunn have portrayed Winters in their own verse.

Raised in Massachusetts and in Maine, Blackmur (1904–65) eventually became a professor at Princeton despite his lack of a college degree. Blackmur's essays ask much of his reader, both in their movement of thought and in their demanding prose style. His stiffly Eliotic and Yeatsian poems have not retained their appeal. *Language as Gesture* (1952) and *Form and Value in Modern Poetry* (1957) gather the important essays, among them appreciations of Yeats and Eliot; an early examination of Stevens; and a famous attack on e e cummings. The retrospective 'Lord Tennyson's Scissors: 1912–1950' rises to a fine if sombre statement of the New Critics' take on their period:

> The general poetry at the centre of our time takes the compact and studiable conceit of Donne with the direct eccentricity, vision and private symbolism of Blake; takes from Hopkins the incalculable . . . freedom of sprung rhythm . . . and from Emily Dickinson takes spontaneous snatched idiom and wooed accidental inductableness. It is a Court poetry, learned at its fingertips and full of a decorous wilfullness called ambiguity. It is, in a mass society, a court poetry without a court. (Blackmur, 1957, p. 382)

A Second Generation

Brooks and Warren's successful textbook *Understanding Poetry* (1938) introduced ways to discuss, analyse and appreciate difficult poems to an expanding population of US undergraduates (*Understanding Fiction* followed in 1943). Ransom's essay 'Criticism, Inc.' proposed that a 'more scientific, or precise and systematic' literary criticism establish itself in academia (Ransom, 1938, p. 329). He got what he wanted; by 1951 Jarrell and others complained of an 'age of criticism'. Bringing modern poetry into the academy, these poet–critics made possible the careful, formal, American poets of the early 1950s, pre-eminent among them Richard Wilbur; they also laid the grounds for the later presence in universities of poets paid to teach the writing of poetry. The New Critics' importance as editors rivals their importance as educators: Ransom's tenure at the *Kenyon Review* (1938–58), which he founded, made it a major venue for poetry and criticism. Blackmur and Winters at *Hound and Horn* (1927–34), Brooks and Warren at the *Southern Review* (1935–42) and Tate at the *Sewanee Review* (1944–6) proved almost as influential.

Sometimes Empson, or Ransom, seems out to introduce new ways of reading poetry; at other times the same critic seems out to codify, transfer or render explicit the already-existing practices of some (best or most-sophisticated) readers. Partly for this reason, New Critics' influence on subsequent poets can seem tacit or even invisible. (Is a poet who learned to read Yeats as Blackmur would influenced by Blackmur, or only by Yeats?) Nevertheless, New Critics helped found an implicit programme and theory for the best American poets who came of age before and during the Second World War, poets with common assumptions who nevertheless 'consistently avoided stating a systematic poetic doctrine' (Travisano, 1999, p. 4). The four major figures in this constellation – Berryman, Bishop, Jarrell and Lowell – display throughout their careers 'elective affinities, mutual influence, and parallel development' (ibid., p. 225). For all four, poems represent persons who describe and enact psychological dilemmas; good poems require closure, incorporate contrasting tones or complex symbols, suggest tragic or unresolvable dilemmas, and evoke moral sentiments only through symbols. Their early poems often adopt seventeenth-century models, whose use marks their clearest debt to New Critical thought.

Brought up in aristocratic Boston, Lowell (1917–77) left Harvard in 1937 to study with Tate in Tennessee, famously camping out in a tent on Tate's lawn. His first published work derives obviously from Tate's. The far more powerful *Lord Weary's Castle* (1946) takes much of its material from New England past and present, its baroque, forceful style from early Milton, and its agenda from Catholic beliefs and Christian eschatology. The book made Lowell the leading poet of his cohort; to call it (as it is often called) a near-perfect realization of American New Critics' hopes should not diminish its latter-day appeal. 'The Quaker Graveyard in Nantucket', a seven-part elegy for a drowned sailor, draws on Thoreau, Marian iconography, 'Lycidas' and *Moby-Dick* to create scenes where 'Sea-gulls blink their heavy lids / Seaward', 'the gulls go round the stoven timbers', and 'The Lord survives the rainbow of His will'. 'Mary Winslow' sets its tenderness for Lowell's dead cousin beside his rage at her social world:

> The bell-rope in King's Chapel Tower unsnarls
> And bells the bestial cow
> From Boston Common; she is dead. But stop,
> Neighbor, these pillows prop
> Her that her terrified and child's cold eyes
> Glass what they're not: our Copley ancestress,
> Grandiloquent, square-jowled and worldly-wise,
> A Cleopatra in her housewife's dress;
> Nothing will go again. The bells cry: 'Come,
> Come home,' the babbling Chapel belfry cries:
> 'Come, Mary Winslow, come; I bell thee home.'

The Mills of the Kavanaughs (1951) used similar rhetoric in overwhelmingly sad dramatic monologues. Its speakers included a meditative Canadian nun, a New York City widower tormented by his Catholic wife's suicide, and an old New Englander 'Falling Asleep Over the Aeneid': where Tate's Aeneas recalled a once-graceful Troy, Lowell's old man can only dream that 'Trojans are singing to their drunken God, / Ares. Their helmets catch on fire'. Lowell would abandon the modes of his first two books in the psychoanalytic, autobiographical work of *Life Studies*. The lessons of his early work may be discerned faintly even in his poems of the 1970s, sometimes as rules to be consciously violated, sometimes as tropisms toward interpretative difficulty, and toward strong, sudden closure.

Berryman (1914–72) preserved throughout most of his work a liking for allusion and ambiguity, creating ever more clearly personal vehicles for those qualities. The poems of *The Dispossessed* (1948) sound like Yeats, or else like puzzles, as in the wintry forest of the title poem: 'My harpsichord weird as a koto drums / *adagio* for twilight, for the storm-worn dove / no more de-iced, and the spidery business of love'. Berryman's major work, the series of eighteen-line poems called *The Dream Songs* (1963, 1968), track the psychological travails of Berryman's alter ego 'Henry' and a never-named friend who calls Henry 'Mr Bones'. Emotionally tumultuous and verbally acrobatic, the several-hundred-poem sequence puts Berryman's darting, polysemous obliquities to purposes ranging from ribaldly comic to intimately diagnostic:

> Henry lay in de netting, wild,
> while the brainfever bird did scales;
> Mr Heartbreak, the New Man,
> come to farm a crazy land;
> an image of the dead on the fingernail
> of a newborn child.

If the Dream Songs are 'confessional poetry' they are also informed (like *Life Studies*) by New Critical senses of achieved difficulty, tension and complex form. Berryman's essays, collected in *The Freedom of the Poet* (1976), cover Yeats, Pound, Whitman, Eliot, Ransom and Hardy, as well as American fiction and Renaissance drama.

In contrast to her peers, Bishop (1911–79) largely avoided writing criticism, declaring in 1950 that 'The analysis of poetry is growing more and more pretentious and deadly. After a session with a few of the highbrow magazines one doesn't want to look at a poem for weeks, much less start writing one' (Ciardi, 1950, p. 267). Bishop's debts to Hopkins and to George Herbert, and her preference for symbol, impersonality and suggestion, all link her aesthetic to New Critical interests. Clear in her first volume, *North and South*, the 'New Critical' elements of Bishop's style reappear transformed in the contained violence of 'The Armadillo' (1957). The poem follows a Brazilian holiday's 'frail, illegal fire balloons'; as some rise towards 'the kite sticks of the Southern Cross', others fall on an alcove of animals, setting the creatures on fire:

> The ancient owls' nest must have burned.
> Hastily, all alone,
> a glistening armadillo left the scene,
> rose-flecked, head down, tail down,

and then a baby rabbit jumped out,
short-eared, to our surprise.
So soft! a handful of intangible ash
with fixed, ignited eyes.

Too pretty, dreamlike mimicry!
O falling fire and a piercing cry
and panic, and a weak, mailed fist
clenched ignorant against the sky!

Jarrell (1914–65) studied with Ransom at Vanderbilt and Kenyon, and modelled his early prose on Empson's. Notably informal and apparently unsystematic compared to his teachers and peers, Jarrell became the best commentator on the literary climate they had produced. (*Poetry and the Age* (1953) includes his best-known essays; ampler posthumous volumes of prose include *No Other Book* (1999) and *Kipling, Auden & Co.* (1980).) Jarrell found his poetic style while writing about the Second World War, in which he served (though never overseas). 'Eighth Air Force' (1948) (which Brooks examined in detail) considers the ambiguous collective guilt of the Allied airmen who bombed Europe from Britain. Watching bomber crews who 'play, before they die / Like puppies with their puppy', Jarrell asks 'shall I say that man / Is not as men have said: a wolf to man?' The taut stanzas (three rhyme twice each on 'man') and the disturbing conflict among allusions (barracks jottings jostle quotes from Pontius Pilate) suspend and weigh Jarrell's contradictory attitudes. Another war poem, the five-line 'The Death of the Ball Turret Gunner', became a classroom favourite.

Jarrell's poems present themselves less as constructed objects than as occasions of speech, by persons, apprehended in time: often they are lonely persons who hope for response. Desiderata of tension, polysemy and closure reappear in Jarrell's later work as protagonists search for terms in which to relate past to present experience and thereby imagine a coherent self. At the end of 'The Player Piano' (1965) an old woman comes to remember, out of her ungoverned life, one scene of ironic control and composure:

The piano's playing something by Chopin
And Mother and Father and their little girl

Listen. Look, the keys go down by themselves!
I go over, hold my hands out, play I play –
If only, somehow, I had learned to live!
The three of us sit watching, as my waltz
Plays itself out a half-inch from my fingers.

At Present

New Critical pedagogy remains irreplaceable in introducing poetry to undergraduates; the label 'New Critical' is – unfortunately – now often pejorative, connoting 'out-of-date', 'narrow' and/or 'right-wing'. The New Critics' own poetry can seem to lack contemporary inheritors – until one remembers Geoffrey Hill, whose metaphysical and historical preoccupations, gnarled density, allusive compression and moral and religious seriousness owe much to Ransom and Tate. Hill's major work has come in sequences, among them the book-length *Mercian Hymns* (1971) and *The Triumph of Love* (1998). 'An Apology for the Revival of Christian Architecture in England' (1979) packs together tightly symbolic language with religious properties: the series of poems seems meant to honour some backward-looking but brilliantly productive effort, one either (Hill preserves the ambiguity) triumphantly finished or prematurely abandoned: one of its thirteen sonnets commemorates

> High voices in domestic chapels; praise;
> praise-worthy feuds; new-burgeoned spires that spring
> crisp-leaved as though from dropping wells. The young
> ferns root among our vitrified tears.

BIBLIOGRAPHY

Bedient, Calvin (1984). *In the Heart's Last Kingdom: Robert Penn Warren's Major Poetry*. Cambridge, MA: Harvard University Press.

Blackmur, R. P. (1957). *Form and Value in Modern Poetry*. New York: Anchor.

Brooks, Cleanth (1939). *Modern Poetry and the Tradition*. Chapel Hill: University of North Carolina Press.

Brooks, Cleanth (1995). *Community, Religion and Literature*. Columbia: University of Missouri Press.

Burt, John (1988). *Robert Penn Warren and American Idealism*. New Haven, CT: Yale University Press.

Ciardi, John (ed.) (1950). *Mid-Century American Poets*. Boston: Twayne.

Eliot, T. S. (1975). *Selected Prose of T. S. Eliot*, ed. Frank Kermode. London: Faber & Faber.

Empson, William (1947). *Seven Types of Ambiguity*, 2nd edn, revd. New York: New Directions.

Empson, William (1987). *Argufying*, ed. John Haffenden. Iowa City: University of Iowa Press.

Fry, Paul (1991). *William Empson: Prophet Against Sacrifice*. London: Routledge.

Gill, Roma (ed.) (1974). *William Empson: The Man and His Work*. London: Routledge.

Guillory, John (1993). *Cultural Capital*. Chicago: University of Chicago Press.

Hammer, Langdon (1993). *Janus-Faced Modernism: Hart Crane and Allen Tate*. Princeton, NJ: Princeton University Press.

Hill, Geoffrey (1984). *The Lords of Limit*. London: Andre Deutsch; New York: Oxford University Press.

Hyman, Stanley Edgar (1955). *The Armed Vision*. New York: Vintage.

Jancovitch, Mark (1993). *The Cultural Politics of the New Criticism*. Cambridge: Cambridge University Press.

Jarrell, Randall (1953). *Poetry and the Age*. New York: Knopf.

Longenbach, James (1998). *Modern Poetry After Modernism*. New York: Oxford University Press.

Norris, Christopher (1978). *William Empson and the Philosophy of Literary Criticism*. London: Athlone Press/University of London.

Ransom, John Crowe (1938). *The World's Body*. New York: Charles Scribner and Sons.

Ransom, John Crowe (1941). *The New Criticism*. Norfolk, CT: New Directions.

Rubin, Louis D. (1978). *The Wary Fugitives: Four Poets and the South*. Baton Rouge: Louisiana State University Press.

Tate, Allen (1968). *Essays of Four Decades*. Chicago: Swallow.

Travisano, Thomas P. (1999). *Mid-Century Quartet: Bishop, Lowell, Jarrell, Berryman, and the Making of a Postmodern Aesthetic.* Charlottesville: University of Virginia Press.

Warren, Robert Penn (1975). *Democracy and Poetry.* Cambridge, MA: Harvard University Press.

Warren, Robert Penn (1989). *New Selected Essays.* New York: Random House.

Young, Thomas Daniel (1976a). *Gentleman in a Dustcoat: A Biography of John Crowe Ransom.* Baton Rouge: Louisiana State University Press.

Young, Thomas Daniel (ed.) (1976b). *The New Criticism and After.* Charlottesville: University of Virginia Press.

13

Black Mountain and Projective Verse

John Osborne

Background

If anyone deserves particular praise for reviving and extending modernist aesthetics in mid-century America, then that person is the poet Charles Olson. Born in Worcester, Massachusetts, in 1910, Olson studied at Wesleyan, Yale and Harvard universities, becoming an acknowledged expert in the work of the nineteenth-century novelist and poet Herman Melville. Abandoning a promising academic career for politics, he held a variety of posts in the third and fourth administrations of President Franklin D. Roosevelt. After the latter's death in 1945, increasingly disenchanted with the USA of Truman and McCarthy, of Cold War paranoia and rampant commodification, Olson reverted to his literary interests with the pent-up energy of a late starter. Erudite, alienated and experimental, his writings were decisively pedagogical, the express intention being to provide a blueprint for an alternative culture. Modernism offered stylistic prototypes for this endeavour, together with the ideology of the avant-garde.

Olson was well equipped to preside over a recrudescence of the movement. As a graduate student he once danced for Diaghilev's Ballet Russe (by then under the direction of Léonide Massine). Through his friend and mentor Edward Dahlberg, he met the photographer Alfred Stieglitz and the painter Marsden Hartley, two great survivors from the first generation of American modernists. In 1946 he was the first person to visit the disgraced Ezra Pound, who had been brought back to the United States to stand trial for treason, and who was to spend twelve years incarcerated in St Elizabeth's lunatic asylum ('Olson saved my life', said Pound). His first book, *Call Me Ishmael* (1947), a critical study of *Moby-Dick*, unveiled the nascent modernism lurking beneath the Romantic surface of Melville's epic novel. A year later he wrote a dance drama for Martha Graham's experimental dance company. His first volume of poems, *Y & X* (1949), was published by the celebrated Black Sun Press, which had specialized since the 1920s in the publication of figures like Proust, Joyce, Pound,

Hart Crane, Lawrence, Hemingway and Faulkner. At a time when *Paterson* was being dismissed in the *Hudson Review* as 'non-sequential babble', Olson was corresponding with and learning from William Carlos Williams. In 1950, when the Objectivists were utterly neglected, Olson was quarrelling with Zukofsky's achievement, praising that of Reznikoff, and commenting generally on the implications of Objectivism for younger practitioners. Hugh MacDiarmid's *In Memoriam James Joyce*, perhaps his most modernist work (though by no means his best), was received with a deafening silence: Olson, however, was drawing his students' attention to it shortly after its publication in 1955. Over and over again, one finds Olson excavating the buried monuments of modernism, and this at a time when many younger Anglo-American poets were reverting to the routine use of regular metres.

The next stage in Olson's project came in 1951, when he joined the faculty of the small liberal arts college of Black Mountain, North Carolina, at which he had been a visiting speaker since 1948 and of which he became the last rector. Until its closure in October 1956, Black Mountain College provided Olson with a suitably isolated site within which to refashion the modernist concept of the avant-garde community. As rector he gathered about him a teaching staff which consisted almost entirely of practising artists. They presented the students, who rarely numbered more than a hundred and at one point less than ten, not with information with which to pass exams, but with the example of what it meant to be seriously engaged in creative activity. At various times the staff included the painters Josef Albers, Franz Kline and Willem de Kooning; the sculptor Richard Lippold; the dancer Merce Cunningham; the composers John Cage and Stefan Wolpe; the architect Buckminster Fuller; and the poets Robert Creeley, Robert Duncan and Olson himself. Students who later became famous include the prose writers Fielding Dawson and Michael Rumaker; the sculptor John Chamberlain; the painters Kenneth Noland and Robert Rauschenberg; the film-maker Stan Vanderbeek; and the poets Ed Dorn, Joel Oppenheimer, John Wieners and Jonathan Williams.

The seven poets named above as having been present at the college would later become known as the 'Black Mountain School'. The designation is misleading, however, for these poets were part of a wider flowering of early 1950s American verse which also involved Denise Levertov, Paul Blackburn, Cid Corman, LeRoi Jones (later known as Amiri Baraka), Larry Eigner and Gilbert Sorrentino (now more famous as a novelist), none of whom set foot on the eponymous mount. This wider grouping had in common: publication in such small magazines as Robert Creeley's *Black Mountain Review* and Cid Corman's *Origin*; book publication through Robert Creeley's Divers Press and Jonathan Williams's Jargon Books; a view of twentieth-century poetics which gave central importance to Pound, Williams, Lawrence, H. D., Cummings, Moore and the Objectivists; and, most especially, an approach to prosody that found its clearest theoretical expression in Olson's celebrated 'Projective Verse' essay. Not all of these poets were directly indebted to Olson: Denise Levertov worked out many of the shared ideals for herself; as did Gary Snyder, a younger poet whose work has some affinities with this group. Yet Olson's role as catalyst in this extraordinary florescence is confirmed in the testimonials of the poets themselves. One thinks of Ed Dorn's *What I See In The Maximus Poems*, Duncan's 'Notes on Poetics Regarding Olson's *Maximus*', and the reviews and articles gathered in Robert Creeley's *A Quick Graph*. As Gilbert Sorrentino put it, 'Olson is our Ezra Pound'.

Theory

Written in 1950, 'Projective Verse' was a theoretical launching-pad from which Olson hoped to propel himself and others into poetic creativity. Herbert Read once said that 'a tradition in art is not a body of beliefs: it is a knowledge of techniques'. Bearing his dictum in mind, we might see the essay as an attempt to identify a prosodic tradition which the author's own verse will later be seen to have forwarded. Even the name 'Projective' may partly have been chosen in order to signify the extending or projecting forward of an existing continuity. Thus, Pound is named seven times, Eliot six, Williams and Hart Crane four times, Cummings twice, and the Objectivists once.

The aim of 'Projective Verse' is to advance 'projective or OPEN verse' as an alternative to 'closed verse'. On one level this is but the familiar, not to say wearisome, opposition between regular and free verse resurrected under new banners. What is unique is Olson's sense that free verse must be thoroughly energized if it is to retain its virtue:

> From the moment (the poet) ventures into FIELD COMPOSITION – puts himself in the open – he can go by no track other than the one the poem underhand declares for itself. . . .
>
> And I think it can be boiled down to one statement (first pounded into my head by Edward Dahlberg): ONE PERCEPTION MUST IMMEDIATELY AND DIRECTLY LEAD TO A FURTHER PERCEPTION. It means exactly what it says, is a matter of, at *all* points . . . get on with it, keep it moving.

There is in this account a great sense of the intensity of the creative process, the poet urgently tracking the poem in its vertiginous procession down the page, seeking to render the successive spurts, lunges and digressions of its fleet unfolding. In keeping with modernist aesthetics, the poem is credited with an autonomous existence, the function of the poet being to facilitate its emergence. This is done by meeting its requirements as, moment by moment, they make themselves known. Poets are obstetricians, presiding over the birth of a living organism; the worst thing they can do is obstruct the process by setting up demands of their own, seeking to guide the poem to a form that has been predetermined. As Olson says, 'the objects which occur at every given moment of composition . . . must be treated exactly as they do occur therein and not by any ideas or preconceptions from outside the poem'.

Having thus indicated the peculiarly energized version of free verse he is dubbing 'projective', Olson enumerates various techniques by means of which to implement it. Of these, by far the most important is the use of the terminal juncture. Quite simply, Olson is proposing that every line should end with a pause; or, to put it the other way round, whenever the poet feels the need for a fresh intake of breath, he or she should signal this fact to the reader by a line-break. Lineation thus becomes a function of respiration: 'the line comes (I swear it) from the breath, from the breathing of the man who writes'. This proposal is easily mistaken for platitude. From the translated psalms of the King James version of the Bible through to the work of the Imagists, free verse had substituted a lineation based on melic cadences for that based on regular syllable counts. What Olson noticed is that in the bulk of this work the lines form complete syntactical units as well as musical phrases, with the result that the terminal pauses are predictable and the transitions from line to line only a little less stately than in regular verse. Olson's injunction that the line should be structured as a breath unit *regardless of whether it also forms a syntactical unit* should be judged against this background. It is true, as he freely acknowledges, that e. e. cummings and William Carlos Williams had already begun to explore this possibility. Yet recorded readings show neither poet to have been diligent in his observation of the terminal juncture, and neither so much as mentions it in his critical and theoretical writings. Olson's greatest coup in 'Projective Verse' is to have brought this matter, towards which the practice of his immediate predecessors had led, into the centre of the debate.

In the manifesto, the structuring of lines by breath patterns is intimately connected with a second contention, which is that contemporary prose and verse would both be improved 'if the syllable, that fine creature, were more allowed to lead the harmony on'. For Olson, breath determines lineation, but the syllable determines the prosody: 'it is the king and pin of versification'.

A third aspect of technique to receive attention is typography. Thanks to the typewriter, the poet now has an equivalent to the stave and bar of the musician. 'It is time we picked the fruit of the experiments of cummings, Pound, Williams, each of whom has, after his way, already used the machine as a scoring to his composing, as a script to its vocalization.' Of these fruits, four are specified: the equating of units of space, whether between lines or between words within a line, with units of silence in the oral delivery of the poem; the use of the oblique, or solidus, when the poet 'wishes a pause so light it hardly separates the words, yet does not want a comma – which is an interruption of the meaning rather than the sounding of the line'; the varying of the left-hand margin, whether on a stanzaic or a line-by-line basis, so as to register minute changes of pace in thought and vocal delivery, progressively greater indentings informing the reader that a more rapid movement from unit to unit is required than in those poems where a single left-hand margin is observed; and, lastly, the opening and then not closing of a parenthesis in those cases, so common in speech and thought but so frequently suppressed in written English, where what began as a temporary digression ends by usurping, rather than returning to, the original subject.

Considered individually, the typographical devices enumerated by Olson may seem trivial, even gimmicky; some were certainly soon abandoned. Considered in combination, however, they are expressive of an extraordinary concern for the scoring of the poem. It is worth remembering that in 1965 Olson withdrew the second volume of *The Maximus Poems* from the Jargon/Corinth press, publishers of the first volume, when they failed to duplicate in print the typographical oddities of his manuscript. Similarly, in 1970 Robert Duncan decided to henceforth publish his own typescript versions of his verse after the New Directions and Black Sparrow presses had muddied his scrupulous notations.

Finally, it might be remarked that although 'Projective Verse' addresses itself to matters of technique rather than of content, the urgent propulsive motion of the sort of verse Olson desiderates peculiarly fits it for dealing with essential ontological processes. Even the agitated compulsive prose in which the manifesto is written is a sign that deep down Olson was searching for a poetics of the emancipation of the self. Whether or not he achieved anything so grandiose, it is certainly the case that in poem after poem the Black Mountaineers use their obsession with the process by which the work unravels as a formal enactment of the self's unfolding. To this extent, they may be said to share a subject as well as a style.

Practice

As Olson first formulated parts of 'Projective Verse' in an exchange of letters with the young Robert Creeley, it is fitting that we begin our textual analysis with one of the latter's poems. These are interior monologues, the *mental* address of a man to a woman. The peculiar intensity of Creeley's work derives precisely from the consequent lack of public address. One approaches the poem with care, for fear of violating a mind in action:

SOMETHING

I approach with such
a careful tremor, always
I feel the finally foolish

question of how it is,
then, supposed to be felt,
and by whom. I remember

once in a rented room on
27th street, the woman I loved
then, literally, after we

had made love on the large
bed sitting across from
a basin with two faucets, she

had to pee but was nervous,
embarrassed I suppose I
would watch her who had but

> a moment ago been completely
> open to me, naked, on
> the same bed. Squatting, her
>
> head reflected in the mirror,
> the hair dark there, the
> full of her face, the shoulders,
>
> sat spread-legged, turned on
> one faucet and shyly pissed. What
> love might learn from such a sight.

This poem fulfils many of the injunctions of the 'Projective Verse' essay. In particular, it confirms Olson's thesis that the structuring of lines as breath units would lead to an increase in pace and dynamicism. The fact that every break is already pointed for the listening ear by a terminal juncture allows Creeley to avoid end-stopping eighteen of the twenty-four lines of the poem. Lacking terminal punctuation, most of the lines end in an unwritten question:

> I remember (*remember what?*)
>
> once in a rented room on (*on what?*)
> 27th street, the woman I loved (*did what?*)
> then, literally, after we (*we what?*)
>
> had made love on the large (*the large what?*)
> bed sitting across from (*from what?*)
> a basin with two faucets, she (*she what?*)
> had to pee . . .

The stranglehold of syntax on lineation is broken, the reader being propelled from line to line by the need to conclude the sentence. The precipitous forward propulsion, momentarily checked by successive terminal pauses, leads to an increase of stress on the first syllable of sequent lines: 'the woman I loved (pause) *then*, literally, after we (pause) *had* made love on the large (pause) *bed* . . .'. With line lengths varying between five and ten syllables, the pumping of these added stresses falls into no predictable periodicity. The result is a kind of syncopation, the inherent rhythm of the phrasing being counterpointed by the intrusive stops and starts arising from the breath patterns. In Creeley's case, this is used to register the nervous garrulity of a timorous narrator forced by the pressure of emotion into reluctant utterance. In the example before us, the stuttering hesitancies of the poem's progress down the page culminate in an apparently confident assertion which, on second thoughts, can only lead to the further question: *what* might love learn from such a sight?

In places, the syncopating of the rhythm is enhanced by inversions, excessive use of the comma, and by the dislocations of syntax consequent upon the depending of innumerable qualifiers from each principal clause. Even written out as prose, a sentence such as the following has an extraordinarily fitful and impulsive movement: 'I remember once in a rented room on 27th street, the woman I loved, then, literally after we had made love on the large bed, sitting across from a basin with two faucets, she had to pee but was nervous, embarrassed I suppose I would watch her, who had but a moment ago been completely open to me, naked, on the same bed'. The tortuous structure bespeaks its author's struggle to bring sensitive matters to exact definition, such awkwardnesses as arise being earnests of the narrator's sincerity. Olson's use of the words 'projectile', 'percussive' and 'prospective' to augment our understanding of the term suggests that it was this propulsive, staccato quality which most prompted the choice of the designation 'projective' for the verse which he had fathered. Certainly, the agitated and compulsive rhythms that result from pausing for breath at the end of every line regardless of punctuation or sense characterize Black Mountain writing as a whole.

This same poem will serve to elucidate the second characteristic of projectivism, the diminishing of the tyranny of the *ictus* by basing the poem's prosody on quantitative or, in this instance, syllabic intensities. Syllabic prosody measures only the number of syllables per line, stress or accent being applied as a device of embellishment and not a criterion of the basic metrical structure. As the syllabic pattern only emerges in integers larger than the individual line, the verse paragraph or stanza tends to be the primary structural unit. Most pertinent of all, it is a convention in syllabic verse to pause at the end of every line in order to point the numerical patterning for the listening ear.

There is no question of Creeley slotting his lines into preconceived grids in the manner preferred by Marianne Moore: his poems are played by ear, not plotted on a graph. Nevertheless, in the poem before us the recurrence of the three-line stanza, the roughly approximate line-lengths, and the predominance of monosyllables (90 of the poem's 125 words), all tempt the attentive ear into trying to descry a syllabic plan. Nor is this a futile activity, for the poem perpetually hovers over, without quite settling into, a fixed permutation based on the seven-syllable line. The seven-syllable line is the most common. The seven-syllable line is the average. Every stanza bar one contains a seven-syllable line. The only stanza which does not contain a seven-syllable line approximates to doing so by being constituted of lines of six and eight syllables. There is no five-, nine- or ten-syllable line which is not adjacent to one of seven syllables. And the last line of the poem is one of seven syllables. Configurations of this kind may be arbitrary, the inevitable consequence of juggling with a few fixed quantities. Nonetheless, what we have here is a syllabic piping which stems from number as surely as does the more calculated carolling of Marianne Moore. As Cid Corman said, 'it is not a matter of counting syllables, but of making syllables count'.

That Creeley's syllables do count is easily demonstrated. Consider, for example, the terrific spinal column of internal rhymes that, vertebra by vertebra, provides the poem with its hidden backbone: stanza one, approach–such; stanzas two and three, whom–room; stanzas three and four, love–love[d]; stanzas four, five and six, she–pee–bee[n]–completely–me; stanza seven, hair–there; stanza eight, turn[ed]–learn, might–sight. To those attuned to its subtle orchestration, such mastery is a source of exquisite pleasure.

Of the comments on typography in 'Projective Verse', the one which had most influence concerned the use of textual spacings to notate silences in oral performance. In the hands of an Olson or a Paul Blackburn this could lead to poems that zigged, not to say zagged, dynamically across the page. For purposes of illustration, however, one might consider a less frenetic work such as 'The Hermit Cackleberry Brown, On Human Vanity' by Jonathan Williams:

> caint call your name
> but your face is easy
>
> come sit
>
> now some folks figure theyre
> bettern
> cowflop they
> aint
>
> not a bit
>
> just good to hold the world together
> like hooved up ground
>
> that's what

This poem has the aforementioned characteristics of projectivism. There is the same use of the terminal juncture to dislocate syntax in a manner that propels the reader from line to line in the attempt to conclude the sentence:

> now some folks figure theyre (*theyre what?*)
> bettern (*bettern what?*)
> cowflop they (*they what?*)
> aint

And there is the same relaxing of accentual patterning by laying down a gritty succession of monosyllables (31 of the 36 words in the poem). But what concerns us here is the function of the spacings. Knowing the poet's love of hitchhiking through the American South, we may take it on trust that the text is a direct transcript of the speech of the hermit named in the title: the poem is an *objet trouvé*. Granted that transcripts of conversation are usually regarded as prose, Williams has cunningly deployed his spacings so as to reveal within the text that more highly patterned utterance we call verse. The poem consists of three main stanzas; each of these stanzas is followed by a typographical space; and after traversing each of these ruptures the reader comes across a terse afterthought to the preceding statements. The sense that the recurrent model of stanza–pause–afterthought constitutes a kind of poetic structuring is added to by the fact that the three terse appendages are near-rhymes: come sit; not a bit; that's what.

At the same time, these spacings neatly augment the poem's scrupulous attention to the speaker's pungent colloquialisms. Consider the first four lines. The opening *distich* records Cackleberry's salutation to our narrator:

> caint call your name
> but your face is easy

Having greeted his visitor, the speaker pauses long enough to decide whether or not to invite him to stay and, having made his decision, offers him a chair:

> caint call your name
> but your face is easy
>
> come sit

Having offered him a seat, Cackleberry pauses again to allow his guest time to get settled, only then launching into his main subject:

> caint call your name
> but your face is easy
>
> come sit
>
> now some folks figure . . .

Each of these typographical rifts is a meaningful hiatus into which we read certain undescribed physical or mental operations; we decipher the spaces as well as the print. And what we glean from the spaces hardens our conviction that this is not a fictive text, but is an authentic rendering of an actual exchange between real people. The erasures in it help lend the text its whiff of authenticity. Jonathan Williams may be a miniaturist, but in a poem such as this he displays a tact and exactitude not always found in the work of those who employ a larger canvas.

The Maximus Poems

With poems as technically adroit as this, Olson, Creeley, Williams and Levertov resuscitated the experimental lyric earlier perfected by the likes of William Carlos Williams. However, the ways in which the shared techniques led on to a shared concern with individuation, the spasmodic process by which we achieve some sort of selfhood, is best explored in relation to Olson's magnum opus. For as early as 1950 he was devoting most of his energies to *The Maximus Poems*, a second-generation modernist long poem after the manner of *The Cantos*, *Paterson* and *Four Quartets*. When he died of cancer in 1970, the work consisted of between three and four hundred passages in verse, prose and assorted amalgams of the two. Set in the small fishing city of Gloucester, Massachusetts, where Olson's parents had holidayed and in which he was eventually to settle, *The Maximus Poems* is one of the most thematically unified and coherent of modernist epics. Despite its surface appearance of bewildering diversity, the work is entirely constructed from the fragments of innumerable tales of coming into being, of beginnings, of origination. The poem is a compilation creation myth, and nothing is included that does not contribute to its account of universal beginnings.

The autobiographical content of the poem provides a clear example of this, for the account of Olson's life in Gloucester dwells almost exclusively on his earliest memories of the city, with remarkably little being said about the Gloucester of the 1950s and 1960s in which the work was largely composed. So marked is the preference for the poet's earliest impressions that the word 'first' runs like a refrain through the many passages of recollection:

> It rained
> the day we arrived . . .
> the first time I saw
> the sea
> (Vol. I)

> I was so young my first memory
> is of a tent . . .
> (Vol. II)

> the bed broke down under
> my mother and father the first night we came to Gloucester
> (Vol. II)

> where the Parsons
> had their first wharf . . .
> And where I first went out,
> in a dory . . .
> and later, moored my own first skiff
> (Vol. III)

It is symptomatic of this bias toward beginnings that Olson's parents are a recurrent subject of discussion, while his own wives and children are hardly mentioned.

The same tendencies are evident in the poem's treatment of Gloucester history. The burden of attention is placed on three origin stories: the city's first founding in 1623; its rebirth in 1642; and the founding of its satellite community, Dogtown, in the early eighteenth century. Around these three principal creation stories a group of subsidiary 'firsts' is arranged: the arrival of Gloucester's first shipwright; the building of Gloucester's first schooner; the establishment of the city's first salt-works, and so on. The historical matter is not fixed and dogmatic, for as each of the three volumes of

The Maximus Poems appeared over a twenty-year period, Olson was to be found pushing each moment of creation back in time as if to enhance its originatory credentials. Thus, the birth of the second Gloucester is dated 1642 in the first volume; early in volume two, after intensive historical research, Olson adjusts the date to 1635; a few pages later this becomes 1632; and in volume three it is pushed back to the late 1620s, thereby linking it, in almost unbroken sequence, to the first Gloucester of 1623. Similarly, the birth of the satellite community of Dogtown is laboriously traced back, over several hundred pages of intermittent documentation and speculation, from 1717 to 1707.

The historian James B. Connolly has said, 'As American history goes, Gloucester in Massachusetts is an ancient port. Of the permanent English settlements here only Jamestown and Plymouth precede it'. Olson is able to trace in fascinating detail how and why a community is born and made to cohere because cities in the United States, unlike those in Europe, were all founded recently enough for a wealth of contemporary evidence to survive. At the same time, by choosing one of the very first English settlements on the North American continent, our poet is able to examine in microcosm the process by which the nation itself came into being. The two creation stories are intimately connected.

This identifying of the founding of Gloucester with the founding of the United States brings us to another constituent of Olson's compilation creation myth – the various waves of exploration, migration and settlement that led to the discovery of the New World. In the first volume the heroes are the expected ones: Columbus, Juan de la Cosa (who made the first map to include the New World), Captain John Smith and Champlain. These figures continue to be celebrated in the subsequent volumes, but it is noticeable that volume two hazards that the Vikings discovered America as early as the tenth century. Volume three, whilst reporting the latest archeological proof that the Vikings had indeed been present in Newfoundland *circa* AD 1006, opens up vastly earlier possibilities by mention of Professor Cyrus Gordon's theory of cultural traffic between ancient Crete and contemporary South American civilization. Once again we find the poet, ever convinced that the key to an event lies in the nature of its genesis, adjusting the date of discovery backwards, as though pushing against the confining walls of known history.

Undergirding all the origin stories so far mentioned are a series of reworkings of those ancient myths, called cosmogonies, that sought to explain how the world was created. In typical modernist style, Olson scavenged the whole of human culture for material, his myth sources including Old Norse, Greek legends, ancient Egyptian religions, the Hindu *Vedas*, and the Hurrian-Hittite civilization of the Mesopotamian Valley. However, his interest in these deposits was extremely selective, the intention being to celebrate the Earth gods of prehistory at the expense of the better-known Sky gods (like the Greek Zeus and the Judaeo-Christian Yahweh, or Jehovah) who later replaced them. Olson is trying to salvage, not the Earth deities as such, but the sacramental view of this planet that has given us life. It is a major purport of *The Maximus Poems* that the cosmic process is natural rather than supernatural, physical rather than abstract, terrestrial rather than sidereal. For Olson, whatever spirit there is informs a body; whatever infinite there is informs the finite; whatever intangibles there are inform the actual; whatever ideal there is informs the real. His continual restitution of archaic Earth gods who have been wrongfully displaced by more abstract Sky gods is therefore an attempt to assert that the human sense perceptions are revelatory, and their revelation is the world:

> nakedness
> is what one means
>
> that all start up
> to the eye and soul
> as though it had never
> happened before
> (Vol. I)

The spiritual trajectory of *The Maximus Poems* is thus identical with that plotted by Eliot in the closing lines of *Four Quartets*:

> We shall not cease from exploration
> And the end of all our exploring
> Will be to arrive where we started
> And know the place for the first time.

By exploring a vast collection of origin stories, Olson is seeking to return the reader to an original experience of now and here and this. He does not ask us to look at a different world, but to look at this same world differently. Even his account of the discovery of the Americas may be interpreted metaphorically as an expression of this desire to experience freshly, as a New World, our battered and abused planet. To achieve this state of innocence after experience is to acquire psychic wholeness; or, to use the term Olson filched from the psychologist Jung, it is to become 'homo Maximus'.

After presiding over the closure and sale of Black Mountain College in 1957, Olson settled in Gloucester. He may have been hoping, by this removal, to break the cultural elitism of the *avant-garde* community, rooting his modernist epic in the lived reality of a working city. It is certainly the case that *The Maximus Poems* honours those citizens whose practice of their trade promotes the general health of Gloucester:

> The brilliant Portuguese owners,
> they do. They pour the money back
> into their engines, into their ships,
> whole families do, put it back
> in. They are but extensions of their own careers
> as mastheadsmen.
> (Vol. I)

Olson especially cherished the fishermen, whose dangerous calling obliged them to develop a physical and mental alertness conspicuously absent from the wielders of public power:

> A fisherman is not a successful man
> he is not a famous man he is not a man
> of power, these are the damned by God
> (Vol. I)

It is also true that Olson became a local celebrity, campaigning in the *Gloucester Times* against the destruction of historic buildings and on occasion being asked by the towns-folk to represent them in their battles with the city council.

Yet it is difficult to credit that the citizenry of Gloucester joyously whiled away winter evenings reading *The Maximus Poems*. That work is *about* them, but it is not *for* them. This is not just because it incorporates so much scholarly material; but also because large parts of it are written in a crabbed and cryptic fashion. It would seem that Olson wished to enact his theme of origination by leaving exposed the means by which his own poetry originates in prose notes. The imperfections that in the earlier modernists were unwilled, are in Olson's case the willed product of a desire to encompass both the flower of art and the compost from which it arises. At times this highly literate poet appears to be returning to a preliterate condition, as though he were trying to complement his vision of a new world with the hieroglyphics of a new speech. Some parts of *The Maximus Poems* have the battered, fragmentary, runic character of the earliest examples of writing. It is the simultaneous coming into being to World and Word that we are offered.

Unfortunately, the fact that Olson had a rationale for incoherence cannot excuse writing like this:

> Cyprus
> the strangled
> Aphrodite – Rhodes
>
> Crete
> – the Mother Goddess
> fr Anatolia
> Phrygian Attis
>
> Malta: Fat Lady
>
> Spain
> (Vol. 11)

This 'poem' (it is quoted entire) can be made sense of: each of the islands named – Cyprus, Crete, Rhodes, Malta – represents a stepping stone in the westward progression of humankind from the Near East through the Mediterranean to Spain, last stop before the Atlantic voyage to the New World. The references to Aphrodite, the Mother Goddess and the Fat Lady, attest that along this route specific matriarchal myths were disseminated. We might even interpret the typography of the poem as a visual equivalent, a verbal map of the itinerary described, each stanza being an island of words in the sea of the page's white. Yet the fact that the piece can be decoded and discovered to belong in the corner of the jigsaw devoted to migration diminishes not one jot the vexation of the reader. Resembling nothing so much as the marginalia the poet habitually scrawled in his favourite source books, this is the recipe for a poem, a preliminary list of ingredients, rather than the finished article; in place of the expected meal, the famished reader is invited to dine on the menu.

Reading *The Maximus Poems* is as exhilarating as riding on a roller-coaster, the work alternately plunging into incoherence and abruptly ascending to the giddiest heights. However, its ragged texturing and formidable range of reference severely limit its appeal. Olson's influence upon other poets has been immense, but his standing with critics is insecure and his readership tiny. (The 1953 Jargon Press edition of *The Maximus Poems, 1–10* had a print-run of 350 copies but was still available in some bookshops at the original price in 1975.) As for his place in literary history, Olson was one of the first to consistently use the term 'Postmodernism' and the whole projectivist tendency represents both a second-generation modernism and a step towards the subsequent aesthetic. In retrospect, the Black Mountain poem that most decisively bespeaks Postmodernity is Ed Dorn's mock epic *Gunslinger*, with its affectionate Pop Art-style guying of the icons of commercial culture (especially Western and Sci-Fi movies). However, this very willingness to incorporate the ad-mass ideology and rampant commodification that Olson deplored may well mean that *Gunslinger* marks not so much the fulfilment of the Black Mountain project as its supercession.

BIBLIOGRAPHY

Bertholf, R. J. and Reid, I. W. (1979), *Robert Duncan: Scales of the Marvellous*, New York: New Directions.

Butterick, G. F. (1978), *A Guide to the Maximus Poems of Charles Olson*, Berkeley, Los Angeles and London: University of California Press.

Butterick, G. F. and Blevins, R. (1980–90), *Charles Olson and Robert Creeley: The Complete Correspondence* (9 vols), Santa Barbara: Black Sparrow Press.

Corrigan, M. (1974), *Boundary 2: A Journal of Postmodern Literature*, Vol. II, Nos 1 & 2 (Olson special double-issue), Binghampton: State University of New York.

Creeley, R. (1970), *A Quick Graph: Collected Notes and Essays*, San Francisco: Four Seasons Foundation.

Dawson, F. (1970), *The Black Mountain Book*, New York: Croton Press.

Duberman, M. (1972), *Black Mountain, An Exploration In Community*, New York: E. P. Dutton.

Duncan, R. (1956), 'Notes on Poetics Regarding Olson's *Maximus*'. *Black Mountain Review*, 6, 201–11.

Levertov, D. (1973), *The Poet in the World*, New York: New Directions.

Olson, C. (1967), 'Projective Verse'. In Charles Olson, *Human Universe and Other Essays* (pp. 51–61), New York: Grove Press.

Paul, S. (1978), *Olson's Push: Origin, Black Mountain and Recent American Poetry*, Baton Rouge and London, Louisiana State University Press.

Spanos, W. V. (1978), *Boundary 2: A Journal of Postmodern Literature*, Vol. VI, No. 3; Vol. VII, No. 1 (Creeley special double-issue), Binghampton: State University of New York.

Von Hallberg, R. (1978), *Charles Olson: The Scholar's Art*, Cambridge and London: Harvard University Press.

Wagner, L. W. (1979), *Denise Levertov: In Her Own Province*, New York: New Directions.

14

The Beats

John Osborne

The Beats: A Problematic Canon

Writers commonly dislike group labels, feeling that their works are being cruelly amputated – an arm off here, a leg there ('the work bleeds', D. H. Lawrence protested) – to fit a communal box. Yet, as David Lodge has pointed out, no text can generate meaning in a vacuum. The meaning of a book is in large part a product of its differences from and similarities to other books. If, say, a novel did not bear some resemblance to other novels, we should not know how to read it, and if it was not different from all other novels we should not want to read it. Any adequate reading of a text, therefore, involves identifying and classifying it in relation to other texts, according to content, genre, mode, period, language, nationality, and so on. Granted the comparative imprecision of literary categories, there is a special onus upon any critic using a group designation to limit the capacity for slither by lending that term a utile definition (though one that must always be held under potential cancellation). And, certainly, of all such terms bandied about in recent decades, the Beat label is one of the oftenest used but least defined.

The source of most of the confusion bedevilling discussion of the Beats is a critical obsession with their lifestyle rather than their literary aesthetic. Emerging in the culturally repressive America of the Cold War era, the Beats sought to counteract a philistine and inhibitive society by exploring the most extreme, potentially ecstatic areas of the self. Characteristic preoccupations of those engaged in this quest were art (Abstract Expressionist painting was especially admired); jazz in its 'Bebop' and 'Cool' phases; drugs (from alcohol to heroin); sex (in Ginsberg's words, with 'whomever come who may'); communal living; frenetic travel; anarchistic drop-out politics; religious experimentation (with various forms of Buddhism, for example); the espousal of an anti-materialist ascetic lifestyle; an infatuation, sometimes consummated, with criminality (archetypal Beat heroes include the murderer Lucien Carr, William Burroughs who 'accidentally' killed his wife, the thief and heroin addict Herbert Huncke, and the car thief and sometime homosexual prostitute Neal Cassady); and, when on the offensive against society, a policy of bugging the squares – or, as it would become known in the 1960s, 'freaking the straights' (a revival of the time-honoured avant-garde tactic of *épater les bourgeois*).

That many Beat authors not only adopted this lifestyle, but also used it as the subject matter of their art is indisputable. Kerouac's novels are heavily fictionalized chronicles of the antics of him and his pals, Allen Ginsberg becoming the Alvah Goldbook of *The Dharma Bums*, Lawrence Ferlinghetti becoming the Lorenzo Monsanto of *Big Sur*, William Burroughs being pseudonymized as Old Bull Lee in *On the Road*, Gregory Corso appearing as Raphael Urso in *Desolation Angels*, and so on, thereby creating the misleading impression that the reader might pierce the text in order to grasp an originatory autobiographical 'truth'. Another problem is that many non-writers adopted the lifestyle, with the result that even the more useful studies of the Beats are apt to be gossipy, sociological tours of one or another of their bohemian haunts with no attempt being made to discriminate the literary praxis from the general behavioural code. Lawrence Lipton's *The Holy Barbarians* (concentrating on Venice West, Los Angeles), *The Real Bohemia* by Francis J. Rigney and L. Douglas Smith (San Francisco), Ned Polsky's *Hustlers, Beats and Others* (Greenwich Village, New York) and Iain Finlayson's *Tangier: City of the Dream*, are examples of this mode. Elsewhere, Jane Kramer's *Paterfamilias*, an account of Allen Ginsberg in the 1960s, sycophantically forebore to comment that his poetic talent was depreciating in inverse ratio to his accession to 'guru' status; Ann Charters and Dennis McNally have written biographies of Kerouac that preposterously assume his novels to be an unmediated transcription of actual events; while major Beat writers have themselves sought to include amongst their number certain friends whose lifestyles they admired, but whose literary talents are irredeemably minor (Herbert Huncke, Carl Solomon, Peter Orlovsky and Neal Cassady are but the most conspicuous instances).

Fifty years after the events, the time has come to set a new agenda for the Beats, and one not based on any of these irresponsible meldings of the biography and the art, the lifestyle and the literature. Alas, this process can hardly be said to be underway, the best recent books in the field still being biographies; especially, perhaps, Gerald Nicosia's *Memory Babe: A Critical Biography of Jack Kerouac* (1983), Barry Miles's *Ginsberg: A Biography* (1989) and Ted Morgan's *Literary Outlaw: The Life and Times of William S. Burroughs* (1991). The most widely available anthology, *The Penguin Book of the Beats* (1992) edited by Ann Charters, is organized on a New York–San Francisco axis based on the personal friendships of Kerouac and Ginsberg. The most recent critical symposium, *The Beat Generation Writers* (1996) edited by A. Robert Lee, contradicts its own title by devoting its longest essay to Huncke and Cassady. And even James Campbell's splendidly ascerbic and undeluded monograph, *This Is The Beat Generation* (1999), crosses the threshold between biography and literary criticism so freely as to blur the distinction between the two. Whatever their virtues, and there are plenty of them, these are not the revisionist studies we so badly need.

Beat Aesthetics

One place where a closer examination of Beat texts might begin is with the Romantic ideology on which their aesthetic is predicated. Quintessential features of this ideology include the attributing of superior value to the individual rather than the collective; the subjective rather than the objective; the irrational rather than the rational; innocence rather than experience, with children, blacks, bums and drug addicts being especially deferred to; nature rather than the city, though with a degree of idealization that is the mark of the urbanite rather than the hardened country dweller (see Ginsberg's 'Sunflower Sutra'); an expressivist poetics in which it is proposed that art should aim for the heart rather than the head, the best way of affecting the reader's emotions being to speak directly from one's own ('I am the substance of my poetry', Corso claims); and, with regard to the act of composition, a privileging of the spontaneous, the epiphanous, the inspirational, over the considered and premeditated (see Kerouac's essay 'Essentials of Spontaneous Prose' and Ginsberg's poem 'On Improvised Poetics' whose axiom 'First thought best thought' might be translated to mean 'First draft, best draft'). With regard to this last point, it is worth remarking the pride with which Kerouac claimed to have written *The Subterraneans* in three nights, Burroughs to have compiled *Naked Lunch* in a few weeks from a vast array of disparate manuscripts, and Ginsberg to have composed 'A Cottage in Berkeley' and 'A Supermarket in California' on the same day, the long first section of 'Howl' in an afternoon, and 'Sunflower Sutra' in twenty minutes.

Granted the insistence with which Ginsberg has acknowledged his debt to Blake and Whitman, Kerouac his admiration for Melville, or Corso his debt to Shelley, it is alarming the unanimity with which champions and detractors of the Beats have alike sought to suppress this pervasive Romanticism, the former in the interests of enhancing the movement's claims to originality, the latter in a desire to dismiss it as an unparalleled plunge into barbarism. However, nothing could be further from the truth than to present the Beats as a naive revival of an indigenous Transcendentalism, unmediated by post-Romantic developments in art and thought. It is hardly possible to read a classic Beat text without being aware of the way in which its Romanticism is contained, qualified and interrogated by the modernism of Stein, Pound, Eliot, Williams, Faulkner, Hart Crane, Thomas Wolfe and Henry Miller; the surrealism of Apollinaire, Prévert, Eluard, Reverdy and Lorca; and the Existentialism of Hemingway, Céline, Artaud, Sartre and Camus. It is precisely the tensions, the dialectics, the electrically precarious negotiations, set up between Romanticism on the one hand and these later developments on the other, that give the best Beat literature its remarkable energy and authority. When their Romanticism is unqualified, the Beats collapse into sentimentality of content and flaccidity of style. It is when Ginsberg places the Romantic poet Whitman in a supermarket in California, or when Kerouac views nature through the plate glass window of a car racing towards the urban delights of Denver, or when Burroughs presents drug states as at once a revelatory expansion of consciousness and the most sickening form of capitalist dependency, that the authentic note is struck. And in this context the polysemic, contradictory term 'Beat' is not as inexact as has sometimes been thought.

Jack Kerouac coined the expression at the close of the 1940s, a fact documented by John Clellon Holmes in his essay 'This is the Beat Generation' in *The New York Times Magazine*, 16 November 1952. The Beats, then, were a phenomenon of the 1940s and the first half of the 1950s. The original nucleus was drawn primarily from the states of Massachusetts (Kerouac, Holmes) and New York (Ginsberg, Corso, Ferlinghetti), attended such East Coast universities as Harvard (Burroughs) and Columbia (Ginsberg, Kerouac, Ferlinghetti), and had its headquarters in New York City. Theirs was the America of Truman, Eisenhower and McCarthy; of the Korean war, the Cold War and the communist witch-hunts; of middle-class values, the work ethic and the sublimated eroticism of Doris Day; of a stultified cultural climate that found its noblest expression in the decent, anguished Liberalism of a Lionel Trilling or Arthur Miller; and of a literary–critical establishment whose house journals (*Hudson Review, Sewanee Review, Partisan Review*) could neither countenance nor accommodate their writings. It is worth reminding ourselves of these matters, for it helps account for that note of psychological extremity, of existential alienation, that is a hallmark of Beat literature.

Kerouac himself insisted that 'the word "beat" originally meant poor, down and out, deadbeat, on the bum, sad, sleeping in subways', and that only secondarily did he have a 'vision of the word Beat as being to mean beatific'. Holmes made the same point when he said that

> Beat means not so much weariness, as rawness of the nerves; not so much 'filled up to *here*', as being emptied out. It describes a state of mind from which all unessentials have been stripped, leaving it receptive to everything around it, but impatient with trivial obstructions. To be beat is to be at the bottom of your personality, looking up; to be existential in the Kierkegaard, rather than the Jean-Paul Sartre sense.

Kerouac's coinage, then, encompasses several levels of meaning: to be Beat is to be defeated, beaten, dead beat, exhausted by the demands of straight society; it is to be hepped up, to have a quickened heart beat, in a high-risk, go for broke, shoot the works, all-or-nothing attitude, such as the writers associated with the best jazz music of the day; and it is to be hungry for beatitude, that epiphanous breakthrough from quotidian norms to an area of ecstatic consciousness in which the self feels itself to have been momentarily eternalized.

Once this complex of ideas has been unravelled, even in some such hasty and reductionist manner as the above, certain correctives to a lax critical orthodoxy immediately present themselves. First, many of the writers included in Beat anthologies (from Denise Levertov to Kenneth Koch) have nothing whatsoever to do with the movement. Second, the fact that this East Coast phenomenon first found a receptive audience when Ginsberg read the unpublished 'Howl' at the Six Gallery, San

Francisco, on 7 October 1955, should not blind us to the fact that the poets of the 'San Francisco Renaissance' differ from the original Beats, lacking their urban angst, their feverishness. To put it another way, the San Franciscans tend towards the beat-itude end of the Beat spectrum at the expense of the bottom-dog, deadbeat, existen-tial end which Kerouac said was primary. Third, certain figures who were neither part of the New York–San Francisco axis nor of Ginsberg's and Kerouac's circle of acquain-tance partake of the Beat aesthetic much more fully than those who were: one thinks of Charles Bukowski living in Los Angeles (it would do no harm to the Beat canon for the profile of Los Angeles to be promoted at some expense to that of San Fran-cisco); of Harold Norse, whose European and North African patrol resembles that of Burroughs; and of William Wantling, whose Midwestern background and long years in prison kept him out of the fashionable coterie.

Finally, the Romantic ideology of Beat literature, when released from the ball and chain of contemporary urban anxiety, has a tendency to recycle classic American myths, often of a quasi-frontier kind, in a way that is politically reactionary. The frantic desire to drop out, hit the road, head for the hills, and share a car with a trusted buddy (like the Lone Ranger and Tonto riding out into the unknown), is fundamen-tally a need to escape domesticity, parenthood, heterosexual commitment – in short, woman. From the Beat perspective, nothing locks one more ruinously into a restric-tive society than a wedding ring, a mortgage and a pile of unwashed nappies (see Corso's poem 'Marriage'). Hence, the prevailing atmosphere of misogyny (often accompanied by mother love); and the lack of any significant women Beat practi-tioners, with the possible exception of Diane Di Prima – though such disenchanted but forgiving memoirs as Carolyn Cassady's *Off the Road*, Joyce Johnson's *Minor Char-acters* and Bonnie Bremser's *Troia: Mexican Memoirs* have their own importance. Simi-larly, one might note that the Romantic privileging of the primitive, uncultured and innocent has sometimes tempted the Beats into racial stereotypes that are uncon-sciously patronizing and demeaning. Kerouac's talk of the 'happy, true-hearted, ecstatic Negroes' is symptomatic. As Ned Polsky has tellingly remarked, to see the Negro as more elemental than the white man is 'an inverted form of keeping the nigger in his place'.

The point at issue is not just that the canon of Beat literature has been falsely founded on biographical rather than literary criteria; but that as a result we are for the immediate future obliged to adopt adversarial reading strategies if we are to avoid entrenching an already stale orthodoxy. The remainder of this essay will endeavour to complicate and enrich usage of the term by focusing on four aspects of Beat mythol-ogy that are particularly in need of redefinition.

A Practised Spontaneity

The Beat writers repeatedly urged spontaneity and anathematized redrafting, as though the latter were the enemy of the former. Hence, in the mini-essay 'The Origins of Joy in Poetry', Kerouac promotes the virtues of 'writing whatever comes into your head as it comes'. In practice, however, the major works in the Beat canon are almost invariably those which benefited from arduous crafting; conversely, the genuinely impromptu pieces are usually the most disposable. This is not to say that the masterpieces exude laboriousness; but that their air of spontaneity has been hard won. Indeed, one of the reasons that academic critics were slow to applaud Beat artistry is that they did not appreciate just how hard it was to make it look that easy.

Ginsberg's 'Howl' is the poem that is usually thought to epitomize Beat aesthetics. When a facsimile edition was published in 1986 it reprinted five drafts of Part I; eighteen of Part II; five of Part III; and seven of Part IV. Other versions, some now lost, are alluded to in the commentary. The variants that are included chronicle the dramatic revisions the poem underwent before assuming its final form. In Part I, for instance, what is now the seventh strophe was the fiftieth in the first version; similarly, the present twenty-second, twenty-third, twenty-seventh and thirtieth strophes all moved fifty or more places in the sequence, often undergoing extensive rewording in the process. Moreover, the facsimile edition concentrates on the period 1955–6, whereas Ginsberg actually met the poem's dedicatee Carl Solomon in 1949, jotting down at the time many of the latter's anecdotes and aphorisms which subsequently found their way into the poem. In other words, 'Howl' was composed over a seven-year period, some parts of it undergoing at least twenty rehearsals before arrival at a persuasively 'improvised' discourse.

Much the same holds true for *On the Road*, usually regarded as the definitive Beat novel. The events it fictionalizes took place in 1947. A year later Kerouac had the title and the basic conception of the narrative. By early 1951 he had completed a 125,000-word version of the novel. By May, 1952, he had entirely rewritten it – though at 530 pages it still needed major surgery. By the mid-1950s he was not only compressing the plot, suppressing libellous passages and excising homosexual episodes at the behest of the novel's eventual publisher, Viking Press, he was also allowing his editor Malcolm Cowley to make his own changes without consultation. 'No emendations in time's reconsidering backstep', Kerouac proclaimed; but when *On the Road* finally appeared in 1957 it was the mature product of ten years' graft by several pairs of hands. The instant celebrity of the novel ensured that Kerouac would never again be under such editorial pressure to revise his work, with the unfortunate consequence that apart from *Visions of Cody* he never again attained such coherence and authority.

Of all the writers who might be considered Beat, it is arguable that only Charles Bukowski extemporized his best work, pressed up against the instantaneity of his inspiration and without the safety net of extensive revision. Two factors made this possible: first, Bukowski perfected his technique, not by redrafting the same text over a ten-year period like Ginsberg and Kerouac, but by drafting different poems and stories for approximately a quarter of a century before arriving at a style a reputable publisher thought worth preserving; and, second, he gave John Martin of the Black Sparrow Press *carte blanche* to select what he wanted from the vast, uneven eruption of material that continued right up until Bukowski's death. Martin rejected half the material that his author sent him, finding much of it close to gibberish: Bukowski, for his part, knowing that he only became blocked if he strove too consciously for perfection, was happy to delegate all editorial functions in this way. Although it does not follow the usual pattern, then, Bukowski's career is further testimony to the virtues of tenacity, dedication and ruthless editing, rather than the expected ones of an anything-goes writing style followed by quick success.

An Educated Barbarism

On the first page of his most famous novel, William Burroughs explains: 'the title means exactly what the words say: NAKED Lunch – a *frozen* moment when everyone sees what is on the end of every fork'. The notion that the writer's duty is to convey experience raw, unmediated by literary convention or good taste, is repeated many times, Burroughs purporting to reject any attempt at novelization and presenting himself as the scientific documentor of his own (and, by extension, the larger culture's) morbid symptoms:

> There is only one thing a writer can write about: *what is in front of his senses at the moment of writing*. . . . I am a recording instrument. . . . I do not presume to impose 'story' 'plot' 'continuity'. . . . Insofar as I succeed in *Direct* recording of certain areas of psychic process I may have limited function. . . . I am not an entertainer.

Paradoxically, in rejecting literature Burroughs simultaneously calls upon it, the title *Naked Lunch* deriving from Kerouac and the clause 'I am a recording instrument' invoking the Berlin stories of Christopher Isherwood together with their theatrical adaptation by John Van Druten, *I Am A Camera* (itself subsequently the inspiration for the stage and screen musical, *Cabaret*). As for the text itself, this scabrous phantasmagoria is densely interwoven with allusions, some admiring, some satirical, to the Bible, Confucius, Lao-Tse, Shakespeare, Webster, Swift, Wordsworth, Coleridge, Keats, Dickens, Rimbaud, Housman, Conrad, Stein, Joyce, Eliot, Kafka and Ginsberg, together with a plethora of popular songs – including, rather incongruously granted the surrounding squalor and mayhem, 'Believe me if all these endearing young charms . . .'!

The truth is that far from stepping outside the mediating frames of culture to get at experience direct, the Beat conceptions of unmediated reality were themselves culturally produced. How typical that when Burroughs murdered his wife it was not in some ghastly explosion of domestic rage and passion, but drunkenly acting out the fictitious William Tell story made famous by Schiller's play and by Rossini's opera *Guillaume Tell* (1829). Similarly, when Ginsberg voluntarily entered Columbia Presbyterian Psychiatric Institute in order to escape imprisonment for possession of stolen goods, he was met by a bespectacled overweight Jewish boy with a towel wrapped around his head. 'Who are you?' the stranger asked. 'I'm Myshkin', Ginsberg said.

'I'm Kirilov', Carl Solomon rejoined. Not even the extreme experience of psychiatric detention was drastic or terrifying enough to be apprehended raw and inchoate, but presented itself pre-processed by the novels of Dostoievsky. (Myshkin is the saintly hero of *The Idiot*, Kirilov the demonic nihilist in *The Possessed*.)

Of course, there is nothing wrong with artists being steeped in their cultural inheritance; nor with the literary stratagem of using intertextual references as a way of foregrounding the fact that all our perceptions of reality are culturally mediated. The trouble is that the Beats themselves keep wobbling between shame and pride in their own scholarliness, lurching from the crudest anti-intellectualism to dandified flauntings of artistic knowingness. In the sixth of the 'Pictures of the Gone World' section of *A Coney Island of the Mind* (1958), Lawrence Ferlinghetti opts for the anti-high art posture:

> walking around in museums always makes me
>   want to
>   'sit down'
> I always feel so
>   constipated
>   in those
>   high altitudes

Yet poem after poem of this same volume (whose very title is an allusion to Henry Miller) begins with some such line as 'In Goya's greatest scenes we seem to see . . .', or 'Kafka's Castle stands above the world . . .', or 'Sarolla's women in their picture hats . . .'. There is no passion so animal, and no animal so bestial, as to elude this web of citations, as when an apparently feral dog waits

> with his head cocked sideways
>   at street corners
>   as if he is just about to have
>   his picture taken
>   for Victor Records
>   listening for
>   His Master's Voice

Despite Ferlinghetti's penchant for lumberjack shirts and mountain boots, his poetry has more in common with Oscar Wilde ('What has nature ever done except copy art?') than *The Call of the Wild* (nature red in tooth and claw, etc).

The same holds true for the other Beats. James Campbell has remarked the extraordinary literary pedigree of Kerouac's title *On the Road*, citing as evidence works of the same name by Douglas Goldring (1910), Gwen John (1920), Langston Hughes (1935) and Cyril Campion (1954). As for Ginsberg, many of his best poems are written over the top of previous works by earlier authors: 'Malest Cornifici Tuo Catullo' translates and adapts a poem by Catullus; 'A Supermarket in California' reworks Lorca's 'Ode to Walt Whitman'; 'Sunflower Sutra' is clearly modelled on Blake's 'Ah, Sunflower!'; 'Kaddish' leans heavily on Edward Marshall's 'Leave the Word Alone'; while in 'Howl' the echoes mutiply, many of them carrying the marks of more than one prior usage (for instance, Ginsberg took Christ's agonized cry 'eli eli lamma sabachthani' – 'My God, my God, why hast thou forsaken me?' – not from its New Testament source in Matthew 27.46, but via Tristan Corbière's 'Cris d'Aveugle', so that both anterior texts are in play in the pertinent passage towards the end of Part I).

There has always been a criticism hostile to the Beats, usually entailing a last-man-on-the-ramparts, end-of-civilization-as-we-know-it tone of hysterical oppositionalism. Thus the poet John Ciardi wrote contemptuously of their 'unwashed eccentricity', while Norman Podhoretz, in 'The Know-Nothing Bohemians', claimed that they stood in opposition to 'intelligence itself'. Yet the Beats are characteristically erudite, bookish, sedentary. As the jam-jar bottom lenses of Ginsberg and Burroughs's spectacles attest, these were men more at home in a library than roughing it 'on the road'.

The Biographical Fallacy

In a 1956 letter to his old college tutor, Lionel Trilling, Allen Ginsberg opined: 'I think what is coming is a romantic period. . . . Eliot & Pound are like Dryden & Pope. What gives now is much more personal.' This speculative neo-Romanticism has latterly been rigidified by sympathetic critics like Ann Charters into something altogether more reductive. In the *Penguin Book of the Beats* she repeatedly asserts that 'Beat literature is predominantly autobiographical' and that 'the Beats insisted on writing directly about events in their own lives'.

Two exhibits will demonstrate the violence done to these texts when they are approached as versified autobiography. The first, 'Pusan Liberty', by the neglected Beat writer William Wantling, is one of the finest English-language poems to come out of the Korean conflict, comparable to the best First World War poetry in its perception of contending soldiers as alike victims of their respective political and military masters. The poem offers a clear example of the way in which Beat literature's defining note of alienated authenticity is artistically constructed rather than being the result of the author vomiting personal experience direct upon the page.

The poem opens with a scene that brilliantly encapsulates the devastation and corruption modern war visits upon its host society:

> the 6 × 6 bounces me down the
> washboard roads, I see the
>
> sun-eaten walls of Korea, my
> girl-wife & child in a mud &
>
> straw hut back in Taegu & here
> I am meeting the SEAL as he

> sits on his roller-skate cart
> minus arms & legs but beneath
>
> his ass a million $'s worth
> of heroin

What initially convinces us of the poem's veracity is not just the precise detailing but also the psychological extremity of the situation, the Wantling protagonist buying and shooting up heroin before selling some on to the enemy:

> 2 Chinese agents come around
>
> to make their buy, 2 young
> boys, they're hooked bad & I
>
> charge them too much – we sit
> there & fix, I fix again, the
>
> so called Enemy & I, but just
> 3 angry boys lost in the immense
>
> absurdity of War & State sudden
> friends who have decided that
>
> our hatred of Government exceeds
> the furthest imaginable limits
>
> of human calculation

We know Wantling was the youngest Marine Sergeant in combat during the winter 1952–3 campaign of the Korean War. We also know that his adult life was in part shaped by his addictions (many of his individual poems and pamphlets have such titles as 'Heroin', *Heroin Haiku*, 'Once You've Been a Dopefiend' and 'For the Peyote Goddess'). Again, the poem's acknowledgement, even as it establishes the momentary camaraderie of '3 angry boys lost in the immense / absurdity of War & State', of the narrator's little betrayal of his 'sudden / friends' by overcharging them for their fix seems like an earnest of psychological candour. As Camus put it in *The Fall*, 'we cannot assert the innocence of anyone, whereas we can state with certainty the guilt of all'.

Yet that use of the word 'absurdity' when describing the situation the three 'boys' find themselves in, invoking as it does Camus' 1942 essay *The Myth of Sisyphus*, in which the existentialist view of the absurdity of the human condition was given definitive formulation, might be interpreted as a sign, not of the poem's veracity, but of its literarity – or, if you prefer, its fictiveness. It is noticeable, for instance, that the protagonist of the poem is given no name: this not only rolls a boulder in the way of our desire to conflate the narrator of this first-person monologue with its author; it may also suggest that, to the contrary, the authorial intention was to present the protagonist as a sort of everyman, his anonymity implying a degree of universality.

(A comparison might be made with Stephen Crane's classic war novel *The Red Badge of Courage*, whose central character, Henry Fleming, remains nameless for most of the story's duration, being referred to simply as 'the youth'.) This is not just a matter of Wantling presenting his experiences as representative so that the subjective or auto-biographical has objective or universal value, for thus far no evidence has come to light confirming that he, like his narrator, had a 'girl-wife & child' in Korea. Most tellingly of all, in a frank letter recounting his life of crime and drug use to Edward Lucie-Smith, Wantling admitted that he actually took up heroin in the United States not Korea, in 1955 not 1952–3, in peace time not in war. However much autobiography infiltrates 'Pusan Liberty', its narrator's experience is not the author's, and the poem's air of extreme authenticity is a fictional construct. In short, the emotional force of the piece is not the result of Wantling baring his soul but of Wantling baring his technique.

Our second exhibit demonstrates by the opposite means the same point – namely, the fictiveness of the Beat text and the absurdity of trying to take its measure in bio-graphical terms. As already noted, Allen Ginsberg met Carl Solomon in the Psychiatric Institute of New York in 1949. Ginsberg dubbed Solomon 'an intuitive Bronx Dadaist and prose-poet', noted down his more memorable anecdotes and turns of phrase, picked up from him Artaud's concept of the artist as a man mad (i.e. sane) in a sane (i.e. mad) society, and six years later brought all these elements together in a poem whose full title is 'Howl for Carl Solomon'. The piece famously begins

> I saw the best minds of my generation destroyed by madness, starving
> > hysterical naked,
> dragging themselves through the negro streets at dawn looking for an angry fix

and Solomon is presented as a prime example, a lunatic–saint cruelly incarcerated in a mental asylum by an uncomprehending society. The pivotal moment of the long first section of the poem begins with a passage particularly reliant on Solomon's stories:

> who threw potato salad at CCNY lecturers on Dadaism and subsequently
> > presented themselves on the granite steps of the madhouse with
> > shaven heads and harlequin speech of suicide, demanding instantaneous lobotomy,
> and who were given instead the concrete void of insulin Metrazol electricity
> > hydrotherapy psychotherapy occupational therapy pingpong & amnesia

and culminates in the direct address: 'ah, Carl, while you are not safe I am not safe'. The third part of 'Howl' opens with a variant of this address – 'Carl Solomon I'm with you in Rockland' – the last five words of this line thereafter being repeated eighteen times as a refrain. (Rockland was one of the mental hospitals in which Solomon was held.) In short, Solomon is the poem's dedicatee, addressee, inspiration and hero–victim. He is to 'Howl' as Neal Cassady is to *On the Road*, the real person whose life the work celebrates.

Once again, however, the case is not what it seems. Solomon left hospital years before the completion of 'Howl' and went to work for Ace books where he accepted Burroughs's *Junky* but rejected the 1951 version of *On the Road* because Kerouac was still refusing to revise. Not only was Ginsberg's plangent identification with his captive buddy ('I'm with you in Rockland') out of date, Solomon being free, but as the latter admitted the wild adventures he had earlier recounted to the poet, and which provide 'Howl' with so much of its vivacity, were largely bogus:

> I gave Allen an apocryphal history of my adventures and pseudo-intellectual deeds of daring. He meticulously took note of everything I said. . . . [H]e published all of the data, compounded partly of truth, but for the most [part] raving self-justification, crypto-bohemian boasting à la Rimbaud, effeminate prancing, and esoteric aphorisms plagiarized from Kierkegaard and others – in the form of *Howl*. Thus he enshrined falsehood as truth and raving as common sense for future generations to ponder over and be misled.

In making this disclosure, Solomon gleefully supposes that he has exposed the poem as worthless. However, just as we found with the Beats' use of improvisation that a spontaneity that has been premeditated, rehearsed and artfully constructed – if you will, a simulated spontaneity – feels more real than genuine extemporization; so the autobiographical 'truth' of Beat literature is most plausible when the product of fictive means. The poet probably thought he was 'telling it like it is'; but by persuading Ginsberg of the truth of his fabulated life, Solomon released him from the treadmill of the biographical into a larger realm of linguistic play. And this, in turn, made the fiction real in the only place that matters, not at the level of the life lived but at the level of the words on the page. To put it another way, the success of Beat literature stems from the fact that even when the authors were trying to be autobiographical they signally failed in the endeavour.

Queering the Canon

In 1996 A. Robert Lee edited a collection of ten essays by British and American scholars under the title *The Beat Generation Writers*. The essays are interesting and provocative, yet all shirk the fundamental task of identifying a Beat aesthetic, preferring, in the usual way, to define the group as a circle of acquaintance on a New York–San Francisco axis. Granted this regrettable dependence upon the biographical, it is paradoxical – though, again, typical – that not one of the essays squarely tackles a subject such an author-centred methodology would seem to make unavoidable: homosexuality. Most of the Beats were either gay (Ginsberg, Burroughs, Norse, Huncke, Wieners) or bisexual (Kerouac, Cassady, Orlovsky); and even those who act macho, like Bukowski, are usually so strident about it that their writings seem rather a theatrical performing of masculinity than a simple affirmation of male power. My own view is that the rise of the feminist movement following the publication of Betty Friedan's *The Feminine Mystique* (1963) swiftly rendered the sexual politics of the Beats suspect, if not mastodontic, and that the only context in which they can still be read as liberational is that of gay rights.

One of the advantages of such an approach is that it can help explain the unusual but shared career trajectory of Beats like Burroughs, Ginsberg and Kerouac. For all began with a decade of false starts and periodic writer's block (roughly 1945–55); then experienced an astonishing uprush of creativity usually entailed to an uninhibited exploration of the homoerotic (1955–60); and thereafter, although prolific, went into a steady qualitative decline with the occasional brief recovery on a generally falling graph. This pattern, I am suggesting, is a product of the mid-century patriarchal order, 'Howl', *On the Road* and *Naked Lunch* all being 'coming out' texts whose liberational intensity is directly proportional to the epistemological constraints of the 1950s' closet. The problem for the authors, of course, is not only that they cannot keep voluntarily returning to the closet so as to reachieve the explosive release of their masterpieces; but that their major works have anyway so transformed the ideological climate that the closet no longer exists in the same way. Their very success, though a long time coming, was decisive enough to swiftly make them obsolete.

Edmund White wrote in his 1997 AIDS novel, *The Farewell Symphony*, 'Never had a group been placed on such a rapid cycle – oppressed in the 1950s, freed in the 1960s, exulted in the 1970s and wiped out in the 1980s'. The Beats are indispensable guides to the first two decades in this abbreviated gay history. Kerouac's *On the Road* and *Visions of Cody* may well be the definitive accounts of what it is like for one man to love another and still be in denial that the romance is erotic as well as companionate. Burroughs is much more outspokenly homosexual, but his Swiftian excrementalism may be read as a sign of self-disgust and his *oeuvre* regarded as transitional. By contrast, Ginsberg's garrulous strophes choreograph most of the vital stages in the progress towards self-acceptance: the stultification of the poems up to 1954 honestly unveils the futility of homosexuals trying to conform to heterosexual norms; by invoking Lorca and Whitman, 'A Supermarket in California' takes crucial, tentative steps towards gay canon-building; 'America' is mock confessional ('America I'm putting my queer shoulder to the wheel'); 'Howl' opts for a 'better blatant than latent' explicitness ('who let themselves be fucked in the ass by saintly motorcyclists, and screamed with joy'); while 'Kaddish', a funeral lament for his mad mother, directly confronts the source of his oedipally driven flight from womankind:

> One time I thought she was trying to make me come lay her – flirting to herself at sink – lay back on huge bed that filled most of the room, dress up around her hips, big slash of hair, scars of operations, pancreas, belly wounds, abortions, appendix, stitching of incisions pulling down in the fat like hideous thick zippers – ragged long lips between her legs – What, even smell of asshole?

Thereafter Ginsberg's erotic poems get steadily duller and ever more lurid, as though driven by an obsessional need to answer the question said to vex the straights – what do gay men do in bed?: see, for instance, the 1968 'PLEASE MASTER' ('& please master make me wiggle my rear to eat up the prick trunk / till my asshalfs cuddle your thighs') or the 1986 'Sphincter' ('active, eager, receptive to phallus / coke bottle, candle, carrot / banana & fingers').

If the Beats are united by a subject as well as an aesthetic, then this surely is it: the mid-century crisis in masculinity; the attempt to establish a male camaraderie that is resolutely anti-patriarchy; the refusal to become a father as a challenge to the Law of the Father. In the process of opening up this new terrain, Beat writings subvert or profane the sacred social discourses of nation (they are particularly good at excavating the latent militarism that undergirds patriotic feeling), family (their work presents the family not as our refuge from the ills of the world but as the place where we are first exposed to them), gender (no contemporaries did as much to unmoor society's sexual certitudes) and normalcy (for the Beats normality is not an edenic given but an ideological aspiration that visibly warps its adherents). If their writings are uneven, and no comparable literary movement has as high a drivel percentage, their achievements are still prodigious and in ways the critical debate has hardly begun to calibrate. Perhaps the recent deaths of Bukowski, Ginsberg, Burroughs and Corso will elicit the reappraisal that is so long overdue.

BIBLIOGRAPHY

Campbell, J. (1999), *This is the Beat Generation*, London: Secker & Warburg.

Charters, A. (1992), *The Penguin Book of the Beats*, London: Penguin Books.

Holmes, J. C. (1988), *Passionate Opinions: The Cultural Essays*, Fayetteville: University of Arkansas Press.

Lee, A. R. (1996), *The Beat Generation Writers*, London and East Haven: Pluto Press.

Lucie-Smith, E. (1968), 'Introduction'. In William Wantling, *The Awakening*, London: Rapp & Whiting.

Miles, B. (1986), *Allen Ginsberg, Howl: Original Draft Facsimile*, New York: Harper & Row.

Miles, B. (1989), *Ginsberg: A Biography*, London and New York: Viking.

Morgan, T. (1991), *Literary Outlaw: The Life and Times of William S. Burroughs*, London: Bodley Head.

Mottram, E. (1977), *William Burroughs: The Algebra of Need*, London: Marion Boyars.

Nicosia, G. (1986), *Memory Babe: A Critical Biography of Jack Kerouac*, London: Penguin Books.

Parkinson, T. (1961), *A Casebook on the Beat*, New York: Crowell.

Peabody, R. (1997), *A Different Beat: Writings by Women of the Beat Generation*, London: Serpent's Tail.

Sounes, H. (1998), *Charles Bukowski: Locked in the Arms of a Crazy Life*, Edinburgh: Rebel Inc.

White, E. (1997), *The Farewell Symphony*, London: Chatto.

15

Confessionalism

Lucy Collins

The considerable difficulty inherent in categorizing literary movements is distinctly evident in the problems surrounding the term 'confessionalism'. Applied retrospectively to the work of a number of mid-century American poets, it was a term which these poets rarely used to describe themselves. Confessionalism has no leader, no manifesto, and in spite of representing an extreme development in modern poetry, it is often difficult to pin-point exactly. It is detected with most accuracy only in a stage of a poet's career, perhaps even in an individual poem or sequence, and because of this its role in the transition of creativity from one stage to another may be a key one. The critic M. L. Rosenthal was the first to explore at length the implications and achievements of the confessional poets and the scope of this essay is somewhat determined by the limits of that study. The poets providing the focus here are those which Rosenthal places centrally, but there are other figures, among them Randall Jarrell and Delmore Schwartz, whose work at times exhibits key characteristics of confessionalism and whose connection to its major figures makes them especially significant. I will concern myself primarily with work written in the 1950s and consider both its collective impact on the progress of modern poetry and its significance in the development of individual poets.

Steven Gould Axelrod cites three essential elements of confessional poetry: 'an undisguised exposure of painful personal event . . . a dialectic of private matter with public matter . . . and an intimate, unornamented style' (Axelrod, 1979, p. 98). In a critical climate which often appears to privilege the first of these definitions at the expense of the others, it is important to consider the relationship between personal and cultural upheaval as well as the formal implications of such poetic change. The expression of personal pain has been regarded as a hallmark of confessional poetry. All its chief proponents suffered from severe personal difficulties: destructive family relationships; traumatic childhoods; broken marriages; recurring mental breakdowns; alcoholism or drug abuse. This was the first generation of poets to be widely affected by the development of psychoanalysis and many dealt with the recesses of the psychological, among them such important writers as Robert Bly, Galway Kinnell and James Wright. The poets conventionally classified as confessional personally faced – and chose as their subject matter – more significant difficulties, however. The connections between these poets were formed in this context and reinforced by the similarities of their unstable lives. The opening of Allen Ginsberg's 'Howl', 'I saw the best minds of my generation destroyed by madness', seems to testify to the feeling of solidarity which these poets experienced. To assume this perspective, though, is to obliterate the aggression and competitiveness which also shaped this generation. Mental suffering could bring with it heightened awareness and at times feelings of omnipotence. As these writers recognized a common predicament, they also tried to assert their individual talent and pre-eminence among their peers.

The validity of personal experience as the matter for art has been the subject of considerable debate but perhaps never so positively and succinctly expressed than by Emerson in his 1844 essay 'The Poet', a text which would prove central to the foundation of American poetry:

> The poet has a new thought: he has a whole new experience to unfold; he will tell us how it was with him, and all men will be the richer in his fortune. For, the experience of each new age requires a new confession. (Emerson, 1983, p. 450)

The idea of the poet courting extremity in order to report the limits of human life is an important aspect of this assertion. That such limits alter with the age makes confessionalism, in spite of its attention to personal trauma, a movement very much of its time which must be examined in the context of 1950s America, where the most enduring of its poems were written. Why it should apply so centrally to American poetry, rather than to any other tradition, is another question which needs to be addressed. In *The American Moment*, Geoffrey Thurley concludes that the New World inevitably mirrored the Old and that 'America was a self-conscious society from the moment of its inception' (Thurley, 1977, p. 4). This self-consciousness is implicated in the concern with Americanness which has preoccupied writers and readers alike. Yet, as Emerson suggests above, transition is crucial to the American poetry scene and the need to document the moment, to report, indeed to embody, cultural change is a key one.

Mid-century America was a country struggling towards readjustment; these were the years in which the Cold War took hold, when nuclear armaments were a developing threat and the disorder left in the wake of the conflict took its toll on both individual and society. It was also a time of economic growth and increasing prosperity for most Americans, though complacency was accompanied by fears for personal and national security, creating the kind of environment in which McCarthyism could flourish. A fractured society, then, was the result both of the traumas of war and of a culture unsure of its own extraordinary progress. If one result of the war was swift technological advancement in subsequent peacetime, it was a form of development which at once benefited and victimized the individual. This sense of becoming a victim was a crucial one, since it would radically alter the status and behaviour of the literary protagonist. The fragmented individual also sought wholeness through aesthetic expression itself, so the act of writing both represented this fragmentation and attempted to reverse it. In a world which seemed increasingly to deprive the individual of meaningful action, the poem became a way of redressing the balance and the poem which spoke directly from troubled experience provided a means of validating feeling in a threatening world.

The personality was clearly under threat in late forties and fifties American life since, as M. L. Rosenthal argues, 'the poetry is a constant struggle to assert the encompassing validity of the feeling personality in the face of depressing realizations' (Rosenthal, 1967, p. 11). This response to the particular stresses and limitations of the time was linked to another form of reaction – to the impersonality of modernism. T. S. Eliot's declaration that 'the more perfect the artist, the more completely separate in him will be the man who suffers and the mind which creates' (Eliot, 1932, p. 8) demands a purely imaginative approach to idealism in art and the ability to withstand comparisons with reality which will be destructive to the spirit. In response to this, the writers of the generation following Eliot's sought to embody the individual perception in direct ways; rather than creating masks or different personae, they began to speak from a position which was unambiguously their own. Yet, at the same time, this position was one re-created by the poets and it is neither true nor useful to imagine that their lives appeared in their poetry unmediated by the creative power to shape and transform.

On the question of style, the informality employed by these poets was both profoundly effective and critically misleading. Again, transition is an important element: the early formalism of Lowell and Berryman, for example, could be seen as a response to cultural uncertainties, but these traditional techniques would later be excised to make way for looser forms. Thematically too, interest in the enduring questions of life was subordinated to an immediate concern with the temporary itself. Abandoning symbolism and complex patterns of imagery in favour of a form akin to, and often incorporating, direct speech, the confessional poets invited the reader to follow closely – indeed to re-experience – the mental processes exposed in their poems. Behind the apparently casual style, however, often lay a finely tuned appreciation of form and an ability to manipulate line and stanza to give the effect of unedited emotion. Not all had the inclination or the capability to achieve this level of mastery however, and confessionalism as a movement gave shelter to such luminous poetic talents as Robert Lowell alongside figures of cultural importance but far less technical sophistication, Allen Ginsberg and Anne Sexton among them. It seems that as a result the movement is in danger of being judged on its weaker moments, rather than on the significance of its achievements for mid-century American literature.

Robert Lowell (1917–77) is widely considered to be the most talented of the middle generation of American poets and is often credited with inaugurating the confessional movement with his influential collection *Life Studies* (1959). The transition was already perceptible, though, in the work of such poets as Allen Ginsberg and in

W. D. Snodgrass, whose first collection *Heart's Needle* would in many ways exemplify
the possibilities of the change. Lowell himself taught Snodgrass and at first was un-
enthusiastic about the personal tendencies of his work; later he recognized its importance and admitted that it may have influenced his own poetic evolution. The key
point here is that while Ginsberg and Snodgrass were just starting their careers, Lowell
was already a much acclaimed and respected poet. The movement away from the
allusive, intellectual and often religious poems which characterized Lowell's earliest
achievement was a brave and decisive one, further precipitated by the sense that his
style was becoming increasingly unwieldy. The extent of the change made Lowell
unsure as to its success and the self-doubt which he exhibited at the publication of
Life Studies could be seen as indicative of a more deep-seated anxiety which this period
of his life heralded.

Uncertainty was in fact a key to much of the work of the confessional poets. As
the relationship between individual and world became more painful and difficult, the
sense of being able to reach a position of intellectual certainty became ever more problematic. All knowledge was conditional and all aspects of life prey to continual change.
In keeping with this tendency Lowell's *Life Studies*, as the title of the collection suggests, can be seen as drafts towards more finished works. This provisional aspect has
important connotations for the autobiographical readings of the poems also, since
what are regarded as factual renderings of family history, for example, or of mental
distress, are similarly open to reinterpretation. Just as confessional poetry as a whole
is a product of its time, these individual poems are the products of a particular stage
in Lowell's career and personal life, when the death of his parents and declining success
of his rather opaque poetic project forced a creative change. This notion of transition
finds expression directly in a number of the poems: 'Waking in the Blue', which recalls
Lowell's time in a mental hospital, begins with a painful movement to consciousness:

> The night attendant, a B.U. sophomore,
> rouses from the mare's-nest of his drowsy head
> propped on *The Meaning of Meaning*.
> He catwalks down our corridor.
> Azure day
> makes my agonized blue window bleaker.
> Crows maunder on the petrified fairway.
> Absence! My heart grows tense
> as though a harpoon were sparring for the kill.
> (This is the house for the 'mentally ill')

The poem's inward movement charts the observing mind turning toward itself, the
language – as well as the speaker's heart – growing tense with inactivity. The period
in hospital is itself a transitional time for Lowell, as he records in such poems as 'Home
After Three Months Away'; removed both from the demands and the pleasures of life,
the poet finds the materials of his art within the confines of the institution and of his
own troubled mind.

The stylistic change which was such a striking feature of Lowell's work can be detected in the poetry of another key figure of the confessional group, John Berryman (1914–72). Closer to Lowell than the others, both personally and in terms of poetic rivalry and achievement, Berryman is most famous for his Dream Songs, published between 1964 and his suicide in 1972. These poems, though written after the main thrust of confessionalism was over, are seen by some critics as exemplifying its private and occasionally impenetrable nature: 'This is not so much confessional poetry', writes Richard Gray, 'as pure confession: moving, sometimes, in the way that the confidences of any stranger might be, but not something in which we can begin to share' (Gray, 1990, p. 260). Yet this assessment takes little account of what Stephen Matterson has called Berryman's persistent fictionalization of the self in his poetry (Matterson, 1988, p. 71). The pain, guilt, confusion and wonder expressed in these works are not just Berryman's own, but those of the age, and if Henry represents the protean self, this fluidity is aptly articulated through the use of a range of voices in the poems. Though Berryman draws extensively on his own life experience, it is a mistake to see the Henry of the Dream Songs as unmediated by an imaginative and creative intelligence. There is discipline to be found, not in the overall structure of the group but in the form of the individual poems (three stanzas of six lines each), though the broken syntax often threatens to distort meaning. The sequence of the Songs, which we might expect to offer an important way of reading the individual's relationship to the world, provides no comforting sense of resolution to this collage of personal pain and cultural displacement. Instead, the cumulative aspect of the poems is emphasized and with it the circumstances of their writing.

M. L. Rosenthal has remarked that Berryman, more than any other confessional poet, has absorbed 'the concerns of his age into his nerve-ends' (Rosenthal, 1967, p. 119) and it is true that the Dream Songs chart the damaging alienation of the individual and the conflict between white Anglo-Saxon and African-American cultures which was increasingly evident in sixties America. Moving ten years back in time to confessionalism's most important decade, we find the poem that decisively marked Berryman's transition from a kind of formalism to a direct personal style. Though his earlier sonnet sequence suggested the changes to come, the delay in its publication probably reflected a culture not yet receptive to that adventurous but flawed project. *Homage to Mistress Bradstreet* presents an extraordinary treatment of Anne Bradstreet, America's first published poet, and in doing so highlights Berryman's use of the voice, how he mingles his own with Bradstreet's until at times the reader has difficulty in telling the two apart. The engagement of present with past is not itself an event in time but a continued intermingling of both contexts. The voices then, while articulating historically specific positions (and ones clearly of literary significance), also partake in a narrative of the divided self, since Berryman not only depicts, but identifies strongly with his female subject. His language, which combines direct, even contemporary, elements with formal and stylized phrasing, moves continually between distance and intimacy:

> – Be kind you, to one unchained eager far & wild
>
> and if, O my love, my heart is breaking, please
> neglect my cries and I will spare you. Deep
> in Time's grave, Love's, you lie still.
> Lie still. – Now? That happy shape
> my forehead had under my most long, rare,
> ravendark, hidden, soft bodiless hair
> you award me still.
> You must not love me, but I do not bid you cease

Allen Ginsberg's (1926–97) language proved as important in establishing his fame, or notoriety, as Berryman's stylized and frequently archaic diction did in determining the direction which his later poetry would take. 'The problem has been to communicate the very spark of life', Ginsberg said, 'and not some opinion about that spark of life' (Howard, 1970, p. 149) and his desire to evoke the immediacy and vibrancy of the human voice was combined with an ear attuned to the changes – particularly in music – which were occurring in mid-century America. As Thurley has pointed out, if Ginsberg were merely interested in rendering the voice realistically, there would be little innovative to remark in his language (Thurley, 1977, p. 174), yet when *Howl and Other Poems* appeared in 1956 it was its vocabulary which startled readers – and the censors – with its unabashed sexual and scatological references and its accelerated wit. Neither this collection, nor Ginsberg's later publications, relied exclusively on linguistic shock-value, however, and the lyricism which in many other writers might have presented an impediment to such extreme experimentation does appear occasionally in Ginsberg's work. His homosexuality and drug addiction made him a social outsider and the crudity of his language reinforced this alienation, yet implicit in the public acceptance of his poetry was an acknowledgement that a new way of evaluating and representing humanity was necessary. By courting extremity, Ginsberg affirms Emerson's idea of the poet 'writing back' from the edge of experience. Likewise, the undisputed influence of Whitman seems to depend not only upon the inclusiveness of 'Howl' or upon its fractured nature and insistent rhythms, but on this sense of the poet as chronicler of the minutiae as well as the breadth of human life; of a combination of earthy realism and spirituality.

> I saw the best minds of my generation destroyed by madness, starving
>   hysterical naked,
> dragging themselves through the negro streets at dawn looking for an angry fix,
> angelheaded hipsters burning for the ancient heavenly connection to the starry
>   dynamo in the machinery of night

The drive to explore experience directly and not merely through the agency of memory makes the moment of writing vitally important to Ginsberg. His choice of form for a later poem, 'Kaddish' (traditionally both a Hebrew lament for the dead and a hymn of praise to God), draws on the elegiac element of confessionalism that has been noted especially in Robert Lowell's work. In this poem Ginsberg explores his ambiguous feelings for his mother by eroticizing his relationship to the disturbed and dying woman. Elsewhere the overt sexuality in his poetry testifies to a search for love and for meaning threatened on one side by a hostile materialist culture and on the other by the soulless nature of the pursuit itself. In spite of the degradation which features frequently in Ginsberg's work, its enduring spiritual concern assured him a cult following.

Spirituality is also an important consideration in any assessment of Theodore Roethke's work. Roethke (1908–63), born and raised in the Midwest, was sensitive to his perceived exclusion from the East Coast poetry scene and was anxious to cultivate critical attention. His first collection showed linguistic competence and a skilled ear but nothing to suggest his later experimental achievements, which were heralded in the 'greenhouse' poems and developed in the 'Lost Son' sequence. The Midwestern landscape was significant for the setting of Roethke's poems and also evoked the open spaces which challenged the individual's sense of identity. His most potent subject matter was the journey inward in search of the evolving self, a concern that had much in common with Wordsworth's *Prelude* and, like the *Prelude*, explored childhood experience as a key to understanding the spiritual and psychic life. Randall Jarrell, though not a poet to exhibit his personal traumas readily, used similar strategies to probe the psychological in his poetry, as did Delmore Schwartz in his acclaimed work *In Dreams Begin Responsibilities* (1938). In keeping with the psychoanalytic developments of the age, these poets began to see childhood as a source of pain and sickness, rather than Wordsworthian joy. This transition was clearly an important one for Roethke, who freed himself to speak with a personal voice – of troubled sexuality, of the early death of his father – for the first time in his career.

The death of the father is at the centre of the 'Lost Son' narratives, but this applies not only to Roethke's real father but also to his loss of belief in a greater spiritual being. His search for identity takes place within this context and the pre-eminence of nature in his poems not only has an autobiographical resonance (his father was a prosperous market gardener) but suggests the impossibility of a single creative power. The poems are deeply involved in mystical experience and often chart a movement towards joyous communion with the cosmos, in marked contrast to the work of other confessional poets whose bleak world-view usually overwhelms the potential for a vigorous appreciation of life. Unlike both Berryman and Lowell, Roethke did not dread his manic episodes but seemed to welcome them as a source of creative renewal. His poetry engages with deeply personal matters while seldom revealing the details of his life, since his use of the child's perspective and his recourse to folk tale and nursery rhyme allow him to broach painful topics within a mythologizing framework.

As the 'greenhouse' poems suggest, Roethke's schemes of imagery are vital to his work and are closely connected to the journey which it enacts, as in the poem 'Cuttings (later)': 'I can hear, underground, that sucking and sobbing, / In my veins, in my bones, I feel it, – / . . . / I quail, lean to beginnings, sheath-wet'. The roots of the plant become the roots of life itself, the primal beginnings to which the poet must return in his search for self. Notable also here is the attention to detail, the microscopic rendering of the natural world which tacitly evokes Roethke's scrutiny of his own inner life. This kind of scrutiny had important formal implications too, and the movement towards a freer verse style did not imply a loss of attention to poetic form: 'If we concern ourselves with more primitive effects in poetry', Roethke argued, 'we come inevitably to the consideration . . . of verse that is closer to prose. . . . The writer must keep his eye on the object, and his rhythm must move as his mind moves' (Roethke, 1965, p. 181). In the most accomplished of Roethke's work, the reader is brought on the journey with him, one which is both mental and emotional:

> Light traveled over the wide field;
> Stayed.
> The weeds stopped swinging.
> The mind moved, not alone,
> Through the clean air, in the silence.
>
> > Was it light?
> > Was it light within?
> > Was it light within light?
> > Stillness becoming alive,
> > Yet still?
> A lively understandable spirit
> Once entertained you.
> It will come again.
> Be still.
> Wait.
> ('The Lost Son')

Sylvia Plath (1932–63), the youngest and most controversial of this confessional group, was significantly influenced by Roethke in style, in subject matter and in her willingness to embrace mental illness as the inspiration for great art. Though younger than the other poets of the group she died before them and anticipated their own fate in many cases. Plath's legacy is hard to assess; she has attracted legions of imitators and her death has been read by feminists as evidence of a female talent destroyed by male oppression. The question of gender is certainly relevant to Plath's work, both in her exploration of familial and sexual relationships and in her concern with the roles of daughter, wife, mother. Her life, as well as her poetry, reflects this concern and rather than representing her traumas unmediated in her work, she to some extent used poetry to overcome or reconstruct relationships which in reality caused her pain and confusion. Always anxious for success and approval, Plath's relationship with her mother was particularly fraught with the difficulties inherent in maintaining a pretence of personal fulfilment and academic excellence during periods of inner turmoil and severe disappointment. Only in her poetry, and then only late in her career, could Plath allow the extremity of her troubled feelings to surface.

In spite of the emotional intensity of Plath's last collection, the posthumously published *Ariel* (1965), which was written in the final year of her life as she struggled with a broken marriage and the care of her two young children, a strong case can be made for the importance of history in this young poet's work. It is a case, however, which polarizes critics: does Plath use the individual life to explore parallels with history, or does she plunder history in order to clarify – or justify – her own private difficulties? The poem 'Daddy' is the one which focuses these issues most clearly: its sustained use of Nazi imagery is certainly uncomfortable for the reader and is fitted together in such a jumbled and at times contradictory way as to be the cause of formal, as well as ethical, dismay. Plath herself, keen to emphasize the public role of the poet, has put this aesthetic decision into context thus:

> I believe that one should be able to control and manipulate experiences, even the most terrifying – like madness, being tortured . . . with an informed and intelligent mind. I think that personal experience shouldn't be a kind of shut box and mirror-looking narcissistic experience. I believe it should be generally relevant, to such things as Hiroshima and Dachau, and so on. (Lane, 1979, p. 35)

So the personal and the public are not merely paralleled in her work but are intermingled in more complex ways. In spite of the estrangement of the individual from public meaning during this period and the repeated rendering of this predicament by other confessional poets, the individual in Plath's work is often an explicit part of history, simultaneously embodying its key concerns and struggling against its apparent omnipotence. What has been termed Plath's obsession with victimhood, then, is not her concern alone, but a crucial preoccupation of the modern sensibility.

The issue of Plath's suicide, of whether dying *is* an art she does exceptionally well, is the source of much of the attention she has attracted and a cause of concern among critics. As Robert Lowell comments in a letter to M. L. Rosenthal: 'Maybe, it's an irrelevant accident that she actually carried out the death she predicted . . . but somehow her death is part of the imaginative risk' (Rosenthal, 1967, p. 68). In describing the genesis and writing of this final collection, however, Plath emphasized the ordered nature of her art, both in terms of setting and arrangement and in an unbroadcast radio interview offered concise and rational comments on her most disturbing and highly wrought poems. Of 'Lady Lazarus' she said: 'The speaker is a woman who has the great and terrible gift of being reborn. The only trouble is, she has to die first. She is the phoenix, the libertarian spirit, what you will. She is also just a good, plain, very resourceful woman' (Rosenthal, 1967, p. 82).

> Dying
> Is an art, like everything else.
> I do it exceptionally well.
>
> I do it so it feels like hell.
> I do it so it feels real.
> I guess you could say I've a call.

Once again process is highlighted and the artificiality of the natural act is pursued in the self-consciously colloquial phrasing here. There is nothing casual about Plath's art at this point, yet in the extremity of her final months she managed to combine emotional tension with a remarkable clarity of purpose.

Plath's last poems, which she claimed were intended 'for the ear, not the eye', 'poems written out loud' (Rosenthal, 1967, p. 88), far outstripped in intensity and in technical achievement the work of Anne Sexton (1928–74). Sexton's art was always more dependent upon her mental illness than was Plath's, or indeed any of the other confessionals. Apart from some poems from her teenage years, she first began writing when in psychoanalysis and this soon flourished in the form of a committed and painstaking art; Sexton worked long hours daily during her most intensely creative periods and would revise poems continually to achieve the effect she desired. With little outside her own life to deeply engage her, she sought stability for her work in particular schemes – fairy-tales, horoscopes, the Psalms – and such striving after form is reflected, though rarely achieved, in the poems themselves. The revelatory style which Sexton preferred worked against containment and her poems, in spite of their intensity, often lack a sustained trajectory.

The immediacy of Sexton's poetry, this desire to render the emotional experiences of her life in intimate detail, makes her perhaps the least historically observant of the confessionals and the flaws that her work exhibits – self-absorption, repetitive themes, overstatement of human truths – are often those which lend weight to the negative criticism levelled at confessional poetry as a whole. Though Sexton rarely manages to transmute the matter of her own life into something universally meaningful, it is clear that she wishes to use it to gain access to hidden emotional territories. If Plath's life-history is appropriated by feminists, in Sexton's case they are attracted by the willingness of her poems to expose taboos of women's experience with unnerving candour. Yet, as Helen Vendler has succinctly observed, 'taboo-breaking is not in itself a poetic task' (Vendler, 1988, p. 301), and many of the aesthetic difficulties which Sexton confronts stem from her insistent and at times indiscriminate exposure of private matters. The voice which she employs to do this is not always recognizably her own, indeed her desire to explore every kind of experience would render this kind of consistency impossible. Voice is of vital importance, however, as the centrality of performance to her reputation affirms, and the poem with which she usually began her readings testifies also to an imaginative use of imagery and to the spirit which kept her writing through a life of continuing emotional and physical pain:

> I have gone out, a possessed witch,
> haunting the black air, braver at night;
> dreaming evil, I have done my hitch
> over the plain houses, light by light:
> lonely thing, twelve-fingered, out of mind.
>   ('Her Kind')

Sexton's popularity is evidence of one kind of cultural importance, yet her inability to connect with America's present or past in more complex ways renders the limitations of her work clearly. Perhaps the most striking thing to observe about her in this context is the persistence of the confessional element in her work. Many other writers adopted these features and transformed or moved beyond them, but Sexton's later work suffered greatly from her entrapment in a limited private world. It is a clear reinforcement of the importance of transition to the confessionals, both as theme and as poetic process, that one of their most distinctive members should be crippled by her own formal and imaginative stasis. In the work of the most impressive and talented of these poets, uncertainty deepens exploration of the human spirit and the merging of private and public worlds provides a moving and enlivening account of cultural change and poetic development; one which helps us to place the work of later American writers in their true context.

BIBLIOGRAPHY

Axelrod, S. (1979). *Robert Lowell: Life and Art*. Princeton, NJ: Princeton University Press.

Brown, D. (1994). *The Poetry of Postmodernity: Anglo/American Encodings*. London: Macmillan.

Eliot, T. S. (1932). *Selected Essays 1917–1932*. London: Faber & Faber.

Emerson, R. W. (1983). *Essays and Lectures*. New York: Literary Classics of America.

Davison, P. (1994). *The Fading Smile: Poets in Boston from Robert Lowell to Sylvia Plath*. London: W. W. Norton.

Gray, R. (1990). *American Poetry of the Twentieth Century*. Essex: Longman.

Haffenden, J. (1980). *John Berryman: A Critical Commentary*. New York: Macmillan.

Howard, R. (1970). *Alone with America: The Art of Poetry in the United States Since 1950*. London: Thames and Hudson.

Kramer, J. (1970). *Allen Ginsberg in America*. New York: Random House.

Lane, G. (1979). *Sylvia Plath: New Views on the Poetry*. London: Johns Hopkins University Press.

McClatchy, J. D. (ed.) (1978). *Anne Sexton: The Artist and Her Critics*. Bloomington: Indiana University Press.

Matterson, S. (1988). *Berryman and Lowell: The Art of Losing*. New Jersey: Barnes and Noble.

Middlebrook, D. W. (1991). *Anne Sexton: A Biography*. Boston: Houghton Mifflin.

Mills, R. J., Jr. (1975). *Cry of the Human: Essays on Contemporary American Poetry*. Chicago: University of Illinois Press.

Packard, W. (ed.) (1970). *The Craft of Poetry: Interviews from the New York Quarterly*. New York: Doubleday.

Plath, S. (1977). *Letters Home: Correspondence 1950–1963*. New York: Bantam.

Roethke, T. (1965). *On the Poet and His Craft: Selected Prose of Theodore Roethke*, R. J. Mills (ed.). Seattle: University of Washington Press.

Rose, J. (1991). *The Haunting of Sylvia Plath*. Cambridge, MA: Harvard University Press.

Rosenthal, M. L. (1967). *The New Poets*. London: Oxford University Press.

Simpson, L. (1978). A *Revolution in Taste: Studies of Dylan Thomas, Allen Ginsberg, Sylvia Plath and Robert Lowell*. New York: Macmillan.

Smith, S. (1982). 'Waist-deep in History: Sylvia Plath'. In *Inviolable Voice: History and Twentieth Century Poetry* (pp. 200–25). Dublin: Gill & Macmillan.

Stiffler, R. (1986). *Theodore Roethke: The Poet and his Critics*. London: American Library Association.

Thurley, G. (1977). *The American Moment: American Poetry in the Mid-Century*. London: Edward Arnold.

Vendler, H. (1988). *The Music of What Happens: Poems, Poets, Critics*. Cambridge, MA: Harvard University Press.

Wolff, G. (1981). *Theodore Roethke*. Boston: Twayne.

16

The Movement

Stephen Regan

In critical studies and literary histories of postwar British poetry, a good deal of discussion has been concerned with the existence – real or imagined – of a group of writers known as the Movement. The common assumption is that the Movement was largely a reaction against the inflated romanticism of the 1940s, a victory of common sense and clarity over obscurity and mystification, of verbal restraint over stylistic excess: in short, the virtues of Philip Larkin over those of Dylan Thomas. Those critics who admire the rationalism of Larkin's verse have been concerned to emphasize the importance of the Movement and its continuing influence in contemporary poetry; some have gone so far as to claim for the Movement a significant place in a tradition of modern poetry – usually dubbed 'the English line' – extending back through Edward Thomas and Thomas Hardy to the poetry of William Wordsworth.

At the same time, there exists a degree of scepticism about the aims and achievements of the Movement. John Press, surveying the poetry of the 1950s, finds the issue unsettling: 'To what extent the Movement was more than a lively journalistic invention is not easy to decide' (Press, 1969, p. 253). Ian Hamilton concludes that the movement was a 'hard-sell' by the literary journals on behalf of a favoured few: 'it was a take-over bid and it brilliantly succeeded' (Hamilton, 1972, p. 71). This critical scepticism is compounded by the reluctance of the writers themselves to acknowledge their membership of a particular group. Philip Larkin, when interviewed by Hamilton, confessed 'no sense at all' of belonging to a movement, and Thom Gunn has said of the Movement: 'I found I was in it before I knew it existed . . . and I have a certain suspicion that it does *not* exist' (Morrison, 1980, p. 4). Elizabeth Jennings was similarly inclined to play down the idea of a movement among a particular generation of postwar poets: 'They may have common aims – but this is something very different from that deliberate practice and promulgation of shared views which a true literary movement implies' (Jennings, 1961, p. 10).

If the Movement did not exist as a coherent literary group, it certainly operated as a significant cultural influence; it was the product of specific views about literature and society, which in turn it helped to establish and disseminate. Those critics who have disputed the idea that the Movement was a well-organized group with a clear and consistent programme of ideas have nevertheless recognized among its alleged participants a shared set of values and assumptions closely related to the moods and conditions of postwar England. Neil Corcoran goes so far as to claim that the preference for traditional forms and methods in Movement poetry was part of a determined effort to rebuild the intellectual culture of the postwar years: 'Syntax, measure and a logic of statement were, in the Movement poem, almost an act of postwar reconstruction: to build the decorous shape of the poem was to provide a defence against barbarism' (Corcoran, 1993, p. 83).

To understand the origins of the Movement it is necessary to return to the autumn of 1954, when the arrival of a new poetic trend was announced in the literary journals. What emerges most forcefully from the early articles and reviews announcing 'the Movement' is not so much a departure from the alleged romanticism of the 1940s, as an awareness of the continuing dominance of W. H. Auden and the poets of the 1930s. In his review article 'Poets of the Fifties' (generally thought to herald the Movement), Anthony Hartley begins by asking 'What do most readers mean when they talk of modern poetry?' He offers the following reply:

> In the eyes of the general reader it is the Thirties that continue to typify the modern movement in verse. . . . Now, however, there are signs that this twenty-year-old domination is coming to an end. New names in the reviews, a fresh atmosphere of controversy, a new spirit of criticism – these are signs that some other group of poets is appearing on the horizon. (Hartley, 1954, p. 260)

At the same time as signalling a shift in direction, the new poetry retains its roots in the work of the 1930s. In Hartley's estimation, 'the return to romanticism which came between was essentially a sport'. Hartley does not consider the new movement to be a school of poets with a specific programme and manifesto, but there is evidence, he argues, 'that the present generation has been sufficiently affected by common influences and circumstances for a not too vague *zeitgeist* to be apparent in their productions' (ibid.). 'Poets of the Fifties' is perhaps the earliest and the most useful description of the Movement as it was perceived in its own time.

Hartley goes some way towards explaining the characteristic features of the new poetry: 'It might roughly be described as "dissenting" and non-conformist, cool, scientific and analytical . . . the poetic equivalent of liberal, dissenting England' (ibid.). It is here that a Movement ideology is first identified. The poetry of Philip Larkin is only briefly mentioned, along with the work of John Wain, Donald Davie, Kingsley Amis and Thom Gunn, but already a group personality is seen to exist. Stylistically, these writers share an avoidance of rhetoric, an austere tone and a colloquial idiom. The importance of Hartley's early review is that it acknowledges the political and cultural contours of a dominant literary tendency in postwar England. The 'liberalism' to which Hartley refers can be traced back to the kind of liberal idealism espoused by E. M. Forster in the early part of the twentieth century: 'A liberalism distrustful of too much fanaticism, austere and sceptical. A liberalism egalitarian and anti-aristocratic. A liberalism profoundly opposed to fashion in the metropolitan sense of the word' (ibid.). This remains one of the best descriptions of Movement ideology.

Hartley's confident remark that 'we are now in the presence of the only considerable movement in English poetry since the Thirties' (ibid., p. 261) is echoed in the title of a later *Spectator* article, 'In the Movement', by its editor J. D. Scott. Scott agrees that 'the English literary scene' has not been transformed in such a way since the 1930s, and contrasts the social, political and moral consciousness of that age with the seeming disengagement of the 1950s. Once again, the Movement is defined in terms of a lost idealism and in terms of a vigilant readjustment to an unsettled postwar England: 'The Movement, as well as being anti-phoney, is anti-wet; sceptical, robust, ironic, prepared to be as comfortable as possible in a wicked, commercial, threatened world which doesn't look, anyway, as if it's going to be changed much by a couple of handfuls of young English writers' (Scott, 1954, p. 400).

It was the appearance of poems by a particular group of writers in several anthologies of the 1950s which gave further impetus to the idea of a movement in English poetry. The editors of *Springtime: An Anthology of Young Poets and Writers* (1953) speak in narrowly technical terms of a poetry which is 'going through a period of consolidation and simplification . . . of reaction against experiment for its own sake', and they further claim that their chosen contributors are 'poets of an analytical habit of mind, whose aim is to clarify, by stating plainly, typical complex situations' (Fraser and Fletcher, 1953, pp. 7–10). The same emphasis on 'honesty of thought and feeling and clarity of expression' can be found in D. J. Enright's introduction to *Poets of the 1950s: An Anthology of New English Verse*, but Enright is clearly alert to the cultural conditions that have prompted this kind of poetic response. Echoing the *Spectator* articles, Enright acknowledges 'a new spirit stirring in contemporary English poetry' (Enright, 1955, p. 15). He presents his anthology *not* as the work of a movement, however, but as a selection of poems by individual writers, some of whom share common attitudes. Like the *Spectator* he stresses the distinction between the political commitment that characterized the poetry of the 1930s and the desired neutrality of the 1950s. Enright offers little explanation for this seeming retreat from political commitment, but his introduction nevertheless registers the disenchantment and general uncertainty of a postwar generation of writers.

The liberal humanist perspective identified by Hartley is given further clarification by Enright, who speaks of the need to 'resuscitate the idea of the dignity of the human individual' and of the way in which 'private responsibility' sometimes outweighs 'social responsibility' (Enright, 1955, pp. 13–14). Despite Enright's disclaimers about a group identity, his poets seem to share a common set of values and assumptions: a vigilant individualism, a careful distancing of the private from the public, and a cautious avoidance of political commitment. Enright's poets are 'moderate': they exemplify 'chastened common sense' and they eschew obscurity 'because they find it unnecessary'. Enright demands from his contemporaries 'a fairly tough intelligence and an unwillingness to be deceived', and in doing so he suggests how closely the poetic ideals of the time were linked to the general scepticism that prevailed in postwar England (ibid., p. 13). In listing these 'virtues' Enright felicitously alludes to the title of Philip Larkin's 1955 volume of poems, *The Less Deceived*.

Had Enright's anthology been more widely distributed, the political and cultural significance of the Movement poets and their anxious relationship with the poetry of the 1930s might have been better understood by a later generation of readers and writers. As it happened, Enright's anthology probably received less attention than it deserved. Instead, the anthology which had the greatest impact and which was generally held to be most representative of the Movement was Robert Conquest's *New Lines* (1956). It was Conquest's introduction to the anthology which was largely responsible for encouraging the idea of a reaction against the excesses of 1940s romanticism. The poets of that decade, he argues, were 'encouraged to produce diffuse and sentimental verbiage', while the new generation holds to 'a rational structure and comprehensible language' (Conquest, 1956, pp. xiv–xv). Conquest shows little concern for the social and historical circumstances of postwar England and instead resorts to dubious cultural metaphors of sickness and health. The 1940s attitude to poetry induced a 'sort of corruption'; it led to 'a rapid collapse of public taste, from which we have not yet recovered'. The poetry of the 1950s, however, represents 'a new and healthy general standpoint . . . the restoration of a sound and fruitful attitude to poetry' (ibid., pp. xii–xiv). Conquest's bombastic description of the new poetry is frequently cited as a manifesto for the Movement poets:

> If one had briefly to distinguish this poetry of the fifties from its predecessors, I believe the most important general point would be that it submits to no great systems of theoretical constructs nor agglomerations of unconscious commands. It is free from both mystical and logical compulsions and – like modern philosophy – is empirical in its attitude to all that comes. This reverence for the real person or event is, indeed, a part of the general intellectual ambience (in so far as that is not blind or retrogressive) of our time. (Ibid., pp. xiv–xv)

What Conquest seems to be saying here is that the poetry of the 1950s is characterized chiefly by its anti-dogmatic ideals, by a kind of aesthetic purity and philosophical detachment. There is an apparent disregard for the poetry of the 1930s in his jibe at 'theoretical constructs', but the principal target would seem to be Dylan Thomas. Conquest assumes that poetry can maintain a 'free' and neutral stance, and that 'empiricism' is, in itself, a guarantee of this neutrality. Even though Conquest defines the new poetry in negative terms – that is, largely in terms of what it is *not* – he cannot conceal the problems of a poetic theory that refuses to recognize its own 'theoretical constructs' and which condemns 'ideology' in the very moment of declaring its own interest and allegiances. A preoccupation with what is 'real' and 'honest' becomes a way of disguising those interests, of positing something 'authentic' against what is merely 'theoretical' and 'false'. These are the problems of a good deal of so-called Movement poetry and they were partly responsible for its eventual demise. The pose of neutrality and objectivity could not be sustained indefinitely; the tensions and conflicts of postwar England continued to disturb the equanimity of such poetry, and what began as something separate and detached was either made to look increasingly defensive and withdrawn, or pushed towards a point of declaration. In the case of Philip Larkin, the fastidious restraint of *The Less Deceived* gradually gave way to a much more confrontational and openly polemical writing, especially in *High Windows*.

Conquest has since strongly denied the charge of having created a Movement manifesto, but what his anthology clearly shows, especially when read in conjunction with Enright's similar offering, is that unmistakable similarities of style and outlook existed among the rising generation of 1950s poets. This is certainly the opinion of Samuel Hynes, writing in the *Times Literary Supplement* in 1980: 'The poems resemble each other enough to suggest that a movement did in fact exist. And the prefaces that the contributors wrote for *Poets of the 1950s* confirm that view: these poets had a programme, they knew what they were for and against' (Hynes, 1980, p. 699). A resemblance in attitudes and techniques is certainly in evidence in much of the Movement poetry that was anthologized in the 1950s and 1960s, and it is useful to compare such poems as Larkin's 'Deceptions' and Amis's 'Alternatives', or Davie's 'A Christening' and Larkin's 'The Whitsun Weddings'. The use of wit and irony is a prominent feature, and this often produces a poetry that seems defensive and guarded. While much of this poetry strives for clarity and intelligibility, it can at times appear tame and trivial.

The prevailing tone of Movement poetry is urbane and academic, and many of the anthologized pieces are too neatly prescriptive or look like pieces of versified literary criticism. Some of the titles provide an indication of a 'bookish' or 'middlebrow' attitude: Kingsley Amis's 'A Bookshop Idyll', D. J. Enright's 'The Verb to Think', Donald Davie's 'Rejoinder to a Critic' and 'Too Late for Satire', and John Wain's 'Reason for not Writing Orthodox Nature Poetry' and 'Poem Without a Main Verb'. One of the shortcomings of Movement poetry is its tendency to make a virtue out of the civilized sensibility, to value intellectual detachment and 'urbanity' above all else. This cool, ironic aloofness can be mildly shocking, as in Amis's 'Shitty', but more often than not it leads to a shallow denial of human potential for change and development, as in Davie's 'A Christening', with its cynical insistence: 'What we do best is breed'. Perhaps the most significant 'manifesto' within Movement poetry is Davie's 'Remembering the Thirties', which in many ways epitomizes the cautious outlook of the Cold War years in its declaration that 'A neutral tone is nowadays preferred'. What the poem demonstrates most forcefully, however, is that the example of Auden and his contemporaries continued to have a powerful impression upon the postwar generation of writers and could never be simply forgotten.

It is also the case, however, that Movement poetry probably displays far more diversity and daring than subsequent critical accounts have given it credit for. Literary history has too readily equated the work of the Movement with parochialism and provincialism. Looking back on Conquest's anthology is to be reminded of the cosmopolitan, international interests of several contributors. Larkin appears resolutely English, but the *New Lines* volume also contains 'Afternoon in Florence' and 'Piazza San Marco' by Elizabeth Jennings; 'Lerici' by Thom Gunn; 'Evening in the Khamsin' and 'Baie des Anges, Nice' by D. J. Enright; 'Nantucket' and 'Near Jakobselv' by Robert Conquest; and 'Woodpigeons at Raheny' by Donald Davie. Davie's *Purity of Diction in English Verse* (1952) is often thought to have set the standard for a neo-Augustan discipline in Movement poetry, promoting a particular kind of English traditional lyricism, but this aspect of Davie's critical endeavours needs to be set against his intense and prolonged engagement with the poetry of Ezra Pound and with post-Poundian poetics in the United States. It is certainly the case that critical appraisals of Movement poetry have tended to repeat the formulas and generalizations associated with 1950s and 1960s anthologies rather than exploring the extent to which the work confounds those familiar summaries.

One of the earliest appraisals of Movement poetry can be found in *Rule and Energy* by John Press (1963). Although Press gives little credence to the publicity surrounding the Movement in the mid-1950s, he nevertheless ventures a critique of its aims and achievements. The new poets 'advance no systematic theory of poetry and offer no rigid set of dogmatic beliefs', but it is possible, Press claims, to summarize the main characteristics of their work:

> They all display a cautious scepticism, favour an empirical attitude, speak in carefully measured accents, and examine a problem with an alert wariness. . . . All of these poets, mistrusting or ignoring the legacy of the Romantics and aiming at colloquial ease, decorum, shapeliness, elegance, are trying to bring back into the currency of the language the precision, the snap, the gravity, the decisive, clinching finality which have been lost since the late Augustan age. (Ibid., pp. 45–6)

Here, Press is referring not just to a reaction against the 'neo-Romanticism' of the 1940s but to the whole trend of English poetry since the early nineteenth century. The Movement poets, in this respect, are seen to represent a new 'classicism' in English poetry. Yet it is clear throughout *Rule and Energy* that this distrust of inflated rhetoric and large emotional gestures is only one aspect of a much broader postwar tendency. The most striking characteristic feature of English poetry in these years, as Press insists at the outset of the book, is 'the general retreat from direct comment on or involvement with any political or social doctrine'. This is particularly noticeable, he adds, 'if we contrast the verse of the past two decades with that of the 1930s' (ibid., p. 5). What disturbs Press is the peculiar passivity of postwar poetry. He speculates that the establishment of the Welfare State may have mitigated some of the more glaring political and social injustices, but continues: 'it is absurd to pretend that in our affluent society a poet can find nothing to arouse his compassion or his savage indignation' (ibid., p. 11). The importance of this statement is that it very accurately identifies the 'neutral tone' of the new poetry and seeks to explain it in terms of its historical context. In 1962, however, Philip Larkin had not yet published *The Whitsun Weddings* and Press was able to offer only a brief and tentative analysis of Larkin's work. Similarly, D. J. Enright's work was to develop in ways that could hardly have been expected in the late 1950s and early 1960s.

In 1980 Blake Morrison produced the first full-length study of the Movement, proposing that it was 'a literary group of considerable importance', as central to the 1950s as 'the Auden generation' was to the 1930s. Morrison asks a number of crucially revealing questions: 'Did the writers know each other? Is there any evidence of mutual admiration, mutual influence, or collaboration? Did the writers come from the same social background? Did they have similar political beliefs? Did they intend to write for the same kind of audience? Was there a common belief about the direction which contemporary literature should take?' (Morrison, 1980, pp. 5–6). To all of these questions Morrison responds positively, and he goes on to argue decisively and persuasively that despite some obvious divisions and contradictions, 'for a time at least, there was considerable agreement and interaction, and that out of these was established a Movement consensus'. 'It is even possible', he suggests, 'to talk of a Movement "ideology" – an identifiable "line" on sex, religion, politics' (ibid., pp. 6, 9). In addition, Morrison offers some illuminating contextual readings of Larkin's poetry (he considers *The Whitsun Weddings* as a Movement collection) and further demonstrates how Larkin 'continued to defend and develop principles central to the Movement programme' (Morrison, 1980, p. 8).

The great strength of Morrison's book lies in its acute analysis of class and culture in the postwar years. What was especially significant, Morrison believes, is that Movement writers were identified by their contemporaries with a spirit of change in postwar British society and were thought to be representative of shifts in power and social structure. They were seen, that is, to have benefited from the new opportunities made available to the lower-middle and working classes and were therefore regarded by some members of the ruling class as a threat to the old order. Evelyn Waugh spoke of 'a new wave of philistinism with which we are threatened by these grim young people coming off the assembly lines in their hundreds every year and finding employment as critics, even as poets and novelists', while Somerset Maugham callously dismissed the same people as 'scum':

> They do not go to university to acquire culture, but to get a job, and when they have got one, scamp it. They have no manners, and are woefully unable to deal with any social predicament. Their idea of a celebration is to go to a public house and drink six beers. They are mean, malicious, and envious. (Morrison, 1980, pp. 58–9)

Morrison, however, finds that the Movement writers were very far from rebellious; they were, in many ways, meekly submissive and often given to compromise and conservatism:

> What emerges in the work of the Movement, then, is an uneasy combination of class-consciousness and acceptance of class division; an acute awareness of privilege, but an

eventual submission to the structure which makes it possible. . . . As spokesmen for the
new self-proclaimed lower-middle-class intelligentsia, the Movement was forced into
an ambivalent position; on the one hand opposed to the 'old order'; on the other hand
indebted to, and respectful towards, its institutions. (Ibid., pp. 74–5)

Morrison attributes this ambivalence to the fact that most of the Movement poets
were scholarship boys in centres of learning still largely dominated by the upper-
middle class and therefore subject to pressures to understate social difference. Larkin
refers to this process in the introduction to his novel *Jill*, where he admits that in
Oxford in 1940 'our impulse was still to minimize social differences rather than exag-
gerate them' (Larkin, 1983, p. 17). Furthermore, the influence of thinkers like F. R.
Leavis, especially in such subjects as English, undoubtedly helped to promote the kind
of conformity and spirit of national unity that Morrison detects.

Despite its mood of dissent and its anti-establishment attitude, the Movement
offered only 'a token rebellion', and did not attempt to change the prevailing social
structure. The ambivalence of Movement politics becomes particularly evident in the
immediate context of the postwar years and manifests itself in a wavering liberal
attitude towards the changing balance of power in the new society. The Movement
poets were clearly influenced by the democratic idealism that accompanied the Labour
victory of 1945, however short-lived that spirit of optimism might have been, and
yet most of them were distrustful of egalitarian political ideals and remained deeply
suspicious of radical change. Blake Morrison diagnoses the Movement predicament
very astutely and shows how it operates in their poetry. Donald Davie's poem 'The
Garden Party', for instance, seems at first sight to be severely critical of both class
division and capitalism, yet the speaker of the poem has benefited too well from the
current social structure to wish to change it. The poem ends in compromise, seeming
to offer a critique of existing social arrangements but carefully maintaining a sense
of distance and neutrality. The Movement, then, for all its initial anti-establishment
fervour, proved to be politically inoffensive. In contrast to the poets of the 1930s,
many of whom were upper-middle-class political activists, the poets of the 1950s were
lower-middle class and politically neutral.

Given this ambivalence in politics, it is not surprising to discover in the work of
Movement writers a sense of nostalgia and regret in the face of Britain's inevitable
decline as a world power. Neil Corcoran claims that 'Some of the most interesting
poetry of the Movement in the 1950s may be read as inscribed with the sense –
anxious, distressed, nostalgic, stoic – of a great national termination and reorientation' (Corcoran, 1993, p. 83). Morrison, too, acknowledges the impact of the end of
empire on Movement poetry and shows how a seemingly innocent lyric poem like
Philip Larkin's 'At Grass' might be read within this context. He claims that the reason
'At Grass' became one of the most popular postwar poems is that 'by allowing the
horses to symbolize loss of power, Larkin manages to tap nostalgia for a past "glory
that was England"'. Accordingly, Morrison identifies 'At Grass' as 'a poem of post-
imperial *tristesse*' (Morrison, 1980, p. 82).

What is particularly impressive about Morrison's thesis is that it demonstrates how the Movement's social and political ambivalence extends into the formal and structural texture of the poetry in terms of hesitations, qualifications and conversational asides. In fact the whole sense of an audience in Movement poetry, Morrison argues, is shaped by questions of socio-political identity, especially by the difficulty of appealing to an academic elite and at the same time being responsible to the general public in a modern democracy. Morrison explains the alleged 'anti-romanticism' of the Movement not as a narrow literary response to the work of Dylan Thomas but as a careful strategy in a Britain more intent on pursuing communal and egalitarian ideals than it had been before the Second World War. In the new Welfare State democracy this amounted to an admission that the poet was not 'a mystic or visionary removed from society' but a 'responsible citizen responsibly employed' (ibid., p. 178).

Further confirmation of the Movement's political caution can be found in Robert Hewison's well-documented account of the postwar years, *In Anger: Culture in the Cold War 1945–60* (1981). Rather comically, Hewison reminds us that 'the movement did not exist' (it was, he believes, an effective piece of stage management), but he himself can hardly avoid using the label (Hewison, 1981, p. 86). His essential point is that the attitudes of the Movement poets reflect the restrictive conditions of the Cold War. In other words, the neutrality, caution and self-limitation of these writers belong to the mood of fear and suspicion created by the continuing opposition among the military and diplomatic forces of East and West after 1945:

> The Cold War tended to freeze public attitudes, and counselled silence about the private ones. It recommended a guarded private life, in which only small gestures were possible, gestures chiefly about the difficulty of making a gesture. Hence the concern of the Movement poets with the problems of perception and expression. (Ibid., p. 122)

As Hewison points out, *literary* history alone does not provide an adequate explanation for what prompted the Movement and determined the kind of poetry it stood for. It was part of a postwar social formation where heightened rhetoric and inflated emotion were likely to be regarded with suspicion.

Most critics writing on the work of Philip Larkin have tended to acknowledge the influence of the Movement on both his poetry and his fiction, while insisting that Larkin ultimately leaves the Movement consensus well behind. The early poetry, in particular, clearly coincides with the Movement ideology described in this chapter, especially in its struggle for neutral ground. The creation of a self-effacing, 'modest' discourse and a self-deprecating, ironic persona is immediately apparent in the poems of *The Less Deceived*; so too is a distrust of large, idealistic gestures and a preference for English provincial settings over those of 'abroad'. Along with the anti-metropolitan and anti-cosmopolitan instincts in Larkin's poetry, there is a sedulous avoidance of any direct treatment of recent history. This does not mean, however, that the poems themselves somehow 'transcend' history. Blake Morrison has shown how well a poem like 'Church Going' fits the Movement 'programme' by carefully balancing agnostic dissent with a susceptibility to tradition and belief. The poem manages to be both reverent and irreverent. In keeping with Movement preferences, 'Church Going' has a traditional iambic structure and a lucid, rational argument; its speaker is presented as an ordinary, fallible and clumsy individual. It is a poem that testifies to the persistence of both the English church and an English poetic tradition (Morrison, 1980, pp. 225–37).

There are, of course, important ways in which Larkin's poetry departs from Movement principles, and these tendencies were evident even before the Movement dissolved into divergent lines. Morrison claims that Larkin is much more astute than his peers in his sense of audience and perhaps more sympathetically attuned to the Romantic influences the Movement poetry professed to scorn. Samuel Hynes in reviewing Morrison's book claims that Larkin's work is more 'expansive' and more 'wide-ranging' than that of other Movement poets (Hynes, 1980, p. 699). Many critics are convinced that Larkin is a 'better' poet than Amis, Wain, Enright and Davie without being entirely sure why. Implicit in their evaluation is a belief that Larkin's poetry, in contrast with the work of other 'Movement' writers, not only exemplifies a deeper imaginative apprehension of social experience and its contradictions, but also exhibits a far greater range of formal and stylistic devices and a more profound sense of the linguistic and aesthetic possibilities of modern colloquial English.

In 1963 Robert Conquest published a second anthology of contemporary poetry, *New Lines II*, in which he once again paid tribute to the persistence and variety of 'the central current of English verse'. Modernist innovations such as might be found in the poetry of Ezra Pound were, for Conquest, little more than 'peripheral additions to the main tradition of English poetry'. Acknowledging the work of Philip Larkin as an essential continuation of this tradition, Conquest continued in a vein of strident anti-modernism:

> One even comes across the impudent assertion that English poets were unaware of the existence of the darker elements in the human personality, and of large-scale suffering, until psychoanalysts and world wars drew attention to them, and this is compounded with transparently spurious logic, by the notion that the way to cope with these forces is to abandon sanity and hope. (Conquest, 1963, pp. xiii–xiv)

Without being explicit about the matter, Conquest was responding to a rival anthology, *The New Poetry* (1962), in which Alfred Alvarez had strongly criticized the work of the Movement (and Larkin in particular) for failing to deal with the full range of human experience. The obvious irritation in Conquest's rejoinder is an indication of the profound impact that Alvarez had made on contemporary literary criticism. By throwing 'tradition' and 'experiment' into sharp relief, *The New Poetry* undoubtedly stimulated one of the liveliest debates in the history of twentieth-century poetry. Alvarez also helped to shape a climate of opinion in which the poetry of Ted Hughes, Sylvia Plath and others – a poetry seemingly at odds with the work of the Movement – might flourish. By 1962, however, any sense of a coherent Movement project had largely dissolved and the writers who were briefly identified with it had already gone their separate ways.

BIBLIOGRAPHY

Alvarez, A. (ed.) (1962). *The New Poetry.* Harmondsworth: Penguin.

Conquest, Robert (ed.) (1956). *New Lines: An Anthology.* London: Macmillan.

Conquest, Robert (ed.) (1963). *New Lines – II: An Anthology.* London: Macmillan.

Corcoran, Neil (1993). *English Poetry Since 1940.* London: Longman.

Davie, Donald (1952). *Purity of Diction in English Verse.* London: Chatto and Windus.

Enright, D. J. (ed.) (1955). *Poets of the 1950s: An Anthology of New English Verse.* Tokyo: Kenkyusha.

Fraser, G. S. and Ian Fletcher (eds) (1953). *Springtime: An Anthology of Young Poets and Writers.* London: Peter Owen.

Hamilton, Ian (1972). 'The Making of the Movement.' In Michael Schmidt and Grevel Lindop (eds), *British Poetry Since 1960: A Critical Survey* (pp. 70–3). Oxford: Carcanet.

Hartley, Anthony (1954). 'Poets of the Fifties.' *Spectator*, 27 August, pp. 260–1.

Hewison, Robert (1981). *In Anger: Culture in the Cold War 1945–60.* London: Weidenfeld and Nicolson.

Hynes, Samuel (1980). 'Sweeping the Empty Stage.' *Times Literary Supplement*, 20 June, p. 699.

Jennings, Elizabeth (1961). *An Anthology of Modern Verse 1940–1960.* London: Methuen.

Larkin, Philip (1983). *Jill.* London: Faber and Faber.

Morrison, Blake (1980). *The Movement: English Poetry and Fiction of the 1950s.* Oxford: Oxford University Press, 1980.

Press, John (1963). *Rule And Energy: Trends in British Poetry Since the Second World War.* London: Oxford University Press.

Press, John (1969). *A Map of Modern English Verse.* Oxford: Oxford University Press.

Scott, J. D. (1954). 'In the Movement.' *Spectator*, 1 October, pp. 399–400.

17

Language Poetry

Simon Perril

'Language writing' or 'Language poetry' emerged in the early 1970s with the appearance of magazines such as *This*, edited by Robert Grenier and Barrett Watten, *Hills*, edited by Bob Perelman, and *L=A=N=G=U=A=G=E* edited by Bruce Andrews and Charles Bernstein. The latter was a solely critical journal that ran from 1978 to 1981 producing a myriad of poetics essays and 'non-normative' reviews that revealed a body of contributors extremely conversant with Marxist and poststructuralist philosophy.

'The Difference is Spreading': Stein

A burgeoning generation of 'language-centred' writers is seen as having offered a materialist critique of the expressivist tendencies of the New American poetry as encapsulated by Robert Grenier's famous pronouncement 'I HATE SPEECH' in the first issue of *This* in 1971. As much as stylistic allegiances, Language poets like Watten, Ron Silliman and Lyn Hejinian are as likely to cite socio-political context as occasioning the formation of the extensive network of publishing, collaboration and reading spaces that have been grouped together under the umbrella term Language poetry. Hejinian explains that the Language generation was emerging from the aftermath of the Vietnam War, and was bonded by exposure to the 'disguised irrationality' of institutions:

> by some coincidence, we all individually had begun to consider language itself as an institution of sorts, determining reasons, and we had individually begun to explore the implications of that. (Hejinian, 1989, p. 34)

For this generation, Olson's heroic 'Field Composition' demanded serious scrutiny. Witnessing the failed war in Indochina and the end of the expansionist optimism underpinning the New American poetry (Silliman, 1986, p. 484), they were particularly sensitive to the masked realities of Olson's mythic poetics of discovery. Of course, the 'SPACE' that Olson saw as an American heritage was populated by natives, and the new continent was not 'discovered' so much as brutally colonized. This is a preoccupation of Susan Howe's work. Howe shares Olson's interest in the use of historical documents within poetry, and has learnt from his projectivist exploration of the use of the typewriter to exploit the space of the page. And yet, countering Olson's rhetoric of discovery, Howe is interested in the American continent as it was necessarily constructed by the emigrants to New England in the Great Migration. Howe is fascinated by the way that the unnerving 'Statelessness' of the American wilderness forced the settlers to fall back on their being united through scripture. As the essay 'Encloser' suggests, the crossing of the ocean was also a leap into the recently translated vernacular Bible, and the myth of themselves as the promised people setting out for a 'virgin garden pre-established for them by the Author and Finisher of creation' (Bernstein, 1993, p. 181). If Olson fetishizes openness, Howe attends to the fear provoked by the prospect of such an experience, and how it forced the emigrants into 'God's Plot' as a protective shield enabling them 'to survive the threat of openness' (ibid., p. 190). Therefore, the experience of the new terrain was mediated by a text:

> Somewhere on the passage they had to convince themselves that the land was holy and that they were on a mission from God as laid down in the Old Testament. These emigrants saw the land through a book. A sacred book. Divinity was tangled in place. *They* were a new typology. They were inside the story. (Ibid.)

In Howe's work the page is always a territory whose white expanse is subject to settlement/invasion by the printed word. She is fascinated by history as discourse; a text marred by what is excluded from it – particularly women and the natives written out of the American story by the myth of the discovery of a virgin land. As she states in the opening text in *The Europe of Trusts*: 'I wish I could tenderly lift from the dark side of history, voices that are anonymous, slighted – inarticulate' (Howe, 1990, p. 14). It is significant that this agenda is carefully acknowledged as a 'wish'; Howe is well aware of the oxymoronic task of voicing the silent, and of articulating the inarticulate.

Olson privileged etymology and the archeological dig into the word's history that would eventually reach the world. This tenet again demanded scrutiny: Language poets began writing in an intellectual climate buzzing with the ideas of continental 'theory' that precisely problematized the 'naturalness' of the relationship between language and world. Hejinian's 'The Rejection of Closure' rejects the assertion that 'FORM IS NEVER MORE THAN AN EXTENSION OF CONTENT' (Olson, 1997, p. 240) and instead proposes celebrating an open text that is not organically inclusive of the world, but is 'formally differentiating' (Perelman, 1985, p. 271). As such she imagines no equal fit between words and things, but sees the very inequality as a necessary gap that pays homage to the 'incomplete' vastness of the world. Instead of Projective verse's bid to blur the distinction between form and content, Hejinian wants to highlight it:

> For me, a central activity of poetic language is formal. In being formal, in making form distinct, it opens – makes variousness and multiplicity and possibility articulate and clear. While failing in the attempt to match the world, we discover structure, distinction, the integrity and separateness of things. (Ibid., p. 285)

The Modernist Gertrude Stein's influence is strongly felt by Language poets, particularly because of its radical upsetting of just the conventions of what proximity words have to things that so concerned Hejinian. *L=A=N=G=U=A=G=E* asked a number of their contributors to respond to three short sections from Stein's 1914 landmark *Tender Buttons*, using it as an exercise in encouraging methods of reading attentive not just to *what* the poems might mean, but to *how* they might do so (Andrews and Bernstein, 1984, pp. 195–207). In Stein's work 'things take place inside the writing, are perceived there, not elsewhere, outside it' (Hejinian, 1986, p. 133). This maintenance of readerly attention at the level of the language itself became a unifying preoccupation of Language writing.

Naturalness and the Illusion of Transparency

What Language writing finds attractive about Stein is her refusal to make her work transparently refer to the world outside of the words. Language poetry's avant-garde lineage is evident in its scrutiny of the naturalness of Realism. Realism, in this instance, refers to the uncomplicated belief that the words on the page offer a transparent window onto the world of everyday life. Such continuity in ideas can be seen in 'The Pacifica Interview' Andrews and Bernstein gave in 1981, which was not subsequently reprinted in *The L=A=N=G=U=A=G=E Book*. Bernstein is adamant about 'seeing language not as a transparency, not as something which simply dissolves as you get a picture of the world in focus, so that, in reading a text, you are hardly aware of the language at all' (unpaginated). What is most contentious in Language writing is some of the political conclusions drawn from a sense of what motivates the promotion of such transparency, and consequently also the political implications awarded to the activity of 'resisting' it. There has been much debate over the extent to which Language writing is 'non-referential'; particularly over whether such a condition for language is possible, or even desirable. Michael Greer uses an example from Bruce Andrews's 'Tizzy Boost' to illustrate how Language writing 'challenges our "shock-proof faith" in the communicability of meaning':

> Cash downy
>   stricture wish looks ratty, the bluff
> basically buried due to games, drugs & pesticides

cashiered glory blood convicted to distance
shockproof faith
(Greer, 1991, p. 153)

How non-referential is this writing? Greer's reading of its challenge forces him back on a phrase from the poem itself, 'shockproof faith', making the poem in some way self-referential. But how accurate is it to claim also that 'we find ourselves unable to construct a single "frame" or "context" capable of resolving individual phrases into a larger, referential whole'? (ibid.). This text is certainly a good example of the way such writing thickens the texture of words into 'material', so as to challenge faith in the transparency of language. And yet this does not necessarily make it non-referential. The materiality on offer can actually be read as a playfully satirical reference to consumer society. 'Cash downy' gives us not only connotations of the cuddly, fetishistic allure of money; but also puns on the cushioning effects of the 'special offer' reduction. The materiality on offer here is in some way literalized by association with a society of the spectacle in which our dreams have become limited to the things that money can buy: commodities. The recognition of such a 'bluff' certainly involves an acknowledgement that 'stricture wish looks ratty': that such a restriction of our horizons makes our hopes cheap and infested. The poem itself is rather 'ratty' as it is seemingly driven by irritation and anger. It functions by punning on the ideolect of the culture it is seemingly attacking. The title can function as a frame or context: to be in a 'tizzy' is to be in a state of nervous agitation, maybe even to the extent of throwing a tantrum. The 'boost' is suitably overdetermined: does it imply that the poem is an inoculating booster – a protective blast? Or is it an acknowledgement of the poem's increase and intensification of the very forces it might claim to be resisting, and therefore a tantrum fuelled by a sense of complicity? Certainly the tension between symptom and critique in Language writing has been noted (Perelman, 1996). But how accurate is this reading of Andrews's poem? In the sense that it is driven by close attention to the words as such, and the web of connotations they weave, then it is following Language writing's agenda for encouraging readerly production. However, how much of this production is actually 'my own'? Such a question opens up an important preoccupation Language writing has with the 'construction' of identity and the resulting scepticism of the extent to which language is ever really the province of individual ownership.

Reader/Writer Relations

The preoccupation with the 'referential fallacy', another term used to indicate the illusion of transparency, was also given a political angle. Capitalism, as Silliman expressed it, involves 'an anaesthetic transformation of the perceived tangibility of the word, with corresponding increases in its descriptive and narrative capacities, preconditions for the invention of "realism," the optical illusion of reality in capitalist thought'

(Andrews and Bernstein, 1984, p. 125). In short, capitalism makes us passive con-
sumers of language as a commodity fetishized for its illusion of transparency. In
response, Andrews and Bernstein call for a poetry that 'involves repossessing the sign
through close attention to, and active participation in, its production' (ibid., p. x).
Therefore, Marxist calls for a seizing of the means of production have been fed through
reader-response criticism's attention to reading as an active process. What emerges is
a bid to redefine reader/writer relations: readerly production is to be freed up from
the jaws of passive consumption. One of Charles Bernstein's most anthologized poems,
'The Klupzy Girl', dramatizes the renegotiation of reader/writer relations. Here are
the first twenty lines:

> Poetry is like a swoon, with this difference:
> it brings you to your senses. Yet his
> parables are not singular. The smoke from
> the boat causes the men to joke. Not
> gymnastic: pyrotechnic. The continuousness
> of a smile – wry, perfume scented. No this
> would go fruity with all these changes
> around. Sense of variety: panic. Like
> my eye takes over from the front
> yard, three pace. Idle gaze – years
> right down the window. Not clairvoyance,
> predictions, deciphering – enacting. Analytically,
> i.e., thoughtlessly. Begin to push and cue
> together. Or I originate out of this
> occurrence, stoop down, bend on. The
> Protest-ant's voice within, calling for
> this to be shepherded, For moment's
> expression's enthroning. Able to be
> alibied (contiguity or vacuity). Or
> telepathetically? . . .
> (Silliman, 1986, p. 285)

Bernstein's poem relishes its uneven surface and the bumpy ride it sets up for the
reader. It is not gracefully gymnastic, but confrontationally pyrotechnic: an explosion
of conflicting discourses unanchored to a single voice; and later incorporating quota-
tions from the leaving speech of a sentimental colleague to co-workers, and the
Frankfurt Marxist Walter Benjamin. Nevertheless, the poem's self-consciously discontinuous wry smile is directed at what our response to it might be. It predicts bewil-
derment at what it envisages as our response to a lack of stable reader–writer relations:
'Sense of variety: panic'. It also seems to map out two possible positions. First, one
where the reader actively enters the text and begins 'to push and cue
/ together' meaning. Second, and slightly more ambiguously, one where 'I originate

out of this / occurrence, stoop down, bend on'. Initially this seems also an emerging emancipated reader, but the status of the 'I' emerging is ambiguated by the follow-ing line's evocation of 'The / Protest-ant's voice within, calling for / this to be shep-herded'. Bernstein's pun 'Protest-ant' unleashes several connotations. As the opposite to readerly autonomy, the 'Protest-ant's voice within' calls for the poem's polyphony to be 'shepherded'; it is a prayer for guidance from the author–god who will emerge as the safely confessional 'I' that will anchor the poem to a stable voice. And yet the pun also plays on a more radical autonomy: the Protestant renegotiation of relations with God as being the realm of personal responsibility rather than institutional mediation – as well as playfully invoking 'ants' protesting as part of a worker's revo-lution. Bernstein's poem therefore enacts a poetics of readerly choice. However, and as several critics have noted, such freedom of choice is also part of the liberatory rhetoric of the capitalist consumerism supposedly being resisted. In relation to this it is worth briefly returning to Bruce Andrews's 'Tizzy Boost'. Alongside Greer's claims for it offering the readerly experience of an inability to construct a single frame or context, I would have to draw attention to how much 'my own' reading of the poem was actually constructed by the frame and context supplied by the very essays espousing the need for readerly emancipation. In the case of Bernstein's 'The Klupzy Girl' the poem harbours a much deeper understanding of the issues than any poetics essay. The 'Protest-ant's voice' acknowledges the necessary complicity of an avant-garde stance through its pun's connotations of a work ethic that made the spread of Protestantism symbiotic with the spread of capitalism's desired economic individualism.

Language poetry's interest in redefining reader/writer relations has also revealed a suspicion of overly simplistic models of communication. Barrett Watten's *Conduit* interrogates the figuring of communication as a simple channelling of message from Addresser to Addressee, pointing out that 'A message may be the bottle' (Watten, 1997a, p. 161). *Conduit*'s interrogation is motivated by an Althusserian awareness of the ideological functioning of language. The book's disjunctive juxtaposition of units of communication explores 'how statement builds in the conditions of its reception' (Watten, 1995, p. 36); a recognition of the subtlety of linguistic coercion that owes something to Althusser's notion of interpellation. The opening section of *Conduit*, 'The XYZ of Reading', sets itself up as an ironic counterpart to Pound's *The ABC of Reading*; part of a didactic modernist act of readerly 'education' that Watten is presumably uncomfortable with. Watten's 'XYZ of Reading' rejects the model of a writer/reader hierarchy, and formulates its distance not as mandarin commentary, but as an enabling space for readerly activity:

> This is precisely the point at which the exemplary rejection structures the reader's involvement in the work. But the meaning of the work has now changed; beginning by deflating its own self-sufficiency, it ends in a form, the limits of a kind of activity that can be identified only at a distance, by another. (Watten, 1997a, p. 153)

More recently, Watten has betrayed dissatisfaction with 'a defunct politics satisfied to claim that the reader is "empowered" to make meaning from material texts' (Watten, 1997b, pp. 3–4) and similarly with the heroic homology between literary and political possibility, so 'that to describe literary possibility is to represent a form of agency, in a circular fashion, as a critique of representation' (ibid., p. 4). Rereading Watten's work, it seems to have always been intent on breaking this 'circular fashion' and on problematizing textual forms of agency through acknowledging the precarious limits between spectatorship and participation. As *Conduit* puts it: 'From which seats to witness?' (Watten, 1997a, p. 169). In *Progress*, the reader is buffeted as much as the writer, and the effect is to disallow the stability of the 'formulated distance' aimed for in *Conduit*. The jolting discontinuities of *Progress* actually achieve a relentless momentum that reflects the coercive drive of its title concept. The excited motion is revealed in the final stanza as a constantly moving 'map of my position'. The pronoun 'I' recurs regularly within the poem, but it is only a provisional locus of utterance; not so much an agent of participation as a drifting marker in the rapids of different discourses. '*Excite I*' italicized, puns on the emptying of the command of first-person address into the turmoil of everyday events; an ongoing process of being buffeted between the poles of spectatorship and participation renders each 'I' an ex cite (Watten, 1985, p. 120).

Nevertheless, it is reductive of the scope of Language poetry to suggest that it always provides the reader with a resistant materiality of language prompting a challenge to the illusion of transparency. Far from being restricted to a feature of language, indeterminacy is very much a feature of the world. As such, many Language writers are preoccupied by dramatizing the experience of being a reader of that world. Stephen Rodefer's *Four Lectures* is a wonderfully high-octane example, managing to be simultaneously honorific and satiric in its overdriven ideolect: 'And pidgeon means business. It carries / messages' (Rodefer, 1982, p. 11). The end of Rae Armantrout's poem 'Fiction' deftly images this empirical indeterminacy: 'A black man in a Union Jack t-shirt was / yelling, "Do you have any idea *what I mean?*"' (Armantrout, 1985a, p. 27).

Armantrout's highly condensed, tensile lyrics couldn't be further from Andrews's work stylistically. And yet they often share similar preoccupations. 'Sit-Calm' is a poem with a title that puns on the genre of the sitcom. And in many respects Armantrout writes a poetry of situation comedy: a wry commentary upon what she has elsewhere termed the 'illegibility' of our environment (Armantrout, 1985b, p. 93). The poem opens her 1995 collection *Made to Seem*, a book title that hints at a possible sense of the ideological coercion underlying the 'natural'. Lines 2–4 of 'Sit-Calm' seem to confirm an allusion to this process: 'we think we want something / we're made up to seem / exaggeratedly unfit for' (Armantrout, 1995, p. 7). To *think* we want something involves problematizing individual control over intention and desire — just as what we *want* figures both that desire and how the media constructs it as a panacea for our lack. The fact that the poem figures us as 'exaggeratedly unfit for' our desires is richly ambiguous; and perhaps indicates the endlessly deferred desire stimulated by consumer culture. An example of what we might be exaggeratedly unfit for is casually rendered at the end of the first stanza as 'touch'. This, as stanza two suggests, is an amusing comment on the sitcom we are 'touched' by; but the humour is also a 'dangerous / moment' of identification from which distraction is needed:

> . . . Right away
> we're talked out of it –
> no harm done –
> by a band of wise-acre friends.
> (Armantrout, 1995, p. 7)

This process of gently being talked out of a reaction by common-sense peer pressure is a touching moment of bonding. But it is also a situation comedy in which the generic humour of characters' difficulties and misunderstandings is redirected to signify the ambivalent cancellation of agency: 'I don't know / what I'm thinking', we say, only to have such awkwardly poignant self-reflection cushioned by the 'spike of merriment' it solicits from the friends. 'Sit-Calm' is awkwardly situated between safety-in-numbers camaraderie, and the violent safety-in-numbness of consumer passivity that allows the poem's title to signify an order.

Charles Altieri has written very suggestively about how Language poetry diminishes 'what in their predecessors had been a much fuller concern with how texts could exemplify powerful models of human agency' (Altieri, 1996, p. 208). He tactfully challenges the rhetoricity of much of the theorizing of readerly passivity and writerly resistance in Language poetics, concluding that such theorists 'feel the need to resist the mainstream interpretative culture so intensely that they lock themselves into oppositional models' (ibid., p. 216). Thankfully, the poetry is not so trapped and frequently – as in the case of Armantrout – presents itself in Altieri's desired role of 'interface between selves and worlds' (ibid., p. 232). Altieri calls for texts that 'exemplify' powerful human agency, but perhaps it is also important to acknowledge those texts that also question the very nature of what agency is in a textual situation. If we look through the smokescreen of what Alan Golding observes as 'the homology (open to debate) between formal and social disruption characteristic of the historical avant-garde' (Golding, 1994, p. 159), then we will find that Language writing has often engaged with just such issues. Frequently, it is dramatized through a problematizing of posture. This can be seen in Armantrout's situation comedy, Bernstein's poetry figured as a swoon that brings you to your senses, or the precarious balance of the 'I' in Watten's *Progress* buffeted by myriad interpellatons and orders: 'Relax, / stand at attention, and' (Watten, 1985, p. 1). Most demonstrably, issues of agency are explored in Language poetry's preoccupation with the notion of the person.

The Person

The concept of the 'Person' in Language writing is very far from confessional. For Lyn Hejinian, author of a sequence of poems entitled 'The Person', personhood inevitably raises the issue of using language for thinking and socializing. She figures the person as

> a radically unstable, wide-ranging, discontinuous construct that is not safely pre-dictable, but rather, within the bounds of mortality, open-ended. (Hejinian and Miller, 1989, p. 35)

Such a concept of the person is heavily informed by contemporary theory's replacement of traditional notions of the self as something stable and autonomous, by the unstable category of an unfixed subjectivity. Hejinian's most famous text, *My Life*, plays out the tension between a subjectivity that is open-ended and yet 'within the bounds of mortality', at a formal level. This prose text strikes a playful dialectic between open and closed forms. It consisted, in its first edition in 1978, of 37 sections each of 37 sentences – to match Hejinian's 37 years. When it was reprinted in 1986, Hejinian added eight new sections, and eight new sentences to each section, so as to preserve the relationship to her then 45 years of age. Nevertheless, the formal arrangement was complicated by the fact that the new material was inserted discontinuously into the existing text; this book is very far from being a straight autobiography. The text exists organically alongside Hejinian's ageing at the same time that its formal numerical constraints contain it. The balance between its being an open and a closed text is played out at the textual level of individual lines, particularly in section two:

> You spill the sugar when you lift the spoon. My father had filled an old apothecary jar with what he called 'sea glass', bits of old bottles rounded and textured by the sea, so abundant on beaches. There is no solitude. It buries itself in veracity. It is as if one splashed in the water lost by one's tears. My mother had climbed into the garbage can in order to stamp down the accumulated trash, but the can was knocked off balance, and when she fell she broke her arm. (Hejinian, 1991, p. 9)

This brief extract from the opening of section two gives a sense of the reading experience the text generates. Sentences are placed next to each other without any overt narrative logic, and the reader has to bridge the resulting gaps. The closer one reads, the more patterns of preoccupation emerge, such as the dialectic of containment and spillage in the above lines. The prose text that refuses to follow overt narrative, and which suspends readerly attention at the level of the individual sentences rather than the overall accumulation of them into 'plot', has been a dominant feature of Language writing and has been named by Ron Silliman the 'New Sentence'. Again, Stein is a major precursor, especially her claim that 'sentences are not emotional but paragraphs are' (Silliman, 1986, p. 570). For Stein, the sentence only becomes emotional when it is incorporated into the higher unit of the paragraph. Silliman reads into this process a violence that he associates with a totalizing – and more problematically a totalitarian – drive to subsume parts into wholes. In the above Hejinian example, this dynamic is subtly present. The mother's violent attempt at stamping down the accumulated trash itself gives way to the violence of her fall and resulting injury. The statement 'There is no solitude' formally maintains its discontinuous independence, even as semantically it is testament to the text's method of making the reader acknowledge the way each sentence is modified and recontextualized by the one that precedes and follows it. The relationship between parts and wholes is obviously of major import for the renegotiation of reading as active labour, but it is also an aspect of the notion of the person as a discontinuous mass of parts.

Bob Perelman's 'The Story of My Life' dramatizes a version of the part and whole conundrum at the level of a problem close to the American psyche: that of the paradox of a democratic collective founded upon the freedom of the individual. The poem opens with characteristic satire:

> I am a moral person, an artificial
> person, made of parts, non-recurrent.
> But if I had been told at birth that I was to have both
> a body and a country, and that
> one would have to be balanced on the other . . .
> (Perelman, 1988, p. 7)

The title of the poem plays upon the construction of subjectivity, just as it also registers the colloquial expression for laughing off bad experiences. This humorous but fatalistic 'story of my life' involves subjection to what poststructuralist psychoanalysis would label the 'symbolic order'; an entry into language, laws, social processes and institutions: 'go sit somewhere and don't come home until you speak the / president's language' (ibid.). It is a 'dead language everyone reads by nature / but no one gets to speak'. This is a major preoccupation of the poem: that entry into language is also a stripping of any autonomy or agency. Charles Bernstein has reiterated his claim that 'You can't fully critique the dominant culture if you are confined to the forms through which it reproduces itself, not because hegemonic forms are compromised "in themselves" but because their criticality has been commandeered' (Bernstein, 1999, p. 4). The problem seems to be one concerning the extent to which one can step outside of hegemonic forms and still be able to communicate with the desired criticality. Perelman's poem wonders whether it is possible to not speak the president's language, when even to desire freedom from it is to fall for a form of the American dream of heroic individualism:

> The citizen is to pry the concrete particulars loose, connect and animate them,
>   freezing them for experience to experience, is that it?

A long-shot self-expressiveness which leads to lifelong self-criticism and serialization,
    movie rights dangling tantalizingly beyond the fingertips?
(Perelman, 1988., p. 8)

One of the earliest, but still most cogent, considerations of the concept of the person
is Bernstein's essay–poem 'Three or Four Things I Know About Him', written in 1977
and later included in *Content's Dream: Essays 1975–1984*. It tackles issues of responsibility, autonomy and agency as they constellate around the experience of the workplace. In particular, it is critical of the consequences of alienation in the workplace as
involving the construction of a 'nine to five self' (Bernstein, 1986, pp. 18–19) that is
actually a 'vacancy of person' (ibid., p. 18). Alienation and dissatisfaction cause a split-
ting of the subject into public and private self. The text questions this, particularly
as the construction of this private self that is the 'real you' distorts the notion of a
person by making the public self 'this sort of neutral gear' that abnegates responsibility for its actions and intentions. Section eight of the essay is a meditation attacking the Romantic cult of the isolated outsider in terms of 'the worship of loneliness
. . . as a way of being whole in the world that demands personal fragmentation as the
price for fitting into society' (ibid., p. 23).

Future Tense

Now that the term 'Language poetry' has academic currency, debate surrounds
whether this loose grouping of writers constitutes a 'moment' or 'movement' – and
whether either formulation is ongoing. If this is a source of tension irresolvable in an
article of this brevity, solace can be found in the fact that it is literally a tense problem
for Bob Perelman. In *The Marginalization of Poetry* Perelman takes on the unenviable
task of attempting to write a history of something in which he is still participating.
As such, in trying to explain the condition of his subject, he has to confide that he is
unsure whether he should write 'Language writing differs' or 'Language writing differed' (Perelman, 1996, p. 15). Treating Language poetry now as a set of generaliz-
able concerns risks caricaturing, rather than characterizing, a large grouping of
individual writers. Now that many are accessible to – and in some cases within – the
Academy as a collective sign, it is hoped that the thinning out of oppositional rhetoric
will enable more detailed reception of individual writers.

BIBLIOGRAPHY

Altieri, Charles (1996). 'Some Problems about
    Agency in the Theories of Radical Poetics.' *Con-*
    temporary Literature 37: 2.
Andrews, Bruce and Charles Bernstein
    (eds) (1984). *The L=A=N=G=U=A=G=E*

Book. Carbondale: Southern Illinois University
    Press.
Andrews, Bruce and Charles Bernstein. 'The
    Pacifica Interview.' *L=A=N=G=U=A=G=E* 3,
    Oct. 1981.

Armantrout, Rae (1985a). *Precedence*. Providence: Burning Deck.

Armantrout, Rae (1985b). 'Chains.' *Poetics Journal* 5, 93–4.

Armantrout, Rae (1995). *Made To Seem*. Los Angeles: Sun & Moon Press.

Bernstein, Charles (1986). *Content's Dream: Essays 1975–1984*. Los Angeles: Sun & Moon Press.

Bernstein, Charles (1993). *The Politics of Poetic Form: Poetry and Public Policy*. New York: Roof Books.

Bernstein, Charles (1999). *My Way: Speeches and Poems*. London: University of Chicago.

Golding, Alan (1994). 'Avant-Gardes and American Poetry.' *Contemporary Literature* 35: 1, spring, 156–70.

Greer, Michael (1991). 'Language Poetry in America: 1971–1991.' *Meanjin* 50: 1, autumn, 149–56.

Hejinian, Lyn (1986). 'Language and Realism.' *Temblor* 3, 128–33.

Hejinian, Lyn (1991). *My Life*. Los Angeles: Sun & Moon Press.

Hejinian, Lyn and Tyrus Miller (1989). 'An Exchange of Letters.' *Paper Air* 4: 2, 33–40.

Howe, Susan (1990). *The Europe of Trusts*. Los Angeles: Sun & Moon Press.

Olson, Charles (1997). *Collected Prose*, ed. Donald Allen and Benjamin Friedlander. Berkeley: University of California Press.

Perelman, Bob (ed.) (1985). *Writing / Talks*. Carbondale: Southern Illinois University Press.

Perelman, Bob (1988). *Face Value*. New York: Roof Books.

Perelman, Bob (1996). *The Marginalization of Poetry: Language Writing and Literary History*. Princeton NJ: Princeton University Press.

Rodefer, Stephen (1982). *Four Lectures*. Berkeley, CA: The Figures.

Silliman, Ron (ed.) (1986). *In The American Tree*. Maine: National Poetry Foundation.

Watten, Barrett (1985). *Progress*. New York: Roof Books.

Watten, Barrett (1995). *Aerial 8: Barrett Watten*, ed. Rod Smith. Washington: Edge Books.

Watten, Barrett (1997a). *Frame (1971–1990)*. Los Angeles: Sun & Moon Press.

Watten, Barrett (1997b). 'The Bride of the Assembly Line: From Material Text to Cultural Poetics.' *The Impercipient Lecture Series* 1: 8, October.

PART III
International and Postcolonial Poetry in English

18

West Indian Poetry

Victor Chang

As far back as 1972 Edward Baugh observed that 'West Indian poetry seems to have come into its own' (Baugh, 1972, p. 1) after the publication of several volumes of poetry by Derek Walcott and Kamau Brathwaite, but when Walcott was awarded the Nobel Prize for Literature in 1992 it could be said that West Indian poetry had reached the height of its achievement. And while it is true that the poetry of the Anglophone Caribbean reveals shifts in approach and variations in style, much as the islands themselves have differences and nuances, still one can discern a similarity and a general pattern which is largely the result of a shared kinship, a shared history and a common heritage of slavery, indentureship and colonialism. One thing is sure and that is that there are recurrent themes and concerns which run throughout the poetry and among these are a concern with Roots, History and the past, national identity, racial prejudice and its effects, a sense and love of place, loss and separation, Love and Death, protest.

From the beginning, the act of writing in the West Indies is marked by a peculiar tension generated by the recognition that it is a product of a colonial society. The West Indian people are not indigenous to the region: they constitute the remnants of what was a slave society and the language they speak is that of their conquerors, since their original tongues have long ceased to have currency. So that the very act of writing forces one to acknowledge that one is using the tongue of the conquerors, and that constitutes a kind of betrayal. Again, it is Walcott who expressed this anguish in an early poem, 'A Far Cry From Africa':

> . . . how choose
> Between this Africa and the English tongue I love?
> Betray them both, or give back what they give?

For the West Indian writer, then, it has always been an issue of language: how to express the colonial experience, how to 'write back' to the conquerors, how to try to come to terms with something 'torn and new', all the while using language which is a part of that colonial heritage. Even Brathwaite, who sees his task as that of retracing African continuities in the New World, has had to write his several trilogies of poems in that conqueror's language.

Brathwaite, in talking about the literature of the region in his keynote address to the 1971 ACLALS conference in Kingston, used the paradigm of the Great House and the plantation to represent, as it were, the split and the uneasy relations between what he has termed 'The Great Tradition' and 'the little tradition' of the folk. Inherent in this paradigm is a dualism that acknowledges the gap between Europe and Africa, the Old World and the New World, the metropolitan centre and the peripheral folk and – above all – the scribal tradition versus the oral. It is a useful paradigm to explore the development of the poetry, but we must keep in mind that this schema does not fully account for the complexity of the situation in the Caribbean. It does not, for example, account for the contribution of the large Indian population in both Trinidad and Guyana.

While some critics have elaborated on this so-called split between the scribal and the oral traditions, it is important to note that in West Indian poetry elements of both coexist and that the too-easy categorization of poets as being in one camp or the other can be misleading. The language continuum in the West Indies covers a wide terrain and we can see elements of creole, of the spoken word, in almost all of the poets currently writing. Even if a line looks like a Standard English line, when it is read we can hear the unmistakable sound of the creole. This is true of Walcott, Brathwaite, Dennis Scott or Lorna Goodison, and we should be cautious of assigning poets to one category or another, based solely on this distinction.

But it is equally misleading to go to the other extreme and claim that the only authentic poetry is that which is couched in the language of the folk because it will communicate directly to the masses. This would be to dismiss the achievement of the scribal tradition and ignore the fact that both aspects make up the totality of the West Indies.

Historically, West Indian poetry has oscillated between the two traditions set out by Brathwaite. The earliest poetry was imitative, written by expatriates who attempted to reproduce as exactly as possible the poetry published in the metropole. It is not surprising that they found the colonies 'barren in incidents for poetical display' (*Midnight Musings in Demerara*, 1832, quoted by Wycliffe Bennett in an unpublished anthology) and so looked at the landscape with alien and, at times, hostile eyes. This eighteenth- and nineteenth-century poetry is only of historical interest and mostly forgettable. We get no insight into the region or the condition of the mass of the people because the writers were seeing through northern eyes, although by the end of the century there were signs that some accommodation was being made. The poets started to look at the landscape which confronted them rather than at alien and distant ones, and took the important step of trying to accept that landscape on its own terms.

In the early twentieth century this expression of love for the landscape would grow and become the vehicle for the first sustained outburst of national feeling in the islands. But the upbringing and education of these writers placed them firmly in the traditions of the central metropolitan culture. In Jamaica, Barbados, Trinidad and Guyana, the pattern was the same. Groups of like-minded, educated people who believed in the study and pursuit of literature set up poetry clubs to encourage each other to write poetry.

Many of them were unashamedly colonial and only concerned with trying to catch 'the fleeting beauties of our land and enshrine them forever in beautiful words and rhythm'. The earliest of these 'clubs' was the Jamaica Poetry League founded in 1923 from an earlier (1908) branch of the Empire Poetry League. David Mitchell's introduction to the first anthology of Jamaican poetry published by the League, *Voices From Summerland* (1929), demonstrates clearly where the loyalties of the League lay and how it institutionalized the writing of poetry. In so doing, it failed to encourage the development of an authentic West Indian voice and excluded those who did not satisfy its preconditions. He writes: 'Once more our restless sea-borne race has explored the wine-dark ocean and founded new homes for the children over not one but many seas. And of its ever-loyal cherishing of our English poetic traditions this volume is proof.' The result, according to Arthur Calder-Marshall in a Caribbean Voices broadcast on 1 February 1948, was that they were unable to find 'the words, the idiom, the rhythms to say what they as individuals, as West Indians, wanted to say'. However much we choose to dismiss the activities and work of the League as inconsequential and see it as having no direct influence on the development of later West Indian poetry, we must not forget that it kept alive the notion that the pursuit of literature was a civilized and civilizing activity and therefore something to be valued.

Unfortunately, with their preconceived notions of what constituted poetry, the members of the League were not innovative or revolutionary in what they wrote and provided little support for the earliest attempts to use the language of the people in verse. Indeed, Claude McKay's two earliest books of verse, *Songs of Jamaica* (*c.* 1911) and *Constab Ballads* (1912), which dealt with the folk and in which he experimented with creole on the printed page, were largely ignored and when he emigrated in 1912 to the USA, McKay left behind no obvious literary heir. Interestingly, when Louise Bennett appeared on the scene in the 1940s she was not so much inheriting a tradition as starting one herself. Bennett has said she was not a member of the League, nor was ever invited to join because what she was doing – rendering in comic verse the events, scenes and characters from the folk culture of Jamaica, using the language of the folk – was not regarded as 'poetry'.

So early practitioners like Tom Redcam (T. H. MacDermot, b. 1870), the first Poet Laureate of Jamaica, would write lines that showed clear affinities with late Victorian verse:

> Now the Lignum Vitae blows;
> Fair-browed April enters here,

In her hand a crimson rose,
In her eye youth's crystal tear.
('Now The Lignum Vitae Blows')

and J. E. Clare McFarlane (b. 1896) produced a 'a strictly colonial poetry' (Baugh, 1972, p. 5). Even though the League had members with real talent like W. Adolphe Roberts (b. 1886) and Vivian Virtue (b. 1911), they both wrote poetry that was private, hermetic and remote from the concerns of the society.

This pattern of conservative writing could be seen throughout the islands and included the work of A. J. Seymour (b. 1914) of Guyana and Frank Collymore (b. 1893) of Barbados. While their talents and abilities were varied, members of this generation were all writing in the Great Tradition, and their notion of what constituted the proper stuff of poetry, and the language of poetry, was shaped by that tradition. Even though Seymour from very early tried to incorporate into his poetry the majestic landscape of South American Guyana as well as the history, myths and legends of the Amerindians, he was not interested only in aboriginal history. In his 'Name Poem', for instance, he tried to incorporate all the strands of the past, Dutch, English, French and Indian, and in this search for spirits of place, he pushes back far beyond Columbus. Even so, he remained very much a link figure poised between the old traditions of writing and the changing demands of the new, a man who was sensitive to the currents of his time but who could not adapt his way of writing to suit those demands.

The 1930s and 1940s were the decades that were crucial in determining far-reaching changes in the political philosophy of the region and consequently the orientation of its creative work in the literary and plastic arts. There was sweeping social change advocated for the islands and everywhere there was agitation for self-government, as the political parties began to emerge and trade unions fought for the right to exist. In this ferment of political agitation and labour riots, there emerged several literary and artistic groups whose agendas were radically different from those of the early poetry groups and which were to have far-reaching consequences for the writing in the region. Not only did they advocate an assertive nationalist approach to everything, they were to provide the only outlets for emergent West Indian writing. As such, they were in a position to shape the kind of writing that they were willing to publish and which fitted in with their philosophy. This is not surprising, for the political movements were centred on a questioning of old perceptions and ways of seeing and on a growing assertion of self-worth and search for some kind of self-definition. Literature was an obvious way by which one could seek to define oneself and one's society. Many of these literary groups saw as part of their programme the establishment of 'little Magazines' which would have a significant impact on the direction in which West Indian poetry was to go.

In Trinidad, the Beacon Group – founded by Albert Gomes, Alfred Mendes and C. L. R. James – issued a periodical, *The Beacon* (1931–9), which was propagandist in nature and which contained prose, verse and polemical pieces as well as discussions of politics. The magazine endorsed the cause of West Indianism, sponsoring and promoting writing that was specifically West Indian. The group also published the first collection of Trinidadian creative writing, *From Trinidad: Fiction & Verse* (1937) edited by Gomes. Though the main focus was on prose fiction, poetry was not neglected and the literature was being nudged in the direction of social awareness and political change. In July 1931, one of Gomes's untitled poems stridently asserted:

> You have to fight the white man's fury
> But you mustn't want to be a white black man
> The real black man wants to be a great
> Black Man and not a great White Man

In June 1933 he editorialized: 'The conscious apeing of another man's culture seems merely a sign of the immaturity of our spirit . . . we look forward to the day when it will be no more'. So the Beacon group explicitly agitated for the development of a uniquely West Indian culture and perspective.

December 1942 saw the appearance of *Bim* in Barbados, edited by Frank Collymore. At first it was strictly a Barbadian magazine, but it quickly became West Indian in scope and Collymore, according to Brathwaite 'the greatest of West Indian literary godfathers', through *Bim* would provide over the years a steady outlet for all West Indian writing. More than that, Collymore himself was a poet and though he wrote more in the conventions of the Great Tradition, it is clear from his work that his sensibility was a West Indian one in the sense that he did not see England as his home nor the English as his people. In 'Triptych' he writes of the slaves as ancestors:

> I see them, ancestors of ours;
> Children of the tribe, ignorant of their doom, innocent
> As cattle, bartered for, captured, beaten, penned,
> Cattle of the slave-ship, less than cattle;
> Sold in the market place, yoked to servitude

In Guyana, *Kyk-over-al* was first published in December 1945 and like the other magazines, started with a nationalist slant. Its editor, Norman Cameron, claimed that 'all other forms of local art and literature should strive' to deal with 'various aspects of local life, and indeed voicing the sentiments and aspirations of the people'. The group would publish the first anthology of *Guyanese Poetry, 1831–1931*. It is from Guyana, too, that we get the work of Martin Carter, who was to be the first to sound a strong note of resistance and protest to the colonial government's treatment of local people in his *Poems of Resistance*.

In Jamaica it was the Focus group – a number of artists, writers and poets led by Edna Manley, wife of Norman Manley, founder and leader of the People's National Party – that would push Jamaican poetry towards expressing concerns about the landscape and people in the first two numbers of the *Focus* magazine published in 1943 and 1948. This was the most consciously literary of the magazines and claimed to provide a complete introduction to the writers of Jamaica, but the magazine was severely restricted and published work only by its members who were all involved in Jamaican politics. Indeed, the title of a Manley carving, 'Negro Aroused', could be seen as a rallying point for the movement. George Campbell was one of the most talented writers in the group and his poem of the same name demonstrates clearly how passionate the feelings of the group were:

> The hot fire of new blood
> Bubbles under this skin; the heart shouts Freedom!
> I lift my face to heaven, awakened, shouting louder, louder
> With triumph, with a new found strength –
> Freedom! We cry only freedom – we were dead when
> Sleeping – now we live! Live! We are aroused.
> ('Negro Aroused', 1945)

The celebration of Africa, the recognition of connections with that continent and a strong sense of pride can also be seen in Philip Sherlock's 'Jamaican Fisherman' (1953), where the lowly fisherman is elevated to the stature of royalty:

> Across the sand I saw a black man stride
> To fetch his fishing gear and broken things,
> And silently that splendid body cried
> Its proud descent from ancient chiefs and kings.

M. G. Smith in his 'Jamaica' achieved a kind of incantatory power and a revolutionary ardour:

> Let the thunder shake
> The old Gods awake
> Past and Future break.
> I saw my land in the morning
> And O but she was fair
> The hills flamed upwards scorning
> Death and failure here.

Throughout the region it is the folk and the folk qualities which are held up for admiration, whether of female beauty as in H. A. Vaughan's 'Revelation':

> Then turn again, and smile, and be
> The perfect answer to those fools
> Who always prate of Greece and Rome

or E. M. Roach of Tobago celebrating the strength of his mother in 'To My Mother':

> I found you strong and tough as guava scrub,
> Hoeing the growing, reaping the ripe corn;
> Kneading and thumping the thick dough for bread . . .
> My poems labour from your blood
> As all my mind burns on our peasant stock
> That cannot be consumed till time is killed.

We have seen that at the beginning of the twentieth century writers were beginning to recognize the differences in their landscape and slowly coming to terms with it, mostly through a passionate declaration of love for its beauty and splendour. The movement continues down into the middle of the century, but there is an increasing maturity of vision which causes poets not simply to celebrate and invoke the beauty of the landscape, but rather to be increasingly concerned with a sober and realistic appraisal of what the society and the land mean to them. They are no longer just declaring themselves ecstatic at the beauty that surrounds them; they are seeing the poverty and the harsh existence demanded by life in the islands and still accepting it as theirs.

In 'We' Owen Campbell recognizes that the lure of big cities can be a chimera:

> So we have decided
> Not to construct hope on continents,
> Or leave lost hearts to rove
> In the quick air on oceans of dream.
> We have decided
> To build here, on our slender soil.

By the end of the decade, though, much of that optimism was replaced by a growing cynicism, and the poetry is marked by a questioning about the whole business of culture and identity. This is best demonstrated by A. N. Forde's 'Across A Fisherman's Net':

> We clap hands wistfully
> At the rhythm of the steel band
> Adjusting our collars into acquiescence
> Of the myth that a new culture pants to the surface.
> On rusty pots and pans
> That bicker in the bleakness of the night
> We blab of a new brotherhood
> Called West Indian . . .
> Forgetting the spite of shade

West Indian poets progressed from attempting to provide their readers with a sense of history and place to probing analyses about the nature of their society. The poetry previous to this, written in the central metropolitan tradition, was more concerned with the surface beauty of things. It was largely a declarative poetry, while the later poetry is concerned with the complexities and ambiguities that lie at the heart of the West Indian experience. The poets do not feel bound by any poetic conventions inherited from a previous tradition, nor do they simply adopt a group stance. In 'I am the Archipelago' Roach paints a bleak vision:

> And now
> I drown in the ground swell of poverty
> No love will quell. I am the shanty town,
> Banana, sugar-cane and cotton man;
> Economies are soldered with my sweat
> Here, everywhere.

Roach sees the shanty town and the poverty, not just the lush exotic growth in the West Indies. His poem suggests just how accommodating the poetry has become because it is no longer limited to a single vision of experience. Instead, it has widened in scope to include a multiplicity of visions: the banana and the sugar cane have become double symbols of sweat and toil, not just lush tropical plants.

No account of West Indian poetry can overlook the contribution to writing made by the BBC Radio programme Caribbean Voices, which was a kind of living literary periodical, broadcast once a week for thirty minutes, starting in March 1945 and continuing until September 1958. Caribbean Voices was important because it helped shape the direction in which the literature of the region was to develop, both by its selection of pieces and also by the critical commentaries. Its first editor, Henry Swanzy, stressed in a broadcast on 21 August 1949 that 'literature is above all a regional thing, rooted in the soil of everyday life'. And this belief guided his selections. It meant, therefore, that if poets wanted to have their poetry selected and broadcast on the programme, they would have to change how they wrote and what they wrote about. We can see then how these 'magazines' were instrumental in charting the direction of change. On a practical level, too, the programme provided recognition for writers and it also paid, however minimally, for work read on the programme.

So what happens in the 1940s and 1950s is a swinging of the pendulum from the Great Tradition that represented the metropolitan, colonizing power to a position of support for what is local, including the language. As yet, though, the changing themes and concerns of the poetry reflect this change in consciousness far more quickly than any corresponding change in the language. What is being written is still very conservative in form and diction and West Indian poetry lagged behind its prose fiction counterparts in drawing on the resources of the creole language of the people. Mendes and C. L. R. James in Trinidad and H. G. deLisser in Jamaica were all using creole registers in their novels and dealing with the realities of urban and rural folk existence long before the change could be discerned in the poetry.

The landscape of the 1960s is dominated by the work of two giant figures: Derek Walcott (St Lucia) and Kamau Brathwaite (Barbados). In a stunning display of talent and virtuosity, between them they have taken the poetry to new heights. Their work shows the multiple strands of influence that have gone into the making of the West Indies and demonstrates the fusion of the tradition of the Great House and the oral tradition at its best. Walcott has always been seen as the traditionalist, writing verse that reveals an immense knowledge of English and European traditions. At no time, however, has he lost his strong sense of place or of his involvement with the history, language and culture of the region. He expresses this clearly in 'At Last':

> And now, let it come to fruit,
> Let me be sure it has flowered
> To break from the bitterest root
> And the earth that soured
> The flower bursts out of my heart,
> The cleft in the rock, at last
> Flowers, the heart-breaking past
> Unforgiven and unforgiving,
> The net of my veins I have cast
> Here flashes with living
> Silver, at last.

Brathwaite, in an unprecedented and totally original trilogy of poems, *Rights of Passage*, *Masks* and *Islands*, wrote what has been termed 'the great poem of the Black Man' (Baugh, 1972, p. 17) and traced in poetry the journeys of the peoples of the Black Diaspora from Africa to the New World and back to ancestral roots. His approach was far-reaching and eclectic and he used a pastiche of styles that ranged from a brilliant evocation of Barbadian and Jamaican creole to rhythms derived from popular dance music and jazz. His poetry encompasses, more than any other, the range of language patterns of the Black Diaspora. His work is crucial too in its emphasis on the centrality of the black experience in the Caribbean and his celebration of the primacy of the folk cultures in the region.

Somewhat overshadowed by the achievement of Brathwaite and Walcott, but important in the development of West Indian poetry, is the work of four Jamaicans: Edward Baugh, Dennis Scott, Mervyn Morris and Anthony McNeill. They form part of a group of young, bright graduates emerging primarily from the University of the West Indies – as was Walcott – whose work reveals a new intellectual toughness, a thorough grounding in traditional English Literature studies, but allied with a strong sense of place and identity and a scathing sense of irony. This is a further development because it means for the first time that we have a number of writers who are schooled in their craft and who are not just dabbling as amateurs. There is a new professionalism and a clear sense of direction charted. The choices they make reflect the fusion of both traditions and it is not something that they stumbled on by accident, but a conscious and deliberate choice.

One of the earliest and most important creole voices in the West Indies is that of Jamaican Louise Bennett, who wrote and performed her work in creole. Some have seen it as a drawback that her work is largely comic, but Bennett's great importance lay in her ability to demonstrate that the folk had a life and vitality and an authenticity that were the proper and fit subjects of poetry. More than that, she captured the earthiness, the spontaneity and the wisdom of her people, and despite her comic mode she was able to provide her readers and listeners with insights into the human condition and into the particular condition of the working class in this society. As such, Bennett starts a powerful and attractive tradition of her own that would spread far beyond Jamaica. It is her work that first exploits the primacy of the oral tradition in the West Indies and her influence can be seen in the work of Paul Keens-Douglas as well as in that of Linton Kwesi Johnson.

If it is true that the oral element in poetry communicates with an immediacy that is appealing to any audience, then it is even more so if the audience is a West Indian one. This is so for a variety of reasons. The first might well be that in a largely illiterate society, orality is of prime importance because all information, all entertainment has to be transmitted orally. It may also be true, as Laurence Breiner (1998) claims in his *An Introduction to West Indian Poetry*, that the practice of poetry is rooted in West Indian societies because of their oral traditions and their organization into relatively small communities. In most cases, the speakers know and are known to their audience. They are accustomed to 'rhetorical improvisation' and 'verbal wit' and to the tradition of preaching and the reading aloud of the King James Version of the Bible in the islands.

Moreover, in an oral setting, audience and performer have a special kind of relationship which does not have to be mediated through print and does not depend on its validation from a metropolitan source as prose fiction seems to, because the whole machinery of publication was controlled by the metropole. What West Indian poetry is doing then is to reach back to its original oral roots and this feeds into and manifests itself in the scribal tradition. So for Louise Bennett no script is necessary because of the primacy of the spoken word. This is clear from the fact that her material was not published in print form until her book *Jamaica Labrish* appeared in 1966, though she had been performing for years.

We must not forget either the special contribution of calypso as an art form in the West Indies. Long before reggae appeared on the scene, as far back as the eighteenth century, the oral poetry of the folk was manifesting itself in the calypso with its verbal wit, playful irony, sexual humour and ridicule that we associate with the best satire. It is this orality which produces in its turn a spate of West Indian poetry that came to be known as 'dub' poetry or performance poetry. Taking its cue from Bennett a whole generation of young writers like Michael Smith, Oku Onuora and Jean Binta Breeze recognized that creole need not be limited to the comic mode, but that it can be employed legitimately to render a range of emotions and feelings which, it had been argued, it could not do and that it can sit comfortably side by side with Standard English, as in Jean Binta Breeze's 'simple tings' (1988):

De simple tings of life, mi dear
De simple tings of life

She rocked the rhythms in her chair
Brushed a hand across her hair
Miles of travel in her stare

De simple tings of life.

Set free from the restrictions of print, the impulse is so powerful that it breaks out of the bounds of the conservative tradition and poetry becomes not just the province of the select few, but is taken over as a vehicle of protest and social commentary, used to engage with the realities of life in the ghettos and with the plight of the marginalized and the underprivileged. Dub poetry was intimately bound up with the emergence of reggae in Jamaica and expanded its boundaries to include the plight of ghetto youths. All of a sudden, the poor and the dispossessed were finding their voice in poetic utterances that encompassed and expressed what it was like to live in their world. This is Michael Smith:

Lawd, mi see some black bud
Livin inna one buildin
But no rent no pay
So dem cyaan stay
Lawd, de oppress an de dispossess
Cyaan get no res
What nex?
('Mi C-YaaN beLieVe iT, 1986')

The most significant force of the appropriation of poetry by the folk was, of course, the dynamic figure of Bob Marley, who would become an icon for the dispossessed and whose lyrics would express the pain and anger of the poor and oppressed as well as the religious fervour of the Rastafarians and the assertion of the African continuities in the region. It was a message that spilled over from the region to envelop the world. But Marley did not just express the pain of dispossession and loss, he also held out a positive message of hope and redemption and a triumphant sense that with the help of Jah we would more than survive. Any consideration of West Indian poetry therefore has to take into account the work of DJs and performance poets. Poetry has now become in a real sense the possession of the mass of the people, so that Brathwaite was right when he said that 'nation language' would reach the masses.

But while that may be true, it fails to recognize that there are also real drawbacks to that type of poetry, since musical accompaniment is an important component. Because dub poetry is meant to be performed, it is always subject to the exigencies of a live performance and the response of an audience that might prove less than attentive. This is so because since the intoning of the poetry is accompanied by an instrumental backing, or 'dub', this poetry frequently suffers from a volume imbalance that is difficult to regulate. This is not a poetry of subtle effects or quiet meditation. It is a poetry of protest and loud rhetoric. It is poetry meant to be shouted to an audience already charged up with emotion. While there is the immediacy there is little chance of the poetry having more than a momentary flash, little chance of it being introspective or tranquil or of leading to insight and inward speculation. But this reggae-oriented poetry has had the most significant international impact because it has travelled with reggae around the world and has acquired scores of imitators.

One other significant aspect of the poetry in the latter part of the twentieth century is that the West Indians, originally unwilling and non-voluntary migrant peoples, have now in turn become colonizers themselves in a real sense. In the 1950s a wave of West Indian immigrants made their way to England. From that diaspora has come a whole new generation of British blacks who try to keep alive their sense of their origin. Children born in England of West Indian parents try to imitate as closely as possible the creole of their grandparents or parents and try to sustain a sense of a living West Indian culture in Britain. The result is a whole set of black British writers who claim rights to the creole of the West Indies, but are using it, as well as every other linguistic means at their disposal, to address the situation of the New World black in Britain. We need only look at the work of Linton Kwesi Johnson to see how he utilizes both the traditions to which he is heir. He has no desire to live in the West Indies and his concerns are those of the blacks living in Britain, but he still draws on his West Indian background.

And it is not only in Britain that this phenomenon has taken place: West Indians have also set up enclaves in Miami, Atlanta and Toronto, so that we are seeing poetry written by the descendants of those immigrants coming out of North America. The notion of what constitutes West Indian poetry has to be considerably enlarged to encompass this phenomenon.

If the earlier centuries of poetry were dominated by men, the last two decades of the twentieth century can rightfully be said to belong to women. In the early years, the poetry clubs were indeed supported by women, but the poetry they wrote was largely sweetly sentimental verse. Only the Jamaican Una Marson in *Heights & Depths* (1931) and *The Moth & The Star* (1937) published anything that was of any interest. Silenced by history and tradition, large numbers of West Indian women are now finding their voice and there is a flood of poetry from all the islands, as well as North America and Britain, as witnessed by the appearance of *Jamaica Woman* (1980), *Creation Fire: A CAFRA Anthology of Caribbean Women's Poetry* (1990) and *Washerwoman Hangs Her Poems in the Sun: Poems by Women of Trinidad & Tobago* (1990). And there is no one single pattern. From all the islands there is this outpouring of poetry that asserts the strong matriarchal presence in the Caribbean, but also poetry that explores the peculiar concerns of the West Indian woman and her anguish and protest at being 'doubly othered' over these years.

The most important of these is probably the Jamaican Lorna Goodison, whose poetry is suffused with her sense of the island and its people but whose sympathies also extend to the poor and suffering wherever she finds them. There are times when she is in what could be termed a mystic, prophetic mode, as evidenced in her poems in *Heartease* (1988).

> In what looked like a black-out last week
> a meteorite burst from the breast of the sky
> smoking like a censer, it spelled out in
> incandescent calligraphy
> a message for all who had deep eyes.
>
> If you did not see it I'll tell you what
> it said:
> Cultivate the search-mi-heart and
> acres of sincerity grass and turn your
> face towards Heartease
> ('Heartease II')

There is no one particular focus in the work of these women writers: their poetry addresses the problems of everyday life, with being wife and mother and daughter. It deals, too, with the difficulties of relationships with men, and with children.

> There's a woman outside singing
> of the wrongs that she endures
> how a man has made her captive,
> fettered, childed, kept, indoors.
>
> One day she cries I'm young, I'm lovely
> I'm on fire like girls must be
> but the man of my desire
> quenched it in a freezing sea.
> (Jane King, 'Sad Mother Ballad', 1988)

But while there is a more interior, quiet tone, this new poetry can also be assertive, as in Jean Binta Breeze's 'soun de abeng fi nanny' (1988):

> an de chant jus a rise, jus a rise
> to de skies
> wid de fervour of freedom
> dat bus up chain
> dat strap de ceaseless itching
> of de sugar cane
>
> We sey wi nah tun back
> we a bus a new track
> dutty tough
> but is enuff
> fi a bite
> fi wi fight

West Indian poetry has come to an astonishing maturity in a short time. When we consider its range, its complexity and the obstacles it had to overcome, we must agree with Edouard Glissant that the twenty-first century belongs to creole cultures because it is that fusion of old and new that generates such strength and the will to triumph.

BIBLIOGRAPHY

Abrahams, Roger (1983). *The Man of Words in the West Indies: Performance and the Emergence of Creole Culture*. Baltimore, MD: Johns Hopkins University Press.

Baugh, Edward (1988). *A Tale From The Rainforest*. Kingston: Sandberry Press.

Baugh, Edward (1972). *West Indian Poetry 1900–1970*. Savacou Publication.

Berry, James (1984). *News for Babylon: The Chatto Book of West Indian-British Poetry*. London: Chatto & Windus.

Brathwaite, Edward Kamau (1984). *History of the Voice: The Development of Nation Language in Anglophone Caribbean Poetry*. London: New Beacon Books.

Breiner, Laurence A. (1998). *An Introduction to West Indian Poetry*. Cambridge: Cambridge University Press.

Brown, Lloyd (1984). *West Indian Poetry*. London: Heinemann.

Brown, Stewart (ed.) (1992). *Caribbean Poetry Now*, 2nd edn. London: Edward Arnold.

Brown, Stewart, Gordon Rohlehr and Mervyn Morris (eds) (1989). *Voiceprint*. London: Longman.

Brown, Wayne (1972). *On the Coast*. London: Andre Deutsch.

Burnett, Paula (1986). *Penguin Book of Caribbean Verse in English*. Harmondsworth: Penguin.

Chamberlin, J. Edward (1993). *Come Back To Me My Language*. Illinois.

Collymore, Frank (1959). *Collected Poems*. Bridgetown.

Dabydeen, Cyril (1987). *A Shapely Fire: Black Writers in Canada*. Oakville: Mosaic Press.

Dabydeen, David (1988). *Coolie Odyssey*. Coventry: Dangaroo Press.

Figueroa, John (1966, 1971). *Caribbean Voices, Vol. I: Dreams & Visions, Vol. II: The Blue Horizons*. London.

Habekost, Christian (ed.) (1986). *Dub Poetry: Nineteen Poets from England and Jamaica*. Neustadt: Michael Schwinn.

Hippolyte, Kendel (1990). *So Much Poetry in We People: An Anthology of Performance Poetry*. Eastern Caribbean Popular Theatre Organization.

Keens-Douglas, Paul (1975). *When Moon Shine*. Port-of-Spain: Keensdee Productions.

King, Bruce (1995). *West Indian Literature*. London: Macmillan.

Kwesi Johnson, Linton (1980). *Inglan is a Bitch*. London: Race Today.

Livingston, J. T. (1974). *Caribbean Rhythms*. New York: Simon & Schuster.

McDonald, Ian (1992). *Mercy Ward*. Manchester: Peterloo Poets.

McNeill, Anthony (1975). *Reel from 'The Life Movie'*. Kingston: Savacou Publications.

Markham, E. A. (1989). *Hinterland: Afro-Caribbean and Black British Poetry*. Newcastle-upon-Tyne: Bloodaxe Books.

Mordecai, Pamela and Betty Wilson (eds) (1972). 'Women Poets of the Caribbean' in *The Literary Review* 35.4 (September).

Morris, Mervyn (1973). *The Pond*. London: New Beacon.

Morris, Mervyn (1979). *Shadowboxing*. London: New Beacon.

Scott, Dennis (1973). *Uncle Time*. Pittsburgh: University of Pittsburgh Press.

Scott, Dennis (1982). *Dreadwalk*. London: New Beacon.

19

African Poetry

Kwadwo Osei-Nyame

> My poetry has exacted a confession
> from me: I will not keep the truth
> from my song and the heartstringed instrument;
> I will not clean the poem to impress the tyrant
> I will not bend my verses into the bow of a praise song.
> I will ask only that the poem watch the world closely;
> Today my poetry has exacted a confession from me.
> (Frank Chipasula, 'Manifesto on Ars Poetica')

Two decades ago Ken Goodwin, in examining the transformations in its formal properties and thematic content that African poetry had undergone since its evolution,
observed in his work *Understanding African Poetry* that '"African poetry in English"'
initially 'meant, in the main, poetry by white South Africans'. Beginning with the
work of the first black Africans to publish poetry, pioneer poets such as Phyllis Wheatley, who wrote in the late eighteenth century, and the Nigerian Dennis Chukude
Osadebay, whose *Africa Sings* (1952) 'was published shortly before the modern revolution in African poetry' (Goodwin, 1982, p. v), Goodwin described early forms of
African poetry as 'derived from English models', 'naïve', and 'sometimes pathetic in
their acceptance, or partial acceptance of the white man's values'. 'Even when they
look forward to national independence, as they often do', he argued,

> it is independence seen largely in terms set by the colonial powers. Much of this poetry
> is based on such models as eighteenth- or nineteenth-century English hymns, the stan-
> zaic poems of the English and American romantics and their successors, or early
> twentieth-century English and American free verse. African names provide little more
> than exotic colour in a way hardly . . . authentic. (Ibid.)

Gerald Moore and Ulli Beier writing in *The Penguin Book of Modern African Poetry*, one
of the first anthologies of African poetry in English to be published in Africa after

independence, also observed that the work of Africa's pioneer poets was 'not only parochial but strangely archaic, with stanzas and diction derived from hymns or Victorian ballads'. Using the Ibadan school of Nigerian poets as an example, they concluded that much African poetry of the early 1960s suffered 'from an overdose of [Ezra] Pound, [Gerard Manley] Hopkins or [T. S.] Eliot (Moore and Beier, 1984, p. 23). A similar viewpoint led Chinweizu, Jemie and Madubuike to argue in their controversial work, *Toward the Decolonisation of African Literature: African Fiction and Poetry and Their Critics*, that both African poetry in English and the criticism of it, especially between the years 1950–75, were 'modernist and eurocentric' (Chinweizu, Jemie and Madubuike, 1980, p. 163).

It is worth mentioning briefly the Négritude movement, which developed in Francophone Africa and the Caribbean as a counter-ideological movement of resistance against the culturally dominant ideology of French colonialism and its policy of assimilation. Négritude poets like Léopold Senghor from Senegal and Aimé Césaire from the Caribbean deployed the philosophy of Négritude 'as the proclamation of African cultural value', and as 'an assertion . . . of the Blackman's right to a culture of his own' (Reed and Wake, 1972, p. vi.) I mention Négritude briefly because a parallel, though less well-known movement emerged in Anglophone Africa, which also aimed at rejecting British colonial domination. This movement was so concerned, in Goodwin's words, with the 'modernization' and then the 'radicalization and indigenization' of African poetry that it ultimately enforced a shift from 'the English nature of the medium to the African nature of the content' (Goodwin, 1982, p. v.). The main characteristic of this mode of African self-assertion was evident in the work of the African poets who had written extensively in

> their mother tongues and then translated their work into English. The Ewe dirges of Kofi Awoonor, the Zulu poems of Mazisi Kunene and the energetic Luo songs of Okot p'Bitek are all examples of this indirect and often fruitful approach to the task of finding an acceptable English 'voice'. (Moore and Beier, 1963, p. 20)

Although it is not easy to outline clear-cut thematic or stylistic patterns in describing the major developments and transitional moments in African poetry, the one poet whose work may be said to most exemplify the evolution of African poetry from a European modernist perspective towards more identifiably African concerns is the Nigerian Christopher Okigbo. In a special collection of essays, *Critical Perspectives on Christopher Okigbo*, the editor describes Okigbo as 'one of the most original, distinctive and important of African poets' (Nwoga, 1984, p. 3). At the beginning of his career Okigbo was adjudged to be eurocentric and modernist in his approach to poetry. For example, one of his earliest critics wrote an article titled 'Ezra Pound in African Poetry: Christopher Okigbo', in which he argued that 'Ezra Pound bulks glaringly' in Okigbo's work (Egudu, 1984, p. 347).

However, Okigbo's poetry was also conspicuous for its blending of both European and African narrative themes and forms. Molara Leslie notes, for example, how in devoting the poem 'The Lament of the Masks' to the English and Irish poet W. B. Yeats, 'Okigbo does not use a modern English style in the poem' but rather 'sings Yeats in the style of the traditional Yoruba praise song in which the attributes of a hero, ancestor or aristocrat are hailed in animal imagery and analogy from nature' (Leslie, 1984, p. 289). Okigbo was, as Leslie observes, later to make a conscious effort to 'speak more and more in an African voice' (ibid., p. 290). This was clearly intended to counter the claims that his poetry was eurocentric and modernist in both content and form. More important perhaps, however, is the fact that Okigbo's African voice was often a critical one, primarily because he saw himself as a nationalist and a patriot of his country Nigeria. This accounts for the jarring, apocalyptic tone of his poems 'Come Thunder', 'Hurrah for Thunder' and 'Elegy for Alto', which are all part of his collection of poems *Paths of Thunder*. These poems prophesied about political strife and war in Nigeria and Africa generally. By 1968, when the first of the poems in *Paths of Thunder* were published, Nigeria had already experienced its first military coup. In 'Come Thunder', for example, the poet warns politicians about the consequences of this continued misuse of power:

> Now that the triumphant march has entered the last street corners,
> Remember, O dancers, the thunder among the clouds . . .
> The death sentence lies in ambush along the corridors of power
> And a great fearful thing already tugs at the cables of the open air
> (Okigbo, 1971, p. 66)

Okigbo was asking politicians not to be complacent about 'the triumphant march' of independence because he had observed the haste with which those in power were clamouring for the nation's resources after Nigeria attained independence from British colonial rule. Likewise, in 'Hurrah for Thunder', the poet warns about the dangers inherent in the actions of politicians and greedy leaders who scramble for the spoils of office:

> Hurrah for thunder –
> Alas the elephant has fallen
> But already the hunters are talking about pumpkins:
> If they share the meat let them remember thunder.
> If I don't learn to shut my mouth I'll soon go to hell,
> I, Okigbo, town-crier, together with my iron bell.
> (Ibid., p. 67)

The elephant in the poem refers to the monolith of colonialism, which had been overthrown. The meat that the hunters or politicians or national leaders share is a euphemism for the corrupt practices of national politicians. The words 'pumpkins' and 'meat' symbolize the extent to which the nation's resources had become food for the consumption of a greedy and powerful few. 'Hurrah for Thunder' is particularly important for its prophetic temperament. Okigbo, watchman, voice and critic of his society, and hence the 'town-crier', was later to die in the service of his community when he fought as a solider on the Biafran side during the Nigerian Civil War of 1967–70. He could not 'shut' his 'mouth'; instead, he took up arms and became the poet–activist who fought for his political convictions.

David Cook's *Origin East Africa: A Makerere Anthology* (1969), which was about the first work in the Heinemann's African writers series to combine short stories and poems, is another interesting collection. This anthology provides instructive background material on the poems. Although the volume contains only a few poems by writers like John Nagenda, Joseph Waiguru and Joseph Gatuiiria, the collection as a whole is an interesting product of Cook's personal interest in developing creative writing at Uganda's Makerere University. There is also Arne Zettersten's *East African Literature: An Anthology* (1983), which combines poems by older East African poets like Okot p'Bitek, Taban lo Liyong and Micere Githae Mugo with those of then lesser-known poets like Stephen Lubega, Amin Kassam, Jared Angira and Yusuf O. Kassam. Poetry anthologies often have introductions which help the reader or critic to set the poems in their social, cultural and political contexts. Thus, it is disappointing to hear David Cook and David Rubadiri contend in their *Poems from East Africa* that they 'are quite sure that critical comment would be out of place from the editors of a volume of *new verse*' (Cook and Rubadiri, 1971, p. xv; emphasis added). This position is unhelpful to the student of African poetry interested in exploring the major issues the poets are addressing.

One of the most attention-grabbing poems in Cook's and Rubadiri's anthology is the self-consciously polemical 'Portrait of an Asian as an East African' by Jagjit Singh. Engaging with black on black racism, the poet bids 'farewell' to his 'beloved illusions' when he realizes that it is not 'only the toes of Africa' that are 'infected' by 'the cancer of colour'. He is a victim of racism, one of the 'malignant cells', who must 'fade away soon' as 'black surgeons, too', have started prescribing 'new drugs' (Singh, in Cook and Rubadiri, 1971, p. 158) – a sign of new forms of racism.

The volume also contains poems like Jim Chaplin's 'Slum Day' which, although documenting the mundane activities of existence in prosaic language, has a certain direct and sombre relevance to life, and as such makes for easy interpretation:

> Partners stretch and yawn,
> Their girls catch up on sleep.
> And children tumble their way to school

Contemporary Lusophone poetry is markedly different from its earlier versions in its combination of the themes of war, liberation, revolution and anti-colonial resistance with other issues considered apolitical. Don Burness's *A Horse of White Clouds: Poems from Lusophone Africa* (1989) is a unique collection, with poems in both the Portuguese original and their English translations, side by side. Burness writes of the collection's composition:

I have chosen poets who sing gently sad songs and poets who cry out ululations of pain. I have included poets who confidently and at times angrily challenge Portuguese domination. I have chosen poets who are friends of understatement, who suggest rather than assert and I have chosen poets who think in political terms and I have chosen poets who see the totality of human experience as appropriate fields for literature – lost dreams of childhood, spiritual love, erotic love, love for the rivers, mountains, clouds, and beautiful landscapes of Africa. (Burness, 1989, 'Introduction')

This is a remarkable departure from earlier collections such as *Poems from Angola*, whose editor Michael Wolfers informed his readers that there was a 'nearly total correlation to be found in Angolan poetry between political commitment and artistic achievement' (Wolfers, 1979, pp. vi–vii).

The poetry of protest, exile, liberation and nationalism of the 1990s, not only from Angola but also throughout Africa, remains highly political. However, although *A Horse of White Clouds* departs in some ways from the thoroughly polemical posture of earlier Lusophone writing, it still has poems of direct relevance to the individual's dilemma in society. The Cape Verdian Joas Rodrigues's 'Synopsis For a Return to Childhood' is a poem in which the child persona yearns nostalgically for a lost childhood:

> It is when the rains come
> That I return to the days of my childhood
> I seek to recapture time.

Though this is another version of 'the return to the African past' which permeates African writing, the poet does not merely crave old values but combines his celebration of the beauty and innocence of youth and childhood with some forcefully rendered, painful reminders of unpleasant experiences in his past:

> I see again in waters turned red running over the red earth
> The blood of my own revenge.

Wole Soyinka's anthology *Poems of Black Africa* (1975) includes poems from major and already-established African poets such as Léopold Senghor, John Pepper-Clark, Dennis Brutus and Okot p'Bitek. The anthology is thematically divided into the following subsections: 'Alien Perspective'; 'Ancestors and Gods'; 'Animistic Phases'; 'Black Thoughts'; 'Captivity'; 'Compatriot'; 'Cosmopolis'; 'Early Passage'; 'Ethics, Mores, Abstractions: Man, the Philosopher'; 'Exile'; 'Indictment and Summons'; 'Land and Liberty'; 'Man in Nature'; 'Mating Cry'; 'Mortality'; 'Poets Passage'; 'Praise-Singer and Critic'; 'Prayers, Invocations' and 'Miscellany'. The anthology includes several poems from West Africa, and has been a popular choice in secondary schools in Africa, having been used as examination material for the West African Examinations Council's GCE 'O' and 'A' Levels. Soyinka writes in his introduction that the poems

he selected 'embrace most of the experience of the African world – modern and historic – though naturally no claim is made' in them 'for an unattainable comprehen-
siveness of themes; or for their mutual exclusiveness' (Soyinka, 1975, p. 13). Especially
from today's perspective, however, a most obvious omission is the collection's lack of
women poets. The only identified woman poet in *Poems of Black Africa* is the Mozambican Noemia de Sousa, though there might be one or two more, given that at least
six of the contributors are not identified by gender.

Another of the better-known publications is Adewale Maja-Pearce's 1990 volume
The Heinemann Book of African Poetry in English, which very much resembles Soyinka's
Poems of Black Africa. Readers already familiar with *Poems of Black Africa* might notice
immediately that such poems as Kofi Awoonor's 'Songs of Sorrow', Dennis Brutus's
'Nightsong City', Odia Ofeimun's 'How Can I Sing', J. P. Clark Bekederemo's 'The
Causalities', Lenrie Peter's 'Isatou Died' and Arthur Nortje's 'Waiting' and 'Autopsy'
and re-anthologized in Maja-Pearce's collection. However, despite the exaspera-
tion caused by the repetition of such well-known poems, Maja-Pearce's volume is a
slight improvement upon *Poems of Black Africa*, particularly where the question of
women's representation is concerned. Maja-Pearce's inclusion of the Nigerians
Molara Ogundipe-Leslie and Catherine Obianuju Acholonu and the Kenyan by marriage Marjorie Oludhe Macgoye gives more space to African women than does *Poems
of Black Africa* and most other anthologies. Ogundipe-Leslie's two poems, 'Song at
the African Middle Class' and 'On Reading an Archaeological Article', capture important aspects of the African experience. 'Song at the African Middle Class' is dedicated
to the Angolan freedom fighter, poet and revolutionary Agostinho Neto. While
Ogundipe-Leslie demonstrates her appreciation of the achievements of pioneer nationalist revolutionaries like Neto, she is critical of the African middle class – those who
led their nations to independence from colonial rule – which Neto represents. Moving
beyond mere adulation, she asks whether, if given another opportunity, this class
would be able to fulfil the great expectations that their people had of them at independence: 'will they be of their people's needs'?

Obviously unsatisfied with the state of affairs, the poet intimates to her readers
that African nationalists have failed their people woefully in many ways. 'On
Reading an Archaeological Article', which celebrates the legendary power of the
poet's African ancestress, the ancient Egyptian queen Nefertiti, offers suggestions
towards resolving the impasse in Africa's leadership crises. Ogundipe-Leslie proposes
another view of power, which questions the sole claim to knowledge by Africa's men
of power:

> How long shall we say another world lives
> not spinned on the axis of maleness

Equal power sharing between men and women is seen as imperative to true democracy. The poem also expresses the view that only such a sense of justice will ensure
that political power in post-independence Africa is put to proper use. It alerts us to

the need to pay attention to gender issues, a subject that I will explore further on in this essay.

In terms of its immediate visibility or topicality, the most striking feature of African poetry in the years after decolonization and national independence in Africa has been its overtly political function. African poets have adopted a radical political tone in confronting dominant ideologies of culture and politics such as neocolonialism and apartheid. South African poetry, one area in which the poetry has been very political, has seen the publication of several collections and anthologies. One can think immediately of such works as Guy Butler and Chris Mann's *A New Book of South African Verse* (1979), Stephen Gray's *The Penguin Book of Southern African Verse* (1989), Michael Chapman's *A Century of South African Poetry* (1981) and the Heinemann collection, *Seven South African Poets*, all of which contain some poems of a highly political nature. Chapman's *A Century of South African Poetry* makes a claim to being the most extensive in historical range, covering 150 years of South African history, and with contributions from the likes of 'Thomas Pringle in the 1820s to the Soweto Poets of the 1970s' (Chapman, 1981, p. 13).

The censorship of the work of leading poets whose ideas are considered dangerous by African statesman and politicians also reflects the directly polemical function of the poetic imagination in Africa. For example, Butler and Mann (1979) inform their readers that 'the South African Minister of Justice . . . refused them permission to print four poems by Dennis Brutus' in spite of their repeated requests to do so. Their progressive political stance notwithstanding, the very composition of their anthology reflects to some extent the dominant cultural and political situation in which black South African languages and cultures have been marginalized from mainstream literary production and publication. Butler and Mann include mainly English and Afrikaans poets, with just a few poems by writers in 'one of the Nguni or Sotho languages' (ibid., p. 15).

Most editors and anthologists are often faced with the problem of choice, or what to include or exclude in collections. Central to this dilemma is the desire to represent and chart specific narrative forms or models of poetry as a means of elucidating how these models emerge in tandem with particular historical movements and ideologies. Thus while some readers may be spurred on by Chapman's and Dangor's (1982) introductory comments regarding the extent to which their

> anthology seeks to convey the extraordinary vitality of black poetry in southern Africa and, by adopting a loose chronological argument, to trace a distinctively black-orientated aesthetic development,

others may question the exclusive politics implicit in the very notion of 'a distinctively black-orientated aesthetic' (ibid., p. 11).

It needs to be pointed out nonetheless that particularly in the context of apartheid South Africa, it is this search for a black aesthetic which led to the emergence of Soweto poetry, alternatively described as the 'New Black poetry or People's

or Participatory poetry'. Soweto poetry is in several respects comparable to the
Négritude poetry of the years of decolonization in Africa, which sought to challenge
white racialist domination. Another South African collection, which sought to represent specifically black voices, was Robert Royston's *Black Poets in South Africa*, which
was first published under the title *To Whom It May Concern: An Anthology of Black South
African Poetry*. Most of the writers in Royston's collection belonged to the Black
Consciousness movement, the liberation movement that was led at one point in time
by Steve Biko. While several of the first wave of black South African writers had,
as Royston explains, been 'made up almost exclusively of essayists, fiction writers
and autobiographers' (Royston, 1974, p. 7), the turn to poetry was a landmark in
the literary history of black South African writing and politics. Jacques Alvarez-
Pereyre, whose *The Poetry of Commitment in South Africa* is probably the most influential study to have discussed South African protest poetry since the Second World War,
explains that

> The late sixties and early seventies saw a veritable flowering of poetry and drama in the
> black community. . . . This poetry revival can be explained in a number of ways. Expe-
> rience had taught blacks that prose was a dangerous instrument because too explicit.
> The government tolerated poetry more readily because it reached a smaller audience.
> But the poem is also a hiding place, and a marvellous short cut to saying what is essen-
> tial with great economy because it expresses the immediacy of emotion in a concen-
> trated form. (Alvarez-Pereyre, 1984, p. 38)

Alvarez-Pereyre's study includes the discussion of older poets of the South African
community such as Dennis Brutus and younger ones like Sipho Sepamla and Mafika
Gwala. His discussion is aimed, among other things, at demonstrating how poetry
for committed black writers 'reveals the "hidden face" of South African society'.

Poetry from central Africa has also been very critical of neocolonial politics and the
politics of nationalism and national liberation in general. The Malawian Steve Chimombo is famous for his collection *Napolo Poems* (1987), and particularly for his appropriation of the symbolism of Malawian myth and folklore in the service of a scathing
scrutiny of that society's politics. A good introduction not only to Chimombo's work
but to poetry from central Africa in general is Mpalive-Hangson Msiska's and Adrian
Roscoe's *The Quiet Chameleon: Modern Poetry from Central Africa* (1992). Frank Chipasula's *When My Brothers Come Home: Poems from Central and Southern Africa* (1985), is
another important collection, which contains poems from Angola, Botswana, Malawi,
Mozambique, Namibia, South Africa and Zimbabwe. Influential Malawian poet Jack
Mapanje engages with contemporary Malawian politics in his poem 'When this carnival finally closes' (in Chipasula, 1985), which addresses a non-identified person,
informing him that the 'very officers' who have been singing his praises

> will burn the scripts of the praises we sang to you
> and shatter the calabashes you drank from.

Unambiguously allegorical, this tale of the 'nation' cautions against the arrogance and egotism associated with the cult of hero-worship in African politics. Mapanje's 'Scrubbing the furious walls of Mikuyu' also emphasizes the roles of custodian and visionary that the writer or critic within society often plays through a series of rhetorical questions:

> Shall I scrub these brave squiggles out
> of human memory then or should I perhaps
> superimpose my own, less caustic; dare I
> overwrite this precious scrawl?

An urgent sense of patriotism requires that the poet preserve the memory of his fellow prisoners, the oppressed, and those who are generally courageous enough to stand up to dictatorship within the society, but who end up being 'liquidated':

> We have liquidated too many
> brave names out of the nation's memory;
> I will not rub out another nor inscribe
> my own, more ignoble

This is a comment on the artistic vocation in which the poet resolves to continue writing on behalf of his people. Mapanje is one of an increasing number of African poets who have been imprisoned and tortured by their governments for being critical. The re-repressive Malawian government under the despotic leadership of Hastings Kamuzu Banda banned his poetry. In *Skipping Without Ropes* Mapanje devotes the poems 'Warm thoughts for Ken Saro-Wiwa' and 'Reply to Ken Saro-Wiwa's letter' to Ken Saro-Wiwa, the Ogoni and Nigerian activist, poet, novelist and playwright, who was executed by the Nigerian junta led by General Sani Abacha for fighting against the exploitation of the land and resources of the Ogoni people by the Nigerian state and multinational companies like Shell. Mapanje's dedication illustrates the extent to which individual poets from different African nations collectively articulate discourses of resistance to counter common experiences of oppression.

Johnson, Ker and Maduka's *New Poetry from Africa* (1996) has the poem 'Night encounter' by Ken Saro-Wiwa. It is a poem which prognosticates the imminent danger Saro-Wiwa faced in confronting brutal dictatorship in his homeland.

> One dark night, I met him
> He laughed gently and I relaxed
> In spite of the gun
> But it was only the low laugh
> Of one who was soon to die

The gun-toting soldier who is 'soon to die' reminds the reader of the late Nigerian dictator General Abacha. The tragedy, however, is that Abacha dies only after ensuring the tragic destruction with his weapon – 'the gun' – of the man (Saro-Wiwa) whom he had met. Anyidoho's (1997) publication on the prison experiences and exile of Africans, *The Word Behind Bars and the Paradox of Exile*, is welcome because long overdue, although it is inadequately representative of the relationship of poetry to prison experience and politics in Africa. It makes an important beginning, however, by testifying to the importance of resisting dictatorship in Africa.

New Poetry from Africa also contains poems by older authors like Soyinka, Okot p'Bitek and Senghor and newer poets like Veronique Tadjo of the Ivory Coast. However, new poets like Tadjo with 'Tell me' are still dealing with the 'old theme' of Mother Africa that Négritude poetry and philosophy dealt with in the 1950s and 1960s. 'Tell me' describes

> the words of the griot
> who sings about Africa
> of time immemorial
> from the depth of . . . memory

A large amount of the existing poetry is by men. Consequently, one of the most disturbing features of contemporary African poetry in English is the invisibility of poems by women poets in general. The need to make women's voices heard inspires Cecily Lockett's significantly titled *Breaking the Silence: A Century of South African Women's Poetry* (1990). This collection is meant to 'break an area of silence in our poetic tradition, to interrupt that tradition and to change it by filling the silence with the voices of our women poets'. As Lockett writes:

> Over a period of more than a hundred years that silence, imposed by anthropologists, literary critics and teachers of literature, has largely blanked out the articulation of women's concerns in poetry. Our literary tradition has been the product of a patriarchal society, which predicates experience as male and suppresses the female. As a result the work of women has been undervalued. (Lockett, 1990, p. 14)

Two important volumes that have appeared since the publication of Lockett's anthology are Stella and Frank Chipasula's *The Heinemann Book of African Poetry* (1995), the first volume of African poetry by women to be published by the major African publisher Heinemann, and Carole Boyce Davies' and Molara Ogundipe-Leslie's *Moving Beyond Boundaries Volume 1: International Dimension of Black Women's Writing* (1995), which is devoted generally to black women's poetry, and has contributions by African women. Both volumes are informed by the awareness that women have been displaced and marginalized from a male-dominated context of poetry production and publication. The Saudi-Arabian and north African woman contributor to *Moving Beyond Boundaries*, Fawzziya Abu Khalid, demonstrates how painful it is for women to be excluded from publication with the following statement to the editors: 'It's a warm and supportive feeling to know poetry from the heart of the desert is included in your collection. Your efforts in *Moving the Boundaries* will be (*inshallah*) appreciated all over the world' (Davies and Ogundipe-Leslie, 1995, p. 243).

The poets in Stella and Frank Chipasula's *The Heinemann Book of African Poetry* celebrate the joys and pains of motherhood, mothering, youth and love, at the same time as they question patriarchy, colonialism and poverty in Africa. Although many of these women have already published important collections, the majority of them are not well known. The editors of the volume therefore hope their anthology will 'redress the balance, bringing to light at least some of the abundant good poetry by women in Africa, which is so conspicuously missing from other collections' (Chipasula and Chipasula, 1995, p. x). The volume is also useful because it draws attention to the important historical roles of women such as Noemia de Sousa and the Sao Tomean Alda do Espirito Santo, who were both active participants in the struggle against colonialism. Readers unfamiliar with the contribution of women poet—activists to the nationalist struggle in Africa learn that 'African women poets are as concerned as the men about colonial oppression, and very often their denunciation of colonial atrocities is more ardent and passionate than the male poets' ' (ibid., pp. xviii—xix).

The Zimbabwean Kristina Rungano's poems 'Labour', 'Mother', 'The woman', 'This morning' and 'After the rain', are powerful and poignant statements on an African woman's experiences, although the self-reflexive 'I' of all the poems except 'Mother' hints that one woman's experiences cannot be easily assimilated to those of an entire group. Nonetheless, a poem like 'Labour' resonates symbolically as a discourse on women's experience. Reflecting on the difficulty of childbirth, the poet asserts:

> For nine months I had borne him in my womb.
> Nine months of disillusionment and pain
> (Ibid., p. 209)

The importance of seeing childbirth as an undertaking as difficult as any other human one, which requires strength of mind, body and character, is conveyed here. The expectant mother anticipates enjoying the fruits of labour with her husband Kit, who looks on with 'warm contemplation' when she is 'borne to the labour ward'. Disappointment soon sets in for the woman, however, as the change in tone from optimism to pessimism in Rungano's narrative makes clear. The expectant mother in 'Labour' becomes a victim of male abuse in 'The woman', a poem whose focus is the harsh treatment some women receive from their husbands:

> A minute ago I came from the well
> My body was weary and my heart tired
> And yet again I heard the sound of duty
> Then I got home and cooked your meal.

The overburdened woman is saddened to see her sacrifices for her husband going unappreciated. As she soon explains, she becomes a victim of domestic violence and abuse. Her husband beats her in his 'drunken lust' after she explains that she is tired and cannot meet his sexual 'demands'. The poem ends on an ambivalent note, however, for the woman says:

> Yet tomorrow I shall again wake up to you
> You shall again be my Lord

The maltreated woman is disinclined to stand up to her man. However, the question she poses at the end: 'For are you not the fruit of the land?', potentially subverts the very idea that she condones male oppression. By framing it as a question, instead of an affirmative statement, Rungano leaves open the question of whether or not male dominance and patriarchy are a man's 'right' in Africa. The concluding sentences of the poem are uttered tongue-in-cheek. Consequently, it cannot be assumed that the oppressed woman is not interested in liberating herself from her husband's insensitive and sexist attitude.

The Heinemann Book of African Poetry also redresses another major imbalance in African anthologies: the obvious omission of writing from North Africa. It seeks, in the words of the editors, to reintegrate 'the Islamic Arab North and Egypt into the rest of the continent as a way of fostering solidarity among diverse cultures' (Chipasula and Chipasula, 1995, p. xvii). This effort at developing a truly international and multicultural portrait of Africa is really worthwhile, and is perhaps complemented by the fact that Leila Aboulela, a Sudanese woman writer based in Scotland, has only recently been named the first recipient of the newly instituted Caine Prize for African Writing for her short story *The Museum*, which is published in another path-breaking anthology of African literature, Yvonne Vera's short story collection *Opening Spaces* (1999).

The Ghanaian Naana Bayniwa-Horne's first volume of poetry, *Sunkwa: Clingings onto Life* (2000), which 'speaks', among other issues, 'to female selfhood and empowerment even as it draws close attention to specific ways in which women's oppression is manifest' (Bayniwa-Horne, 2000, preface), is another important recent publication. Bayniwa-Horne's volume represents one of the most powerful, articulate and fervent of the up-and-coming individual voices in African women's poetry. Her passionate voice complements that of her Ghanaian colleagues Abena Busia and Ama Ata Aidoo, whose *Testimonies of Exile* (1990) and *An Angry Letter in January and Other Poems* (1992), respectively, are already well-known collections in African poetry studies. In 'Who am I' Bayniwa-Horne asserts:

> I am no Job
> to be bound in allegiance
> I am a *Fantse* woman
> He is a freak hooked on pain
> And I thrive on sunshine and rain.
> (Bayniwa-Horne, 2000, p. 57)

While expressing the poet's personal and individual will not to be put down by the trials and tribulations she faces as a woman, the poem can also be seen as testifying to women's refusal to remain an eternally oppressed group, be it in relation to racism or patriarchy, or any other form of oppression. Bayniwa-Horne's collection resounds with black women's experiences, especially in the context of what Carole Boyce Davies describes as the 'common imperative' for them 'of resistance, *in different ways* and *on different levels*, to a variety of oppressive situations in a variety of contexts' (Davies, 1995, p. xv).

Stewart Brown's anthology *African New Voices* (1997), which contains short stories and poems from nine African countries – Benin, Nigeria, Zimbabwe, South Africa, Ghana, The Gambia, Kenya, Tanzania and Botswana – is 'intended to serve as a kind of showcase for African writers who are, for the most part, at the beginning of their literary careers, having published very little previously'. For Brown, 'the range of styles, concerns and voices to be found in even this brief selection does suggest something of the continuing vigour and linguistic cunning that characterizes the work of African authors using the English language as their primary medium of literary expression' (Brown, 1997, p. 138). Tijan M. Sallah's poem 'Bosnia Hercegovina', although addressing the perennial topic of war, is innovative and experimental in style and form. Ostensibly about civil war in Eastern Europe, it reverberates with lessons for Africa's troubled warring nations:

> He watched his siblings crumble to ashes.
> His world is brittle; Serbs, Moslems, Croats;
> Turf and counter-turf: Generals with instincts
> For erasing tolerance and tenderness.
> The Generals are drunk in their hearts.

'Bosnia Hercegovina' evokes the traumatized landscape of Yugoslavia and Bosnia as war zones, but only to use that foreign locale to discuss issues also largely African. Sallah's native Gambia has witnessed some of the multiple military coups in Africa led by army men who soon transform themselves into 'Generals'. The word 'siblings' in the first stanza refers to Sallah's African neighbours and the people from Sierra Leone, Liberia, Somalia, Eritrea and Ethiopia who have recently experienced 'civil war', as it is often wrongly described.

Sallah's own edited collection, *New Poets of West Africa* (1995), deals with the subject of the everyday, an increasingly important trope in recent African poetry. Thus Dick Dawson declares that the poems in *Revival: An Anthology of African Poetry*, though 'peculiarly African' in 'their protest against exploitation' and 'the conflict of the traditional and the modern', also include 'themes like love, friendship, conservation and nature' which are universal (Dawson, 1989, introduction). An apparently apolitical poem in *Revival*, 'Drat you, mosquito', reads:

> I'm after your blood
> I wish you . . . and all
> Your kind
> Had perished in the flood

Anonymously written and animated by the picture of a child, the poet is probably after the mosquito's blood because it carries a disease – malaria – that has had deadly consequences (especially for children) in Africa. Malaria is curable, but if we consider that the devastation caused by the mosquito in under-resourced areas could be alleviated through improved preventive resources and medical care in Africa, then even this poem can ultimately be read as political, since it is governments which are in the final event among those most responsible for providing the resources for their people to combat such diseases.

Alongside the critique of all kinds of oppressive and totalitarian regimes, ideologies and discourses, African poetry has not abandoned the debate over language and form and its search for the most appropriate narrative style and aesthetics. Thus, Chipasula asserts of *When My Brothers Come Home* that

> those who are concerned about whether this collection of African poetry fits in with Western literary tradition must bear in mind that it is in the nature of syncretic literatures to partake of both worlds, although it may or may not retain the original constituent traits in the pure form. This anthology has its place in world literature, of which Western literature is only a small part, because the poems deal with universal human concerns and values. This poetry is not, however, a mere extension of Western literary traditions; instead it reflects in its major themes and attitudes the contentious relationship between Europe and Africa. (Chipasula, 1985, pp. 3–4)

Unquestionably, much African poetry is concerned with the oppositional relationship between Europe and Africa, but it is not *always* as concerned, particularly at the present moment, with negating colonial identity as it once was. Among the most stimulating poetry is that which engages with the internal dynamics of African history and politics. African poetry has a remarkable historical pedigree in the life and work of such poet–activists and anti-colonial agitators as South Africa's Dennis Brutus, the Angolans Agostinho Neto and Antonio Jacinto, the Mozambican woman freedom fighter Noemia de Sousa, and the Sao Tomean heroine Alda do Espirito Santo; yet a contemporary generation of writers and poet–activists like Malawi's Mapanje, Kenya's Micere Mugo and Nigeria's Ken Saro-Wiwa have demonstrated the extent to which to be political is also to write about or critique the contradictions inherent within the often dominant discourses of nationalism, and other narratives of 'community' and 'nation'.

BIBLIOGRAPHY

Abena Busia (1990). *Testimonies of Exile*. Trenton, NJ: Africa World Press.

Aidoo, Ama Ata (1992). *An Angry Letter in January and Other Poems*. Coventry: Dangaroo.

Alvarez-Pereyre, Jacques (1984). *The Poetry of Commitment in South Africa*, trans. Clive Wake. London: Heinemann; orig. 1979.

Anyidoho, Kofi (ed.) (1997). *The Word Behind Bars and the Paradox of Exile*. Evanston, IL: Northwestern University Press.

Bayniwa-Horne, Naana (2000). *Sunkwa: Clingings onto Life*. Trenton, NJ: Africa World Press.

Brown, Stewart (ed.) (1997). *African New Voices*. Harlow: Longman.

Burness, Don (trans. and ed.) (1989). *A Horse of White Clouds: Poems from Lusophone Africa.* Athens, Ohio: Ohio University Center for International Studies: Monographs in International Studies, Africa Series Number 55: xv–xix.

Butler, Guy and Chris Mann (eds) (1979). *A New Book of South African Verse.* Cape Town: Oxford University Press.

Chapman, Michael (ed.) (1981). *A Century of South African Poetry.* Johannesburg: Ad Donker.

Chapman, Michael and Achmat Dangor (eds) (1982). *Voices from Within: Black Poetry from Southern Africa.* Johannesburg: Ad Donker.

Chimombo, Steve (1987). *Napolo Poems.* Zomba: Manchichi.

Chinweizu, Onwuchekwa Jemie and Ihechukwu Madubuike (1980). *Toward the Decolonisation of African Literature: African Fiction and Poetry and their Critics.* London: KPI.

Chipasula, Frank Mkalawile (ed.) (1985). *When My Brothers Come Home: Poems from Central and Southern Africa.* Middletown, CT: Wesleyan University Press.

Chipasula, Stella and Frank Chipasula (eds) (1995). *The Heinemann Book of African Poetry.* London: Heinemann.

Cook, David (ed.) (1969). *Origin East Africa: A Makerere Anthology.* London: Heinemann.

Cook, David and David Rubadiri (eds) (1971). *Poems from East Africa.* London: Heinemann.

Davies, Carole Boyce and Molara Ogundipe-Leslie (eds) (1995). *Moving Beyond Boundaries Volume 1: International Dimension of Black Women's Writing.* London: Pluto Press.

Dawson, Dick (ed.) (1989). *Revival: An Anthology of African Poetry.* Harare: College Press.

Egudu, Romanus (1984). 'Ezra Pound in African Poetry: Christopher Okigbo.' Nwoga, *Critical Perspectives*: 337–48.

Goodwin, Ken (ed.) (1982). *Understanding African Poetry: A Study of Ten Poets.* London; Heinemann.

Gray, Stephen (ed.) (1989). *The Penguin Book of Southern African Verse.* London: Penguin.

Johnson, R. D., C. Ker and O. Obafemi Maduka (eds) (1996). *New Poetry from Africa.* Ibadan: University Press.

Leslie, Omolara (1984). 'The Poetry of Christopher Okigbo: Its Evolution and Significance.' Nwoga, *Critical Perspectives*: 288–99.

Lockett, Cecily (ed.) (1990). *Breaking the Silence: A Century of South African Women's Poetry.* Cape Town: Ad Donker.

Maja-Pearce, Adewale (1990). *The Heinemann Book of African Poetry in English.* London: Heinemann.

Mapanje, Jack (1993). *The Chattering Wagtails of Mikuyu Prison.* London: Heinemann.

Moore, Gerald and Ulli Beier (eds) (1963). *Modern Poetry from Africa.* London: Heinemann.

Moore, Gerald and Ulli Beier (eds) (1984). *The Penguin Book of Modern African Poetry.* London: Penguin.

Moore, Gerald and Ulli Beier (1998). *Skipping Without Ropes.* Newcastle upon Tyne: Bloodaxe.

Msiska, Mpalive-Hangson and Adrian Roscoe (1992). *The Quiet Chameleon: Modern Poetry from Central Africa.* London: Hans Zell.

Nwoga, Donatus Ibe (ed.) (1984). *Critical Perspectives on Christopher Okigbo.* Washington, DC: Three Continents Press.

Okigbo, Christopher (1971). *Labyrinths: With Path of Thunder.* London: Heinemann.

Reed, John and Clive Wake (trans and eds) (1972). *French African Verse.* London: Heinemann Educational.

Royston, Robert (1973). *To Whom It May Concern: An Anthology of Black South African Poetry.* Johannesburg: Ad Donker.

Royston, Robert (ed.) (1974). *Black Poets in South Africa.* London: Heinemann.

Sallah, Tijan M. (1971). *Seven South African Poets.* London: Heinemann.

Sallah, Tijan M. (1995). *New Poets of West Africa.* Lagos: Malthouse Press.

Soyinka, Wole (1975). *Poems of Black Africa.* London: Heinemann.

Vera, Yvonne (ed.) (1999). *Opening Spaces: An Anthology of Contemporary African Women's Writing.* Oxford: Heinemann; Harare: Baobab Books.

Wolfers, Michael (ed.) (1979). *Poems from Angola.* London: Heinemann.

Zettersten, Arne (ed.) (1983). *East African Literature: An Anthology.* London and New York: Longman.

20

Poetry of the Indian Subcontinent

Vinay Dharwadker

The Indian subcontinent's poetry in English was the first body of verse composed in a European language by writers of non-European origin to enter print outside the Western hemisphere. Between the second quarter of the nineteenth century and the middle of the twentieth, it emerged as a relatively small but cohesive order of works modelled mostly on Romantic and post-Romantic British poetry in closed forms, much like the English poetry of the colonial period produced in Australia, New Zealand, Canada, and several parts of the Caribbean and Africa. Starting with the partition and decolonization of the subcontinent in 1947–8, however, the region's poetry in English – like its poetry in Urdu, Bengali, Punjabi and Sindhi, but on a larger scale – split up into distinct national canons. Throughout the post-Independence decades these new bodies of writing in English have diverged steadily from each other, as also from their counterparts in Britain, the British Commonwealth, and other Anglophone and Anglicized regions around the globe. Viewed as a whole at the beginning of the twenty-first century, the map of subcontinental poetry in English therefore looks larger, more crowded, and more diverse than its map at any time in the first one hundred and fifty years of its existence.

Beginnings

Subcontinental writing in English is now a literature in the comprehensive sense of the term, but it started at the end of the eighteenth century without a core of poetry, narrative fiction or drama. Among its inaugural texts, Dean Mahomet's *Travels* (1794) was a combination of autobiography, professional memoir and cultural exposition in the form of an epistolary travel-narrative; C. V. Boriah's 'Account of the Jains' (completed in 1803, but published posthumously in 1809) was an ethnographic field-report based on an oral history; and Rammohun Roy's multiform *oeuvre*, produced between 1817 and 1833, consisted of works of journalism, social and political criticism, philosophical explication, religious debate, scriptural translation and learned commentary. The surprising fact is that Dean Mahomet was a connoisseur of Persian poetry and probably learnt to write English verse after his migration to Ireland in 1784; that Boriah was trained in Sanskrit poetics and composed poetry in Telugu; and that Roy published texts in Sanskrit, Arabic and Persian and left behind a body of lyrical poems in Bengali. Despite their skills, however, these innovators did not highlight the aesthetic dimension of their works in English: instead, they emphasized the functional use of language and the instrumentality of prose, creating a literature of persuasion rather than a literature of the imagination.

The reasons for this rhetorical disposition were complex. Raised in the subcontinent's multilingual culture with multiple literatures and script-systems, Dean Mahomet, Boriah and Roy acquired their literacy in English 'on the job' in and around the East India Company, without the benefit of a formal Western-style education. They published their first writings in English for limited practical purposes but, as unprecedented participants in the colonial print-sphere, they found themselves engaged in a specific form of cross-cultural exchange. In this dynamic, their texts represented Indian understandings of India that stood at an angle to the representations of the British experience of India that had already accumulated in large quantities by the end of the eighteenth century. While Dean Mahomet and Boriah grappled with British critiques of subcontinental 'customs and manners' and developed tactful counter-critiques, Roy complicated the 'East–West dialectic' by combining aggressive, self-reflexive criticism of Indian society with trenchant criticism of Protestant theology and the finances of British India, among other things. Thus, their stress on the instrumentality of prose and their suppression of its imaginative dimension were linked to their efforts to change the epistemological basis of the representations and interpretations of India prevalent in this language. Such a change, as Roy argued, was itself part of the process by which Indians had to carry out a self-transformation and a counter-transformation in response to the changes that the East India Company had initiated on the subcontinent.

Indigenous poetry in English was born in this textual–political environment early in the first quarter of the nineteenth century, and developed two distinct orientations towards it. In one direction, the poetry remained embedded within the larger subcontinental literature in English, and hence reproduced within its own textual formation the dynamic of critique, counter-critique and self-reflexive critique that had preceded it. In the other direction, however, it reacted to its antecedents by devaluing prose and elevating verse as the vehicle of indigenous expression, and launching an ambitious aestheticization of subcontinental discourse and experience, which transposed the conflicts between India and Britain (or East and West) from the social, economic and political planes onto the poetic plane. These two orientations proved to be seminal, because they shaped much of the development of poetry in the high colonial and postcolonial periods. But the objects of criticism and aestheticization turned out to be variable over time, changing with successive generations of poets, entering into new combinations, and even cancelling each other. The history of the poetry therefore became inseparable from the story of a series of aesthetic and critical positions that individual poets and groups of poets invented in order to deal with their particular circumstances and with the material and cultural conditions of the nineteenth and twentieth centuries. As the following discussion indicates, these positions opened up the poetry to a range of historical ironies and cultural ambiguities, as also to a variety of conflicts over language, literariness, identity, representation and originality.

Between 1825 and 1830, however, the incipient critical and aesthetic orientations of subcontinental poetry in English were entangled in ambiguous, multiple beginnings. Chronologically, the first indigenous writer to attempt a representation of the Indian poetic imagination in this language was C. V. Ramaswami, but his text, published in 1825, was explicitly a translation of an early seventeenth-century Sanskrit poem, Arashanipala Venkatadhvarin's *Vishwagunadarshana*. As a translation, it could not claim to be the first 'Indian poem in English', since such a category implicitly equates poetry with originality and associates the medium of poetry with acts of original composition in it. By these criteria, the first indigenous author to compose his own poems directly in English was Kashi Prosad Ghose, who published *The Shair, or Minstrel and Other Poems* in 1830. While Kashi Prosad's work was original in one sense, however, it imitated minor Elizabethan verse so closely that, in another sense, as Theodore O. Dunn noted retrospectively in *Bengali Writers of English Verse* (1918), it possessed 'no real originality either in the form of the poems or in their themes' (cited in Alphonso-Karkala, 1970, p. 45). In fact, *The Shair* failed to become the decisive inaugural text in the tradition for two contrary reasons: its originality in English was at best nominal and, at the same time, its textual attributes were not sufficiently Indian.

Placed historically between Ramaswami and Kashi Prosad, Henry Louis Vivian Derozio displayed greater originality than either, and a firmer command of English and its prosody. But whereas Ramaswami (like his brother, C. V. Boriah) was a Vaishnava brahman from the Andhra region, and Kashi Prosad was a well-to-do, high-ranking brahman from Bengal, and both therefore were indisputably indigenous, Derozio's identity proved to be equivocal. Although he was born and lived all his life on the subcontinent, his father was half-Portuguese and half-Indian, whereas his mother was wholly English – which made him predominantly European by blood. Moreover, he was raised in an English-speaking, Christian household, and was educated at a Scottish school in Bengal, where he learnt English and French and some German, Latin and Greek, and received a rigorous introduction to the literature of the European Enlightenment. In British India – as contrasted to the Dutch and French colonies in Asia, or the English colonies in the Americas – Eurasians, Christians of indeterminate descent, and even upper-caste Hindu converts to Christianity were often identified more closely with the European colonial community than with indigenous society. This made British critics reluctant to categorize Derozio as an 'Indian': E. F. Oaten, for example, in *A Sketch of Anglo-Indian Literature* (1908), suggested that he be treated as a figure in the British Romantic tradition, rather than as an Indian original.

But Derozio himself seems to have undercut the deterministic logic and black-and-white politics of racial identity. By the age of sixteen he had set about passionately Indianizing himself, conceiving original poems around Indian stories, characters and experiences, celebrating Indian 'ways of feeling', and building up more ambitious lyric and narrative pieces for inclusion in *Poems* (1827) and *The Fakir of Jungheera, a Metrical Tale, and Other Poems* (1828). Although he died before turning twenty-three, in a few years of astonishing creativity as a writer and a teacher (at Hindu College, Calcutta) he constructed a more complex and influential critical–aesthetic vision than most of his contemporaries. His poetry contained some of the earliest articulations of Indian nationalism (he was the first to use the phrase 'Mother India'); he developed an extended critique of Indian traditions (he was an outspoken critic of *sati* before Lord William Bentinck outlawed it); and he urged his students to transform themselves as well as their indigenous society radically (most of them became famous in the Bengal Renaissance). At the same time, he deployed a wide variety of metres and verse forms in short as well as long poems, and invented distinctive images, comparisons and analogies to naturalize and aestheticize the Indian landscape in the English language. Derozio probably failed to fulfil his potential and may be overrated as an original poet, but his innovations became models for the next two generations of subcontinental writers in English. The double irony was that a *mestizo* invented Indian poetry in English more successfully than his authentically Indian contemporaries; and that the indigenous poetic tradition in this language could launch itself only through his supposedly inauthentic racial–cultural hybridity.

The Long Nineteenth Century

The invention of poetry in this tradition preceded that of the short story (1835), the play (1848–9) and the novel (1864), and poetry became the paradigmatic genre and testing-ground for indigenous creativity in English for several decades. The ascendancy of poetry and imaginative writing was the result of one altered circumstance: whereas the first prose writers had learnt English informally, most of the poets received a formal education in the language, which became available to Indians widely after the Charter Act of 1813 and familiarized them with the English and European classics as well as contemporary *belles lettres* in England. Under this stimulus, in the course of the long literary nineteenth century on the subcontinent – which lasted until about 1925 – indigenous poetry in English passed through several critical and aesthetic variations on the positions developed by the first poets.

The first variation surfaced in the two generations after Derozio, in the form of a gradual shift from racial hybridization to the kind of cultural hybridization involved in religious conversion. The most famous instance of his time was Michael Madhusudan Dutt, a student of Derozio's, who converted to the Church of England at age nineteen, broke off from his devastated Hindu family, and married twice across racial lines: his first wife was an English girl who had grown up in the Anglican orphanage in Madras, whereas his second wife was a middle-class French woman who had migrated to Calcutta in the 1850s. Madhusudan's *The Captive Ladie* (1849) and uncollected poems in English were technically more varied and inventive than Derozio's, and he also became the first Indian dramatist in English, when he published *Rizia, Empress of Ind* (1848–9), a full-length play in verse. Where Derozio echoed Shelley and Keats, and Ramaswami and Kashi Prosad Ghose imitated Samuel Johnson and minor Elizabethan poets, respectively, Madhusudan alluded more ambitiously to Homer, Spenser, Shakespeare, Milton, Scott, Byron and Wordsworth, and audaciously dedicated individual poems to his living contemporaries, Wordsworth and Hugo.

Madhusudan remains central to nineteenth-century subcontinental poetry for at least two aesthetic and critical innovations. On the one hand, he was the first to go beyond a mere fusion of English prosody and Indian content, attempting to bend the language itself so that it could convey the verbal and syntactic 'flavour' of Sanskrit, Persian and Bengali poetic sensibilities as precisely as possible. In this, he was the direct precursor of the twentieth-century Indian–English novelists, from Raja Rao, R. K. Narayan and G. V. Desani to Anita Desai, Salman Rushdie and 'the children of *Midnight's Children*', who have modulated standard English to capture Indian cadences, verbal habits, feelings and thought-patterns. On the other hand, Madhusudan remains the paradigm of the colonial subject riven by linguistic and cultural schizophrenia. After his early success in English, he switched abruptly at age thirty-four to writing literary works exclusively in Bengali, becoming the first great modern playwright and poet – and an immediate precursor of Rabindranath Tagore – in that language. As a young poet recently converted to Christianity, Madhusudan Indianized English verse; in middle age, as a lapsed Christian married to a Bengali-speaking Frenchwoman, he simultaneously Europeanized Bengali prosody, poetics, lyric, and drama and Indianized Europe by absorbing it into Bengali literature.

In its time, the second major example of the transformative connection between conversion to Christianity and poetry in English was the extended family of Govin Chunder Dutt, which included his brothers Hur and Giris and his cousins Oomesh, Ishan and Soshee, as well as his daughters Aru and Toru and Ishan's son Romesh. Unrelated to Madhusudan but sharing the same famous Bengali caste-name, several members of this Dutt family converted to Christianity in 1862, and collectively produced a large body of English poetry in the second half of the nineteenth century, from Soshee Chunder Dutt's *Miscellaneous Verses* (1848) to Romesh Chunder Dutt's condensed retellings in verse of the *Mahabharata* (1898) and the *Ramayana* (1899). One remarkable text by the clan was *The Dutt Family Album* (1870), printed for private circulation during an extended family visit to England, France and Italy, which contained 198 poems by Oomesh (73), Govin (67), Giris (47), and Hur (11). The most notable individual books were Toru Dutt's *A Sheaf Gleaned in French Fields* (1875, 1878) and *Ancient Ballads and Legends of Hindustan* (posthumous, 1882). The former contained her metrical English translations of nearly 200 classic French poems, whereas the latter (assembled by Govin after Toru's death at age twenty-one) brought together her versions in the ballad form of myths and legends from Sanskrit sources, as well as her own poems in English. Edmund Gosse, an influential literary figure in Victorian and Edwardian England, read Toru's *Sheaf* with 'surprise and almost rapture', finding it 'a wonderful mixture . . . of genius overriding great obstacles and of talent succumbing to ignorance and inexperience. That it should have been performed at all is so extra-ordinary that we forget to be surprised by its inequality' (cited in Alphonso-Karkala, 1970, pp. 113, 114). In the posthumous *Ancient Ballads* Toru succeeded better than either Derozio or Madhusudan in combining prosodic mastery and English mellifluousness with Indian subject matter and an Indian sensibility, Indianizing European form and Europeanizing Indian voice in equal measure – an accomplishment she replicated in prose in her unfinished English novel *Bianca* (1879), as well as her original novel in French, *Le Journal de Madmoiselle d'Arvers* (1879).

Michael Madhusudan Dutt and the other Dutt clan enacted a far-reaching cultural hybridization of India and Europe, of Hinduism and Christianity, without themselves being racial hybrids. The next two generations of indigenous poets in English – in the last quarter of the nineteenth century and in the first quarter of the twentieth – then developed some of the varieties of Anglicization and nationalism first imagined by Ramaswami, Derozio and Kashi Prosad Ghose. Two brothers, Manmohan and Aurobindo Ghose (unrelated to Kashi Prosad), played complementary and contradictory roles as they moved in diametrically opposite directions. Manmohan, educated in England at Manchester Grammar School and St Paul's School, London, won a scholarship to Christ Church College, Oxford, where his companions included the poet Lionel Johnson, writer and actor Stephen Phillips, and poet, translator and art critic Laurence Binyon. When Manmohan returned to Calcutta after eighteen years in 1892, to begin teaching English literature at Presidency College (formerly Hindu College), he found that he had become a stranger in his homeland and among fellow Bengalis, 'denationalized' by his love of England and European (especially Greek) literature and art. His suffering was exacerbated by his wife's long paralysis and painful death, by the harsh treatment he received from the British colonial government because of his brother's political activities, by the hostility of his nationalistic colleagues at the college, and by poor health and increasing blindness in his final years. Under these circumstances, in works such as 'Perseus – The Gorgon Slayer' (written 1898–1916), 'Nollo and Damayanti', (a mystery play in verse, 1916–18), 'Orphic Mysteries' (1918–23) and 'Adam Alarmed in Paradise' (1918–23) – in the last of which Adam appeared as a patriotic early twentieth-century Englishman – he produced a deeply Anglicized and Hellenized poetry that disconnected him emotionally, intellectually and politically from the actual India around him. As the philosopher George Santayana noted of Manmohan's poems, an Anglo-American reader 'would readily take them as the work of an English poet trained in the classical tradition' (cited in Srinivasa Iyengar, 1973, p. 89).

Aurobindo, the younger brother, was also schooled in Manchester and London but went up to King's College, Cambridge. On his return to India he worked in the progressive native state of Baroda for thirteen years, before plunging into radical nationalist politics in the first decade of the twentieth century. In 1907 and 1908 he was arrested and prosecuted for anti-British activities, first for seditious journalism and then for conspiring in an insurrectionary bombing in Muzaffarpur, in the Bengal Presidency. In 1910 he migrated permanently to Pondicherry, a French protectorate south of Madras, where over the next four decades he became a spiritual practitioner, mystic and guru known honorifically as Sri Aurobindo. Between 1895 and 1950, the year of his death, he produced a massive body of prose and verse in English which now fills thirty large volumes in the standard edition. His poetry was philosophical, theological, mythological and epic, drawing on an eclectic mix of ancient Hindu tradition, modern European universalism, several varieties of mysticism, and even contemporary science. Intended to 'divinise humanity', it remains controversial: his spiritual followers admire and defend it strenuously, whereas his critics find it vapid and unreadable. Despite its failure as an aesthetic–imaginative artefact, however, it seeks to capture the essence of India on a scale that no other indigenous poet in English has attempted so far. If Manmohan died a broken man in British India mourning his loss of the 'sweet' England of his idealistic youth, then Aurobindo lived long on French–Indian soil constructing a timeless and transcendent version of the India from which he had been banished for life for the violent idealism of his early adulthood. In effect, the older brother aestheticized modern England and Anglicized ancient India (in a style that was already latent in Derozio), while the younger one absorbed the aesthetic into the moral and the mystical, spiritualizing both Europe and the East.

In the first quarter of the twentieth century, a weaker variation on these positions appeared in the poetic *oeuvre* of Sarojini Naidu. Raised in a Bengali family of cosmopolitan professionals living in the native state of Hyderabad, Naidu had a precocious gift for lyrical expression in English that resembled Toru Dutt's. Between 1896 and 1898, supported by a scholarship from the Nizam of Hyderabad, she studied at King's College, London, and Girton College, Cambridge, and established literary connections with Arthur Symons, Edmund Gosse and the Rhymers' Club (which led Jack B. Yeats to paint a famous portrait of her). In the 1910s she travelled to England again, socialized with the Bloomsbury group, and was noticed for a while by the modernists: it was at Naidu's London residence that Ezra Pound first met the widow of Ernest Fenollosa, and learnt of the existence of the notebooks that were to draw him into the intricacies of Chinese poetry for the next several decades. Naidu published four volumes of poetry between 1905 and 1917, but recognized the limitations of her talent and devoted her later years to nationalist politics. However, she could not escape her early fame: promoted by Mahatma Gandhi and Jawaharlal Nehru in the Indian National Congress (of which she served as the party president), she became the unofficial poet laureate of the freedom movement, prized for her lyrical evocations of a picturesque, orientalized India.

India After Partition and Independence

The history and the aesthetic formation of the subcontinent's English poetry are both inseparable from its geography and geopolitics. Between about 1757 and 1947, the subcontinent was coextensive with today's South Asia, and British India, which at its largest covered about one-third of the area, was divided into three Presidencies centred administratively around Calcutta, Bombay and Madras. The remaining two-thirds of the subcontinent was made up of approximately 625 'native states', which retained their independent political status but gradually came under indirect colonial rule, as Britain asserted its paramountcy over the entire region. This geopolitical order meant that the Presidencies were more Anglicized than most of the native states, and within the Presidencies the cities were more Westernized than the countryside. Particularly between the so-called Mutiny of 1857 and the end of the Raj in 1947, indigenous literary culture in English emerged as a predominantly urban phenomenon, dotted across the subcontinent in a network of colonial cities, from Lahore and Delhi to Calcutta, Madras and Bombay.

This unity of Anglicized (as distinct from Anglophone) subcontinental culture was violently and irreparably fractured in 1947–8. When the British left, they divided the mainland into India and East and West Pakistan, with Nepal, Sikkim and Bhutan as independent kingdoms, and Ceylon (now Sri Lanka) as a separate island-nation. The Republic of India emerged from this balkanization as a union of the old British Presidencies and 601 native states; in 1971 East Pakistan liberated itself from West Pakistan and became Bangladesh; and in 1982 India absorbed Sikkim for reasons of strategic defence, thus creating South Asia as it exists at present. The prolonged dismemberment and redistribution of the subcontinent into sovereign postcolonial nation-states has had far-reaching consequences for the region's literary cultures: what seemed to be a cohesive indigenous literary culture in English before 1947 has since been broken up into distinct national traditions, each with its own history, canon, multilingual and multi-ethnic socio-economic order, politics and aesthetics. Of these, the new canons of India, Pakistan and Sri Lanka have overshadowed the output of Nepal and Bangladesh, and Indian–English poetry has achieved greater international visibility than the poetry of Pakistan and Sri Lanka.

In the first two decades after Independence most Indian–English poets developed a depoliticized aesthetics, focusing strategically on self-expression or self-exploration and thematically on self, sensibility and personal experience, and hence turning away from the larger critical and self-critical positions of the nineteenth-century poets. However, attacks by Indian-language writers and nationalists on the foreignness, colonial complicity and cultural irrelevance of English forced many of them to reconsider their conceptions of Indianness. Between about 1960 and 1990 this reconsideration generated two important bodies of Indian–English poetry with distinct orientations toward India and Indian materials and themes, as reconceived critically in a post-Partition frame of reference.

The first kind of construction of Indianness appears paradigmatically in the poetry of Nissim Ezekiel, which has affinities in this regard with the poetry of Dom Moraes, Adil Jussawalla, Keki Daruwalla, Eunice de Souza, Meena Alexander and Vikram Seth, among others. Ezekiel is practically monolingual in English and therefore has not been in a position to choose an alternative Indian literary language. As his *Collected Poems* (1989) show, after the late 1950s Ezekiel tried to invent ways of poetically representing India and Indians – characters, situations, motives, desires, beliefs, behaviour-patterns, and even speech – that are firmly anchored in actual individual and collective experience and, at the same time, accessible transparently through the medium of English. Such representations, however, cannot adopt a merely positive stance towards India and things Indian, since Ezekiel's monolingualism in English as well as his ethnic and social background tend to alienate him from his immediate environment: he was born into a prosperous, secular Bene–Israeli Jewish family in Bombay, was educated in philosophy and literature in England, and hence almost always views India from a cultural and intellectual distance, which is troped as irony and ambiguity in his poetry. The same is broadly true, with adjustments, of Moraes and de Souza, both of whom come from a Luso-Indian, Goan–Christian background; of Alexander, who is linked genealogically to an English-speaking community in Kerala converted to Christianity; and of Jussawalla and Daruwalla, both Parsis who are practically monolingual so far as their writing is concerned (though Jussawalla has collaborated on translations from several languages). Taken together, these poets appear to have limited access to the Indian-language worlds around them, and therefore have to construct ironic, ambiguous, even alienated visions of the subcontinent through the filters of their own monolingual, Anglicized sensibilities. In retrospect, the situations of these postcolonial poets seem closer to those of Derozio and Manmohan Ghose than those of Madhusudan or Toru Dutt in the nineteenth century.

The second main type of construction of Indianness surfaces in the work of those post-Independence poets who actively read and/or write in English as well as at least one indigenous language. The paradigmatic position here is that of A. K. Ramanujan, who lived in the United States after 1959 (until his death in 1993) but cultivated a complex of literary languages: he wrote original poetry and fiction in English and Kannada, and extensively translated verse and prose from Tamil and Kannada into English as well as from English into Kannada. Other bilingual or multilingual postcolonial Indian–English poets and their respective indigenous languages include Kamala Das (Malayalam), Arun Kolatkar (Marathi), Dilip Chitre (Marathi), Jayanta Mahapatra (Oriya), R. Parthasarathy (Tamil), Arvind Krishna Mehrotra (Hindi), Mamta Kalia (Hindi), Agha Shahid Ali (Urdu), Vinay Dharwadker (Hindi and Marathi), Sujata Bhatt (Gujarati) and Chitra Divakaruni Banerjee (Bengali). Whereas Das, Kolatkar, Chitre, Mahapatra and Kalia are important writers in two languages each, the others practise their literary ambidexterity mainly in the form of translation into English.

Ramanujan's literate multilingualism – more complex than Madhusudan's in the third quarter of the nineteenth century – gave him remarkable access to Indian-language sensibilities and experiences, enabling him to construct a poetic Indianness that was in much closer contact with subcontinental realities than the Indianness of, say, Ezekiel or Moraes. However, like the poets of the first postcolonial paradigm, Ramanujan did not merely celebrate an authentic, unmediated Indian national identity. Instead, as his *Collected Poems* (1995) indicate, his interest in and representation of Indianness were constantly modified by his long domicile abroad, which introduced a critical distance between his perceptions, feelings and emotions and his objects of poetic representation. This critical distance again manifested itself in the trope of irony, which ambiguated Ramanujan's attitudes towards Indian history, society and culture. A similar critical distance – expressed as doubt, scepticism and even aversion towards specific aspects of life in modern India – also asserts itself in Kolatkar's satirical and subversive poetry in two languages. Other bilinguals, however, prefer to represent their mother-tongues and native cultures more positively: Mahapatra, for example, mythologizes Orissa, whereas Parthasarathy nostalgically celebrates the precolonial Tamil world.

In contrast to the poets who concentrate on one or another version of Indianness, poets belonging to a smaller group have developed postcolonial critiques of their British-colonial heritage. Adil Jussawalla, for example, offers a comprehensive appraisal of the subjection of Indians in colonial as well as postcolonial regimes of power. In *Missing Person* (1976), a book-length sequence of political–psychological poems marked by the influence of Frantz Fanon, he attempts to dismantle the conventional (modernist and New Critical) aestheticism of his contemporaries to such an extent that he seems sometimes to lose sight altogether of poetry and the poetic. Risking an extreme form of political anti-poetry, Jussawalla constructs the postcolonial Indian citizen and intellectual as a 'missing person', who is missing precisely because his subjectivity and agency have been substantially evacuated by the colonial past and the postcolonial present. Jussawalla's anti-heroic persona or protagonist in the sequence experiences and represents himself, as well as his overall social and cultural situation, as a series of unrelatable, unrecoverable fragments. His mind, or the zone of postcolonial consciousness he represents as a type, has been reduced to schizophrenia, incoherence and possibly even madness. If this character is to restore himself to health, sanity and wholeness, then he can do so only by erasing the colonial and postcolonial conflicts and contradictions which have produced him and which he still embodies. In hinting at this strategy of hypothetical recovery, Jussawalla comes closest among the Indian English poets to representing a full-fledged anti-colonial postcolonialism of the kind familiar from African and Caribbean literature and theory, especially in Fanon, Aimé Césaire, Ngugi wa Thiongo', and the later Derek Walcott.

In contrast to Jussawalla, many post-Independence Indian–English poets view English and Indian–English writing as phenomena that cannot (and perhaps should not) be erased or reversed. For them, English in India has had a devastating and destructive effect on Indian culture but, at the same time, has also proved to be an undeniably productive influence. Since the late 1940s such poets have resolved the acute tensions within and around themselves between modernity and tradition, and between Westernization and Indianness, by adopting a manifold cosmopolitanism. This cosmopolitanism, which combines European, Islamic and Hindu cultural perspectives, opposes non-ironic forms of nationalism as well as unilateral and unambiguous forms of anti-colonialism. In the first quarter-century after Independence, such poets as Ezekiel, Ramanujan, Moraes, Jussawalla, Das, Kolatkar, Chitre, Mahapatra, Mehrotra, de Souza and Daruwalla represent a spectrum of cosmopolitan positions, in which numerous explicitly Indian elements interact with Western ones, and traditional subcontinental conventions and codes modify and are modified by modern ones.

Among the poets of the last quarter of the twentieth century, however, this cosmopolitanism is rarefied and aestheticized into a postmodernist internationalism from which national identities, nationalistic concerns, and Indianness sometimes vanish altogether. Thus, Vikram Seth, Agha Shahid Ali, Meena Alexander, Sujata Bhatt and Chitra Divakaruni Banerjee can write important poems that do not reflect in any way (except in their authors' obviously Indian names) on India or things Indian. Seth's self-styled 'pure poetry' in *The Humble Administrator's Garden* (1985) and in his Pushkinesque verse-novel *The Golden Gate* (1987), Ali's longing for a male American lover in *A Nostalgist's Map of America* (1991), and Bhatt's aesthetic exoticization of Europe – especially Ireland, Germany and Russia – in *Brunizem* (1988) and *The Monkey Shadows* (1992), for instance, do not question or explore their authors' national identities. In contrast to the older poets who seek to Indianize themselves or to develop a post-Independence anti-colonial stance, many of the younger cosmopolitans simply ignore the themes of colonialism, postcolonialism and anti-colonialism, and seem to accept, even celebrate, the world order that has emerged in the neocolonial global economy, without either criticism or self-criticism to ambiguate their positions.

The single most significant critical and aesthetic development in post-Independence India, however, may be the formation of a unique body of women's poetry in English, which has important parallels in the contemporary indigenous languages. In such collections as *Summer in Calcutta* (1965), *The Descendants* (1967) and *The Old Playhouse and Other Poems* (1973), Kamala Das sparked off a scandal by using free verse boldly to explore female desire within and outside a conventional arranged marriage, questioning male power as well as covert male bisexuality and homosexuality in the middle-class Indian domestic sphere, and playing simultaneously with female infidelity, women's bisexuality and lesbian identity. Between the 1970s and the 1990s the poetry of Eunice de Souza, Mamta Kalia, Melanie Silgardo, Charmayne D'Souza, Suniti Namjoshi, Sujata Bhatt and Imtiaz Dharker, among others, broadened and deepened the reach of women's experimentation, linking the female psyche to its economic and social conditions, re-examining the structures of Indian extended and nuclear families, raising questions about race and ethnicity in subcontinental society, exploring issues concerning property, law, motherhood, social class and religion, and renewing the gender-based solidarity among women writers and readers. De Souza (in *New and Selected Poems*, 1994), followed independently by Silgardo and D'Souza, has richly documented and dramatized the collective life of the Luso-Indian and Anglo-Indian Christian communities in the Bombay–Goa coastal region, improvising an unprecedented poetic dialect based on local creoles. Dharker (especially in *Postcards from God*, 1997) has devised a thicker, darker and more formal language for Muslim minorities and Muslim women on the subcontinent, without flinching from the psychic and public violence involved. In the diaspora, Namjoshi (who has lived in Canada and now lives in England) experiments with sexual identity, whereas Alexander (in the United States) and Bhatt (in Germany) explore the nature of female memory, both collective and individual, in relation to a range of disparate elements: cultural identity, homeland and migration, the complexities of assimilation in a foreign society, and the special pleasures of an unconstrained female cosmopolitanism.

Pakistan and Sri Lanka

Since 1947–8, Pakistani–English poetry and Sri Lankan–English poetry have diverged from Indian–English poetry and each other in their aesthetic and critical functions chiefly because of their specific national situations. When Pakistan was created in 1947 it was defined as an aggregate of two regions – West Pakistan and East Pakistan – separated by nearly one thousand miles; in 1971, helped by India's military intervention, East Pakistan broke away to form the independent nation of Bangladesh. Pakistan was originally conceived of as an autonomous homeland for the subcontinent's Muslim population, consisting of the descendants of immigrants from West and Central Asia and of Indian converts to Islam since the eighth century. It was launched as a constitutional parliamentary democracy, but its new constitution in 1956 characterized it as an Islamic republic. Before, as well as after, 1971, Pakistan's population has been almost entirely Muslim, but beneath this religious unity it is irrevocably multilingual and multi-ethnic. The most widespread mediums of communication are Urdu (the republic's official language) and Punjabi, while Sindhi, Pashto, Baluchi and Brahui serve as mother-tongues for regionalized ethnic minorities. In this mix, English is the preferred language of Westernized professionals, businessmen, educators, artists, journalists and bureaucrats, who make up a postcolonial elite that is far more cohesive and exclusive than its counterparts in India and Sri Lanka. Given this background, the contemporary Pakistani writer tends to be a bilingual Muslim: as Alamgir Hashmi has noted, his identity is now equally entangled in English and an indigenous language.

For many poets in English, the search for a distinctive national identity in the past fifty years has led to a new literary archeology. Daud Kamal and Taufiq Rafat in particular, and Zulfikar Ghose, Hashmi and Adrian Hussain more broadly, have directed their verbal excavations at Pakistan's rugged landscape, which changes rapidly from icy mountain and fertile river-valley to desert and seashore; and at its extraordinary pre-colonial history, from the first Indus civilization to Alexander's march, Greek colonization, classical Buddhist art, and multiple Muslim conquests. In unearthing a buried land as well as buried past, Kamal confronts the ruins of Mohenjo-daro; Ghose celebrates the cultural diversity of the ancient period, suppressed in the present; Rafat and Hussain build symbolic spaces filled with animals and animal violence; and Hashmi dramatizes epic journeys and migrations from the Caucasus, Anatolia and the Trans-Oxus region.

At the same time, some Pakistani–English poets have pushed this national landscape into a more cosmopolitan frame. Among the cosmopolitans are Hashmi, who travels frequently to the West; Hussain, who was born in India, was educated in Europe, and is a *muhajir* or immigrant in Pakistan; Salman Tarik Kureshi, whose father is a Pakistani Muslim, but whose mother is an Australian of mixed Kashmiri and German descent; and Shuja Nawaz who, like Ghose, is a diasporic writer living in the United States but also, unlike him, is an enthusiastic 'born-again expat[riate] Pakistani' (Coppola, 1998, p. 217). In his *Landscapes of the Mind* (1997), for instance, Kureshi re-examines the legacies of British colonial rule from the viewpoint of a biracial Pakistani, like the diasporic Pakistani–Welsh scholar and autobiographer, Sara Suleri; whereas Ghose, Hashmi (in *A Choice of Hashmi's Verse*, 1997), Hussain (in *Desert Album*, 1997) and Nawaz (in *Journeys*, 1998) explore the experience of dislocation, itinerancy, emigration and nostalgia in different perspectives, pitting the divided self against anchored memory and indeterminate identity against the certitude of knowledge in a transnational context. In this elaboration, however, Pakistani–English literary culture has been dominated by male writers to a much greater extent than either the Indian–English or the Sri Lankan canon. In *The Far Thing* (1997) Maki Kureishi – who, like the novelist Bapsi Sidhwa, is a woman from the tiny minority of Parsis in Pakistan, and is married to a Muslim – focuses on gender issues within the dialectic of tradition and modernization in her immediate domestic, social and political environments. Like other Anglicized women writers in her situation, however, she continues to be relegated to the margins of the contemporary Pakistani literary economy.

Separated geographically from the mainland but connected intimately to it by 2,500 years of history, Sri Lanka has a multicultural society in which racial, ethnic, religious and linguistic boundaries coincide to a greater degree than in Pakistan. The demographic majority on the island-nation consists of Sinhalas, almost all of whom are Buddhists in the Theravada tradition, and whose mother-tongue is Sinhala, an Indo-European language that has been the republic's official language since 1956. The largest minority is made up of the descendants of old and new immigrants from southern India (going back to the thirteenth century), whose mother-tongue is Tamil, and most of whom are Hindus. One small minority consists of Muslims, who also speak Tamil, and whose religion has been a presence on the island since the first Arab traders landed there in the eighth century. Another small minority is made up of Sinhalas and Tamils who have converted to Christianity: it includes old converts to Roman Catholicism, who appeared under Portuguese domination between about 1510 and 1658; and later converts to various Protestant denominations, who emerged first during the Dutch ascendancy of 1658–1795, and then during the British colonization of 1795–1948. The tiniest minority consists of Eurasians – called Burghers in this context – who are descended from Portuguese, Dutch and British intermixtures with Sinhala, Tamil and other indigenous populations, and are predominantly Christian.

In the decades since the decolonization of Sri Lanka in 1948, this distribution of identities has contributed to the formation of three large bodies of writing, in which the size of a community is not necessarily proportionate to its share of power in the social, economic, political and cultural spheres. One is a literature in Tamil, mostly linked to Tamil nationalism in the northernmost portions of the island; another is a literature in Sinhala, which unifies the Sinhala–Buddhist majority; and the third is a literature in English, produced and consumed by a relatively secular and cosmopolitan community of Burghers, Christians and Anglicized Sinhalas and Tamils, most of whom come from the landowning and professional classes in and around the island's urban centres and port-cities, and many of whom are now scattered in the Sri Lankan diaspora around the globe.

If post-Partition Pakistani (and now Bangladeshi) writing in Urdu, Punjabi, Bengali and English has been shaped by adversity under a series of military dictatorships and turbulent civilian regimes, then the new literatures in Sri Lanka have been stimulated by a series of violent populist upheavals in its democratic-socialist system. Four moments have left a particularly deep mark on Sri Lankan literary consciousness in the second half of the twentieth century: communal riots between Sinhalas and Tamils in 1958; discriminatory changes in national policy in the early 1960s that triggered an exodus of the Burghers to the West; an armed insurrection against the state in 1971, engineered by an extremist left-wing organization that included both Sinhalas and Tamils; and the beginning of a civil war in 1983, between Tamil nationalists around Jaffna and the Sinhala-majority national government, which has continued into the new millennium. Separately and together, these events have influenced the lives, careers and imaginations of such Anglicized writers of Sri Lankan origin as Michael Ondaatje, Rienzi Crusz and Jean Arasanayagam (all Burghers), Yasmine Gooneratne, Rajiva Wijesinha and Romesh Gunesekera (all Sinhala), and Shyam Selvadurai and Ambalavaner Sivanandan (both Tamil).

Where early post-Independence Pakistani poets in English seem to excavate an uninscribed proto-historical landscape in order to domesticate it in a modern Muslim national imagination, the Sri Lankan poets mostly confront a natural environment that is always already too thickly covered with the discourse, mythology and architecture of the island's long-standing, disparate religions. Thus, between the 1940s and the 1970s, Patrick Fernando (a Luso-Lankan of Catholic background) meditates on a richly Christianized topography; George Keyt and Jean Arasanayagam (both Burghers, the latter married to a Colombo Tamil man) explore the light and dark contours of a Hindu landscape; and Lakdasa Wikkramasinha (an Anglicized Sinhala) maps out the Buddhist hinterlands of history as well as the imagination. At the same time, such poets as Fernando (in his *Selected Poems*, 1984), David Craig and Yasmine Gooneratne also chart the social and economic landscape of the first quarter-century since Independence, in which a modern, urban and secular prospect is imprinted all over with traces of Victorian, Edwardian and Georgian England – reminding readers that the first modern novel in Anglicized Sri Lanka was by Leonard Woolf, written while he worked there as a British civil servant between 1904 and 1911.

Until the late 1970s much of this poetry emphasized control, decorum and aesthetic balance in closed metrical forms. With the eruption of the civil war in 1983 and the continuation of the insurrection begun in 1971, however, it gave way to a more omnivorous, experimental and ambitious literature, much of which grapples aesthetically and critically with the violence and terror unleashed on ordinary citizens by 'two incompatible ideologies, both seeking legitimation', one affirming 'a Sinhala, Buddhist nation' and the other an independent Tamil diasporic homeland (Kanaganayakam, 1998, p. 54). While the prose and fiction of this phase have justly received most of the international attention – from Romesh Gunesekera's *Reef* (1994) and Yasmine Gooneratne's *Pleasures of Conquest* (1995) to Ambalavaner Sivanandan's *When Memory Dies* (1997) and Michael Ondaatje's *Anil's Ghost* (2000) – the poetry, such as Derek de Silva's or Jean Arasanayagam's, especially the latter's *Trial by Terror* (1987) and *Reddened Water Flows Clear* (1991), has been no less consequential. Ondaatje's poetry is discussed in chapter 23 on Canadian poetry. But the civic turmoil may have overshadowed important literary aspects of this body of writing in the final years of the twentieth century, such as the singular contribution of Sri Lankan women writers to the national canon. While Arasanayagam and Gooneratne are well recognized now, such figures as Anne Ranasinghe – who was born in Germany between the wars, escaped to England as a child, lost her family in the Nazi death camps, but survived to write poems from a hybrid Sinhala–Christian position that are unique in modern South Asian literature – remain unjustly in the shadows.

Since 1947–8, Indian, Pakistani and Sri Lankan poets have quarrelled intensely with the English language. As late as 1976, R. Parthasarathy complained about his 'tongue in English chains' (Parthasarathy, 1976, p. 80); and, as early as 1965, Lakdasa Wikkramasinha foreshadowed both Parthasarathy and the Kenyan writer Ngugi wa Thiongo' when he professed angrily:

> I have come to realize that I am using the language of the most despicable and loathsome people on earth; I have no wish to extend its life and range, or enrich its tonality.
>
> To write in English is a form of cultural treason. I have had for the future to think of a way of circumventing this treason; I propose to do this by making my writing entirely immoralist and destructive. (Gooneratne, 1979, p. 6)

Nevertheless, these writers have continued to produce poetry and prose in English, even when their bilingualism or multilingualism has offered them alternative literary mediums. On a parallel plane, many postcolonial South Asian poets have also rejected the colonial origins of their writing, and have dismissed their predecessors of the pre-1947 period. Arvind Krishna Mehrotra, for instance, has argued that the subcontinental poetry in English 'written between 1825 and 1945 . . . is truly dead. Later poets have found no use for it, and a literary tradition is of no use to anyone else', so that, in his view, 'The origins of modern Indian poetry in English go no further back than' the moment of Independence (Mehrotra, 1992, p. 1). But the writers who deny the continuity between the colonial past and the postcolonial present practise the very aestheticization of South Asian discourse and experience in English that their precursors in British India invented more than a century ago. What is equally remarkable is that, consciously or unconsciously, they also continue to engage in the dialectic of critique, counter-critique and self-reflexive critique launched by early nineteenth-century prose writers, even though the objects of their critical–poetic imaginations are now very different: ethnic identities rather than racial divisions, male dominance rather than European colonization, civil war rather than religious conversion, separatism rather than balkanization, and self-contained nations rather than expanding empires.

BIBLIOGRAPHY

Alphonso-Karkala, John B. (1970). *Indo-English Literature in the Nineteenth Century*. Mysore, India: Literary Half-Yearly, University of Mysore.

Biddle, Arthur W., Gloria Bien and Vinay Dharwadker (eds) (1996). *Contemporary Literature of Asia*. Upper Saddle River, NJ: Blair Press, Prentice Hall.

Coppola, Carlo (1998). 'Some Recent English-language Poetry from Pakistan.' *Ariel: A Review of International English Literature*, 29: 203–20.

Das, Sisir Kumar (1991). *A History of Indian Literature, 1800–1910. Western Impact: Indian Response*. New Delhi: Sahitya Akademi.

Das, Sisir Kumar (1995). *A History of Indian Literature, 1911–1956. Struggle for Freedom: Triumph and Tragedy*. New Delhi: Sahitya Akademi.

De Souza, Eunice (ed.) (1997). *Nine Indian Women Poets: An Anthology*. Delhi: Oxford University Press.

Dharwadker, Aparna, and Vinay Dharwadker (1996). 'Language, Identity, and Nation in Postcolonial Indian English Literature.' In Radika Mohanram and Gita Rajan (eds), *English Postcoloniality: Literatures from Around the World*. Westwood, CT: Greenwood Press.

Dharwadker, Vinay (2001). 'The Historical Formation of Indian–English Literature.' In Sheldon Pollock (ed.), *Literary Cultures in History: Reconstructions from South Asia*. Berkeley: University of California Press.

Dharwadker, Vinay, and A. K. Ramanujan (eds) (1994). *The Oxford Anthology of Modern Indian Poetry*. Delhi: Oxford University Press.

Gooneratne, Yasmine (ed.) (1979). *Poems from India, Sri Lanka, Malaysia and Singapore*. Hong Kong: Heinemann Asia.

Haq, Kaiser (ed.) (1990). *Contemporary Indian Poetry*. Columbus, Ohio: Ohio State University Press.

Hashmi, Alamgir (1996). 'Prolegomena to the Study of Pakistani English and Pakistani Literature in English.' In Radika Mohanram and Gita Rajan (eds), *English Postcoloniality: Literatures from Around the World*. Westwood, CT: Greenwood Press.

Hashmi, Alamgir and Malashri Lal (eds) (1998). 'Postindependence Voices in South Asian Writings.' Special issue of *Ariel: A Review of International English Literature*, 29.

Kadir, Djelal and Vinay Dharwadker (eds) (1994). 'Indian Literatures: In the Fifth Decade of Independence.' Special issue of *World Literature Today*, 68.

Kanaganayakam, Chelva (1998) 'Dancing in the Rarefied Air: Reading Contemporary Sri Lankan Literature.' *Ariel: A Review of International English Literature*, 29: 51–65.

King, Bruce (1987). *Modern Indian Poetry in English*. Delhi: Oxford University Press.

King, Bruce (1991). *Three Indian Poets: Nissim Ezekiel, A. K. Ramanujan, Dom Moraes*. Madras: Oxford University Press.

King, Bruce (ed.) (1996). *New National and Post-Colonial Literatures: An Introduction*. Oxford: Clarendon Press.

Kulshrestha, Chirantan (ed.) (1980). *Contemporary Indian English Verse: An Evaluation*. New Delhi: Arnold-Heinemann.

McCutchion, David (1969). *Indian Writing in English: Critical Essays*. Calcutta: Writers Workshop.

Mehrotra, Arvind Krishna (ed.) (1992). *The Oxford India Anthology of Twelve Modern Indian Poets*. Delhi: Oxford University Press.

Naik, M. K. (1982). *A History of Indian English Literature*. New Delhi: Sahitya Akademi.

Nelson, Emmanuel S. (ed.) (1993). *Writers of the Indian Diaspora: A Bio-bibliographical Critical Sourcebook*. Westport, CT: Greenwood Press.

Parthasarathy, R. (ed.) (1976). *Ten Twentieth Century Indian Poets*. Delhi: Oxford University Press.

Srinivasa Iyengar, K. R. (1973). *Indian Writing in English*, 2nd edn. New York: Asia Publishing House.

21

Australian Poetry

Livio Dobrez

These days, in the shadow of postmodern anti-essentialisms, many Australian scholars will profess not to know what 'Australian poetry' is. What can one say except that, in Andrew Taylor's Foucauldian formulation, it must be what 'we' (itself problematical) *say* it is. What else could 'Australian' (or 'American' or 'Japanese') possibly mean? But this is only the beginning of the difficulty. Why 'poetry' (and not, more broadly, 'discourse')? And what about 'history of'? Without totalizing narrative, can one retain the idea of a 'history'? For the present writer this is the least of it. The most immediate problem here is not intellectual, that is, textually-political, but straightforwardly political. 'Australian poetry in English' is itself a tendentious entity. It is certainly not synonymous with 'Australian', since it excludes the *poesie australiane* of Maria Valli (in Italian) or the poetry of Dimitris Tsaloumas (in Greek), not to mention material in Aboriginal languages. Thus in its way perpetuating colonial dependence, 'Australian' but 'in English' – 'English' which at once functions as something other than neutral linguistic referent. I can only note this fact and move on.

The present essay is not a descriptive survey, but an argument about twentieth-century Australian history, more concerned with its conceptual logic than chronology. If the combination of history and logic sounds Hegelian, it does so with heuristic intent. The historical logic which concerns me is mediated and to that extent constructed by discourse, and in *Identifying Australia in Postmodern Times* I sought to name five such discourses, three of which are relevant here. It may be that such discourses occur wherever colonial settlement has taken place in the last few hundred years. When the British came to Australia in 1788 they encountered puzzling novelty, marvelled and observed. After which they appropriated. What I term 'contact discourse' corresponds to low-level economic exploitation; 'appropriation discourse' comes with high-level exploitation which, I have argued, transforms the land and the colonial subject, generating local identity, the beginnings of national consciousness. Australianness, that is, nationalism proper, does not arrive until the (fundamentally economic) process is consolidated towards the end of the nineteenth century. Nationalist discourse in Australia is a text in which possession of the land, a certain taming, may be taken for granted. Australia no longer appears as exotic (as at contact) or as obstacle (as in the process of appropriation). Colonial Australians see themselves, indeed construct themselves as Australian, that is, as belonging to the land. Any hint of contradiction is excluded along with the presence of Aboriginal people.

Nationalist Discourse

It is in this highly specific context that poetry, like any discourse, locates itself, both passively and actively. If it might be said of twentieth-century Western poetry in general that its project is to come to terms with the historical phenomenon of modernity, that is, technology, then the same is true in Australia. But with the difference that more local-historical issues, fundamentally those of belonging or identity-formation, come into play as well. Thus where nineteenth-century poetry in Australia takes the successive forms of discourses of contact (say in Barron Field) and of appropriation (in Charles Harpur), twentieth-century poetry comes into being alongside varieties of discourses of nationalism. Celebrated by diversely patriotic bards such as James Brunton Stephens, George Essex Evans and Bernard O'Dowd, the federation of the Australian colonies into a single independent nation became fact on 1 January 1901. What I term 'nationalist discourse' is not necessarily explicitly so. Rather, I have in mind a culture of self-assertion, of triumphalist confidence, especially in its identity which, however, contains unexamined contradictions, since what is generally asserted is identity within the further identity of empire: empire nationalism.

What Australians want to celebrate at the turn of the century is what bourgeois Europeans also celebrate: the progress of modernization. In Australia this takes the specific frontier form of celebrating the transformation and adaptation of a continent to Europeans – and vice versa. Poetic voices variously approach this nexus. Henry Lawson and A. B. Paterson do so by recourse to an *en plein air* ballad tradition and in apparently different ways. Lawson, now better known for his prose writing, praises the stoic suffering of the country poor; Paterson, with a more middle-class background, the achievement. Yet both write as natives, taking their place in Australia for granted, like their contemporaries, Tom Roberts and Arthur Streeton (implicit nationalists in landscape painting) or the early film-makers who, in the first decade of the century, stress country settings and the bushranger motif. At the same time the local note is inevitably sounded in a borrowed key, adapted for the purpose: Paterson echoing Kipling, and Lawson the European realist tradition. Nor did Lawson's local patriotism or his socialism prevent him from producing jingoistic verse during the First World War ('The Song of the Dardanelles').

Lawson and Paterson wrote much of their best verse before 1900, though both wrote well into the new century (Paterson's 1921 *Collected Verse* set the seal on his reputation). Mary Gilmore and O'Dowd, both patriotic socialists (the first finally reconciling this with a DBE), belong to the new century but express nineteenth-century optimisms, in particular about Australia. O'Dowd, now regarded as an unreadable autodidact, was influential in his day, proposing politicized poetry in *Poetry Militant* (1909) and utopian humanism in the antipodes from *Dawnward?* (1903) to *The Bush* (1912). He corresponded with Whitman and had this in common with Australian and empire patriots of the left and right, that he felt a distinctive national identity had come into being. Perhaps no one expressed this identity with more influential naïveté than Dorothea Mackellar, who could eulogize the 'wide brown land' in her 1908 'My Country' while elsewhere writing of England as Mother, Priestess, Nurse and Queen.

To assert native identity in the most explicit terms and to have the luxury of ignoring it altogether must be seen as two sides of the same discursive coin. No poet in the bulk of the nineteenth century could have written credibly without reference to place; Christopher Brennan, whose *Poems 1913* represented a large poetic task undertaken in the 1890s, could do so. 1914 and its backward-looking inspiration made Brennan's text irrelevant, but it is one of the most ambitious recent poetic works written in the West and has been much commented upon in the last fifty years. *Poems 1913* is a *livre composé* which aims at a coherent philosophic and aesthetic statement. As a well-read academic (who corresponded with Mallarmé at a time when Symbolism was little known) familiar with the classics, French and English Romanticism and theological and hermetic traditions, Brennan could modulate from the lyricism of 'Towards the Source' (with its Symbolist evocation of 'silence after bells') to the dense Aestheticism of 'The Forest of Night' to, finally, the God-is-dead, Arnoldian-in-tone synthesis of 'The Wanderer'. Others who likewise appealed to explicitly European inspiration were antipodean representatives of the Celtic Twilight like Victor Daley and Roderic Quinn (whose painting contemporary, Sydney Long, filled Art Nouveau eucalypt glades with nymphs and satyrs). Once more, however, place-identity, the reality of the Australian environment, asserts itself unambiguously. John Shaw Neilson, with Brennan the most interesting poetic figure of the time, wrote subtle *fin de siècle* lyrics with open-air naturalness in the tough Mallee district of western Victoria. His muse had to be natural. Though he has been called a Symbolist, he had little education and worked all his life as a poverty-dogged bush worker. His lyrics – visionary, engrossed in the cycles of plant and animal life, the seasons, the fundamentals of love and death – combine without apparent tension effete beauty and the harshest of environmental and existential realities, European and Australian fact. That this combination is possible in Australia signals precisely the easy identification, on the face of it unproblematical, of twin identities.

Perhaps Aestheticism, which in Europe both challenges industrial bourgeois capitalism and, in its apoliticism, supports it; which in its focus on the immediacy of sensation equally collaborates with bourgeois secular empiricism, serves, in Australia, the function of further Europeanizing the raw data of frontier experience. In this way it helps to forge the Janus-faced nationalism of Federation. Nationalist discourse in Australia generates poetry that either knows itself as distinctly Australian or glosses over this knowledge, in each case unproblematically, confidently. This is so in its second phase, into the 1920s and 1930s.

Hugh McCrae's lyrics, beginning with *Satyrs and Sunlight* (1909), have been seen as Art Nouveau, but comparison with Neilson suggests a different assessment. Neilson, in classics like 'The Orange Tree' or 'Love's Coming', treads very softly, whereas McCrae's nymphs and centaurs have a rollicking testosterone muscularity about them. Violence and sex and rape-in-Arcady coexist with a forced assertiveness. Using the term broadly to indicate a between-the-wars phenomenon, I want to call this 'Deco poetry'. Where the *fin de siècle*, following Pater, focused on the fine point of sense, this is a poetry of the body in a more sculptural, indeed quasi-fascist mood. Its context is a complex of ideas not restricted to Italy or Germany at the time and noted in Australia when Lawrence visited the place to write *Kangaroo* (1922). The list might run as follows: a cult of bodily health and of unthinking action; an optimism akin to that of the Futurists; a Nietzschean celebration of will, achievement; a tendency to racism connected with notions of evolution (anti-semitism, White Australia, the belief that Aborigines are dying out); a radical conservatism, anti-modernity but itself modern. All this may be summed up by the term Vitalism, which I read here as a nationalism gone to seed. Vitalism represents a form of modernism. Its major Australian impulse came from Norman Lindsay and his circle in the twenties, its manifesto being Lindsay's *Creative Effort* (1920) and its organ the journal *Vision*. The Lindsayites were avowedly anti-nationalist but proudly provincial, believing in a southern renaissance. They were anti-modernist but of their time. Their Aestheticism took the Deco form of Lindsay's pictures: adolescently male, historically fantastic, brashly optimistic, anti-puritan, politically reactionary.

It was a smug cultural note evident in the music of Percy Grainger and the films of Charles Chauvel, sometimes more, sometimes less explicitly of the right. Its local message was one of confident belonging to a white (British-race) continent now in the process of final transformation, wilderness not merely into pastoral run but into National Park, possessed in the symbolic social act of hiking. McCrae's lyrics vacuously exalt precisely this final-phase nationalism in which nationalism and Australia need never be mentioned, as they were in the verse of the left-nationalists. Triumphalist assertion could occupy itself fully with poetic equivalents of Lindsay's jolly erotica, classical, renaissance or medieval, as in McCrae's 'Ambuscade' or the more complex, ultimately self-deconstructing early poems of Kenneth Slessor, or the earlier verse of Kenneth Mackenzie – overtly right-wing philosophical Vitalism occurring at the same time in the unwieldy poetry of William Baylebridge.

Only escapist nostalgia can explain the protracted Australian fascination for Vitalist themes, often directly referrable to the influence of Lindsay. Or perhaps political conservatism. The list of offenders is practically the post-twenties canon of Australian poetry. In addition to Slessor, who never entirely outgrew Lindsay and whose own influence came from his editing of *Southerly* (1956–61), there were, among others, Robert FitzGerald, Douglas Stewart, A. D. Hope and, more recently, Les Murray and

Geoffrey Lehmann. Stewart edited the literary page of the Sydney *Bulletin* (originally a vehicle for radical publication) from 1939 to 1961, thus fostering generations of poets; Hope dominated his university environment for some time. FitzGerald's rugged ruminations on the historical process led him to explicit concern with place; his most highly regarded work being *Moonlight Acre* (1938), which contains 'The Hidden Bole' and 'Essay on Memory', and *Heemskerck Shoals* (1944). Stewart, currently as eclipsed as FitzGerald, is thought to have done his best work in *Rutherford* (1962). Hope, still writing under the spell of the original aesthetic in the 1980s, though with a mellower muse, has been a politically conservative critic of modernist forms since the thirties and this to the point of absurdity. His anachronistic style, fluent and urbane, has, however, assured him an international audience. More than anyone else he elaborated, in late-forties, early-fifties verse such as 'Pyramis' and 'Imperial Adam' and in the 1959 'An Epistle: Edward Sackville to Venetia Digby' and the 1962 'Conversation with Calliope', a manifesto of Vitalist assumptions. More crassly in the earlier poems, more lyrically and reflectively in the later, Hope writes of the (female) life-force and the sex-drive which builds pyramids of the will. In this mythology, the male/female pair (day to night, lamp to jar) function to promote evolutionary progress, the one – as artist – making, the other inspiring. At its least offensive this story is told in 'On an Engraving by Casserius' and 'Vivaldi, Bird and Angel'.

Hope embodies some of the major contradictions of the Lindsayites: local, yet anti-nationalist inspiration; provincial scorn of modernism coupled with internationalism; anti-feminist obsession with the, ultimately mothering, female. Mother earth which is not *Heimat*, however, but that ambivalent presence evoked in 'Australia' (1939). In Murray the mix is more radical, though still radically conservative: populist, promoting the clean air of the country and country values (idealized) as against the rot of city intellectual life; stubbornly local but willing to adopt experimental modes; apparently pro-Aboriginal but only (Pauline Hanson logic) if poor country whites count as Aborigines. What makes Murray a true Vitalist, however, as I have argued elsewhere, is his fast pace, the whoosh of fast-talking. Compared to this Lehmann's mannered, articulate pieces about ancient Romans, straight from a Lindsay etching, look rather thin. Interestingly, a strain of unease – to the point of incipient despair – is evident in many of the Vitalists, from Slessor to Murray, like a surfacing awareness of the trajectory from *élan vital* to *Götterdämmerung*.

The Australian right dominated between-the-wars poetry as the left dominated the novel. The famous city-ballad doggerel-versifier of the period, C. J. Dennis, best known for *The Songs of a Sentimental Bloke* (1915) which became a fine Raymond Longford film, charted the process of *embourgeoisement* and respectability for his larrikin hero. The Jindyworobak poets, Adelaide-based and led by Rex Ingamells, sought to localize their inspiration by appeal to Aboriginal themes. Even this well-meant movement could not avoid reproducing the hollow vigour of a Deco nationalism, in this case explicit and not, as with the Vitalists, generally implicit and obscured.

Discourse of 'Consciousness'

By the earlier decades of the century the position of Europeans in a place which had not originally belonged to them had been strengthened to the point of complacency, bolstered by race and empire complacencies. Australia was a modern nation and in cities or the industrialized pastoral landscape one could forget recent origins. In the nature of things, though, such confidence had to ring hollow, as it does indeed at the heart of Vitalist assertions. But it is worth grasping that anxiety had local as well as international-modern roots. The mechanism operated as follows. Possessing the land and the new (complex) identity it conferred had to be confirmed by inward possession. In Hegelian terms we could say Australians felt the need to raise their Australianness to the level of the idea, to make it matter for consciousness. My term for this is 'discourse of consciousness', which may be dated from the 1930s to the 1960s and which signals renewed anxiety after a phase of triumphalism. This anxiety is self-generating but its rationale is to consolidate in the very act of questioning. Necessary historical triggers come in the form of the Depression, the war and the subsequent shake-up produced by unprecedented non-Anglo immigration.

Modernism enters the cultural stream, understandably, at precisely this point. It enters in the verse of Frank Wilmot with city inspiration in *Melbourne Odes* (1934) and more momentously in the late-twenties and the thirties verse of Slessor, who maintains Lindsayite loyalties but in poetic practice develops well beyond Lindsay. I have referred to Slessor as a Man of Sentiment in the eighteenth-century sense. His sensibility is neurasthenic, awake to the fragility of fantasies (including Lindsayite ones), ultimately bound to face the reality of solipsistic void. In 'Captain Dobbin' (which adapts Eliot rhythms to the requirements of life on Sydney Harbour), in the later 'Sleep', 'Last Trams' and above all 'Five Bells' (regarded by some as the finest Australian poem), Slessor gathers up the disillusioned voices of the First War (Owen especially) and gives them an expressionist edge – what I elsewhere term 'soft' expressionism because I want to stress that its *Angst*-ridden modernity serves specific local historical-political ends.

This is more readily apparent in the historical revisionism of the thirties to sixties, a time which sees the establishment of Australian Literature in the universities, increased Australian publication in Australia, H. M. Green's 1961 history of Australian writing, Manning Clark's historical volumes, the renewal of radical nationalist traditions via the work of Vance Palmer and Russel Ward, Judith Wright's 1965 *Preoccupations in Australian Poetry* and a great deal more. In particular self-consciousness could at last readmit the neglected Aboriginal presence to white culture. Unobligingly, black people had refused to die out as a master race had fondly hoped. Now – and this too seems a part of historical logic – even as Australians sought to grasp that elusive identity of theirs, they had to re-encounter Aboriginality. From Margaret Preston to Russell Drysdale, Aborigines reappear in art; they reappear on the screen in Chauvel's *Jedda*; they reappear in the novel and in the early poems of Judith Wright.

If Wright, beginning with *The Moving Image* (1946) and *Woman to Man* (1949), more than any other postwar poet made herself a consciously ambivalent voice for the land and its first-nation inhabitants, the note of reassessment is ubiquitous. It emerges as a querying, surrealist-expressionist rewriting of place and self, as if Australia, romping, muscular in the Deco decades, now presented itself as dreamlike, once more alien, though with an alienness which has been internalized, made one's own. Defamiliarization serves local ends. It overwhelms the novels of Patrick White and the canvases of Sidney Nolan and Arthur Boyd. In poetry it crops up where one would least expect it, in the early work of Hope and James McAuley. Hope's style may be antiquarian but in *The Wandering Islands* (1955) the content, and the psychology, is modern. Moderated, of course, by irony. McAuley's *Under Aldebaran* (1946) contained grotesque and nightmarish pieces like 'Gnostic Prelude' or, more subtly, the oneiric questionings of 'Envoi'. This when Judith Wright was reinterpreting Australian history in 'Bullocky' with doubt and unease, and even the ballad, in the hands of David Campbell, turned into revelations of strangeness. Somewhat later, as if the traditional realism of Australian writing were being turned inside-out, this same quality emerges in the poems of Randolph Stow. But nowhere is the pulse of the times captured more intensely than in the poetry of a man who spent most of his time in asylums, obsessed by the fear that the communists might overcome the Blue Army of Mary. Francis Webb borrowed the modernism of Slessor and the knotty style of FitzGerald to produce a wrestling with the word unique in Australian letters. He too rewrote local history in the lurid light of the surreal, epitomizing better than anyone the problematizing process I have termed consciousness discourse. And sometimes breaking out into uninhibited lyricism. This from *A Drum for Ben Boyd* (1948) to *Leichhardt in Theatre* (1952) to 'Eyre All Alone' (1961) and the still later 'Ward Two' poems.

Postwar modernism and the problematizing of discourses of identity and belonging, the renewal, as always in borrowed European clothing, of the fundamental 'who are we?', 'what are we doing here?' did not go unchallenged. The uncritical Vitalist muse had, as argued above, a long life (it could take more thoughtful form, of course, from FitzGerald to Lehmann, and more tormented form, as in Murray). McAuley converted to a conservative Catholicism (celebrated in *A Vision of Ceremony*, 1956) and went on to edit the reactionary journal *Quadrant* – though he showed lyrical poetic resilience and a truly surprising, and touching, turn to the autobiographical in *Surprises of the Sun* (1969). Hope elaborated on the subject of the penis and the pen articulately and in heroic couplets. Poets like Rosemary Dobson wrote admired verse and John Manifold kept ballad traditions alive, with sophistication and concern born of political idealism. Perhaps the clearest sign of cultural ferment and, in this case, challenge to modernism appeared with the Ern Malley hoax. Malley was a modernist genius invented by McAuley and others in 1944 to make a fool of Max Harris, editor of *Angry Penguins*. It worked, more or less, though now the fictional genius is included in anthologies and regarded as after all talented. Which doubtless serves McAuley right.

In many ways the late fifties and early sixties represent a transition between the heroic modernism of the postwar – uncertain, myth-making, grasping and failing to grasp the slippery essence of being-Australian which was its Grail – and the revolution of 1968. To its national and international anxieties history added the Cold War. Fifties poetry, if we may loosely term it that, differs from the earlier product in its detached stance, Audenish in Chris Wallace-Crabbe's 'A Wintry Manifesto' (1959) with its call for a knowing, limited precision, closer to the confessional Lowell in the darker poetry of Vincent Buckley. Like the later McAuley, Buckley (very much a Melbourne voice), keeps the fearful subject-I in check, releasing him with care as one might a dangerous lunatic. Inhibition is conscious and often tormented, all the way to Buckley's major achievement, *Golden Builders* (1976). In Wallace-Crabbe there are partial thaws and developments up to the present. Perhaps it was not coincidental that most poets of the time were, for the first time in Australian history, academics – who moreover, like Hope, McAuley and Buckley, moulded opinion through their writing on poetry. (Buckley also edited poetry for the *Bulletin*.) In a situation of political impasse, existentialist unease mingled with Bogart, or Camus, cool. Again, Wallace-Crabbe said it all in a 1961 article on the 'habit of irony'. Diverse poets, the middle-of-the-road Grace Perry with her *Poetry Australia* magazine (launched in 1964), high-profile practitioners like Gwen Harwood, Andrew Taylor, the expatriate Peter Porter and the popular and populist Bruce Dawe, as well as Rodney Hall, Thomas Shapcott and the early David Malouf, all adopted a temperate, cautious manner. This fact was especially underlined in Hall's and Shapcott's anthology, *New Impulses* (1968), though the content of the anthology was more varied than its manifesto suggests.

Postmodernity

I discussed Australian poetry post-1968 in *Parnassus Mad Ward* where, however, I made little direct reference to postmodernity. The revolution which ushered in the so-called generation of '68 and which overtook *New Impulses* as the war overtook Brennan's *Poems 1913*, seems to me to mark the postmodern moment in Australia. Postmodernism, triggered by the communications revolution theorized by Baudrillard and by the late consumer capitalism identified by Jameson, brought affluence, advertising, television, then computer, virtuality. Its utopian phase, linked to drugs, pop culture and Vietnam protests and, more fundamentally, to the postcolonial emergence of the Third World, barely outlived the early seventies. Its economic-rationalist, greed-is-good phase continues vigorously to this day. Whether utopian or reactionary, this generated quite new discursive formations. In Australia its globalizing capitalism, as well as its well-meaning French-left gurus, spelled the death of nationalism. The sixties generation took their Australianness, and their internationalism, for granted. There simply was no issue left to discuss, after the agonizing of the consciousness-phase myth-makers. Or if there was, it had little to do with being in Australia, or anywhere else, since virtual place had no specificity.

Three anthologies, Shapcott's *Australian Poetry Now* (1970), the Melbourne *Applestealers* (1974), edited by Robert Kenny and C. Talbot, and Sydney's *The New Australian Poetry* (1979), edited by John Tranter, established the fact of a generation of '68. Broadly it followed international, in particular, American trends, those of Donald Allen's *The New American Poetry*. It also coincided with renewed cultural vitality in and following the sixties spring: a new Australian drama, the painting of Brett Whiteley, the resurgence of the local film industry. Overseas poetic mentors could vary, though the Beats, the New York school and Black Mountain played prominent roles. Older Australian mentors included Ken Taylor in Melbourne, whose 'At Valentine's' provided a new model, and Bruce Beaver in Sydney (in particular the Beaver of *Letters to Live Poets*, 1969). The effect, as many commentators have noted, was to make substantial difference to the writing of older poets, both the generation of McAuley and that of Wallace-Crabbe. There was a massive explosion in readings and publication; readings in Balmain and Carlton (at La Mama with Kris Hemensley presiding), at Monash (with the poets Laurie Duggan, Alan Wearne and John Scott); publications in a rush of little underground magazines. But the underground also affected established publishing: Hemensley became poetry editor of *Meanjin* in the mid-to-late seventies, and Robert Adamson led a coup which took over *Poetry Magazine*, subsequently *New Poetry*.

In *Parnassus Mad Ward* I divided '68 poetry into three poetics strands: one in which the subject and language function transparently; one in which subjectivity is mediated by language; one in which subjectivity dies in the play of linguistic signifiers. In each case, however, I noted a new immediacy in the verse and an easy stance towards the subject-I quite different from the ironist, self-conscious distancing of subjectivity in fifties verse. Michael Dransfield, Nigel Roberts and Vicki Viidikas exemplified the poetic of transparency; John Forbes and Tranter that of hard-edge play of signifiers; Hemensley tended to shift between a Beat (*Children of Albion*) transparency and a field poetics, a projectivism of sorts (in *The Poem of the Clear Eye*, 1975); as did the Adelaide poet Richard Tipping, from *Soft Riots* (1972) to *Domestic Hardcore* (1975); Adamson moved between the most straightforwardly autobiographical verse (*Where I Come From*, 1979) to a Duncanesque projectivism in 'The Rumour'. Others, like Charles Buckmaster, Jennifer Maiden, Jan Harry, Susan Hampton or the next generation of '68 poets (Pi O, Steve Kelen, Gig Ryan) worked out further variations. Two of the promising stars of the generation, Dransfield and Buckmaster, died very early deaths. Dransfield, a major figure in Australian writing, scribbled carelessly and sometimes brilliantly in the midst of addiction, combining the easy nonchalance of the times with biting ironies and sensitive intelligence, a delicacy reminiscent of, but more spontaneous than, Slessor's – perhaps most memorably in his Courland Penders poems, his drug verse ('Fix', 'Bums' Rush', 'Miss Havisham') and his M Ward Canberra poems. The self-taught, Dylan-driven Adamson managed a kinetic verse that could project something of his hard life and his survival-of-the-fittest experiences on the Hawkesbury river. Tranter experimented with self-referentiality to the point of (highly readable) degree zero in 'The Alphabet Murders' and his *Crying in Early Infancy* sonnets.

Post-'68 did not belong to a single group of poets, even one as diverse as the above. Many older poets continued to write and young poets unconnected with the New Poetry emerged. Hall and Shapcott turned to the novel; Malouf concentrated, though not exclusively, on prose; Dorothy Hewett wrote verse and plays; Roger McDonald, editor of the timely Paperback Poets series, also wrote prose; Judith Rodriguez, Antigone Kefala, Rhyll McMaster, Geoff Page, Fay Zwicky and many others simply wrote. The attack on the New Poetry, which I have termed a Battle of the Books and characterized as a clash between a poetic of praxis and the 'reflective' mode, was headed by Robert Gray and Lehmann in their 1983 anthology *The Younger Australian Poets*. Rivalries continued when both Tranter (with Philip Mead) and Gray and Lehmann issued antagonistic anthologies in 1991. But no one could continue by-now jaded traditions in the seventies and eighties. Gray, like Dransfield and Whiteley, sought Asian inspiration; Lehmann developed to the reflections of *Ross's Poems*. There were also younger followers of talent such as Philip Hodgins. Above all, there was the larger-than-life Les Murray. Murray defended hillbilly Boeotia against Peter Porter's suave Athens; he asserted a visionary Catholicism; committed imitations of Aboriginal oral songs; foolishly involved himself in the reactionary attack on the left-wing historian Manning Clark; suffered existentially; generated a 'vernacular republic' of poetry with experimental verve that the generation of '68 might envy. Gradually, he received the praise of a conservative academy still withheld from the poets of '68.

Postmodern fragmentation brought about the demise of class as much as of nation. What remained was 'pluralpolitics', that of gender or the environment. It was a sign of the change that women's and minority writing began to gain recognition. The first women's anthology, *Mother I'm Rooted*, was edited in 1975 by Kate Jennings, to be followed by Susan Hampton's and Kate Llewellyn's *The Penguin Book of Australian Women Poets* in 1986. Pi O's 1985 *Off the Record* anthology contained twenty-three women to thirty men and a substantial non-Anglo presence. It also showed that much of the populist revolution of the New Poetry and the sixties Happening had been channelled into Performance Poetry, a vogue thus far preserved from academic appropriation. At the same time, Aboriginal politics had been active since the sixties and a large cultural flowering (best known for its visual arts achievement but extending to every field) had established itself. Kath Walker (Oodgeroo) wrote her ground-breaking *We Are Going* in 1964 and there have been many who followed the example, including Jack Davis, Kevin Gilbert, Archie Weller, Lionel Fogarty and Lisa Bellear. Gilbert's 1988 *Inside Black Australia* brought most of these together. Likewise, oral traditions have continued and recent collections of translations include *The Honey-Ant Men's Love Song* and *Little Eva at Moonlight Creek*.

It is customary to conclude an essay like this one on a note of open-ended pluralism, given the difficulty of attempting any totalization of the present. In this case it seems to me plurality is structurally historical and one of the legacies of postmodernity. I myself have not sought to evade synthesis, to present a mere catalogue of Australian poetry, though cataloguing has been necessary to a degree. Rather, focus has been on three historically successive discursive formations, those of national consolidation, questioning self-consciousness and, finally, the postmodern retirement of the question. In a recently colonized country the question is inescapably one of ownership, belonging, identity. All else, including this century's modernization, must be interpreted in its light. Australian poetry in the first three decades of the century celebrates conquest, either overtly or covertly. From the thirties to the sixties it seeks the ultimate conquest: to gain by loss, query, doubt, to escape historical-geographical contingency by entertaining and so overcoming the idea of it. By the seventies the entire project is made meaningless by globalization. The question ceases, though it has not been answered. In Tranter's poetry the death of the question is matter for congratulation, in Dransfield's it is a problematical fact to be lived out and to die by. At any rate just this crisis precipitated by postmodernity shakes the foundations of the present essay. Why 'poetry'? Why 'Australian'? How 'history of'?

BIBLIOGRAPHY

Histories

Dutton, G. (ed.) (1964). *The Literature of Australia*. Harmondsworth: Penguin.

Hergenhan, L. (ed.) (1988). *The Penguin New Literary History of Australia*. Ringwood: Penguin.

Kramer, L. (ed.) (1981). *The Oxford History of Australian Literature*. Oxford: Oxford University Press.

Wilde, W. H., Hooton, J. and Andrews, B. (eds) (1995). *The Oxford Companion to Australian Literature*. Melbourne: Oxford University Press.

Anthologies

Campbell, D. (ed.) (1970). *Modern Australian Poetry*. Melbourne: Sun Books.

Duwell, M. and Dixon, R. M. W. (eds) (1990). *The Honey-Ant Men's Love Song and Other Aboriginal Song Poems*. St Lucia: University of Queensland Press.

Duwell, M. and Dixon, R. M. W. (eds) (1994). *Little Eva at Moonlight Creek and Other Aboriginal Song Poems*. St Lucia: University of Queensland Press.

Gilbert, K. (ed.) (1988). *Inside Black Australia: An Anthology of Aboriginal Poetry*. Ringwood: Penguin.

Gray, R. and Lehmann, G. (eds) (1983). *The Younger Australian Poets*. Sydney: Hale & Iremonger.

Gray, R. and Lehmann, G. (eds) (1991). *Australian Poetry in the Twentieth Century*. Melbourne: Heinemann.

Hall, R. and Shapcott, T. W. (eds) (1968). *New Impulses in Australian Poetry*. St Lucia: University of Queensland Press.

Hampton, S. and Llewellyn, K. (eds) (1986). *The Penguin Book of Australian Women Poets*. Ringwood: Penguin.

Heseltine, H. (ed.) (1981). *The Penguin Book of Modern Australian Verse*. Ringwood: Penguin.

McDonald, R. (ed.) (1974). *The First Paperback Poets Anthology*. St Lucia: University of Queensland Press.

Pi O (ed.) (1985). *Off the Record*. Ringwood: Penguin.

Shapcott, T. W. (ed.) (1970). *Australian Poetry Now*. Melbourne: Sun Books.

Tranter, J. (ed.) (1979). *The New Australian Poetry*. St Lucia: Makar Press.

Tranter, J. and Mead, P. (eds) (1991). *The Penguin Book of Modern Australian Poetry*. Ringwood: Penguin.

Criticism

Brooks, D. and Walker, B. (eds) (1989). *Poetry and Gender: Statements and Essays in Australian Women's Poetry and Poetics*. St Lucia: University of Queensland Press.

Buckley, V. (1957). *Essays in Poetry, Mainly Australian*. Melbourne: Melbourne University Press.

Dobrez, L. A. C. (1990). *Parnassus Mad Ward: Michael Dransfield and the New Australian Poetry*. St Lucia: University of Queensland Press.

Duwell, M. (ed.) (1982). *A Possible Contemporary Poetry*. St Lucia: Makar Press.

Kirkby, J. (ed.) (1982). *The American Model: Influence and Independence in Australian Poetry*. Sydney: Hale & Iremonger.

Taylor, A. (1987). *Reading Australian Poetry*. St Lucia: University of Queensland Press.

Wright, J. (1965). *Preoccupations in Australian Poetry*. Melbourne: Melbourne University Press.

22

New Zealand Poetry

Terry Sturm

A generation ago there would have been widespread agreement about the general shape an account of New Zealand poetry would take. It would have confined itself to poetry in English, and identified a development in two phases: a colonial period of largely Anglophile mimic-verse, lasting from the beginnings of European settlement in the 1840s until the early decades of the twentieth century, followed, in the key decade of the 1930s, by the emergence of powerful nationalist impulses, aligned to modernist developments overseas. These transformed the direction of poetry, establishing a local tradition and the beginnings of a canon. In the later 1960s, however, this dominant cultural nationalist paradigm, buttressed as it often was by romanticist organic metaphors of the birth and maturing of colonies into nations, began to crumble, unable to contain the sheer diversity of poetic impulses – experimental, postmodern, postcolonial, feminist, indigenous – which characterized the practice of poets during the last three decades of the century. This new work has in turn prompted new readings, new mappings, of the past, problematizing the very notion of 'New Zealand poetry', as well as the apparent stabilities of nation, location and language on which it had been based.

None of the shifts identified above occurred without protracted and lively debates – about particular authors, about the nature of poetry itself (in particular, about what its proper subject matter in New Zealand should be), about the broader context of the kind of society New Zealand was, its history, its 'place in the world', and its future. In fact throughout the twentieth century New Zealand produced an unusually rich discourse of *poetics*, articulated through influential anthologies and the arguments they generated, as well as through lively, if often shortlived, literary magazines and the small presses which supported them. Although other forms of New Zealand writing, including non-fiction, began to attract attention within the ambit of postcolonial, postmodernist and feminist theory in the 1980s, poetics has remained a key *instance* of discourse about the culture as a whole. For these reasons it provides the starting point for this account of 'New Zealand poetry'.

The Colonial Inheritance

It was the poet Allen Curnow, in his most considered foray into poetics, the introduction to his anthology, *The Penguin Book of New Zealand Verse* (1960), who articulated most persuasively the notion of a 'historical divide' separating the first eight decades of the country's 'literature' (1840–1920) from the subsequent three or four decades (1920/1930–60), asserting that this was 'the most significant fact to be regarded in any realistic retrospect' on the country's literary history (Curnow, 1987, p. 137). The historical divide marked a huge social and cultural shift, 'away from colonialism and on towards the island nation of the past three or four decades' (ibid., p. 135). It also involved a redrawing of boundaries, an anti-colonialist breaking of New Zealand's direct cultural line to England and a nationalist redrawing of that line as a circle around and containing 'New Zealand', the demarcation of an internal space whose characterizing feature – the signature of the national – is geographical, locational and historical 'difference': 'peculiar pressures . . . arising from the isolation of the country, its physical character, and its history' (ibid., p. 133).

Curnow's reading of colonial poetry focused on the destructive psychic effects of colonial dislocation and dependence, and on a growing split between 'imagination' and 'culture' on the one hand (the province of what had been formed in England, and become increasingly fossilized) and on the other the practical work of colonization and settlement which by the early twentieth century had hardened into an obstinate, philistine materialism and conformism. Few of the scores of colonial poets who inhabited New Zealand's first significant national anthology (Alexander and Currie's *New Zealand Verse*, 1906) escaped critical scrutiny. What survived was, rather, a handful of *poems*, read as in some way avoiding the general cultural malaise and offering glimpses of the real experience of colonization: accurate reflections of the strangenesses of landscape and seascape, renderings of sensibility less strident or sentimental than the standard rhymed genuflexions to Empire and colonial Destiny. In this respect at least Curnow's project was entirely successful. Neither of the two national anthologies which appeared after the 1960 *Penguin* – a new Penguin anthology, edited by Ian Wedde and Harvey McQueen, in 1985, and *The Oxford Anthology of New Zealand Poetry in English*, edited by Jenny Bornholdt, Gregory O'Brien and Mark Williams, in 1997 – included more than a handful of nineteenth-century poems.

The Maori Tradition

Alexander and Currie, like most critics at the turn of the century, had singled out as a potentially distinctive feature of New Zealand poetry the 'colourful' narrative possibilities of Maori myths and legends. The vast colonial body of poeticized Maori myths and legends was almost wholly drawn from Sir George Grey's collection, *Polynesian Mythology* (1855). Grey's preface to that volume, which explained why, as governor of the colony, he had undertaken the project – 'I could neither successfully govern, nor hope to conciliate, a numerous and turbulent people, with whose language, manners, customs, religion, and modes of thought I was quite unacquainted' – indicates how indivisible the project's political and cultural motives were. The prototype of the many poetic appropriations of Maori myth that followed in the wake of Grey's collection was Alfred Domett's *Ranolf and Amohia: A South-Sea Day-Dream*, an epic of twenty-five cantos published in London in 1872 and (revised) in 1883. Domett, also a leading political figure in the colony, derived the form of his poem from the high European tradition of epic, much of his versification from Longfellow's treatment of the Hiawatha legend in the United States, and his philosophy from the discourse of religious belief and doubt in Victorian England. The elaborateness and intricacy of its format and versification – a distinctive feature of almost all colonial verse – was primarily a demonstrative act of affiliation with Britishness, epitomizing local anxieties about colonial identity in a country remote from the centre of High Culture.

Perhaps by way of reaction against the wholesale appropriation of Maori culture by their precursors, poets of the nationalist period tended to avoid or evade the complications of indigenous/settler relations, in their explorations of identity. Indeed, although the nationalist paradigm emphasized 'difference' from England, *internal* cultural differences were relegated to the margins in order to promote the construction of an inclusive settler/national identity in an essentially unpeopled, unhistoried landscape. Such gestures, in the poetry of Charles Brasch and others, in their search, as Alex Calder puts it, 'for a deeper relation of settler to place' often 'repeat colonial patterns' which they otherwise condemn (Calder, 1998, p. 172), and in the process Maori poetry itself was relegated to an earlier pre-settlement era, as if belonging to a museum of the past.

The tradition of poetry composed in the Maori language is in fact rich, copious and *ongoing* into the present. Much of it has not been committed to print, and remains vested in tribal memory. However, from among the thousands of texts in archives and libraries an exceptional record of 400 waiata (sung poems) of many kinds and from many different tribal sources – the product of decades of scholarly work by Sir Apirana Ngata between the 1920s and 1950, and by his successor Pei Te Hurunui Jones – appeared in four volumes under the title *Nga Moteatea* ('The Songs') in 1959, 1961, 1970 and 1990. Numerous other collections of translations began to appear after the 1960s, notably Mervyn McLean and Margaret Orbell's *Traditional Songs of the Maori* and Orbell's *Waiata: Maori Songs in History*, a collection which illustrated the ways in which nineteenth-century waiata represented the transformations (political, religious, linguistic) wrought by colonization and settlement. In the wake of this growing awareness of the indigenous inheritance, the editors of the new 1985 *Penguin Book of New Zealand Verse* controversially included representations of the ongoing Maori-language tradition (including sixteen twentieth-century poets), accompanied by translations and interspersed among the English-language poems. The poets were presented chronologically, but the editors were also interested to emphasize differences of cultural perspective. One of Curnow's best-known early poems of settler alienation, 'House and Land' (1941), appeared beside a waiata tangi (elegy) by Arapeta Awatere in which the sense of personal loss is contained within an indigenous frame of explanatory myth of precisely the kind that seemed unavailable to Curnow's displaced settlers, 'with never a soul at home'.

In fact, the intersections of English and Maori traditions became increasingly complex from the 1950s onwards. James K. Baxter, in his later poetry especially, was able to achieve an inwardness of reference to Maori values and spirituality, as if he had at last found the master narrative whose absence had driven him to poetry throughout his life. His contemporary, Alistair Campbell – of mixed Rarotongan and Scottish descent – drew strongly on Polynesian rhythms and metaphors in his earlier poems of the 1950s, and later moved increasingly into Maori and Pacific subject matter. In the late 1950s, also, New Zealand's first major Maori poet writing in English, Hone Tuwhare, began publishing, and his voice immediately cut across the polarized poetic debates of the time, which were both generational and regional, and focused on what was felt to be the narrowness of cultural nationalism's emphasis on geographical isolation, landscape and history. Initially a poet of formal lyric eloquence with a rich vein of allusiveness to Maori metaphors, myths and distinctive cultural knowledge, his poetry became increasingly freer and more hybrid, increasingly a mode of highly skilled, subtly charged conversation in which formal and informal registers of New Zealand English and Maori speech meet, collide, mix and comment on each other. By the 1980s the term 'Maori poetry' covered a wide range of practice, some poets composing wholly in the traditional forms of waiata, some writing wholly in English, and others writing in varying proportions in both languages.

Expatriatism

The phenomenon of expatriatism, invariably significant in *all* colonial societies, as settler writers seek to negotiate their peripheral relationship to the cultural 'centre', could be accommodated *within* nationalism provided that the writer could be interpreted as 'discovering' his or her nationality through absence. New Zealand's cultural icon of such self-discovery in the earlier part of the century is Katherine Mansfield, but nationalism was also able to read other writers this way – most notably the 1930s poet, Robin Hyde, for whom the final eighteen months of her life, travelling in China and then to London, seemed to crystallize the discovery of a poetic identity which had largely eluded her as long as she stayed in New Zealand. However, there was always a problem of identification: when was an expatriate poet *so* expatriate as to cease to be a New Zealand poet?

One of the major tests for cultural nationalism's construction of its own pre-history was the turn-of-the-century phenomenon of literary expatriatism to Australia. The issue was of moment because the Sydney *Bulletin*, to which many New Zealand poets were attracted, was itself the source, in the 1890s and after, of *Australian* cultural nationalism. The question often asked, 'Was there a *Bulletin* school of New Zealand poetry?', entailed a more fundamental question, 'Did New Zealand's cultural nationalism begin much earlier than the 1930s (at least a generation earlier, in fact), and was it in fact not "internally generated" but simply an Australian export?' The orthodox answer, that New Zealand contributors to the *Bulletin* belonged largely to a genteel colonial poetic tradition in decay, needs considerable modification. The *Bulletin* published a huge amount of New Zealand verse between the later 1890s and 1960 – more than 4,000 items according to a recent estimate – and it was a major outlet for at least a dozen New Zealand poets, three of whom – A. H. Adams, David McKee Wright and Douglas Stewart – were in fact literary editors of the magazine for more than half the period to 1960.

A considerable number of these and other early twentieth-century poets, most of them New Zealand-born and struggling to survive by making professional careers as journalists, are best seen as transitional figures, striving to articulate questions about nation and location a generation before the fully-fledged cultural nationalism of the 1930s and 1940s. Some, like Will Lawson and McKee Wright, attempted a local balladry; Jessie Mackay and Constance Clyde were influenced by the turn-of-the-century women's movement; Adams and Frank Morton attempted a more urban-based poetry, influenced by Decadent and early modernist models in England and Europe. All, in different ways, sought to question the puritanism, materialism and conformism of the new society which was emerging in the wake of colonialism. At its best the poetry also began to draw on the new variety of English that began to be noticed (and deplored by Anglophile educationists) from the 1890s onwards. Blanche Baughan's 'A Bush Section' offered a paradigm of this shift occurring in the language of New Zealand poetry.

In the later twentieth century the increasing mobility of writers across national boundaries remains a phenomenon generating unresolved postcolonial problems of identity, location, and the interpretation of texts. Douglas Stewart disappeared from New Zealand anthologies after the 1950s, as did William Hart-Smith, another distinguished *Bulletin* contributor. The editors of the 1985 Penguin anthology excluded Hart-Smith and a number of younger New Zealand expatriate poets in Australia ('with regret'), as well as the established poets Peter Bland (living in England) and Charles Doyle (living in Canada). However, they *included* Alan Brunton, Fleur Adcock and Kevin Ireland because of 'their continued connection' and because they drew 'sustenance from location' (Wedde and McQueen, 1985, p. 45). Quite what principles underlay these differentiations is unclear.

The Nationalist Canon, 1920–1960

The canon which Allen Curnow established in the 1960 Penguin anthology, if one were to list the poets who received selections of ten or more pages, consisted of nine poets, eight male and one female, all of whom belonged to the near side of his 'historical divide', the decades between 1920 and 1960. They were Ursula Bethell, A. R. D. Fairburn, R. A. K. Mason, Charles Brasch, Curnow himself, Denis Glover, Keith Sinclair, Kendrick Smithyman and James K. Baxter. Women fared better if the grouping were extended to include a further six poets given six or eight pages: Blanche Baughan (the only poet from the far side of the historical divide), Robin Hyde and Gloria Rawlinson, alongside D'Arcy Cresswell, Charles Spear and C. K. Stead. Eileen Duggan, whose work Curnow wished to include, refused permission. With the exception of Cresswell, and a more generous evaluation by others of a number of 1950s poets – Alistair Campbell, M. K. Joseph and Louis Johnson – these assessments were very largely confirmed, for the period up to the 1950s, in the anthologies which appeared after 1960. Curnow's singling out of Kendrick Smithyman and C. K. Stead in addition to Baxter, among the newer post-Second World War poets, was also strikingly confirmed by their later development. In the later anthologies there has also been a general consensus about the new figures to be added to the 'canon' in the decades following: from the 1960s, Hone Tuwhare, Fleur Adcock and Vincent O'Sullivan, and from the early 1970s to the mid-1980s, Ian Wedde, Bill Manhire, Lauris Edmond and Elizabeth Smither.

League tables are one thing, of course, but how the poets are discussed by powerful anthologists is another, and often a great deal of cultural debate is generated around the edges of the main figures: in the weightings given to lesser figures and in the nature of the selections made from the more substantial figures. Much of the initial controversy which greeted Curnow's 1960 Penguin centred on its sparse selection of 1950s poets (the so-called 'Baxter generation'), and Baxter himself produced numerous anti-nationalist counter-readings of poets whom Curnow had under-represented, readings which spoke as eloquently of his own mytho-poetic and psychological interests as Curnow's readings reflected his own investment in cultural nationalist adaptations of modernist principles.

Curnow's subtle readings of his canonical poets recognized individual distinctions of tone, technique and thematic emphasis, but carefully assembled generalizations around a number of key formalist and modernist terms of approbation: 'tension' and ambivalence of attitude, a critical slant on colonial history and its still-active traces in contemporary society, a carefully wrought metaphoric or symbolic response to landscape (beyond colonial scenic pictorialism), complexity of language. All of these qualities functioned as markers of, as he put it in his discussion of Mansfield's 'To Stanislaw Wyspianski', 'the emergence of New Zealand as a characterizing emotional force in the work of a native poet', a sign of the inward engagement of 'the whole personality' in the problems of being a poet in New Zealand. Although the language of postcolonial theory was not available to Curnow, his emphasis on inward, unresolved tensions fits closely Stephen Slemon's argument that 'ambivalence of emplacement' – outside the '*illusion* of a stable self/other, here/there binary division' – is 'the "always already" condition of Second-World settler and post-colonial literary writing', the source of its particular importance within the field of postcolonial analysis: '[In] the white literatures of Australia, or New Zealand, or Canada, or southern Africa, anti-colonialist resistance has *never* been directed at an object or a discursive structure which can be seen as purely external to the self' (Slemon, 1996, p. 80).

It was nevertheless the case that some poets, and some poems, fitted the terms of cultural nationalism better than others. Fairburn, Glover, Brasch and Bethell – later, Baxter and Smithyman (but only in some of their poems) – lent themselves to the charting of a sophisticated iconography of New Zealand landscape, including its regional differences, which at the same time respected the varieties of preoccupation explored through their landscape meditations: Fairburn's love poetry and poetry of social comment; Glover's interest in the kiwi 'common man' explored though his lone 'Harry' and 'Arawata Bill' personae; Brasch's sense of alienation from landscape and history, and the same concern (though more personally focused) in some of Baxter's poetry; Bethell's religious meditations, grounded in the Canterbury landscape; and Smithyman's use of Northland landscapes to explore epistemological issues. However, poetry and poems whose personal, domestic or psychological interests could not be immediately anchored in an identifiable landscape or history, tended to move out of focus. A great deal of women's poetry fell into this category, as well as significant work by Baxter, Louis Johnson, Alistair Campbell and M. K. Joseph. Similarly, R. A. K. Mason's intense psychological questionings of sexuality and relationships, and his agnostic probings of religious belief, were downplayed in their own terms in order to reinforce the notion of an 'essential' New Zealand isolation as the *formative, originary condition* of his poetry (and thus an appropriate starting point for the nationalist tradition); Mason's emergent commitment to Marxism in the late 1920s, ambivalent though its relationship was to his development as a poet, was also largely ignored.

In his introduction to the 1985 Penguin anthology Wedde drew attention to the possibility of alternative, gender-inflected readings of the nationalist canon, proposing a 'structural line' of women's poetry, from Baughan, through Bethell, Duggan, Hyde and Rawlinson, as 'one of the great strengths' of New Zealand poetry. He identified this strength – somewhat vaguely – as an 'upwelling vigour of original language' and as 'a code of alert irony' (including here, as well, the later poets, Janet Frame, Fleur Adcock and Elizabeth Smither) in contradistinction to the 'celebrated humour' of the male poets. (Wedde and McQueen, 1985, p. 36). A more vigorously gender-inflected reading of New Zealand poetry, underpinned by a sustained polemic against Curnow's earlier readings and strongly focused on defining an alternative female poetics and its cultural implications, was advanced a decade later by Michele Leggott, herself an experimental poet exploring much of the territory identified in her reading of women poets in New Zealand. Focusing on Hyde and Duggan, Leggott placed them within 'a lost matrix of women poets', including Jessie Mackay (and Baughan and Bethell), who 'shaped New Zealand poetry in the first half of the century as a politically alert, humanitarian enterprise, diverse in its subjects and styles but run on sympathetic and highly reticulated energies that took as their point of departure the socially progressive atmosphere of the late colonial period'. Leggott's feminist reading thus also worked to break down the notion of a 'historical divide' located in the 1920s: the concerns of this matrix of women poets were rooted in the 'hope of cultural continuity' and 'the complications of endurance', rather than the 'carefully anatomized alienation of the male poets'. Her reading of Hyde and Duggan draws continuing attention to 'metamorphic, control-eluding figures' in their work, to coded representations of female experience (especially, female sexuality) in a culture that 'refused all talk of the body' (Leggott, 1995, pp. 267ff.).

The 1960s and After

By the mid-1960s poetry itself was also moving in significantly different directions. One of these directions was a movement among the older poets to break out of fixed forms, to develop a more personal mode of expression which drew flexibly from a variety of formal and informal speech registers and explored a wide range of personal, domestic and social concerns in a style which exploited shifts and contrasts of tone, mood and emotional intensity. Its immediate model was the confessional poetry of Americans like Robert Lowell, but it had distinguished New Zealand precursors in Robin Hyde's sequence, 'Houses by the Sea', and in Mary Stanley's slim output in the 1950s. Apart from Baxter its most skilled exponents in the 1960s were Fleur Adcock, Peter Bland and Louis Johnson, and variations of it were later to appear in the substantial *oeuvres* of Vincent O'Sullivan, Kevin Ireland, Brian Turner, Lauris Edmond and Anne French. By the early 1980s it seemed so ubiquitous a mode among a host of minor poets that Roger Horrocks could caricature it as a form of local mass-production and draw attention to the irony that its 'studied spontaneity', based on the notion that 'poetry is an exemplary defence of individuality', had itself hardened into a set of predictable conventions. (Horrocks, 1985, pp. 101–2). Nevertheless it has remained a significant form in New Zealand, especially among women poets – perhaps because of the special claims it makes for the authenticity of personal experience.

    The other major shift in the mid-1960s was an explosion of writing by a new generation, mainly students, youthful, iconoclastic, involved variously in the counter-culture of political protest, drugs and rock music. They were deeply suspicious of authority in any form (including the literary–cultural establishment and its privileged voices), hostile to High Culture (especially its Anglo-European exemplars and icons), but receptive to the wide variety of new energies emerging in the United States (Donald M. Allen's anthology, *The New American Poetry: 1945–1960*, was widely read and influential), and to the language and iconography of popular culture. The practice of the many poets whose work began to appear at this time, in student magazines (including *Freed*, the best known, which appeared from Auckland in five issues between 1969 and 1972) and in new small presses, varied widely, and – as elsewhere – such labels as 'open form' and 'postmodern' soon began to be applied to it. As a group they were more readily identifiable by what they opposed than by what, collectively, they might 'stand for', and indeed were resistant to the practice of attaching labels to traditions and trends. What proved most durable – in the work of those who went on to produce substantial bodies of work and in turn influence younger poets (Wedde, Bill Manhire, Alan Brunton, Alan Loney, Murray Edmond) – was the *nature* of their attention to language and to the authority of the poetic voice. Behind the often exuberant display of verbal and typographical virtuosity lay a deep scepticism about the capacity of language to represent any special truth thought to be accessible to the authority of the poetic voice, and a celebration instead of the contingency of language, its strategic possibilities for hugely more various, allusive and performative deployment on the page – ranging from the fragment to the most elaborate patterning – as well as in spoken performance.

Such a poetics, with its postmodern tendency to abolish the distinction between surface and depth, lay at the opposite pole to the poetics of the personal poem, which retains a kind of epistemological faith in the continuity of 'mind', 'self', 'language' and 'the world', despite the often elaborate casualness and indirection of the movement of the poem's thought and language. However, Wedde's key terms and strategies of selection, later, for the 1985 Penguin, belonged less to the poetics of either postmodernism or the personal poem than to the new critical discourse of postcolonialism: language, location and the ongoing *processes* of cultural exchange and translation, both within the country and in its outward global relations. Despite his emphasis on these questions, he did not entirely avoid the teleological, prescriptive cast of the older nationalism, and in this sense shared the latter's ambivalence.

Whereas the earlier model was modernist-derived, Wedde suggestively adapted a model invented by the Canadian critic, Northrop Frye, premised on a distinction between 'hieratic' and 'demotic' modes of writing. Wedde emphasized the linguistic and cultural implications of the model: 'Hieratic describes language that is received, self-referential, encoded *elect*, with a "high" social threshold emphasizing cultural and historical continuity. . . . [Whereas] "demotic" describes language with a spoken base, adaptable and exploratory codes, and a "lower" and more inclusive social threshold emphasizing cultural mobility and immediacy' (Wedde and McQueen, 1985, p. 25). Although he strives to avoid applying the terms normatively to New Zealand poetry, they do in fact often function that way, producing a narrative of the *progressive* development of poetry in English from the (implicitly colonialist) hieratic to the (implicitly postcolonial) demotic. The nationalist period (1920s–1950s) becomes, in this progression, a deeply ambivalent, 'transitional' period, compromised by its backward-looking colonialist/hieratic affiliations to High Culture (the province, always, of 'some distantly-located spring') in the practice of figures like Brasch, but at other times (in some of the work of Glover, Baxter and the women poets, drawing on other elements in modernism) marking the beginnings of the 'growth of the language into its location', and looking forward to 'the consummation of a sense of relation' (ibid., pp. 23, 26) apparent, diversely, in poetry from the 1960s onwards. Wedde's argument is itself deeply ambivalent in this respect, locked into a binary opposition of alienation/relation which elides, or leaves unresolved, the key issue, for postcolonial analysis, of settler/indigenous power relations. An 'ease' of relation to location, if that is indeed what post-sixties New Zealand poetry in English reflects, might simply suggest that the cultural colonization of the country has been, at last, achieved.

Wedde's emphasis on the inescapably linguistic character of the cultural issues he addressed was nevertheless both highly original and deeply suggestive as a way of reading New Zealand poetry, especially poetry written after the 1960s. A highly significant development in the poetry itself was the emergence of language as a driving preoccupation in the work of many poets. In no other respect, it might be argued, has poetry in New Zealand (in English and in Maori) signalled more strongly its participation in the international discourse of postcolonialism. Among the older poets, Curnow, Smithyman and Stead moved increasingly self-consciously into the epistemological issues raised by the transactions between language and location. The focus of Manhire, Wedde, Brunton, Leggott and others was less self-conscious, more celebratory, but every poem they wrote exhibits an implicit knowingness about language as offering a rich repertoire of strategic possibilities for cultural interventions. Tuwhare's poetry increasingly shared the same impulse. Other poets, like Alan Loney and Graham Lindsay, wrote with a more deliberate sense of the instrumental possibilities of language. The line of women's poetry extending from Elizabeth Smither in the mid-1970s to – after the mid-1980s – Leggott, Dinah Hawken, Anne French and Jenny Bornholdt carried the same kinds of linguistic sophistication, and in many of their poems they explored and exploited, as well, the gendered nature of language.

Manhire, the major poetic voice of his generation, and highly influential as a creative writing teacher and mentor of many emerging poets of the 1980s and 1990s, is also notable as a critic for his foregrounding of issues of language. 'A whole range of contemporary New Zealand poetry', he argues, is characterized by the linguistic habit of 'code-switching' – the deployment of multiple voices, multiple registers, producing texts 'crammed with voices, locations, and perspectives', in order to break down, move beyond, 'the control of a single homogenizing voice . . . the achieved, inviolable voice of the poet' (Manhire, 1991, pp. 149, 151–2). The distinction he makes between 'pure' and 'impure' language is related to Wedde's distinction between the hieratic and the demotic. Some of Manhire's examples of 'impurity' – Glover's 'The Magpies' and Curnow's 'House and Land' – survive from the earlier modernist–nationalist period, and he draws attention to key shifts in a poet like Baxter, who 'begins as the elevated poet of a single voice, but becomes a far more interesting poet when he opens his work – in *Pig Island Letters* and the Jerusalem poems – to a range of tones and registers', as well as to Curnow's development into 'the master of code-switching in our writing' (ibid., p. 152). However, most of his examples are drawn from the 1970s and after: Tuwhare in particular, but also Smither, O'Sullivan and his own work.

There is always a temptation to invoke undifferentiated notions of diversity or plurality when confronted by the sheer plethora of generations, styles, individual voices and languages, which seemed to characterize New Zealand poetry in the last two decades of the twentieth century. Such notions, however, tend to ignore or downplay the 'disputed ground' which remains central to the energies of poetry. The sites of contestation are many and various, and in that sense different from the older single-issue literary politics of cultural nationalism. Furthermore, every site has its own complex cultural dynamics, whether the issues are generational, gender- or ethnicity-focused, locational (a refiguring of notions of the national or regional, revisions of the canon), or global (new international configurations of power and influence). Fortunately, there seems little prospect of a diminution in the vigour with which poetry, and poetics, engage with these key postcolonial issues.

BIBLIOGRAPHY

Alley, E. and Williams, M. (eds) (1992). *In the Same Room: Conversations with New Zealand Writers.* Auckland: Auckland University Press.

Baxter, J. K. (1955). *The Fire and the Anvil: Notes on Modern Poetry.* Wellington: New Zealand University Press.

Baxter, J. K. (1967). *Aspects of Poetry in New Zeland.* Christchurch: Caxton Press.

Bornholdt, J, O'Brien, G. and Williams, M. (eds) (1997). *An Anthology of New Zealand Poetry in English.* Auckland: Oxford University Press.

Calder, A. (1998). 'Unsettling Settlement: Poetry and Nationalism in Aotearoa/New Zealand.' *REAL: Yearbook of Research in English and American Literature,* 14: 165–81.

Curnow, A. (ed.) (1960). *The Penguin Book of New Zealand Verse.* Harmondsworth: Penguin.

Curnow, A. (1987). *Look Back Harder: Critical Writings 1935–84.* Auckland: Auckland University Press.

Grey, G. (1855). *Polynesian Mythology.* London: John Murray.

Horrocks, R. (1985). '"Natural" as only you can be": Some Readings of Contemporary NZ poetry.' *And,* 4: 101–23.

Ihimaera, W. (ed.) (1992–6). *Te Ao Marama: Contemporary Maori Writing,* 5 vols. Auckland: Reed.

Leggott, M. (1995). 'Opening the Archive: Robin Hyde, Eileen Duggan and the Persistence of Record.' In M. Williams and M. Leggott (eds), *Opening the Book: New Essays on New Zealand Writing.* Auckland: Auckland University Press.

McLean, M. and Orbell, M. (eds) (1975). *Traditional Songs of the Maori.* Revd edn 1990. Wellington: Reed.

Manhire, W. (1991). 'Dirty Silence: Impure Sounds in New Zealand Poetry.' In G. McGregor and M. Williams (eds), *Dirty Silence: Aspects of Language and Literature in New Zealand.* Auckland: Oxford University Press.

Murray, S. (1998). *Never a Soul at Home: New Zealand Literary Nationalism and the 1930s.* Wellington: Victoria University Press.

Ngata, Sir A. and Jones, P. Te H. (eds) (1959–90). *Nga Moteatea (The Songs): A Selection of Annotated Tribal Songs of the Maori with English Translations,* 4 vols. Wellington: Polynesian Society with A. H. & A. W. Reed.

Orbell, M. (ed. and trans.) (1991). *Waiata: Maori Songs in History.* Auckland: Reed.

O'Sullivan, V. (ed.) (1970, 1976, 1987). *An Anthology of Twentieth Century New Zealand Poetry.* Auckland: Oxford University Press.

Ricketts. H. (ed.) (1986). *Talking About Ourselves: Twelve New Zealand Poets in Conversation with Harry Ricketts.* Wellington: Mallinson Rendell.

Robinson, R. and Wattie, N. (eds) (1998). *The Oxford Companion to New Zealand Literature.* Auckland: Oxford University Press.

Slemon, S. (1996). 'Unsettling the Empire: Resistance Theory for the Second World.' In P. Mongia (ed.), *Contemporary Postcolonial Theory: A Reader.* London: Arnold.

Smithyman, K. (1965). *A Way of Saying: A Study of New Zealand Poetry.* Auckland and London: Collins.

Stead, C. K. (1981). *In the Glass Case: Essays on New Zealand Literature.* Auckland: Auckland University Press and Oxford University Press.

Sturm, T. (ed.) (1991, 1998). *The Oxford History of New Zealand Literature in English.* Auckland: Oxford University Press. See M. P. Jackson and E. Caffin, 'Poetry' (pp. 394–524); J. Thomson, 'Bibliography' (pp. 737–865).

Wedde, I. (1995). *How to be Nowhere: Essays and Texts 1971–1994.* Wellington: Victoria University Press.

Wedde, I. and McQueen, H. (eds) (1985). *The Penguin Book of New Zealand Verse.* Auckland: Penguin.

23
Canadian Poetry
Cynthia Messenger

English–Canadian poetry of the twentieth century is not easily characterized, mainly because it is notable less for its schools or movements than for a small number of writers of singular talent and vision. This essay cannot attempt to be comprehensive but will discuss Canada's most accomplished and historically significant poets.

Archibald Lampman (1861–99), Duncan Campbell Scott (1862–1947), Sir Charles G. D. Roberts (1860–1943), and his cousin Bliss Carman (1861–1929), together referred to as the Confederation poets, were Canada's best-known writers in the thirty years after 1880. In the early decades of the twentieth century, 'lyrics' and 'ballads' by these writers appeared, sometimes posthumously, on themes related to the poet's confrontation with an idealized Canadian landscape. The Confederation poets were steeped in the English Romantic and Victorian traditions, and they are often dismissed as inadequate imitators of the art of the mother country. But they were also interested in Emersonian transcendentalism, and their encounters with the challenging natural world of a new country caused them to seek inventive rhetorical solutions to the artistic problems before them. Their attempts to write about Aboriginal peoples (Scott's 'The Forsaken'), to engage in social protest (Lampman's 'The City of the End of Things'), and to re-create the Canadian landscape in metaphysical terms (Roberts's 'Tantramar Revisited'), shaped the direction of at least the subsequent two generations of Canadian writers.

Isabella Valancy Crawford (1850–87), a writer of classical training, was another influential, even if sentimental, poet who was read in Canada in the early twentieth century; her collected poems were published in 1905. Pauline Johnson (1861–1913), daughter of a Mohawk father and an English mother, published volumes with titles such as *Flint and Feather* (1912) and was internationally known as a performer of her popular poetry, which blended indigenous traditions with the verse forms of Byron, Longfellow and Keats, among others.

Even though the poetry of E. J. Pratt (1882–1964) in several respects reflects the nineteenth-century poetic traditions of his national predecessors, the Confederation poets, it also signals the beginnings of modernism in English–Canadian poetry. Pratt's engagement with the landscape is modelled, at least in part, on the romanticism of his poetic forebears (both British and Canadian), and his sense of the poet's prophetic role is also theirs. His well-received first volume, *Newfoundland Verse* (1923), depicts a fierce but also mythical Canadian landscape that refuses the imported rhetoric of the Edenic new world of more traditional verse. Pratt's almost brutal realism is in part what defines his verse as modern, but his tendency to create myth in his depiction of the settler's struggle with his environment ties him to the previous century.

Pratt was a Christian in a time and culture that would not condemn him for grounding his art in his faith, and he was also a humanist and a student of Darwin's theories. Pratt infused his epic verse narratives with the principles of his expansive faith, which he felt were not incompatible with those of science. His humanism exhibited itself in a belief in humankind's ability to triumph through reason; when British and American poets were doubting, Pratt believed. Sandra Djwa and R. G. Moyles suggest in their introduction to the two-volume *E. J. Pratt: Complete Poems* that *The Titanic* (1953) (one of Pratt's best-known works) challenges Hardy's fatalism in 'The Convergence of the Twain, Lines on the Loss of the Titanic'. Pratt's other well-known works include *Brébeuf and His Brethren* (1940) and *Towards the Last Spike* (1952), both widely read and influential narratives that dramatized Canadian historical events.

The early modern period in Canada, like later phases of its literary history, is remarkable for the diversity of work its poets produced. The imagist poet W. W. E. Ross (1894–1966), who published two volumes in the 1930s and one in the 1950s, wrote on a smaller scale than Pratt and was one of Canada's first important practitioners of free verse. Other poets whose work shows traces of American imagism include Dorothy Livesay (1909–96), perhaps the only Canadian female poet of the 1920s and 1930s with a substantial reputation. Over approximately seven decades Livesay wrote and published verse on a wide range of topics, including social protest and erotica, but her strongest work was derived from the same imagist movement that shaped Ross. Livesay's *Call My People Home* (1950), a long poem written for radio in protest over the internment of Japanese-Canadians during the Second World War, was one of many volumes published by Lorne Pierce, editor for the Ryerson Press (Toronto), an important vehicle for the development of Canadian poetry between 1920 and 1960.

Farther east, in the 1940s and 1950s, a group of poets who met in Montreal were writing verse that would dramatically alter literary history in Canada. These poets published their early work in two little magazines called *Preview* (1942–5) and *First Statement* (1942–5), which eventually amalgamated to become *Northern Review* (1945–56). These magazines, although they were in some cases circulating for only a few years, have taken on a literary–historical importance that is perhaps exaggerated. They went some way, however, to transfiguring the very early modernism of E. J. Pratt, and they expanded on the varieties of modernism that would characterize the century.

The *Preview* poets, including F. R. Scott (1899–1985), A. J. M. Smith (1902–80), A. M. Klein (1909–72) and P. K. Page (b. 1916), were led by English poet and travel writer Patrick Anderson (1915–79), who encouraged his group to read and imitate foreign poets such as T. S. Eliot, W. H. Auden and Dylan Thomas. Irving Layton, Louis Dudek and John Sutherland (1919–56) published in *First Statement*. The cultural influences that shaped the writing of the Montreal poets were common to artists and intellectuals in 1940s Europe and America: Freudian psychology, anti-war sentiment, socialism and communism, to name only a few. The Canadian early modernist movement echoes but does not shadow similar movements in twentieth-century America and Britain. It follows trends in a somewhat zigzag pattern, some poets moving towards experimentation in verse form, while often simultaneously retreating to the poetic traditions of the pre-modernist period in English-language poetry.

F. R. Scott and A. J. M. Smith were for decades the most celebrated writers of the Montreal group. Brian Trehearne, in *Aestheticism and the Canadian Modernists: Aspects of a Poetic Influence* (1989), explores the myths that have grown up around the Canadian moderns and persuasively argues for a more nuanced appreciation of the strains of old traditions, especially aestheticism, identifiable in their work. Even while Scott and Smith (and others in their circle) often echoed nineteenth-century English traditions, they nevertheless successfully reflected the social upheaval Canada experienced during and after the Second World War and were undeniable leaders in Canadian modernism.

A. M. Klein was in the 1940s Canada's most highly acclaimed poet of Jewish life and social protest. The extraordinary poem 'Out of the Pulver and the Polished Lens', published in *Hath Not a Jew* (1940), is considered by many to be among Klein's finest poems and one of the most philosophically challenging of the era. His *The Rocking Chair and Other Poems* won the Governor General's Award for 1948.

P. K. Page, who has written her best poems in recent years, emerged from the Montreal era to become one of Canada's most highly regarded writers. The admiration her work has attracted and her influence on younger writers cannot be adequately articulated here. Page's early verse protested the Second World War and the stultifying conditions of the female office workers who were left behind. Her first two books, an anthology, *Unit of Five* (1944), and a solo volume, *As Ten As Twenty* (1946), set out some of the themes and concerns that define her work into the present. She was typical of the 1940s poets in her refusal of the religious faith one finds in E. J. Pratt and his predecessors. Page's poetry moved increasingly inward in the 1950s; social protest gave way to a preoccupation with the self and the mind. In 1954 she won the Governor General's Award for *The Metal and Flower*.

In the late 1950s, living in Brazil as wife of the Canadian ambassador there, Page began to paint, under her married name, P. K. Irwin. After this turning point,

Page's poetry and visual art revealed her growing interest in mysticism, particularly sufism. (Her artistic transformation is recorded decades after the fact in the prose of *Brazilian Journal*, 1987.) *Cry Ararat!: Poems New and Selected* appeared in 1967, her first volume to feature her drawings prominently (both within the book and on the jacket). This volume hints at the link between her poetry and visual art. Page's Klee-inspired drawings of the early 1960s, with their careful attention to slivers of lineation, complement poems that depend on favourite metaphors for infinity: air molecules and atoms. These small points of connection suggest the invisible barrier between the realm we experience and a fourth dimension. In one of her finest poems, 'Another Space', published in *P. K. Page: Poems Selected and New* in 1974 (a volume selected and edited by Margaret Atwood), Page creates a notional world in which a vitalism conveyed through geometric configurations links the cosmos to humanity:

> Those people in a circle on the sand
> are dark against its gold
> turn like a wheel
> revolving in a horizontal plane
> whose axis – do I dream it? –
> vertical
> invisible
> immeasurably tall
> rotates a starry spool.

This poem features all of the recurring symbology in Page's verse: the mandalas of circles and wheels; the colour 'gold', consistently signifying transcendence; ekphrastic images that express the metaphysical power of the sister arts; and metaphors of vision and inner sight. The thesis in this, and indeed in most of Page's work, is that art – be it poetry, music or visual art – is the only vehicle through which human beings may transcend the quotidian. Page's sense of the interconnectedness of the cosmos has led to a return, in some of her later poems, to social protest, particularly in the form of environmental advocacy.

Evening Dance of the Grey Flies (1981), in part through its innovative juxtaposition of poetry and prose, reveals some of the sources of Page's ideas. Doris Lessing's notions of social justice, for example, play a role in this volume's central prose piece, 'Unless the Eye Catch Fire . . .'. The next volume of uncollected poems did not appear until 1994, when Page published *Hologram: A Book of Glosas*, in which she adapts the fourteenth-century Spanish stanzaic form to produce stunning intertexts that acknowledge her indebtedness to poets as diverse as T. S. Eliot, Mark Strand and Sappho. Page's work has remained in print over the years in collections, including *The Glass Air: Selected Poems* (1985 and 1991, expanded) and *The Hidden Room: Collected Poems* (1997, two volumes).

Although, like Page, Irving Layton (b. 1912) writes verse that could be described as metaphysical, he eschews any aestheticizing of experience. One of the most internationally renowned of the poets who thrived in the never-duplicated milieu of English-speaking Montreal in the first half of the twentieth century, Layton has had a remarkable impact. At his best, Layton produced difficult, allusive poems that suggest an intellectual cast of mind thoroughly educated in Western culture. His good poems are poems of ideas; the figure of the poet is fairly consistently depicted as a prophet. Most of his poetry is well known, however, for its vehemence and directness and daring. Some of his major themes are the Holocaust, sex and art.

Layton has never been interested in linguistic experiment for its own sake, and he is not the kind of poet who reflects the trends and practices of his time, except that the preoccupation with themes Nietzschean one observes in his work was more fashionable in the 1950s and 1960s than it is now. One of his most widely studied poems is 'Tall Man Executes a Jig'. In it Layton creates the lone male artist figure that resides in much verbal art of the twentieth century; he is burdened, heavily burdened, by art, history and human misery:

> And the man wept because pity was useless.
> 'Your jig's up; the flies come like kites,' he said
> And watched the grass snake crawl towards the hedge,
> Convulsing and dragging into the dark
> The satchel filled with curses for the earth,
> For the odours of warm sedge, and the sun,
> A blood-red organ in the dying sky.

In *Butterfly on Rock* (1970), for years a cornerstone in Canada of the now-unpopular thematic criticism, D. G. Jones writes, 'The grass snake is transformed, becomes the cosmic serpent, the ambiguous symbol of the universal power which is both dark and light, the speaker's identification with a cosmic power that comprehends both life and death' (Jones, 1970, p. 133). This notion of a 'cosmic power' could be found in a great deal of poetry and criticism in the 1960s and 1970s and was in fact endemic in popular culture, a not-surprising result of the refusal of both conventional belief and total scepticism that characterized the last forty years of the twentieth century. A metaphysical poetry, diffuse in nature, was the by-product of these profound changes in culture.

The metaphysical nature of the dense early verse of Margaret Avison (b. 1918), published in *Winter Sun* to much praise (1960, Governor General's Award), grew out of the poetic traditions that prevailed in mid-century. Avison asks the big questions in her early work and creates appropriately complex conceits in order to pose them:

> Nobody stuffs the world in at your eyes.
> The optic heart must venture: a jail-break
> And re-creation . . .
> ('Snow', 1960)

This kind of verse was transmuted into the language of Christian faith by the time she published *The Dumbfounding* (1966) and *Sunblue* (1978). *No Time* (1989, Governor General's Award) is one of her strongest and most accessible volumes, its elegiac tone not surprising from a poet born in 1918.

Writing on the West Coast, Phyllis Webb (b. 1927) is separated by more than just vast distance from the writers of her generation, writers such as Layton, even though they began publishing in roughly the same period and moved in some of the same literary circles for a time. Webb's near-isolation on an island off the coast is an index of her need to work alone. She is a poet with no obvious literary debts, so singular is her vision. Like other writers who published in the turning-point sixties, she is interested in cosmic power, in left-leaning politics, in social justice, etc., but Webb has consistently demonstrated a meticulous devotion to a continual rethinking of the line. She is therefore often called a poet's poet, and in spite of her relatively infrequent publications, is revered. One of her most stunning works is *Naked Poems* (1965), a volume that can be interpreted as a reworking of the haiku in an era fascinated by minimalism and the haiku in particular. In the 1980s Webb published many of her best works, among them *Wilson's Bowl* (1980) and *The Vision Tree: Selected Poems* (1982). Her most recent volume, *Hanging Fire*, appeared in 1990.

Earle Birney (1904–95), also a West Coast poet, was a mentor figure for Webb and for many others and a major poetic voice well into the 1980s. He founded the first creative writing programme in Canada at the University of British Columbia (Vancouver) and went on to become a celebrated innovator on the contemporary scene. He was particularly interested in unusual verse forms. Birney wrote concrete poetry, narrative and travel verse, and he embraced the experimentation of younger writers more readily than his contemporaries. His long narrative poem 'David' (1942) was for decades one of the most frequently taught poems in Canadian schools. Light echoes of Birney's work can perhaps be heard in the poetry of George Johnston (b. 1913), the well-known scholar of Icelandic sagas. Johnston's poems show a careful attention to rhythm and syllabification that has influenced many poets, including P. K. Page. Johnston's *Endeared by Dark: The Collected Poems* was published in 1990.

Margaret Atwood (b. 1939), who is today considered a major English-language poet (with awards and honours too numerous to list here), began her career in Canada as one of the leading voices in the vibrant 1960s. This was a period that saw a sudden and enormous increase in the production of poetry, partly encouraged by government grants and the rise of small presses. Atwood is a writer of considerable integrity, who has consistently demonstrated a strong personal commitment to social justice. The political climate in which she wrote in the late sixties encouraged dissent (and made possible Dennis Lee's unprecedented *Civil Elegies* (1968); read more widely in its revised version of 1972, this long poem shows the influence of the Canadian thinker George Grant in its extended consideration of nation and community). Like Lee's, Atwood's poetry of the 1960s and 1970s is political in tone; gender politics and national mythologies are her themes. *Circle Game* (1966), Atwood's first major poetry publication, was immediately recognized with a Governor General's Award. 'This is a Photograph of Me' from that collection is representative of this period in Atwood's development for its arch new take on introspection.

In *The Animals in that Country* (1968) and *The Journals of Susanna Moodie* (1970) Atwood reveals the influence of Northrop Frye (whose ideas about myth in Western literature could also be detected in the work of Jay Macpherson, author of *The Boatman* (1957, Governor General's Award), a poet, once Atwood's professor, whom Atwood greatly admires). Atwood, reflecting Frye's notion of the garrison mentality, reconstructs the pioneer's fearful sensibility using the vernacular of the twentieth century. Through extended metaphors related to descent and re-emergence and through a lean, terse, even barbed poetic language, Atwood dissects the psyche of a colonial culture. *Procedures for Underground* (1970) invokes Aboriginal myth, in a manner fashionable during the period, to explore many of the same concerns, fear of the unknown a central one. 'Further Arrivals', from *The Journals of Susanna Moodie* – based on the life of an English pioneer who immigrated in 1832 to Upper Canada (Ontario) – is typical of the poems in this outstanding and highly lauded collection in its tight evocation of paranoia:

> My brain gropes nervous
> tentacles in the night, sends out
> fears hairy as bears,
> demands lamps; or waiting
>
> for my shadowy husband, hears
> malice in the trees' whispers.

The poems of *Power Politics* (1971) have come to embody, for many readers, Atwood's stance on gender relations. The point-blank delivery of these lines was sharpened into a powerful feminist weapon, and Atwood used it to advantage in *You are Happy* (1974). *Two-Headed Poems* (1978), *True Stories* (1981) and *Interlunar* (1984) deal with various issues to which Atwood returns periodically, including the problematics of Canadian nationalism, foreign politics, and the poet's relationships to family and the natural world.

Morning in the Burned House (1995) marks a deepening of Atwood's writing and a departure from her early persona. Her poems in honour of her father are particularly moving:

> In the daylight we know
> what's gone is gone,
> but at night it's different.
> Nothing gets finished,
> not dying, not mourning;

the dead repeat themselves, like clumsy drunks
lurching sideways through the doors
we open to them in sleep;
('Two Dreams, 2')

Experimentation in 1960s Vancouver was associated with a group of young writers (born between 1935 and the early 1940s) called the Tish poets, who, like the Montreal poets more than a generation before them, published their work and their ideas in a literary magazine. *Tish* (1961–9, intermittent publication) was small in scale and mimeographed. It was heavily influenced by America's Black Mountain poets, especially Robert Duncan and Charles Olson. Largely a regional movement, Tish maintained loose ties between the West Coast and the Toronto–Montreal axis through Raymond Souster and Louis Dudek. Colloquial speech and the use of breath in free-verse prosody were all-important principles of composition. The Tish editors that went on to establish national reputations include Frank Davey, Fred Wah and George Bowering. Sharon Thesen, influenced by this movement, nevertheless emerged an extraordinary poet who shows none of the weaknesses generated by Tish orthodoxies. The verse of Roger Greenwald, a Toronto poet with no connection to Tish, provides a compelling example of the best use of the rhythms of breath.

The Toronto poet bpNichol (1944–88) was associated briefly with Tish when he lived in Vancouver; his concrete poetry, his performance work, and his lifelong interest in word-play complement the work of the Tish writers. He became a widely admired mentor, editor and leader in avant-garde verse, with especially strong ties to Coach House Press. His most famous work is the multi-volume *The Martyrology* (1972–90).

Robert Kroetsch (b. 1927), a prairie poet of considerable distinction, echoes some of Nichol's textual strategies in the compilation of his various long poems into one project called *Completed Field Notes* (1989). His serious engagement with post-structuralist literary theory has meant that his readership tends to be university students and critics who are familiar with the theoretical foundations of his writing. Writers such as Patrick Lane (b. 1939) and Lorna Crozier (b. 1941) embody the changes that occurred in poetry in the 1960s and 1970s while also resisting innovation for the sake of it. These two popular writers – often identified, like Kroetsch, with western Canada – have acted as unofficial ambassadors of free verse and the poetry of personal experience in their various roles as writers-in-residence across the country.

Al Purdy (1918–2000), considered by many to be one of Canada's greatest poets, was remarkable for his ability to write about labouring in rural Ontario while also drawing on his wide reading in poetry and fiction. He wore his learning lightly and was embraced by readers across the country for his openness and lack of pretense. He published many volumes and is perhaps best known for *The Cariboo Horses* (1965,

Governor General's Award) and an often-anthologized poem, 'The Country North of Belleville'. Sam Solecki's *The Last Canadian Poet: An Essay on Al Purdy* (1999) demonstrates, through its ample research, the allusiveness and impressive learning that runs throughout Purdy's work.

The novel *The English Patient* (1992) made the novelist Michael Ondaatje (b. 1943) internationally famous, particularly after it was turned into an Oscar-winning film. Many readers, however, believe that Ondaatje should be better known as a poet. In his poems, Ondaatje's genius for provocative images and sharp verbal patterning is unencumbered by the constraints of narrative and the delineation of character.

Each of Ondaatje's volumes of poetry is an innovation on the one before: *The Dainty Monsters* (1967), *The Man with Seven Toes* (1969), *The Collected Works of Billy the Kid* (1970, Governor General's Award) *Rat Jelly* (1973), *There's a Trick With a Knife I'm Learning To Do: Poems 1973–1978* (1979, Governor General's Award), *Elimination Dance* (1980), *Tin Roof* (1982), *Secular Love* (1984), *The Cinnamon Peeler: Selected Poems* (1989; 1994) and *Handwriting* (1998). Born in Sri Lanka in 1943 (then Ceylon), Ondaatje arrived in Canada in 1962 after spending his early years in Sri Lanka and England. After the publication of *The Collected Works of Billy the Kid* he was embraced as the Golden Boy of Canadian letters; the outpouring of love and admiration that came his way from local poets and Can. Lit. academics cannot be overstated. His books were regarded as the work of an astonishing new voice with no Canadian antecedents. And he was handsome, shy and mysterious, attributes that fostered the cult of personality that grew up around him and, in a peculiar ripple effect, spread to other writers in the 1970s and 1980s.

Many readers believe that Ondaatje's early poems are among his best. One of his most frequently anthologized poems, 'Letter & Other Worlds', about his alcoholic father, is a 1973 narrative full of lines that, despite their use of metaphor, depend on a confrontation with his subject that is one of Ondaatje's trademarks:

> He came to death with his mind drowning.
> On the last day he enclosed himself
> in a room with two bottles of gin, later
> fell the length of his body
> so that brain blood moved
> to new compartments
> that never knew the wash of fluid
> and he died in minutes of a new equilibrium.

Secular Love was written out of the anguish of a disintegrating marriage and produced some of the most moving poems in the Canadian canon, poems that embody the authenticity of experience espoused by British and American late modernists. Perhaps no network of images demonstrates more clearly this poet's capacity to turn experience into art than that of the underwater world of the brilliant 'Claude Glass', a central poem thematically in *Secular Love*. Almost ten years after meditating on his father in verse, the poet creates strikingly similar imagery to castigate himself:

> from now on I will drink only landscapes
> – here, pour me a cup of Spain.
>
> Opens the gate and stumbles
> blood like a cassette through the body
> away from the lights, unbuttoning,
> this desire to be riverman.

Ondaatje's greatest writing has always involved an intensely private quest. In *Handwriting* he searches, as he did in the prose and poetry of *Running in the Family*, for a past that has disappeared:

> The last Sinhala word I lost
> was *vatura*.
> The word for water.
> ('Wells')

In contemplating Sri Lanka, as he does in *Handwriting* (1998), Ondaatje faces social pressure to focus on and somehow to illuminate – or at least condemn – all the violence in that terrorized part of the world. He approaches this problem in what is for him a completely new way: by writing about religious faith. He is, in this latest volume, and for the first time in his published work, quite obviously fascinated by Buddhism. 'Buried' which describes the local priests' efforts to preserve their religion and culture by burying statues of the Buddha during violent conflict, agonizes over the history of political turmoil in Sri Lanka without didacticism or agenda. The graphic violence of his poetry of the late 1960s and 1970s is somewhat subsumed in *Handwriting* by soulful contemplation. This is not to say that Ondaatje shrinks from confronting horror when he must. In 'Buried', images of 'the large stone heads' of statues about to be hidden, 'surrounded by flares', are mirrored in the closing lines, where the shock is created almost through the virtuosity of the recognizably Ondaatjean conceit:

> Above ground, massacre and race.
> A heart silenced.
> The tongue removed.
> The human body merged into burning tire.
> Mud glaring back
> into a stare.

The powerful images of 'Buried' reflect but do not overwhelm the devastating issues they explore. Equally moving are poems in a completely different register that offer cinematic frames, and epigrammatic tercets and couplets on the themes of love and passion.

If the cult of the personality played a role in Ondaatje's fame, it was everything in the career of Leonard Cohen (b. 1934), whose persona as the contemplative renegade in search of fulfilment is at the centre of all his work. The ideas in Cohen's poetry tend to oppose those of the dominant culture and range over sexual freedom, saint-hood, madness, suicide, violence and pornography. It was these themes, the disarm-ing directness of his voice, and his self-presentation that won him a large following as a poet and singer in the 1960s. His song albums outnumber his small number of poetry books. His most famous poem, 'Suzanne Takes You Down', is a version of his most famous song, 'Suzanne'. Cohen's first volume of poetry, *Let Us Compare Mythologies*, was published in 1956, and he maintained his poetic stance until the publication of one of his most widely read volumes, *Death of a Lady's Man*, which appeared in 1978. His dark, sardonic early volumes are somewhat relieved by *Book of Mercy* (1984), a collection of devotional and meditative verse that draws on Cohen's Jewish heritage.

The poetry of Gwendolyn MacEwen (1941–87) grew out of the same coffee-house culture as Cohen's, even if MacEwen's coffee-house was in Toronto. Like Cohen, MacEwen developed ties to Greece, and she also acquired a persona that mirrored the counter-culture. The multilingual MacEwen, however, was more interested in mysti-cal ideas and in adventuresome historical figures than Cohen. Both MacEwen and Cohen represent Canadian poets attempting to develop a profile as writers and yet also, because of the dictates of the period, exiling themselves as anti-heroes, if not always in fact then in the rebelliousness of their verse. MacEwen's *The Shadow-Maker* won a Governor General's Award for 1969, but a late book, *The T. E. Lawrence Poems* (1982), might well offer the best of MacEwen for its skilful execution of the male narrative voice she seemed to favour.

Of the Canadian poets who rose to prominence in the 1980s, Anne Michaels (b. 1958) has received some of the highest praise. Internationally known as the author of the Holocaust novel *Fugitive Pieces*, she was awarded the Commonwealth Poetry Prize for the Americas for her strongest collection of verse, *The Weight of Oranges* (1985). She is the most skilful of a whole body of Canadian poets whose work is a distant out-growth of the imagist movement. These poets depend heavily on the distillation of a mood. In Michaels's case this mood is achieved largely through imagery associated with the manipulation of light, through an intense lyricism, and through the uncanny ability to produce a variety of dramatic voices.

Other notable poets whose work will carry Canadian literature into the next century include the following: Sharon Thesen (b. 1946), a poet who consistently produces outstanding verse; Richard Outram (b. 1930), whose *Benedict Abroad* (1998) won the City of Toronto Book Award for 1999; Dionne Brand (b. 1953), George Elliott Clarke (b. 1960) and Daniel David Moses (b. 1952), who use their considerable art as an expression of social conscience; Christian Bök (b. 1966), whose experimentation with poststructuralist ideas has opened up exciting possibilities for verse; Jan Zwicky (b. 1955), whose poems on music and philosophy reflect a contemporary trend towards greater erudition; and Stephanie Bolster (b. 1969), whose allusive poetic forms include a modern form of ekphrasis (roughly defined as poetry about visual art).

It is somehow fitting to reserve the last segment of this essay for a discussion of poets who do not fit easily into any of the traditions, trends or movements discussed so far. Anne Carson (b. 1950) is perhaps the most successful English-language poet Canada has ever produced. Her poetry does not resemble the work of any other Canadian writer, except perhaps that of Michael Ondaatje, whose imagery and phrasing the reader occasionally 'hears' in her lines. In June, 2000, she was awarded a MacArthur Foundation Grant, commonly called the 'Genius Prize', in recognition of her fine body of poetry and prose. In 1996 she received the Lannan Literary Award (US). A professor of classics at McGill University in Montreal, she earned her B.A., M.A. and Ph.D. at the University of Toronto. Often taken to be an American poet because her work has been published and celebrated largely in the United States, Carson is an important exemplar of a cross-border culture between the US and Canada that is broadening and gaining in power. Increasingly, partly as a result of both a weakened literary regionalism and the absence of discernible poetic movements, Canadian poets are finding their influences in American and British writers, a trend that has on the whole strengthened Canadian poetry. When a poet of the first rank, such as Carson, decides to publish in the US, that country will not only readily embrace her but also claim her as one of its own.

Anne Carson's publications include *Short Talks* (1992), a collection of prose poems, the only book to date published in Canada; *Plainwater: Essays and Poetry* (1995); *Glass, Irony and God* (1995, poetry), a New Directions book, released as *Glass and God* in England, in the Cape Poetry series; the widely acclaimed *Eros the Bittersweet: An Essay* (1996, literary criticism); *Autobiography of Red* (1998, a novel in verse); *Men in the Off Hours* (2000, poetry and prose); *Economy of the Unlost: Reading Simonides of Keos with Paul Celan* (2000, literary criticism).

Carson's poetry holds a central place in the contemporary canon partly because it exhibits a breadth of learning almost unprecedented in the work of her peers. Carson uses her education, as she should, to ponder what it means to feel. She re-sees her own experience through many, often dense allusions to classical myth, biblical history, metaphysics, modernist verse, nineteenth- and twentieth-century English fiction, and Christian theology (to cite only a partial list of the crucial intertexts). Her best poems recover a role for wisdom in verse, for humour and for faith.

One of her greatest works, a long poem titled 'The Glass Essay' (in *Glass, Irony and God*), is a kind of Yeatsian 'dialogue', written out of the tradition of the duality of soul and body. Carson's context is, as it must be in this kind of poem, personal – a lost relationship. Like all poems that leave one reeling, 'The Glass Essay' offers sensuous and bold surfaces that also call up unutterable subtexts. 'First Chaldaic Oracle', published in *Men in the Off Hours*, a collection that demonstrates the impressive range of Carson's formal skill as a poet, engages in word-play that lightly echoes John Ashbery's. Carson's poem showcases her ability to move in the undercurrents of the language, but some might say that accessibility succumbs in these swift-moving waters:

> keep Praguing the eye
>
> of your soul and reach –
> mind empty
> towards that thing you should know
>
> until you get it.
> That thing you should know.
> Because it is out there (orchid) outside your *and*, it is.

In its allusiveness and in its moral seriousness, Carson's work signals a new dimension in Canadian poetry observable in other very able poets writing at the turn of the millennium. Several of these poets teach in universities and, even if they do not intend to, write against the anti-intellectualism of the 1960s. A. F. Moritz (b. 1947) is one of the most accomplished and prolific of this group. His work has been featured in the Princeton Series of Contemporary Poets, and he has held a Guggenheim Fellowship in poetry. American-born, Moritz has been living and writing in Canada since the 1970s; some of his best work has emerged in the last decade. His fine book *Mahoning* (1994), indebted to William Carlos Williams's *Paterson*, acknowledges – through its structure, echoes and parallels – not just Williams, but the role literary ancestry plays in the work of contemporary poets who read. Moritz's extended consideration of a river in his home state is a sophisticated dialectic on the tension between the natural world and the mechanized one that reflects the questioning of a late-century sensibility. Other titles by Moritz include *The Ruined Cottage* (1993), *Phantoms in the Ark* (1994) and *Rest on the Flight into Egypt* (1999).

John Reibetanz (b. 1944) and Jeffery Donaldson (b. 1960) are part of this group that is more likely to echo Elizabeth Bishop than Margaret Atwood, a group that has rekindled interest in traditional forms and in modernist forebears such as W. H. Auden, W. B. Yeats, Wallace Stevens and T. S. Eliot. Reibetanz's faith and his deep reading in theology give him the authority in some of the poems of *Near Finisterre* (1996) to consider the moral failings of practising Christians in their neglect of those who suffer. Peremptory dismissals of religion abounded in the anti-establishment poetry in the 1960s and 1970s, making it difficult for devotional poetry to find an audience until late century, when the political movements that propelled a still-gestating canon finally dissipated. The late 1990s were a productive period for Reibetanz; among his titles published in this decade are *Morning Watch* (1995) and *Midland Swimmer* (1996).

Donaldson's verse is formalist in nature, his use of the tercet particularly effective. *Once out of Nature* (1991) and *Waterglass* (1999) show the influence of American writers such as James Merrill and Richard Howard in the reconciliation of a highly cultivated sensibility with the language of conversation. Urbane and affectionate references to modernist art and European cultural figures depart entirely from the concerns of earlier Canadian poets who faced the daunting task of establishing a local voice.

BIBLIOGRAPHY

Atwood, M. (1982). Introduction. *The New Oxford Book of Canadian Verse in English.* Toronto: Oxford University Press.

Bayard, Caroline (1989). *The New Poetics in Canada and Québec: From Concretism to Post-Modernism.* Toronto: University of Toronto Press.

Benson, E. and W. Toye (eds) (1997). *The Oxford Companion to Canadian Literature*, 2nd edn. Toronto: Oxford University Press.

Bentley, D. M. R. (1992). *The Gay Grey Moose: Essays on the Ecologies and Mythologies of Canadian Poetry, 1690–1990.* Ottawa: University of Ottawa Press.

Davidson, A. E. and C. N. Davidson (eds) (1981) *The Art of Margaret Atwood: Essays in Criticism.* Toronto: Anansi.

Dwja, S. and R. G. Moyles (eds) (1989). Introduction. *E. J. Pratt: Complete Poems: Parts 1 & 2.* Toronto: University of Toronto Press.

Fass, E. and S. Reed (eds) (1990). *Irving Layton and Robert Creeley: The Complete Correspondence, 1953–1978.* Kingston and Montreal: McGill-Queen's University Press.

Frye, N. (1971). *The Bush Garden: Essays on the Canadian Imagination.* Toronto: Anansi.

Howells, C. A. (1996). *Margaret Atwood.* New York: St Martin's Press.

Jones, D. G. (1970). *Butterfly on Rock: A Study of Themes and Images in Canadian Literature.* Toronto: University of Toronto Press.

Keith, W. J. (1985). *Canadian Literature in English.* London and New York: Longman.

Kent, D. (1987). *Lighting Up the Terrain: The Poetry of Margaret Avison.* Toronto: ECW Press.

Mandel, E. (1971). *Contexts of Canadian Criticism.* Chicago: University of Chicago Press.

Nadel, I. (1996). *Various Positions: A Life of Leonard Cohen.* Toronto: Random House of Canada.

Neuman, S. and S. Kamboureli (eds) (1986). *A Mazing Space: Writing Canadian Women Writing.* Edmonton: Longspoon Press, NeWest Press.

Pollock, Z. (1994). *A. M. Klein: The Story of the Poet.* Toronto: University of Toronto Press.

Solecki, S. (ed.) (1985). *Spider Blues: Essays on Michael Ondaatje.* Montreal: Véhicule Press.

Solecki, S. (1999). *The Last Canadian Poet: An Essay on Al Purdy.* Toronto: University of Toronto Press.

Sullivan, R. (1995). *Shadow Maker: The Life of Gwendolyn MacEwen.* Toronto: HarperCollins.

Sullivan, R. (1998). *The Red Shoes: Margaret Atwood Starting Out.* Toronto: HarperCollins.

Trehearne, B. (1989). *Aestheticism and the Canadian Modernists: Aspects of a Poetic Influence.* Kingston and Montreal: McGill-Queen's University Press.

Trehearne, B. (1999). *The Montreal Forties: Modernist Poetry in Transition.* Toronto: University of Toronto Press.

Webb, P. (1982). *Talking.* Dunvegan, Ontario: Quadrant Editions.

Williamson, J. (ed.) (1993). *Sounding Differences: Conversations with Seventeen Canadian Women Writers.* Toronto: University of Toronto Press.

Woodcock, G. (1993). *George Woodcock's Introduction to Canadian Literature.* Toronto: ECW Press.

24
Scottish Poetry
Jeffrey Skoblow

No doubt the first observation to make about twentieth-century Scottish poetry is that to consider this material under the heading of 'poetry in English' is, at best, problematic. Scotland and England share a long and vexed history, and the vexations have been as much linguistic as political (if, indeed, these categories are distinguishable at all). With the joining of the Scottish and English thrones under King James VI in 1603, and the Union of Parliaments of the two nations in 1707, Scotland effectively ceased to exist as an independent entity on the geopolitical scene, and much of the story of Scottish literature over the past three hundred years or so has concerned the ins and outs and ups and downs of coping with that fact, embracing and/or resisting the subsumption of Scotland within Great Britain, and the ascension of English over Scots and Gaelic (previously the two most widespread languages in those parts).

And so perhaps the second observation to make about Scottish poetry in our period is that it has been more than usually preoccupied with questions of history and cultural identity – with the weight of the past upon the present, with claims of nationalism and self-conscious efforts at the preservation of heritage, including linguistic heritage. The literature of Scotland, in other words, is the literature of a kind of prolonged cultural crisis, framing all other considerations – even the most personal, lyrical or mundane – in the context of a broadly social, problematically national experience.

As Kevin Lynch puts it in *Scotland: A New History* (1991): '*We arra peepull!* is the strange, defiant cry heard from some of Scotland's football terraces in the late twentieth century. But which people? A foreign visitor might well feel confused.' In terms of language alone, the tale of national identity is a tangled one. With the rise of English power over Scotland centuries ago, the Gaelic and Scots tongues begin their long decline into marginality, near extinction, and radical uncertainty. At the start of the twentieth century, both tongues have given way largely to English as the language of literature, as increasingly of common life – although both Scots and Gaelic continue to pursue their own distinct survival strategies, and to carve out their own histories, with different niches successfully occupied and the emergence of sustaining figures here and there. Scottish poetry in our century is a story of these three tongues – English, Scots, and Gaelic – their separate and related fortunes, and the cultural politics of their claims to a hearing.

At the end of the twentieth century all three languages display robust poetic life, if not an unparalleled multilingual situation at least a distinctive one (on a national scale), which a quick look at any anthology will reveal. The Scots line has produced one major figure (among several others of high achievement) in the period – Hugh MacDiarmid (the pen-name of Christopher Murray Grieve, 1892–1978), a figure too of considerable international reputation; the Gaelic line has as well found a kind of defining voice in Sorley MacLean/Somhairle Macgill-Eain (1911–96), a figure read in the original hardly at all, perhaps, outside the Hebrides; while the English line has produced no comparable figure, although on the whole perhaps a broader and deeper body of verse than either Scots or Gaelic, and many distinctive figures.

To say as much is to simplify things, of course, and though these basic parameters will do by way of orientation, the picture is rather more complicated than perhaps I make it seem here. Much of MacDiarmid's work is in English, for instance, or in varying degrees of Scots mixed with English – the two tongues closely related after all, the line between them not always plain – and this is true as well of many other poets who work in Scots. Scots itself as an instrument of poetic language has given itself to many forms of revival: a range of orthographies and approaches to vocabulary, sometimes neologized, sometimes raided from old dictionaries like Jamieson's *Etymological Dictionary of the Scottish Language* (1879–82), sometimes caught on the fly from common speech – so Scots itself can hardly be said to be a single language. Many poets working in Gaelic work in English as well, primarily or occasionally, and most, whatever their working tongue, write to varying degrees in the context of all three languages' relative currency, drawing from the national tradition as a whole (with Gaelic in translation, largely, and Scots often laden with glossary) and carrying it forward in this or that linguistic channel.

MacDiarmid is probably the best place to begin our survey, as the most prominent figure to emerge from this welter of divergent impulses, and as plainly the major figure in the reinvention of Scots as a modern poetic language. With Gaelic a closed book to most readers, and English a kind of interloper (of however long standing and current dominion), Scots – in large part through MacDiarmid's work and the subsequent work it made possible – makes a strong claim to representing Scottish poetry's signature mode. (But this may merely be my own prejudice.)

There were poets working in Scots alongside MacDiarmid, earlier in the century too, and back into the previous one. Violet Jacob and Helen B. Cruikshank, for instance, Lewis Spence, Bessie J. B. MacArthur, and Margaret Winefride Simpson – vivid voices all – carry the tradition forward, along with innumerable other more narrowly known and ephemeral poets working through the period. That many of these transitional, turn-of-the-century voices belong to women is a striking feature of the Scots line, but female voices of note are scarce thereafter, until much more recently –

another striking feature, which gives to modern Scottish poetry a distinctly masculinist air, a kind of burden which grows increasingly problematic as the century unfolds. In any case, the loudest voice in Scots as the century opens comes from the so-called Kailyard School – less a school than a tendency or reflex – a poetry of a kind of antique charm. 'Och hey! for the splendour of tartans!': this opening line of Pittendrigh MacGillivray's 'The Return', although a song of attack against the 'Sasunnach' English, a poem of political engagement, nevertheless shows the tendency well. Scots early in the century lives a subsistence existence, in an impoverished, often sentimental landscape.

In this cultural context, MacDiarmid's first three books in Scots, *Sangschaw* (1925), *Penny Wheep* and *A Drunk Man Looks at the Thistle* (both 1926), appear as a veritable explosion. The first two are collections of lyrics, and the *Drunk Man* one continuous poem (of some 2,600 lines) stitched together out of many shorter ones, lyrical, exhortatory, cosmic, political, philosophical, scabrous, and otherwise by turns, revolving around the meditations of the title character on the thistle, the moon beyond, Scotland, and the state of his soul as he lies flat on his back in a ditch. It is an extraordinary *tour de force* which, together with the two books of lyrics, reclaims for Scots a full range of poetic effects, subjects and ambitions.

'The Watergaw' (in *Sangschaw*) for instance, has the force and feeling of one of Wordsworth's Lucy poems, reclaimed for freshly vivid, modern use. It begins:

> Ae weet forenicht i' the yow-trummle
> I saw yon antrin thing,
> A watergaw wi' its chitterin' licht
> Ayont the on-ding;
> An' I thocht o' the last wild look ye gied
> Afore ye deed![1]

Even such a private poem as this speaks to broader concerns, too, with its faith in the persistence of the antrin and of something wild, indistinct yet not to be extinguished in the on-ding: a figure for Scotland itself. (This is, again, a common concern of MacDiarmid's as of the Scottish tradition generally: the pursuit of metaphorical relations between personal and national experience.) MacDiarmid is drawn to such figures of unaccountable persistence (like a drunk man, or a thistle), and mines the vein with endless variability. In a related poem, 'The Eemis Stane', for instance, the canvas is less intimate, more historical, even cosmic. Here the earth itself is (as glossed) an unsteady stone floating in space, with words cut into it and covered in a 'yow-dendrift' (blizzard) of 'eerie memories', making the inscriptions unreadable 'had the fug o' fame / An' history's hazelraw / No' yirdit thaim'.[2] Here memory obscures and burial preserves, and such paradoxes are par for the Scottish course.

These early poems reclaim old words and old forms and make them new, in good modernist fashion. 'Empty Vessel', a poem of two four-line stanzas, begins in ballad measure and then shifts – with an abrupt rhythmic breakdown – into a different, more discursive rhetoric, signalling both the persistence and exhaustion of the traditional form. 'The Innumerable Christ' at once celebrates and relativizes the Christian miracle ('On coontless stars the Babe maun cry / An' the Crucified maun bleed'), another paradoxical move perhaps characteristic of Scottish poetic sensibility – the relativizing vision at work even here upon the most conceptually universal material.

That English hegemony over Scotland, always an important frame of reference, is never far from explicit in MacDiarmid, who declares in his tangled and obstreperous autobiography *Lucky Poet* (1943) that 'Anglophobia' is 'more than a mere hobby' but 'my very life'. To seek the relative – to seek limits on the absolute – is a Scottish political imperative, even if the form it takes here in the early lyrics seems far from politics indeed. (Cultural crisis means that nothing is far from politics.) MacDiarmid is zealous as anyone for 'all that the Gael holds dear' against the 'Sasunnach thieves and their laws' (as MacGillivray puts it in 'The Return', noted above), but his approach to the problem is more various and subtle than any Kailyard apostrophe. Often it is not so subtle, either, as in 'Crowdieknowe', a vision of a day 'the deid come loupin' owre / the auld grey wa's' of the local graveyard:

> Muckle men wi' tousled beards,
> I grat at as a bairn
> 'll scramble frae the croodit clay
> Wi feck o' swearin'
>
> An' glower at God an' a' his gang
> O' angels i' the lift
> – Thae trashy bleezin' French-like folk
> Wha gar'd them shift![3]

The dark underside of nationalism – xenophobia – is handled here with (perhaps) a humorous touch, but elsewhere the hand is heavier, the tone more bilious, and the effect less lovely. This rage and contumely – descent into scorn, isolation, hermetic pride – is as essential to MacDiarmid's verse as the breezy vigour, vivid directness, sharp music, and vision of Scottish souls uprising vengeful and heroic also exhibited here.

In the *Drunk Man* all these matters are more explicit still. The poem takes as premise that 'He canna Scotland see wha yet / Canna see the Infinite / And Scotland in true scale to it' and proceeds via endless series of thematic oppositions and substitutions and formal and rhetorical variations both to explore and explode the notion of national identity. The drunk, the drink, the thistle, the rose, the phallus, the moon and stars, wisdom and folly, Time and Eternity, Scotland and Infinity . . . all circle round and through the poem, for (as a nameless voice tells the drunk man near the end) 'A Scottish poet maun assume / The burden o' his people's doom, / And dee to brak' their livin' tomb', and this is a task that requires a wide-ranging poetic language.

The *Drunk Man* is an attempt to provide that language in a single poem – a kind of mad, quasi-encyclopedic, stunted epic – and as such defies description in no uncertain terms. It is a powerfully witty and ambitious piece of work, a signal achievement. MacDiarmid would continue his efforts in this direction in later Scots poems, including the long and rather more chaotic collage of *To Circumjack Cencrastus* (1930); and he would begin writing increasingly in English, in a range of forms including the grim cosmic meditation of 'On a Raised Beach' (1934), with its language of 'lithogenesis', 'epanadiplosis' and 'old Norn words', and the sprawling experiments of *In Memoriam James Joyce* (1955). These later works represent the most immediate aftershocks of that initial explosion – the reclamation of a literary Scots tongue – and, among other things, they show the difficulty of sustaining the project.

But Scots persists in other mouths, by other hands, as well. Younger contemporaries like William Soutar (1898–1943), Robert Garioch (1909–81) and Sydney Goodsir Smith (1915–75) expand the poetic uses of the language in different directions, walking (like MacDiarmid) the line between traditional and as yet unimagined forms. Of the three, Soutar's work tends most heavily towards the auld forms and themes; still, even here, the sense of a modern context impinges, as in the shock of strangeness thematized in 'The Tryst', or more explicitly in 'The Makar' (or Maker, an old Scots term roughly equivalent to 'bard'), in which 'Nae man wha loves the lawland tongue / But warsles wi' the thocht – / There are mair sangs that bide unsung / Nor a' that hae been wrocht', 'Though a' his feres were fremmit men'.[4]

Garioch is a more complex figure. More formally adventurous – he borrows stanza forms from Robert Burns (the centre of an earlier, late eighteenth-century explosion of Scots verse, a problematic predecessor, guide and obstacle to MacDiarmid and the whole latter tradition as well), some of which Burns himself had borrowed from still earlier figures; and he writes numerous sonnets, among other traditional forms – Garioch brings to these more or less long-lost vessels a distinctly modern eye and tongue. 'Embro to the Ploy' (Edinburgh to the Frolic is one way to gloss this) is a poem that begins right out of the old Burnsian mode ('In simmer, whan aa sorts foregether / in Embro to the ploy, / fowk seek out friens to hae a blether') and goes on in that same mode gathering in the most modern details:

> Whan day's anomalies are cled
> in decent shades of nicht,
> the Castle is transmogrified
> by braw electric licht.
> The toure that bields the Bruce's croun
> presents an unco sicht
> mair sib to Wardour Street nor Scone,
> wae's me for Scotland's micht,
>   says I
> in Embro to the ploy.

An Edinburgh poet, Garioch writes (in what is known as the Burns stanza, a six-line form also known as Standard Habbie, after an old antecedent) 'To Robert Fergusson', drawing this other Edinburgh poet (another eighteenth-century figure, immediate predecessor and hero of Burns's) fully into modern light, where 'the flicker-pictur on the screen / bursts as by boomb-blast, and is gane', and 'our life's a bogle-hauntit dream / owre thrang wi wirrikows to seem / quite real'.

Garioch moves between the documentary and the visionary, as in 'The Wire', a horrific vision of extreme desolation and helplessness in a Second World War prison camp, with 'guns gaun aff, and pouther-reik / and yappin packs of foetid dugs, / and blobs of cramosie, like blebs / of bluid' – or in 'Heard in the Cougate' (one of the 'Edinburgh Sonnets'), a mellifluous yawp in which 'the Queen's t'meet / The King o Norway' and we hear about it from one of the locals ('Chwoich! Ptt! Hechyuch! Ab-boannie cairry-on'), who declares: 'Ah ddae-ken whu' the pplace is comin tae / wi aw thae, hechyuch! fforeign po'entates'. As ever, the subject is Scotland (and here, its place in the world).

For Goodsir Smith the subject is always Scotland as well, and his reach even wider than Garioch's in formal, rhetorical and thematic terms. Conversational modern poems like 'Under the Eildon Tree' in which he sees himself 'scrievan the last great coronach / O' the westren flickeran bourgeois world', auld mode or quasi-Elizabethan pieces like 'Time Be Brief' and 'The Ineffable Dou' ('White Dou o Truth / Black Dou of Luve / Perpend, incline / My sang to pruve'), social commentary, lyric: on subjects ranging from personal love to the Libyan desert in the Second World War, Goodsir Smith demonstrates the flexibility of a Scots poetic, and pursues his own and his nation's demons. In 'The Grace of God and the Meth-Drinker', a vision of 'a mercifu omnipotent majestic God / Superne eterne and sceptred in the firmament', both the self and the state are figured as, at once, utterly crushed by and impervious to Imperial power: paradoxical image of the Scottish condition.

Other, younger Scots poets have followed, although without the programmatic edge of the mid-century generation, and with perhaps an even more local audience. Both subject matter and poetic style have moved further from the auld mode into fully modern (or postmodern) language. The best of this new material, the most ambitious reinvention of a Scots poetic, is in *Sharawaggi* (1990), a collaborative book of poems by Robert Crawford and W. N. Herbert, and in Herbert's books *Dundee Doldrums* (1991) and *Forked Tongue* (1994), among others. (Crawford has continued to publish poems in Scots, too, although he works more regularly in English – as in *Spirit Machines* (1999), which contains only one poem in Scots, but which also carries odd, faint Scots echoes of syntax or rhythm in its English. Herbert too has worked frequently in English.) In Herbert's 'Mappamundi' 'Eh've wurkt oot a poetic map o thi warld', in which 'vass tracts o land ur penntit reid tae shaw / Englan kens naethin aboot um', and in which 'scenario Eh'm a bittern stoarm aff Ulm'. Scotland persists – 'Scoatlan's braith draggin lyk a serpint owre / thi causie o ma spine' (in 'Cormundum', Confession, from *Sharawaggi*) – and Herbert at once celebrates and challenges the fact:

> this Disnaeland, this
> Brokendoon, Eh breath ut,
> aynd withoot end, Eh am
> thi coontircheck that cuts thi groove
> oan whilk oor severt heid an erse o gless
> sall open til thir celsitudes o noth, thi stern.[5]

Scotland clearly is a problem for Scottish poets: it can be a nourishing problem or a crippling one, sometimes both at once. Edwin Morgan (b. 1920), a Glasgow poet, identifies this problem as an 'incubus' in his essay 'The Beatnik in the Kailyard' (1962):

> I think it is clear that the language problem, the problem of Scottishness, has proved something of an incubus, and the fact that it is a real and unavoidable incubus (shake it off, and you leave scars and puncture marks) makes it all the more difficult for the Scottish writer to develop integrally.

Or as Herbert puts it, in 'Owre Mony Nemms' (Over Many Names, a poem 'After Neruda', *Sharawaggi*):

> Thuv harpit oan at me aboot Britain,
> o Scoatlan and Englan;
> Eh huvnae a clue whut thur oan aboot.
> Eh ken anely thi peelreestie o thi yirth
> an thon's no gote a nemm.[6]

Herbert, like MacDiarmid often, both breathes the very air of national identity anxiety and wishes merely to be done with it. For many Scottish poets writing in English throughout the century, the problem is the same, though caressed by a different tongue.

Here the foundational figure is Edwin Muir (1887–1959), although perhaps less for his poetic achievement (which is considerable) than for his articulation of the necessity for a Scottish poetry in English. In *Scott and Scotland* (1936) Muir claims that

> a Scottish writer who wishes to achieve some approximation to completeness has no choice except to absorb the English tradition, and that if he thoroughly does so his work belongs not merely to Scottish literature but to English literature as well. On the other hand, if he wishes to add to an indigenous Scottish literature, and roots himself deliberately in Scotland, he will find there, no matter how long he may search, neither an organic community to round off his conceptions, nor a major literary tradition to support him, nor even a faith among the people themselves that a Scottish literature is possible or desirable.

Many Scottish poets before and since have assumed as much, or, at any rate, have recognized English as their native tongue (or among their native tongues), and have sought their bargain with the incubus in those alternative terms.

If Muir thinks he has solved the language problem, the problem of Scottishness remains in full force: he is preoccupied throughout with the nation. His verse too tries to bring to Scottish poetry the perspective of modern experience – his English is itself a programmatic gesture in this direction – and his tone is for the most part sober and quietly elevated, though not without stern and graceful force, and with a mythic reach as well. 'Childhood' conflates personal history, geography and political history; in 'Scotland 1941' 'We, fanatics of the frustrate and the brave', inhabit 'a sham nation' with our 'mummified housegods in their musty niches'; many other poems, like 'The Castle' and 'The Labyrinth', elaborate emblems of Scotland, inquire into 'the long-forgotten word' ('The Ring') or the 'earth still left forlorn, / An exile or a prisoner' ('The Transfiguration'); in 'The Horses', 'Sometimes we think of the nations lying asleep'.

Other poets have more distinctive voices, bringing the problem of Scottishness into English, not only (as in Muir) thematically, but in more broadly conceptual ways as well, by means of various odd rhetorical and formal strategies. W. S. Graham (1919–86) and Morgan (mentioned above) are poets of precise and striking achievement. Graham's subject is often explicitly, as in 'Malcolm Mooney's Land', 'the obstacle of language' and the power of silence, as in 'Johann Joachim Quantz's Five Lessons': 'Here where I am to speak on the other side / Of language'. The language is both philosophical and intimately emotional, 'through / Each word you make between / Each word I burn bright in' ('Seven Letters'): 'From wherever it is I urge these words / To find their subtle vents, the northern dazzle / Of silence cranes to watch. Footprint on foot / Print, word on word and each on a fool's errand' ('Malcolm Mooney's Land'). The language problem here cuts deeper than English, Scots or Gaelic, to the roots of human communication, as Graham pitches his English (and all language) at an extremity of unlikelihood: 'I walk the dead water / Burning language towards / You where you lie in the dark / Ascension of all words' ('Seven Letters'). If Muir solved the language problem but could not shake the nation, it may be Graham's distinction to have escaped, in some measure, the incubus of Scottishness (he lived for many years in Cornwall, later in life, and wrote only in his own idiosyncratic English) without, however, having escaped the incubus of language. His work is beautifully vigorous and quiet.

Morgan's work is something else: extreme variation of form and subject is its immediate impression. Although he does work in various Scots idioms (see especially his translations of Mayakovsky into Scots, *Wi the Haill Voice*, 1972), his customary tongue is English – but this English encompasses a wild diversity of tongues over the course of his career, from Concrete Poetry ('Dialeck Piece', 'Centaur', many others) to 'Allairblue beauheaven ablove / Avlanchbloomfondshowed brrumalljove' ('Verses for a Christmas Card') to remarkable science-fictional meditations. like Scottish parables, on exile, alienation and contradiction ('In Sobieski's Shield', 'From the Domain of Arnheim', 'The First Men on Mercury') to social commentary of various kinds, as in 'Glasgow Sonnets' ('A shilpit dog fucks grimly by the close') to quieter reflections, lighter caprices, poems in many voices. The restlessness of his work, and its formal and rhetorical energy, has been an important force in opening the possibilities of modern Scottish poetry in English.

An older contemporary of Graham and Morgan, Norman MacCaig (1910–96) has produced an extensive body of work that perhaps most successfully finds a middle ground between the lean stringencies of the one and the mad excesses of the other. Scotland is as ever a preoccupation, sometimes explicitly but more often in MacCaig underlying other, more personal and immediate concerns. 'A hen stares at nothing with one eye, / Then picks it up' ('Farm') I would call a very Scottish line (though its subject nominally and centrally is *not* national identity), in its economical movement and humour, and its wry concern with states of diminishment, silence and redemption from the brink of nothing. MacCaig writes a largely conversational, subtly flexible, contemporary idiom – a poet at home assuming an audience, quite without fuss (and as such, quite an anomaly among Scottish writers of early and mid-century) – observing and reflecting upon the contemporary Scottish cultural landscape, imagining the life of the land and of the individual in one shifting focus: 'Farm within farm, and in the centre, me'.

In 'The Shore Road', 'As though things were / Perpetual chronicles of themselves, / He sounded his small history', but this small history is never his alone; 'Feeding Ducks' begins 'One duck stood on my toes' and ends 'Till my gestures enlarged, wide over the darkening land'. 'Only men's minds could ever have unmapped / Into abstraction such a territory' ('Celtic Cross'), and MacCaig's sometimes ironic visions of the material present of Scotland, seek to re-map it out of abstraction into closely observed detail and careful reflection. His project in this regard resembles Muir's, though it feels considerably less programmatic in MacCaig, and makes for a more supple and fully developed poetic language, intelligent and graceful.

Another figure of stature is Iain Crichton Smith (b. 1928), who writes in Gaelic (he is from Lewis, the outermost of the Outer Hebrides) and in a wide range of English verse and prose forms. He too is often explicitly concerned with Scotland itself, Scottish cultural institutions and national landscape, and with finding ways of circumventing or banishing the burden of this preoccupation. 'The White Air of March' tells of 'Culloden' (site of the last decisive battle – 1745 – in the struggle for Scottish independence from England): 'where the sun shone / on the feeding raven. / Let it be forgotten!' 'The Clearances' begins: 'The thistles climb the thatch. Forever / this sharp scale in our poems, / as also the waste music of the sea'. Crichton Smith seeks continually fresh ground upon which to stand, honouring the thistle and the waste while pursuing something else as well. His verse shows an admirably wide range, from 'orphans rejected from our Welfare State' and 'the marble and carnations of Elysium' (in 'By the Sea'), to 'a conversation / between a wellington / and a herring' ('Gaelic Stories', translated from his own Gaelic), to his mother, 'her voyage . . . / to truthful Lewis rising, / most loved though most bare' ('For My Mother'). Throughout, his modernist precision, rhetorical vigour, and laconic humour map out a modern Scotland of considerable achievement in English.

Thus my quick sketch of twentieth-century Scottish poetry in English, from which I have omitted much. I have neglected Gaelic almost entirely, including the powerful and extensive poetry of Sorley MacLean, because I do not know the language and because it can by no stretch of the imagination be considered poetry in English. (I have drawn the line between the gloss of Scots and the translation of Gaelic, however arbitrary this may ultimately be: as noted earlier, the relation between English and Scottish is always problematic.) Among MacLean's other achievements is a rich body of work (even in translation) on the Second World War, a subject which forms a rich thread throughout the Scottish tradition, in whatever language, and which I have only glanced at here. (Hamish Henderson, William Montgomerie, Norman Cameron, among many others, deal directly with the war, often with reference to North Africa.) I have largely omitted, too, the literature of the Islands, like George Mackay Brown's work from Orkney in the far north, in English mostly, Scots occasionally, with a savour of Norse tongues: 'No more ballads in Eynhallow. / The schoolmaster / Opens a box of grammars' ('Runes from a Holy Island'). I have neglected Douglas Dunn's quietly various work in English, full of local detail and wide-ranging meditation. And I have omitted idiosyncratic figures of powerful interest like Tom Leonard, a Glaswegian, whose work ('stick thi bootnyi good style / so ah wull', 'goaty learna new langwij / sumhm ihnturnashnl' ('Six Glasgow Poems', 'Paroakial')) has given a hard shove to the Scottish idiom, and been an influential voice of strong licence; and I have said nothing of the Scottish tradition's strong interest in modes of performance (with its roots, however unrecognizable, in the old ballad culture), as in the spoken recordings of Ivor Cutler or the public performances of Liz Lochhead, as well as in the rhetorical self-consciousness of Scottish poetry in general, even in print.

Poets of younger generations, still active or just rising, continue the work sustained by those throughout my historical sketch. Many are concerned, in varying ways and to various degrees, 'tae wak a' Scoatlan's stour o deid' (Crawford, *Sharawaggi*, 'Semi-conductors') – to wake all Scotland's dusty dead – although the inclination has been increasingly to turn in other directions, in whatever language, to shake somewhat free of the incubus, to tell it: No. Women in particular – Lochhead (b. 1947) and Veronica Forrest-Thomson (1947–75), and younger poets like Carol Ann Duffy, Elizabeth Burns, Jackie Kay, Kathleen Jamie, among many others, and men as well – have looked for ways to turn their backs on the problem of Scottishness, as part of a general counter-attack on the more macho elements and self-importance of the national tradition. Forrest-Thomson's brief body of work is particularly distinctive: 'the only art where failure is renowned' ('Strike') – but even here Poetry itself is figured as yet another emblem of Scotland: the incubus is tenacious.

The issue of gender itself rhymes in manifold ways with issues of national identity: dominations and submissions, dichotomized social orders, anxieties of powerlessness, assertions of abiding strength, and questions of silence pervade the one as the other. It seems that if gender can provide, in part, a fresh perspective, it will be by means of transforming our understanding of issues long familiar through other – nationalist – terms of oppression and liberation. As the century ends, contemporary

Scottish poets move both more fully still to the roots of their traditions, and with unprecedented range over the modern landscape. The signs are hopeful for continued poetic vigour and growth, the scene is lively; and 1999 has seen, for the first time in almost three hundred years, the convening of an independent Scottish parliament.

Notes

1   *Watergaw* indistinct rainbow; *ae weet* one wet; *forenicht* early evening; *yow-trummle* cold weather in July after sheep-shearing; *antrin* rare; *chitterin'* shivering; *on-ding* downpour.

2   *Fug* moss; *hazelraw* lichen; *yirdit* buried; *thaim* them.

3   *Crowdieknowe* graveyard near Langholm; *loupin'* leaping; *grat* wept; *bairn* child; *feck* plenty; *lift* sky; *thae* those; *bleezin'* blazing; *gar'd* made.

4   *Feres* comrades; *fremmit* foreign.

5   *Disnaeland* Disneyland, Does Not Land; *Brokendoon* Brigadoon, brokendown; *Eh* I; *aynd* breath; *coontircheck* tool for cutting the groove that unites two sashes of a window (Herbert's gloss); *oan whilk oor severt heid an erse o gless* on which our severed head and glass arse; *noth* nothing; *stern* stars.

6   *Peelreestie* the restless, youthful skin (Herbert's gloss); *yirth* earth.

Bibliography

Crawford, Robert (1999). *Spirit Machines*. London: Cape Poetry.

Crawford, Robert and W. N. Herbert (1990). *Sharawaggi: Poems in Scots*. Edinburgh: Polygon.

Crichton Smith, Iain (1985). *Selected Poems*. Manchester: Carcanet.

Dunn, Douglas (ed.) (1992). *The Faber Book of Twentieth-Century Scottish Poetry*. London: Faber & Faber.

Goodsir Smith, Sydney (1975). *Collected Poems*. London: John Calder.

Graham, W. S. (1996). *Selected Poems*. London: Faber & Faber.

Herbert, W. N. (1991). *Dundee Doldrums*. Edinburgh: Galliard.

Herbert, W. N. (1994). *Forked Tongue*. Newcastle upon Tyne: Bloodaxe.

Leonard, Tom (1984). *Intimate Voices*. Newcastle upon Tyne: Galloping Dog Press.

Lynch, Kevin (1992). *Scotland: A New History*. London: Pimlico.

MacCaig, Norman (1990). *Collected Poems*. London: Chatto & Windus.

MacDiarmid, Hugh (1972). *Lucky Poet: A Self-* *Study in Literature and Political Ideas*. London: Jonathan Cape.

MacDiarmid, Hugh (1987). *A Drunk Man Looks at the Thistle*, ed. Kenneth Buthlay. Edinburgh: Scottish Academic Press.

MacDiarmid, Hugh (1992). *Selected Poetry*, ed. Alan Riach and Michael Grieve. Manchester: Carcanet.

MacLean, Sorley (1991). *From Wood to Ridge: Collected Poems in Gaelic and English*. London: Vintage.

MacQueen, John and Tom Scott (eds) (1989). *The Oxford Book of Scottish Verse*. Oxford: Oxford University Press.

Morgan, Edwin (1972). *Wi the Haill Voice*. Oxford: Carcanet.

Morgan, Edwin (1974). *Essays*. Cheadle Hulme: Carcanet.

Morgan, Edwin (1985). *Selected Poems*. Manchester: Carcanet.

Muir, Edwin (1936). *Scott and Scotland: The Predicament of the Scottish Writer*. London: Routledge.

O'Rourke, Daniel (ed.) (1994). *Dream State: The New Scottish Poets*. Edinburgh: Polygon.

25

Welsh Poetry

Douglas Houston

With regard to the internal cultural identity of Wales, the canon of Welsh poetry in English, or Anglo-Welsh poetry as it is often termed, has emerged during the twentieth century. Such earlier poets as Henry Vaughan, George Herbert and John Dyer have strong claims to being Welsh, but their works belong primarily in the English poetic tradition. Welsh remained the pre-eminent language of poetry within Wales until the end of the nineteenth century. The establishment of Welsh poetry in English as an internal literature of Wales followed the fading of the social and cultural order initiated in the mid-eighteenth century by the Methodist Awakening. Industrialism and the demographic shifts it effected displaced Welsh as the language of the majority in the more densely populated regions. The chapel-dominated and politically Liberal consensus was supplanted by the socialist ethos in the south and elsewhere.

This background to the corpus of twentieth-century Welsh poetry in English is discussed in detail by Anthony Conran in his *Frontiers in Anglo-Welsh Poetry*, one of two studies by that author forming the best available critical account of the subject. Conran notes that 'English in the families of . . . Dylan Thomas and Idris Davies was no more than a generation or two old. Before that, people no doubt spoke it, but it was a foreign speech to them' (Conran, 1997, p. 51). The poetic impulse, while still imaginatively nourished by the Welsh language's rich legacy, had to be accommodated in English and adapt itself to the social and psychological contexts of modernity. For Conran, the defining characteristic of Anglo-Welsh poetry is a complex awareness of the cultural situation it occupies. It stands apart from but is conditioned by Welsh-language traditions that, following the upsurge of linguistic nationalism in the 1960s, are energetically maintained in the politics as well as in the poetry of the Principality.

Dannie Abse's edition of *Twentieth Century Anglo-Welsh Poetry* (1997) forms a useful text for the present discussion. In addition to the six major figures considered below, some sixty other poets are represented, some of whom, like Edward Thomas and Wilfred Owen, have rather peripheral claims to Welshness. Abse also provides a useful anthology of critical observations on the nature of Anglo-Welsh poetry. Local particularity, emotional intensity, rhetorical energy, and historical and political contexts are among its suggested attributes. Abse himself believes accessibility is a characteristic feature, writing that 'the Welsh poet with his sense of community, while recognizing that the language of poetry differs from the language of logic, acknowledges his or her duty to communicate person to person' (Abse, 1997, p. 15). The accessibility of Anglo-Welsh poetry is akin to the generously communicative manner evident in the work of Seamus Heaney, Derek Walcott and Les Murray, which runs counter to the narcissistic privacies of much *soi disant* postmodernism.

Anglo-Welsh poetry has emotional and stylistic qualities relating to its sense of cultural displacement and the need to negotiate between past and present that Conran describes. Modernity gives rise to its own particular strain of *hiraeth*. This definitively Welsh state of longing is perhaps nearer the German *Sehnsucht* than the English nostalgia, but seems deeper in affective intensity and more spiritually elevated than either. Present in the passionately elegiac quality of much Welsh verse in English from earlier decades of the twentieth century, it fades to more muted registrations of an absent community of values in later Anglo-Welsh writing. As such, the Anglo-Welsh descendant of *hiraeth* is linked with the widespread acknowledgement of a missing moral term that is part of the modern yearning for a more knowable past and a less alienating present.

Stylistically, Welshness is manifest in the rhetorical and musical character of Welsh poetry in English. The sound and authority of *yr iaith hen* ('the old language') survive, as Roland Mathias notes, in the work of Dylan Thomas and his contemporaries:

> The uninhibited eloquence of older Welsh speakers – what is too often loosely called the *hwyl* – had its echo in the extraordinary richness and profusion of language which was common in this first twentieth-century generation of Anglo-Welsh writers. (In Abse, 1997, p. 17)

In terms of its syllabic textures, Dylan Thomas's verse, like that of Hopkins before him and of various notable Anglo-Welsh poets since, displays a heightened musicality. Much Welsh verse in English is rich in assonance, alliteration and forms of internal rhyme which loosely simulate *cynghanedd*, the structural system of corresponding sounds in much Welsh poetry. The Welsh tradition's close concern with rhythm and metre is also reflected in the work of many Anglo-Welsh poets.

For the purposes of this essay, Anglo-Welsh poetry suffers an embarrassment of riches. Space must be reserved for Dylan Thomas, R. S. Thomas, Vernon Watkins and Alun Lewis, each indubitably Anglo-Welsh and generally accorded some importance in discussing twentieth-century poetry in English. David Jones's ambitiously modernist project does not fit neatly into an introductory treatment, though Welsh materials are central to his work. The shrewd and naive lyric poetry of W. H. Davies is also problematic. While there is very little explicit Welshness about his verse, it originates in the linguistic dispossession and social displacement experienced in South

Wales with the fading of the old cultural order. With regard to contemporary writing, the number of noteworthy poets who have formed reputations from the 1980s onward is too great to allow adequate commentary. The contribution of women poets like Jean Earle, Gillian Clarke, Ruth Bidgood and Sheenagh Pugh to more recent Anglo-Welsh writing compensates for the slender representation of women in earlier decades. While Lynette Roberts and Brenda Chamberlain, the best-known Anglo-Welsh women poets of the 1940s and 1950s, both produced outstanding poems, the comparative slenderness of their overall achievements excludes them from a general survey such as this.

What follows is therefore limited to introductory accounts of the works of Idris Davies (1905–53), Dylan Thomas (1914–53), Vernon Watkins (1906–67), Alun Lewis (1915–44), R. S. Thomas (1913–2000) and Dannie Abse (1923–), the six poets whom consensus already acknowledges as the principal contributors to twentieth-century Welsh poetry in English. Readers are referred to Abse's anthology for a broader view, taking in much fine poetry that is necessarily neglected here.

Idris Davies's work exhibits clearly most of the attributes of Welsh poetry in English identified above. At best, his writing is richly musical, accessible and rooted very specifically in the South Wales valleys. For Conran, Davies's poetry in English (he also wrote in Welsh) marks the final collapse of the unified culture whose eighteenth-century beginnings had their *bardd* in the great revivalist William Williams (Pantycelyn). The last vestiges of that era's visionary pieties underwent industrial burn-out during the long struggle of the General Strike of 1926 and the hardship of its aftermath. Davies quit the mine where he had worked since the age of fourteen in the year of the strike, and, after achieving that exile from origins conferred by education, spent much of the 1930s as a teacher in London.

At the centre of his poetry stand the title-sequences of *Gwalia Deserta* (1938) and *The Angry Summer* (1943). Both works amount to vivid montages of the mining valleys up to the onset of the depression of the 1930s. They offer vignettes of social and domestic situations, sharply satirical commentaries on religious and political pretensions, and memorable treatments of conditions among the miners, whether unemployed or at the coal-face:

> There are countless tons of rock above his head,
> And gases wait in secret corners for a spark;
> And his lamp shows dimly in the dust.
> His leather belt is warm and moist with sweat,
> And he crouches against the hanging coal,
> And the pick swings to and fro . . .
> (Davies, 1972, p. 29)

Running intermittently through the poetry is an elegiac invocation of personal and communal senses of innocence and prosperity recalled from before the catastrophe of the First World War and the hardships of the 1920s and 1930s.

Like his collected poems as a whole, his major sequences alternate between traditional forms of versification, chiefly Housmanesque ballad stanzas, and rhythmically
enhanced free verse. Davies's free verse has considerable originality in combining conversational directness with rhythmical fluency. His characteristic tendency to parataxis
increases the effect of smooth continuity and sets up biblical resonances that function
ironically in many of the poems:

> The Commissioners depart with all their papers
> And the pit-heads grin in the evening rain;
> The white deacons dream of Gilead in the Methodist vestry
> And the unemployed stare at the winter trees.
> (Ibid., p. 26)

The lines open *Gwalia Deserta*, configuring oppressive capitalism, impotent chapel
and hapless proletariat in the relative positions they emblematically occupy throughout Davies's poetry. While this sequence has an open historical focus covering the
period from the late nineteenth-century heyday of King Coal in South Wales to the
onset of the depression, the fifty poems making up *The Angry Summer* deal exclusively
with events of 1926. Davies's free verse takes on a heightened colloquial vigour in
poetic reportage of the social and commercial demarcations set up by the strike. His
use of distinctively Anglo-Welsh speech idioms in *The Angry Summer* is poised inci-
sively between affection and the satiric mood of many poems:

> Mrs. Evans fach, you want butter again.
> How will you pay for it now, little woman
> With your husband out on strike, and full
> Of the fiery language?
> (Ibid., p. 88)

Throughout both these sequences a tension is maintained between the relaxed
fluency of his free-verse and the rhetorical heightening of his rhymed forms, which
can be fiercely impressive in the heraldic simplicity of their imagery:

> From wandering in Worcester,
>   In Merthyr, and in Bow,
> This is the truth I gather,
>   As naked as the snow;
>
> The cur shall be in clover,
>   The poet in the sleet,
> Till Christ comes into Dover
>   With fire at his feet.
> (Ibid., p. 117)

Davies's achievement lies in the formal originality with which he manipulates his
contrasting modes to maintain a tone of humane detachment from the social, moral

and political urgency of his concerns. His verse engages his native place with a thoroughness and sensitivity equalling that of John Clare's poetry of Helpstone. The long poem 'I was Born in Rhymney', an experimental autobiography in ballad form, is notable for its luminous economy of narrative. In other work, like 'September 1940' and 'Air Raid', his London experiences give rise to graphic civilian poems of the Second World War. Of the major contributors to Welsh poetry in English of the twentieth century, he remains at present the least well known beyond his Welsh home ground.

There is something of a disparity between the enduring popularity with an international readership Dylan Thomas continues to enjoy and the comparative neglect of his work by the critical mainstream. For the orthodoxy established by the Movement in the 1950s, Thomas's poetry exemplified the neo-romanticism such rationally sceptical poets as Philip Larkin and Donald Davie sought to supersede. There is no doubt that Thomas's imaginative audacity and sonorously vatic tone were intoxicating influences for poets associated with the New Apocalypse in the 1940s. Such work, however, lacks the impact and cohesion conferred on Thomas's poetry by his outstanding technical abilities.

The intelligibility of his verse with regard to its delivery of paraphrasable meanings varies widely. He often writes with the elevated straightforwardness of 'Do not go gentle into that good night', his celebrated elegy for his father. On the other hand, in many poems cataracts of imagery offer up their own imaginative modes of continuity, with taut musical regulation through metre and effects of rhyme, assonance and alliteration supplying structural integrity:

> Dawn breaks behind the eyes;
> From poles of skull and toe the windy blood
> Slides like a sea;
> Nor fenced, nor staked, the gushers of the sky
> Spout to the rod
> Divining in a smile the oil of tears.
> ('Light breaks where no sun shines')

The stanza is an example of the affirmation of unities between nature and human experience made in many of his earlier poems. Much of Thomas's imagery at this stage in his career is strongly charged with sexual and generative connotations in poems that draw on his conceptions of 'symbolism derived . . . from the cosmic significance of the human anatomy' (Thomas, 1985, p. 98).

His most successful work finds its level of meaning somewhere between his plainly comprehensible manner and the opacities of his more reckless raids on the emotionally and psychologically inarticulate. 'The force that through the green fuse drives the flower' is an early poem in which the visionary thrust of the afflatus is held in working tension with a prevailing logic of exposition. Poems like the popular 'Fern Hill' are easily assimilated in terms of their narrative and descriptive development once the reader adjusts to the long casts of Thomas's parataxis, a hallmark of the Anglicized approximations to *hwyl* remarked on by Roland Mathias above. The poem also instances the rich textures of sound Thomas carries over from the Welsh traditions. *Cynghanedd* effects are heard throughout in such internally distributed sound correspondences as 'swallow/shadow', 'rising/riding', 'fly/high' and 'easy/means/green/chains':

> Nothing I cared, in the lamb white days, that time would take me
> Up to the swallow thronged loft by the shadow of my hand,
>> In the moon that is always rising,
>>> Nor that riding to sleep
>> I should hear him fly with the high fields
> And wake to the farm forever fled from the childless land.
> Oh as I was young and easy in the mercy of his means,
>> Time held me green and dying
>> Though I sang in my chains like the sea.

'Fern Hill' is one of a number of Thomas's later poems in which direct sensory experience of landscape and locality supports an emotionally energized lyricism. Broadly speaking, there is a development discernible from the cryptic intensities of the early verse towards the more accessible and accommodating tone of *Deaths and Entrances* (1946) and later writing.

Regardless of his stock's fluctuation among postwar critics, he is clearly located on the large-scale map of English verse through his strong representation in Helen Gardner's *New Oxford Book of English Verse* (1972) and Philip Larkin's *Oxford Book of Twentieth-Century English Verse* (1973). His spectacular verbal dexterity in poetry, in various prose forms, and in the idiosyncratic triumph of his 'play for voices' *Under Milk Wood* (1954) is inseparable from the generous humanity and imaginative vitality that continue to ensure his work an active readership.

Vernon Watkins was a life-long friend of Dylan Thomas's. Watkins's admiration for the younger poet, whom he recurrently addressed in his work, was equalled only by his passionate regard for Yeats, whom he met and made the subject of numerous poems. Both represented to him the revelatory ideals of poethood his own writing strongly reflects. For Watkins, they stand alongside the ancient Welsh poet Taliesin, a figure in whom myth and history are confused, as exponents of the hieratic and magical conception of poetry. Several times Watkins assumes the persona of Taliesin to press poetry's transcendent claims:

> Before men walked
> I was in these places.
> I was here
> When the mountains were laid.
>
> I am as light
> To eyes long blind,

I, the stone
Upon every grave.
('Taliesin and the Mockers')

Classical mythology, biblical material and neoplatonism fuse with Welsh legend and lore in the metaphysically ambitious project of Watkins's verse. Throughout his long and prolific career, he continued drawing on the natural world, history and myth to affirm by image and exposition an order in which time and transience are denied ultimate significance.

He is a poet of consequence and originality through the opulence of his lyric intuitions, his keen technical skill, and the restlessly intelligent imagination evident in much of his writing. The close of 'Egyptian Burial: Resurrection in Wales', the second of his 'Pledges to Darkness', illustrates his eclectic historical and imaginative manner, the suppleness of his verse, and the affirmative power with which he concludes many poems:

Dear love, could my true soul believe
The wide heavens merciless, I still would not forsake
The man-tilled earth to which bones cleave
While horses race across
The neighbouring field, and their hooves shine
Scattering a starlike wake.
Magnanimous morning, if we change no line,
Shall pierce stone, leaf and moss,
And the true creature at light's bidding wake.

Watkins frequently produces such elevated effects, contriving the sounds and images of his poetry with innate virtuosity.

His high style is complemented by masterful use of ballad forms for many poems. The best known of these, and arguably his most impressive single achievement, is the long poem 'The Ballad of the Mari Lwyd', based on childhood memories of a Welsh folk tradition in which a mare's skull is carried from house to house on a pole. The poem's imaginative power, borne on its insistent rhythm and refrain, draws the reader into a liminal dimension where the sinister dead plead with the living for a share in life:

'Hell curse this house for a badger's holt
If we find no man devout.
God singe this doorway, hinge and bolt,
If you keep our evil out.
Long-limbed we hung in the taunting trees
And cried in our great thirst:
Give us a drink, light breaks our knees.
Give, or the house is cursed.'

The persistence of Watkins's visionary concerns tends to preclude thematic development in his work. His verse, however, is distinguished by a clarity and precision of imagery that work in conjunction with its acutely judged musicality. He is a refreshingly readable poet, whose Welshness is self-evidently at home in the English language.

The Welshness of Alun Lewis is also readily apparent through the invocations of Welsh myth and history that recur in his earlier verse and through the local specificity of such documentary poems as 'The Mountain Over Aberdare':

> The drab streets strung across the cwm,
> Derelict workings, tips of slag
> The gospellers and gamblers use
> And children scrutting for the coal
> That winter dole cannot purvey.

The majority of his collected poems were written after the outbreak of the Second World War in 1939 and much of his finest work is deeply preoccupied with the themes of love and war. *Raider's Dawn* (1942), the only collection published in his lifetime, recurrently reflects the brutalizing diminution of individuality effected by military training and anticipates action with imaginative inventiveness:

> We are the little men grown huge with death.
> Stolid in squads or grumbling on fatigues,
> We held the honour of the regiment
> And stifled our antipathies.
> Stiff-backed and parrot-wise with pamphlet learning,
> We officiated at the slaughter of the riverine peoples
> In butcheries beyond the scope of our pamphlets.

The sequences 'Threnody for a Starry Night' and 'War Wedding' engage the abnegation wrought on social, cultural and personal levels by the experience of war, reaching for shards of humane values amid the destruction:

> We were the daylight but we could not see.
>
> Yet now at last, in shelter, tube and street,
> Communal anguish banishes
> Individual defeat.
> Now in the crowded deadly places
> Indifferent profiles have become
> Beautiful tormented faces.
> ('Threnody for a Starry Night', VIII)

Ha! Ha! Among the Trumpets (1945) has a narrative inevitability running through its three sections, 'England', 'The Voyage' and 'India', which progress towards the heart of darkness confronted in the poems Lewis composed before his death in Burma. 'Goodbye', which closes the first section, is arguably the finest love poem of the Second World War, playing off bleak realism against limpid romanticism in a manner characteristic of Lewis's poetry:

> I put a final shilling in the gas,
> And watch you slip your dress below your knees
> And lie so still I hear your rustling comb
> Modulate the autumn in the trees.

'Karanje Village' states 'I am seeking less and less of the world' (Lewis, 1994, p. 130), indicating the fatalistic withdrawal registered in the substantial body of poetry Lewis produced after arriving in India. 'The Jungle', the longest of these poems, meditates on the moral and existential impasse of war in traumatically alienating surroundings and extends its apologia for the loss of humanity undergone:

> Oh you who want us for ourselves,
> Whose love can start the snow-rush in the woods
> And melt the glacier in the dark coulisse,
> Forgive this strange inconstancy of soul,
> The face distorted in a jungle pool
> That drowns its image in a mort of leaves.

'The Maharatta Ghats', 'Indian Day' and the two parts of 'In Hospital: Poona' are further striking examples of Lewis's Indian poetry. In such work brilliantly focused detail gives structure and substance to blank realizations of the distance war has brought him and his fellow soldiers from their former moral and psychological environments.

There is much else in Lewis's work, including the unsettlingly dead-pan treatment of the terror and banality of warfare in 'The Run-In', to underwrite the distinction he shares with Keith Douglas of producing the finest British poetry of the Second World War.

R. S. Thomas, the pre-eminent Anglo-Welsh poet of the postwar era, configures in much of his earlier work a remote Welsh landscape of spiritual and material privation, whose benighted representatives command recognition as types of the modern everyman:

> I am the farmer, stripped of love
> And thought and grace by the land's hardness;
> But what I am saying over the fields'
> Desolate acres, rough with dew,
> Is, Listen, listen, I am a man like you.
> ('The Hill Farmer Speaks')

For over forty years Thomas was vicar of a succession of rural Welsh parishes. Many of his poems focus with disquieting intensity on domestic and social instancings of life and death in which the theological problem of evil and the terrible challenge of faith are implicit. 'Death of a Peasant' is one of several poems which can offer no consolation in the face of the brute facts of poverty and ignorance:

> I remember . . . //
> . . . neighbours crossing the uneasy boards
> To peer at Davies with gruff words
> Of meaningless comfort, before they turned
> Heartless away from the stale smell
> Of death in league with those dank walls.

The sure metrical tread and rugged syllabic music typical of Thomas's verse are in those lines, his plain diction habitually resonant with the conviction of considered utterance. His early work's bare landscapes have their analogue in the pared-down and scrupulous style that has always distinguished his verse. One effect of such economy is to concentrate images in poems that combine qualities of fable and realist particularity, as in 'Meet the Family', where a life-denying meanness of spirit is presented with chilling starkness:

> John All and his lean wife,
> Whose forced complicity gave life
> To each loathed foetus, stare from the wall,
> Dead not absent. The night falls.

'Here' exemplifies his ability to shape poetry from a simplicity of statement that disconcerts through the very blankness of its factuality:

> I am a man now.
> Pass your hand over my brow,
> You can feel the place where the brains grow.

A harshly unsentimental Welsh nationalism is intermittently present throughout Thomas's work in such poems as 'The Old Language', 'Welsh History' and 'Reservoirs'. For Thomas, the enemy is not only 'the English / Scavenging among the remains / Of our culture' (Thomas, 1993, p. 194), but equally the parvanimity of his own people. The dry humour his laconically precise tone can support so well is frequently aimed at the Welsh. In 'Welcome to Wales' the tourist is urged to 'Come to Wales / To be buried; the undertaker / Will arrange it for you', while 'Walter Llywarch' opens with a tautological twist mocking a circumspect retreat into terminal social stagnation:

> I am, as you know, Walter Llywarch,
> Born in Wales of approved parents,
> Well goitred, round in the bum,
> Sure prey of the slow virus
> Bred in quarries of grey rain.

The affirmatives in Thomas's poetry are hard-won from the bleakness of vision often encountered in his work. He is, however, capable of putting his uncompromising talent to memorably epiphanic use:

> There were no prayers said. But stillness
> Of the heart's passions – that was praise
> Enough; and the mind's cession
> Of its kingdom. I walked on,
> Simple and poor, while the air crumbled
> And broke on me generously as bread.

The lines are from 'The Moor', one of the poems of the early 1960s in which religious and theological elements begin to assume ascendancy in Thomas's work. Faith and doubt, logic and intuition, joy and terror are brought urgently into play in his poetry's search to know the God with whom it struggles, acknowledging that 'we die / with the knowledge that your resistance / is endless at the frontier of the great poem' (Thomas, 1993, p. 291). Some of his later work steps through the deep space of the great abstractions on an idiosyncratic exactitude of metre and diction that conveys the tension of the engagement:

> God, it is not your reflections
> we seek, wonderful as they are
> in the live fibre; it is the possibility
> of your presence at the cone's
> point towards which we soar
> in hope to arrive at the still
> centre, where love operates
> on all those frequencies
> that are set up by the spinning
> of two minds, the one on the other.
> ('Cones')

Throughout his work's profound and extensive involvement over more than fifty years with social, cultural, theological and personal themes, the same clear and rigorous voice is heard. He is as capable of provoking with quirky humour as he is of fixing attention to the dark and brutal places of the psyche, or of striking new chords of rarefied praise from his solitary broodings on God. The two greatest Welsh poets in English of the twentieth century will be found in the reference books under 'T' for 'Thomas'.

The careers of R. S. Thomas and Dannie Abse have a parallel chronology, Thomas's first collection having appeared in 1946, Abse's in 1948. While they are equally concerned to make poetic sense of the human condition, Abse's hospitably communicative manner is very different from the craggy singularity with which Thomas pursues his major themes. Abse, whose Welshness is reflected clearly in his work, unites the Anglo-Welsh idiom with the dominant metropolitan modes of postwar British poetry as shaped by the Movement and succeeding developments. From 1943 onward he lived in London, where he studied medicine and subsequently practised as a doctor. In Abse the peculiarity of being 'London Welsh' coexists with his distinctness of cultural identity as a Jew, which is acutely registered at many points in his work:

> The eyes open:
> the German earth is made of helmets;
> the wind seeps through a deep
> frost hole that is somewhere else
> carrying the far Jew-sounds of railway trucks.
> ('No More Mozart')

While such notes of historical and moral gravity are periodically heard, Abse more characteristically displays a relaxed urbanity of tone and an attractive mobility across a wide range of themes and occasions: family, medicine, sport, love, art, religion, landscape and suburbia are recurrent sources of poetry. He can be the poet of social situations whose abject ordinariness becomes something almost loved through the gentle strength of his cadences and subtle heightenings of imagery:

> Who, in the public library, one evening after rain,
> amongst the polished tables and linoleum,
> stands bored under blank light to glance at these pages?
> Whose absent mood, like neon glowing in the night,
> is conversant with wet pavements, nothing to do?
> ('Public Library')

Abse's capacity for intense lyricism is one of his clearest Anglo-Welsh traits. 'Epithalamion', the best known of his early poems, is a ritualized effusion celebrating marriage that reflects stylistically his admiration for Dylan Thomas. In the much later 'Letter from Ogmore' the Anglo-Welsh lyrical surge breaks through the poem's grim survey of modern history. The lines quoted have a characteristic technical adroitness in combining tautness of form and heightened musicality with an informal openness of tone:

> But here, this mellow evening,
> on these high cliffs I look down
> to read the unrolling

holy scrolls of the sea. They are
blank. The enigma is alive
and, for the Present, I boast,
thumbs in lapels, I survive.

'In the Theatre', 'The Smile Was' and 'Case History' are among the poems in which Abse draws on his professional experience of medicine and surgery to produce compelling and occasionally harrowing poetry. The sureness of touch and humane tact he brings to such work is frequently encountered elsewhere in his writing, which is much concerned with mortality and death:

> For that night his wife brought him a peach,
> his favourite fruit, while the sick light glowed,
> and his slack, dry mouth sucked, sucked, sucked,
> with dying eyes closed – perhaps for her sake –
> till bright as blood the peachstone showed.
> ('The Peachstone')

The satisfactions of his work range from such moving achievements to the sophisticated ribaldry of 'The Ballad of Oedipus Sex' – 'some like girls contemporary / but I like them antique' – and other memorably amusing poems. Abse's example suggested a stimulating variety of new stylistic and formal possibilities for younger poets contributing to Welsh writing in English. While he continues his own mature development, his facilitating influence is discernible in the work of Tony Curtis, Robert Minhinnick and others of their generation. With such talents as Gwyneth Lewis, Duncan Bush, Paul Henry, Christine Evans, Stephen Knight and Catherine Fisher working alongside them, contemporary Welsh poetry in English seems in capable hands.

BIBLIOGRAPHY

Abse, Dannie (1989). *White Coat, Purple Coat: Collected Poems, 1948–1988*. London: Century Hutchinson.

Abse, Dannie (1997). *Welsh Retrospective*. Bridgend: Seren.

Abse, Dannie (ed.) (1997). *Twentieth Century Anglo-Welsh Poetry*. Bridgend: Seren.

Bush, Duncan (1994). *Masks*. Bridgend: Seren.

Clarke, Gillian (1996). *Selected Poems*. Manchester: Carcanet.

Conran, Anthony (1982). *The Cost of Strangeness*. Llandysul: Gwasg Gomer.

Conran, Anthony (1997). *Frontiers in Anglo-Welsh Poetry*. Cardiff: University of Wales Press.

Curtis Tony (1986). *Selected Poems, 1970–1985*. Bridgend: Poetry Wales.

Davies, Idris (1972). *Collected Poems*. Llandysul: Gwasg Gomer.

Henry, Paul (1998). *The Milk Thief*. Bridgend: Seren.

Jones, Gwyn (ed.) (1983). *The Oxford Book of Welsh Verse in English*. Oxford: Oxford University Press.

Knight, Stephen (1996). *Dream City Cinema*. Newcastle upon Tyne: Bloodaxe.

Lewis, Alun (1994). *Collected Poems*. Bridgend: Seren.

Lewis, Gwyneth (1995). *Parables and Faxes*. Newcastle upon Tyne: Bloodaxe.

Minhinnick, Robert (1999). *Selected Poems*. Manchester: Carcanet.

Pugh, Shenagh (1990). *Selected Poems*. Bridgend: Seren.

Stephens, Meic (ed.) (1991). *The Bright Field: An Anthology of Contemporary Poetry From Wales*. Manchester: Carcanet.

Stephens, Meic (ed.) (1998). *The New Companion to the Literature of Wales*. Cardiff: University of Wales Press.

Thomas, Dylan (1985). *Collected Letters*. London: Dent.

Thomas, Dylan (1988). *Collected Poems, 1934–1953*. London: Dent.

Thomas, R. S. (1993). *Collected Poems, 1945–1990*. London: Dent.

Watkins, Vernon (1986). *Collected Poems*. Ipswich: Golgonooza Press.

'Writers of Wales' series (monographs by various authors). Cardiff: University of Wales Press.

26

Irish Poetry to 1966

Alex Davis

A few days before Christmas 1900, Augusta Gregory was delighted to receive a copy of Yeats's dramatic poem *The Shadowy Waters*, from its author (Yeats, 1997, p. 610). The linguistic opulence and static quality of Gregory's 'best Xmas box' would soon come into conflict with Yeats's theatrical ambitions in the early years of the century, prompting him to revise it twice in an attempt to discard its 'needless symbols' (Yeats, 1954, p. 453). As a poetic text, the 1900 version reads as a lengthy postscript to the symbolist poems collected in Yeats's quintessentially *fin-de-siècle* volume of the preceding year, *The Wind Among the Reeds*. In his introduction to *The Oxford Book of Modern Verse* (1936), Yeats famously declared that 'in 1900 everybody got down off his stilts' (Yeats, 1994, p. 185); but, on the evidence of *The Shadowy Waters*, he himself was still riding high at the turn of the century. Yeats's poetic trajectory up to the First World War, and the publication of *Responsibilities*, can be viewed as a prolonged effort to come down to earth, as it were. Turning away from the introspective, dreamy Celticism of his 1890s verse, he sought a more public and declamatory poetry, the rhythms of which, to his gender-fixated mind, would be more 'masculine' than those of his early work.

Yeats's characteristic refashioning of his poetic identity in this period is representative of the general trend in Irish poetry from the turn of the century to independence, as poets increasingly found the ethereal qualities of the poetry of the 1890s turning ersatz. Aestheticism did survive the nineteenth century in Irish poetry: it is discernible, in a self-consciously manipulated form, in Joyce's *Chamber Music* (1907), and traces linger as late as Oliver St John Gogarty's urbane *An Offering of Swans* (1923). Yet the poetry of Joyce and Gogarty equally signals an impatience with the dreamy mood of the *symboliste* twilight of the Literary Revival. Joyce and Gogarty's fraught relationship is, of course, famously recast by Joyce as that of Stephen Dedalus and Buck Mulligan in *Ulysses*; and in the latter's 'Ballad of Joking Jesus' (in the 'Telemachus' section of Joyce's novel) Joyce rescued for posterity an example of the kind of scurrilous poetry for which Gogarty was famous among his peers, the mildly ribald quality of which informs the poems he subsequently gathered together as 'Satires and Facetiae' in his *Collected Poems* (1954). Joyce's mischief-making reveals his own taste for verse of this kind. In his satirical broadside of 1904, 'The Holy Office', Joyce lampoons the work of Yeats and the Revival in the name of a rude 'Katharsis-Purgative': 'That they may dream their dreamy dreams / I carry off their filthy streams' (Joyce, 1992, pp. 103, 104). One of Joyce's targets in this poem is George Russell (AE), whose *Collected Poems* of 1913 illustrates well the persistent afterglow of the Celtic Twilight in the first decade or so of the new century. Nevertheless, George Russell was instrumental in the shift in Irish poetry towards a sharper focus and rhythmic firmness through his role in the publication, in 1904, of *New Songs*, a volume of poetry by a younger generation than his and Yeats's (though he chose to exclude Joyce, a possible slight remembered by the author of *Ulysses*). Although Richard Fallis makes *New Songs* sound more programmatic than it actually was, he is right to note the manner in which many of its contributors 'replace the mazy rhythms of the poetry of the nineties with an energy which came from folk song' (Fallis, 1977, p. 119), and their concomitant rejection of mythical material largely in favour of ruralist preoccupations.

New Songs' shift away from Celticism is imbricated in the literary phenomenon of these years which Seamus Deane adroitly dubs 'Irish Elizabethanism' (Deane, 1991, p. 721). The importance of Elizabethan lyricism to the poets of the 1890s is, in an Irish context, most palpable in the work of the English-born Celtophile, and self-styled Irish patriot, Lionel Johnson, whose dissipation and premature death in 1902 would guarantee him a prominent place in Yeats's account of his 'tragic generation'. Johnson's poetry, however, is far from dissolute; its astringency was admired by Ezra Pound, who saw in his 'small slabs of ivory, firmly combined and contrived' (Johnson, 1915, p. ix) something lost to English-language poetry since the Elizabethans. Irish Elizabethanism in the early years of the twentieth century attempts to reinflect Johnson's 'hard energy', as Yeats described it (Yeats, 1999, p. 241), into 'the vigour, fullness of speech, energy' which Deane believes Synge for one found in Elizabethan poetry (Deane, 1991, p. 721); and which Synge and other poets descried in the culture of rural Ireland, specifically its traditional folksongs. In another revision of 1890s Celticism, urban experience finds a place in a small body of Irish poetry at this date: in James Stephens's irate and disturbingly vivid depictions of Dublin's poor in *Insurrections* (1909), and in a number of wistful, impressionistic poems about city life by a contributor to *New Songs*, Seamus O'Sullivan. (O'Sullivan would latterly become an important figure in the dissemination of Irish poetry through his editorship, from 1923 to 1958, of the highly eclectic literary periodical, *The Dublin Magazine*.) In Synge's poems and those of two slightly younger writers encouraged by Russell, Joseph Campbell and Padraic Colum, Celticism gives way to an earthier representation of rural Ireland and the lives of its inhabitants. As Austin Clarke later observed, 'our poetry had passed into what we might call the folk phase' (Clarke, 1967, p. 30), a transformation he traced to the importance for younger poets of Douglas Hyde's bilingual anthologies, *The Love Songs of Connacht* (1893) and *Religious Songs of Connacht* (1906).

Colum's strength, in his poems included in *New Songs* and in his first and finest collection, *Wild Earth* (1907), resides in his pastiche-folksongs: his well-known 'She Moved Through the Fair', for instance, pours new lyrics into the bottle of an old air. Similarly, the Ulsterman Campbell published, in the same year as *New Songs* appeared, a collaborative venture with Herbert Hughes, *Songs of Uladh*, in which Campbell provided the words to traditional Donegal tunes collected by Hughes, their most successful result the popular 'My Lagan Love'. Colum's ruralist subject matter, wedded to his verbal and rhythmic simplicity, can border on sentimentality. Campbell's intense preoccupation with the Irish landscape, conveyed through an increasingly evocative and, in *Earth of Cualann* (1917), allusive language, is richer fare; and shows the influence of literary modernism, principally Imagism, with which he came into contact in London early in the century. The cultural nationalism of the two poets was at one with their militant politics: both were involved with the Irish Volunteers, and Campbell's anti-Treaty position would find him interned during the Irish Civil War. Indeed, Campbell played a part in the Easter Rising, the repercussions of which included the execution of three of his poetic contemporaries, Thomas MacDonagh, Patrick Pearse and Joseph Mary Plunkett. Of these, MacDonagh most thoughtfully addressed, from a nationalist standpoint, the vexed issue of an Irish poetry in English. His *Literature in Ireland* (1916) seeks to discredit the notion of a 'Celtic Note' in Irish literature, arguing instead that there is an essentially 'Irish Mode' of writing in English, which shows 'the influence of Gaelic versification, of Irish music or the Irish way of speech' (MacDonagh, 1996, p. xiv). Provocatively, MacDonagh links 'the element of disturbance, of revolution' he identifies in this Anglo-Irish hybrid to Futurism and experiments in *vers libre* (ibid., p. 5). While his own poems are anything but disturbing, some of his versions of Irish poems, such as 'The Yellow Bittern', impressively deploy assonantal patterns derived from their Irish originals. Such a device, in Russian Formalist parlance, defamiliarizes the English-language lyric, generating mildly disjunctive sound-patterns in its new linguistic context. In this respect, MacDonagh's translations can be profitably considered alongside those of Pound – an admirer of MacDonagh's thesis in *Literature in Ireland* – whose revolutionary 'translations' from Chinese poetry, *Cathay*, had appeared in 1915.

MacDonagh's exercises in this manner were important for Francis Ledwidge, whose elegy for the insurrectionist, 'Lament for Thomas MacDonagh', begins by echoing 'The Yellow Bittern'. Ledwidge died a year after MacDonagh was shot – blown to pieces at Ypres in 1917 while serving for the imperial power the Easter Rising had contested. Seamus Heaney has memorably described Ledwidge as 'our dead enigma', a figure in whom 'all the strains / Criss-cross in useless equilibrium' (Heaney, 1998, p. 186). Criss-crossing Ledwidge's later poetry are a number of 'strains': the atrophied lyricism familiar to readers of Edward Marsh's anthologies of contemporary British poetry, a mythological allusiveness after the example of the Revival, and a number of essays in the kind of 'Irish Mode' argued for by MacDonagh (of which this 'Lament' is one instance). Haunted by the violence of 1916, Ledwidge's poignant pastoralism contains no overt attempt to accommodate his own traumatic experiences at Gallipoli and in the Western trenches. Unlike Wilfred Owen's, his Georgianism is not forced to implode under the pressure of modern warfare. By way of contrast, the poetry of another combatant, Thomas MacGreevy, does address the representation of warfare, both that of the Great War and the struggles in Ireland prior to and attendant upon the formation of the Irish Free State in 1922. Yet MacGreevy chooses to approach his subject matter by means of techniques derived from high modernism rather than John Masefield, producing a fragmentary textual patina most fully developed in his middle-length poem, *Crón Tráth na nDéithe*, a work which owes as much to T. S. Eliot's *The Waste Land* as to its acknowledged model, *Ulysses*.

MacGreevy, along with his younger friend Samuel Beckett, and Beckett's contemporaries Brian Coffey and Denis Devlin, rejected not only Celticism, but also much of the poetry which in various ways had sought to create an 'Irish Mode' distinct from that of Revival. Beckett's *Echo's Bones and Other Precipitates* (1936) is aggressively modernist in its disorientating dislocations. Well-apprised of Joyce's linguistic bravado in *Work in Progress*, and temperamentally inclined towards the sense of cultural malaise permeating *The Waste Land*, Beckett's early poems edgily atomize concerns developed at greater length in his prose and drama. With his turn to French, the overdetermined nature of the early verse modulates into an evocation of 'strangely gentle apocalypse', as Hugh Kenner felicitously describes the quality of a poem such as 'je suis ce cours de sable qui glisse/my way is in the sand flowing' (Kenner, 1996, p. 45). Beckett's increasingly minimalist poetic contrasts with Devlin's linguistic *jouissance*, in Barthes's sense of the word. Devlin's *Intercessions* (1937) is unique in Irish poetry, being saturated with the example of French surrealism, specifically the love poetry of Paul Éluard. Devlin's career as a diplomat in the civil service would take him to the United States during the Second World War, and into a creative relationship with the New Critical poetics of Allan Tate and Robert Penn Warren, the results of which are evident in a number of poems included in *Lough Derg and Other Poems* (1946). But surrealist images continue to spot the densely symbolic patterning of these works, just as the libido's urges inform and direct the Mariology of Devlin's religious outlook in his late masterpiece, *The Heavenly Foreigner* (1950).

An indigenous modernist aesthetics is, if not absent, then a fitful presence in the literary landscape of Ireland in the interwar years, though, with the notable exception of the novelist Flann O'Brien, Irish writers drawn to experimental modes of writing gravitated in the early 1930s to London and continental Europe, specifically Paris. In Terence Brown's view, 'An almost Stalinist antagonism to modernism' is evident in much of the media during the years leading up to the Emergency; antipathy towards 'surrealism, free verse, symbolism and the modern cinema . . . combined with prudery (the 1930s saw opposition to paintings of nudes being exhibited in the National Gallery in Dublin) and a deep reverence for the Irish past' (Brown, 1985, p. 147). What can be overlooked in such a dispirited portrayal of the period is the liberating influence of modernist poetics on certain women poets, specifically, Mary Devenport O'Neill and Sheila Wingfield, and to a lesser extent Rhoda Coghill (just as a number of Irish women painters were inspired by abstraction in the visual arts). O'Neill's and Wingfield's adoption of what are basically Imagistic procedures in some of their poems comes long after Imagism, as a coherent movement, had expired. Such belatedness is indicative of the extent to which O'Neill and, to a greater extent, Wingfield, wrote in relative isolation, though O'Neill's Thursday *salon* was frequented by such literary luminaries as Yeats and Russell. Despite this connection, O'Neill's poetry is anti-revivalist in its refusal to idealize rural Ireland; its Imagistic clarity, as Anne Fogarty suggests, is governed by an attentiveness to the world that bears some comparison with Laura (Riding) Jackson's emphasis on poetic purity. Wingfield's poetry also possesses a quality of objectivism, though her most achieved work is the discursive long poem *Beat Drum, Beat Heart* (1946), a sustained meditation in four parts on the effects of war on men and women. It is one of the major Irish long poems of the century, and, in its complex and scrupulous attention to the activities and behaviour of men and women during military conflict, is comparable with the blitz novels of fellow Ascendancy writer Elizabeth Bowen.

Writers who stood opposed to the cultural insularity of the 1930s and 1940s made various attempts to demystify the ideology originally developed by the Irish Ireland movement in the early decades of the century, particularly in the work of D. P. Moran and Daniel Corkery, which achieved its most notorious formulation in Éamon de Valera's St Patrick's Day speech of 1943, with its vision of an Ireland of 'frugal comfort', 'joyous with the sounds of industry, the romping of sturdy children, the contests of athletic youths, the laughter of comely maidens' (quoted in Brown, 1985, p. 146). Patrick Kavanagh's unflinching *exposé* of the hardships underpinning the 'frugal comfort' of de Valera's Ireland in *The Great Hunger* (1942) is the poetic counterpart to the critique of mid-century Ireland mounted in the pages of Seán Ó Faoláin's robustly uncompromising journal, *The Bell*. Like *The Bell*, Kavanagh's long poem engages with some of the grimmer realities of Ireland after independence and during the Second World War. Targeting the country's conservative and patriarchal social order, it provides an alternatively fierce and poignant analysis of the hardships suffered by those who lived in a relatively unmechanized, underdeveloped rural economy. Centring on the life of a subsistence farmer, Kavanagh deals a realist rebuke to de Valeran notions of rural Ireland as well as denouncing the Revivalists' treatment of the Irish 'peasantry', giving the lie to their idealized representations of a mode of life which few of the Revivalists knew at first hand.

Louis MacNeice served briefly as poetry editor for *The Bell* during the late 1940s; his earlier long poem *Autumn Journal* (1938) had in part dealt with the insularity of Ireland, north and south of the border, as MacNeice perceived it. The documentary style of the poem makes good the thesis adumbrated in MacNeice's *Modern Poetry* (1938) of the current need for 'impure' poetry (a demand which *The Great Hunger* and *Beat Drum, Beat Heart* equally fulfil): a verse form that registers the vagaries of experience, shaping its recalcitrant material into patterns without transmuting existential lead into spurious poetic gold. The intensity of MacNeice's response to the dross, as he sees it, of post-partition Ireland prefigures his sensitivity, a decade later, to the experience of the Indian subcontinent on the cusp of independence and partition. But his unflinching poetic does contain an idealistic dimension, an innocence to weigh against the bifurcated sense of being felt by the Anglo-Irish MacNeice, and which finds its imaginative locus in the west of Ireland. This aspect of MacNeice, coupled to his preoccupation with divisiveness, both of the self and recent European and Irish history, suggests an affinity with Yeats, on whom MacNeice wrote one of the first and best full-length studies. *Autumn Journal's* splenetic reaction to Ireland also recalls another hyphenated Anglo-Irishman's polemics of this period – Beckett's swingeing 1934 essay, 'Recent Irish Poetry'. Whereas MacNeice's socio-political critique targets, in the south, the 'round tower' of de Valera's Ireland, Beckett's essay lambastes the poetry of 'our leading twilighters' (Beckett, 1983, p. 71) – that of Austin Clarke, Colum, Monk Gibbon, F. R. Higgins and James Stephens – and the deleterious effects, to Beckett's eye, of Yeats's *The Tower* and *The Winding Stair and Other Poems* on contemporary Irish poetry.

It needs to be said that Beckett's 'younger antiquarians' are largely straw men, his depiction of Yeats a burlesque. As John P. Harrington has observed, Beckett's 'critique of cut-and-dried Ossianic goods [is] virtually as old as those goods themselves' (Harrington, 1991, p. 33); and Yeats's later poetry constitutes its own 'critique' of various currents within Irish political and cultural nationalism, including it needs to be said, the political and social efficacy of his own work. His misgivings, in this regard, are apparent in the recognition of the gulf that separates his literary activity from the lives of the combatants in 'The Road at my Door', one of the 'Meditations in Time of Civil War': trying to 'silence the envy in [his] thought', the poet 'turns towards [his] chamber, caught / in the cold snows of a dream' (Yeats, 1957, p. 424). This is a worry that gnaws at the vitals of Yeats's work, and informs the self-interrogative mood of his late poem 'Man and the Echo'. In the course of that poem, Yeats famously asks, 'Did that play of mine send out / Certain men the English shot' (Yeats, 1957, p. 632); and it is hard to determine whether an answer in the negative would not disturb the speaker more than a positive reply. The play in question, the nationalist allegory *Cathleen ni Houlihan* (as much Augusta Gregory's play as Yeats's, it should be said), exemplifies an important element of the Revival's modernism, that which Terry Eagleton terms its '*non-realist* representation, art faithful to an action which is itself realistically improbable, or one which represents it in a non-realist way' (Eagleton, 1995, p. 305). *Cathleen ni Houlihan* undermines realist theatrical conventions, not, as in Yeats's later Noh-inspired drama, by rejecting them, but by means of the introduction of the symbolic figure of Cathleen into a representational drama set in Mayo, 1798, on the eve of rebellion. 'Man and the Echo' questions the political import of the play's modernist form and, by extension, the entire Literary Revival's contribution to the nationalist cause in the run-up to 1916 and the War of Independence.

This is not to downplay the importance of the Revivalists' nationalist intentions and respective political agendas: *pace* the revisionist historian R. F. Foster, *Cathleen ni Houlihan* and the cultural nationalism of the Revival as a whole may well have been formative in the politicizing of some of its audience. After all, one of the casualties of the Easter Rising was Seán Connolly, an actor at the Abbey Theatre from 1913, whom Yeats memorializes in another late poem, 'Three Songs to the One Burden': 'Who was the first man shot that day? / The player Connolly' (Yeats, 1957, p. 608). Perhaps the player's actions owed something to the Abbey's plays. My point is rather that the Revival's modernism is apparent in Yeats's later anxiety with regard to the *relationship* between his literary output and the social and political conjuncture in which it is produced. While the cultural nationalism of the Revival is informed by a desire to *re-present* Ireland to itself in literary form, the 'Ireland' constructed to this end took on its own autonomous existence. Hence the antipathy it generated in later writers, several of whom, including Beckett and Kavanagh, tended to conflate the Revival's representation of Ireland with the more obviously ideological national self-images promoted by Irish Ireland and de Valera. The older Yeats admits to the free-floating nature of the Revival's Ireland in several contexts: in 'The Municipal Gallery Re-visited' the portraits among which the speaker stands, 'the images of thirty years', have precisely that property of '*non-realist* representation' Eagleton identifies in the Revival. 'This is not', the persona declares, 'The dead Ireland of my youth, but an Ireland / The poets have imagined, terrible and gay' (Yeats, 1957, pp. 601–2). Like-wise, in 'The Circus Animals' Desertion' Yeats confesses that 'Players and painted stage took all my love / And not those things that they were emblems of' (Yeats, 1957, p. 630). Partially unhinged from its referent, Yeats's Ireland, 'terrible and gay', is an *emblematic* Ireland; that is, it relates to its horizon of production in the manner of an 'emblem' or moral fable. The autonomy of these images is that of the high mod-ernist artwork, which can never attain the closeness to lived experience enjoyed by the folk artefact.

Yeats flirted with the apparent immediacy of the ballad in several late poems, and issued a number of these from the Cuala Press in a collaborative venture with F. R. Higgins. Higgins's preoccupation with the folksong predated his acquaintance with Yeats, and has its origins in his reading in Hyde's *Love Songs*, as is apparent from the poetry collected in *Island Blood* (1925) and *The Dark Breed* (1927). As the titles of these two collections suggest, Higgins's early poetry is concerned with racial identity, an issue over which he came into conflict with MacNeice in a radio broadcast of 1939, an exchange which has since achieved minor notoriety due to its strategic deployment by Paul Muldoon as the 'Prologue' to his *Faber Book of Contemporary Poetry*. Higgins's poetry delimits a notion of Irishness which it locates in the western seaboard, in 'the dark men from the glenside / And bare-limbed girls with creels', who populate the title poem of his first collection (Higgins, 1925, p. 65). Such a portrayal of the 'dark breed' of Connacht is, of course, the kind of poetic representation ridiculed by Beckett in 'Recent Irish Poetry' and lampooned by Devlin as the 'Eternally emerald pastures of Ireland . . . and brown men of Connaught' (Devlin, 1989, p. 13). But the darkness explored in Higgins's poetry is as much that of his melancholic lyric subject as it is a racial property. His speaker's valedictions to the rapidly eroding customs of rural Ireland are reinforced by evocative exercises in the kind of 'Irish Mode' argued for by MacDonagh. As his friend Austin Clarke noted, the sound-patterns of Higgins's poetry possess remarkable 'subtlety in tune rhythm', his 'use of end-assonance has the same effect as diminished intervals in music' (Clarke, 1967, p. 46). In Higgins's final volume, *The Gap of Brightness* (1940), the insistent rhythms of the ballad dominate, their urgency helping to convey his anxiety over the changing face of the rural landscape. As a number of critics have remarked, some of these poems bear more than a trace of Yeats's late hauteur; but, as is also the case with the poetry of Padraic Fallon, rather than merely imitating Yeats's preoccupations and mannerisms, Higgins, at his best, maintains a dialogue with the older poet. In 'Auction!' for instance, Higgins turns a rueful eye on his own Protestant background, as he places that heritage, and its glamorization in Yeats's hands, under the hammer of the auctioneer: 'Now, I'll knock down to this fine throng / The spacious park – once great and grand – / That Higgins mortgaged for a song' (Higgins, 1940, p. 83).

Fallon has often been read as though he mortgaged his poetry to Yeats; and a poem such as 'Yeats's Tower at Ballylee' does indeed, as Robert F. Garratt observes, succumb to the very Yeatsian rhetoric it seeks to circumnavigate. Yet elsewhere Fallon shows how the incorporation of Irish-language poetic devices and elements drawn from folksong can be fruitfully combined with a more disjunctive modernist mode of writing, thus destabilizing the conventional lyric form from within. In a related fashion, John Goodby has cogently argued that Fallon's deployment of archetypal female figures, in a problematic attempt to critique Yeats's phallocentrism, resembles the interspersion of mythic female presences in Pound's *Cantos*. The sensuality of much of Fallon's writing resembles that of W. R. Rodgers's, though the latter's linguistic *brio* owes more to Dylan Thomas and the Neo-Romantics of the 1940s than the preceding generation of high modernists. The conjoining of sexuality and spirituality in the title poem of Rodgers's *Europa and the Bull* (1942) is reinforced by a rhetorical excess that Gregory A. Schirmer sees as functioning in a compensatory fashion, as a reaction to his Northern Presbyterianism culture. If that is the case, Rodgers's style stands in marked contrast to that of his fellow Ulsterman, John Hewitt, whose monologic, pentameter-based voice can be heard to attempt a more rational and comprehensive interrogation of the realities of the Northern Irish Protestant. The great strength of Hewitt's meditations on the place and roots of his poetic persona lies in their ability to deconstruct the very regionalist ideology on which they are based. His forays into the nature of Irishness, underpinned by the desire for liberal tolerance, are forced into quiet self-rebuke, as his aspirations for Ulster are made to confront the dispossessions of the past.

Hewitt's emphasis on the particularities of place finds an echo in Austin Clarke's localism. Clarke's attentiveness to the events and personages of Ireland after independence developed out of his growing antipathy to the haziness of what he called 'the Twilight mood': 'all that is vague, wistful and dreamful was assumed to be characteristic of the Celtic race here and elsewhere' (Clarke, 1995, p. 153). From the 1920s on his work can be read, at least in part, as a series of strategic moves to free himself of the influence of Revival, in particular Yeats, though the movement's cultural nationalism and idealism remained with Clarke throughout his life, leading to his intense dissatisfaction with the often far from ideal realities of the Free State and, later, the Republic. Indeed, Robert F. Garratt has argued that Clarke saw himself as inheriting the tradition of the Literary Revival, which he was compelled to 'extend and develop' (Garratt, 1986, p. 107). His first work, a long narrative poem, *The Vengeance of Fionn* (1917), is heavily indebted to the Revival's interest in Irish mythology, retelling the story of the relationship between Diarmuid and Grainne in vivid English. Well-received by reviewers, Clarke was unable to repeat either the critical success or artistic achievement of this work in his following long poems. Concurrent with Clarke's poetic tribulations were the Anglo-Irish war and the Irish Civil War. Clarke, a republican sympathizer, was deeply troubled by the fierce reprisals exacted by the Free State government on republicans. In self-imposed exile in London, Clarke responded to this betrayal, as he saw it, of the ideals of 1916 in *Pilgrimage and Other Poems* (1929), which, aside from its striking experiments in the 'Irish Mode', drew for its subject matter upon the Celto-Romanesque period in Irish history, an era which it implicitly deploys as a yardstick against which to measure the shortcomings of the present.

Throughout the early stages of his life, Clarke was troubled by mental illness, a topic which was finally explored in his long poem of 1966, *Mnemosyne Lay in Dust*. But emotional and intellectual crisis is to be found in Clarke's poetry as early as the thirties, in *Night and Morning* (1938), a collection in which Clarke began to examine an issue to which he would return obsessively for the next thirty or so years: the relationship between the oppressive and arrogant Church and the subjected, suffering individual. With his resumption of poetic writing in the 1950s, after a period devoted principally to verse drama, a new satirical voice emerges in Clarke's work, one which is unflinching in its criticism of what Clarke dubbed the 'Ill-fare State' of Ireland at this time (Clarke, 1968, p. 52). In these poems, Clarke scores his points through irony, wit and word-play; and it thus comes as little surprise that Jonathan Swift, the eighteenth-century Irish – indeed, Dublin – satirist, became an increasingly important figure for Clarke in his later years. Finally, Clarke turned his back on such sporadic forays into the fields of politics and topical social questions. His late work marks a return to the mythological, though his sources are Classical as well as Irish. In a fashion which again asks to be read as an attempt to swerve away from Yeats, he analysed sexuality from the position of enlightened old age, a theme evident in his 1971 comic–erotic masterpiece, *Tiresias*.

Kavanagh did not see any connection between his own work and that of Clarke, viewing the slightly older figure as a hang-over from the Revival; and Clarke is among those lambasted in the 1949 satire 'The Paddidad' (after Pope's *The Dunciad*), as 'Paddy of the Celtic West' (Kavanagh, 1996, p. 85). The work of these 'Paddies' Kavanagh called the 'Irish thing', which he viewed as suitable for export only, particularly to the United States. Unquestionably, the identification of Clarke with the Paddies-for-export is erroneous. Kavanagh never recognized – or refused to recognize – the similarity between aspects of his work and Clarke's in their respective turns to the local: Clarke to Dublin, its society, politics and culture; Kavanagh to memories of the rural parish, its life and people, a world that he left behind in 1939 when he moved to Dublin. Clarke, the fairer critic of the two, admired *The Great Hunger*, describing it as 'a realistic study of country life, almost Joycean in its intensity' (Clarke, 1995, p. 109). Kavanagh's 'realism' is equally evident in the wilful parochialism of the poetry he wrote subsequent to *The Great Hunger*. The 'parochial', for Kavanagh, is distinct from the 'provincial' mindset, the latter defining itself solely in relation to 'the metropolis':

> The parochial mentality on the other hand is never in any doubt about the social and artistic validity of his parish. All great civilizations are based on parochialism – Greek, Israelite, English. In Ireland we are inclined to be provincial not parochial, for it requires a great deal of courage to be parochial. When we do attempt having the courage of our parish we are inclined to go false and play up to the larger parish on the other side of the Irish Sea. In recent times we have had two great Irish parishioners – James Joyce and George Moore. (Kavanagh, 1988, p. 206)

Kavanagh's conceptual opposition degrades Irish writers who perpetuate imperial stereotypes of Irishness, and who thus are complicit in a form of cultural neocolonialism (a charge he levelled against his own 1938 quasi-autobiographical novel *The Green Fool*). Writers like Joyce, in *Ulysses*, and Moore, in *Hail and Farewell*, successfully resist this temptation; and, in making the city of Dublin their parish, they equally reject any idealized monolithic conception of Irish culture, either that of the Revivalists or that of Irish Ireland and de Valera. As Antoinette Quinn suggestively argues, Kavanagh follows Joyce and Moore in deconstructing the idea of Ireland possessing an essential identity, thus eschewing the idea that there should be a national literature that embodies this essence. In Homi Bhabha's terminology, such a postcolonial strategy emphasizes the *hybrid* nature of modern Ireland – it has no spiritual core because it is a 'mosaic' of cultures.

During the 1960s the effects of Sean Lemass's economic policies drew Ireland out of the social and economic stagnation that Clarke's satires and Kavanagh's *The Great Hunger* had addressed. It is a critical commonplace to see a similar 'expansionism', on the level of culture, in the poetry of Thomas Kinsella, John Montague and, to a lesser extent, Richard Murphy, in which Irish poetry is seen to become more open to Anglo-American and other poetic influences. In their shared preface to the *Dolmen Miscellany of Irish Writing* (1962) Montague and Kinsella write that, linking the work of the writers therein, was the 'desire to avoid the forms of "Irishism" . . . exploited in the past' (Kinsella and Montague, 1962). Montague and Kinsella were, however, preceded by several poets in this desire: in the North, Robert Greacen had absorbed successfully much from the Neo-Romantic poets of the early 1940s; while in the South, Valentin Iremonger, in *Reservations* (1950), showed the possibilities for Irish poetry through going to school with Auden. Similarly, preceding Kinsella's, Montague's and Murphy's experiments in the long-poem, Eugene Watters's extraordinary *The Weekend of Dermot and Grace* (1964) combined the mythic structuration of *The Waste Land* with the linguistic fluidities of *Finnegans Wake*. But there is a sense in which these earlier 'expansionist' poetic projects failed, or petered out. Greacen lapsed into silence in the late 1940s, his poetic hiatus lasting well into the 1970s; twenty years separate Iremonger's first and second collections, the latter slim volume reprinting much of the first; and Watters wrote, at least in English, no other poem comparable to *The Week-end*. (In Irish, he wrote 'Aifreann na Marbh', a poem which, like *The Week-end*, deals with the bombing of Hiroshima.) With Montague and Kinsella, by way of contrast to these three slightly older poets, ambition finds itself matched by achievement.

Montague's early poetry is informed by a tension between traditionalism and experimentation, the parochial and the cosmopolitan. The roots of this tension are biographical: born in New York of emigrant parents, Montague spent his childhood in Tyrone; as an adult he was educated at University College, Dublin, and thence spent time in Paris and the States, before returning to Ireland. His poetry explores this 'tangle, a turmoil of contradictory allegiance it would take a lifetime to unravel' (Montague, 1989, pp. 8–9). Hence Montague's obsession with returning to origins, sites, memories, ancestral figures, which or whom he attempts to imaginatively reconstruct, aware that, in doing so, he is partly recomposing them precisely as images. Montague's most sustained 'backward look' is his exploration of personal and Ulster history in *The Rough Field* (1972), a sequence of poems which reworks, in part, material from the 1960s, bringing together pre-existing lyrics and modernist formal devices. Mapping the rough field of the townland of Garvaghey, Montague intersperses meditative and autobiographical poems with Elizabethan woodcuts and accounts of Ireland, political pamphlets and letters, in a fashion reminiscent of William Carlos Williams's and Charles Olson's deployment of found materials in *Paterson* and *The Maximus Poems*. In 'The Bread God' section of the sequence, for instance, Montague interlards his lyrics with loyalist documents and letters from his Jesuit uncle to produce 'A Collage of Religious Misunderstandings' (Montague, 1979, p. 25). This use of montage has 'the effect', in Dillon Johnson's view, of 'dissolv[ing] any sense of an authoritative causal history into separate documents defining sectarian histories' (Johnson, 1997, p. 193); and, in this respect, the open form of *The Rough Field* is a brilliantly realized extension of its densely conflictual content.

Such a problematic relationship to familial and national origins also marks the poetry of Kinsella. Kinsella can be interpreted as heralding many of the concerns of contemporary Irish poets in his concern with, in Deane's words, 'the need to break, however reluctantly, out of a deep insulation from the actual, and to take on again the burden of history and thereby to come to a recognition of horror and violence, the imposition of such forces upon an isolated, peripheral consciousness' (Deane, 1985, p. 137). Kinsella's trademark emphasis on suffering and brutality is coupled to the need to find in these intensely negative experiences their positive contraries. Throughout his poetry, early and late, is the belief, in his words: 'We're surrounded and penetrated by squalor, disorder and the insignificant, and I believe the artistic impulse has a great deal to do with our trying to make sense out of that' (Kinsella, 1981, p. 101). In both his poetry and literary–critical prose is the conviction that Irish history, Irish identity, and the Irish literary tradition are not givens, but must be sought out, due to the turbulent history of Ireland from the seventeenth century on. Kinsella has spoken of the 'great inheritance' that Irish-language literature bequeaths to the modern Irish writer; but it is also a 'great loss' because the 'inheritance' is only available 'at two enormous removes – across a century's silence and through an exchange of worlds' (Kinsella, 1970, p. 60). Such a double-remove is the result of the eclipse of the Irish language through the imposition and adoption of the English tongue. The modern Irish writer thus works in what Kinsella calls a 'dual tradition'; he or she has a necessarily 'divided mind', and is thus distinct from the modern English or French poet, say, whose tradition is basically monolingual, and relatively unaffected by linguistic and other forms of colonization. Hence the enormous importance that Kinsella ascribes to Joyce and his enabling downplaying of Yeats. Joyce provides a connection between the two halves of Ireland's 'divided mind' – his realism and his sense of alienation look back, argues Kinsella, to the seventeenth- and eighteenth-century Gaelic poets, whose old order had collapsed after Kinsale. Yet Joyce's modern concerns, those of the urban Catholic bourgeoisie, tie him to this side, our side, of the broken tradition. He thus, in Kinsella's thought, stands opposed to Yeats who, for all his magnificence, is not part of the Irish tradition as Joyce is: he is a magnificent, but solitary figure. Joyce, by way of contrast, and despite his rejection of nationalism, religion and the Irish language, is central to the – in Kinsella's word – 'healing' of the rupture in the divided Irish psyche: 'He is the first major Irish voice to speak for Irish reality since the death-blow to the Irish language' (ibid., p. 65).

What is particularly interesting about these remarks, which Kinsella has reiterated from the mid-1960s on, is that they occlude the obviously Yeatsian qualities of much of Kinsella's early poetry. These verbal tics reveal the dependence of the poetry collected in *Another September* (1957) and *Downstream* (1962) on the lyric form that Yeats adhered to throughout his career. Kinsella's lyric subject, however, is closer to the humdrum persona of the British Movement poem than to any of Yeats's many selves; and in such reach-me-down existential *angst* Kinsella finds a surprising vehicle for his exploration of what is posited as an unbridgeable divide between consciousness and the object-world. The early poems read as a defensive reaction to a world which seems chaotic; reality resists the poet's rage for order, obdurately refusing to yield any epistemological certainty. Kinsella's later poetry, beginning with *Nightwalker* (1968), will bypass this dualism by a subtle change in approach, in which the binary oppositions between self and world, poet and reality, give way to a more phenomenological interaction in which the mind, itself *part* of reality, seeks to find, in an endless process of tentative searchings, momentary and transitory order rather than the possibility of fixed and determinate bearings.

In this respect, Kinsella's poetry reflects at the level of form the sea-change in the social fabric of Ireland during the 1960s. His modernist constructivism, beginning in the late 1960s, is implicated in, even as it takes an explicit stance against, the effects of economic expansion satirized in the figure of 'Productive Investment' in 'Nightwalker', who 'beckons the nations through our gold half-door' (Kinsella, 1968, p. 59). While the decade saw economic recovery and growth reduce emigration and raise living standards, it also witnessed industrial unrest and botched housing and commercial developments, particularly in Dublin. The gradual emergence, in the late 1960s, of group politics, most significantly that of the civil rights movement in the North, followed hard on the heels of the nationalist obeisance shown in the commemorations for the revolutionaries of the Easter Rising in 1966. The immense popularity of showbands in the decade, the influence of television after Radio Telefís Éireann began broadcasting in 1961, a sharp growth in tourism, are all indices of the radical alterations in Irish culture and society during these years, as the country's economy increasingly interpenetrated with multinational capitalism. In Kinsella and Montague, among others, Irish poetry had found voices capable of articulating this new 'Irish reality'.

BIBLIOGRAPHY

Beckett, Samuel (1983). *Disjecta: Miscellaneous Writings and a Dramatic Fragment*, ed. Ruby Cohn. London: John Calder.

Brown, Terence (1985). *Ireland: A Social and Cultural History 1922–1985*. London: Fontana.

Clarke, Austin (1967). *Poetry In Modern Ireland*. Cork: Mercier.

Clarke, Austin (1968). *The Echo at Coole and Other Poems*. Dublin: Dolmen.

Clarke, Austin (1995). *Reviews and Essays of Austin Clarke*, ed. Gregory A. Schirmer. Gerrards Cross: Colin Smythe.

Corcoran, Neil (1997). *After Yeats and Joyce: Reading Modern Irish Literature*. Oxford: Oxford University Press.

Coughlan, Patricia and Alex Davis (eds) (1995). *Modernism and Ireland: The Poetry of the 1930s*. Cork: Cork University Press.

Deane, Seamus (1985). *Celtic Revivals: Essays in Modern Irish Literature 1880–1980*. London: Faber.

Deane, Seamus (1991). 'Poetry 1890–1930.' In Seamus Deane (ed.), *The Field Day Anthology of Irish Writing*, vol. II, pp. 720–3. Derry: Field Day.

Devlin, Denis (1989). *Collected Poems of Denis Devlin*, ed. J. C. C. Mays. Dublin: Dedalus.

Eagleton, Terry (1995). *Heathcliff and the Great Hunger: Studies in Irish Culture*. London: Verso.

Fallis, Richard (1977). *The Irish Renaissance*. Syracuse: Syracuse University Press.

Fallon, Brian (1998). *An Age of Innocence: Irish Culture 1930–1960*. Dublin: Gill and Macmillan.

Fogarty, Anne (1999). 'Outside the Mainstream: Irish Women Poets of the 1930s.' *Angel Exhaust*, 17: 87–92.

Garratt, Robert F. (1986). *Modern Irish Poetry: Tradition and Continuity from Yeats to Heaney*. Berkeley: University of California Press.

Goodby, John (2000). *From Stillness into History: Irish Poetry since 1950*. Manchester: Manchester University Press.

Harrington, John P. (1991). *The Irish Beckett*. Syracuse: Syracuse University Press.

Heaney, Seamus (1998). *Opened Ground: Poems 1966–1996*. London: Faber.

Higgins, F. R. (1925). *Island Blood*. Plaistow: Curwen.

Higgins, F. R. (1940). *The Gap of Brightness*. London: Macmillan.

Johnson, Lionel (1915). *Poetical Works of Lionel Johnson*. London: Elkin Mathews.

Johnston, Dillon (1997). *Irish Poetry after Joyce*. Syracuse: Syracuse University Press.

Joyce, James (1992). *Poems and Exiles*, ed. J. C. C. Mays. Harmondsworth: Penguin.

Kavanagh, Patrick (1988). 'The Parish and the Universe.' In Mark Storey (ed.), *Poetry and Ireland Since 1800: A Source Book*. London: Routledge.

Kinsella, Thomas (1968). *Nightwalker*. Dublin: Dolmen.

Kinsella, Thomas (1970). 'The Irish Writer.' In Roger McHugh (ed.), *Davis, Mangan, Ferguson? Tradition and the Irish Writer*. Dublin: Dolmen.

Kinsella, Thomas (1981). 'Interview.' In John Haffenden, *Viewpoints: Poets in Conversation*. London: Faber.

Kinsella, Thomas and John Montague (eds) (1962). *The Dolmen Miscellany of Irish Writing*. Dublin: Dolmen.

Kavanagh, Patrick (1996). *Selected Poems*, ed. Antoinette Quinn. Harmondsworth: Penguin.

Kenner, Hugh (1996). *A Reader's Guide to Samuel Beckett*. Syracuse: Syracuse University Press.

MacDonagh, Thomas (1996). *Literature in Ireland: Studies Irish and Anglo-Irish*. Dublin: Talbot.

Montague, John (1979). *The Rough Field*. Dublin: Dolmen.

Montague, John (1989). *The Figure in the Cave and Other Essays*, ed. Antoinette Quinn. Dublin: Lilliput.

Schirmer, Gregory A. (1998). *Out of What Began: A History of Irish Poetry in English*. Ithaca, NY: Cornell University Press.

Yeats, W. B. (1954). *The Letters of W. B. Yeats*, ed. Allan Wade. London: Rupert Hart-Davis.

Yeats, W. B. (1957). *The Variorum Edition of the Poems of W. B. Yeats*, ed. Peter Allt and Russell K. Alspach. New York: Macmillan.

Yeats, W. B. (1994). *Later Essays*, ed. William H. O'Donnell. New York: Scribners.

Yeats, W. B. (1997). *The Collected Letters of W. B. Yeats. Volume II: 1896–1900*, ed. Warwick Gould, John Kelly and Deirdre Toomey. Oxford: Oxford University Press.

Yeats, W. B. (1999). *Autobiographies*, ed. William H. O'Donnell and Douglas N. Archibald. New York: Scribner.

PART IV
Readings

27

Thomas Hardy: *Poems of 1912–13*

Tim Armstrong

The 'Poems of 1912–13' are a sequence of elegies which Thomas Hardy wrote after the sudden death of his first wife Emma on the morning of 27 November 1912. They describe her death, Hardy's reaction, and his visit to the scenes of their courtship in Cornwall the following March. The original sequence, published with other groups of poems in the first edition of *Satires of Circumstance* (1914), comprised eighteen poems. Five years later, in the Wessex Edition and *Collected Poems* (1919) Hardy altered the sequence, placing three poems which had previously been outside it at its end, as well as making a number of other small revisions cumulatively suggestive of a greater distance from the material. If *Satires of Circumstance* is arguably not, overall, Hardy's strongest volume of poems – most critics would award that prize to *Moments of Vision*, which followed in 1917 – the 21-poem arrangement which crystallized as the 'Poems of 1912–13' remains one of the greatest and most personal elegiac sequences written in English, offering a substantial revision of the elegiac tradition for the twentieth century, as well as a uniquely honest image of the poet struggling with his own grief and remorse.

Love's Ashes

Emma Hardy died suddenly, though given how little he and his wife seemed to have had to do with each other by 1912, Thomas Hardy may well have been inattentive to signs of just how serious the illness arising from her gall-bladder complaint was. And that is one of the problems that the sequence addresses: Emma's death forced Hardy to confront not just death, but the extent to which, over the course of a long marriage, the passionate early love celebrated in his romance novel *A Pair of Blue Eyes* (1872) had itself cooled. In the 1890s, in particular, the couple had drifted apart, Emma becoming increasingly religious and scandalized by his iconoclastic late novels, and Hardy enjoying flirtations with other women (at the point of Emma's death he had a clandestine connection with Florence Dugdale, who was to become the second Mrs Hardy in early 1914). Emma's death thus represented a double challenge and a double grief, confronting Hardy with the truth of his marriage. This is reflected in the structure of the sequence (discussed below), in Hardy's use of both Emma's auto-biographical writings (later published as *Some Recollections*) and *A Pair of Blue Eyes* to recall the sites of his courtship, and in the richly suggestive Virgilian context which Hardy evokes in the sequence's epigraph, *Veteris vestigia flammae*.

Veteris vestigia flammae are the words spoken by Dido, Queen of Carthage, in Book IV of Virgil's *Aeneid*, describing how the capacity to love which had died with her husband Sychaeus is reawakened by the visiting Trojan hero Aeneas – who is, of course, shortly to abandon her, prompting her suicide. Her words have been variously trans-lated: 'the sparkles of my former flame' (Dryden); 'the signs of the old flame' (Man-delbaum); but perhaps also 'the traces of an old fire', since *flammae* can mean either fire or ashes, and *vestigia* can signify a mark, trace, even the track of a footstep. Hardy's epigraph itself asks questions about the status of remembered passion. The words posi-tion Hardy as Dido, falling in love again. But they also imply an accusation in which he stands in the place of Aeneas, standing before Dido's mute accusing shade during his visit to the underworld in Book VI. The underworld motif suggests another mythic subtext, more explicitly alluded to in a later poem, 'The Shadow on the Stone': the story of Orpheus and Eurydice, of the singer who must attempt to rescue his beloved from death. This in turn suggests one of the greatest mysteries of these poems: the question of just *why* Hardy feels such passion for the dead? – a question which seems to refer us to his individual psychopathology, the unique mixture of 'distance and desire' described by J. Hillis Miller, but which also surely relates to the fact that he had already written the story of his romance into *A Pair of Blue Eyes*, and given it there a tragic ending, and was now confronted by his own plotting.

As Donald Davie brilliantly pointed out, the Virgilian context is also evoked by the 'purples' which 'prink' the main in 'Beeny Cliff', the poem in the sequence in which Hardy most explicitly returns to the scenes of courtship (it is subtitled 'March 1870–March 1913'):

> A little cloud then cloaked us, and there flew an irised rain,
> And the Atlantic dyed its levels with a dull misfeatured stain,
> And then the sun burst out again, and purples prinked the main.

In the 1895 preface to *A Pair of Blue Eyes* the same 'bloom of dark purple cast' is described, and in chapter 4 (in quotation marks) Hardy writes of 'the purple light' which surrounds its protagonists, referring, Davie argues, to the *purpureus* of Virgil's underworld. Later commentators have argued that this is more directly the 'purple light of love' of Thomas Gray's ode 'The Progress of Poesy'. But Virgil lies behind that reference as well, and Davie is right to stress that the Virgilian context pervades the novel and the sequence, and that the epigraph echoes across Western tradition. Virgil's words are translated by Dante at the climactic moment of the *Purgatorio* in which Beatrice replaces Virgil as Dante's guide: recognizing her, Dante says *conosco i segni dell' antica fiamma*. Hardy as Dido driven wild by passion; Hardy as the Aeneas who betrays; Hardy as Aeneas/Orpheus in the underworld; Emma as the lamentable ghost of Dido/Eurydice or as the redemptive guide Beatrice leading him through the topography of the past – all these positions are called up and interrogated. When Hardy writes 'Through the years, through the dead scenes I have tracked you; / What have you now found to say of our past – / Scanned across the dark space wherein I have lacked you?' ('After a Journey') he evokes the *vestigia* (tracks) of the epigraph, Aeneas's confrontation with the unanswering ghost of Dido, and Dante's passage through Hell and Purgatory.

The most important question raised by the epigraph, for Davie, is whether the space which the epigraph opens for us is metaphysical or psychological. For Davie the three poems added at the end of the sequence in 1919 represent a betrayal of the powerful affirmative vision of 'At Castle Boterel', turning metaphysical insights into mere moments in the psychology of grief. Other commentators on the sequence have seen this process as inevitable, as necessitated by the rhythms of mourning. But Davie's own scheme also implies a counter to the visionary Platonism he sees in Hardy: the *vestigia* of the epigraph are worked into the formal closure of 'Where the Picnic Was', when Hardy returns to the Ridgeway above Portland and stands in the circle of charred embers – the ashes from an old fire – and sees the devastation for what it is. Moreover Hardy's eros is imbued with death, its 'dark space' recalling the tormented topography of Dante's hell – the purple and black air which Dante calls *perso*, and the sleety rain of Canto 6 (which Hardy marked in his *Inferno*) – as well as the Elysian Fields of classical epic.

Hardy and the Elegiac Tradition

Davie's claims about the 'Poems of 1912–13' hinge on two issues: on the question of what elegy is *for*; and on the valency attached to particular moments in the sequence rather than on its total shape. Recent criticism on the elegy has focused on the way in which it completes what Freud terms 'the work of mourning', that is a complex process in which the experience of death, initially overwhelming, is worked-through to a point of resolution and achieved distance. That process is typically seen as involving a repeated confrontation of loss; anger and perhaps denial; a recapitulation of the relationship with the dead; the creation of a satisfactory internal image of the dead; and a giving up of the dead to the larger forces of nature – with each of these moments of mourning having formal or topical equivalents in the elegy. The point of a poetic sequence, rather than a single elegy, is that it 'freezes' moments in the mourning process, allowing them to be explored.

This psychological reading – which Davie rejects, as we have seen – is exemplified by Peter Sacks in *The English Elegy*. Sacks represents the 'Poems of 1912–13' as marking a break with the traditions of the genre, refusing or at least substantially deferring the consolation it offers: 'In few other elegies', he writes, 'has the poet gone so far to undermine his own identity or had to fight so desperately for his own survival' (Sacks, 1985, p. 244). Sacks points out that the difficulty is partly the ground on which memory must be recovered: in fictionalizing Emma in *A Pair of Blue Eyes*, Hardy had in a sense already displaced her – and indeed his two protagonists see her dead at the end of the novel, mourned by her husband. Moreover if the elegist must do battle with Time, which takes away the dead, Hardy's own typical poetic stance is uncomfortably close to Time's. How can he seek 'That time's renewal' ('The Going') if he depicts himself as simply an isolated observer of 'Time's derision' ('After a Journey'), and as an atheist without even Tennyson's attenuated hope of an audience with the dead?

Another problem is simply the difficulty of Emma's legacy. When she died, Hardy found a vituperative diary reportedly called 'What I Think of My Husband'. He burnt it. What of *these* ashes? We might see them as haunting the second poem of the sequence, which ends 'Yet abides the fact, indeed, the same, – / You are past love, praise, indifference, blame.' The halting penultimate line stutters into a truncated series: if 'indifference' is the middle term and 'praise' and 'blame' are conventionally balanced, then the occluded final term of the series is 'hate'. If he refuses the word here, there is nevertheless a great deal of aggression in some of the poems: in the projected anger of the opening complaint, 'Why did you give no hint that night . . . ?'; in the depiction of Emma 'shut' and 'powerless' in her grave in 'Lament'; in the bitter irony of a fashion circular addressed to one 'costumed in a shroud' in 'A Circular' (though in this poem the irony also rebounds on the author sending his letters to the dead); even in the trampling of the sticks of the fire in the closing poem. Those we mourn for take themselves violently from us, and one response for the elegist is the exercise of power over the dead or over a portion of the self attached to them. The bitter shift in tone at the conclusion of 'St Launce's Revisited' – 'Why waste thought, / When I know them vanished / Under earth; yea, banished / Ever into nought!' – represents this impulse, and the negatives here are echoed throughout the sequence (the words 'not', 'nought', 'nobody', 'never', 'none' constantly return).

The 'Poems of 1912–13' also incorporate and trope on elements of elegiac tradition. The sub-genre of the 'domestic elegy' has origins in the seventeenth century, but it is only in the nineteenth century that it loses its theological frame and takes on a personal specificity and a psychological realism. Hardy's immediate precursor is Coventry Patmore in *To the Unknown Eros* (1877), a sequence addressed to a dead wife (his opening poem directly borrows from Patmore's 'Departure'). Tennyson's *In Memoriam* is also, clearly, a model, with its sense of mourning as extended struggle. But Hardy's elegies are harsher than most of his models, as Sacks points out. Where he uses the traditional elements of elegy, for example references to the cycle of the seasons, flowers on a grave, and Emma as a child in 'Rain on a Grave' and 'I Found Her Out There' (all recalling Wordsworth's 'Lucy' poems), these references are followed by the stilted and almost parodic formality of 'Without Ceremony', with its bland suggestion that Emma's sudden death was simply a form of bad manners. Where he finds memories of Emma written in the landscape of some of the central poems of the sequence, he also registers the Cornish landscape's indifference in 'A Death-Day Recalled' and points out that Emma's ghost will itself have to 'creep underground' from Dorset to Cornwall. The gaps which the elegist must close are always on display in Hardy, and most strikingly of all, it is only very late in the sequence, with its thirteenth poem, 'After a Journey', that he moves unequivocally beyond the depressive position of the man who mourns without hope.

One other way in which Hardy shifts the emphasis of elegy is in his use of a hugely varied metrical and technical repertoire, in contrast to the measured and solemn stanzas of Gray and Tennyson. The metres of the 'Poems of 1912–13' range from the labouring fourteeners of 'Beeny Cliff' 's rhyming triplets, seeming to imitate the waves of 'that wandering western sea', to the tripping pitter-patter of the irregular two-beat lines of 'Rain on a Grave', littered with feminine endings and double-rhymes. 'The Voice' is a brilliant exploration of carefully adjusted (and revised) sonic effects, from its echoing triple-rhymes ('call to me / all to me') to the broken metre of the final stanza, marking the poem's collapse into solipsism and doubt. 'After a Journey' is, Dennis Taylor suggests, 'perhaps his most metrically interesting poem', with its ambiguous scansion and its complex rhyme-scheme (Taylor, 1988, p. 82). To expend such poetic labours on the dead is not a matter of tribute or self-display; rather it implies a sense of form close to that of modernist poetry, in which that which is described or expressed dictates the mode of expression. The poet's restless dealings with loss and landscape and his sense of the inadequacy of all formal consolation are both reflected in the variations in form, even within individual poems.

The Structure of the Sequence: Time and Place, Voice and Vision

The other important issue in Hardy's sequence is its overall shape. The sequence is structured around a series of geographical, temporal and perspectival 'contrasts' (the harsh word used in 'His Visitor'). Those include the contrast between Dorset ('here') and Cornwall ('there'), with Plymouth, the setting of 'Places', as a point of mediation; and the corresponding contrast between present or recent past (in Dorset and then the trip to Cornwall) and the distant past (in Cornwall). There is a contrast between old-Emma and young-Emma in their respective places, and (less marked) between Hardy and his younger self. Finally, in terms of perspective the poems in Hardy's voice are occasionally replaced by those in which he ventriloquizes Emma's – though in a ventriloquy which never moves from soliloquy to dialogue. These contrasts are not static: the sequence develops *through* them, moving from Dorset to Cornwall and back, from present to past and back, and shifts its emphasis in other ways:

from collapse and stasis to distance and movement; from voice (or the absence of voice) to vision and the memorialized image of the beloved.

In the early poems Emma's death and its aftermath are treated, and the poems represent the frozen and fractured states of grief. Death is alternately denied, internalized ('I seem but a dead man held on end'); the self alternately vacated or wounded and defended. The poems restlessly move between the recent past and the present, seeking to trace clues of Emma's death. When Hardy does move on, it is in the conventionalities of 'Rain on a Grave' (the only poem in the sequence with no negative terms), followed by 'I Found Her Out There', in which the possibility of a shift in focus to Cornwall is broached for the first time. But that move is delayed as Hardy returns to poems dealing with the aftermath of Emma's death, including for the first time poems in which her voice is imagined. 'The Haunter' represents a ghost whom the poet cannot see, who must beg the reader to act as intermediary: 'Tell him a faithful one is doing / All that love can do'. 'All that love can do' is a line from Swinburne's cynical 'Félise', which Hardy knew very well indeed. Swinburne writes: 'Though love do all that love can do, / My heart will never ache or break / For your heart's sake.' The old Emma appears, then, deflecting the possibility of a harsher voice, insisting on love's endurance. But hers is a voice which, as the next poem demonstrates, is uncertain in status, too close to the fluttering sounds of the wind. 'The Voice' contrasts a dubious sound ('Can it be you that I hear?') with a desired image of an earlier self ('Let me view you, then'). The Emma it wishes to recover is described in a temporally convoluted phrase as 'Saying that now you are not as you were / When you had changed from the one who was all to me'. But the voice of an earlier self is not easily imagined, and seems to dissolve into the poem's windy sound effects, leaving the poet 'faltering forward' in the halting final stanza. It is unsurprising that the next poem, 'His Visitor', returns to the everyday voice of the older Emma making a final visit to Max Gate: with her departure to join the 'mute' voices of the dead, Hardy is finally free to imagine a move to Cornwall in 'A Dream or No'.

He arrives there in 'After a Journey', the fulcrum-point of the sequence, and surely in itself one of the greatest elegies of the twentieth century. The poem as we have it begins with an abandoning of voice. 'Hereto I come to interview a ghost', he wrote in early versions, before crossing out this opening line and substituting 'Hereto I come to view a voiceless ghost', reducing even the possibility of interchange. Voice here bound up with image and landscape:

> Yes: I have re-entered your olden haunts at last;
>   Through the years, through the dead scenes I have tracked you;
> What have you now found to say of our past –
>   Scanned across the dark space wherein I have lacked you?

A voice which must be 'scanned' is a textualized voice; and Hardy was reading *Some Recollections* and *A Pair of Blue Eyes* as he wrote. But 'scanned' also suggests scansion, and as Matthew Campbell argues, the poem's heavy rhymes suggest a poet who must recognize a non-responsiveness in the dead, and move on (Campbell, 1999, p. 230). 'After a Journey' is a poem which admits the loss and damage which comprise the 'dark space' of experience; indeed that loss is carried in its cruel rhymes ('tracked you/lacked you'; 'division/derision'). But grief can be mastered, partly because what he seeks is two ghosts, not just one: the young Emma, and the ghost of his own earlier self in 'the spots we knew when we haunted here together'. After the uncertainty of the first stanzas, Emma becomes his guide, and the ashes of love are rekindled as he hears the cave

> with a voice still so hollow
> That it seems to call out to me from forty years ago,
> When you were all aglow,
> And not the thin ghost that I now fraitly follow.

This is to admit that both he and the ghost are frail, transient; and even to admit that what he sees is a willed illusion (what is this but another version of Plato's parable of the cave?). But movement has finally replaced stasis, and a negotiation of past and present has replaced their frozen opposition. In the opening poem Hardy had asked why they did not revisit Cornwall when Emma was still alive, 'And ere your vanishing strive to seek / That time's renewal?' There he had declared 'All's past amend / Unchangeable'. Here, he says 'Soon you will have, Dear, to vanish from me', restaging her departure and declaring that he is willing to experience this encounter again, that in this place he is 'the same' as he once was, and can carry that continuity within himself.

The extent to which this vision is tied to place is underscored by both 'Beeny Cliff' and 'At Castle Boterel', the latter Hardy's most impassioned recollection of the young Emma and himself on his early visits to St Juliot. Here he can assert the absolute significance of what he remembers:

> It filled but a minute. But was there ever
> A time of such quality, since or before,
> In that hill's story? To one mind never,
> Though it has been climbed, foot-swift, foot-sore,
> By thousands more.

The next stanza inscribes that memory, as if into the fossil record, in the 'primaeval rocks' which border the road. As Sacks notes, he has again forgone voice ('what we talked of / Matters not much') for a memorial sign, 'recorded' in the stone like the memorial which Hardy later had erected in the church at St Juliot. The poem acknowledges that the rocks have seen much of 'the transitory', but Hardy is nonetheless willing to assert the *quality* of what he experienced, and what he now records. The vision of Emma here is his last: it is Orphic, over the shoulder ('I look behind at the fading byway'), finally leaving Emma's image amidst the rainy gloom of what seems close to an underworld.

The original sequence ended with 'The Phantom Horsewoman', which offers an externalized description of Hardy which some readers mistakenly see as being in Emma's voice. But that voice, as we have seen, has vanished from the sequence (even if it returns in the distanced allegory of one of the three added poems, 'The Spell of the Rose'), and what we are offered in 'The Phantom Horsewoman' is a distanced view of Hardy himself. The vision of Emma here is more psychologically located ('in his brain'), but the poem's main function is to complete the turning away initiated by 'At Castle Boterel': Hardy 'turns to go' in the opening stanza, carrying his vision with him 'far from this shore'; Emma, at the end, 'Draws rein and sings to the swing of the tide'. The poem is replete with closure and reversal: in its final reference to a stabilized and portable image of Emma; in its top-and-tailed form; but also in its reversal of figures seen earlier in the sequence. In the opening poem he had recalled that she 'reining nigh me / Would muse and eye me'; here it is she who is seen 'as when first eyed'. In 'After a Journey' he insisted that he remained 'the same'; now we read 'He withers daily / Time touches her not / But she still rides gaily / In his rapt thought'.

These reversals suggest an important truth about the poems: that the closest that they can get to interchange is the rhetoric of chiasmus, of crossing and reversal. As David Gewanter (1991) has pointed out, Hardy often had to settle for the dead letter of Emma's notebook where he would have wished for a live voice ('Places', the poem between the visionary pairing of 'At Castle Boterel' and 'The Phantom Horsewoman', is quite directly worked up from *Some Recollections*; 'Beeny Cliff' borrows most of its details and descriptive adjectives – purples, rain-showers, bulking cliff, nether sky – from chapter 21 of *A Pair of Blue Eyes*). Moreover the 'frail ghost' he follows is contaminated with old-Emma, with lost time. 'Calling for the girl by means of the woman', a compromised voice entwines itself through his discourse. Radically, Gewanter suggests it is the encounter with old-Emma rather than the wispy ghost which provides the real energy of the sequence. It is perhaps for this reason that the first poem added in the sequence in 1919, 'The Spell of the Rose', is in the voice of the mature Emma, using the figure of the memorial rose to call for a posthumous understanding and reconciliation in a way which is reminiscent of the artful ghosts and oppositional rhetoric of Christina Rossetti. This version of Emma seems to understand at least as much as the poet does.

The final two poems reinforce the sense of closure; 'St Launce's Revisited' admits a previously suppressed negative moment into the original pilgrimage to the Cornish coast. Finally, 'Where the Picnic Was' returns to the winter scene in Dorset and, as we have seen, surveys the burnt stick-ends, ritually closing the eyes of the dead. Hardy describes himself as 'last relic of the band / Who came that day', making himself one of the *vestigia*, a carrier of traces (and a 'band' is also a circle, like the 'burnt circle' of fire). The cycle of experience represented in the sequence is closed in a final act of reading, completed with a wintry stoicism.

Within Hardy's corpus, it is Emma's death which is the event which makes him as a poet, which is at the core of what Dennis Taylor calls his 'apocalypse', including as well the Great War – an apocalypse in which the pattern of his loss is preinscribed and fulfilled in a pattern of belated recognition. Some of the issues raised in the sequence are only resolved in later poems, notably the great wind-and-water series of *Moments of Vision*. The late Hardy achieves a freer relation to memory and the dead. But it is the intensity and immediacy of the 'Poems of 1912–13' which give them their power, as well as the honesty with which Hardy faces up to his own evasions. He may dissemble in saying that he had no hint that Emma was unwell, he may efface his own duplicities in his marriage, but that dissembling is presented to us for judgement; like the 'look of a room on returning thence' described in 'The Walk', the empty spaces and negations of the poems speak to us.

The final significance of 'Poems of 1912–13' is in its legacy. Hardy engages in a dialogue with the elegiac tradition, but in such a way that the limitations of its formulae are exposed, its redemptive baggage cast aside. In the elegiacs of the poets who follow – in Owen, Auden, Berryman, Lowell, Sexton, Hughes, Heaney, Douglas Dunn, Thom Gunn, Amy Clampitt, Sharon Olds and many others – the elegy is more varied in form and tone, whether ironic, confessional, reticent, or gothic; whether addressing the dead or the reader. The Victorian spectacle of Tennyson reading the rolling, consoling stanzas of *In Memoriam* to his monarch is banished, and death's rituals are rendered a more personal, and more problematic quest.

BIBLIOGRAPHY

Armstrong, T. (2000). *Haunted Hardy: Poetry, History, Memory.* Basingstoke: Macmillan.

Austin, L. (1998). 'Reading Depression in Hardy's "Poems of 1912–13."' *Victorian Poetry* 36: 1–17.

Brooks, J. (1971). *Thomas Hardy: The Poetic Structure.* Ithaca, NY: Cornell University Press.

Buckler, W. H. (1979). 'The Dark Space Illumined: A Reading of Hardy's "Poems of 1912–1913."' *Victorian Poetry* 17: 98–107.

Campbell, M. (1999). *Rhythm and Will in Victorian Poetry.* Cambridge: Cambridge University Press.

Davie, D. (1972). 'Hardy's Virgilian Purples.' *Agenda* 10: 2–3, 138–56. Reprinted in *With the Grain: Essays on Thomas Hardy and Modern British Poetry.* Manchester: Carcanet, 1999.

Edmond, R. (1981). 'Death Sequences: Hardy, Patmore and the New Domestic Elegy.' *Victorian Poetry* 19: 151–65. Reprinted in *Affairs of the*

Hearth: Victorian Poetry, Domestic Ideology and Narrative Form. London: Routledge, 1988.

Gewanter, D. (1991). '"Undervoicings of Loss" in Hardy's Elegies to his Wife.' *Victorian Poetry* 29: 193–207.

Green, B. (1996). *Hardy's Lyrics: Pearls of Pity.* Basingstoke: Macmillan.

Griffiths, E. (1989). *The Printed Voice of Victorian Poetry.* Oxford: Clarendon Press.

Miller, J. H. (1970). *Thomas Hardy: Distance and Desire.* Cambridge, MA: Harvard University Press.

Morgan, W. W. (1974). 'Form, Tradition and Consolation in Hardy's "Poems of 1912–13",' *PMLA* 89: 496–505.

Ramazani, J. (1994). *Poetry of Mourning: The Modern Elegy from Hardy to Heaney.* Chicago: Chicago University Press.

Robinson, P. (1982). 'In Another's Words: Thomas Hardy's Poetry.' *English* 31: 221–46.

Rosenthal, M. and S. M. Gall (1983). *The Modern Poetic Sequence, Genius of Modern Poetry.* Oxford: Oxford University Press.

Sacks, P. (1985). *The English Elegy: Studies in the Genre from Spencer to Yeats.* Baltimore, MD: Johns Hopkins University Press.

Sexton, M. (1991). 'Phantoms of His Own Figuring: The Movement Toward Recovery in Hardy's "Poems of 1912–13." ' *Victorian Poetry* 29: 209–26.

Taylor, D. (1988). *Hardy's Metres and Victorian Prosody.* Oxford: Clarendon Press.

Taylor, D. (1989). *Hardy's Poetry, 1860–1928,* 2nd edn. Basingstoke: Macmillan.

28

Robert Frost: *North of Boston*

Alex Calder

'Fred, where is north?'
('West-Running Brook')

North of Boston, Frost's second book, came out in England in 1914. A few poems go back a decade to Frost's years as a chicken farmer in New Hampshire ('The Death of a Hired Man', 'The Black Cottage', 'The Housekeeper'); others ('The Mountain', 'After Apple-Picking', 'The Woodpile') were largely completed before Frost left for England in 1912, where the remaining ten poems were written 'on an inspiration compounded of homesickness and the delight of new friendships' (Cramer, 1996, pp. 28–9). It is striking how early in the century these poems appear. The major work of the first-generation modernists is still years off, yet Frost is already writing in his mature style and has found his own way through to the directness valued by Pound and the Imagists. There is another reason why these poems might seem to have arrived early: Frost does not develop as a poet after the publication of this book. He would often write as well, but he would seldom write differently. Other poets would experiment and make breakthroughs, but from 1914 through to 1962, as Jay Parini puts it, each new volume has him adding rings 'like a tree' (Parini 1999, p. 262). The lyric and narrative norms of this collection are the cornerstone of a remarkably homogeneous body of work.

It is curious, too, that Frost would stick with much the same setting in the fifty or so years left to him as a writer. 'The Pasture', a prefatory poem to this and other volumes, begins with a farmer's everyday tasks – 'I'm going out to clean the pasture spring' – and an invitation: 'I shan't be gone long. – You come too'. It has sometimes been urged that a paucity of interest beyond such places and occasions reveals the poet as hayseed. An established response to these reservations has been to look beyond the apparent simplicities of setting to the psychological depth of Frost's 'Landscapes of the Self' (Lentricchia, 1975), or to the epistemological sophistication of the 'Work of Knowing' (Poirier, 1977) his poems perform. These are key insights, but it is also the case that the restricted setting of Frost's poems is as much of its time, and as similarly codified, as their popular counterpart, the Western.

Not that there are cowboys or Indians, gunslingers or sheriffs, in Frost. But there are desert places where a lone human being confronts nature in its immensity and is tested; there are outposts where hopeless farms grind people down; there are arenas where men value physical skill and emotional reserve – and women go mad. Even so, it may go against the grain to locate 'Westerns' north of Boston. That city is reputedly strait-laced, civilized, old. Americans say it's East. We know that forever rolling west of Boston is the new: the promising empty (emptied) space of settlement, 'the land vaguely realizing westward, / but still unstoried, artless, unenhanced' ('The Gift Outright'). There is also a South of antebellum mansions, slaves, rafts and riverboats, a mental co-ordinate from which one might say that North is puritanical, self-reliant, earnest . . . Bostonian. But north of Boston? In a way, it is like saying north of North: surely, as Gertrude Stein might say, there is no there there. The poems themselves suggest a map where roads peter out and towns with far-off names like Lunenburg give way to ominous legends: frozen swamp, dark woods, dead house. Frost's own guide to these tumble-down spaces of America – to the north of the North – is a poem written much later in life called 'Directive'.

> Back out of all this now too much for us,
> Back in a time made simple by the loss
> Of detail, burned, dissolved, and broken off
> Like graveyard marble sculpture in the weather,
> There is a house that is no more a house
> Upon a farm that is no more a farm
> And in a town that is no more a town.

People who live in out of the way places whose names begin with 'new' (New Hampshire, New Zealand) know those oxymorons well. In *North of Boston* Frost is a poet of settlement as ruin.

A dedication note commends 'This book of people' to Frost's wife, but this is not a populous work. We meet people on lonely journeys, people in lonely houses, people for whom the project of making a life and home for themselves has come unstuck. If 'North of Boston' is a place where nature has the upper hand, it is not simply because the climate is cruel and the soil poor, but also because this is a place where the promise of America is exhausted and exposed. The new is *blasted* in this environment.

'The Black Cottage' concerns a dwelling so run down, 'the warping boards pull out their own old nails / With none to tread and put them in their place'. A Civil War widow used to live there, and the narrator's talkative companion, a minister, tries to explain why the cottage – first glimpsed as a picture framed by cherry trees – seems to him so singularly forsaken. It is not simply 'the lives / That had gone out of it', but something he can't quite put his finger on, and will later misconstrue, even as he senses that it involves unsettling familiar relations between old and new. The widow's husband fell at Gettysburg or Fredericksburg; the minister knows it ought to matter which, but cannot recall whether the carnage in question was the famous Union victory or the famous defeat. He does remember that the woman maintained a touching faith in the proposition that all men are created free and equal, a difficult saying 'each age will have to reconsider', but which she holds to with simple fervour.

> What are you going to do with such a person?
> Strange how such innocence gets its own way.
> I shouldn't be surprised if in this world
> It were the force that would at last prevail.

The minister feels tender towards this quality in her and goes on to indulge a fantasy:

> As I sit here, and oftentimes, I wish
> I could be monarch of a desert land
> I could devote and dedicate forever
> To the truths we keep coming back and back to.
> So desert it would have to be, so walled
> By mountain ranges half in summer snow,
> No one would covet it or think it worth
> The pains of conquering to force change on.

The minister imagines a citadel in the wilderness, a place so desert, so wild, that no one would wish to conquer it. He sounds like a founding father. The settlement of any new world requires visions of empty space even as indigenous peoples are conquered and change is imposed: it is another example of how ironclad innocence 'gets its own way'. Frost underlines this by having the minister overreach himself – he imagines sand grains turning to sugar in 'the natal dew' – and then pull up short:

> 'There are bees in this wall'. He struck the clapboards,
> Fierce heads looked out; small bodies pivoted.
> We rose to go. Sunset blazed on the windows.

The bees are where the honey is – they may suggest a more natural or original mode of habitation in contrast to the minister's arid and solipsistic ideal. Yet because those 'fierce' recolonizing bees have made themselves a home where they will not be wanted, Frost's natural image also catches on the ferocity of human patterns of settlement. In 'The Black Cottage' the American past is housed in a kind of anti-monument that not only yields to time but makes any saving act of commemoration ambivalent and unsure.

Other houses in *North of Boston* are more private, but also encrypt dead or half-living things. 'Home Burial', perhaps the best known, is motivated by the death, at age three and a half, of Robert and Elinor Frost's first child, and the distressingly different ways each parent responded to this loss. According to one biographer, Amy, the woman in the poem, in her implacable grief speaks words spoken repeatedly at the time by Elinor ('the world's evil'), while Frost once said of himself: 'And I suppose I am a brute in that my nature refuses to carry sympathy to the point of going crazy just because someone else goes crazy, or of dying just because someone else dies' (Cramer, 1996, pp. 35–6). In the poem, she goes quiet, he copes; he wants to penetrate her envelope of silence, she feels he is too brutish to be let in. Every line elaborates the double-binds and tightens the drama another notch. There is a virtuoso close reading by Joseph Brodsky that should not be missed, but it might also be said that few poems permit beginning readers to make their own 'close-reading' discoveries quite so readily. I think this is because the compelling human drama at the centre of the poem fits so well with practical or new critical styles of reading that 'see' through language, as it were, to the human consciousness at the heart of the poem. How does the husband feel? How does Amy feel? What does the poet make of them both?

One answers such questions by being sensitive to image, subtext and tone, and by allowing the detail of the poem to sharpen one's perceptions of emotional states. The woman says:

> I saw you from that very window there,
> Making the gravel leap and leap in air,
> Leap up, like that, like that, and land so lightly
> And roll back down the mound beside the hole.

What we are hearing is not only words in sequence but also a 'sentence sound' – Frost's 1913 term for the way voice carries extra-semantic meaning. In these lines, the repetitions of 'leap and leap in air, / Leap up, like that, like that' signify more than just what is said – it is as if we also hear an unspoken grievance jolted into hostility. Or consider the way Brodsky draws the reader into the poem (and into his performance of it) by elaborating the visual implications of the first line and a half.

> He saw her from the bottom of the stairs
> Before she saw him.

. . . It is an extremely loaded scene – or, better yet, a frame. . . . He's looking up at her; she, for all we know thus far, doesn't register his presence at all. Also, you've got to remember that it's in black and white. The staircase dividing them suggests a hierarchy of significances. It is a pedestal with her atop (at least, in his eyes) and him at the bottom (in our eyes and, eventually, in hers). The angle is sharp. Place yourself here in either position – better in his – and you'll see what I mean. Imagine yourself observing, watching somebody, or imagine yourself being watched. Imagine yourself interpreting someone's movements – or immobility – unbeknownst to that person. That's what turns you into a hunter, or into Pygmalion. (Brodsky, Heaney and Walcott, 1997, p. 21)

Frost is especially amenable to this quality of attention, and that may be one reason why his poetry is sometimes patronized by poets and critics who have 'moved on' from expressive realism. Yet, as Brodsky goes on to explain, 'Home Burial' is a poem that is sceptical of the very empathy its reading would seem to invite. The reader, like the husband, ought to be able to say 'I see', but in the poem this little verb and its cognates (understand, ask, speak . . . 'let me in') lose their standard meaning through repetition; instead, they either perform his wish to 'explicate' her as a form of violence or become instances of the sound one makes when one is, as Brodsky puts it, 'reeling from the unnameable' (ibid., p. 27). In his view, 'Home Burial' is not about the couple's tragic failure to communicate, about their not finding the right words, but 'a tragedy of communication' in which each would like to imprint their understanding on the other, and each has words to bludgeon the other. 'This is a poem about language's terrifying success', he adds, 'for language, in the final analysis, is alien to the sentiments it articulates' (ibid., p. 39).

At first sight, 'The Death of a Hired Man' might seem to offer a radical contrast to 'Home Burial'. It is another dialogue between husband and wife, between the practical man and the woman of feeling, but rather than assail each other as they air these differences, they build relationship as they talk. But their conversation on the front porch is in counterpoint with what happens off stage, inside the house. Silas, an old farmhand, like a hound 'worn out upon the trail', has returned to Mary and Warren's farm. In the past he has done a little unpaid work for them in return for food and lodging. Times are hard, there is not enough money to pay him, but at haying time, when there is real farm work to be done, Silas always finds he can work for cash somewhere else. This time, Warren has vowed not to take him back. Silas is waiting in the parlour, where he has been reminiscing about the time he and a young college boy named Harold were haying together. They used to argue over such things as the good of learning Latin, and Silas, concerned the young man is becoming 'the fool of books', aims to teach him the practical art of building a haystack, his 'one accomplishment'. This opposition between the practical and the impractical is in keeping with another: Mary and Warren's different understandings of home. He shrewdly reckons, 'home is the place where, when you have to go there, / They have to take you in'; and she counters, 'I should have called it / Something you somehow haven't to deserve'.

Norman Holland, in *The Brain of Robert Frost*, comments: 'Frost conceives his poem, his thought really, in twos. He pairs man and wife, father and mother, Republican and Democrat, hardness and nurturing, obligation and lack of obligation' (Holland, 1988, p. 31). We could add talk and action, volubility and bluntness, to that list of twos. Which side wins? I expect it seems to most readers that Mary has the best of the argument, that her husband's attitude softens over the course of the poem. He goes in to talk to Silas:

> . . . returned – too soon, it seemed to her,
> Slipped to her side, caught up her hand and waited.
> 'Warren?' she questioned.
> > 'Dead', was all he answered.

Their whole conversation is overshadowed by that one stark word. In so far as Silas dies while they are talking, it is as if death were itself a kind of home, a finality that dwarfs both their human concerns. The balance between Warren's and Mary's view of things is probably intended to settle back toward even with this ending, but I would say the scales tip all the way over onto the man's side. What is at stake is a secular, masculine, pared-down view of life and language, versus a feminine, Christian and sentimental one.

Frost differs from Pound in that his modernism is nativist rather than cosmopolitan, but he is as opposed to the 'Aunt Hepsy' strain in turn-of-the-century American poetry as Pound had ever been. He once said that with *North of Boston* he 'dropped to an everyday level of diction even Wordsworth kept above' (Thompson, 1965, pp. 83–4). It is a kind of manly anti-writing that proves one is not 'the fool of books'. Frank Lentricchia puts it this way:

> Frost's struggle against canonical forces was a struggle carried out on behalf of a new lyric diction . . . for the purpose of reengendering lyric for 'masculinity', a word in Frost's and other modernists' lexicons signifying, not a literal opening of the lyric to actual male voices and subjects, but a symbolic shattering of a constrictive lyric decorum that had the effect, in Frost's America, of denigrating poetry as the province of leisured women. (Lentricchia 1994, pp. 86–7)

I would add that this 'reengendering' is not only, and not mainly, the work of high culture. It also defines the difference between turn-of-the-century novels of morality and sentiment and emergent popular forms like the Western. 'There are times in life when the fancy words and pretty actions don't count for much', says the Western, 'when it's blood and death and a cold wind blowing and a gun in your hand and you know suddenly you're just an animal with guts and blood that wants to live, love and mate, and die in your own good time' (cited in Tompkins, 1992, p. 47). In 'The Death of a Hired Man' something like that view brings questions of home into final perspective.

People who are away from home, or whose homes have become 'buried' in one way or another, allow Frost to examine some of the adventures and misadventures that can befall the self. 'The Fear', a study in paranoia, begins:

> A lantern light from deeper in the barn
> Shone on a man and woman in the door
> And threw their lurching shadows on a house
> Nearby, all dark in every glossy window.

Imagine the movie: lights and camera are placed behind the actors, whose long shadows are thrown on the wall of a house nearby. It could only be a horror film. A generic example might start with the heroine safe inside the house, and a lurching menace outside, wanting to get in. Soon enough, the ghoul, monster, axe-murderer gets inside, and the film is likely to end with the expulsion of a threat, with an inner sanctum safely restored. But compare the situation of the woman in this poem. She is alarmed because she feels she is being watched – if not by her previous husband then someone he has sent. Yet her companion, Joel, has seen no one and her behaviour seems out of proportion as she takes the lantern and prepares to confront this supposed menace. Oddly, and in contrast to the usual conventions, her sense of threat is first associated with something inside the house, with the spooky feeling that a 'key rattled loudly into place' could warn an intruder 'to be getting out / At one door as we entered at another'. This chasing out then leaves a residue of fear:

> Let him get off and he'll be everywhere
> Around us, looking out of trees and bushes
> 'Till I sha'n't dare to set a foot outdoors.
> And I can't stand it.

Something bad that was in the house is sent outside the house; once outside, it terrorizes the one who sent it out. This is the logic of projection: something bad inside me is sent outside me; once outside, it terrorizes me.

It turns out, however, that there really was someone there, a father with a child, out for a 'long-after-bedtime walk'. But rather than be relieved that her anxieties had a cause and were not just imagined, the woman continues to be agitated:

> 'But if that's all – Joel – you realize –
> You won't think anything. You understand?
> You understand that we have to be careful.
> This is a very, very lonely place.
> Joel!' She spoke as if she couldn't turn.
> The swinging lantern lengthened to the ground,
> It touched, it struck, it clattered and went out.

In the darkness, the woman has no object for her fear. It is as if she has lost her sense of having borders – as if the fear, now, is both inside and outside the house. Why is she like this? Frost gives the reader one or two hints to work on. Joel doesn't believe the watcher could really be her former lover – 'It's nonsense to think he'd care enough'. Her reply suggests that Joel is actually speaking about himself – 'You mean you couldn't understand his caring' – but when she adds: 'Oh, but you see, he hadn't had enough' it is herself she gives away. She has not been loved but used. Her delusion that someone once loved her enough to watch her jealously has been the fragile refuge of her self-esteem. If I may borrow from one of Frost's later, famous definitions of poetry, it is her 'momentary stay against confusion'.

In 'A Servant to Servants', in another house haunted by the past, a depressed and bone-tired farmer's wife complains:

> It seems to me
> I can't express my feelings any more
> Than I can raise my voice or want to lift
> My hand (oh, I can lift it when I have to).
> Did you ever feel so? I hope you never.
> It's got so I don't even know for sure
> Whether I *am* glad, sorry, or anything.
> There's nothing but a voice-like left inside
> That seems to tell me how I ought to feel,
> And would feel if I wasn't all gone wrong.

The 'sentence sound' conveys a heavy sort of lassitude as she describes a feeling of emptiness or hollowness where the self should be; it is as if the part of her that knows how she ought to feel is out of touch with anything that can do the feeling. Her husband, Len, has a more common affliction: the part of him that knows how he *ought* to feel, fully defines his emotional range. Like the neighbour in 'Mending Wall' he is a fount of bright pithy sayings like, 'One steady pull more ought to do it / . . . the best way out is always through'. A pathological optimist, 'he looks on the bright side of everything', his wife notes mordantly, 'including me'.

Mary, in 'The Death of a Hired Man', stresses the psychological need for houses that are safe enclosures, that offer sanctuary, as it were. But this woman's house is not only a place where there is a never-ending round of work, it is also an environment where she can feel neither private nor safe. She is the servant of her husband's hired men and, prompted in part by the sexual menace they represent to her, she goes on to explain how her mother, as a new bride, had to care for her husband's mad brother, who was kept in a cage in the attic of the house.

> That was what marrying father meant to her.
> She had to lie and hear love things made dreadful
> By his shouts in the night. He'd shout and shout
> Until the strength was shouted out of him,
> And his voice died down slowly from exhaustion.

> He'd pull his bars apart like bow and bowstring,
> And let them go and make them twang until
> His hands had worn them smooth as any oxbow.

Initially the woman sees herself repeating her mother's situation, but as she goes on the energy of her voice changes, and she seems to identify rather more with her uncle.

> I often think of the smooth hickory bars.
> It got so I would say – you know, half-fooling –
> 'It's time I took my turn upstairs in jail' –
> Just as you will till it becomes a habit.

Why might the uncle's situation be appealing? For one critic, his room within a room is 'a horrifying metaphor for the enemy lurking within the sanctuary of self – not really lurking, but more horrible, having a place there of its own' (Lentricchia, 1975, p. 68). In this line of interpretation, 'A Servant to Servants' – like many of Frost's poems of madness – illustrates a dark possibility of imagination, in which a person (usually a woman) risks losing all touch with reality in preferring constructs of her own making. It might be argued, however, that the speaker of this poem has a firm grip on the horrors of her world, and that her taking time off work to talk is a means of warding off emotional collapse. In fancying herself in her uncle's place, she identifies with what she knows she needs: a room of her own, as it were, or, as 'Directive' would have it, a ruined place of which one could say:

> Here are your waters and your watering place.
> Drink and be whole again beyond confusion.

The uncle in his attic, it should also be said, is as naked as Huck Finn on his island, and his twanging the hickory bars like 'bow and bowstring' has a boyish, playful quality to it. It is deeply American of Frost to imagine this attic room as an oasis of the primitive.

'The Wood-Pile' begins where many of Frost's hemmed-in people would like to be: somewhere else, 'just far from home'. The speaker has gone for a winter's-day walk: rather than turn back at an accustomed point, he has kept on walking and finds himself a little out of his depth, in surroundings he does not recognize. It is just scary enough to wonder if he should be frightened. This is evident in his anthropomorphic dealings with a small bird that flits ahead of him, which he imagines imagining him as a threat to tail feathers, 'like one who takes / Everything said as personal to himself'. But is it possible not to? Frost is staging a philosophical conundrum to do with the human subject and its objects in his rural vernacular. He is wondering what it would be like to encounter nature as object on its own terms, purely and simply, without our human overlay of perception and thought. Like the bird, he necessarily takes things as 'personal to himself', even as he postulates a 'view' with no trace of human presence beyond the sweep of his perceptual field, advancing, bird-like, a step ahead of consciousness, into undifferentiated nature.

This little epistemological drama not only informs the speaker's dealings with the bird, but also with the next object he encounters: 'a cord of maple, cut and split / And piled – and measured, four by four by eight'. The woodpile has been abandoned long enough for it to seem neither a human structure nor yet a wholly natural one. It is the handiwork of both the person who 'cut and split and piled' the logs and his supplementary helper, clematis, that 'wound strings round and round it like a bundle'. It seems that an effort to imagine nature on its own terms produces a cluster of defences: anthropomorphic projection most obviously and, beyond an inevitable impulse to order, to measure something out in human terms, a more subtle and instinctive need: camouflage or mimicry. Whenever you feel too visible in your environment, chances are you try to fit in, you copy others, you become like the environment. Rather like the bird, the speaker can imagine himself being seen by something bigger than himself – call it Nature, the Real itself, what you will. The result is that the subject is now an object. The sensation of being seen like this is spooky – perhaps the skin creeps or prickles – but there is some protection from Nature's view of the subject in the prospect of camouflage, of somehow blending into the environment. This is what draws the speaker to the woodpile.

> I thought that only
> Someone who lived in turning to fresh tasks
> Could so forget his handiwork on which
> He spent himself, the labour of his ax,
> And leave it there far from a useful fireplace
> To warm the frozen swamp as best it could
> With the slow smokeless burning of decay.

The final image places human doings in an inhuman perspective and makes the prospect seem almost homely. I am reminded of the power of the word 'downy' in a later poem, 'Stopping by Woods on a Snowy Evening', where another cold and inhuman scene invites the possibility of merger:

> . . . The only other sound's the sweep
> Of easy wind and downy flake.
>
> The woods are lovely, dark and deep,
> But I have promises to keep,
> And miles to go before I sleep,
> And miles to go before I sleep.

In *North of Boston* the role of that repeated last line is the work of the poem that follows 'The Woodpile' in the collection, the very last poem, 'Good Hours', in which the speaker has walked 'till there were no cottages found' and as he returns, it is as if he is trailing the land's emptiness alongside him.

In another season, and in a more plangent mood, the game of imagining the absence of human boundaries is also the concern of 'After Apple Picking' – 'Essence of winter sleep is on the night, / The scent of apples: I am drowsing off' – while the importance of maintaining them is the theme of the collection's opening poem, 'Mending Wall'. This poem recounts an exchange between the speaker and his neighbour as they go about the spring chore of repairing fences knocked about by the winter. The neighbour repeats the old saw, 'good fences make good neighbours' and preserves a stolid silence as they work. The speaker would like to plant a notion in his head: something mischievous, something unsettling. He conceives his own work of boundary-making to be like, rather than opposed to, the 'Something there is that doesn't love a wall, / That wants it down'. The force of that contradiction – to simultaneously make a boundary and outreach it – is what drives manifest destiny. Yet whatever the 'something' that doesn't love a wall is, its most resonant location is not the new horizon (where it would be imperceptible) but what I have called 'north of the North': the ruined or blighted place, the interstitial crypt of settlement. It is 'something' that likes to dwell in 'gaps' opened out in what is left behind, knocked over, or run down. One of the names for it is Frost.

BIBLIOGRAPHY

Books

Barry, Elaine (1973). *Robert Frost on Writing*. New Brunswick: Rutgers University Press.

Brodsky, Joseph, Seamus Heaney and Derek Walcott (1997). *Homage to Robert Frost*. New York: Farrar, Strauss and Giroux.

Cady, Edwin H. and Louis J. Budd (eds) (1991). *On Frost: The Best from American Literature*. Durham, NC and London: Duke University Press.

Cox James M. (1962). *Robert Frost: A Collection of Critical Essays*. Englewood Cliffs, NJ: Prentice-Hall.

Cramer, Jeffrey S. (1996). *Robert Frost Among His Poems: A Literary Companion to the Poet's Own Biographical Contexts and Associations*. Jefferson, NC, and London: McFarland.

Frost, Robert (1995). *Collected Poems, Prose, & Plays*. New York: Library of America.

Holland, Norman N. (1988). *The Brain of Robert Frost*. London: Routledge.

Jarrell, Randall (1973). *Poetry and the Age*. London: Faber and Faber.

Kearns, Katherine (1994). *Robert Frost and a Poetics of Appetite*. New York: Cambridge University Press.

Lentricchia, Frank (1975). *Robert Frost: Modern Poetics and the Landscapes of the Self*. Durham, NC: Duke University Press.

Lentricchia, Frank (1994). *Modernist Quartet*. New York: Cambridge University Press.

Meyers, Jeffrey (ed.) (1996). *Early Frost: The First Three Books*. Hopewell. NJ: Ecco Press.

Parini, Jay (1999). *Robert Frost: A Life*. New York: Henry Holt.

Pearce, Roy Harvey (1961). *The Continuity of American Poetry*. Princeton, NJ: Princeton University Press.

Poirier, Richard (1977). *Robert Frost: The Work of Knowing*. New York: Oxford University Press.

Thompson, Lawrence (ed.) (1965). *Selected Letters of Robert Frost*. London: Jonathan Cape.

Tompkins, Jane (1992). *West of Everything*. New York: Oxford University Press.

Vendler Helen (ed.) (1987). *Voices & Visions: The Poet in America*. New York: Random House.

Articles in journals

Costello, Bonnie (1998). 'What to Make of a Diminished Thing: Modern Nature and Poetic Response.' *American Literary History*, 10 (4) 569–605.

Muldoon, Paul (1998). 'Getting Round: Notes Towards an Ars Poetica.' *Essays in Criticism*, 48 (2) 107–29.

29

T. S. Eliot: *The Waste Land*

John Haffenden

The Waste Land runs to 434 lines in length, so it is not really the 'long poem' that Eliot planned or anticipated ('the longest poem in the English langwidge', as Ezra Pound once jokingly applauded it). First published in *The Criterion* (London, October 1922) and *The Dial* (New York, November 1922), it has been the cause of more consternation and controversy than any other poem of the twentieth century. To some readers it appears to be staggeringly esoteric; a medley of voices; a 'music of allusions' and a 'palimpsest or layered mixture of historical times' (Smith, 1983, pp. 23, 50); or, if you prefer, a hotchpotch, a piece of elitist eclecticism appealing principally to those who appear to have access, like Eliot, to a swathe of European literary history: perhaps in particular Dante, Shakespeare and other sixteenth- and seventeenth-century dramatists, the English metaphysical poets, and the French symbolists, as well as philosophical and anthropological lore – much of it stemming from Sir James Frazer's digest of primitive vegetative ritual, *The Golden Bough* (12 vols, 1890–1915) – of an equally arcane kind.

Yet the poem, though it may look like an arbitrary assemblage, does comprise five distinct sections in a specific sequence; and it aspires to a mythical structure rather than to any other kind of 'narrative method' ('Ulysses, Order, and Myth', 1923, p. 483). While it may resemble a cut-and-paste job, a collage, it runs deliberately, as Ezra Pound said, from 'April . . . to Shantih', and was duly signed and published by Eliot himself – and so 'authorized' in every sense.

'Various critics have done me the honour to interpret the poem in terms of criticism of the contemporary world, have considered it, indeed, as an important bit of social criticism. To me it was only the relief of a personal and wholly insignificant grouse against life; it is just a piece of rhythmical grumbling' (Eliot, 1971, p. 1). So said Eliot, according to his brother: it is an astonishing observation from the poet and critic who is famed for his insistence on impersonality; who coined the useful locution 'objective correlative'; who laid down decrees about the importance of 'objectification' in art, the need to escape from 'personality', to transform felt life into literary form. Whenever he said those words, he had evidently forgotten the pointer he had given in one of the curious notes which were added to the Boni & Liveright (New York) edition of *The Waste Land* in December 1922, to the effect that one of the themes of section V, 'What the Thunder Said', is 'the present decay of eastern Europe' – which was as much as to say that certain passages of the poem, as he framed them, were indeed intended to express some mode of 'criticism of the contemporary world'.

Did Eliot understand his own poem? Maybe not in any sense that greatly helps us in the work of interpreting it. Even after he supplied a number of teasing and occasionally tendentious notes to the poem, he came to lament, in 'The Frontiers of Criticism' (1956), what he styled his 'exposition of bogus scholarship' (Eliot, 1957, p. 109). In 'The Function of Criticism' (1923) he seemed to describe himself as much in terms of the harrowed critic as the inspired poet: 'Probably . . . the larger part of an author in composing his work is critical labour; the labour of sifting, combining, constructing, expunging, correcting, testing: this frightful toil is as much critical as it is creative' (Eliot, 1951, p. 30). We know too that Eliot made grateful use of the services of a fellow poet and critic, Ezra Pound, who sifted, corrected and expunged a fair part of the original critical mass of the poem. Since 1971, when Eliot's widow, Mrs Valerie Eliot, published a facsimile of the drafts that were lost for many years, we have been able to enjoy insights into the process of composition, and the work which Pound undertook: the painful breech-birth by a nerveless 'midwife'. (Probably the best essay to date on the question of 'co-authorship' is that by Jack Stillinger, 1991.)

At least in his later years, Eliot disparaged the centrality, the supposed moment, of the poem. In 1959 he was asked if Pound's 'excisions' had changed the original 'intellectual structure' of the work? 'No', he responded, 'I think it was just as structureless, only in a more futile way, in the longer version' (Hall, 1959, pp. 53–4). (The 'longer version' seems to have extended to the inclusion of at least four other short sections or quasi-autonomous poems: 'Exequy', 'Dirge', 'The Death of the Duchess', 'Elegy'; Eliot wondered too whether another difficult poem about the defeated psyche, the plangent 'Gerontion', should feature as a 'prelude' to *The Waste Land*.) Perhaps we should take Eliot's words as the last word, and not look for structure or purposive meaning in the poem. Should we accept what often seems to be the case, that it is a jumble, a writhing rag-bag? Is it simply the last gasp of the epic aspirations of poetry in our age – 'a kind of epic in a walnut shell' (as Eliot's friend Conrad Aiken once dubbed it)?

This is not to say that Eliot had no sense of what he had achieved, or any original or progressive intention, whether conscious or unconscious. Originally, for example, he chose as his epigraph to the work this passage from Conrad's *Heart of Darkness* (1899): 'Did he live his life again in every detail of desire, temptation, and surrender during that supreme moment of complete knowledge? He cried in a whisper at some image, at some vision, – he cried out twice, a cry that was no more than a breath – "The horror! the horror!"' According to contemporary correspondence, Eliot considered that passage 'much the most appropriate I can find, and somewhat elucidative'. Whereas most readers today would find that quotation not only 'somewhat elucidative' but rather brayingly prescriptive and even reductive, Pound urged Eliot to drop it on the grounds that Conrad was simply not 'weighty enough to stand the citation' (Eliot, 1971, p. 125). Thereupon Eliot turned instead to a much more obscure passage, a sentence in Latin and Greek from a satire by Petronius, *Satyricon*; Brian Southam, in his *Student's Guide to the Selected Poems of T. S. Eliot* (1974, p. 71), translates the passage thus: 'For once I saw with my very own eyes the Sibyl at Cumae hanging in a cage, and when the boys said to her, "Sibyl, what do you want?" she answered, "I want to die."' Granted the gift of foreseeing all, the Sibyl neglected to look to her own future: she forgot to ask for eternal youth and so turned into an aged crone yearning for the release of death from a prospect that was always immediately apparent to her. Prevision could do nothing to solve her particular problem of the everlasting, ever-present pains of existence. ('In the Cage', adverting both to a story by Henry James and to Stravinsky's ballet *The Firebird*, was the original title of the second section of the poem, which eventually hung by another stolen citation, from the dramatist Thomas Middleton: 'A Game of Chess'.) But the Latin original for the word given as 'cage' is actually *ampulla*, an ampoule or glass vessel: the Sibyl is jammed into a kind of bell jar, that is to say, and longs, quite like Sylvia Plath, to escape a suffocating existence, her death-in-life.

How appropriate it then seems that the first of the five sections of the poem is called 'The Burial of the Dead' (the title taken from the Anglican funeral service); and how chillingly apt that the burden of this section is a congeries of markedly different voices speaking of the horror of the living dead, that what seemed satisfactorily dead is 'stirring' back to the surface, the return of remembrance and pain. The world invoked and evoked here is literally ghastly: we are presented with a series of zombies finding voice alongside images of a dessicated landscape – 'stony rubbish . . . A heap of broken images . . . fear in a handful of dust' (the last phrase being ultimately derived from a sermon by John Donne). The point is grisly horror; not decent, blessed burial but the utterly unwilling resuscitation of memory and desire, failed love, betrayed love. The section includes the ghoulish suggestion that last year's corpse might 'sprout' back into life, and it ends by quoting Baudelaire's shocking refusal of any safe ironic distance on the part of the reader: 'You! hypocrite lecteur! – mon semblable, – mon frère!' Eliot's readers are denied the prerogative of standing in judgement; we are trapped in complicity, in misery, suffering with those we see suffer.

This opening section includes a latter-day Sibyl in decadent modern dress: 'Madame Sosostris' is a 'famous clairvoyante', alias fortune-teller, who can't get the hang of her Tarot cards and so is unable to comprehend the counsel she hands out. A perverse, catch-as-catch-can and decadent prophetess, she suborns her own authority when she ends up by voicing her very own anxieties in this form:

> Thank you. If you see dear Mrs Equitone,
> Tell her I bring the horoscope myself:
> One must be so careful these days.

This portrait of Mrs Equitone's phoney personal trainer is of course comic, but it has serious implications, most obviously by begging this question: for want of any author-ized, received teacher or visionary, who is to lead us to the world of the spirit? This waste land is a place bereft of certain symbols; the sanction of received religious wisdom.

The theme of deathliness, decadence and claustrophobia is continued into section II of the poem, which features three major instances of bad gender relations – begin-ning with the well-known description of a kind of chokingly baroque bordello, and moving on to the fraught, staccato, neurotic, non-communicative exchange between man and wife that is often thought to be modelled on the dealings between Eliot and his own wife Vivienne, and concluding with another, though related, piece of pas-tiche conversation, the dire pub scene focusing on a vulgar conversation about the overburdened Lil's understandable unwillingness to meet the sexual demands of her husband Albert. As one of Eliot's biographers has remarked, '"A Game of Chess" is hell itself, the diabolical routines of marital powerplay' (Gordon, 1977, p. 111). These portraits turn out to be all the more sick when you realize a couple of features about the first of this series of scenes, in the stiflingly over-ornate brothel: while usually reckoned to borrow from the description of Cleopatra's barge in Shakespeare's tragedy, it actually owes just as much, possibly more, to the scene in *Cymbeline* in which the voyeuristic Iachimo, the dirty trickster, tells over the detail of the pure and faithful Imogen's chamber (Smith, 1983, pp. 122–3), including the observation that:

> She hath been reading late
> The tale of Tereus; here the leaf's turned down
> Where Philomel gave up.

Eliot provides a frame within a frame. His nameless woman's chamber is adorned with pictures depicting rape and other barbarities; it exhibits a glut of polyperverse grati-fication, most notably:

> Above the antique mantel was displayed
> As though a window gave upon the sylvan scene
> The change of Philomel, by the barbarous king
> So rudely forced; yet there the nightingale
> Filled all the desert with inviolable voice
> And still she cried, and still the world pursues,
> 'Jug jug' to dirty ears.

(The story of the violation of Philomel by King Tereus is best known in the version retailed by Ovid in *Metamorphoses* VI.)

What is most surprising to discover from the drafts of the poem about these opening sections – given that they represent a linked series of painful memories, regret, loss, resistance to life, and sordid sex – is that originally they went under the title 'He Do The Police in Different Voices' (Eliot, 1971, pp. 5, 11, 17). That curious title, with its seeming echoes of a music-hall turn, is taken from an incidental remark in Dickens's *Our Mutual Friend* (I, ch. 16), in which a foundling named Sloppy is complimented for his skill as a mimic: the widow Higden says 'I do love a newspaper. . . . You mightn't think it, but Sloppy is a beautiful reader of a newspaper. He do the Police in different voices.' Such an allusion might suggest that Eliot thought he was undertaking a piece of social satire in a vein not unlike some of his own, and Pound's, earlier verses. In any event, the idea of ventriloquism, of 'sending up' – often with feelings of revulsion – the various figures of his poem, may have been a primary force behind the work; and elements of that initial stance survive in the finished poem. As much as there is pain, remorse and horror in this waste land, there is also contempt.

Sexual rapaciousness and abuse (as well as sordid indifference), exploitation, violation, mutilation, abandonment and voicelessness, all figure again in the following section, 'The Fire Sermon', which includes the notorious – and, ironically, formally rhyming – quatrains describing a wretched, dissociated encounter: the casual, indifferent coupling of the typist and 'the young man carbuncular . . . A small house agent's clerk'. It represents a snatch of sex without joy or comfort. (Eliot's scorn for the figures he thus delineates may be deduced from a phrase in the original draft which calls the clerk and typist 'these crawling bugs'.) This section significantly closes with baleful lines convoking St Augustine's appeal for redemptive grace and the gospel of purgation according to the Buddha's most famous sermon, *Maha-Vagga* (Kearns, 1987, p. 75):

> Burning burning burning burning
> O Lord Thou pluckest me out
> O Lord Thou pluckest
>
> burning

Typographically, the passage represents a kind of expressionist motif: the broken syntax is in key with the prevalent disjunctions, the anti-discursive strategy, the ellipses, the upsetting dislocations and incompletions, of the poem as a whole. Yet the apostrophized appeal to the Lord is unavailing: we are left with a dangling gerund, 'burning', which may suggest either a satisfactory purgation, the burning-out of sin, in the divine fire that transforms and purifies, or a sense of being continuously consumed by one's own burning desires. Harriet Davidson, in the *Cambridge Companion to T. S. Eliot*, mistakenly observes: ' "The Fire Sermon" refers to Buddha's sermon on the purification of sexual desire' (Davidson, 1994, p. 129). In truth, the Fire Sermon is by no means confined to sex; it is a terrifying, incantatory exhortation to purge oneself of *all* desires and attachments, in accordance with the Buddhist teaching that earthly existence is evil: one must pass through a series of reincarnations with the object of refining oneself out of existence, of attaining Nirvana or Nothingness. It is a paradoxical doctrine, and has really little in common with Christianity except for the notion that both creeds seek fulfilment beyond death. Eliot would have it in his notes to *The Waste Land* that the Fire Sermon 'corresponds in importance to the Sermon on the Mount' (Eliot, 1971, p. 148); and yet the correspondence is in fact figured only by Eliot in *this* poem. The poet is concerned with the necessary, painful process of dying, the purgation; not with the life after death, of which he cannot here conceive. 'The collocation of these two representatives of eastern and western *asceticism*, as the culmination of this part of the poem, is not an accident', Eliot frankly observed (ibid.).

It then follows, if one is seeking a configuration, a shape, for the work as a whole, that the next, and briefest, part of the poem, section IV, is a *memento mori* entitled 'Death by Water': a beautiful, lyrical evocation of a merchant, 'Phlebas the Phoenician', revisiting his life and surrendering his worldly concerns:

> A current under sea
> Picked his bones in whispers. As he rose and fell
> He passed the stages of his age and youth
> Entering the whirlpool.

The lines ironically hark back to the earlier account of Madame Sosostris and her ill-informed (unwitting) fortune-telling – 'Here, said she, / Is *your* card, the drowned Phoenician sailor' – and likewise, '*Fear* death by water'.

The base note of the whole poem is dread, which might be said to be relieved, but only equivocally, or ambiguously, in the final section, 'What the Thunder Said', which undertakes a nightmare journey through a hallucinatory landscape – 'agony in stony places', sterile rocks, hideous apparitions. It is in fact a veritable apocalypse; 'I John saw these things, and heard them' reads a cancelled line in the draft of the first section, 'The Burial of the Dead', referring to the appalling and yet splendid Revelation of St John the Divine: the terrifying Apocalypse or End of the World News. But perhaps most interestingly of all, the poem now moves decisively beyond Eurocentrism, beyond the segment of the world dominated by the dispensation of Judaeo-Christianity, and clearly locates itself in the Himalayas, and by the River Ganges. Hinduism is invoked, and quoted, and Eliot cites a specific holy text, the *Brihadaranyaka Upanishad* – a fable, which has a moral design upon the auditor – in which the thunder booms 'DA', and again 'DA', and again 'DA', and is interpreted to be urging generosity, charity, order – Datta, Dayadhvam, Damyata – Give, Sympathize, Control (as Eliot renders the exhortations which are given in his sources as 'Be liberal, be clement, be restrained'). In this Upanishad, it is further interesting to know, the supplicant hears also the word of godhead, the logos, speaking out the mantra 'OM' and again 'OM' and again 'OM', the word of assent. The point is that to ask the right questions is at once to receive the right response: you hear in the voice, the word, of the thunder what you are fit to hear. But Eliot omits the 'OM', presumably with intent, since he had studied the Sanskrit (Kearns, 1987, pp. 228–9). In place of a pacific conclusion, the poem explodes into fragments, a cacophony of juxtaposed voices, a babble, a Babel, or what Stephen Spender called a hysteria (Spender, 1975, p. 119) – citing here the figure of the Provençal poet Arnaut Daniel out of Dante's *Purgatorio* XXVI who wishes to be remembered as he plunges into the painfully refining fire of Purgatory (*Sovegna vos a temps de ma dolor*: 'Be mindful in due season of my pain'); here, 'O swallow swallow', a reference to the transmogrification of Procne in Ovid's version of the violation of Philomel; and here (to take just one further instance) a famous citation from *The Spanish Tragedy* by Thomas Kyd, 'Why then Ile fit you [oblige you]. Hieronymo's mad againe' (which is not actually an authentic quotation from the play, since the latter phrase is in fact the subtitle of the play itself), referring to the hideous way in which Hieronymo, driven to dementia, avenges his murdered son. Hieronymo makes up a play out of a jumble of languages, and under cover of this riddling, distracting device he slaughters his enemies. Critics often take this allusion to Hieronymo and his multilingual play as Eliot's blackly comic piece of meta-poetry: Hieronymo's creation is a mélange of languages, and so is *The Waste Land* itself. Yet Eliot may have been ahead of such an intertextual game, with an ironic double bluff, since the following lines give the context in Kyd of Eliot's first terse phrase:

> Why then Ile fit you, say no more.
> When I was yong I gave my minde,
> And plide my selfe to fruitles poetrie:
> Which though it profite the professor naught,
> Yet it is passing pleasing to the world   [IV, i. 67–72]

Many critics like to think too that the poem ends up with a quiescent or quasi-religious closure – as in citing the Sanskrit 'Shantih shantih shantih' – the 'formal ending to an Upanishad'. But while Eliot was evidently deeply moved by the significance and the sound of the Sanskrit term 'Shantih' – in the first version of his notes he deferentially suggests that the Christian formulation ' "The Peace which passeth understanding" is *a feeble translation of the content* of this word' (Eliot, 1971, p. 149), and in so doing seems to exalt the ineffable wonder of the Sanskrit at the expense of the comfortable Christian locution – I still do not think it possible to suggest that *The Waste Land* concludes with an assent to peace and well-wishing. On the contrary, what happens in the final lines of the poem is that Eliot's splurge of allusions – citing violence, horror, murderous vengeance, purgatorial pain, self-mutilation and ultimate voicelessness – is left in open confrontation with the voice of order, self-control and peace as expressed in the Upanishad. 'These fragments I have shored against my ruins', runs the famous line 430, three lines from the end; but a fine variant occurs in the drafts, 'These fragments I have *spelt into* my ruins', which I happen to think is even better than the final version. 'Spelt' is such a reverberant word, with connotations not only of piecing together language and ideas but also of conjuring magic, runes or spirits. At any rate, the end of the poem cannot be said to represent a solution or resolution; it is just 'a formal ending' (Eliot, 1971, p. 149). Grover Smith has I think correctly noted: 'Neither grace nor self-reliance is invoked, only endurance'; and Eliot's 'thrice-repeated "Shantih" ' must 'be taken as heavily ironic. If it is hopeful it is the first word of the poem which is' (Smith, 1983, p. 55).

What I have been describing is what I see as the implicit schema of the poem, which is less a narrative or plot than an impulsion, an emotional purposiveness, a quest, starting out from a living death and its attendant horrors, moving on by way of a commemoration of death in the figure of Phlebas, and ending up by soliciting a spiritual explanation, perhaps even transcendence, but assuredly not attaining it. Eliot's strategy is not just to juxtapose voices through ventriloquism and allusiveness, nor to synthesize anything, but to engage us in a process of interplay and cross-play: a play of interconnection and interpenetration.

William Empson wrote about *The Waste Land*: 'The poem is inherently a mystery; I would never have believed that the Symbolist programme could be made to work at all, if it had not scored a few resounding triumphs, such as this. Many people, when the poem was new, felt greatly affected by it without understanding why; and even if you decide that the effect was an accident you cannot help wanting to know how it happened' (Empson, 1984, p. 190). Well-disposed contemporary critics were quick to apply to Eliot's poetry the vocabulary of his own running commentary as supplied by his prose, as well as to distil the sources and influences of the mode Eliot brought to fruition in England. In *Axel's Castle* (1931), for example, Edmund Wilson happily placed Eliot in the tradition of French Symbolist poetry, pointing out that 'The Symbolist Movement . . . finally succeeded in throwing overboard completely the clarity and logic of the French classical tradition . . . [T]o approximate the indefiniteness of music was to become one of the principal aims of Symbolism. . . . To intimate things rather than state them plainly was thus one of the primary aims of the Symbolists' (Wilson, 1961, pp. 18, 20, 23). With specific reference to *The Waste Land*, Wilson observed that Eliot 'succeeds in conveying his meaning, in communicating his emotion, in spite of all his learned or mysterious allusions, and whether we understand them or not' (ibid., p. 94). In view of the fact that he then praises what he calls Eliot's 'trenchant rationalism', his comments might well be taken as a kind of backhanded compliment.

Archibald MacLeish's poeticized dictum that 'A poem should not mean but be' (which Wimsatt and Beardsley happily endorse in 'The Intentional Fallacy') obviously challenges us either to surrender critical analysis or to approach the poem in terms of itself and as referring to itself. The latter is the New Critical position, and its logic is anti-rational: it accords more or less directly with the Imagist tenet 'No ideas but in things', which is itself an anti-intellectual blow against what Ezra Pound and other poets took to be the moribund self-indulgence of Romantic subjectivity. On those terms, of course, the poem is jealously guarded against the excrescences of 'meaning' which the poet might otherwise have considered himself to be proposing. Put simply, the argument is that to realize an emotion in images is to have interpreted that emotion, without the interposition of the poet's ego: the poet is the agent of his vision, not the active proponent; images are a self-sufficient mediation to which the deliberative consciousness of the author would be an irrelevance.

In 1935 F. O. Matthiessen published the first full-length study of Eliot, *The Achievement of T. S. Eliot*, a book which is still most valuable as a loyal exposition of Eliot's ideas. It certainly helped further to ensure that what Eliot wrote about poetry rapidly became orthodoxy, and that his critical pronouncements should be seen as matching the achievement of his poetry. In spite of the book's high usefulness, therefore, it does have the character of answering for Eliot rather than of enquiring of him. Using more or less the same phrasing as Wilson in *Axel's Castle*, Matthiessen reports Eliot's conviction that 'a poem should be constructed deliberately with the aim of producing a unified effect' (Matthiessen, 1958, p. 41). (Wilson wrote 'a certain effect', which has a marginally but not materially different implication.) Matthiessen went on, 'consequently, after composing the first draft of *The Waste Land*, [Eliot's] revisions shortened it to less than two-thirds of its original length, in order that he might best create a dramatic structure that would possess at the same time a lyrical intensity'. Having thus praised *The Waste Land* as both drama and lyric, as well as Eliot's capacity for deliberate construction, he for some reason chooses to defend the poet against any reader who might then feel that Eliot had been what he calls 'a too conscious artist' (ibid., p. 44). In other words, even while praising Eliot's *deliberateness* in structuring the poem, he anticipates the possible objection that he might seem to have been over-intellectualized: 'it is now apparent', Matthiessen wrote, 'that [Eliot's] principal desire is not for intellectual density but for richness and subtlety of emotional impression' (ibid., p. 57).

Since the publication of the drafts of *The Waste Land* we have been given cause for surprise to find that Matthiessen felt so confident in talking about the poem's 'deliberate construction'. It is instructive, I think, to look briefly at the first draft of the section 'Death by Water', which (in both holograph (fair copy) and typescript versions) describes a seafaring narrative to the Arctic circle; the haunting lyric about Phlebas the Phoenician occurs as a coda. Ezra Pound insisted on cutting the main narrative passage, with the consequence that Eliot could see little point to the passage about Phlebas if the allegorical narrative was set aside. Eliot asked, 'Perhaps better omit Phlebas also???' Pound's response was definite: 'I DO advise keeping Phlebas. In fact I more'n advise. Phlebas is an integral part of the poem; the card pack introduces him, the drowned phoen. sailor. And he is needed ABSOlootly where he is. Must stay in' (Eliot, 1971, p. 129; Eliot, 1988, pp. 504–5). In short, Pound had discerned a major motif which gave the poem some coherence as he determined it, a linking figure that Eliot seems to have been unaware of.

However, when we turn to a good recent study of Eliot, *Thomas Stearns Eliot, Poet*, we find A. D. Moody asserting that 'There is nothing to suggest that [Pound] tried to understand the poem, in the sense of seeking an interpretation or explanation of its meaning' (Moody, 1980, p. 317). Yet Valerie Eliot's notes to her edition of the poem helpfully draw attention to the fact that Eliot's original seafaring narrative was 'rather inspired' by the Ulysses Canto (XXVI), about the ultimate voyage, in Dante's *Inferno* – which suggests that even at the time of writing *The Waste Land* Eliot was strongly drawn to philosophical narrative, and not just to the 'lyrical formulation'

(Moody's term for what remained of 'Phlebas the Phoenician') that Pound chose to carve out of the drafts. Some seven or eight years later, when he wrote his essay on Dante, Eliot finally formulated what had been his earlier predilection. He praised the simple philosophical lucidity of Dante's allegory, and especially commended the Ulysses episode as being 'particularly "readable" because of its straightforward narrative' (Eliot, 1971, p. 128). So, in excising Eliot's seafaring narrative, Pound had substituted his own lyric ideal for Eliot's inclination towards philosophical and allegorical narrative (we know that Pound abhorred allegory). It therefore seems likely that Eliot himself could not find enough cohesion in the parts of the work he had drafted, and that – far from Pound *not* seeking an interpretation of the poem, as Moody asserts – Pound's suggestion that Phlebas was integral gave Eliot his cue for his note on line 218: 'Tiresias, although a mere spectator and not indeed a "character", is yet the most important personage in the poem, uniting all the rest. . . . What Tiresias *sees*, in fact, is the substance of the poem.' Eliot's explanation that the bisexual Tiresias unites 'all the rest' of the characters might well be regarded as the one piece of genuine exposition he afforded in the notes, but I would suggest that any such co-inherence came mostly *after* the 'event' of the poem, by way of Pound's construction of its meaning. It was therefore fitting that in his *Poems 1909–1925* Eliot paid tribute to Pound by adding to *The Waste Land* the famous dedication: *il miglior fabbro* ('the better craftsman').

BIBLIOGRAPHY

Davidson, Harriet (1994), 'Improper Desire: Reading *The Waste Land*', in *The Cambridge Companion to T. S. Eliot*, Cambridge: Cambridge University Press.

Deussen, Paul (1897), *Sechzig Upanishad's des Veda*, Leipzig: F. A. Brockhaus.

Eliot, T. S. (1951), *Selected Essays*, 3rd edn, London: Faber & Faber.

Eliot, T. S. (1957), *On Poetry and Poets*, London: Faber & Faber.

Eliot, T. S. (1971), *The Waste Land: A Facsimile and Transcript of the Original Drafts including the Annotations of Ezra Pound*, ed. Valerie Eliot, London: Faber & Faber.

Eliot, T. S. (1988), *The Letters of T. S. Eliot, I: 1898–1922*, ed. Valerie Eliot, London: Faber & Faber.

Empson, William (1984), 'My God, Man, There's Bears On It', *Using Biography*, London: Chatto & Windus.

Gordon, Lyndall (1977), *Eliot's Early Years*, Oxford: Oxford University Press.

Hall, Donald (1959), 'The Art of Poetry, I: T. S. Eliot', *Paris Review*, 21: 47–70.

Harwood, John (1995), '"These Fragments You Have Shelved (Shored)": Pound, Eliot and *The Waste Land*', in *Eliot to Derrida: The Poverty of Interpretation*, Basingstoke: Macmillan.

Kearns, Cleo McNelly (1987), *T. S. Eliot and Indic Traditions: A Study in Poetry and Beliefs*, Cambridge: Cambridge University Press.

Matthiessen, F. O. (1958) [1935], *The Achievement of T. S. Eliot*, 3rd edn, New York and London: Oxford University Press.

Moody, A. D. (1980), *Thomas Stearns Eliot, Poet*, Cambridge: Cambridge University Press.

Müller, F. Max (1884), *The Upanishads*, part II, Oxford: Clarendon Press.

Smith, Grover (1983), '*The Waste Land*' (Unwin Critical Library), London: Allen & Unwin.

Southam, B. C. (1974), *A Student's Guide to the Selected Poems of T. S. Eliot*, 2nd edn, London: Faber & Faber.

Spender, Stephen (1975), *Eliot*, London: Fontana/
Collins.

Sri, P. S. (1985), *T. S. Eliot, Vedanta and Buddhism*,
Vancouver: University of British Columbia
Press.

Stillinger, Jack (1991), 'Pound's *Waste Land*', in
*Multiple Authorship and the Myth of Solitary
Genius*, New York and Oxford: Oxford Univer-
sity Press.

Trivedi, Harish (1992), ' "Ganga was Sunken . . .":
T. S. Eliot's Use of India', in *The Fire and
the Rose: New Essays on T. S. Eliot*, ed. Venod
Sena and Rajiva Verma, New Delhi: Oxford
University Press.

Wilson, Edmund (1961) [1931], *Axel's Castle: A
Study in the Imaginative Literature of 1870–1930*,
London: Collins Fontana.

30

D. H. Lawrence: *Birds, Beasts and Flowers*

David Ellis

D. H. Lawrence is an anomaly among the great literary figures of the early twentieth century. Although there are many ways in which he is a distinctively modern writer, the attempts periodically made to drag him into the modernist camp are never wholly convincing. This is as true of his poetry as it is of his fiction. Generally acknowledged as his strongest collection, *Birds, Beasts and Flowers* was published in 1923, only a year or two after *Hugh Selwyn Mauberley* and *The Wasteland*; yet the difference from the contemporary work of Eliot and Pound is enormous.

One major aspect of this difference could be described as 'voice': an implicit but nonetheless total rejection of Eliot's doctrine of impersonality. A principal target in 'Tradition and the Individual Talent' is the direct expression of personal feeling in the traditional Romantic mode, and Eliot ends one section of his essay with,

> Poetry is not a turning loose of emotion, but an escape from emotion: it is not the expression of personality, but an escape from personality. But, of course, only those who have personality and emotions know what it means to want to escape from these things. (Eliot, 1932, p. 21)

In his own early poetry, there is an absence of any voice which might be identified as directly autobiographical, even if that absence sometimes appears to have been partly achieved (as in the magnificent 'Portrait of a Lady') through a deliberately confusing manipulation of personal pronouns.

Anyone who opens *Birds, Beasts and Flowers* for the first time, and reads the first lines of the first poem ('Pomegranate'), immediately encounters a 'personality':

> You tell me I am wrong.
> Who are you, who is anybody to tell me I am wrong?
> I am not wrong.

This is the Whitmanesque Lawrence, deliberately aggressive and provocative. As we continue to read 'Pomegranate' it turns out that these lines are not addressed to us but to a supposed listener whose responses, at various moments in the poem, are not recorded and have to be inferred from what the poet himself says (a favourite way Lawrence has in this collection of driving a poem forward and making it dramatic). Yet the first impression they make is of direct challenge to the reader – 'Who are *you* to tell me I am wrong?' – and since, like 'Pomegranate', both 'Peach' and 'Fig' are also concerned to associate various features of these fruits with the female genitalia, it is not only in their tone that the opening three poems in the first, American edition of *Birds, Beasts and Flowers* are a challenge. The fourth startles by describing the 'delicious rottenness' which the poet loves to 'suck out' from 'Medlars and Sorb-Apples' as 'Autumnal excrementa'. Well before *Lady Chatterley's Lover*, here is the Lawrence who is not only quite prepared to shock, but seems to take a good deal of pleasure in doing so.

The challenging, aggressive voice which opens *Birds, Beasts and Flowers* is far from the only one we hear in it. Lawrence can be gently reflective in a traditional Romantic manner, the tone is frequently humorous and, although he is often interrogative, he is not always defiantly so. There is a great variety of voice, yet everything we hear gives the impression of emanating from the same 'personality' (to use Eliot's word once more). Of course, no one who speaks in public – and the quietest, most reflective of poems are public performances – does so without adopting a persona; but Lawrence's use of various narrative voices in *Birds, Beasts and Flowers* is quite different from the ventriloquism Pound practises in his *Personae* (1926), in that they all seem to lead back to the same individual. The communication is indirect only to the extent that we are occasionally addressed through his own putative interlocutor. That this is the poet himself speaking is an impression reinforced by various stylistic devices Lawrence has for conveying immediacy, a sense of the here-and-now. 'Bare Fig-Trees', for example, begins with the suggestion that their wood seems like 'sweet untarnished silver', but in the fourth line Lawrence pulls himself up:

> I say untarnished, but I mean opaque –
> Thick, smooth-fleshed silver, dull as human limbs are dull
> With the life-lustre . . .

This self-correction draws the reader into the process of composition, the effort to find exactly the right word for what the poet implies he is at that very moment contemplating or remembering. Its apparent willingness to reveal Lawrence making a mistake contributes to a general impression in the collection of an author unafraid to put himself on show, to display both the strengths and weaknesses of his nature.

Quite unlike Eliot, Lawrence is often himself his own subject and, with their otherwise gratuitous details of daily living, several of the poems signal themselves as poetic transcripts from his daily life. A good example here would be 'Bibbles', which describes a dog, living with Lawrence on a ranch in New Mexico, whose indiscriminately affectionate nature he both laments and attempts to control, especially after she has gone on heat. The autobiographical status of this poem is established early on when Lawrence describes Bibbles as the 'First live thing I've "owned" since the lop-eared rabbits when I was a lad / And those over-prolific white mice, and Adolph, and Rex whom I didn't own'. This is typical in that anyone unfamiliar with Lawrence's life or work could have no way of realizing that Adolph was a rabbit and Rex a dog (for all the general reader knows they might both have been guinea pigs!). Far from erecting barriers against biographical intrusion, this way of writing accepts that it will happen, invites it or takes it for granted. The rest of 'Bibbles' is self-explanatory and needs no biographical gloss to be comprehensible, but that it is what it seems – a record of personal experience – can be established with certainty by reference to con-temporary letters and memoirs. We know from those that Bibbles, and the episodes involving her which are described in the poem, were not invented.

This kind of link is one which cannot always be made, either because the docu-mentation is unavailable or the impression Lawrence usually gives of actually being, or having recently been, in the presence of whatever he is talking about may some-times be no more than that. The much-anthologized 'Humming-Bird', for example, is still followed in most editions of *Birds, Beasts and Flowers* by 'Española' (the name of a town in New Mexico), but the poem was in fact written in Italy before Lawrence had moved to North America and before he had seen a live humming-bird – he based the poem on a written description (Sagar, 1985, pp. 215–16). His work is not always quite what it might seem, yet there are no words in this poem to suggest that, at the time of writing, he was or had been in the actual presence of its subject. That is an impression a reader might glean from 'Española', but then this word would have been appended to the poem when Lawrence was in New Mexico revising *Birds, Beasts and Flowers* for publication, and when he could establish that there was nothing in it which the opportunities he had recently enjoyed for seeing humming-birds in places like Española contradicted. To make that point risks suggesting that it would be to Lawrence's discredit if it could be shown that there were encounters with the natural world which he had entirely invented. Invention is not something Lawrence or any other poet needs to be defended against, yet it simply happens to be the case that many of his poems can be shown to be directly autobiographical. Certainly there are no contradictions between the story of Bibbles which can be followed in the poem and the similar or additional details concerning the dog to be found in various letters and memoirs, so that here we can be sure that what we are being offered is not merely a simulated record of a poet's day-to-day existence. These things happened to Lawrence and he is registering his responses to them more or less directly.

Does then the continual self-exposure or self-display in *Birds, Beasts and Flowers*, its continual reliance on details from the poet's own experience, mean that, far from having a personality and emotions from which he wanted to escape, Lawrence was always comfortable with both? Not perhaps entirely. It can be argued that, like Wordsworth, Lawrence was aware of how the strength of his personality, or more pre-cisely here his imagination, so imposed itself on his surroundings that it was in danger of condemning him to solipsism: to being trapped in a world so dependent on, or subservient to, his own concepts and imaginings that there was no challenge to him from outside. His fear was then the madness which can ensue from inhabiting a world where there is no genuine other (Ellis, 1994, pp. 233–6). Many previous critics of his poetry have implicitly endorsed this notion when attempting to explain why *Birds, Beasts and Flowers* is his strongest collection. As its title suggests, most (although by no means all) of the poems it contains concern the natural world and its non-human inhabitants. It is encounters within this realm, the argument goes, which allowed Lawrence to demonstrate his remarkable sensitivity to Nature, but also mark the boundaries between his own powerful personality or emotions and what needs, for the sake of mental health and balance, to escape their grasp. What he has often been praised for is the powerful poetic presentation of 'otherness' in an area where (the accompanying assumption is) he found it easier to recognize than he did in the human world. In his 'Introduction' to the *Complete Poems*, for example, Vivian de Sola Pinto claimed (rather surprisingly) that in *Birds, Beasts and Flowers* Lawrence had 'found a new theme which freed him from the trammels of autobiography'. What he presumably meant was not that these were poems in which Lawrence did not talk about his own doings (that he continually does so is what I have just been attempting to establish), but that in them he is not so much concerned as he is elsewhere with his own thoughts and feelings, the record (as it were) of his own *spiritual* autobiography. In Pinto's view this was because the 'new theme' he had found was an 'exploration of what may be called the divine otherness of non-human life' (Pinto and Roberts, 1964, pp. 11–12).

In his early poetry Lawrence can frequently be found using features of the natural world to express his own feelings; he imposes himself on it, infiltrates its every nook and cranny as if he had completely forgotten Ruskin's strictures on the pathetic fallacy in the third book of *Modern Painters* (which he must surely have read). His own awareness of this habit emerges in 'New Heaven and Earth' from the collection *Look! We Have Come Through!* (1917). This is a poem chiefly concerned with the way his wife has at last allowed him to escape solipsism in his *human* relations, but at one point he looks back on his past and says,

> I was so weary of the world,
> I was so sick of it,
> everything was tainted with myself,
> skies, trees, flowers, birds, water . . .

and he goes on to refer to the 'maniacal horror . . . when everything was me'. What he is deploring is the way that, in the past, he has allowed his mood to appropriate features of the outside world for the purposes of its own self-expression. He is recognizing in what he once was that 'merging' of the self into its environment which he came to deplore in Whitman, in part because it resulted not in forgetfulness (lapsing out) but a swollen, ubiquitous self into which everything extraneous had been incorporated. 'I embrace ALL', he derisively quotes Whitman as claiming in his essay on that poet in *Studies in Classic American Literature*, 'I weave all things into myself' (Lawrence, 1971, p. 174).

Moving from Lawrence's early poetry to *Birds, Beasts and Flowers* it is not always clear that, in this matter of appropriations, a reader would be aware of dramatic change. Signs of merging may here have virtually disappeared, but there is still a tendency to treat a natural object as a pretext. 'Cypresses', for example, is really not about the cypress as such but how these trees in the Tuscan landscape recall for Lawrence the lost civilization of the Etruscans; and although 'Medlars and Sorb-Apples' begins with several striking phenomenological observations, it quickly moves on to reflections on the 'river of dissolution' theme so prominent in *Women in Love* and (by a complicated chain of associations) to a celebration of being alone. That the natural objects which are the ostensible subjects in each of these poems rapidly retreat into the background does not make them *necessarily* inferior. It isn't necessarily against them that what they begin by purporting to describe has not brought the poet further out of himself but rather driven him further in. And in any case there is the vital issue here of quite how the natural world a poet sets out to describe can ever avoid being appropriated by human beings when it is described in human language. To talk about the non-human is almost inevitably to tailor it to our own human concerns.

One remarkable feature of *Birds, Beasts and Flowers* which allows some temporary resistance to that process is the frequent sharpness and delicacy of Lawrence's observation. Having previously described the branches of almond trees as 'Like iron sticking grimly out of earth', for example, allows him to say in 'Almond Blossom': 'Upon the iron, and upon the steel, / Odd flakes as if of snow, odd bits of snow, / Odd crumbs of melting snow.' The wattles of the 'Turkey-Cock' are described in the poem of that name as 'the colour of steel-slag which has been red hot / And is going cold, / Cooling to a powdery, pale-oxidised sky-blue'; and 'Bat' has some fine phrases about this creature as it swoops under the bridges of the Arno at twilight, its wings 'like bits of umbrella'.

Partly because they encourage visualization, descriptions like this remind the reader vividly that these non-human features of the world also exist outside the landscape of the poet's mind; to a minor extent they restore their independence. We are made aware of the poet in his *interchange* with an environment which presents characteristics sharply enough realized to suggest that he cannot always have everything his own way. To be this alert to its particularities is to be simultaneously aware of its challenge, of the difference of the natural world from our own. And yet at the same time the imagery Lawrence often employs – tree branches like iron, a turkey's wattles like steel-slag, and especially a bat's wings like an umbrella – tends to emphasize how easily and naturally we make our own, human measure the measure of all things.

Yet if language is so inevitably anthropomorphic in its tendencies, continually approximating the world of nature to human concerns, how is it that critics have been able to praise Lawrence for his ability to convey in *Birds, Beasts and Flowers* an impression of otherness (divine or otherwise)? The answer partly lies in three or four of the more well-known poems and in particular perhaps in 'Fish'. A very determined and impressive effort is made in the first part of 'Fish' to imagine what it would be like to live in water (to 'wash in oneness / And never emerge' as Lawrence puts it), and to reproduce without any contact with the opposite sex: 'Who is it ejects his sperm to the naked flood? / In the wave-mother? / Who swims enwombed?' But moving on to describe himself sitting in a boat and looking down to identify the fish beneath the surface of a lake, Lawrence writes:

> A slim young pike, with smart fins
> And grey-striped suit, a young cub of a pike
> Slouching along away below, half out of sight,
> Like a lout on an obscure pavement . . .
> Aha, there's somebody in the know!
>
> But watching closer
> That motionless deadly motion,
> That unnatural barrel body, that long ghoul nose, . . .
> I left off hailing him.
>
> I had made a mistake, I didn't know him,
> This grey, monotonous soul in the water,
> This intense individual in shadow,
> Fish-alive.
>
> I didn't know his God,
> I didn't know his God.

What may have made these lines so influential is their explicit rejection of simile and metaphor. The pike as a slouching pavement lout is unusually fanciful for the Lawrence of this collection, a comparison far enough removed from the actual physical features of what he is attempting to describe that one could say that it is not surprising he rejects it. Yet what is also involved in his confession that the pike's god is unknown to him is the implicit discrediting of his immediately previous description of the pike as an 'intense individual', or of its soul as 'monotonous'. In confessing to his ignorance of the god of fish Lawrence is recognizing the limits of human understanding: the impossibility of so standing aside from the human condition that we could ever imagine what it is really like to be a fish. In one sense they are part of our universe, incorporated into it; but in another their world is quite different and separate, with other gods. In associating them with intensity or monotony, we make the characteristic error of imagining that, if we were fish, we would somehow nevertheless retain our human attributes.

Although not so conveniently explicit, there is the same recognition of the mystery of otherness in 'Snake' (the fact that snakes excite fear and hostility in most individuals makes them less easy to assimilate into the human world). It can also be found in what is probably the finest achievement in *Birds, Beasts and Flowers*, the six poems about tortoises, absent from the first edition because they had already been published separately in the United States, but included in the one which appeared in England. Lawrence is wonderfully alert in this sequence to the strangeness and peculiarity of tortoise life and yet, in marvelling at the independence of the baby tortoise as soon as it is born ('Alone, with no sense of being alone'), and in noting the indifference tortoises show towards one another in what the title of one of the poems refers to as 'Tortoise Family Connections', he is of course applying human standards to creatures for whom they could mean nothing at all. The main theme of the sequence, moreover, is regret at how the tortoise loses its independence through being 'crucified into sex'. The metaphor betrays clearly enough that the regret belongs not to the tortoise (who would hardly know what to do with it), but to Lawrence himself. What however prevents the treatment of the creatures in these poems from making it seem that they are only there for the purposes of convenient illustration is an acuity of observation which continually reminds us of their strangeness. The point could be made by a comparison with 'The Ass', where that animal's present ignominious position is attributed to his having fallen 'into the rut of love'. There is not enough particularity in that poem to persuade us that several other animals or creatures might not have illustrated the point just as well, and the consequence is that we have less a sense of an interchange between the poet and his surroundings than the exploration of a private mental universe. In the introduction to an anthology of 'animal verse' George Macbeth once pointed out that 'All good poems about animals are about something else as well'. He went on to suggest however that, whatever the other concerns of such poems, they 'should be seen *through* the nature of animals. The apparent content of the poem should at least be a part of the real content' (Macbeth, 1965, p. 7). This could never be a hard-and-fast rule: it would hardly do for the vast majority of seventeenth-century poems about animals; but it provides a useful line of approach to the poems in *Birds, Beasts and Flowers*, which would not be as interesting as they are if any other choice of subjects could have served just as well for the expression of Lawrence's sexual concerns.

For poets to recognize fully and continually the otherness of the natural world and its inhabitants would leave them with very little to say. Since language condemns us to anthropomorphizing both, the only real issue is one of degree. It is a question of what devices human beings have at their disposal for both moderating the extent of their appropriations and making themselves aware that, in the last resort, they can never know what it is to be other than human. Sharpness of observation is certainly one of these, but another brings us back to that question of 'voice' with which I began. In many of the poems Lawrence directly addresses birds, trees, flowers and creatures of all kinds, either assuming their replies or supplying some for them. This is a familiar activity, best known to us from our relationships with domestic animals. A *locus classicus* here would be the clown Launce talking in *Two Gentlemen of Verona* to his dog Crab (sometimes described as the most interesting character in that play). In his second great soliloquy Launce describes how ashamed he was of Crab when he took him as an offering to his own master's inamorata, Silvia: 'O, 'tis a foul thing, when a cur cannot keep himself in all companies' he complains in the Elizabethan equivalent of, 'You can't take him anywhere'. After cataloguing for the benefit of the audience the dog's misdemeanours, and his lack of gratitude for the kindness with which he has been treated in the past, Launce turns to Crab and addresses him directly: 'did I not bid thee mark me, and do as I do? When did'st thou see me heave up my leg, and make water against a gentlewoman's farthingale?' (IV, iv).

Most of us talk to our animals, but Shakespeare's treatment shows both how natural these conversations are and, at the same time, how fundamentally absurd. Something similar might be said of the tone Lawrence adopts in one of the single most successful poems in *Birds, Beasts and Flowers*, 'Mosquito'. He certainly speaks to its subject here, and in a tone not without a certain understandable belligerence as he tries to protect himself from being bitten:

> But I know your game now, streaky sorcerer.
> Queer, how you stalk and prowl the air
> In circles and evasions, enveloping me,
> Ghoul on wings
> Winged Victory.
> Settle, and stand on long thin shanks
> Eyeing me sideways, and cunningly conscious that I am aware,
> You speck.
>
> I hate the way you lurch off sideways into air
> Having read my thoughts against you.

The attribution of this degree of anthropomorphic intention (a mosquito reading our thoughts) is certainly moderated in this fine poem by descriptive brio. The insect is a 'translucent phantom shred / Of a frail corpus'; with 'thin wings' and 'streaming legs' it sails through the air 'like a heron'; and after it has bitten Lawrence, it staggers with the gorged blood but then, because of its 'hairy frailty', 'imponderable weightlessness', wafts away 'on the very draught my anger makes in its snatching'. But what moderates it also of course is a certain mock-heroic mode in which Lawrence can operate: it was after all one of the poets he most admired, Robert Burns, who wrote 'To a Louse'. There is an inevitable comedy, on which Lawrence is able to rely in this poem, in the disparity between the attributed feelings and its tiny subject. Because of that subject, he is in no danger of conveying the impression that he has deluded himself into believing communication between a human being and a mosquito belongs anywhere but with the former's powers of make-believe. What helps him to avoid that danger also is the fact that, like many other poems in the collection, and somewhat on the model of Donne's 'The Flea', 'Mosquito' is a rounded drama with a finale in which Lawrence wonders at the 'dim dark smudge' his antagonist has disappeared into. In dramas people play their parts, enact a role, and this is what we are made conscious the poet is doing as he converses so intimately with an insect.

There are analogies between the tone of Launce in *Two Gentlemen of Verona* and Lawrence's in 'Mosquito', but to move from humankind's four-legged friend to a tiny creature with six could well seem strange and an evasion of the issue. If there is no very strict ratio between the danger of anthropomorphic delusion and a creature's size, it is certainly the case that it is likely to be at its most extreme with domestic animals. The intimacy in which we live with certain members of the animal world can easily lure us into thinking they share our concerns and preoccupations. Shakespeare's comedy is a barrier against that mistake. When Launce addresses us, we know from his tone that he knows Crab cannot really be judged by human standards. This is a truth Lawrence might be said to lose sight of in 'Bibbles'. The poem is vivid in its evocation of the 'Little black snub-nosed bitch with a shoved-out jaw / And a wrinkled reproachful look', and it catalogues with precision many of the dog's habits; but Lawrence becomes so preoccupied with Bibbles as a representative of promiscuity (especially in its female manifestations), that he tends to lose the tone, the voice, that would remind us of the gulf there is between human beings and even such an honorary member of the human race as a dog. As Lawrence complains that Bibbles makes no distinction between himself and 'the Mexican who comes to chop wood', and ends the poem with 'All right, my little bitch / You learn loyalty rather than loving, / And I'll protect you', he forgets the fact that, like fish, dogs also have gods who are different from ours and that, as a result, it would be foolish to expect from them too much social discrimination or impose upon them our forms of contractual arrangement.

This judgement might well be a consequence of the impossibility some of us have in reading 'Bibbles' without the letters and memoirs in mind: to avoid the feeling that the poem after all only gives a part of the story. We know from other sources how strangely exercised Lawrence continued to be by his dog's behaviour, and that the poem's conclusion represents only one stage in his hopeless and sometimes violent efforts to change her nature. The openly autobiographical poet, whose manner invites the reader to enquire beyond or behind the text (and how otherwise could we establish the identity of Adolph and Rex?), is much more likely than someone such as Eliot to be a victim of what used to be known as the biographical fallacy – yet why it is a fallacy when we all bring a variety of information to the reading of a poem which it is impossible for us not to remember we know, is not clear. In so far as this reading of 'Bibbles' implies a criticism, however, it is one which would seem to be corroborated by comparison with 'She-Goat'. The subject of this poem is certainly a domestic animal in that, as Lawrence informs us with typical circumstantial detail, she has been bought 'at Giardini fair, on the sands, for six hundred lire' and is now tied up at night 'in the shed at the back of the broken Greek tomb in the garden'. There are impressively acute and striking descriptions of the goat's behaviour. 'Come down, crapa, out of that almond tree', the poet shouts at one moment, in one of several addresses to, and indeed conversations with, the goat:

> Instead of which she strangely rears on her perch in the air, vast beast,
> And strangely paws the air, delicate,

And reaches her black-striped face up like a snake, far up,
Subtly, to the twigs overhead, far up, vast beast,
And snaps them sharp, with a little twist of her anaconda head;
All her great hairy shaggy belly open against the morning.

'Bibbles' shows that sharp descriptive power, accompanied as it is here by impressive rhythmic control, is sometimes not enough to prevent the slide into the extremes of anthropomorphic delusion, but in 'She-Goat' there is a wondering, sub-humorous tone throughout that inhibits the suggestion that goats can really be measured by our standards. Partly through the strangeness here of a goat standing in a tree, otherness is implied in a way it isn't always in 'Bibbles', even though Lawrence is also preoccupied in this poem with an animal's sexuality. But then the very physical appearance of a goat, somewhat like that of a tortoise, a snake or a fish, reminds us of strangeness, whereas we are so accustomed to seeing dogs in the company of humans that we easily forget that their world is strangely alien also.

In emphasizing the separation between our world and that of birds, beasts and flowers, I am not of course interested in contending that animals never experience what we would be entitled to call feelings, only that the language in which humans describe those feelings tends to be full of inappropriate human implications. Why this should be so could be deduced from Wittgenstein's famous remark that if a lion could talk, we wouldn't understand it. Lion talk would be so dependent on all those aspects of communication which lions would understand instinctively through living together that an outsider would not be able to grasp enough of its context to make it fully comprehensible. Human life is likewise so shot through with human concerns that it creates a gulf between our lives and those who share the planet with us. Not that one is dealing here with realms that are completely distinct (Wittgenstein's dictum would not have the same force if it began, 'If a chimpanzee could talk . . .'). There are ways of talking about animals, some of which Lawrence shares, which are much less anthropomorphic than others. No one could object to describing a dog as frightened, but problems will arise if we want to describe them as experiencing love, nostalgia, regret. In 'Bibbles' Lawrence says that his dog hates having the dust brushed out of her face because that makes her look undignified ('How you hate being laughed at, Miss Superb!'); and he talks of her 'conceit', her 'unblemished belief' in her own perfection. It is not too hard to visualize the expressions on a dog's face to which these attributions could correspond; but there needs to be something in the general tone to remind us that they are after all only *façons de parler*, ways of talking that we humans have evolved. That is what one finds in 'She-Goat' when Lawrence describes its subject as a 'canny listener', or suggests that the manner in which 'invariably she crouches her rear and makes water' is 'her way of answer if I speak to her'.

As human beings, we leave our taint everywhere. Sola Pinto's suggestion that Lawrence's concern with otherness in *Birds, Beasts and Flowers* allowed him to escape the trammels of autobiography may be true at various superficial levels (although I doubt in fact that it is), but at the deepest one it must be false. Through language at least, there is no escape for us from what Eliot called our personality and emotions. Whatever we do, and however much we twist and turn, that 'vile self' which Burns's Holy Willie made a point of deploring always gets in. Although he may have occasionally lost sight of this truth in his dealings with the natural world, Lawrence relied on it in working out his attitude to Flaubert's impersonality and what he came to regard as Eliot's 'classicism'. The devices these two writers employed to give the impression that they were not there, in or behind their work, seem to him too transparent to be worth the trouble, and in Eliot's case merely cowardice (Ellis, 1998, p. 383n). The only path to impersonality, in his view, involved a deeper delving into the self rather than futile efforts to escape it. Yet the dangers of self-exploration needed to be countered by continual reminders that there is a world which exists independently of the self and its imaginings. If in many of the best poems in *Birds, Beasts and Flowers*, Lawrence's endeavours to encounter that world do not reveal an essentially irrecoverable 'otherness', with their felicity of description and their alertness of tone they at least go further than most other 'nature poetry' has to indicate the directions in which it might lie.

BIBLIOGRAPHY

Eliot, T. S. (1932). 'Tradition and the Individual Talent' in *Selected Essays*. London: Faber and Faber.

Ellis, David (1994). 'Lawrence, Wordsworth and "Anthropomorphic Lust"' in *The Cambridge Quarterly*, xxiii: 3, pp. 230–42.

Ellis, David (1998). *D. H. Lawrence 1922–1930: Dying Game*. Cambridge: Cambridge University Press.

Lawrence, David Herbert (1971). *Studies in Classic American Literature*. Harmonddsworth: Penguin.

Macbeth, George (ed.) (1965). *The Penguin Book of Animal Verse*. Harmondsworth; Penguin.

Sagar, Keith (1985). *D. H. Lawrence: Life Into Art*. Harmondsworth: Penguin.

Pinto, Vivian de Sola and Roberts, Warren (eds) (1964). *The Complete Poems of D. H. Lawrence*, 2 vols. London: Heinemann.

Useful writings on Lawrence's poetry not cited in the text

Auden, W. H. (1948). 'D. H. Lawrence' in *The Dyer's Hand and Other Essays*. London: Faber and Faber.

Blackmuir, R. P. (1954). 'D. H. Lawrence and Expressive Form' in *Language as Gesture: Essays in Poetry*. London: Allen and Unwin.

Draper, R. P. (1974). *D. H. Lawrence: The Critical Heritage*. London: Routledge.

Ellis David, and De Zordo, Ornella (eds) (1992). 'The Poetry' in vol. 4 of *D. H. Lawrence: Critical Assessments*. London: Croom Helm.

Gilbert, Sandra (1972). *Acts of Attention: The Poems of D. H. Lawrence*. Ithaca, NY: Cornell University Press.

Kalnins, Mara (1992). 'Introduction' to *D. H. Lawrence: Selected Poems*. London: Everyman's Library.

Oates, Joyce Carol (1973). *The Hostile Sun: The Poetry of D. H. Lawrence*. Los Angeles: Black Sparrow Press.

Pollnitz, Christopher (1982). '"I Don't Know his God": The Epistemology of "Fish"' in *D. H. Lawrence Review*, 15: 1, spring, pp. 1–50.

31

William Carlos Williams:
Spring and All
Lisa M. Steinman

There are many fruitful ways to approach *Spring and All*. I want here to start with its historical and textual beginnings. The book was published in Paris by Robert McAlmon's Contact Publishing Company after William Carlos Williams failed to find an American publisher. It was a landmark year for modernist writing by Americans: T. S. Eliot's *The Waste Land* appeared late in 1922; 1923 saw the publication of Wallace Stevens's *Harmonium* and Gertrude Stein's *The Making of Americans*, along with two books by Williams: *Spring and All* and *The Great American Novel*. Marianne Moore's *Observations* would appear by 1924. Although much of *Spring and All* was written before Williams could have read Eliot's much-touted poem, their poems appeared only seven months apart in *The Dial*, and Williams can be seen to be responding to Eliot when he writes in *Spring and All*: 'If I could say what is in my mind in Sanscrit or even Latin I would do so. But I cannot' (Weaver, 1971, p. 44; Williams, *Collected Poems*, 1986 [hereafter, *CP*], p. 179). Injunctions to 'imagine the New World' and announcements that 'we the people of the United States are going to Europe armed to kill' (*CP*, p. 178) make clear *Spring and All*'s engagement and identification with American national culture and resistance to the kind of erudition of which Williams disapproved in Eliot's work.

As Williams would write in his *Autobiography*, 'Eliot returned us to the classroom' (Williams, 1951, p. 174). *Spring and All* is unequivocal about 'the academic tape-worm [that] hoard[s] its excrementa in books' (*CP*, p. 215), parodied in Williams's proclamation that the re-creation of the world 'begins to near a new day. (More of this in Chapter XIX)' (*CP*, p. 181), or his image of his book as 'notes jotted down in the midst of the action, under distracting circumstance – to remind [him]self (see p. 177, paragraph 6) of the truth' (*CP*, p. 186). The scholarly notes clearly defer and interrupt the very renewal of which the book speaks, making truth always memory or prolepsis, but never present. Williams's spring is thus deliberately set against Eliot's April. By implication, *Spring and All* will not look to the past, but will be a New World presence, albeit one Williams suggests will not be warmly received.

The first sentences of the book read: 'If anything of moment results – so much the better. And so much the more likely will it be that no one will want to see it' (*CP*, p. 177). Throughout, Williams returns to the concept of the 'immediate', the 'moment' and 'the present', making clear that there is a pun in that first sentence, which introduces a quest for something 'of moment' in the sense of being a fleeting, living practice – 'notes jotted down in the midst of the action' – rather than in the sense of being important or consequential. Yet a defensiveness about how the public generally dismissed poetry ('no one will want to see it') also runs throughout, a somewhat different response to Eliot – and to the modernists among whom Williams placed himself. Williams's challenge to Eliot is edgy in part because his American spring is not finally (or perhaps not historically) so different from other wastelands: just two years earlier, in an editorial comment for the journal *Contact*, on which he worked with McAlmon, Williams had written of 'the ignorance which has made America an artistic desert' (Williams, 1954, p. 29).

There is a further, if an anticipated, irony in Williams's association of the United States with the site of his new poetics, when the book had little company and less circulation in the land where he lived. In fact, it had little circulation anywhere, with only three hundred copies printed, most of which were not distributed. There was only one review of any length, in *Poetry*, and that reviewer (Marjorie Allen Seiffert) found the poetry, as opposed to the prose, difficult. The voice that in Poem XXV proclaims 'To hell with you and your poetry' is identifiably American, even without Williams's late (1950s) comment to John C. Thirlwall explaining that he was interested in 'a presentation of the language as it actually is used' (*CP*, pp. 231, 505). Obviously, Williams's use of an American language does not entail accepting the typical American's evaluation of art. The popular dismissal of modernist poetry and art in America is further underlined by the later publishing history of the volume, from which the poems were extracted (by Williams himself), and not restored to their context in the full volume until 1970. As Burton Hatlen has nicely pointed out, when Williams reprinted the poems from the volume for circulation in the United States, he not only extracted what his audience could read as poems (rather than the more avant-garde mixture of prose and poetry that forms the 1923 text), he also added final punctuation to the poems, with the effect of offering closed, more traditional, poetic structures to his local readers, suggesting that openness is not, in terms of any historical readership, a characteristic American aesthetic, images of the New World notwithstanding (Hatlen, 1994).

However, in his consideration of poetry's place in modern America, Williams's eye is not only on Eliot, but also on modernist experiments in the visual arts: the book is dedicated to the American artist Charles Demuth; it mentions the work of Paul Cézanne and Juan Gris; it refers readers to the painter Marsden Hartley's chapter on Dada in the 1921 *Adventures in the Arts* (the one cross-reference that is not obviously ironic) in the penultimate prose paragraph; and it is indebted to Dadaism with its opening destruction of the world, its typographical experimentation, and its arrangement of the prose sections of the book in chapters that are not numbered sequentially (the first subheading we meet is, for instance, 'chapter 19'). Williams may attempt to resist European culture, but he also invokes and emulates it. The opening destruction of the world, read in this context, is no declaration of independence at all, but a clear echo of Dadaist (and Futurist) iconoclasm; its repetition of European avant-garde gestures, a 'perfect plagiarism' (*CP*, p. 181). The references to plagiarism and the repetitious manner in which the prose keeps announcing the destruction of the world and the intimations of spring approaching (over and over) indicate Williams's self-consciousness about not only the ways in which iconoclastic gestures themselves can become icons – domesticated or codified, imaged as 'the handcuffs of "art"' (*CP*, p. 185, see pp. 181, 235) – but also about his debts to European modernist movements. When it dismisses ideas of art as 'the beautiful illusion' (*CP*, p. 178, see pp. 194, 199), or renounces art that seeks 'refuge in fantasy' (*CP,* p. 177) – or when it more positively appeals to art as 'design' (*CP*, pp. 186, 188, 209), or 'vitality' (*CP*, p. 188), defining poetry as not '"like" life' (*CP*, p. 215), but 'its own reality' (*CP*, p. 235) – Williams's book becomes as much an uneasy tribute to a transnational avant-garde as an American artistic revolution. At least, Williams posits a less geographically or temporally rooted search for, as he puts it, '"something" [found] in the [best] writing' (*CP*, p. 230).

The status of *Spring and All*'s central 'something' (the spring, truth or presence to which Williams lays claim) and the definition of what, precisely, poetry makes present, is not easily described, as J. Hillis Miller, Marjorie Perloff and Terence Diggory, among others (including Williams himself) have pointed out. The nature of Williams's claims – even whether they are at heart ethical or epistemological or ontological claims for art – is a subject of continued debate. Yet most critics agree that Williams's poetics are related to his knowledge of modern painters, especially in those passages where he insists that what *Spring and All* has to offer is linguistic, a reference neither to the world of nature nor to some realm beyond the page. As the book puts it, 'writing deals with words and words only' (*CP*, p. 231), a point underlined when we are told: 'Meanwhile, SPRING, which has been approaching *for several pages*, is at last here' (*CP*, p. 186, emphasis added). We are also told: 'In imagination, we are henceforth (so long as you read) locked in a fraternal embrace, the classic caress of author and reader' (*CP*, p. 178). 'So long as you read' similarly emphasizes the reader's engagement with words on a page; the motion or activity in question is that of our eyes, reading 'the word . . . not as a symbol of nature but a part" (*CP*, p. 189).

Such critiques of representation draw on Williams's understanding of Cubist practices in particular. Specifically, he cites Juan Gris on the need for art to 'be real, not "realism" but reality itself – . . . It is not a matter of "representation" – . . . but of separate existence' (*CP*, p. 204). However, precisely how to read *Spring and All*'s poems as linguistic artefacts, comparable to Cubist collage, is puzzling. The first poem a reader encounters does attempt a new poetic language for an old topic, spring. But in what way is Willams's 'spring' language as such, rather than being symbolic or representational? One could answer this question, as John Lowney does, by noticing that the enjambments and lack of punctuation in Poem I involve constant shifts in subject position, one way of enacting empirical examination and clarity of vision in a renamed 'new world naked', using language largely stripped of its conventional associations (Lowney, 1997, pp. 62–4). Or one could look at how Henry Sayre more specifically links Williams's spring with Dadaism, noting both the rhetoric of renewal and rebirth used by the visual artists and the actual season – spring – in which the Armory Show, the American Independents Exhibition in which Williams participated (and to which Marcel Duchamp submitted his famous urinal), and the inaugural issues of a number of avant-garde magazines appeared (Sayre, 1984, pp. 16–17). Yet both readings depend in part on reading spring as representational; indeed, as Lowney concludes, the contagious hospital of Poem I is a New World (and thus metaphoric) equivalent of Eliot's wasteland. This is not to dismiss such readings, but to point out that the poems present themselves as both the new linguistic world of *Spring and All* and as images of the historical world of 1923.

Poems VI to VIII present similar difficulties when read in light of the claims *Spring and All* makes about poems as objects made of words. Poem VIII ('At the Faucet of June'), for instance, finds spring – most obviously a figure for renewal and creativity – in the stuff of American modernity (tires, faucets or steel). The poem also translates the rape of classical figures for spring, Persephone or Kora, into the rape of art by American business and industry, in the figure of J. Pierpont Morgan, who

> solve[s] the core
> of whirling flywheels
> by cutting
>
> the Gordian knot
> with a Veronese or
> perhaps a Rubens –

Williams offers J. Pierpont Morgan's art collecting as an example of Gilded Age wealth used to collect 'art' as trophy; in the poem, Morgan neither supports living art (and artists) nor solves the difficulties of how to value modernity (flywheels, with 'core' containing perhaps a slight punning reference to the Corliss engine as well as to the Latin 'Kora'). Morgan instead turns to a European art of the past, art already commodified and codified. Against this kind of art collecting and perhaps against the poem's own reliance on classical myth, Williams then calls attention to language freed from 'demoded words and shapes' (*CP*, p. 188), recasting 'son' (Morgan's industrialist son) as 'song' 'leaving off the g' (*CP*, p. 197), much the way Poem VI (after a note on how difficult it is to resist 'the old mode') proclaims 'I have done / nothing' and then recasts its proclamation as

> the diphthong
>
> ae
> together with

the first person
singular
indicative

of the auxiliary
verb

so that one must understand the phrase 'I have done nothing' as syntax, mood (indicative), tense and sound, not reference. Critics like Marjorie Perloff and Henry Sayre have read the thirteenth and seventh poems similarly (Perloff, 1981, pp. 125–9; Sayre, 1984, pp. 19–20). The latter begins:

The rose is obsolete
but each petal ends in
an edge, the double facet
cementing the grooved
columns of air – The edge
cuts without cutting

Williams takes Cubism – and presumably Gertrude Stein – to 'engage roses', not through 'obsolete' literary or iconographic associations, not even as an ekphrastic replaying of Gris's or Demuth's Cubist or Precisionist flowers, but as a model for his production of a Cubist poem. On this view, 'The Rose' is not about botanical roses; its structure (dashes and line breaks, sentence fragments, oxymoron) is the object of our attention. The poem's meaning *is* its spatial and material arrangements. Or so Williams's invitations to us to take the language of poems as words, lifted out of context, equivalent to Cubist collage, would lead us to say.

In the prose just before and just after 'The Rose' Williams alludes specifically to Gris's painting 'Open Window', which he would have seen reproduced in the January 1922 issue of *Broom* (Sayre, 1979). His uses of the painters, moreover, are as often through their theories and rhetoric as through their art. Thus, he also refers his readers to Marsden Hartley's comment on a poem by Francis Picabia, where Hartley writes that Picabia's Dadaist litany 'is too edifying for proper expression. It is like a window opened upon a wide cool place where all parts of one's exhausted being may receive the kind of air that is imperative to it' (Hartley, 1921, p. 250). Drawing on Gris's and Hartley's open windows, *Spring and All* implies that the place to which poems lead us is not the historical world, although it is worth noting that Hartley's figure has art represent an opening to something off the canvas or page.

Similarly, in *Spring and All* the poems and especially the prose consistently refer us elsewhere: to what generates or is unleashed by the poems – 'imagination [as] an actual force comparable to electricity or steam' (*CP*, p. 207) – to the historical world of both politics and artistic manifestos, to Williams's position as a modernist in a culture of Morgans and hostile readers. We might, then, attempt to answer the question of how poems can be only words and also be representations of the world by reading the larger structure of *Spring and All* – its mixture of prose and poetry – as an enactment of just this relationship between poems and world. After Poem I the volume no longer numbers the prose 'chapters', but lets the poetry run into the following prose (only the second poem has a final punctuation mark), while the poems are consecutively numbered. The prose, then, at first seems to figure that from which the clarity or crystallization of the poetry arises; the consecutively numbered poems seem illustrations of the prose statement that 'every flake of truth [is] . . . numbered' (*CP*, p. 199). The figure of 'isolate flecks [where] / something / is given off' (*CP*, p. 219) is repeated with variations throughout the book, as when Williams speaks of life as 'a hell of repression lit by flashes of inspiration, when a poem . . . appear[s]' (*CP*, p. 203). Again, the image is of spring, Persephone, released from the underworld of the everyday or the habitual, while Williams's *Autobiography* repeats the image of the poetic 'release' of some 'thing' in a vocabulary that invites a more Freudian narrative: 'The poem is a capsule where we wrap up our punishable secrets', we are told, and at times a 'thing . . . may for a moment be freed to fly for a moment guiltily about the room' (Williams, 1951, pp. 343, 289). Although sometimes described as a formal design or structure, sometimes as a psychological release, Williams's '(some)thing' or 'moment' is regularly aligned with poetry, not prose. Even the typography of *Spring and All* offers the poems as analogues of such moments. That is, the prose is full of ellipses or parodies of the derivative (and proleptic) gestures of scholarship, and the connections between prose passages are mocked, or conspicuously absent, while the poems stand out because of their lineation, as if connected in a different matrix. They seem, then, to figure as the epiphanic moments or glimpses for which the book calls, themselves figured alternately as the separate reality of the imagination or as defamiliarized visions of reality or as moments of more personal confession.

I suspect it is obvious that to read the entire structure of *Spring and All* as I have just proposed begs the question with which I began, namely what poems are said to be or offer. Indeed, the one certainty is that we are consistently invited to reread the poem in different registers, an invitation accepted in the structure of my own essay. To take a final example, returning briefly to Williams's references to 'release', the text opens by discussing how the imagination is 'intoxicated by prohibitions' (*CP*, p. 179), and thus aligns a psychological figure of repression and release not only with avant-garde practices and poetry's access to some truth or presence or force, but also with the fact of American Prohibition, a more socio-political repression that bred outlaw practices more literal than the verbal or psychological intoxication, the disregard for logic or set forms, the violence and appropriations of production imaginatively figured throughout the book. And to align Prohibition with the individual psyche's sources of creativity, the prose (as genre or language), and the conventions from which art breaks free, at best invites precisely the connection between 'things of the imagination' and 'life' (*CP*, p. 194) that the book dismisses. One may, borrowing Williams's vocabulary, propose that these registers are 'not opposed . . . but apposed' (*CP*, p. 208), but this only defers the question of how to discuss the significance of apposition, or to understand what Williams thinks is at stake in such a practice.

Moreover, *Spring and All* strongly suggests that Williams believes something is at stake. One cannot, that is, simply short-circuit the various registers in which the book invites readings to conclude that it is (although it is) a 'montage of genres' (Lowney, 1997, p. 61) or a 'metonymic network' (Perloff, 1981, p. 137). To reinforce this point I would like to point out, briefly, two further registers in which *Spring and All* may be read, turning first to a 1921 article by Lewis Mumford, 'Machinery and the Modern Style', on architecture and city planning. Mumford's basic argument is straightforward. To be living, architecture must not simply look to traditionally sanctioned 'art' (to repeat the quotation marks Williams and Hartley, from whom Williams takes the idea, use). Greek columns or Roman facades, Mumford argues, cannot be misappropriated from a long-dead cultural system and transplanted to modern America. Yet Mumford also has qualms about functional architecture. The problem, he suggests, is not with any inherent lack in functional or machine design. But his analysis of what is required, framed in organicist language, remains vague: modern design is wrong because not 'living', not infused by 'vivifying human imagination'. His description of the interior of a Child's restaurant is telling: 'Lured into the void of a modern lunchroom by the vision of thick disks of golden batter basking on the griddle, one is struck immediately upon entrance by a cacophonous chorus of china and metal' (Mumford, 1921, p. 264). Mumford's language aestheticizes the geometry and the sounds of industrial materials (disks, chorus, china, cacophonous) but he adds 'golden batter basking'. As an image of industry feeding people, this makes sense, but one wonders why 'golden' is not an adjective drawn from a different, more classical, age in just the way Mumford finds objectionable. I introduce Mumford's cultural criticism because its problems are repeated in Williams's attempt to locate the central claims of art in modern culture. That neither Williams nor Mumford could yet see how Morrisite views of the arts would be used in America to provide a rationale for therapeutic weekends, renewing people for the work week, is not surprising. Even so, how art, even architecture, might integrally serve culture proved difficult to describe. Moreover, unlike Mumford in 1921, Williams saw that his American readers were not looking to modernism to solve either their practical or their aesthetic needs. They were reading Keats or Edgar Guest, not Eliot, let alone Stein or Williams. New Yorkers may have been eating in Child's restaurants, but they were not looking to industrial design to place 'value upon experience' (*CP*, p. 215).

Perhaps the most obvious places where *Spring and All* focuses on such questions about how social history and aesthetics are related are Poems XVII ('Shoot it Jimmy!') and XVIII ('To Elsie'). The first, a dramatic monologue, which draws on jazz and on the vernacular speech of urban African-America, concludes: 'Nobody else / but me — / They can't copy it'. In another context, the poem would be a celebration of the artist's originality. But it is not clear how the inimitable can be reconciled with the appeal to community speech in the first line ('*Our* orchestra / is the cat's nuts') (*CP*, p. 216, emphasis added), despite the echo of the volume's initial appeal to an intersubjective 'embrace' between reader and writer. In particular, it is unclear what it means for Williams to appropriate speech from Harlem: is this Williams in black face? As reporter or tourist? The last line of the poem brings home, as well, *Spring and All*'s self-consciousness about its appropriation of speech. The writer by definition 'can't copy' certain forms of speech, namely spoken language, African-American vernacular, and jazz rhythms in poetry. The inclusive first-person plural that opens the poem ultimately emphasizes how speech communities operate sociologically and suggests the status of the poetic transcription as approximation. That is, speech lifted out of social context is not simply imaginatively charged, but changed in a way that is difficult to reconcile with *Spring and All*'s more celebratory Cubist gestures towards separating 'things of the imagination from life' (*CP*, p. 194).

This is not to deny there is some connection between linguistic and social codes, but it is to say the connection is uneasy. The same sort of tension is rehearsed in the following poem, 'To Elsie' (*CP*, pp. 217–19), a poem critics like David Frail or cultural anthropologists like James Clifford characterize as a self-conscious diagnosis of the failure, not only of social welfare agencies, but of Williams's poetry of 'contact' to find the common meeting place between stark social reality and poetry. The poem's language, on one level, lifts for inspection the language of advertising – commercial goods ('gauds') are seen as a poor substitute foisted on those like the 'Elsie' whose needs and circumstances are hardly answered by mass cultural goods. The poem itself, if ironically, reads Elsie herself as one of America's 'pure products'. That is, she is not so much home grown as manufactured (a product), and offered in the language of the advertisement for Ivory soap (99.9 per cent pure). To separate language, even advertising language or public rhetoric, from the world-as-usual, 'to detach [words] from ordinary existence' (*CP*, p. 197) and lift them into a separate formal or imaginative sphere, is one thing in a collage by Gris, another when it is a person – 'some Elsie' – taken by a welfare agency and deposited in 'some doctor's family'.

My point is that whenever we attempt to take the poem as not enmeshed in history, as a kind of Cubist detachment from context, we find it is always also engaged in the contemporary history of its day, and this simultaneity is discomforting, most specifically in the images of violence and of grimmer social realities, which work quite differently on the page as avant-garde practice and in the world, Williams's or our own. The discomfort is comparable to that set in motion by the opening pages of *Spring and All* when we read an attack on Europe as an aesthetic equivalent of a Wilsonian crusade. That is, we may take 'Kill kill kill' playfully, as a Dadaist figure of imaginative decreation; more literally, the invading Americans figure the flood of artists and writers – including the dedicatee and the publisher of *Spring and All* (Demuth and McAlmon) – who left the country for Europe in 1921, an exodus about which Williams's prose indicates he had mixed feelings. At the same time, the American attack also seems more serious and less inviting as a political commentary on the United States's role in the First World War and political events in postwar Europe.

I have already mentioned how *Spring and All* draws from Hartley and Gris the figure of open windows – suggesting the text's openness to European and American avant-garde practices from Cubism to Dada; to history; and to contradictions. The book is self-conscious about the way it mixes diction and positions, poetry and paint-ing, spontaneity and craft, history and interiority, urban or suburban and rural, bour-geois and avant-garde, speech acts and representations. The penultimate page claims the right to mix figures, acknowledging the book's images of imagination 'as a force, . . . a medium, a place' (*CP*, p. 235). *Spring and All* offers and as quickly replaces similar figures for itself throughout: it is an open window; it is the release of repressed energy or forces; it is a rapid transit – glimpses from a speeding car – or a Cubist collage, or a Dadaist jeu. Like the 'girl with one leg / over the rail of a balcony' in Poem XI, the multiple, and multivalenced, often unreconcilable figures it offers of itself remain suspended (Lowney, 1997, p. 69). What results is neither a tidy dialec-tic, nor a set of evenly balanced tensions.

I have rehearsed here a variety of figures that might provide a reader with footing from which to approach *Spring and All*. On the one hand, it should be clear that not all of these readings – cultural criticism, avant-gardism, a claim to an American poetics, an investigation of issues of representation and appropriation – can serve as the text's centre; on the other hand, all are certainly avenues of investigation toward which Williams's language points. To privilege for a moment the figure of openness, it seems *Spring and All* leaves open the questions it raises, and its initial invitation to the reader to re-enter the book's processes or performance of openness becomes the one gesture it does not seriously undercut. The final question may be not how to choose between thematic concerns and discursive registers, but to ask why or in what sense we are asked to adopt openness itself: is this the openness of art to experience, Williams's 'contact' versus Eliot's retrenchment? Or is this an answer to the felt chal-lenge of the European avant-garde? Nine years earlier, Williams's 'The Wanderer' had asked how he could 'be a mirror to this modernity' (*CP*, p. 28) and – from advertis-ing to Elsie, from Cubism to Harlem – *Spring and All* does mirror the various facets of modernity and the fractured nature – the fact of various facets – of modernity. Although the one figure it disclaims is that of mirrors (*CP*, p. 208), it also plays with the alliances and differences between mirrors (representations) and open windows (framed but unmediated sight). In short, the book itself 'opens' questions about the significance of its own openness.

We do know that Williams had been closely following the exchanges in the pages of *The New Republic* and *The Dial* between McAlmon and John Dewey on education. Dewey's emphasis on 'creative thought' (Dewey, 1918, p. 334) and his insistence that thinking always involves doubt, suspension and process so that '*ac*quiring is always secondary' (Dewey, 1916, p. 173), informs not only *Spring and All*'s rejection of 'the acquisitive' (*CP*, p. 220) but also the open-endedness of the book's structure. And Williams does make a pitch for Deweyan education, claiming that knowledge is 'not . . . dead dissections', and that the 'whole field of education is affected' (*CP*, p. 224) by the imagination. Still, finally, it seems too tidy to say that it is Dewey who autho-rizes the structure of *Spring and All*. After all, Dewey is arguing about public educa-tion, hardly an arena in which Williams thought a limited edition of experimental literature published in Paris would have significant impact. Of course, one of *Spring* *and All*'s central concerns is the difficulty of relating the realities of America in 1923 to the modern and the real in the realm of art. Both art and history clearly inform the book. The question is which is figure; which, ground. If I have voiced scepticism over taking the book's open-endedness as a purely Cubist or Dadaist gesture, it is at least as difficult to suggest that the significance of *Spring and All*'s openness is singular, simply a demonstration, if a rich one, of Dewey's creative intelligence.

Critically, *Spring and All* has attracted ever-increasing interest, in part because it invites and yields to multiple technologies of reading. I would suggest that no single procedure will gather all the threads of the book; no one figure, however interpreted, serves as *the* central emblem – not 'calculated indeterminacy' (Perloff, 1981, p. 129) nor the 'desire to connect art to social reality' (Sayre, 1984, p. 18), nor a 'dance' of the intellect (Whitaker, 1984), nor my own appeals to Mumford and Dewey as critics of American culture. Yet perhaps it is not too much to suggest that *Spring and All* does provides a window on the pressing issues of the 1920s, from the redefinitions of modern art by way of Eliot, the French and the Americans, to the social, political and philosophical questions under debate not only in publications from small arts publishers, but equally in the pages of newspapers, in the American Congress, on the streets of Chicago and New York, and in the backwoods of New Jersey. The volume also forces any reader to frame and reframe sets of questions about the place of poetry in the world, and to take seriously the multiple answers tested within Williams's pages. *Spring and All*, at least in these ways, results in something of moment.

BIBLIOGRAPHY

Breslin, James E. (1977). 'William Carlos Williams and Charles Demuth: Cross-Fertilization in the Arts.' *Journal of Modern Literature*, 6, 248–63.

Clifford, James (1988). *The Predicament of Culture: Twentieth-Century Ethnography, Literature, and Art*. Cambridge, MA: Harvard University Press.

Dewey, John (1916). *Democracy and Education*. New York: Macmillan.

Dewey, John (1918). 'Education and Social Direction.' *The Dial*, 64, 333–5.

Diggory, Terence (1991). *William Carlos Williams and the Ethics of Painting*. Princeton, NJ: Princeton University Press.

Dijkstra, Bram (1969). *The Hieroglyphics of a New Speech: Cubism, Stieglitz, and the Early Poetry of William Carlos Williams*. Princeton, NJ: Princeton University Press.

Frail, David (1987). *The Early Politics and Poetics of William Carlos Williams*. Ann Arbor, MI: UMI Research Press.

Hartley, Marsden (1921). *Adventures in the Arts*. New York: Boni and Liveright.

Hatlen, Burton (1994). 'Openness and Closure in Williams's *Spring and All*.' *William Carlos Williams Review*, 20, 15–29.

Lowney, John (1997). *The American Avant-Garde Tradition: William Carlos Williams, Postmodern Poetry, and the Politics of Cultural Memory*. Lewisburg: Bucknell University Press.

MacGowan, Christopher (1984). *William Carlos Williams's Early Poetry: The Visual Arts Background*. Ann Arbor, MI: UMI Research Press.

Miller, J. Hillis (1970). 'Williams's *Spring and All* and the Progress of Poetry.' *Daedalus*, 99, 405–34.

Mumford, Lewis (1921). 'Machinery and the Modern Style.' *The New Republic*, 27, 263–5.

Palattella, John (1995). 'But If It Ends The Start Is Begun: *Spring and All*, Americanism, and Postwar Apocalypse.' *William Carlos Williams Review*, 21, 1–22.

Perloff, Marjorie (1981). *The Poetics of Indeterminacy: Rimbaud to Cage.* Princeton, NJ: Princeton University Press.

Sayre, Henry (1979). 'Distancing "The Rose" from *Roses.' William Carlos Williams Newsletter,* 5, 18–19.

Sayre, Henry (1984). 'Avant-Garde Dispositions: Placing *Spring and All* in Context.' *William Carlos Williams Review,* 10, 13–24.

Schmidt, Peter (1988). *William Carlos Williams, The Arts, and Literary Tradition.* Baton Rouge: Louisiana State University Press.

Steinman, Lisa M. (1984). 'Once More with Feeling: Teaching *Spring and All.' William Carlos Williams Review,* 10, 7–12.

Steinman, Lisa M. (1987). *Made in America: Science, Technology and American Modernist Poets.* New Haven, CT: Yale University Press.

Weaver, Mike (1971). *William Carlos Williams: The American Background.* Cambridge: Cambridge University Press.

Whitaker, Thomas R. (1984). *'Spring and All:* Teaching Us the Figures of the Dance.' *William Carlos Williams Review,* 10, 1–6.

Williams, William Carlos (1951). *The Autobiography of William Carlos Williams.* New York: Random House.

Williams, William Carlos (1954). 'Comment.' In *Selected Essays of William Carlos Williams.* New York: Random House.

Williams, William Carlos (1986). *The Collected Poems of William Carlos Williams,* Vol. 1, ed. A. Walton Litz and Christopher MacGowan. New York: New Directions.

32

Wallace Stevens: *Harmonium*

Philip Hobsbaum

Wallace Stevens, of Pennsylvania Dutch descent, was born in 1879 and died in 1955. He read a General Arts course at Harvard, freelanced for a time as a journalist in New York, then qualified in Law and spent most of his life working as an insurance man. He excelled especially in sorting out defaults and bankruptcies, and did well out of the Depression of 1929.

Stevens began his literary career as one of a number of Harvard undergraduates in the 1890s who sought to create an American poetry. Previous attempts towards that end seem to have been beneath their attention. An influential lecturer at Harvard in those days was George Santayana (1863–1952), who wrote a patronizing essay *Interpretations of Poetry and Religion* (1900) which adversely criticized 'the poetry of barbarism'; that is to say, the poetry of Walt Whitman (1819–92), with whom he associated Robert Browning (1812–89). There may have been a class-differential here, at least as regards Whitman. Instead, Stevens and his contemporaries looked to what was the *dernier cri* of poetry in those days, a series of English verse-writers most of them published in the USA by the firm of T. B. Mosher. These, in their turn, were derivative from the French symbolist poets boosted by the lectures, delivered in 1900 at Harvard and elsewhere, of Henri de Régnier (1864–1936), a late symbolist whose poetry dwelt on the fading glories of pre-Revolutionary France.

Contemporaries of Stevens at Harvard, with whom he later associated in New York, included Pitts Sanborn (1879–1941), author of *Vie de Bordeaux* (1916), Walter C. Arensberg (1876–1954) and Donald Evans (1884–1921). Sanborn became noted as an opera aficionado, and Arensberg as an art connoisseur. Evans persisted as a poet, and produced five collections of verse, as well as a pseudonymous pamphlet explaining his artistry to an unheeding world. All these writers published their respective first volumes a decade or so ahead of Stevens. His first book, *Harmonium*, appeared in 1923, when he was already forty-four.

Stevens took his time to find his feet, publishing effusions under such pseudonyms as Hillary Harness and R. Jerries between 1898 and 1900 in *The Harvard Monthly* and *The Harvard Advocate*, the governing committee of which latter he chaired for a while. However, he was to develop far beyond the mannered rhetoric of this period. The Frenchified poets whom his contemporaries saw as modern included Ernest Dowson (1867–1900), W. E. Henley (1849–1903) and Austin Dobson (1840–1921). They specialized in an affected notion of the eighteenth century, even going so far as to adopt some metrical forms of that period, and indeed earlier. Henley has 'Ballade Made in the Hot Weather', beginning 'Fountains that frisk and sprinkle / The moss they overspill; / Pools that the breezes crinkle' (*Poems*, 1921), while Austin Dobson has 'On a Fan that Belonged to the Marquise of Pompadour': 'Chicken-skin, delicate, white, / Painted by Carlo Vanloo, / Loves in a riot of light' (*Complete Poetical Works*, 1923).

The 'ballade' that these poets favoured has little in common with English works favoured with that title. Theirs is a French form, requiring a plethora of rhyming. In a language conspicuously short of rhymes, this demanded a degree of ingenuity. Arensberg has 'A Ballade to my Lady Moonlight':

> Listen, my Moonlight, to my plea!
> Because I have not half defined
> Thy beauties in these stanzas three,
> Beloved, do not call me blind!
> (*Poems*, 1914)

Early Stevens is surprisingly like this. 'Ballade of the Pink Parasol' appeared in *The Harvard Advocate* of 23 May 1900 and seems to be an ironic lament for a more ordered age:

> I pray thee where is the old-time wig,
>   And where is the lofty hat?
> Where is the maid on the road with her gig,
>   And where is the fire-side cat?
>   Never was sight more fair than that,
> Outshining, outreaching them all,
>   There in the night where the lovers sat –
>   But where is the pink parasol?
> (Stevens, 1977)

This, for all its mannerism, looks forward to *Harmonium*, whose properties included umbrellas, hats and wigs. One reason why Stevens, even at the age of twenty-one, could carry off this kind of pastiche was his sense of humour – a quality lacking in some of his contemporaries.

Also, he grew up to read the French symbolists for himself, and not through the spectacles of their English imitators. An obvious source of reference is Jules Laforgue (1860–87), with whom both the young Stevens and his contemporary Donald Evans shared, apparently, an unappeasable ennui. This surfaces in those poems by Laforgue centred upon the *commedia del arte* figure, Pierrot. As translated by Walter Arensberg, one of these pieces begins:

> She that must put me wise about the Feminine!
> We'll tell her firstly, with my air least impolite:
> 'The angles of a triangle, O sweetheart mine,
> Are equal to two right'.

It is a way of showing a detached view of the world, distinct from simple romanticism. Donald Evans, addressing a woman who is unappealingly self-controlled, writes, 'Your hat was of an angle, and the veil / Was impudent with seven maddening spots' (*Two Deaths in the Bronx*, 1916).

In Stevens, such geometrical language is used as a means to indicate the restricted capacities of reason:

> Rationalists, wearing square hats,
> Think, in square rooms,
> Looking at the floor,
> Looking at the ceiling.
> They confine themselves
> To right-angled triangles.
> If they tried rhomboids,
> Cones, waving lines, ellipses –
> As, for example, the ellipse of the half-moon –
> Rationalists would wear sombreros.
> ('Six Significant Landscapes', VI; *Collected Poems*)

Here the square hat betokens the plain direct man, while the sombrero suggests the beauty of extravagance and unrest.

Even more School of Laforgue is Stevens's 'Disillusionment of Ten O'clock'. Here, he complains of simplicity in a town where folk go to bed early, and invokes by way of contrast an extravagant and seemingly more attractive mode of being:

> The houses are haunted
> By white night-gowns.
> None are green,
> Or purple with green rings,
> Or green with yellow rings.

Alongside the sense of incongruity found in Laforgue is the euphony associated with Paul Verlaine (1844–96). A whole sequence by this poet is named 'Ariettes Oubliées' ('Forgotten Songs'), and deploys imagery evocative of music. Number Five, especially, begins with a piano which, in kissing a frail hand, shines through the pink and grey of evening. Evans seeks to encapsulate Verlaine in a piece called, after that poet's sequence, 'Jadis et Naguere': 'When disillusionment was fiercely new . . . I longed for a numbed sense to ease my pain' (*Discords*, 1911). Arensberg has, in 'Music to Hear', 'A little longer let thy fingers fall / Upon the keys'.

However, Stevens picks up the attitude and makes it his own, chiefly through the mellifluousness of his verse. This, none of his contemporaries could equal:

> Just as my fingers on these keys
> Make music, so the selfsame sounds
> On my spirit make a music, too.
> Music is feeling, then, not sound;
> And thus it is that what I feel,
> Here in this room, desiring you,
>
> Thinking of your blue-shadowed silk,
> Is music.
> ('Peter Quince at the Clavier')

There are other echoes, too, mostly from the French. Stéphane Mallarmé (1842–98), as translated by Arensberg, has, in his famous 'L'Après-Midi d'un Faune':

> The large and double reed . . .
> Dreams, in a long extended solo, of amusing
> The beauty of the neighbourhood by a confusing
> False of that beauty.
> (Arensberg, *Idols*, 1916)

Of course, one can understand and enjoy Stevens putting on the mask of Peter Quince – a bumpkin from *A Midsummer Night's Dream* – without necessarily recognizing all the allusions. They are cited here as a means of showing how Stevens developed from the frivolities and pastiches of his college days to what Randall Jarrell (1914–65), in his book *Poetry and the Age* (1955), finely called 'the last purity and refinement of the grand style'. 'Peter Quince at the Clavier' attests the power of art to dissolve disagreeables and immortalize beauty. The poem ends:

> The body dies; the body's beauty lives.
> So evenings die, in their green going,
> A wave interminably flowing . . .
> . . . Susanna's music touched the bawdy strings
> Of those white elders; but, escaping,
> Left only Death's ironic scraping.
> Now, in its immortality, it plays
> On the clear viol of her memory,
> And makes a constant sacrament of praise.

One does not need to know Verlaine and Mallarmé to appreciate this poetry, but it is as well to understand that, without Verlaine and Mallarmé, this poetry would not be what it is.

The distinction between Stevens and his contemporaries can be phrased in linguistic terms. Whatever his antecedents, he absorbed and developed them to produce a style at once characteristic and flexible. This points to a prolonged study of language and literature.

It has been said that Stevens owed one of his characteristic images to Donald Evans. Evans had written a poem, ostensibly about one of their poetic contemporaries, Allen Norton (1888–1945). It is a sonnet, and the octave runs thus:

> Born with a monocle he stares at life,
> And sends his soul on pensive promenades;
> He pays a high price for discarded gods,
> And then regilds them to renew their strife.
> His calm moustache points to the ironies,
> And a fawn-coloured laugh sucks in the night,
> Full of the riant mists that turn to white
> In brief lost battles with banalities.
> (*Sonnets from the Patagonian*, 1914)

This is tainted with something of the self-regarding dandyism out of which Stevens managed to develop.

The influence, however, may have been as much biographical as literary. In his *Letters* (Stevens, 1967) – which form an indispensable commentary on the poems – he writes to Elsie Moll, his future wife: 'Sometimes an uncle from Saint Paul visited us. He could talk French and had big dollars in his pockets, some of which went into mine' (21 January 1909). There is a photograph of this uncle, James Van Sant Stevens, reproduced in Joan Richardson's (1986, vol. 1) biography of the poet, looking decidedly cocky. Apparently he was a bachelor, and dealt in art. However that may be, something of this personality went into Stevens's poem about middle-aged love, ingeniously titled, 'Le Monocle de Mon Oncle':

> 'Mother of heaven, regina of the clouds,
> O sceptre of the sun, crown of the moon,
> There is not nothing, no, no never nothing,
> Like the clashed edges of two words that kill.'
> And so I mocked her in magnificent measure.
> Or was it that I mocked myself alone?
> I wish that I might be a thinking stone.
> The sea of spuming thought foists up again
> The radiant bubble that she was. And then
> A deep up-pouring from some saltier well
> Within me, bursts its watery syllable.

Barbara Fisher suggested (in the *Wallace Stevens Journal*, IX: 1, spring 1985) that the 'magnificent measure' of the first four lines is based upon a French poet, earlier than any of those previously mentioned. In his 'Ballade: pour prier Notre Dame', François Villon (1431–?63) begins, as translated by an American poet of a vintage more recent than that of Stevens, Galway Kinnell (b. 1927):

> Lady of heaven, regent of earth,
> Empress over the swamps of hell,
> Receive me your humble Christian
> That I may be counted among your elect.

However, Stevens's invocation is likely to owe at least as much to 'Hymne', by Charles Baudelaire (1821–67), which starts by dedicating the poem 'to the very dear, to the very beautiful, to the angel, to the immortal idol'. This tone of extravagant praise may lead us to doubt the straightforwardness of Baudelaire. Certainly, it would seem that Stevens's invocation is ironic.

For the 'uncle' of his poem is a one-eyed visionary in mind as well as eyesight, even though he seems astigmatically aware that his 'mockery' tells us more about himself than about the passive beauty he eulogizes. The poem moves via qualitative progression – the association of thoughts – and not by any logic of narrative. Through 'Le Monocle de Mon Oncle' we observe an ageing body harbouring the passions of youth, particularly absurd when these are directed at an equally ageing inamorata:

> Our bloom is gone. We are the fruit thereof.
> Two golden gourds distended on our vines,
> Into the autumn weather, splashed with frost,
> Distorted by hale fatness, turned grotesque.
> We hang like warty squashes, streaked and rayed,
> The laughing sky will see the two of us
> Washed into rinds by rotting winter rains.

Though the elements laugh at the dear old fruits, the uncle laughs at himself and his love, too, and, presumably, so does the poet behind him, conscious of thinning hair and thickening waistline. Unlike his contemporaries, who take themselves rather solemnly, Stevens is almost always the comedian, quite capable of self-mockery in an almost finical diction: 'the sea of spuming thought', 'the fruit thereof', 'we hang like warty squashes'. It is this fastidiousness in speech whereby the passions that shake an Ernest Dowson or a Donald Evans – 'I am sick of empty trumpetings' (*Discords*) – are held up by Stevens to ironic contemplation.

Consider the registers of language deployed by Stevens. It is his vocabulary that renders him so distinctive:

caracole ('The Jack-Rabbit'): 'A half-turn to the right or left executed by a horseman; a succession of such; (loosely) to caper about' (*Oxford English Dictionary*, hereafter, *OED*)

coquelicot ('Cy Est Pourtraicte, Madame Ste Ursule, et Les Unze Mille Vierges'): 'The red poppy, the colour of which is a brilliant red with an admixture of orange' (*OED*)

cabildo ('The Comedian as the Letter C'): 'cabilliau, codfish that has been salted and hung for a few days but not thoroughly dried' (*OED*)

clickering ('The Comedian as the Letter C'): 'distribution, dividing up (of syllables); derived from the practice of the printer's foreman, or clicker, who distributes type among his juniors' (*OED*)

– or, 'clickering' may be a neologism, constructed from the association with the word 'click', meaning a short sharp sound. Stevens is quite capable of making up words. In this same poem, 'The Comedian as the Letter C', he has, for example, 'nincompate', which finds no definition in the *OED*. Since the run of the vocabulary is on the letter 'C', as the title indicates, it is not accidental that 'nincompate', presumably meaning 'to talk like a ninny (or fool)', contains that letter. Stevens himself wrote, 'I ought to confess that by the letter C I meant the sound of the letter C; what was in my mind was to play on that sound throughout the poem. While the sound of that letter has more or less variety, and includes, for instance, K and S, all its shades may be said to have a comic aspect. Consequently, the letter C is a comedian' (letter to Ronald Lane Latimer, 15 November 1935).

And why did Stevens choose to dilate on the letter 'C'? Crucial is the fact that the hero is a comedian, but also in the comic vein is a letter which Stevens's father sent to him when the boy wrote home, innocently boasting of having been elected to the Signet Club, a sort of academic society: 'Just what the election to the *Signet signifies* I have no *sign*. It is *signi*ficant that your letter is a *sign*al to *sign* another cheque that you may *sigh* no more' (21 May 1899; Stevens senior's italics). It is clear that Garret Stevens, a middle-aged lawyer, was a little concerned that his son might become the 'nincompated pedagogue' represented some twenty-two years later in 'The Comedian as the Letter C'.

Because, for all his efforts as a glossator, Stevens uncovered something very deep in exposing the pedagogue Crispin. What is betokened in the narrative of 'The Comedian . . .' is fear on the poet's part. The poem, somewhat after the plan of 'Le Bateau Ivre' by Arthur Rimbaud (1854–91), tells of a failed venture in the jungle and a voyage back to domesticity. Stevens seems to have been afraid that the necessity of establishing himself in the world, in order to support a home and family, would mean the sacrifice of his poetry.

Writing seems to have been connected with his very survival. It was a way to make sense of a denuded planet. One may feel it therefore symptomatic that, on completing 'The Comedian . . .', one of the latest to be written of the poems that appeared in *Harmonium*, he produced very little verse in the next decade, and published hardly anything. 'The Comedian . . .' is therefore prophetic:

How many poems he denied himself
In his observant progress, lesser things
Than the relentless contact he desired;
How many sea-masks he ignored; what sounds
He shut out from his tempering ear . . .

                     . . . Prolong

His active force in an inactive dirge,
Which, let the tall musicians call and call,
Should merely call him dead? Pronouce amen
Through choirs infolded to the outmost clouds?
Because he built a cabin who once planned
Loquacious columns by the ructive sea.

'Ructive', a word not defined by the *OED*, would appear to be associated with insurrection; in this context, an 'insurgent' sea. There is, then, a caricature element in this most ambitious of all Stevens's poems. Its bomphiologia, an embracing of inflated speech, arises out of the worry that he would have to forsake the romantic sombrero of the artist for the square hat of the rationalist. During this period of building a cabin, his income grew, his relationship with his wife deteriorated, and the volume he at length squeezed out thirteen years after *Harmonium*, *Ideas of Order* (1936), proved to be the weakest of them all.

It is true that Stevens went on to consolidate his work, and built impressively on that consolidation. Some think that 'Notes Towards a Supreme Fiction' in *Transport to Summer* (1947) is his single greatest work, though it is a series of philosophical lyrics rather than a concerted philosophical statement. The true Stevens *aficionado* would probably opt for the late sequence, 'The Rock', incorporated in the *Collected Poems* of 1955.

However, for many, *Harmonium* is the most attractive of all the books. It can be read, quite lazily, for the snap, crackle and pop of its words; or it may be studied as representing the first major phase of one of the very few genuinely philosophical poets in English.

There are a number of lyrics which represent moments of perception. 'Invective against Swans' reproaches the great birds for looking like souls but being confined to the parks and not taking advantage of their wings to fly to the skies, as souls are feigned to do. In 'Domination of Black' the cries of peacocks amid the falling leaves replicate themselves in the firelight, striking fear into the imagination of the lone watcher. 'The Snow Man', a finely tuned piece of free verse, enacts the concept of empathy. You have to feel like the snow to appreciate the snow, but then it may be found that you have reduced yourself to nothing. 'The Ordinary Women' shows an incursion of the poor into the sybaritic luxuries of a palace which is quite likely to be a product of their imagination: 'The lacquered loges huddled there / Mumbled zay-zay and a-zay, a-zay'. Similarly, in 'Tea at the Palaz of Hoon', luxuries bestowed upon the guest, such as 'ointment sprinkled on my beard', are all products of his imagination: 'I was the world in which I walked . . . And there I found myself more truly and more strange'. 'Metaphors of a Magnifico' shows the power of the mind to create a reality, in which twenty men crossing a bridge into a village can be twenty men crossing twenty bridges, or, indeed, one man crossing one bridge. In 'Hibiscus on the Sleeping Shores' the mind is turned by metaphor into a moth that leaves the lazy sea for the fertile land and the pollen of the flowers. As a contrast, in 'The Doctor of Geneva' the protagonist without imagination has lost out through being only mildly disturbed by the savagery and majesty of the sea.

'Last Looks at the Lilacs' tells of a prosaic anti-hero, 'poor buffo', being superseded in the affection of 'the divine ingenue' by a swaggering figure straight out of the Don Juan legends. 'The Worms at Heaven's Gate', a perfectly voiced piece of blank verse, tells of the worms dutifully escorting the body of an Arabian princess bit by bit from her tomb into a fallacious immortality. 'Floral Decorations for Bananas' is one of several exhortations to render the plain world more exotic. 'Anecdote of Canna' shows someone great in earthly terms, such as the president whose ceaseless thoughts never encounter any other thoughts, regaling himself by the sight of the brightly coloured flowers on his terrace. 'On the Manner of Addressing Clouds' suggests that, if clouds could speak, they would sound like the thoughts of philosophers preoccupied with death; but in reality they are silent, and alone. 'Of Heaven Considered as a Tomb' sets, against the conventional notion of ghosts wandering, the more horrific possibility that there is nothing after death at all.

'Anecdote of the Prince of Peacocks' has the protagonist meeting with a warrior called 'Berserk', whose environment is created by his own disordered imagination. The character addressed in 'A High-Toned Old Christian Woman' is, quite possibly, based upon Stevens's own pious mother and is told that poetry can create an alternative universe – 'tink and tank and tunk-a-tunk-tunk' – far other than her received morality. The chief properties in 'The Curtains in the House of the Metaphysician', the curtains themselves, contain in their own being the qualities which are conventionally ascribed to the external universe. 'Banal Sojourn' is a statement of ennui. In Stevens's prose gloss, culled from a letter to Hi Simons dated 18 April 1944: 'a poem of (exhaustion in August!). The mildew of any late season, of any experience that has grown monotonous as, for instance, the experience of life'. The inference may be, that is why one needs poetry.

'The Emperor of Ice Cream' is an answer to marriage poems, such as the 'Epithalamion' of Edmund Spenser (1552–99). It is a funeral song in mock-honour of one withered and dead. Whereas in a marriage poem, preparations are made for a ceremony, here Stevens requires nothing to be changed. 'His command merely orders what already is to continue being' (Maureen Kravec, 'Let Arcade Be Finale of Arcade', *The Wallace Stevens Journal*, III: 1 & 2, spring 1979; an article to which the present interpretation owes much). The 'concupiscent curds' are in lieu of a wedding feast and are probably ice cream, not the most nourishing of comestibles. Instead of flowers of rhetoric, here you get 'last month's newspapers'. Spenser says 'Now bring the Bryde into the brydall boures. / Now night is come, now soone her disaray, / And in her bed her lay'. Stevens says 'Take from the dresser of deal . . . that sheet . . . And spread it so as to cover her face'. The poem is an ironic parody; an anti-wedding song, and also a stand against the concept of immortality.

'Bantams in Pine-Woods' exhibits the rhetoric of Stevens at its most extravagant:

> Chieftain Iffucan of Azcan in caftan
> Of tan with henna hackles halt!
>
> Damned universal cock, as if the sun
> Was blackamoor to bear your blazing tail.
>
> Fat! Fat! Fat! Fat! I am the personal.
> Your world is you. I am my world.

The poem is spoken, so to say, by tiny bantam chickens who are angrily confronting a very large poet, dressed, as 'Iffucan' and 'Azcan' may assure us, like a Red Indian. It is the poet who is addressed as 'Damned universal cock' and who is admonished (four times over) for being 'Fat'. In this joke poem, as elsewhere, a characteristic theme is asserted. Even a tiny chicken has to make his world out of the imagination, in order to be master of himself.

For all the variegation of the poems in *Harmonium*, a discernible theme runs through. It is that there is no life without the imagination; that, without the enlivening vision of poetry, the world is a waste and terrible place. Verlaine, Laforgue and Donald Evans may have succumbed to their ennui, but Stevens is piloted out of it by his recourse to verse. However, he shows by poignant metaphor what happens when one cannot write; it is like being seized with acute laryngitis. The protagonist of 'The Man Whose Pharynx Was Bad' has fallen victim to the climate of his time. As Stevens puts it in this atmospheric poem (with its echoing internal rhymes, one of his best), 'I am too dumbly in my being pent'. A crucial stanza has been dropped from the poem as printed. Readers may care to insert it, between the existing lines nine and ten:

> Perhaps if summer ever came to rest
> And lengthened, deepened, comforted, caressed
> Through days like oceans in obsidian
> Horizons, full of night's midsummer blaze . . .

Since it is imagination that creates the world as a living entity, it therefore follows that the world can vary according to the play of the imagination. Anyone but Stevens would have written a poem about a blackbird. He writes one called 'Thirteen Ways of Looking at a Blackbird'. So the poem does not concern what is perceived so much as various ways of perceiving it. Further, it is the inferred melodies that may be the sweeter:

> I do not know which to prefer,
> The beauty of inflections
> Or the beauty of innuendoes,
> The blackbird whistling
> Or just after.

On a grander scale, 'Sea Surface Full of Clouds' describes the same scene over and over, not so much at different times but as experienced with different degrees of sensibility. Thus, in the first section, 'paradisal green / Gave suavity to the perplexed machine / Of ocean'; in the second, 'a sham-like green / Capped summer-seeming on the tense machine / Of ocean'; in the third, 'an uncertain green, / piano-polished, held the tranced machine / Of ocean' – and right through all five sections in a symphonic effect of reiteration, patterning and development. This wonderful piece ends with a celebration of life in a resolution of all the imagistic charades that have been played before us, as the rhythm opens out:

> Then the sea
> And heaven rolled as one and from the two
> Came fresh transfigurings of freshest blue.

This, a truly happy poem, derived from one of the very few trips Stevens took abroad. He and Elsie, his wife, cruised past Mexico, through the Panama Canal and on to California. During that voyage, according to Joan Richardson's biography (Richardson, 1988, vol. 2), their only child, their daughter Holly, was conceived. One does not need to know that fact in order to appreciate the poem, but it helps to explain the celebratory tone of the finale.

The crown jewel of *Harmonium*, however, is 'Sunday Morning'. Not only does it sum up many of the separate perceptions of that volume, to do with the way in which thought remakes reality, but it looks forward to the great philosophy propounded in the later works of Stevens. This has many analogies with the distinction propounded by Martin Heidegger (1889–1976). He makes the distinction between 'earth', which is matter not infiltrated by perception, and 'world', which is matter perceived by humanity – indeed, created in art ('The Origin of the Work of Art', 1915, in *Poetry, Language, Thought*).

Without this quality of human perception the world would be meaningless. Stevens had been brought up as a Presbyterian, and he was not prepared to sacrifice the certainties of that religion for an atheism which would draw meaning out of the world. Follower of Matthew Arnold as he was, Stevens seems to have seen imagination, and more precisely poetry, as a substitute for religion.

The protagonist of 'Sunday Morning' is a woman who has decided not to go to church. Instead, her meditation creates its own sabbath. A clue to the poem is a voice crying, near the end:

> 'The tomb in Palestine
> Is not the porch of spirits lingering.
> It is the grave of Jesus where he lay.'

The woman, meditating, has rejected organized religion. She has rejected the concept of 'life after death': 'why should she give her bounty to the dead?' Rejected, also, is pagan mythology: 'Jove in the clouds had his inhuman birth'. This does not, as a Christian might suppose, leave her with mere sensuality: 'But when the birds are gone, and their warm fields / Return no more, where, then, is paradise?'

The woman recognizes the potential arbitrariness to which her thoughts give rise: 'We live in an old chaos of the sun'. However, that chaos is rendered meaningful by her perceptions of natural beauty. It is not that she is proposing some never-changing paradise. On the contrary – and this is the key sentence of the poem – 'Death is the mother of beauty'. Because her perception has a term, it is all the more keenly felt, and this gives it meaning. Her understanding irradiates that upon which she gazes. This is implied in the nature imagery which has been developing throughout the poem. It is fulfilled in the resolution at the end, which is one of the loveliest passages in modern poetry:

> Deer walk upon our mountains, and the quail
> Whistle about us their spontaneous cries;
> Sweet berries ripen in the wilderness;
> And, in the isolation of the sky,
> At evening, casual flocks of pigeons make
> Ambiguous undulations as they sink,
> Downward to darkness, on extended wings.

It is not the wonder of this natural world that is the meaning. It is the woman's perception of that wonder, which has given rise to the poem which communicates her perception. Hence, the meaning of life is in poetry.

If the poet's hand had faltered, his creed would have failed. But here is an original rehandling of blank verse; a remarkable achievement, aesthetic as well as technical, for this late stage in the history of literature. The working out of this great poem guarantees its philosophy. It is at the centre of *Harmonium*, and, hence, at the centre of Stevens's art. That art is, as Arnold might have said, a creation of the brain, woven of poetry and philosophy.

BIBLIOGRAPHY

Blackmur, R. P. (1954). *Language as Gesture*, London: George Allen and Unwin.

Brazeau, Peter (1983). *Parts of a World: Wallace Stevens Remembered*, New York: Random House.

Buttel, Robert (1967). *The Making of Harmonium*, Princeton NJ: Princeton University Press.

Doyle, Charles (ed.) (1985). *Wallace Stevens: The Critical Heritage*, London: Routledge.

Jarrell, Randall (1973). *Poetry and the Age*, London: Faber and Faber.

Lensing, George S. (1986). *Wallace Stevens: A Poet's Growth*, Baton Rouge: Louisiana State University Press.

Richardson, Joan (1986). *Wallace Stevens: The Early Years, 1879–1923*, New York: Beech Tree Books.

Richardson, Joan (1988). *Wallace Stevens: The Later Years, 1923–1955*, New York: Beech Tree Books.

Stevens, Holly (1977). *Souvenirs and Prophecies: The Young Wallace Stevens*, New York: Alfred A. Knopf.

Stevens, Wallace (1955). *Collected Poems*, London: Faber and Faber.

Stevens, Wallace (1960). *The Necessary Angel: Essays on Reality and the Imagination*, London: Faber and Faber.

Stevens, Wallace (1967). *Letters*, ed. Holly Stevens, London: Faber and Faber.

Stevens, Wallace (1989). *Opus Posthumous*, revd edn, ed. Milton J. Bates, New York: Alfred A. Knopf.

33

Marianne Moore: *Observations*

Elizabeth Wilson

Observations, published in 1924 in New York by the Dial Press, was Marianne Moore's second book of poems. It was, nevertheless, the book Moore considered her first legitimate collection. It was reprinted a year later in 1925, by which time it had won the Dial Award for Poetry, and wide critical acclaim. Moore's first collection, *Poems*, was published in London in 1921, by the Egoist Press. The selection had been put together by H. D., Winifred Bryher and Robert McAlmon, H. D.'s husband, ostensibly without Moore's permission. *Poems*, with its patterned brown-paper cover and hand-glued title sticker, is a small delight, yet Moore's reaction to its publication was complex. In her letters she both acknowledges and disowns it. To her brother, Warner, Moore wrote that she was 'startled to receive from Miss Weaver of *The Egoist*' her first book of poems: 'a little book of poems of mine collected and published by Hilda, Winifred Bryher and Mr. McAlmon. I will send you a copy as soon as I have decided on, and made, some corrections' (Costello, 1981, p. 170) and

> Miss Weaver wrote to me three months ago to know would I be willing to publish something 'before the reviewers scatter for the summer' and I said no. I had also told T. S. Eliot I didn't wish to publish a book and Ezra [Pound] and Hilda [H. D.] and Bryher herself. Several poems could have been put in that aren't in – many should be left out that are in and I would make changes in half the poems that are in. (Ibid.)

Moore's discomfort seems as much to do with the situation she found herself in, of appearing to be less than honest with Eliot, whose offer of help with publication she had refused not long before. She is at pains to reassure Eliot that she knew nothing of the venture and to express her hesitancies as to the quality of the book:

> Its publication was a tremendous surprise to me. . . . I felt that it was not to my literary advantage to publish work. . . . I am aware that everything has been done to give the dignity of size and a beautiful construction and as the act of a friend it is a testi-

mony of affection but if it were the act of an enemy, I should realize that it was an attempt to show how little I had accomplished. (Ibid., p. 171)

Observations carries, after its title page, a note, in effect a disclaimer: 'With additions this book is a reprint of *Poems* published in London in 1921 by The Egoist Press, that collection being made and arranged by H. D. and Mr and Mrs Robert MacAlmon [sic].' The note inscribes formally the gestures of distancing with which Moore had greeted the publication of *Poems*. It attributes editorship of the first book and asserts ownership of the new volume. Moore never again (unless we think of her mother in such terms) relinquished editorial control of her texts to any other person. Even after her death, her dictum 'omissions are not accidents' continues to haunt with its constraints the publication of Moore's work. Much of her poetry still remains uncollected.

The note also asserts a set of relationships. For Moore, the community of artists was vital. She worked hard to sustain links with those whose friendship she valued. The circle within which she moved in New York was crucial to her sense of her own identity as a writer, as too were the contacts she kept with people in Europe like Pound and Eliot, and H. D. and Bryher, with whom she maintained a lifelong friendship and correspondence.

Observations, then, still seen as Moore herself saw it, as her first substantial work, marks that moment when Moore, having been granted the luxury of a first sortie into print, took back control of her publication and editorial decisions. It is the moment of 'putting the record straight'. While much else changed and developed, the first imperative, the issue of writerly control and volition, was established once and for all.

Moore's response to *Poems*, that there were deletions, emendations and additions she would wish to make, shows her desire continually to re-examine her writing as new work is added, modifying the *oeuvre*. This careful process of modification, emendation and displacement continued throughout Moore's publishing career and provides a rich set of variations for our perusal. Indeed, the notion of a sequence of work steadily under revision, steadily contesting itself and its methods, is crucial to an understanding of Moore's work. Twenty-one of *Poems'* twenty-four texts were carried forward. A range of typographical changes were made and the order in which the poems appear was altered, though some remain grouped in relationships as they were in *Poems*. Thirty-four poems were added, only four of which were previously unpublished. 'Poetry' began its contraction towards the famed three-line version of the *Complete Poems*: 'I, too, dislike it. / Reading it, however, with a perfect contempt for it, one dis- / covers in / it, after all, a place for the genuine' (Moore, 1990, p. 36).

A volume of poems, particularly one where the writer controls editorial process, always allows that the poems be read conjunctively as well as discretely. Such sequential or horizontal reading sees the poems gathering collective momentum. Throughout *Observations* it is the relationship between things that Moore interrogates, between ideas, images, tropes, and between poems. The poems establish ongoing, complex, episodic conversations that branch out, are left, returned to and extended. 'Like a

Bulrush', for example, evokes the image of an amphibious creature, a predator. His effectiveness has to do with his ability to maintain an initial perfect stillness and a misleading similitude that masks his capacity to move between two *milieux*, the land and the water. His predatory, self-interested restraint is underscored by the *double entendre* of the stanza break: 'he did not strike // them at the / time as being differ-ent'. Often thought of as a crane, the subject of the poem establishes an analogue with a particular behaviour, a recurrent approach of Moore's in which animals take on, not only totemic value, but also act as *exempla* for actions or kinds of behaviour in spe-cific circumstances. From its earliest moments Moore's writing has about it the dis-cursive air of the fable, the allegory, and the panoply of animals in her work invariably demonstrates human action.

Images of land and water and an amphibious predator figure also in 'Sojourn in the Whale', neighbour to 'Like a Bulrush'. Its subject, in fact, is Ireland; surrounded by sea, with its struggles and pain, its mythic dimension and its capacity in the face of appalling difficulty to prevail miraculously, like Jonah, and to survive. The predator's adversarial voice is quoted. Defining Ireland's heritage as 'blindness and native / incompetence', he predicts her demise, coercively equating wisdom with submission: 'she will become wise and will be forced / to give / in'. Water works here as analogy for two very different kinds of action. It is the figure used by the adversary to under-score Ireland's 'inevitable' defeat; it is then turned by the speaker towards the idea of uprising. Voice answers voice and the adversary is refuted. 'You have seen it [water] when obstacles happened / to bar / the path – rise automatically.' Ireland's capacity for miraculous deliverance in the face of seemingly insurmountable odds is reinscribed. Moore took her Irish ancestry most seriously. That she also described her first visit to New York as her 'sojourn in the whale' gives some idea of the impact the experience had upon her.

Animals recur as key figures in 'My Apish Cousins', paramount among them an astringently predatory 'cat', savage in its disdain for the uncomprehending, 'inarti-culate frenzy' of 'fledglings' for whom art remains a mystery. Recurrent here too is the image of the sea. 'My Apish Cousins' ends, in one of Moore's fast shifts of atten-tion, with the idea of an ocean capable of swallowing anything that might traverse its surface in the interests of commerce: 'deeper / than the sea when it proffers flat-tery in exchange / for hemp, / rye, flax, horses, platinum, timber, and fir'.

Moore's connective gestures, her sequential echoes such as the accumulating images of ocean and water, and those of commercial activity, operate throughout the collection. In this sense the end of 'My Apish Cousins' prefigures 'A Grave', as does, most tellingly, the end of 'Reinforcements' which asserts that 'the future of time is determined by the power of volition'. 'Roses Only', which extends the debate on 'the predatory hand', also evokes the issue of beauty ('You do not seem to realize that beauty is a liability rather / than / an asset') which is returned to in 'Marriage'.

Moore's writing was a vocation; it was her life's work. Having determined to make her living by writing and to locate herself within a particular cultural *milieu*, she set about constructing a self that would 'enable' writing, while also responding to the complexities of her family life. Her brother Warner, an ordained Presbyterian minister, and her mother saw Moore's writing as an act of pietas. Moore constructed her literary persona within this environment. Into these plans marriage did not enter. Her brother's idea for the family to be together 'in service' may well, at least until his own marriage, have been an added imperative.

Richard Aldington described Moore as 'a poet whose mixture of whimsicality, subtlety, cool intelligence, wit, nimbleness of apprehension and old maidenly priggishness is something quite original' (Molesworth, 1990, p. 170). Charles Molesworth, Moore's biographer, sees descriptions such as Aldington's as influential in shaping public perception of Moore. Molesworth translates 'old maidenly priggishness' as 'fastidiousness' (ibid.) – a change in terminology which does not escape the vague inference of dysfunction, sexual or otherwise. R. P. Blackmur links the assertion that Moore is sexless with a comment on her 'chaste poetry' which he sees as evincing 'a special chastity aside from the flesh, not a chastity that arises from an awareness of the flesh. A purity by birth and from the void' (Blackmur). Gilbert Sorrentino remarks of Moore's work that 'restraint is like continence', and speaks of the 'really juiceless phenomena' (Sorrentino, 1984, pp. 157–66) of her poetry. Commentators persistently find her 'spinsterhood' troubling, and over the decades have returned to Moore's sexuality or perceived lack of it as a key feature of her poetics and in so doing have neglected her engagement with ontological and theological issues arising from her Protestant framework. That Moore never married has meant that her long poem 'Marriage' has been read attentively, as apologia, by those interested in her 'singularity'. 'Marriage' does construct a debate between male and female. It also frames that debate in primal terms, configuring the man as Adam and the woman as Eve, living now after the Fall, outside the Garden, in the world of time and of death: 'See her, see her in this common world'.

'Marriage' both asserts and resists the beauty of the material, post-lapsarian world where, first and foremost, consciousness is that of separation: 'Below the incandescent stars / below the incandescent fruit, / the strange experience of beauty; / its existence is too much; / it tears one to pieces / and each fresh wave of consciousness / is poison'. Aesthetic experience arises out of a consciousness that is both the consequence of and the awareness of the Fall. It is both pleasure and pain. Beauty, in all its diverse attraction, inscribes loss as it also provides the artist's *raison d'être*. In some notes for a public lecture, tentatively entitled 'The Creative Use of Influence', Moore says:

> When one is attracted to a thing one is subject to its influence. The influence however should be assimilated. In my own case I seem to import (incorporate bodily) what is too unbearably valuable to let alone – dominates my imagination or ear – haunting and takes charge of me.

The fragmented lines and breathless breaks give a sense of being overwhelmed. The things that are too 'unbearably valuable' to let alone are countered imaginatively by a process of 'bodily incorporation'. Moore's tautology underscores the crucial physicality of the process. What takes place is a kind of transubstantiation: the threat of domination, but also the unbearable pain of separation from 'the thing', are answered by an act of assimilation or incorporation. Yet the irrevocable outsideness of the thing leaves her always subject to its power. The pull of attraction exerted by the thing is such that volition is threatened and control undermined.

Moore's sense of commitment to a profound theological loss is always balanced by a belief in the restored, multitudinous condition of the natural world. Moore's theology, however, in which desire characterizes the post-lapsarian condition, works in conjunction with a second way of reading. Desire also becomes a positive force of production, an act of volition capable of creating links between objects, forging alliances and establishing connections. Thus Moore catalogues, collects and, above all, names and makes. Separation from the *causa prima* and 'first object' is the lapsarian condition, the starting point of differentiation. But the emptiness filled with things is both fundamental deficiency and sign of a transcendental potentiality. Moore's poetry sets up a dialectic of mourning while also raising the question of a libidinal investment in a finite world.

In 'Marriage' the pun on 'common', meaning (as in 'common grave') anonymous or without name, defines the world's condition. It was the firm belief of George Herbert, whose work Moore knew and loved, or indeed his predecessor Sir Philip Sidney, that it became the Christian, consequent upon the Fall, to name things and in that act of making which is poetry, to reinscribe them. Sidney in *The Defence of Poetry* defended such a stance from the orthodox Calvinist who averred that the appropriating of naming to oneself, the act of writing poetry, was an act of hubris, of pride against God. Moore's writing supported this rich convention of heterodoxy. She often obliquely interrogates Protestant theology, seemingly unnoticed by her brother and mother, despite their steady readership of her work, suggesting a 'heretical' reinscription of a personal faith in the face of the familial constraints that were the concomitant of her artistic selfhood and its vocational commitment to remaining 'unattached'.

The poem 'Black Earth', which before disappearing from the published '*oeuvre*' was renamed 'Melanchthon' making explicit the link with Philip Melanchthon, Luther's insurgent contemporary (whose name means 'black earth'), underscores the idea of Moore's own heterodoxy. In 'Black Earth' the experiential nature of existence makes problematic the possibility of a baptismal cleansing. The 'patina of circumstance' and 'unpreventable experience' are part of a process of enrichment that contradicts the notion of washing away such experience. The layers of the sediment add to the complexity of the elephant's thick skin. In a world defined by things and by doing, the elephant epitomizes the limited sight (for now I see through a glass darkly) of 'black glass'. This condition, however, with its 'beautiful element of unreason', is affirmed. It is not to be repudiated but is cause for a calm certainty.

That certainty is arrived at again in 'When I Buy Pictures'. The title operates as a first line and signals the onset of the discursive voice. Moore uses such run-on titles frequently, as entry points marking the onset of utterance. Within the space of a line, however, qualification begins as the poem moves towards the precision of 'truth': 'When I buy pictures / Or what is closer to the truth, / when I look at that of which I may regard myself as / the imaginary possessor . . .'.

Possession is seen as imaginary, a shift that arises from a looking which almost immediately becomes self-reflexive, where to look at (regard) is to value (have regard for). The distancing is from actual ownership, though buying and possessing remain at issue here as elsewhere. Moore returns repeatedly to the problematic of ownership, even in its relation to description, to naming and to writing itself. To own or to possess is to appropriate with authority. The issue is side-stepped, however, in 'When I Buy Pictures'. The focus shifts to the pleasure gained from the scopic relationship between perceiver and thing perceived. Pleasure arises from a thing capable of giving pleasure 'in my average moments'. The engagement is not out of the ordinary. It is with mundane things, the things of 'the world', this everyday life. A catalogue, a list ensues, a tendency underscored throughout *Observations* by Moore's wry and delightful inclusion of an index to the whole work. The 'things' in this poem that pleasure range from an artichoke, a square of parquet, a hieroglyph, a decorated hatbox, a photograph, a painting.

To 'fix upon' things, close looking, observation, is required. Focused visual perception is the crucial means of engagement with the material world, a looking/finding which has the capacity to engender pleasure in the perceiver. But the 'taking' of pleasure is conditional and the conditions of constraint upon that 'enjoyment' are defined: 'Too stern an intellectual emphasis upon this quality or that, / detracts from one's enjoyment'. Nor can pleasure be taken where there is the desire to exercise power. One 'must not wish to disarm anything'. Pleasure cannot be had through an inequitable relation of cause and effect, through diminishment, through predation, or at the 'expense' of any other thing, 'that which is great because something else is small'.

'When I Buy Pictures' asserts that the capacity for pleasure exists in the willed, direct relationship between perceiver and thing perceived. Yet the poem does not present its most pertinent points directly but itself operates reflexively as a 'satire upon curiosity'. Moore's poetry, abounding with things that are the objects of her attention, often deals wryly with its own scopic curiosity. It evokes collection and connoisseurship. It establishes taxonomies. It takes pleasure in these things. Yet it also negotiates constantly with the problematic of such writing, questioning how to describe without owning, how to write of things without implication in the authority of definition, how to write but not at the expense of the autonomous things upon which the writing focuses. Imaginary possession still carries the risk of definitive, unsubtle and proscriptive relations, tendencies which Moore counters often through formal strategies. Her collage technique, for example, demonstrates not only a wish to question the univocal, as does her multiple naming, but to assert the materiality and constructedness of her art. Even her notes, which after *Observations* were always a part of her collections, offer over time less guidance to the reader, as if resisting explication while valuing the increased readerly effort that less explanation encourages.

Since mutability and transience define the post-lapsarian condition, however, the world of things must itself always exist as a paradox. In all its complexity, with all its capacity to engender pleasure, it is shadowed. 'When I Buy Pictures' lists the things in which one might delight, those that give particular pleasure. But delight in 'the silver fence protecting Adam's grave' must intersect with the notion of Adam's mortality, the dire consequence of his expulsion into time itself. That expulsion is figured by the final item on Moore's list, the representation of 'Michael taking / Adam by the wrist' to lead him from The Garden. These are the concomitants of Moore's 'average moments'. It becomes very noticeable that time is figured elsewhere in the poem; the 'old thing', the 'hour-glass' and its associated 'diminishing'.

The final lines of the poem return to the one vital act of attention which must inform the relationship with the temporal, plenitudinous world. Enjoyment must be 'lit with piercing glances into the life of things'; one's pleasure in a thing must be based on 'acknowledg[ing] the spiritual forces which have made it'. Making, in Moore's terms, at its best is always aligned with an act of grace.

Moore's poems, then, frequently begin with one thing but end somewhere else altogether. Reading entails movement, being moved, through a thought process. An argument is articulated and its shifts are demonstrated one after the other, though there are often shifts that feel disjunctive. Invariably, however, there is a logic to them. Often negation is used to establish important information by saying what a thing is not. In 'New York', which explores settlement and trade, a series of negatives details while stretching beyond to some other meaning altogether: 'it is not the atmosphere of ingenuity'; 'it is not the plunder'.

In 'A Grave' the sea is likewise defined by its ability not to be owned. Though the look of the spectator is rapacious, and his gaze one of appropriation, the sea cannot be claimed as part of a collection, cannot be claimed as can the land by conquest or settlement. The sea matches human rapacity with an equivalent capacity. It answers claim with claim. That which we are is here mirrored and bested. The fir trees, marking the edge of the land, process funereal towards the sea's edge. They are reserved, saying nothing. This, however, is termed 'repression'. That which might be spoken is not articulated but is repressed. The sea does not share this characteristic. It will match desire, to claim a thing for one's own, with desire.

'A Grave' acts as warning, as cautionary tale. The 'others' whose gaze also once evinced rapacity are now beyond being even bones. 'There are others besides you who have worn that look − / whose expression is no longer a protest; the fish no longer / investigate them / for their bones have not lasted'. The knowledge of such things is repressed. Those who work the sea are oblivious of the dead for whom the sea is a grave. The quick rowing of the fishermen indicates their repressed awareness of the sea as the figure par excellence of death. The rowers' position upon the surface is one of denial: 'as if there were no such thing as death'. Transient life is a disturbance upon the surface, about which we are warned: 'the pulsation of lighthouse and noise / of bell-buoys'. And while the sea is implacable in its ordinary advance, it dissembles, proffering a surface of daily ordinariness that masks the fact and presence of death, the 'nothingness' of the grave.

That ocean of time into which Adam and Eve first were dropped is also, of course, the grave. 'Dropped things are bound to sink'; the fall was always into time, a descent as it was for Adam and Eve, towards death. For Moore, the greatest hubris is thinking that we can, in time, by what ever means, own anything. In fact time entirely owns us. To deny our temporality, which is to deny our mortality, is a repression of knowledge, and of death itself. It renders us unconscious of our condition and unconscious we are stripped of will and volition. We turn and twist, unknowingly.

Yet how can one 'turn and twist' with volition and consciousness? The answer lies in making poetry itself. Moore's writing from its earliest moments systematically seeks to undo unknowing and loss of volition. While silence is repression, speech is a bringing into consciousness through tropaic activity. Through writing, thought is brought into the consciousness of language. Writing is the crucial act of volition, that which constructs as trope the vessel of grace whose construction and capacity is an act of grace, whether it be empty of things or not. And so in the old Protestant conundrum between fallen nature and free will, the heterodox Moore comes down firmly on the side of will.

'A Grave', then, crucially identifies the condition of the fallen world with figurative activity. Figurative activity, in turn, frames Moore's attitude to the physical world, in that the things of the world function tropically, function as tropes. The Greek meaning of *tropein*, 'to turn or twist', is the phrase towards which 'A Grave' moves: 'looking as if it were not that ocean in / which dropped things are bound to sink – / in which if they turn and twist, it is neither with volition / nor consciousness'. To 'turn and twist without volition or consciousness' is to be caught unknowingly in post-lapsarian experience. Only consciousness entails will. Moore's Calvinist heritage asserts that because we are fallen, we are figured; the world itself is figured, and our stories, our very lives operate primarily as trope.

'In the Days of Prismatic Colour', the 'days of Adam' are differentiated from 'the days of Adam and Eve', and both are differentiated from a present now: 'it is no / longer that'. Colour signifies a process of loss, from an originary, prismatic, unmodified condition of 'original plainness' where plainness, as it did so often for Herbert and his contemporaries, intends both openness and fullness. The 'original plainness' thus carries the sense of unfallen plenitude. The fullness and primariness of unfallen colour becomes, in the fallen world, a fraught complexity which risks murkiness where 'nothing is plain', that is, obvious and full, and both perception and 'account' are modified. Darkness and pestilence shadow this kind of complexity, which 'moves all a- / bout as if to bewilder us'. Sophistication, defined sibilantly, in snake-like terms as 'principally throat', exists at a far remove from originality, 'the init- / ial great truths', as Lucifer comes to exist removed from and entirely opposed to grace as its antithesis, and 'antipodes'.

The insistence on sophistication's location as being 'principally throat' suggests that vocal disputation, insistence as persuasion, stand at a remove from truth. The poem addresses a particular rhetoric of construction, a style of writing, 'the gurgling and all the minutiae', the 'multitude of feet'. The approach is seen as purposeless, fruitless. Neither fixed nor formal, truth transcends the constraints of a 'classics' formality of style, epitomized by the Apollo Belvedere, which accounts itself as 'sophisticated'. Truth transcends the dark complexities of a world where any account, any writing without exception, must necessarily stretch towards an absent clarity. The transcendental nature of truth, however, is such that it is impervious to cataclysm. The language of pestilence and of flood, 'the wave may go over it if it likes', must be read together here, and be framed in turn by the prismatic evocation of the rainbow, signalling in its 'plain intent' the possibility of grace.

Thus Moore's writing establishes an insistent materiality which is the site and source of our visionary capacity. The natural world, in which Moore is complicit, encourages a complex libidinal investment in things. Moore's persona is 'the subject sustaining [herself] in a function of desire', implicating her in as complex a sensual and moral system as sexuality itself. Desire and pleasure, violence, both intellectual and physical, and power, both political and personal, permeate her writing. The irresistible thing is unbearably valuable, and the problematic of possession and ownership is always also that of colonization. Amongst the colonial imperatives explored by Moore's poetry, none is more pressing than that of America. Discomforted by its history, and like Williams, committed to its nationhood, Moore subjects America itself to scrutiny.

The title of 'England' misleads in seeming to suggest a subject. Instead it begins a catalogue. A set of geographical locations each has its defining factors listed. England is framed imaginatively, 'one voice perhaps, echoing through the tran / sept'. The narrative voice, marked by the 'perhaps', demonstrates both the control and the construction of a fiction. Each geographical definition is underscored by this narrative fictiveness which is the fictiveness of established knowledge, of assumption. The poem's geography establishes a cumulative force and each place is attributed virtue: England is defined by its criteria of suitability and convenience; Italy contrives an epicureanism without grossness; Greece nurtures the modification of illusion, hatches philosophical inquiry; France has its complex products; the East is imperturbable. England, Italy, France, Greece and the East are afforded separation each from the others. America comes last. Not England, but America, by coming last in the list, appended with paratactic ease, becomes the focus of the poem's differentiations. America is the reason for the text's comparative laudations, and is the actual subject of the poem entitled 'England'. If last arrived at, then America is set contrapuntally against those in the poem that came earlier; Europe and Asia are established that they might be departed from. The continent of arrival is America.

The poem's procedure mimics the process of settlement: pre-established terms of reference, deferred arrival, the slow, often problematic movement towards defining a different entity. 'England' also critiques the habit of generalizing from a few misapprehended particulars: 'To have misapprehended the mat- / ter, is to have confessed / that one has not looked far enough'. Or carefully enough. Though the collective value of the old continents is acknowledged: sublimated wisdom; discernment; emotion compressed; self-containment; self-fulfilment even: 'I envy nobody but him and him only, who catches / more fish than / I do' (Walton, *The Compleat Angler*), the danger of generalizing from an already-established knowledge-base remains. Difference established by generalization arising from prior knowledge, such a commonplace of the colonial experience, fails to apprehend crucial distinctions and overlooks the capacity for other knowledge, other excellence.

Locality is the term with which one is left in 'England', and the assertion that excellence has the capacity to present itself in any location. It is not confined by the exigencies of any one geography, nor by the specificity of a particular culture, nor disallowed by the phenomenon of 'newness'. To think that any 'new world' exists as lacking is to assert one's own inattention. One must not imagine that just because one has not found the flower and the fruit they are not there. A different and further knowing is always possible. Moore's dictum, in which of course her own writing is implicated, turns outward to the reader and in the end, throughout *Observations*, it is the reader in whom she most seeks to engender attentiveness and receptiveness, the reader whose eyes she most desires, in her particular way, to open.

BIBLIOGRAPHY

Bloom, Harold (ed.) (1987). *Modern Critical Views: Marianne Moore*. New York: Chelsea House.

Costello, Bonnie (1981). *Marianne Moore: Imaginary Possessions*. Cambridge, MA: Harvard University Press.

Heuving, Jeanne (1992). *Omissions Are Not Accidents: Gender in the Art of Marianne Moore*. Detroit: Wayne State University Press.

Holley, Margaret (1987). *The Poetry of Marianne Moore: A Study in Voice and Value*: Cambridge: Cambridge University Press.

Molesworth, Charles (1990). *Marianne Moore: A Literary Life*. Boston: Northeastern University Press.

Moore, Marianne (1921). *Poems*. London: Egoist Press.

Moore, Marianne (1924, 1925). *Observations*. New York: Dial Press.

Moore, Marianne (1951). *Collected Poems*. New York: Macmillan.

Moore, Marianne (1967, 1990). *Complete Poems*. London: Faber and Faber.

Schultze, Robin G. (1995). *The Web of Friendship: Marianne Moore and Wallace Stevens*. Ann Arbor: Michigan University Press.

Sorrentino, Gilbert (1984). *Something Said*. North Point Press.

34

W. B. Yeats: *The Tower*

Terence Brown

When W. B. Yeats's *The Tower* (a collection of twenty-one poems, including some of his greatest achievements as a poet) was published in London on 14 February 1928 he was a renowned literary figure and public man. His distinction as poet and man of letters, who had contributed by his cultural work to the independence movement in his native Ireland, had received the ultimate accolade in the award of the Nobel Prize for literature in December 1923. His life-long engagement in Irish cultural politics had also brought him to the significant office of Senator in the upper house of a new Dublin parliament, founded in 1922 after a bitter guerrilla war between a volunteer Irish Republican Army and the forces of the British Crown. He was in his sixty-third year when *The Tower* appeared, the husband of a much younger woman whom he had married in 1917. Georgie Hyde-Lees had borne him a daughter and a son and given him a family life in a splendid town-house on a noble square in the Irish capital, after many years of difficult bachelorhood in which unrequited love for a beauty of the age had involved much frustration and great despair. He was at a time of life at which many men might have been content to rest on their laurels, happy to bask in the kind of critical regard the symbolist love lyrics of his youth and young manhood (such poems as 'The Sorrow of Love', 'He Wishes for the Cloths of Heaven', 'The White Birds') had won for him in the English-speaking world. That *The Tower* was the volume which secured Yeats's reputation as a major poet who addressed in boldly dramatic terms some of the central experiences of the twentieth century, is a testament to the way its author had been strenuously remaking himself as man and writer since at least the date of his marriage.

Two reviews give a clear indication of the transformation which was perceived to have taken place in Yeats's poetic in the decade since his marriage.

In April 1919 in *The Athenaeum* the influential English critic Middleton Murry had reviewed an earlier collection of Yeats poems – *The Wild Swans at Coole* (an expanded version of a book the poet had first published in Dublin shortly after his marriage). He reached a damning conclusion: 'He is empty, now. He has the apparatus of enchantment, but no potency in his soul'. In September 1928, by contrast, John Gould Fletcher concluded of *The Tower* in T. S. Eliot's *The Criterion*: 'He corresponds, or will correspond, when the true literary history of our epoch is written, to what we moderns mean by a great poet'.

These widely differing estimates of the poetic success of two individual Yeatsian volumes, published within a decade of each other do, significantly, share a preoccupation. Murry's review had reflected tellingly on the poet's use of myth in *The Wild Swans at Coole*. He believed that 'the structural possibilities' of myth in poetry depend on 'intelligibility'. He observed:

> The poet turns to myth as a foundation upon which he can explicate his imagination. He may take his myth from legend or familiar history, or he may create one for himself anew; but the function it fulfils is always the same. It supplies the elements, upon which he can build the structure of his parable, upon which he can make it elaborate enough to convey the multitudinous reactions of his soul to the world.

Yeats, in Murry's view, had failed as a mythologist, for his myths remained the 'phantoms' of an 'individual brain'. He insists: 'the poet himself must move securely among his visions; they must not be less certain and steadfast than men are. To anchor them needs intelligent myth'. In 1928 Fletcher was convinced that it was Yeats's use of myth that indeed accounted for his achievement in *The Tower*. He observed: 'To Mr Yeats, the world of myth and legend and the world of objective fact are extraordinarily close to each other. He sees the whole of outward phenomena and the whole of subjective fantasy as being in some senses like the creations of man'. Where Murry had sensed myth floating free of history and the perceived world of ordinary human experience in the volume of 1919, Fletcher found them knit together in *The Tower*, where a 'subrational love for the undisciplined world of imagination' coexists 'alongside of Greek epic fatalism of contemplation directed to the outer world of fact'.

In the light of Yeats's development as a poet in the 1920s it is now possible to see how Murry's judgement in 1919 was unduly harsh. There were poems in that volume, as there had been in earlier volumes (pre-eminently 'No Second Troy' in *The Green Helmet and Other Poems*, 1910) which might have alerted him to the way in which Yeats could bring myth and actuality into fruitful relationship. Fletcher is right, however, in identifying *The Tower* as the book where that dynamic functions in Yeats's *oeuvre* with the greatest power.

Events both in Yeats's personal life and in the public sphere played their part in making *The Tower* a book in which myth, history and lived experience traffic with one another in a verse of dramatic intensity.

When Yeats married Georgie Hyde-Lees in October 1917 the world was at war. Yeats had spent his days since 1914 in London and Sussex, with occasional visits to the west of Ireland to visit his friend and patron Lady Gregory at Coole Park in County Galway. As an Irish nationalist he had felt in the war years somewhat remote from the concerns of the English men and women among whom he lived. He had only been profoundly moved by a public event when acquaintances in Dublin had seized a chance in war-time to rise in rebellion against British rule in Ireland in April 1916. The execution of the ring-leaders had drawn from him the pained, doubting but ultimately nobly commemorative poem 'Easter 1916' (which was not made fully public until October, 1920). He had felt then that he might forsake London for Dublin as his main place of residence, the better to be able to rebuild that unity of national purpose that his cultural activism had for so long sponsored and which political violence and oppression had cast terribly in doubt. Instead of a Dublin house or apartment, however, Yeats in March 1917 chose to purchase a semi-ruined Norman keep at Ballylee in County Galway (near Lady Gregory's house and estate) which he hoped to make habitable again. It is this tower in its symbolic aspects which is the setting for a number of the poems in the 1928 volume, including the title poem itself.

The dwelling that Yeats had purchased and to which he introduced his new bride in the summer of 1918 possessed undoubted symbolic attributes. As a military redoubt in the countryside erected by the Norman conquerors of Gaelic Ireland it bespoke a history of warfare and conquest. It was a visible sign in the landscape of the power England had exercised over the island of Ireland since the middle ages. That Yeats chose to own such an edifice in the years when Ireland sought to overturn that colonial inheritance suggests both his awareness of how violence is a constant in human affairs and the anomalous position he occupied as a Nationalist whose forebears were all Protestants with their roots in England.

The Anglo-Irish war was fought with intensifying viciousness (the British government augmented the Irish police in the countryside with undisciplined recruits from Britain who committed gross atrocities, some indeed in Gort close to Lady Gregory's Coole estate) on both sides between January 1919 and the summer of 1921. Following a truce an agreement was negotiated which gave partial independence to twenty-six counties of southern Ireland and established the parliament in which Yeats served as Senator until September 1928. In the early summer of 1922 a faction of those who had fought for Irish freedom in the Anglo-Irish war rose in arms to attack the new administration. They believed the republic declared by the rebels of 1916 with its putative all-Ireland jurisdiction had been betrayed by a settlement which still required Irish parliamentarians to swear an oath of allegiance to the English sovereign and acquiesced to partition.

Hostilities ended by spring 1923 with the government victorious. Casualties were not numerous (about a thousand died in all), but the war fought between former comrades planted bitter seeds of enmity in the Irish body politic. The government had responded to guerrilla tactics with summary executions of prisoners. Seventy-seven men faced firing squads, their death warrants signed by the young minister for Home Affairs, Kevin O'Higgins, whom Yeats came to admire and know. O'Higgins met his death at the hands of an avenging assassin in July 1927 as Yeats was finalizing the contents of the book of poems he would publish in 1928.

The poet and his family did not escape the dangers and stresses of these troubled times in Ireland. Georgie and he spent the summer of 1922 at work on the renovation of the tower which Yeats always referred to as Thor Ballylee. In August, anti-government forces blew up the bridge over their stream, isolating them from the world for a time. In December of the same year, when Yeats had accepted his sena-torship, bullets were fired into his Dublin residence and an armed guard was placed at his door to deter assassins and bombers. Such intimacy with peril may account for the way in *The Tower* the poems which deal directly with the years of struggle and violence in Ireland express real fear and are alertly horrified by the local immediacies of history in the making, in a way Yeats's poetry had never quite been before.

> Now days are dragon-ridden, the nightmare
> Rides upon sleep: a drunken soldiery
> Can leave the mother, murdered at her door,
> To crawl in her own blood, and go scot free;
> The night can sweat with terror as before
> We pieced our thoughts into philosophy
> And planned to bring the world under a rule,
> Who are but weasels fighting in a hole.
> ('Nineteen Hundred and Nineteen')

The Anglo-Irish war and the civil war were indisputably fought in the name of ideologies and specific Irish aims. They could be seen, however, as Irish mani-festations of a more general disorder in Europe and the world which had followed the mass slaughter of the Great War. Revolutions in Russia and Germany, imperial disintegration in Central and Eastern Europe, were changing the map of the globe in the years in which Ireland wrestled with its own fraught destiny. So Yeats's poem 'Nineteen Hundred and Nineteen', with its precise references to the atrocity which took place in Gort nearby Coole and Ballylee, engages broad historical perspectives and rises to magisterial generality of utterance before the spectacle of epochal change:

> Man is in love and loves what vanishes,
> What more is there to say?

Yeats's consciousness that he was living through a period of profound universal change (a note of general crisis as well as particular horror resounds in *The Tower*), as well as a crucial phase of Irish history, was given strange authority in the years in which these events, to which *The Tower* in part responds, took place. For since October 1917, in an extended experiment in spiritualist communication which bore fruit at the end of 1925 in the publication of the first version of *A Vision*, Yeats had, with the help of his spouse, been assembling a myth of human personality and of history which could account for the turbulence of contemporary events in which Ireland was caught up. In all of this, Yeats's wife George (as he called her) played a pivotal role. It was her talent for automatic writing (discovered to distract her husband during an unsatisfactory honeymoon) which brought messages, apparently from the spirit world, which Yeats, guided by her communicators, made the basis of the system (an 'intelligent myth' in Middleton Murry's term) of psychology and historicism he made public in *A Vision* in 1925.

The most systematic sections of *A Vision* (an obscure, elaborate book in prose with which Yeats quickly became dissatisfied) are those which categorize types of human personality in terms of a series of complex permutations based on twenty-eight phases of the moon. These phases (which Yeats employed simply as a schema and without astrological import) he called the Great Wheel. In this a principle of opposition was permanently at work, between solar and lunar aspects of the psyche, objective and subjective. History is read more loosely in *A Vision* as a manifestation in time of a similar process of thesis and antithesis, with periods succeeding one another in an endless cycle governed by change from primary (solar) to antithetical (lunar) periods. To express this dynamic visually Yeats employed a symbol of two interpenetrating cones (or 'gyres' as he called them). The moment of fundamental transition in this resolutely historicist vision of things is reckoned to be a kind of annunciation in which forces in opposition to the spirit of the age reveal themselves in all their shocking novelty. A new age coming to birth cannot escape the violence of a terrible parturition, nor the fear of what is to come to term – strange and incomprehensible as it must be to contemporary thought and feeling.

The section of *A Vision* titled 'Dove or Swan' makes clear that Yeats believed that he was living through just such a period of transition. A democratic world that had been in thrall since the scientific revolution of the seventeenth century to primary, reductive and desacralizing accounts of reality – rational and superficially progressive in outlook – was giving way to an antithetical era in which imagination and established authority would once again hold sway in history. It will be, Yeats avers, 'the reversal of what we know'. One of the starkly dramatic of the poems collected in *The Tower* had an earlier printing as an introduction to 'Dove or Swan' in *A Vision*. There simply titled 'Leda' it appears in the 1928 volume as 'Leda and the Swan', to contextualize the contemporary violence and terror that the volume registers elsewhere, in the metaphysical and mythic dimensions of understanding that *A Vision* had explored in detail.

'Leda and the Swan' is a fractured sonnet. Line eleven breaks into two lines at the caesura to suggest poetic form coming under destructive violence, as the poem itself dramatizes a moment of brutal assault and rape. Zeus in Greek myth lusted after the mortal Leda, daughter of the King of Sparta and, taking the form of a swan, raped her. From that intercourse came the twins Castor and Pollux and the Helen whose kidnap provoked the Trojan war: 'The broken wall, the burning roof and tower'. Leda's daughter Clytaemnestra also helped to murder Agamemnon on his return from Troy. An impregnatory moment had, therefore, untold consequences, making Zeus's act a blasphemous version of the Christian Annunciation, when the wingèd Angel Gabriel had appeared to the Virgin Mary to announce the birth of Jesus and to change history.

What makes 'Leda and the Swan' so convincing a dramatization of myth, and what allows it to seem in truth an interpretation of contemporary experience with its own broken walls and burning roofs and towers, its own slaughtered warriors, is the graphic physicality of its imagery and the mood created of appalled fascination before the spectacle of power unleashing terror. What is represented here is no mere stylized revisitation of classical antiquity, but a febrile, near-pornographic representation of lust, repulsion, sado-masochistic acquiescence, power exercised, knowledge desired, of sated indifference. And that is to say that the forces at work in bringing to birth an antithetical age are as remote from the values of Christianity Jesus introduced to the world as they are from the later ameliorist hopes of scientific, progressive rationalism.

Poem Two of 'Nineteen Hundred and Nineteen' (originally titled 'Thoughts Upon the Present State of the World') makes clear how 'Leda and the Swan' is included in *The Tower* as a mythic version of current reality. For there the dragon-ridden days of Anglo-Irish warfare are given symbolic meaning in an image that anticipates Leda's fate later in the volume. A troupe of Chinese dancers is seen unwinding a 'shining, a floating ribbon of cloth':

> It seemed that a dragon of air
> Had fallen among the dancers, had whirled them round
> Or hurried them off on its own furious path;
> So the platonic year
> Whirls out new right and wrong;
> Whirls in the old instead

It is not only historical transition to which Yeats responds in *The Tower*, but personal. Since the end of 1924 Yeats had been suffering recurrent bouts of ill health and as he turned sixty in 1925 he knew old age was definitely at hand ('Among School Children', completed in 1926, had him self-mockingly 'A sixty year old smiling public man'). Accordingly the volume takes fast-encroaching old age as its primary perspective, a point of view identified in the opening poem 'Sailing to Byzantium', with its bitterly regretful acknowledgement that only aesthetic pleasures remain for 'an aged man' zealous of the 'sensual music' enjoyed 'all summer long' by the 'young in one anothers' arms'. The title poem further reckons that abstract philosophy ('Plato and Plotinus for a friend') may be the appropriate accompaniment of an impotent old age in which only recollected, not actual, passion is possible, before the deepening shades close in. And the volume concludes in 'All Souls' Night' with the poet summoning the ghosts of dead friends and associates, as if the aged man who had opened the book is now awaiting translation himself 'To where the damned have howled away their hearts, / And where the blessed dance'.

Some poems in *The Tower* hint that personal and historical crises may have their resolution in eternity (the 'artifice of eternity' as 'Sailing to Byzantium' has it). For Book Four of *A Vision*, 'The Gates of Pluto', had been a Yeatsian Book of the Dead which revealed that the soul after death in a purgatory of its own, dreams back the events of the life it has lived, before returning once again to the cycle of life. Yet even in the holy city of Byzantium, an image of life lived 'out of nature', the poet is driven to sing of process, of the natural order of time's progression: 'What is past, or passing, or to come'. There can be no transcendental escape from the challenges of history and individual life in the body. This is the burden of the first four poems in the book, which constitute a kind of poetic suite at the head of the volume, since they are each dated in an order which suggests an intensifying retrospection which carries the poet from 1927, the year in which O'Higgins was assassinated, back to 1919 (in fact the fourth poem 'Nineteen Hundred and Nineteen' was finished in 1921 and refers to the atrocity which took place at Gort, Country Galway in 1920), when the Anglo-Irish war broke out. In each poem various emotional stances are tested by the poet as possible bulwarks against the personal and public horrors they also invoke and each is found wanting. In 'The Tower', for example, philosophy cannot assuage the suffering occasioned by passionate memory of erotic entanglements recalled from the frustration of old age. The poet is driven back in the isolation of his tower on racial pride, denunciatory rage, faith in creativity. The tone is of mingled heroism and desperation.

'Meditations in Time of Civil War' sets in question the very art of poetry at a time when the turning gyres have unleashed the fury of fratricidal violence in the countryside. In 'Ancestral Houses', the first poem of the sequence, poetry's intimacy with the free graciousness of aristocracy is read as a complicity with foundational Anglo-Irish violence (though the poem was begun as an evocation of an English country house the ambiguous 'planted' in the first line involves Irish implications of Protestant conquest and plantation). Poem two ponders the poet's role as Platonic mage, whose work might serve as moral beacon in a benighted community. But the military associations of a Norman castle in the Irish landscape overwhelm such naive hopes. All the poet can aspire to is a familial legacy in offering to his descendants 'befitting emblems of adversity'. Poem three broods on a Keatsian dialectic whereby pain is necessary to a spiritually elevated art which can moralize the social order. This dream of humanized aestheticism is definitively interrupted by the scream of Juno's peacock. Poems four and five dramatize the poet in the troubled times as anxious founder of a dynasty which may fall into desuetude, or as non-combant envying activists who can sink their doubts in action. Poem six offers the poet as shaman, who can invoke the beneficent powers of nature to overcome the evil of warfare:

> We had fed the heart on fantasies,
> The heart's grown brutal from the fare,
> More substance in our enmities
> Than in our love; oh, honey-bees
> Come build in the empty house of the stare.

Yet even these mesmeric lines are inadequate as response to civil war; for poem seven unfolds a vision of terror and awesome sublimity that throws the poet, at the last, back on the private resources of occult knowledge if he is to survive the knowledge the vision imparts of age succeeding age in an orgy of levelling violence:

> Nothing but grip of claw, and the eye's complacency,
> The innumerable clanging wings that have put out the moon.

'Nineteen Hundred and Nineteen' concludes this suite of poems in the volume. Local horror is set on a stage of general European crisis in which the long peace of nineteenth-century imperial hegemony gives way to feral, predatory conflict: 'The weasel's twist, the weasel's tooth'. The final poem of this sequence poem, like 'Meditations', consorts with nightmare. Demonic possession through sexual coupling is the foul version of annunciation (it is a grotesque anticipation of 'Leda and the Swan' later in the volume) this poem admits to the book, in lines that recoil from as they also relish the horror they invoke. Poetry can do little (the poem as a whole is a threnody for the aesthetic in a time of war) when the fiend is loose in the land.

It is not that *The Tower* lacks poetic ambition. Its dominant tones are authoritative, its voice assumes poetic powers, rhetorical capacities of a high order. It moves easily between symbolic and real orders of being, between image and lived experience, myth and moment, in a manner which suggests a poet conscious that he is writing at the height of his powers. He unembarrassedly names precursors – Homer, Chaucer – as if to serve notice that he knows his book, with its grandeur of manner, does not lack the kinds of theme great art must engage. Shakespeare, Wordsworth, Coleridge, Keats, the Irish folk poet Raftery are also present in allusion and reference. Yet a major impression of the book, for all its resonance of statement, is of a poet haunted by fear of failing physical energies and horrified at the incapacity of poetry to achieve anything momentous in an age of social disintegration. The sequence poem, accordingly (as in 'The Tower', 'Meditations in Time of Civil War' and 'Nineteen Hundred and Nineteen'), with its various parts contributing as fragments to a possible rather an actual finality of statement, seems the appropriate poetic kind for a poet so aware of dissolution and disintegration at a transitional time in public as in his personal history.

Which is to say that *The Tower* is a work of modernist anxiety, for all the high romanticism of some of its indulgence of the figure of the poet in his solitary elevation in his tower. Tradition lives in echoes and allusion, in tones of presumed poetic authority, but everywhere is assaulted, humiliated by 'the multitude' and 'the barbarous clangour of [a] gong' (the 'a' was added in later printings).

Yet an alternative to the poet's primary tone of heroic utterance *in extremis* does find expression in *The Tower*. For this is a book which admits to its male arena of dramatic introspection ('that is no country for old men' it bitterly opens; in 'The Tower' the poet leaves 'both faith and pride / To young upstanding men') the accents of a feminine wisdom of the body. The lyrical sequence 'A Man Young and Old' tells its tale of sexual frustration, release and ultimate resignation to his erotic fate in the jaunty metrics of traditional balladry, with its savage directness of statement. Yet this elliptical narrative of sexual suffering also includes genial communion between the sexes in bawdy recollection, while the ballad form gives a sense of timelessness to its observations in a volume which is so obsessed with dates and epochs. In sexuality and now in conversation with old women the weight of history can be laid aside:

> I have old women's secrets now
> That had those of the young;
> Madge tells me what I dared not think
> When my blood was strong,
> And what had drowned a lover once
> Sounds like an old song.
> ....
> Stories of the bed of straw
> Or of the bed of down.

Female visionary power is also celebrated in this volume as a counterweight to the male poet's haunted consciousness of apocalypse and nightmare. For in 1928 Yeats included in *The Tower* a narrative poem in Browningesque mode (it was excluded by the poet from the volume in collected editions of his work; Albright has restored it in his *W. B. Yeats: The Poems*), in which an elderly Arab philosopher named Kusta Ben Luka writes to a friend about the young bride he has been gifted by the great prince Harun Al-Rashid. A piece of obvious costume drama, this poem allowed Yeats to dramatize how his wife's automatic writing lay behind the mythology which gives to *The Tower* its charged atmosphere of revelatory occasions. Ben Luka's young bride speaks in her sleep and her husband questions: 'was it she that spoke or some great Djinn?' For a time she seemed 'the learned man' and he 'the child'. The 'Truths without father' the young woman speaks, as if from a source beyond male tradition, do, however, in their 'implacable straight lines', remind of the geometric symbols Yeats had elaborated so painstakingly in *A Vision*. 'The Gift of Harun Al-Rashid' suggests what their true import might be:

> All, all those gyres and cubes and midnight things
>
> Are but the expression of her body
> Drunk with the bitter sweetness of her youth.
> And now my utmost mystery is out.
> A woman's beauty is a storm-tossed banner;
> Under it wisdom stands

In *A Vision* Yeats had cryptically confessed that in its pages he had not 'dealt with the whole' of his subject, 'perhaps not even with what is most important, writing nothing about the Beatific Vision, little of sexual love'. The publication in 1992 (as the *Vision Notebooks*) of much of the automatic writing and of the sleep and dream record which served as the basis of *A Vision*, has now revealed how Ben Luka's 'utmost mystery' was Yeats's own. For many phases of the curious transaction the poet and his wife enacted with one another in the years of George's mediumship were marked by intense explorations of erotic destiny and of their shared sexual life. Consequently critics, among them Daniel Albright, have been able to read *A Vision* as a kind of Cubist experiment in which the body and its life in the world and in history is represented in the stark abstractions of geometry. 'The Gift of Harun Al-Rashid' hints at a similar relationship between the body and the gyres, cubes and midnight things which derive from female 'wisdom', from the revelations of a spiritualist wife. To exploit an intelligent mythology, as *The Tower* does, is not therefore to transpose history or personal experience into some abstract zone of pure forms, but to seek to comprehend reality in terms of a system that has female, bodily origins.

This might then be taken as relating to the central theme of 'Among School Children', one of Yeats's greatest poems, which he also included in *The Tower*. In this poem the poet dramatizes himself as an elderly public man, inspecting a school as part of his public, senatorial duties. The presence of the schoolchildren provokes in him a brooding reverie on his own youth and on the youth and childhood of a beloved beautiful woman, who like himself has suffered the depredations of old age. The poem is a work of fluid recall as memory ranges back through time, juxtaposing past and present, as if the mind could transcend time itself. Yet it is also a poem of palpable physicality – of fingers, eyes, cheeks, hair, a mother's lap, even 'the bottom of a king of kings' – as if to remind that the mind cannot escape its entrapment in mutable flesh. Philosophy with its vision of transcendence of the material world cannot offer comfort in face of such bleak knowledge, nor can certain kinds of religiously inspired art forms 'that all heavenly glory symbolize'. Only an art centred in the truths of earthly, bodily existence can offer any credible alternative to the vision of personal and historical disintegration that *The Tower* so powerfully unfolds:

> Labour is blossoming or dancing where
> The body is not bruised to pleasure soul,
> Nor beauty born out of its own despair;
> Nor blear-eyed wisdom out of midnight oil.
> O chestnut tree, great rooted blossomer,
> Are you the leaf, the blossom or the bole?
> O body swayed to music, O brightening glance,
> How can we know the dancer from the dance?

BIBLIOGRAPHY

Adams, Hazard (1995). *The Book of Yeats's Vision: Romantic Modernism and Antithetical Tradition*, Ann Arbor, MI: University of Michigan Press.

Albright, Daniel (1997). *Quantum Poetics: Yeats, Pound and the Science of Modernism*, Cambridge: Cambridge University Press.

Archibald, Douglas (1986). *Yeats*, New York: Syracuse University Press.

Bloom, Harold (1970). *Yeats*, New York: Oxford University Press.

Cullingford, Elizabeth (1993). *Gender and History in Yeats's Love Poetry*, Cambridge: Cambridge University Press.

Cullingford, Elizabeth (1981). *Yeats, Ireland and Fascism,* London and Basingstoke: Macmillan.

Donoghue, Denis (1971). *William Butler Yeats,* New York: Viking Press; Glasgow: Fontana.

Ellmann, Richard (1964). *The Identity of Yeats,* London: Faber and Faber.

Ellmann, Richard (1987). *Yeats: The Man and the Masks,* London: Penguin.

Emig, Rainer (1995). *Modernism in Poetry: Motivations, Structures, and Limits.* London and New York: Longman.

Henn, T. R. (1965). *The Lonely Tower,* revd edn. London: Methuen.

Hough, Graham (1984). *The Mystery Religion of W. B. Yeats,* Sussex: Harvester Press; New Jersey: Barnes and Noble.

Howes, Marjorie (1996). *Yeats's Nations,* Cambridge: Cambridge University Press.

Jeffares, A. N. (ed.) (1977). *W. B. Yeats: The Critical Heritage,* London, Henley and Boston: Routledge and Kegan Paul.

Jeffares, A. N. (1988). *W. B. Yeats: A New Biography,* London: Hutchinson.

Kermode, Frank (1957). *Romantic Image,* London: Routledge and Kegan Paul.

Larrissey, Edward (1994). *Yeats the Poet: The Measures of Difference,* London and New York: Harvester/Wheatsheaf.

MacNeice, Louis (1967). *The Poetry of W. B. Yeats,* London: Faber and Faber.

Smith, Stan (1994). *The Origins of Modernism: Eliot, Pound, Yeats and the Rhetoric of Renewal,* New York and London: Harvester/Wheatsheaf.

Stock, A. G. (1961). *W. B. Yeats: His Poetry and Thought,* Cambridge: Cambridge University Press.

Torchiana, Donald (1966). *W. B. Yeats and Georgian Ireland,* Evanston, IL: Northwestern University Press; London: Oxford University Press.

Tratner, Michael (1995). *Modernism and Mass Politics; Joyce, Woolf, Eliot, and Yeats,* Stanford, CA: Stanford University Press.

35

W. H. Auden: *Poems*

Peter McDonald

The book which appeared under the plain title *Poems* from Faber and Faber in September, 1930, was not only W. H. Auden's first commercially published volume, but also the most significant collection, in terms of its immediate and its longer-term impact, of his entire career as a poet. This is not to propose a reading of that career as an abnormally drawn-out decline; quite apart from any of the later critical arguments on whether Auden got better or worse as a writer in the course of his life, the impact of *Poems* was such that no poet might wish for — even if he were to be capable of — more than one such success. It was *Poems* which established, with remarkable completeness, a whole style of writing that was recognizable as 'Audenesque', and that spread like a contagion through both the poetry and the prose of a generation in the literary Britain of the 1930s. It crept unhelpfully into some of the poetry of its own author at times in the 1930s, and he subsequently tried, through retrospective revision and deletion, to curtail the worst of its effects; this was a style which it became Auden's own creative task, and artistic challenge, to outgrow in the years and decades that followed. However, the artistic integrity and success of *Poems* itself should not be confused with the subsequent coarsenings of stylistic affectation: although the older Auden was notably severe in his dealings with his work from later in the 1930s, he retained much of *Poems* in subsequent collected editions. For generations after Auden's, too, *Poems* has remained a potent example of immediate and transforming poetic impact, to which many would-be successors have aspired but which none, in the event, has managed to equal.

The stylistic originality of *Poems* is, like any kind of artistic breakthrough, not without either its influences or parallels: at this stage of his career, Auden had already learned much by absorbing poets like Edward Thomas, Thomas Hardy and Gerard Manley Hopkins in his schoolboy and university writing; T. S. Eliot's work, and that of Laura Riding, are parts of the stylistic mix, which includes also elements of popular culture — the spy-story, the cinema, the language of headline-writers or the telegram office. But to list the ingredients is not to

describe the dish. One of the thirty poems making up the book's second part
begins like this:

> From the very first coming down
> Into a new valley with a frown
> Because of the sun and a lost way,
> You certainly remain: to-day
> I, crouching behind a sheep-pen, heard
> Travel across a sudden bird,
> Cry out against the storm, and found
> The year's arc a completed round
> And love's worn circuit re-begun,
> Endless with no dissenting turn.

The landscape which this poem inhabits is something established before the syntactic contours of what is being said are allowed to become clear: it takes three lines for
'You' to emerge as the poem's addressee, and even then it is not clear whether 'You'
or 'I' is the person who has come down into the valley. This valley is 'new', but its
strangeness inheres largely in the slight strangeness of the language through which
the poem occupies it: 'certainly', for instance, is more than a casual intensifier, and
hints at some degree of certainty involved in the act of remaining; 'sudden' becomes
an adjective for the bird rather than a 'suddenly' which would more conventionally
be the adverb attached to the narrator's act of hearing; 'Travel' (not 'Travelling') stiff-
ens the syntax into a slightly clipped formality, then makes this altogether more rigid
by starting the next line with 'Cry out' (the bird again, with a word like 'then' suppressed), but immediately after this 'and found', where the verb now is in the first
person (it is 'I', and not now the bird, doing the finding). The landscape's simplicity
and definiteness – a valley, the sun, a sheep-pen, a bird – are countered by the ensuing
metaphors: expressions like 'The year's arc' and 'love's worn circuit' are as bare in their
outlines as anything that comes before, but this seems to make more apparent their
air of abstraction. It is easy to read 'The year's arc' as a conventional expression of the
passing of a year, but the development of this into the image of 'love's worn circuit',
something now 're-begun / Endless with no dissenting turn' appears to take for
granted comprehension which the reader will not, in fact, possess. A 'circuit' is not,
or not necessarily, and not quite, the same thing as an arc, and a 'worn circuit' begins
to sound more like a piece of equipment than an image of the seasons; 'dissenting',
also, seems less to denote a pattern of motion than a tendency to disagreement: what,
and how, is a reader to understand by such unforthcoming, and yet self-confident
strangenesses in expression?

Uncertainties like these are not obstacles to the poem's progression, but rather its
means. Like many other poems in the volume, this one makes uncertainty, unease and
puzzlement the elements of a situation in which the poetry's meaning is carried in
syntax that is itself both compressed and baffled. 'I' can speak to 'You', but the lines

of that communication generally seem unclear to a reader who, as it were, eavesdrops on the exchange:

> But now
> To interrupt the homely brow,
> Thought warmed to evening through and through
> Your letter comes, speaking as you,
> Speaking of much but not to come.

The difficulties of interpretation are manifold, and build on the poem's initial oddness of expression without the least sign of self-consciousness. Auden generates, and maintains, a state of protracted and unresolved ambiguity by such methods, and the poetry's stylistic distinctiveness is its capacity to raise questions of interpretation relentlessly, without pausing to relish or explain them, and without allowing the poem's situation to either wallow in a mire of obscurity or fall into the bathos of over-obvious solutions. By this stage in the poem, in fact, the reader is aware that 'I' and 'You' are apart, are in written communication, and are not perhaps likely to be reunited; beyond that, reading is done mainly *between* the lines. Yet Auden's concluding lines take this situation somewhere else again:

> Nor speech is close nor fingers numb,
> If love not seldom has received
> An unjust answer, was deceived.
> I, decent with the seasons, move
> Different or with a different love,
> Nor question overmuch the nod,
> The stone smile of this country god
> That never was more reticent,
> Always afraid to say more than it meant.

By now, the syntax is capable of moving entirely beyond anything speakable or writable in even the oddest contexts: 'If love not seldom has received / An unjust answer' reads like a literal translation from some heavily inflected foreign language, while 'decent with the seasons' seems to speak Latin as much as English ('decent' as fitting, or in keeping with something, rather than a generalized agreeableness). If the poem has been about the parting of ways between lovers, then the awkwardness of the situation has been transfused into its expression. The complicitous 'nod' of that garden-ornament deity becomes an image for the ease of exclusion which private communication must preserve: intimacies do not translate to public clarity, but just as they cut off the public realm from their shared meanings, they can also be themselves cut off just as abruptly: one party can suddenly be on the receiving end of a reticence that will not give ground.

Evidently, the poem's conclusion gives an account of its own workings, for questions of reticence, of how much, and how, things said are 'meant', are to the fore in this poem, as they are in *Poems* as a whole. There is a strapped formality about the writing, and an insistence about the rhymes, which presents itself as a form of reticence, and does not loosen its grip for a moment. For a poem which is finally a report from the wrong side of an emotional or communicative exclusion, this is itself a remarkably elliptical and tight-lipped piece of writing. Again, this is a paradox which emerges from many of the volume's individual pieces, where an urgency of communication is time and again at odds with an opacity of intent.

But much of the original impact of *Poems*, and much of the book's continuing interest, lies in the effectiveness of this very sense of opacity. It is important to distinguish Auden's characteristic mode in this writing from other kinds of apparent obscurity – from the slightly mandarin 'difficulty' of Eliot or Pound, for example, or from the elaborations of the hermetic in Yeats and other contemporary writers. In Auden, readers discovered a voice which sent out messages of urgent import: these were clear in their expression, though inscrutable in their intent, yet they established a register in which different kinds of anxiety (the political, the sexual, the psychological) could all seem to find persuasive expression. Auden's lyrics were hard to translate into clear statement; but they spoke to their earliest admirers with the force and the inevitability of a new language.

In poem XI ('Who stands, the crux left of the watershed'), Auden begins by presenting his characteristic Northern landscape complete with all the detritus of 'An industry already comatose': the inhabitants are shown in an heroic light, as figures from legend without names ('two there were / Cleaned out a damaged shaft by hand' . . . one died / During a storm, the fells impassable'). After this grim chronicle, and the impressive sternness of its telling, the poet's voice addresses itself to the reader – someone who is emphatically a 'stranger' to the poem's world. In these lines, the urgency and opacity of Auden's new register work together, creating a kind of poetry in which a verbal world, and the world of its images, collaborate with both the voice's insistence and the reader's desire to understand the message. It reflects, perhaps, an aesthetic of estrangement:

> Go home, now, stranger, proud of your young stock,
> Stranger, turn back again, frustrate and vexed:
> This land, cut off, will not communicate,
> Be no accessory content to one
> Aimless for faces rather there than here.
> Beams from your car may cross a bedroom wall,
> They wake no sleeper; you may hear the wind
> Arriving driven from the ignorant sea
> To hurt itself on pane, on bark of elm
> Where sap unbaffled rises, being spring;
> But seldom this. Near you, taller than grass,
> Ears poise before decision, scenting danger.

'This land, cut off, will not communicate': Auden's line is the opposite of Eliot's ven-triloquised 'You! hypocrite lecteur! – mon semblable, – mon frere!' in *The Waste Land*, turning on the reader as it does with an equanimity of denial, not making a chal-lenge, but delivering information. Even so, this is information with a particular poetic charge, for all its surface flatness. If the poem addresses a 'stranger' (the urban sophis-ticate, perhaps, 'frustrate and vexed' in trying to comprehend a world of heroic isola-tion and courage), it gives him images for his own estrangement, and provides images for the powers with which he remains out of touch: 'the wind / Arriving driven from the ignorant sea', 'bark of elm / Where sap unbaffled rises', the 'Ears' that 'poise before decision, scenting danger'. A great deal depends on what, or how sharply, the reader can *hear*, and the poem's last line presents, without any sign of strain, an image of hearing so acute it can *smell* things. Auden's style does not pause to let the reader decide whether this is a metaphorical 'scenting' or plain synaesthesia, any more than the pace of the lines lets up to explain 'But seldom this'. To ask 'seldom what?' is to fail to keep up with the alternative speed and order of perceptions which the poem sends its 'stranger' away from: 'this' is the 'poise', not only of the scenting ears, but of the poetry's entire pitch of acute perception and attentiveness, 'On the wet road between the chafing grass'.

It is not without importance that the stranger/reader is told to 'Go home'. One of the most pervasive and unnerving elements in the thematic content of *Poems* is the focus on what 'home' might be, as a site on which are concentrated intense (and sometimes malign) energies of love, anger, fear and possessiveness. As against a conventional understanding of 'home' as the scene of belonging and security, and as a place in which emotions may be experienced or celebrated in a comparatively unquestioned way, the 'home' of *Poems* is an arena of psychological, and perhaps literal carnage.

The first part of *Poems* is taken up entirely by 'Paid on Both Sides: A Charade', a strange, quasi-surrealistic verse play in which the landscape of the shorter poems is inhabited by characters from two families locked in generations of violence and attrition. The Nowers of Lintzgarth, and the Shaws of Nattrass, like some bizarrely transplanted Montagues and Capulets, are the parties to an immemorial feud, which the Charade arms with modern weaponry, but which is played out in the stark, uncommunicative world of Auden's Northern landscapes, permanently 'cut off' from the layers of civilization which might obscure the contours of atavistic hatred and violence. John Nower, whose father is murdered at the beginning, grows into his inheritance, under the tuition of his unforgiving mother, and avenges his father's death by killing a Shaw; his eventual realization of the futility of the age-old quarrel, and his attempts to end it through marriage with Anne Shaw, are ulti-mately in vain, for he is assassinated at his wedding-party by another son of the Shaw family, himself spurred on by his own mother. At the close, it is clear that the feud will continue.

Reduced to the outline of its plot, then, 'Paid on Both Sides' seems grim enough; in fact, Auden brings to this scenario elements of broad humour and farce, along with an insistence on psychological investigation and exposure, which make the charade into a kind of intensified exposition of the symbolic world of *Poems* as a whole. The story itself veers between the tight-lipped, matter-of-fact presentation of violence of the Icelandic Sagas or Anglo-Saxon poetry, to the hectic action of a gangster movie; in addition, the meaning of the events is investigated both by the high seriousness of the choric verse, and the high unseriousness of Father Christmas, who arrives as a psychological master of ceremonies half-way through, to conduct a mock-trial. The effort which all this seeks to articulate (or at least, to present) is that of the break with the past, the leaving of 'home'. It is an effort which, like so much else in the book, is doomed to be 'frustrate and vexed', but the poetry's task is in part to help imagine the condition of newness or freedom which might be implicit in the dangers and uncertainties of a situation which is now subject to an unnerving acuteness of observation. This seems, at any rate, to be the function of some of the choric writing, and the act of imagination in such passages provides an initiation into the kinds of reading which the shorter lyrics in *Poems* will require:

> But there are still to tempt; areas not seen
> Because of blizzards or an erring sign
> Whose guessed at wonders would be worth alleging,
> And lies about the cost of a night's lodging.
> Travellers may sleep at inns but not attach,
> They sleep one night together, not asked to touch;
> Receive no normal welcome, not the pressed lip,
> Children to lift, nor the assuaging lap.
> Crossing the pass descend the growing stream
> Too tired to hear except the pulses' strum,
> Reach villages to ask for a bed in
> Rock shutting out the sky, the old life done.

The plot of 'Paid on Both Sides' suggests that an abandonment of the old life is doomed to be, from one point of view, an escapist fantasy; from another perspective, however, this determination 'To throw away the key and walk away' is something which the poetry's acts of imagination can themselves figure, and which an aesthetic of estrangement can enact. The half-rhymes of the lines above (indebted, not by accident, to Wilfred Owen's example in poems like 'Strange Meeting') establish the cautious contact, implicitly sexual contact, which leads away from 'the old life': 'attach', 'touch', 'lip', 'lap'.

However, the conditions for the imagining of intimacy are not those which the dramatic world of the charade will long permit, and it is the mothers, above all, who in this play make sure that their sons will die rather than be party to a communicative erosion of 'the old life'. The final chorus takes on the tones of Greek tragedy in its summary:

> Though he believe it, no man is strong.
> He thinks to be called the fortunate,
> To bring home a wife, to live long.
>
> But he is defeated; let the son
> Sell the farm lest the mountain fall;
> His mother and her mother won.
>
> His fields are used up where the moles visit,
> The contours worn flat; if there show
> Passage for water he will miss it:
>
> Give up his breath, his woman, his team;
> No life to touch, though later there be
> Big fruit, eagles above the stream.

The victory of the mothers is acknowledged in this compelling hymn of defeat; but the means of its imaginative subversion are here too, in the poetry's mole-like undermining of the certain signs of home. The hope of 'touch', and in what will come 'later', provides the poetry with its horizon of expectation.

It is this which helps to establish the feeling of urgency in the style of *Poems*, and which certainly enabled early readers to interpret Auden's tone as in some sense a prophetic one. In the final section of poem XVI ('It was Easter as I walked in the public gardens') this air of diagnostic observation seems to mark for destruction the larger bourgeois society which grows out of the tensions and repressions of the kind of 'home' from which so much of the poetry is determined to walk away. To read such lines with a political slant was not difficult, and it remains tempting:

> It is time for the destruction of error.
> The chairs are being brought in from the garden,
> The summer talk stopped on that savage coast
> Before the storms, after the guests and birds:
> In sanatoriums they laugh less and less,
> Less certain of cure; and the loud madman
> Sinks now into a more terrible calm.

The note of clinical authority suggests that some clear social analysis is about to form; many early readers were to find such an analysis in communism, and it is possible that Auden himself, for a very brief period in the later 1930s, entertained this as a clue to his own interpretative puzzles. But such solutions were not solutions for long, and in fact they oversimplify the complexity of the different problems and competing analyses which go into *Poems*. More productive than an explicitly political line of interpretation, and closer indeed to the kinds of interest which Auden himself cultivated while the poems were being written, is the concern with the meanings, for both the individual and society, of psychological analysis. The poems return again and again to problems of strength and weakness, independence and attachment and, above all perhaps, sexual repression and desire.

In poem III ('Since you are going to begin to-day') a voice which may be that of Nature speaks of a grimly deterministic state of things; anxiety in the face of crisis or disaster is here not unique to the individual who experiences it ('Nor even is despair your own, when swiftly / Comes general assault on your ideas of safety'):

> Your shutting up the house and taking prow
> To go into the wilderness to pray,
> Means that I wish to leave and to pass on,
> Select another form, perhaps your son;
> Though he reject you, join opposing team
> Be late or early at another time,
> My treatment will not differ – he will be tipped,
> Found weeping, signed for, made to answer, topped.

The cycle which this poem proposes is similar to that explored dramatically in 'Paid on Both Sides', and its victim is depicted as a brilliant son, stricken with incommunicable sorrow or guilt, and subjected to an obscure, and probably sexual, sense of shame. It is important to the effect that the final violent end ('topped', to mean hanged) is reported so briskly and coldly, since the chill here is that of a whole analysis of a sick society:

> Do not imagine you can abdicate;
> Before you reach the frontier you are caught;
> Others have tried it and will try again
> To finish that which they did not begin:
> Their fate must always be the same as yours,
> To suffer the loss they were afraid of, yes,
> Holders of one position, wrong for years.

This 'frontier' (which occurs often in Auden's poetry of the period) is primarily a frontier in the mind, although the poems give it some sharply realized physical locations; crossing is possible only at cost, a cost for which death is, at least sometimes, Auden's metaphor ('death, death of the grain, our death, / Death of the old gang'). This identification of what has been 'wrong for years' is, however, less a call to revolutionary violence than it is the experiencing of a thrill: the need for 'destruction of error' carries, in this poetry, the charged excitement of being in on a scandalous secret.

The extent to which *Poems* relies on secrets of various kinds is an essential element in the poetic style which the book so successfully establishes. Auden's writing is full of private references and intimate jokes, but these are made parts of poems that are finally impersonal in their effects, where the reader's role as interpreter is partly that of collaborator in an undercover investigation of the psyche, and the society, in a distorted, and possibly a doomed, world. At one extreme, this issues in the cod-

Tennyson sound of 'Get there if you can . . .' (Poem XXII), with its exhortations to 'Drop those priggish ways for ever, stop behaving like a stone: / Throw the bath-chairs right away, and learn to leave ourselves alone', and its conclusion that 'If we really want to live, we'd better start at once to try; / If we don't, it doesn't matter, but we'd better start to die'. At another extreme of *Poems*, the need to leave behind the old life is imagined in terms of an acceptance of estrangement and alienation, a process which is inseparable from the new and estranging sounds made in the verse itself. In one of the seven poems added by Auden for the second edition in 1933 (where seven poems from the first edition were withdrawn), 'Doom is dark and deeper than any sea-dingle', the voice inhabits beautifully the register of Anglo-Saxon elegiac verse, to see its hero as 'A stranger to strangers over undried sea' who, though he 'dreams of home', must go on to encounter 'Bird-flocks nameless to him, through doorway voices / Of new men making another love'. The prayer with which this poem ends, to 'Protect his house / . . . From gradual ruin spreading like a stain', and its final image of a man 'Lucky with day approaching, with leaning dawn', might also, perhaps, serve to describe the secret hope with which *Poems* counterbalances its secret fears.

The adventurousness and originality of *Poems* are bound up with the book's stylistic capacities; Auden's distinctiveness was established immediately by the book, and it remained for many readers one of his most important achievements. While Auden himself developed in some respects away from the voice of *Poems*, that voice became for a generation in the 1930s the sound of an inevitable poetic authority. Subsequently, and perhaps just as remarkably, the voice of this poetry has retained its power to dazzle and convince.

BIBLIOGRAPHY

Auden, W. H. (1977). *The English Auden: Poems, Essays and Dramatic Writings 1927–1939*, ed. E. Mendelson. London: Faber and Faber.

Auden, W. H. (1994). *Juvenilia: Poems 1922–28*, ed. K. Bucknell. London: Faber and Faber.

Callan, E. (1983). *Auden: A Carnival of Intellect*. New York: Oxford University Press.

Carpenter, H. (1981). *W. H. Auden: A Biography*. London: Allen and Unwin.

Davenport-Hines, R. (1995). *Auden*. London: Heinemann.

Emig, R. (1999). *W. H. Auden: Towards a Postmodern Poetics*. Basingstoke: Macmillan.

Fuller, J. (1998). *W. H. Auden: A Commentary*. London: Faber and Faber.

Hecht, A. (1993). *The Hidden Law: The Poetry of W. H. Auden*. Cambridge, MA: Harvard University Press.

Mendelson, E. (1981). *Early Auden*. London: Faber and Faber.

O'Neill, M. and Reeves, G. (1992). *Auden, MacNeice, Spender: The Thirties Poetry*. Basingstoke: Macmillan.

Smith, S. (1985). *W. H. Auden*. Oxford: Blackwell Publishers.

36

Elizabeth Bishop: *North & South*
Jonathan Ellis

His beak is focussed; he is preoccupied,

looking for something, something, something.
Poor bird, he is obsessed!
The millions of grains are black, white, tan, and gray,
mixed with quartz grains, rose and amethyst.
('Sandpiper', 1955)

North & South, published in 1946, was Elizabeth Bishop's first collection of poems. It took its thirty-five-year-old author more than a decade to complete and is the product of half a lifetime's travelling, both literally between places and figuratively in her writing. A close friend of Marianne Moore and Robert Lowell, Bishop nonetheless finds a unique poetic voice. Her poems remain difficult to place within the poetic tradition. Truant from any one school or movement, her poetry continually changes as she experiments with different registers, tones and voices. In a sense she runs along one of the faultlines of twentieth-century poetry, between the Modernists (Eliot, Stevens, Moore) on the one hand and the Confessionals (Berryman, Lowell, Sexton) on the other. Her observations are less abstract than the formers', just as her life studies are less direct than the latters'.

The first reviewers of *North & South* were nearly all poets. Each came to Bishop's work with a mixture of envy and excitement. Marianne Moore was Bishop's first and most important critic. The two poets met in 1934, on a bench outside the reading room of the New York Public Library. They went to the circus together and corresponded for over thirty years. Moore, as the older poet, is often seen as Bishop's mentor. In David Kalstone's *Becoming A Poet* she is a 'wise, eccentric aunt' to Bishop's 'wayward niece' (Kalstone, 1989, p. 109). In Victoria Harrison's *Poetics of Intimacy* she is an artistic 'mother' to Bishop's 'terrified child' (Harrison, 1993, p. 50). The problem with these interpretations lies in their emphasis on Moore's seniority and Bishop's immaturity. Moore may have wished to become Bishop's mentor, but she was never allowed to. Bishop was willing to accept occasional editorial assistance from her. She did not need lessons on how to write. Moore admired these assertions of artistic independence, though her reviews of Bishop's poetry betray a degree of censure too. Her praise tends to be qualified by her use of oxymoronic phrases. Bishop is 'archaically new' (Schwartz and Estess, 1983, p. 175). She is a 'modest expert' (ibid., p. 177). Her poetry is 'spectacular in being unspectacular' (ibid.). *North & South* is a 'small-large book of beautifully formulated aesthetic-moral mathematics' (ibid., p. 179). Moore celebrates her friend's work in terms that consistently appear begrudging. She was both jealous and proud of Bishop's achievements.

Randall Jarrell was a more disinterested critic than Moore. He drew attention to Bishop's avoidance of despair, recognizing the importance of observation in her work:

> Instead of crying, with justice, 'This is a world in which no one can get along', Miss Bishop's poems show that it is barely but perfectly possible – has been, that is, for her . . . all her poems have written underneath, *I have seen it.* (Ibid., p. 181)

Robert Lowell took Jarrell's comments a stage further when he noticed the movement within *North & South* between different poetic traditions. His description of the book's 'shifting speech-tones' (ibid., p. 187) was the only review with which Bishop agreed, presumably because he was also the only critic to judge her poetry on its own terms. Lowell compared her scrutiny of the world to Kafka's, praising her 'humorous, commanding genius for picking up the unnoticed' (ibid., p. 206). He underlines the jittery nature of Bishop's voice, showing how she switches perspective between 'sorrowing amusement' and 'grave tenderness' (ibid.). In doing so, he often invokes the language of travel central to an understanding of all Bishop's work. For Lowell:

> There are two opposing factors. The first is something in motion, weary but always persisting, almost always failing and on the point of disintegrating, and yet, for the most part, stoically maintained. This is morality, memory. . . . The second factor is a terminus: rest, sleep, fulfilment or death. (Ibid., pp. 186–7)

In Bishop's opinion, there were only 'two kinds of poetry, that . . . at *rest*, and that which is in action, within itself' (Bishop, 1996a, p. 11). She associated a poetry of action with writers like Donne, Herbert and Hopkins, celebrating their ability 'to portray, not a thought, but a mind thinking' (ibid., p. 12). Bishop clearly wanted to follow in this tradition. Her poetry is more in motion than at rest, as Lowell perceived. It rarely arrives at an emotional conclusion or intellectual 'terminus'.

Bishop had few theories about poetry and discouraged others from adopting them. The closest she came to defining her aesthetic was in a notebook entry from the mid-1930s. In it, she carefully explores the relationship between imagination and reality:

> If I stretch my thought to Egypt, to Africa, downtown, it is in my thought that I see them and they are not, at the time, reality for me. If I go to these places, it is a different matter. Reality, then is something like a huge circus tent, folding, adjustable, which

we carry around with us and set up wherever we are. It possesses the magical property of being able to take on characteristics of whatever place we are in, in fact it can become identical with it. (Costello, 1991, p. 129)

For Bishop, reality is always something 'adjustable'. Her poetry shifts in line with the place she is in. She alters perspective, style and tone according to her changing perception of reality. The choice of a 'huge circus tent' to explain her understanding of reality underlines Bishop's sense of humour. She makes fun of the idea that poetry 'can become identical' with the place it describes. As she says in the poem 'Santarém', there is always a gap between the literal 'place' and the poet's 'idea of the place' later (Bishop, 1991, p. 185). Inside the circus tent of her poetry, she has room in which to play.

Bishop's actual movements prior to the publication of *North & South* were similarly changeable. In the spring of 1946 she travelled north along the Atlantic coast from Key West to Nova Scotia. She was literally on the move on the day *North & South* was published, returning south by bus to Boston, the journey which would later become the setting for one of her greatest poems, 'The Moose'. The image of the poet moving between places is an appropriate one. Her journeys north and south show her actually living out the shifting geography of the book's title. Travelling, in all its senses, clearly lies at the heart of Bishop's art and life. The runaway poet, cannily evading neat categorization or capture by the reader, is obviously related to the traveller, running away from her editors and public.

Bishop's life prior to 1946 is full of similar journeys north and south. Born in Worcester, Massachusetts, in 1911, she learnt 'the art of losing' (Bishop, 1991, p. 178) and, related to it, the art of travelling, early in life. She lost her father to Bright's disease when she was eight months old and her mother to schizophrenia shortly after. In 1913 she was taken in by her maternal grandparents in Great Village, Nova Scotia, where her mother also stayed between breakdowns. Her mother was permanently hospitalized when she was only five years old. Bishop lived for a further two years in Great Village before being suddenly taken to live in New England again with her paternal grandparents. She later remembered feeling as if 'she was being kidnapped' (Bishop, 1994, p. 14). Bishop attributed her alcoholism, her asthma and her constant search for home to the displacements and traumas of these first seven years of life. Her mother died in 1934, sixteen years after the poet left Nova Scotia for the States. Even though Bishop visited her maternal grandparents every summer, she never saw her mother again, whether by choice or not is uncertain.

North & South does not reflect any of these events directly, though it is often a witness to their consequences. Its very title speaks of the two directions in which the poet moved as a child, propelled like a pinball between opposing sets of grandparents, north and south of the American–Canadian border. From her paternal relatives in New England Bishop received an education at Vassar College (where she studied music and English), as well as financial independence well into her sixties. But from her maternal relatives in Great Village she received the experiences, tragic and restorative, which are central to an understanding of her poetry. Bishop called Nova Scotia 'the richest, saddest, simplest landscape in the world' (Bishop, 1996a, p. 139). Her childhood there, and later on her poetry, copied its various colours, contours and folds, being rich, sad and simple too.

The importance of biography in *North & South* has been at issue ever since Bishop's reputation began to grow in the mid-1980s. Although she always maintained that autobiography was not something she practised, at least not consciously, the publication of her biography and letters suggested more links between art and life than she herself had acknowledged. Critics had known most of the biographical facts before, but they had taken on trust the poet's insistence that a 'good dictionary' (Gioia, 1986, p. 101) was a more useful guide to her poetry than her life. An awareness of Bishop's life does not discredit her advice, though it does weaken the assumption that she is a totally impersonal poet. Biography is a kind of guest inhabiting many of the poems in the collection. As Sandra Barry argues, 'this time and place and these people were not merely subjects in her poetry and prose, but conditioners of her poetic development and aesthetic sensibilities' (Barry, 1996, p. 193). Thus we can see how her love of poetry came from her grandfather's reading of Burns each night, just as her fascination with travel first grew out of stories of an uncle's shipwreck. 'Casabianca' alludes both to this memory of reciting poetry (in this case, a popular poem by Felicia Hemans), as well as to the story of a relative's loss at sea. 'Seascape' and 'Little Exercise' also bear the imprint of Bishop's use of oral history. Her interest in primitive painting similarly takes the reader back to Nova Scotia, to her Great Uncle Hutchinson. A portrait painter in London and the first illustrator of *Treasure Island*, his is the landscape she remembers fondly in 'Large Bad Picture'. In 'Poem' Bishop called this maternal inheritance her 'earthly trust' (Bishop, 1991, p. 177). She used art to close and reopen it.

The place of this 'earthly trust' within *North & South* is always discreet. Autobiography pressures rather than punctuates the surface of her poetry, which is why she seems intimate without ever being confessional. As David Bromwich states, 'her work is a conversation which never quite takes place but whose possibility always beckons' (Bloom, 1985, p. 160). Bishop's poetic evasiveness is a symptom of, and perhaps a way of dealing with, her life. Certainly, few poets have had quite as many poet fans as Bishop. Anne Sexton read her work for its sanity of tone and beauty of forms. Sylvia Plath admired her 'fine originality' (Plath, 1982, p. 319). She was Robert Lowell's favourite poet. Mark Strand was fascinated by her 'ghoulish humour' (Schwartz and Estess, 1983, p. 210). Octavio Paz drew attention to her 'enormous power of reticence' (ibid., p. 213). Adrienne Rich learnt to 'connect the themes of outsiderhood and marginality in her work . . . with a lesbian identity' (Rich, 1987, p. 125). Tom Paulin recently praised her 'puritan temperament' (Paulin, 1996, p. 222). Seamus Heaney keeps returning to her poetry, celebrating her ability to write in a way that helps us to 'enjoy' and 'endure' life (Heaney, 1995, p. 185). It is not surprising that Bishop is seen by James Fenton as the 'poet's poet' (Fenton, 1997, p. 12). At the same time, in spite of its evasive nature, hers is a poetry accessible to many readers.

Many of the poems in *North & South* experiment with the poetic tradition. Bishop's playful regendering of Tennyson's 'The Lady of Shalott' into her 'The Gentleman of Shalott' is perhaps the most obvious case. 'The Weed', 'Florida' and 'The Fish' draw on Herbert's 'Love Unknown', Stevens's 'The Idea of Order at Key West' and Moore's 'The Fish', respectively. Bishop is not a particularly respectful student of these poets. She tends to mimic rather than imitate their styles and voices. Tennyson's lady, 'half-sick of shadows' (Tennyson, 1994, p. 45), becomes a kind of Chaplinesque tramp, fooling about in front of the looking-glass. Herbert's anguished parable about Christian salvation twists into a far more disturbing nightmare about the desperate dreams which divide the heart. Stevens uses art to order nature, whereas Bishop seems to take pleasure in its chaos. Moore's fish is always secondary to the poet's delight in describing it, while in Bishop's poem, the fish remains resistant to its author's full comprehension. Bishop sees the tradition not as a dead monument, but as a living house to be reinhabited and reinvented. Moore called this her 'flicker of impudence' (Schwartz and Estess, 1983, p. 175). Bishop, in a more telling phrase, speaks of a 'slight transvestite twist' (Bishop, 1991, p. 200). The image of an artist audaciously dressing up in another poet's clothes is an appropriate one. Bishop's fondness for mimicry stems from her desire to write like other poets and to make fun of their work. Such 'impudence' had a serious side too. Bishop may have been trying to enter the poetic tradition, but she ended up by subverting it.

Mary McCarthy once compared reading Bishop's poetry to a game of hide-and-seek: 'I envy the mind hiding in her words, like an "I" counting up to a hundred and waiting to be found' (Schwartz and Estess, 1983, p. 267). Bishop's aesthetic remains 'waiting to be found'. We can never be sure where (or even whether) the poet's 'I' lies within the poem. Does art mirror life, or run away from it? As the speaker in 'The Gentleman of Shalott' warns us:

> Which eye's his eye?
> Which limb lies
> next the mirror?
> For neither is clearer
> nor a different color
> than the other,
> nor meets a stranger
> in this arrangement
> of leg and leg and
> arm and so on.

Bishop confuses art and life by stressing the similarity of the two 'eyes' in the poem, for 'neither is clearer / nor a different color / than the other'. Which 'eye' is the poet's, if either? How do we separate Tennyson's perspective from Bishop's? How does a male character in a poem relate to the female poet writing it? Bishop sets up similar riddles throughout *North & South*. She shows how poems move between art and life, neither concealing nor revealing the poet's secrets. The game of hide-and-seek never really comes to an end, for the poet or for her gentleman:

> The uncertainty
> he says he
> finds exhilarating. He loves
> that sense of constant re-adjustment.
> He wishes to be quoted as saying at present:
> 'Half is enough.'

The 'uncertainty' principle in her poems requires of the reader a 'sense of constant readjustment' which can become 'exhilarating.' Half is always 'enough' for Bishop because half-truths about the self are perhaps the only truths she can face.

Yet these half-truths usually exist inside perfectly finished poems. Creating a balance between emotion and form was never an easy task for Bishop. She may have been a prolific letter writer, but she was never a prolific poet. Plath completed half of her *Ariel* poems in a month. Bishop rarely finished more than a couple of poems a year. She took eleven years to complete *North & South*, though even this was a comparatively short time compared with the twenty-six years that passed between the first and last draft of 'The Moose'. Bishop compared composing poetry to the experience of having an aneurism or stroke:

> I have that uncomfortable feeling of 'things' in the head, like icebergs or rocks or awkwardly placed pieces of furniture. It's as if the nouns were there but the verbs were lacking . . . I can't help having the theory that if they are joggled around hard enough and long enough some kind of electricity will arrange everything. (Bishop, 1996a, p. 94)

The 'things' in the head, like 'icebergs or rocks or awkwardly placed pieces of furniture', hint at Bishop's 'earthly trust' of accumulated childhood feelings. The metaphors she uses to describe these feelings recur throughout *North & South*, particularly the sense of coldness and frigidity associated with the iceberg. Bishop's problem in her poetry is how to dissolve certain emotions into language whilst at the same time freezing others. It is of course impossible to melt one half of an iceberg without threatening the rest at the same time. The 'electricity' that transforms feeling into language runs the risk of charging the wrong emotions. Whilst it may be risky to keep these emotions inside the head, it seems just as hazardous to release them in a poem.

Bishop's desire to control awkward emotion can certainly be heard in a letter to Moore from 1937:

> 'Mother-love' – isn't it awful. I long for an Arctic climate where no emotions of any sort can possibly grow, – always excepting disinterested 'friendship' of course. (Millier, 1995, p. 125)

Bishop is actually referring to the cloying love of a friend's mother, but it is difficult not to imagine the phrase also alluding to the poet's own mother. Whereas here she seems overwhelmed by too much 'mother-love', Bishop had in fact complained of receiving too little during her childhood. By placing 'mother-love' within an 'Arctic climate' of cool containment, the poet attempts to prevent its being exposed.

Bishop has several poems which use ice or snow as a metaphor. These include 'The Imaginary Iceberg', 'The Colder the Air', 'The Weed', 'Paris, 7 A.M.' and 'Cirque d'Hiver'. In each of these poems, distress shows through a frigid geographical land-scape. In 'The Weed' the leaves which grow out of the dreamer's chest suggest the poet's 'nervous roots'. In 'Paris, 7 A.M.' the wintry suburbs mutate into a series of 'star-splintered hearts'. In 'Cirque d'Hiver' the mechanical toy has a 'melancholy soul'. Bishop cannot keep the expression of awkward emotion on ice forever, nor does she wish to do so. Her poetry's 'Arctic climate' controls the growth of difficult feeling, it does not deny its existence.

In 'The Imaginary Iceberg' for instance, icebergs seem to stand in for aspects of Bishop's life. Nature's 'shifting stage' corresponds to the poet's 'shifting' travels. The iceberg is always fracturing and changing shape, but the ship has to get used to moving on:

> Good-bye, we say, good-bye, the ship steers off
> where waves give in to one another's waves
> and clouds run in a warmer sky.
> Icebergs behoove the soul
> (both being self-made from elements least visible)
> to see them so: fleshed, fair, erected indivisible.

Bishop was similarly practised in the art of waving good-bye. The iceberg 'behoove[s] the soul' because of its reticent nature. It is 'self-made from elements least visible' as Bishop's poetry is constructed out of a life largely hidden from the reader.

Bishop's notorious emotional reticence marks in particular her attitudes to gender and sexuality. She conceals her own losses behind a genderless narrator or an ambigu-ous 'we'. She hated being classed as a woman poet and was extremely secretive about her lesbianism. What Bishop wanted from art was 'the same thing that is necessary for its creation, a self-forgetful, perfectly useless concentration' (Goldensohn, 1992, p. 130). The poet's gender and sexuality were some of the first things to be forgotten when she began writing. Bishop is a mid-century aesthete. Her definition of art as 'perfectly useless' is a restatement of Wilde's 'All art is quite useless' (Wilde, 1994, p. 17). Bishop thought it better to be considered ' "the 16ᵗʰ poet" with no reference to my sex, than one of 4 women – even if the other 3 are pretty good' (Harrison, 1993, p. 33). She objected to being in all-female anthologies on 'feminist' grounds, considering it 'nonsense' to separate the sexes (Bishop, 1996b, p. 90). A close friend to several women writers (including Flannery O'Connor and May Swenson), she still associated woman's writing negatively with domesticity and class snobbery:

Male poets often seem to be taking walks when they write poems. . . . Women, unfortunately, seem to stay at home a lot to write theirs. There is no reason why the home,
houses, apartment, or furnished room, can't produce good poems, but almost all women
poets seem to fall occasionally into the 'Order is a lovely thing' . . . category, and one
wishes they wouldn't. (Harrison, 1993, p. 31)

Bishop does not object to writing about home, houses and rooms. In fact they are
some of her most recurrent themes. What she objects to is the 'order[ed]'containment
and domestication of these spaces by some women poets. She writes *from* rather than
about these spaces, doing so in a way that makes it very difficult to locate her writing
within a specific female or lesbian tradition.

Bishop mentions 'home' on only three occasions in *North & South*, in 'The Man-
Moth', 'The Monument' and 'Jerónimo's House'. In these it is respectively a subway,
a series of piled-up boxes and a house made of chewed-up paper and spit. Each of
these homes is subject to adjustment, collapse or disruption, mirroring the poet's own
sense of dislocation. Cities, houses and the relationships that often go with them, are
always considered potentially insecure: 'filled with the intent / to be lost' as Bishop
remarks in the late poem, 'One Art'. Bishop felt more at home when she was on the
move, travelling away from disaster. In 1929 she hitchhiked back to boarding school
a month before term began to avoid staying with cousins. At Vassar College her solution for despair was again found in running away. She was arrested at three in the
morning by police who believed she was a prostitute, except for the Greek notes they
found in her pocket. In 1935 she ended an affair by leaving New York for Europe, a
move which possibly prompted her rejected lover's subsequent suicide. She evaded
another crisis in 1937 and left a seriously injured friend in a Paris hospital. In 1940
she ran away from a different lover, accusing her of infidelity. Finally, in the 1960s,
she left her home in Brazil twice, prompting another companion's suicide.

Her poetic homes are constructed on similar lines to her biographical experiences.
They provide shelter for their inhabitants on a guest basis only, though each might
be abandoned or threatened at any point. In 'The Man-Moth', for example, home
becomes not only part of the 'pale subways of cement', but also a potential trap:

> Each night he must
> be carried through artificial tunnels and dream recurrent dreams.
> Just as the ties recur beneath his train, these underlie
> his rushing brain. He does not dare look out the window,
> for the third rail, the unbroken draught of poison,
> runs there beside him. He regards it as a disease
> he has inherited the susceptibility to. He has to keep
> his hands in his pockets, as others must wear mufflers.

The 'unbroken draught of poison', whether madness or suicide, is a disease the Man-
Moth has 'inherited the susceptibility to'. It is the 'third rail' that threatens and underpins his meaning of 'home'. The poem was written shortly after the death of Bishop's

mother in 1934, an event that must have emphasized her already intense sense of isolation. Bishop's worries about inheriting her mother's madness run through the poem,
much as 'the third rail' underlies the Man-Moth's 'rushing brain'. Her only resort is
to run away from any thought of 'Mother-love', just as the Man-Moth 'dare not look
out of the window'. Avoiding the past inevitably leads to being haunted by it, as the
poem's 'recurrent dreams' imply. The Man-Moth 'keep[s] / his hands in his pockets'.
Though he avoids touching the 'third rail', he is always conscious of its threatening
presence.

In 'The Monument' Bishop is more successful in travelling away from biographical 'ties'. The monument is made 'homelier' by 'all the conditions of its existence'. It
is a house literally built on sand, subject to 'the strong sunlight, the wind from the
sea', the ebb and flow of the tide. The monument on the shore, which may or may
not conceal the 'artist-prince', is Bishop's preferred poetic home. It is safer than any
other place of refuge because:

> . . . roughly but adequately it can shelter
> what is within (which after all
> cannot have been intended to be seen).
> It is the beginning of a painting,
> a piece of sculpture, or poem, or monument,
> and all of wood. Watch it closely.

The monument is a shut-up house that might hide the artist. It 'roughly but adequately shelter[s] / what is within'. That 'within' is not 'intended to be seen', yet the
poet leaves enough clues for us to presume that some part of the monument's secrets
relate to her own life. The poem's main subject is its own construction, particularly
the way it both exposes and conceals the poet inside. Its last line seems to offer the
reader an important piece of advice on how to understand all Bishop's poetry. 'Watch
it closely', she teases. To follow the poet we have first to pay close attention to the
poem. Bishop replaces the domesticated home of the female poet with the frightening subway of the Man-Moth and the ambiguous refuge of the artist-prince. The
monument is, in a sense, the poetic home she escapes to. It shelters Bishop more
securely from 'what is within', while also allowing her to fly 'far away'.

Other poems set on the shoreline include 'The Map', 'Large Bad Picture', 'The
Unbeliever', 'Florida', 'Seascape', 'Little Exercise' and 'The Fish'. The shoreline is
nearly always seen positively by Bishop. Its pink light is 'consoling' for the observer
of 'Large Bad Picture'. Its 'sagging coast line / is delicately ornamented' in 'Florida'.
It looks a little 'like heaven' in 'Seascape'. This playhouse by the sea is one of the few
places in *North & South* where the 'third rail' is deactivated. Free from the negative
associations of childhood removal, houses built on sand paradoxically stand for recovery and refuge in Bishop's poetry, however unstable their foundations.

Less safe are the relationships which take place within these imaginary houses.
Almost a third of the poems begin or end with the speaker or speakers in bed, their

gender and sexuality hidden. These include 'A Miracle for Breakfast', 'Love Lies Sleeping', 'The Weed', 'Paris, 7 A.M.', 'Sleeping On the Ceiling', 'Sleeping Standing Up', 'Roosters' and 'Anaphora'. All share a distrust of human relationships, balanced by a desire to wake up to the world within them. Bishop's belief in 'closets, closets and more closets' (Fountain and Brazeau, 1994, p. 327) keeps her lesbianism concealed, though this does not prevent her from writing about love and sexuality.

In 'Love Lies Sleeping' she focuses on 'the queer cupids of all persons getting up'. Queerness may stand in for homosexuality, but it seems more likely that Bishop is commenting on the strangeness of love in itself. This is particularly apparent in 'Roosters', where the birds' 'traditional cries' suggest military bravado and sexual violence. The roosters' behaviour seems to offer an ironic commentary on the nature of human relationships, defined in the poem by 'unwanted love, conceit, and war'. Bishop's scepticism about the character and permanence of human love can be felt throughout the collection. In 'Casabianca', 'love's the burning boy' who dies reciting poetry. In 'Chemin de Fer', 'love should be put into action' but never is. In 'Florida', 'love' is one of the alligator's 'five distinct calls'. It follows 'friendliness' but leads only to 'mating, war, and a warning'. Bishop's love poems are written from the perspective of affairs and relationships breaking down. Her lesbianism remains hidden, but not her anxious fascination with love.

This negative outlook may also have its source in historical events. Bishop composed *North & South* on the move between cities, countries and war zones. She spent the mid-1930s in a New York still recovering from the Depression. She was in Spain when the civil war began in 1936 and in Italy watching a Fascist rally the year after. In the early 1940s she lived in Key West while the navy base was being extended, witnessing the military build-up nearby. Bishop's distrust of political propaganda (left or right, pro- or anti-war) keeps these events off-stage, though they still trouble the language she uses. There is 'Danger' and 'Death' in 'Love Lies Sleeping', 'armored cars' and 'ugly tanks' in 'Sleeping Standing Up', 'sallies' and 'commands' in 'Roosters', the 'rage' and 'fall' of nations in 'Songs for a Colored Singer'. Yet none of these images ever names its source outside the poem. Bishop's refusal to take sides in her poetry means that she never specifies a clear enemy or target. The aggressors in *North & South* are more likely to be found inside the speaker's room than outside in the world.

Bishop's poetry frequently blurs the edge of categories that seem clear-cut. She is fascinated by meeting-places, literal and figurative, where boundaries melt or overlap. She begins crossing lines in 'The Map', the very first poem in *North & South*. In doing so, she sets in motion many of the aesthetic questions that preoccupy her in this and in subsequent collections. 'The Map' is primarily a poem about art. The problems faced by the map-maker are the same as those faced by the poet. The map-maker can choose to draw several types of map: small-scale, large-scale, out-of-scale, political, geographical, historical. The poet has the same bewildering choice of perspective and palette. Bishop shows how impossible it is for the map-maker and the poet not to transgress the boundaries of his or her project.

The speaker switches voice in the opening stanza between flat description and surreal interrogation, much as the map represents and distorts the world it stands for:

> Land lies in water; it is shadowed green.
> Shadows, or are they shallows, at its edges
> showing the line of long sea-weeded ledges
> where weeds hang to the simple blue from green.
> Or does the land lean down to lift the sea from under,
> drawing it unperturbed around itself?
> Along the fine tan sandy shelf
> is the land tugging at the sea from under?

Bishop is drawn to the sea again and its relationship to the land. This geographical question – does the sea or the land define the contours and movements of the earth? – is in its own turn undermined by the language the poet uses. The metaphors of touch by which she evokes the push-and-shove of sea and land suggest a lovers' gentle playfight. Their bodies lie in shadow. Their interaction is ambiguous. Who 'lean[s] down to lift' the other from under? Who is 'drawing' who, 'unperturbed around itself'? Who is 'tugging' at the other? The poem's odd fusion of maps and bodies is reminiscent of Donne's *Songs and Sonnets*, which Bishop admired. If anything, 'The Map' is a little more coy than some of its Metaphysical predecessors, though it manages to say more about the literal map and the places it describes than a conceit might ordinarily allow. Bishop shows how the map's meaning shifts according to the perspective of the viewer. For her, 'reality goes with one' (Costello, 1991, p. 130). It is as fluctuating and unstable as the sea's relationship to the land. This is again reminiscent of her description of reality as a 'huge circus tent . . . which we carry around with us and set up wherever we are'. In her poetry, Bishop very often takes reality for a circus ride, consistently drawing attention to what she termed 'the surrealism of everyday life' (Goldensohn, 1992, p. 129).

As a poet, Bishop is clearly preoccupied by thresholds, as the map, the melting iceberg and the shifting seascape show. Within these tropes lie many of the tensions that characterize *North & South*: the continual shift between reticence and intimacy, the awkward game of biographical hide-and-seek, the conflict between home and that which underpins it, love and its loss. Bishop is an awkward poet to pin down because she never really takes sides. She makes an entire aesthetic out of a refusal to settle down in any one place or with any one set of views. Although she writes frequently about geography, she is not a geographical poet in the sense that Frost or Wordsworth are. She is fascinated not by place itself, but by the movement between places.

Questions of home, of place and of travel, are still preoccupying subjects in subsequent collections of prose and verse, particularly in her last and most intimate volume, *Geography III*. Bishop is a poet in transit from artistic schools, sects and political positions. She is in search not only of an aesthetic, but also of a way of writing safely about life's losses. When Bishop won the Neustadt International Prize for

Literature in 1976, she compared her habit of travelling to the frantic movements of her sandpiper: 'Yes, all my life I have lived and behaved very much like that sandpiper – just running along the edges of different countries and continents, "looking for something"' (Millier, 1995, p. 17). In art, as in life, she was always running on, skirting the edges of movements and groups, endlessly on the lookout for that elusive something else.

BIBLIOGRAPHY

Barry, Sandra (1996), *Elizabeth Bishop: An Archival Guide to her Life in Nova Scotia*, Hantsport (Nova Scotia): Lancelot Press.

Bishop, Elizabeth (1991) [1983], *Complete Poems*, London: Chatto & Windus.

Bishop, Elizabeth (1994) [1984], *Collected Prose*, London: Chatto & Windus.

Bishop, Elizabeth (1996(a)) [1994], *One Art: The Selected Letters*, ed. Robert Giroux, London: Pimlico.

Bishop, Elizabeth (1996(b)), *Conversations with Elizabeth Bishop*, ed. George Monteiro, Jackson: University Press of Mississippi.

Bishop, Elizabeth (1997) [1996], *Exchanging Hats*, ed. William Benton, Manchester: Carcanet Press.

Bloom, Harold (ed.) (1985), *Modern Critical Views: Elizabeth Bishop*, New York: Chelsea House Publishers.

Costello, Bonnie (1991), *Questions of Mastery*, Cambridge, MA and London: Harvard University Press.

Fenton, James (1997), 'The Many Arts of Elizabeth Bishop', in *The New York Review of Books*, 15 May, pp. 12–15.

Fountain, Gary and Brazeau, Peter (eds) (1994), *Remembering Elizabeth Bishop: An Oral Biography*, Amherst: University of Massachusetts Press.

Gioia, Dana (1986), 'Studying with Miss Bishop', in *The New Yorker*, 15 September, pp. 90–101.

Goldensohn, Lorrie (1992), *Elizabeth Bishop: The Biography of a Poetry*, Chichester and New York: University of Columbia Press.

Harrison, Victoria (1993), *Poetics of Intimacy*, Cambridge, New York and Victoria (Australia): Cambridge University Press.

Heaney, Seamus (1995) [1992], 'Counting Up to a Hundred: On Elizabeth Bishop', in *The Redress of Poetry: Oxford Lectures*, London: Faber & Faber, pp. 164–85.

Kalstone, David (1989), *Becoming A Poet: Elizabeth Bishop with Marianne Moore and Robert Lowell*, New York: Farrar, Straus & Giroux.

Lombardi, Marilyn May (ed.) (1993), *The Geography of Gender*, Charlottesville and London: University Press of Virginia.

McCabe, Susan (1994), *Elizabeth Bishop: Her Poetics of Loss*, Pennsylvania: Pennsylvania State University Press.

Millier, Brett C. (1995) [1993], *Elizabeth Bishop: Life and the Memory of It*, Berkeley, CA and London: University of California Press.

Paulin, Tom (1996), 'Writing to the Moment', in *Writing to the Moment*, London: Faber & Faber, pp. 215–37.

Plath, Sylvia (1982), *The Journals of Sylvia Plath*, ed. Ted Hughes and Frances McCullough, New York: Ballantine Books.

Rich, Adrienne (1987) [1993], 'The Eye of the Outsider: The Poetry of Elizabeth Bishop', in *Selected Prose*, London: Virago, pp. 124–35.

Schwartz, Lloyd and Estess, Sybil P. (eds) (1983), *Elizabeth Bishop and Her Art*, Ann Arbor: University of Michigan Press.

Stevenson, Anne (1998), *Five Looks at Elizabeth Bishop*, London: Bellow.

Tennyson, Alfred (1994) [1842], *The Works of Alfred Lord Tennyson*, Ware (Worcestershire): Wordsworth Editions.

Wilde, Oscar (1994) [1890], *The Picture of Dorian Gray*, in *The Complete Works of Oscar Wilde*, London: Paragon.

Ezra Pound: *The Pisan Cantos*

A. David Moody

Basil Bunting saw Pound's *Cantos* as the Alps – 'you will have to go a long way round / if you want to avoid them' (Bunting, 1968, p. 110). To continue his metaphor, *The Pisan Cantos* might be seen as the Mont Blanc range, possibly more accessible than the rest, but immense in themselves and rising to a majestic summit. There is no way my 6,000 words can contain them, unless by turning the telescope round I can show them in miniature. However, that could mean losing the detail, and these cantos are nothing if not a composition of detail, 3,500 lines of detail upon detail. So somehow they must be entered into by way of the detail, taking a few for the many.

'What is there to say about them?', Bunting wondered, and began, where most of us must, 'They don't make sense'. Certainly they do not make sense in any accustomed way. Even Yeats, a great poet in his own manner and a close friend of Pound, had to confess that, like other readers, he could discover 'merely exquisite and grotesque fragments' (Yeats, 1936, p. xxiv). He went on, however, to give an invaluable lead into the difficult art of *The Cantos* by asking, though altogether sceptically, 'Can impressions that are in part visual, in part metrical, be related like the notes of a symphony?' Hard as it may be to read them in that way, nevertheless that does indicate the only way in which the flow of statements, observations, images and thoughts presented to us in *The Pisan Cantos* can be followed intelligently. They are, as *canto* (from the Italian *cantare*, to sing) signals, a music made of words.

The analogy with a symphony is a very loose one, and it would be better to think of Bach than of Beethoven in this connection. Further, a music made of words has very different possibilities and conditions as compared with a music of sound only. Its harmonic system will be based on the energies of words and images, and on the accords and torsions of their meanings and associations. Where it may differ from our customary way with words is in not observing the grammar, syntax and logic of rationalized expression. Things may relate to each other in other ways, as in the play of likeness and counterpointed difference in LXXIX:

> Moon,   cloud,   tower,   a patch of the battistero
> all of a whiteness,
> dirt pile as per the Del Cossa inset
> (79/498)

The next fifteen lines develop the theme or subject of whiteness and womankind; then the counter-subject of (male) 'shades' is developed, with a mixture of seriousness and humour, through a further eighteen lines. An extended ring-composed passage of counterpoint follows, beginning 'with 8 birds on a wire' – answered at the end by '4 birds on 3 wires, one bird on one' – and with its centre the explicit statement 'some minds take pleasure in counterpoint / pleasure in counterpoint'.

It has to be recognized that to perceive the musical relations between one thing and another in the apparently rather random flow demands not only an alert but an analytic attention. This is no mere flow of sense-impressions and mental associations as in a passive 'stream of consciousness'. The 'things' being presented are, characteristically, things that have been sorted out by an intelligence. 'All of a whiteness' is a simple instance. The connection is less obvious between

> Guard's cap quattrocento passes *a cavallo*
> on horseback thru landscape Cosimo Tura
> or, as some think, Del Cossa

and

> what castrum romanum, what
> 'went into winter quarters'
> is under us?
> as the young horse whinnies against the tubas

The full meaning of these and the other relations built up in that thirty-line passage has to do with 'contending for certain values', but one reaches towards this understanding only by way, first, of an intellectual perception of the nature of each thing in turn, and then by perceiving how they interact with each other. This calls for the critical intelligence to be exercised in a manner nearly the opposite to that now dominant in Anglophone and European culture. Our advanced intellectual practice subsumes details into generalizations and generalizations into theory; but the method of *The Cantos* is designed to escape generalization and theory while being intelligent about things in particular, and while arranging the perceptions of them into an order which will yield their full relations or harmonies. It is not an escape from intelligence, only from the tendency to abstraction. But minds trained to think in abstractions and to take their stand on theories may well feel overwhelmed when offered the plenitude of intelligently perceived particularity.

That plenitude is Pound's great resource throughout *The Cantos*, but most of all in *The Pisan Cantos*, and in a very long one such as **LXXIV** it is difficult at first to see 'the rose in the steel dust'. As with any sustained composition it helps to distinguish the various themes or thematic materials, and to make out the parts and divisions. The latter, it must be said, can generally be made out only on the basis of the former, since the breaks are rarely marked by a line space or even by a full-stop. The main divisions of LXXIV, for example, are: (1) ll. 1–243 ('surrounded by herds and by cohorts . . .'); (2) ll. 244–487 ('of no fortune and with a name to come'); (3) ll. 488–566 ('all of which leads to the death-cells'); (4) ll. 567–811 ('searching every house . . .'); (5) ll. 812–28 (coda). It will be seen that parts 1, 2 and 4 are nearly identical in length, while part 3, on the theme of usury as against a just economy, is much shorter. There is nothing at all to mark off part 3 from part 2 or part 4 – except of course the shifts of thematic material.

The three principal themes of LXXIV, and of the entire Pisan sequence, are stated in the opening lines (ll. 1–52). First, 'The enormous tragedy' – a tragedy beyond the norms of tragedy – seems an end of the world without prospect of a rebirth. Yet Manes's doctrine of light could be found in twelfth-century Provence a millennium after his death; and the myth of Dionysus figures the self-renewals of nature. The dream of a just republic which Pound hoped Mussolini might realize has ended ingloriously, yet he remains defiantly committed to the idea of building the visionary city, modelled upon the mandate of heaven, where the peasant's dream of abundance and justice will be fulfilled. Those first ten lines give the motive, the driving intention, of the entire sequence: to build in the music of words 'the city of Dioce whose terraces are the colour of stars'.

The second passage (ll. 11–25), a response to the first, gives a basis for the continuing effort to achieve a right order, in setting against those tragic endings the endless process of nature. 'The suave eyes' might be a retort to the merciless eyes of 'Possum' Eliot's 'The Hollow Men' – they will recur through these cantos as the eyes of Kuanon the merciful and of other divinities of nature. Here they accord with sister moon, and with the rain and wind. The sun is implicit in '[his] great periplum brings in the stars to our shore' – the stars mirrored in Dioce's terraces. Lucifer too is a light-bearer, though an exceeder of limits, as was Dante's Ulysses in venturing beyond the known world. Are these discords, as they contrast with the faithful adherence of Confucius's disciples to the way, sympathetic or warning? The poet resolves them by identifying himself with Homer's canny Odysseus when he escaped the one-eyed Cyclops (and a tragic end) by giving the name of his family as Ou Tis, Noman. In LXXXI, under the spell of divine eyes, he will write 'It is not man / Made courage, or made order, or made grace . . . Learn of the green world what can be thy place' (81/535). The just city or *paradiso terrestre* is not a solely human creation.

But humanity has its place and its part to play in the universal process – 'man, earth: two halves of the tally' (82/540). This is the third theme, introduced through ll. 26–52. The human contribution is enlightened intelligence. It can produce in the works of men of unusual genius – artists or the framers of the Constitution of the United States – the precise definitions of the nature of things which shape right action and so build a just society. But the unenlightened go against nature, seeking to exploit its abundance for private profit, as by usurious loans to Indian farmers. A key idea here is that of measure, the gold standard being a false measure as against the true measure of need. There is also the implication, to be developed in the course of these cantos, that usury causes wars (which destroy works of art) and puts the Constitution in jeopardy. It will emerge that for Pound the real war, the perennial war underlying the particular one which has just come to its end, is the war between the greedy and the enlightened. In this war his weapon is his art, an art dedicated to constructing in words a world true to nature, even 'from the death cells in sight of Mt. Taishan @ Pisa'.

How Pound came to be in a prison camp, and how this part of *The Cantos* came to be written there, is deeply, tragically, ironic, for he had become the victim of his (not always precisely conceived) effort to save the world from usury. In the decade before the outbreak of the 1939–45 war he had been fighting his own war on two fronts, in prose propaganda intended to have immediate political effect, and in his poem designed to create a new mindset by the very different and rather slower process of art. By 1939 he had brought the poem to the point where he was ready 'to write paradise', that is, to write the governing ideas of the just society. The war, however, meant to him that the usurers were creating hell and that he must devote himself to direct action against them. His propaganda against usury had always been directed against the financial systems of France, England and the United States of America, and especially against the USA, his own country which in his judgement was failing, by its complicity in usurious banking practices, to honour a fundamental principle of its Constitution. At the same time he placed his hopes for the realization of Jeffersonian principles of social justice in Mussolini and his Fascist regime in Italy (where he had been resident since 1924). Moreover, he thought Hitler had the right idea about money, and that his anti-semitism was a justifiable strategy in the war on usury. To support the Hitler–Mussolini Axis against France, Great Britain and their Allies was therefore a straightforward course for him to take when the war broke out in Europe in 1939. He broadcast talks over Rome Radio as a way of continuing his propaganda war against usury, telling the Allies that they were fighting on the wrong side, and urging the USA not to get involved. When America was drawn into the war on the side of the Allies he stridently denounced its leaders, maintaining that they were betraying the Constitution which he as a true Jeffersonian democrat was trying to defend. From the American point of view of course his broadcasts were seen as giving aid and comfort to the enemy, and he was indicted as a traitor. Thus shortly after the war ended in 1945 he found himself held in a US Army prison camp near Pisa while the FBI gathered evidence to bring him to trial. He was facing a death sentence for having attempted, as he was convinced in his own mind, to save America from its real enemy.

The camp, set up on the bare plain within sight of Pisa, was the 6677th DTC, or Detention Training Center. High barbed-wire fences, army huts, tents, wire cages on death row; a bare, dusty drill-field where the ordinary prisoners – US soldiers, many of them Afro-American, condemned for civil crimes by military courts – underwent an extreme course of basic military (re)training. Pound was not an ordinary prisoner. Admitted on 24 May 1945, he was initially treated as high risk and kept in a specially reinforced wire cage on death row: concrete floor, flat roofcover, wire and metal landing-strip on all four sides leaving him exposed to rain, wind, sun, dust. The order was given that no one should speak to him. After three or four weeks it was recognized that he was not in fact dangerous and that his physical and mental health was being stressed unnecessarily, and he was transferred to a tent in the medical compound. He composed *The Pisan Cantos* there, ten of them, LXXIV to LXXXIII, in the two months between mid-July and mid-September, adding LXXXIV as coda in October. He was taken from the camp to be flown to Washington DC for trial on 16 November 1945. Perceived by the US authorities as a traitor, he still saw himself as a loyal defender of the Constitution.

It was his American publisher, James Laughlin, who fixed the title *The Pisan Cantos* upon cantos LXXIV–LXXXIV. Pound himself had wanted their title to be just those numbers, in line with the titling of the previous volumes, though he was prepared to accept 'The Pisan Cantos' as a subtitle. Laughlin, as a good publisher, was emphasizing what set this group of cantos apart from the rest; while Pound wanted them to be seen as a continuation of the still-growing work. The difference goes deeper. Laughlin's title has directed attention upon Pound's personal tragedy, upon the prisoner paying for his mistakes. It encourages a reading of these cantos as elegiac and lyrical. But Pound had refused the role of tragic victim and had elected to be of the family of Ou Tis, Noman, and to turn his intelligence not upon his merely personal feelings but upon the state of the world. By a reversal of the tragic irony of his indictment and imprisonment for his propaganda, the US Army DTC proved to be a perfectly suitable place for him to continue his effort as an epic poet. As Mephistopheles could say of Faustus's world, 'This is hell, nor am I out of it', Pound might have said of the Pisan prison camp, 'This is the world as it really is, nor am I out of it'.

Though he was a prisoner, Pound's mind was free. Though in the hands of the US authorities, whom he saw as the servants not of the public good but of its enemy *Usura*, and surrounded by US Army guards and prisoners in a hell of usury's making, he could yet look out to a small mountain near Pisa and think of it as Taishan, a sacred mountain in China. Or knowing that some of those alongside him in the death cells were to be hung, he could think of the words Villon had imagined for himself and his fellow thieves when on the gallows, 'Absoudre . . .', absolve us all – words he had set to haunting music in his early opera, *Le Testament*. He could overhear Mr K.'s 'If we weren't dumb, we wouldn't be here', rhyme it with his own comment, 'the voiceless with bumm drum and banners', and notice in passing 'Butterflies, mint and Lesbia's sparrows'. By the end of LXXVI the dumb prisoners will have become poor devils, 'po'eri di'aoli sent to the slaughter / [slave against slave] / to the sound of the bumm drum, to eat remnants / for a usurer's holiday' (76/477). Against that, butterflies, mint and other herbs, and birds and other creatures will become figures of the sustaining process of nature, as will 'Mt Taishan' with its clouds.

The phrase from Villon would be (in translation) in the 'R.C. chaplain's field book' to be said *after* confession (compare 74/440), and that appears to be followed shortly by the chaplain's performing a Mass (seen in his vestments as 'the great scarab is bowed at the altar'). Later, at the end of the first part of LXXIV, is a phrase said at the close of the Mass, 'Est consummatum, Ite' (74/446), to suggest that through the preceding 240 or so lines Pound has been composing his own service in counterpoint to the priest's confession and communion. Pound's rite is extravagantly oecumenical, bringing together 'a lizard upheld me' – 'Mt Taishan' – Kuanon of the merciful eyes – Catholic saints invoked at the start of the Mass – the Egyptian sacred scarab symbolizing rebirth and the sun – Chinese emperors and their wives performing the rites to connect heaven and earth to ensure abundance – and uniting them all Scotus Erigena's 'OMNIA, / all things that are are lights' (74/442–3). Pound's revelation, his 'paraclete or the verbum perfectum', is the light that is in all things and that makes them what they are. Against this light is the 'thickness and fatness' which makes war for 'the profits of usurers', thus leading to the death cells and 'slaves learning slavery / and the dull driven back toward the jungle' (74/445–6). And the poet is down among these victims of *Usura* even as he affirms what is 'in the mind indestructible'.

But not everything in the mind is of permanent value. There are memories of past experiences which preserve only what has passed away, and which bring backward-looking feelings of sadness and loss. The elegiac note was sounded briefly in the twelve lines before 'A lizard upheld me', beginning 'el triste pensier si volge / ad Ussel' (74/442). It comes again at the beginning of the second part, most fully in 'Lordly men are to earth o'ergiven', and again in 'où sont les heurs of that year' (74/446–70). This will become a major concern, especially in LXXVI and LXXX, as what is merely of its era is winnowed out from what will endure indestructibly. Here in LXXIV there is a turn from elegy to actuality at 'and they have bitched the Adelphi / niggers scaling the obstacle fence'; and then a return to the permanent in some of its various forms and intimations in the long passage beginning at 'Cloud over mountain' and going down to 'rain, Ussel' (74/448–50).

The main episode of this second part, from 'To the left of la bella Torre' to its end at 'of no fortune and with a name to come' (74/450–3), is a descent into his actual hell in the form of a variation upon the dark night of the soul. The variation amounts to a radical revision of what that phrase would mean in the context of John of the Cross or 'Possum' Eliot. In their accounts the soul experiences desolation and despair while feeling itself separated from the divine light, and must learn to accept this as a preparation for its union with God: 'So the darkness shall be the light', as Eliot put it in *East Coker*. Pound puns and mocks his way out of that:

is it blacker? was it blacker? Νύξ animae?
is there a blacker or was it merely San Juan with a belly ache
writing ad posteros
in short shall we look for a deeper or is this the bottom?
(74/452)

Earlier he has termed his own experience 'magna NUX animae', not a dark night of the soul but the great nut of the soul, a phrase which Terrell helpfully associates with 'the great acorn of light' (116/809). (Recent editions of *The Cantos* mistakenly print 'NOX' for 'NUX'.) The implication would be that the light is in the soul or mind itself, as its 'intelligence' is within the acorn. In the same way 'paradise' or union with the divine exists in the enlightened mind, not as 'a painted paradise at the end of it' but 'in fragments . . . the smell of mint, for example'. It is always open to the mind that can perceive it, 'in the dwarf morning-glory [that] twines round the grass blade', in 'filial, fraternal affection' – a Confucian principle – and also where there is 'no vestige save in the air . . . under the olives / saeculorum Athenae', and in 'the sharp song with sun under its radiance'. There is no hint of the poet's despairing of this paradise.

He sees himself among the prisoners as among slaves packed between decks in a slave-ship, or as Odysseus's men changed by Circe's spell into swine. But, like Odysseus aided by Hermes – or like Tiresias enlightened by Persephone in hell – he still has 'his mind entire' (47/236) and so is proof against the blind lust which makes men enslavers of others, or thieves or rapists, or bankers 'robbing the public for private individual's gain'. Yet the poison of greed flows 'in all the veins of the commonweal / if on high, will flow downward all thru them'. And here, at the exact mid-point of the canto, is a hint of a desperate doubt: 'if on the forge at Predappio?' Mussolini was born at Predappio, son of a blacksmith – was even he infected at birth with the poison? (And was the whole Fascist experiment therefore infected?) The response is an invocation of Allen Upward, an enlightened intelligence driven to suicide by the prevailing lack of comprehension in his own Circe's swine-sty, in spite of having as his seal Sitalkas, 'a precise definition' of the divine power in the grain, to be his Hermes or Persephone. Is Pound to despair as he did, to 'destroy himself ere others destroy him' (74/444)? 'For praise of intaglios' and what follows shows him moving from Upward's black mood back to the light of humaneness, of 'la Luna', of the flash of Athene's eyes 'as the [olive] leaf turns in the air' – Upward had seen that in her epithet γλαυκῶπις – and of 'the sharp song with sun under its radiance'. His power to resist is the power of intelligence, specifically the intelligence which perceives and defines things with precision.

That theme is developed in the fourth part, following the eighty-line summary of Pound's economic thought (74/453–5). There are three main sections: (a) 'each in the name of its god' to 'as the green blade under Apeliota' (ll. 567–644, 74/455–8); (b) 'Time is not, Time is the evil, beloved' to 'to forge Achaia' (ll. 645–745,

74/458–61); (c) 'and as for playing chequers' to 'searching every house' (ll. 746–811, 74/461–2). The vision that has *virtù*, the force of divine light, must be 'born from a sufficient phalanx of particulars', but 'not to a schema', rather 'as grass under Zephyrus'. Here, out of a specific phalanx of particulars, he summons up first Kore/Persephone 'under Taishan'; then the 'ΧΑΡΙΤΕΣ', the Graces who accompany Venus, 'in the soft air . . . as of Kuanon'; then the spirit of love herself, along with others including the particular beloved who said 'Io son la Luna' (cf. 74/452). It is perhaps she who is seen 'against the half-light of the window' at the start of the next section as a cameo or 'profile "to carve Achaia" ' – an image to inspire a civilization. Pound's poetic persona of 1919/20, Hugh Selwyn Mauberley, had been an artist in profile only, 'lacking the skill / To forge Achaia'. The 'beauty is difficult' passage which follows (ll. 654–724) might be a descent into Mauberley's milieu, among more or less ineffectual lovers of beauty for whom the air does not come alive with the light of the beloved ('fa di clarità l'aer tremare'). Beauty is difficult, but it exists, and this section concludes with a twenty-one line passage which moves swiftly to restate the theme of a precise definition transmitted in works of art, mosaics or medallions, 'to forge Achaia'. This is what drives the poet, 'that certain images be formed in the mind . . . to remain there, resurgent ΕΙΚΟΝΕΣ'. And it is by this that he comes forth 'out of hell, the pit / out of the dust and glare evil'.

LXXIV is the overture to *The Pisan Cantos*. In it the main thematic materials have been sorted out into what the Confucian *Great Digest* terms their 'organic categories', that is, according to their values for right living. At the same time the main form for the full development of the materials has been established. The rest of these notes will trace the outlines of their form through LXXV–LXXXIV.

LXXV presents the score of Gerhart Munch's 1933 transcription for Olga Rudge's solo violin of Francesco da Milano's sixteenth-century setting for lute of Clement Janequin's chorus for several voices imitating the songs of many birds. Terrell's notes remind us that for Pound this was an instance of a formative conception, a 'rose in the steel dust', taking 'a third life in our time' (Terrell, 1984, p. 389). More than that, it is an instance of human intelligence attending to nature, and of a series of refinements in the accurate registration of nature in human art. The canto stands then as a purely musical statement of what Pound is attempting.

The following eight cantos subdivide into two groups, each of four cantos: LXXVI–LXXIX and LXXX–LXXXIII. In the first group the emphasis is upon nature, or upon human living in its natural setting; in the second group the emphasis is rather upon the contribution to nature of what the human intelligence makes of it in art. The first group culminates in a hymn to Dionysus as lynx; the second culminates in Pound's observing a wasp building a nest in his tent and making a ritual ode of it, and in a celebration of Yeats composing 'The Peacock' in 1914:

> What's riches to him
> That has made a great peacock
> With the pride of his eye?

These of course are very broad and simplified indications. It is not to be forgotten that the life and music of the cantos is all in the detailed working out and continuous interweaving of their thematic materials.

Much of the thematic material of LXXVI is carried over from LXXIV, though with significant variations. The dominant location is now Sant' Ambrogio above Rapallo, Pound's beloved landscape associated with Olga Rudge and affording intimations and visions of a paradise on earth. The DTC is still present but rather in the background, and the *usura* theme is repeated but not much developed. 'Nothing matters but the quality / of the affection – / in the end – that has carved the trace in the mind' (76/471). Yet while the visionary presence of loving spirits may comfort and restore, the end of the canto recognizes that *usura* and all its works remain to be confronted.

LXXVII is concerned with government, with the process or natural law of things, and with the art of precise definition necessary to keep the former in accord with the latter. Precise definition comes in many forms, notably the variety of ways of perceiving breasts, from Eliot's Grishkin and 'Gaudier's eye on the telluric mass of Miss Lowell' to the breasts of life-giving earth ('Tellus, γέα'). In contrast there is the poverty and coarseness of the army vocabulary, as in its 'one phrase sexless that is / used as sort of pronoun / from a watchman's club to a vamp or fair lady'. A major motif is the recognition of the earth as life-giving (as against 'the mass graves at Katin'), from 'men rose out of χθόνος' with the variant 'the forms of men rose out of γέα', to the final naming of Zagreus, that is Dionysus conceived as the life-force within the earth.

The emphasis in LXXVIII is upon the perennial 'economic war', more particularly as it was waged in his own time in Italy between the forces of usury and Mussolini. The fall of the Fascist regime is recorded as Pound himself experienced it, when he left Rome on foot and made his way north to where his daughter was in the Tyrol. Mussolini's achievements – 'Put down the slave trade, made the desert to yield / and menaced the loan swine' – are seen as placing him with Sitalkas (and therefore also Zagreus) as a force for the abundance of nature, opposed to the usury that is *contra naturam* (45/230). Nevertheless he 'was hang'd dead by the heels before his thought in proposito / came into action efficiently'.

LXXIX is a composition of the mind of the poem towards efficient action. 'Can't move 'em with / a cold thing like economics' (78/495) – what then will move people to act in accord with nature? The answer might be 'Athene cd / have done with more sex appeal' (79/500). Invocations and visions of the powers of nature are what this canto offers, a religious rite based on Greek and Latin myth. This is prepared for by a summary treatment in counterpoint of the themes of the preceding cantos. Counterpoint demands discriminations of likeness and difference, of likeness in difference and difference in likeness. Here (as already indicated) the discriminations are at first aesthetic, then the aesthetic becomes the basis for ethical discriminations. In the fifty-line passage of ring-composed counterpoint from 'the imprint of the intaglio' to '2 cups for three altars. Tellus γέα feconda' (79/500–1), there is an acceleration creating a vortex of discriminations, and calling for an answering quickness of mind in perceiving their interrelations. Closing the first part of the canto there are then five lines (down to 'in memoriam') affording a kind of resolution, or at least a rest. In the second part, the seventy lines from ' "Hell! . . ." ' to 'Kyrie eleison', counterpoint gives way to division, as what has 'root in the equities' is opposed to iniquities. Then follows the Lynx hymn proper, exactly a hundred lines long. In this fashion, as culmination of the first half of *The Pisan Cantos*, the inspiration of right living is affirmed to be in the (divine) abundance of nature.

The second group of four cantos builds on that. There are indications of the governing concerns in the opening lines of LXXX: 'our rising θέμις' – a phrase John Adams might have used, meaning the making of an American civilization based on natural law and approved custom – as against 'the end of an era', signifying whatever is merely of its time and fated to pass away with it; and between the possible *Themis* and the actual passings away comes the affirmation 'Amo ergo sum, and in just that proportion', an anticipation of 'What thou lovest well remains / the rest is dross / What thou lov'st well shall not be reft from thee' (81/535). LXXX deals mainly with things merely of their era, its keynote being 'Les moeurs passent et la douleur reste' – a way of life disappears, the regrets remain. Pound's England provides most of the material typifying a lack of staying power due, as previously indicated in the 'Beauty is difficult' passage of LXXIV, to a failure of vision and volition – to the absence from English life of the 'Zagreus' principle. Pound was saved from it, and is saved again now, by 'the eternal moods' and their records in myth, paintings – and the poems in *The Pocket Book of Verse* left on the seat in the camp latrine. (There are echoes from that anthology at the end of LXXX and in LXXXI.) The final section, from 'Oh to be in England now that Winston's out', is a finely wrought homage and farewell, much as *Hugh Selwyn Mauberley* had been, to a gone England unable 'to forge Achaia'. That condition is what Pound needed to make his escape from, as an intelligence, rather than from the DTC.

'To have gathered from the air a live tradition' is the key phrase in LXXXI. After the opening chord (three lines) there is a ninety-line 'phalanx of particulars' rounding out a concept of tradition; then an eighty-line passage of intensifying lyric writing gathering from the tradition and from the air a live vision of the spirit of what he has loved, and giving it voice. It is a merciless beauty, as in Chaucer's poem or like Artemis in canto XXX, demanding a love purged of vanity, of 'mean . . . hates / Fostered in falsity' and of the urge to destroy. (Here the propagandist is subdued to the poetic vision.) At the same time, 'error is all in the not done, / all in the diffidence that faltered'.

That too-often anthologized passage of traditional lyric does not stand in isolation from what precedes and what follows it, nor is it the climax or summit of the sequence.

'Swinburne my only miss', in **LXXXII**, picks up from 'faltered . . .', and begins a sixty-three line passage giving further details of what Pound had to get through in London, concluding with an affirmation of Ford's 'humanitas'. The ideogram 'jen' alongside 'humanitas' was interpreted by Pound as representing man in touch with both earth and sky, that is holding together the light of intelligence and the fecundity of the biosphere. The second half of the canto (again sixty-three lines) celebrates a ritual marriage of man and earth, taking leads from Whitman's 'Out Of The Cradle Endlessly Rocking', from Kipling's *Kim*, and from Aeschylus's Clytemnaestra. This is to put into practice the wisdom of 'learn of the green world what can be thy place', and to follow the example of 'Zeus lies in Ceres' bosom' (81/531).

The true climax of the Pisan sequence is **LXXXIII**. Here a full humanity and a just social order are first conceived in terms of combinations of light and water in air and in art. 'Mermaids, that carving' is a fine grace note. The music is everywhere connecting and integrating perceptions of natural energies and human ideas, as if to prove that 'Le Paradis n'est pas artificiel'. So 'The roots go down to the river's edge / and the hidden city moves upward'; and (this is out of Mencius) the sun's breath 'nourishes by its rectitude'; or again, 'that he eat of the barley corn / and move with the seed's breath'. There is a new lightness and aerial fluidity in the writing – to the reader's eye the words float in the white spaces of the page – and an evident impulse to form lyric strophes. Moreover, in several places 'the virtue *hilaritas*' is manifest. There is no mention of usury, and while his 'month in the death cells' is not forgotten, still he sees even the world of the camp with the eyes of his spirits of love. Just now his divinity is upon him, not merely wished for in the phantasms of classical myth. At the same time his mood is as much Confucian as Eleusinian. Thus 'the humane man has amity with the hills'; and it is a real infant wasp descending to earth from the mud nest on his tent roof 'that shall sing in the bower' of Persephone. Again, there is a down-to-earth, lived humanity in his recollection of Yeats composing his 'great Peeeeacock'. The entire canto is a celebration of 'humanitas', of man as the live intelligence of the cosmos.

The work of *The Pisan Cantos*, it now appears, has not been to recover 'Italia tradita' (74/444) or to save the Constitution, at least not immediately and directly. It has been rather to reconstitute the poet's own mind, to bring it out of chaos into enlightenment, and so to fit it for a renewed effort to realize in whatever way he can the natural order of things. The final canto, **LXXXIV** – in three sections, each of exactly forty lines – re-enters the problematic realm of action, with the USA now in the foreground. An instance of how problematic this can be is the associating of Mussolini and Pierre Laval and Vidkun Quisling, the last two leading collaborators with the Nazi invaders of their countries, with 'men full of humanitas (manhood)' (84/553). The bracketed addition indicates in this context a failure to maintain 'distinctions in clarity' and a politicizing and coarsening of language characteristic of Pound in his wartime propaganda. This is disconcerting – as it is disconcerting to look into a galaxy and come upon a black hole amid its great spiral of stars. How they can coexist is beyond our comprehension, and nonetheless they do somehow coexist.

Bibliography

Bunting, Basil (1968). *Collected Poems*. Oxford: Oxford University Press.

Cookson, William (1985). *A Guide to The Cantos of Ezra Pound*. London: Croom Helm. New enlarged edition in preparation.

Davis, Kay (1984). *Fugue and Fresco: Structures in Pound's Cantos*. Orono, ME: National Poetry Foundation.

De Rachewiltz, Mary (1971). *Discretions*. London: Faber & Faber.

Eliot, T. S. (1963). *Collected Poems 1909–1962*. London: Faber & Faber.

Furia, Philip (1984). *Pound's Cantos Declassified*. University Park: Pennsylvania State University Press.

Kearns, George (1980). *Guide to Ezra Pound's 'Selected Cantos'*. Folkestone: Dawson.

Kearns, George (1989). *Ezra Pound: The Cantos*. Cambridge: Cambridge University Press.

Kenner, Hugh (1951). *The Poetry of Ezra Pound*. Norfolk. CT: New Directions.

Kenner, Hugh (1972). *The Pound Era*. London: Faber & Faber.

Makin, Peter (1985). *Pound's Cantos*. London: George Allen & Unwin.

Marsh, Alec (1998). *Money and Modernity: Pound, Williams, and the Spirit of Jefferson*. Tuscaloosa: University of Alabama Press.

Pound, Ezra (1935). *Jefferson and/or Mussolini: L'Idea Statale – Fascism as I Have Seen It*. London: Stanley Nott.

Pound, Ezra (1938). *Guide to Kulchur*. London: Faber & Faber.

Pound, Ezra (1951). *Confucius: The Great Digest & The Unwobbling Pivot*. New York: New Directions.

Pound, Ezra (1956). *Confucian Analects*. London: Peter Owen.

Pound, Ezra (1973). *Selected Prose 1909–1965*, ed. William Cookson. London: Faber & Faber.

Pound, Ezra (1978). *'Ezra Pound Speaking': Radio Speeches of World War II*, ed. Leonard W. Doob. Westport, CT: Greenwood Press.

Pound, Ezra (1987). *The Cantos of Ezra Pound*, 4th collected edn. London: Faber & Faber. [Note: 74/498 signifies canto 74, page 498 of this edition.]

Pound, Ezra (1990). *Personae: The Shorter Poems of Ezra Pound*, a revd edn, ed. Lea Baechler and A. Walton Litz. New York: New Directions.

Pound, Ezra (1991). *Ezra Pound's Poetry and Prose Contributions to Periodicals*, vols 5–8, ed. Lea Baechler, A. Walton Litz and James Longenbach. New York: Garland.

Pound, Ezra (1998). *Ezra and Dorothy Pound: Letters in Captivity, 1945–1946*, ed. Omar Pound and Robert Spoo. New York: Oxford University Press.

Rabaté, Jean-Michel (1986). *Language, Sexuality and Ideology in Ezra Pound's 'Cantos'*. London: Macmillan.

Redman, Tim (1991). *Ezra Pound and Italian Fascism*. Cambridge: Cambridge University Press.

Terrell, Carroll F. (1984). *A Companion to the Cantos of Ezra Pound*. Berkeley: University of California Press.

Yeats, W. B. (ed.) (1936). *The Oxford Book of Modern Verse*. Oxford: Oxford University Press.

Yeats, W. B. (1983). *The Poems*, ed. Richard J. Finneran. London: Macmillan.

38

Robert Lowell: *Life Studies*

Stephen Matterson

Life Studies has been one of the most acclaimed and influential single books in American poetry. It exists alongside *Leaves of Grass*, *Prufrock and Other Observations*, *Harmonium*, *Spring and All*, *Howl and Other Poems*, *77 Dream Songs* and *Ariel* as a work through which a distinctive American poetic tradition has been defined. In spite of subsequent acclaim, however, *Life Studies* was a book which its author regarded on its publication in 1959 with a remarkable degree of uncertainty concerning its worth and status. Lowell lacked the self-assured belief, characteristic of a Whitman or a Williams or a Ginsberg, in the revolutionary originality of his work and indeed he wondered whether the poems were any good at all. *Life Studies*, he thought, could either be a dead end, an aberration in his poetic career, or it could open up a fresh way of writing. He did not know which. 'When I finished *Life Studies*', Lowell said in 1960, 'I was left hanging on a question mark. I am still hanging there. I don't know whether it is a death-rope or a lifeline' (Price, 1974, p. 80).

The reasons for Lowell's self-doubt are not hard to find, and indeed self-doubt itself is a telling trope in *Life Studies*, from the envy of the lofty confidence of the Victorians expressed in its first poem 'Beyond the Alps', to the potential annihilation of the self in the final one, 'Skunk Hour'. Appropriately, *Life Studies* does not exhibit any Whitmanesque exuberant self-belief, in either thematic or technical terms. That it was not Lowell's first book points to a significant contrast with Whitman, Eliot, Stevens and Ginsberg, for whom there was a strong element of self-conscious innovation in their first publications. For over a decade before 1959, since the publication of his first volumes, *Land of Unlikeness* (1944) and *Lord Weary's Castle* (1946), Lowell had held a formidable reputation in American poetry. He developed a particular style of poetry which was well suited to the climate in which New Criticism was institutionalized. Technically his work was dazzling in its formal effects. Stylistically it was dense, allusive, impersonal and 'difficult' in the ways that New Criticism encouraged. Thematically it was deeply religious, even Puritanical, in its judgement of the modern world, informed as it was by the stabilizing world view offered by the Roman Catholicism to which Lowell had converted in 1940. The poems in *Life Studies* are so different that they virtually represent Lowell's poetic self-reinvention since the book that preceded it eight years earlier, *The Mills of the Kavanaughs*. *Life Studies* is prosy, the poems loose, decentred, lacking precision, concision, density. They seem anecdotal, seem to be drafts towards more finished, achieved poems (the 'studies' of the title reinforcing this impression). Most significantly in terms of the book's immediate influence, these poems came across as naked representations of personal experiences. In the second half of *Life Studies* the self was either the subject or the inescapable mediating presence, undisguised by the masking convention of the poetic persona. What he wanted, Lowell said later, was readers to feel they were getting 'the real Robert Lowell' (Seidel, 1961, p. 247).

More than anything else, it was this feature of *Life Studies* which accounted for the immediate influence that it had on other writers. But perhaps the longer-term influence of the book will prove to be stylistic rather than thematic, as we come to accept decentred non-symbolic writing as the foundation of postmodern poetry. However, at the end of the 1950s it was the use of the self, 'the real Robert Lowell', which stimulated the acclaim for *Life Studies* and contributed to the sense that there really was a poetic revolution underway as the authority of the Modernist generation and of that most influenced by New Criticism began to decline. In stating this, though, it needs immediately to be emphasized that *Life Studies* by itself did not initiate the revolution in taste which led to the so-called 'confessional' movement and to postmodern poetics. It was the middle of the 1950s that had marked the beginning of that change and certainly the work of Ginsberg (*Howl and Other Poems*, 1956), Charles Olson ('The Kingfishers', 1950) and W. D. Snodgrass (*Heart's Needle*, 1959) did much to change the prevailing poetic climate. Along with those writers, there were other crucial factors. These include the growing acceptance of the work of William Carlos Williams during the 1950s, the re-emergence of Whitman's poetry after New Critical-led neglect (the centenary of the first publication of *Leaves of Grass* was celebrated in 1955), and even the 1955 publication of Thomas Johnson's edition of Emily Dickinson which made her work available in a completely new way. From this larger perspective *Life Studies* was not unique in representing an individual self interacting with a public world. It drew upon fresh work in the 1950s but also on an older tradition of American writing in which individual experience is validated, and in which the poem is valued for being authentically grounded in the personal. *Life Studies* demanded attention as something fresh, though, because Lowell was an established poet whose work was fundamentally and demonstrably revised with this book. He was not virtually unknown like Snodgrass or Olson or Ginsberg. When Lowell's work changed, it was time to acknowledge a shift in American poetry.

Nor of course does literary history exist somehow apart from larger public history. *Life Studies* is a book for the end of the 1950s in the United States. Norman Mailer called the 1950s 'one of the worst decades in the history of man' (Montgomery, 1965, p. 5), and certainly the decade was seen as anti-intellectual, a time when American life seemed to demand more conformity than ever before, perhaps as a reaction against the loosening of social roles during the Second World War. This was the decade characterized by the build-up of nuclear weaponry, the Cold War, McCarthyism, the reinforcement of gender roles in which women were situated (during the postwar 'baby boom') as wives and mothers in the (suburban) domestic sphere, while men 'in the grey flannel suit' were uniformed as corporate entities. The 'tranquillized *Fifties*' Lowell calls the decade in 'Memories of West Street and Lepke' and the sharply double-edged phrase indicates the demand for uniformity on the surface of American life and suggests the cost of that conformity, cost leading to public and private stresses that demanded treatment in the form of the tranquillizer, 'tamed by *Miltown*'.

The fifties were 'tranquillized' but far from tranquil, and one of the paradoxes of the decade is that under a supposedly calm surface, repressed energies were developing a power that would utterly transform American life. It was during the 1950s that the roots of the public transformative movements of the 1960s in areas such as the civil rights movement and women's liberation were laid down. The task of identifying this duality of a public 'tranquillized' surface and a buried dissatisfaction holding crucial forces is an important element of *Life Studies*, and one in danger of being overlooked if we privilege only the book's private and autobiographical aspects. *Life Studies* inscribes both paralysis and undirected, potentially destructive forces; there is no readily available compromise between these. Recurring images of stasis, paralysis and death become metonyms for a public state that is frozen and unbending. Such images coalesce now and then in individual poems; they do so very powerfully in 'Inauguration Day: January 1953', with its terrible clinching image of 'the mausoleum in her heart' as Eisenhower is sworn in as president. Immobility is appalling but also somehow desirable – being 'buried' by snow perhaps a paradoxically comforting, warming image. By contrast *Life Studies* includes images of violent energies. These may be hot, colourful and vibrant, welcoming in contrast to cold and paralysis, but they represent destabilization, unharnessed and misdirected forces. Thus in 'Sailing Home From Rapallo' there are jumbles of images representing energy, but these are 'clashing colours'; brilliant and animated but, paradoxically, unwelcome because they are not amenable to stabilization.

The originality of *Life Studies* and the terms of the influence it has exerted are both thematic and technical. Of course, theme and technique cannot exist separately and one of the book's principal characteristics is the way that they are made to be especially appropriate to each other. 'It was a book without symbols' Lowell once said and in many ways this provides a helpful key to *Life Studies* (Lowell, 1969, p. 304). For one thing the statement precisely directs us towards the basic difference between *Life Studies* and his earlier poetry and, since Lowell did not make such a transition alone, it also indicates something of the direction that American poetry took after Modernism.

As a technique, symbolism involves centring the poem on a symbol, making a series of connections radiating from that centre. Technically it involves a spatialization of the poem, a gesture perfectly appropriate to New Critical emphasis on the poem as an object. In broader terms, and ones which were especially appropriate to

Lowell's poetry before *Life Studies*, the capacity to symbolize represents creative mastery over material. It is rooted in the imagination's transformation of reality that romanticism celebrated. For a religious poet, symbolism implicitly involves the recognition of some numinous aspect to surface reality. Gerard Manley Hopkins, for instance, a crucial influence on Lowell's early work, often expresses in his poems the discovery of a pre-existent symbolic order which brings him closer to witnessing God's otherwise abstract presence in concrete reality.

In contrast to Lowell's earlier style, the poems in *Life Studies* generally appear to lack formal design that involves a symbolic centre. Again, this is thematically appropriate since *Life Studies* is very much concerned with the lack of order and meaning in reality and about the inability of the individual either to locate or formulate a coherent stable satisfying pattern. Tellingly, Lowell said that he wanted each poem in *Life Studies* to be 'as open and single surfaced as a photograph' (Lowell, 1971, p. 272). Images of looking into flat surfaces recur, particularly in 'My Last Afternoon with Uncle Devereux Winslow', suggesting a separation of surface from substance, a loss of weight and meaning. Often the surface of an individual poem is disrupted, its images disconnected from each other, and the poems often lack exactly the kind of stabilizing, symbolic centre that would give them the internal coherence that we usually expect to find in poetry.

As well as developing a non-symbolist technique, Lowell in *Life Studies* also worked away from the sense of the autonomous lyric poem as a unit of meaning. In part this has to do with his sense of the possibilities offered by prose narrative sequence. As its first reviewers often noted (and not usually with approval), the book had a casual quality which was in sharp contrast to the heightened language, even Yeatsian grandiloquence, of Lowell's earlier style. This is evident not only in the fact that a large and crucial part of it, '91 Revere Street', is autobiographical prose (unfortunately omitted from the book's first edition, published in England), but also in the prosaic, almost casual, improvisational quality of some of the poems. It should be emphasized though that the prose of '91 Revere Street' is highly crafted and charged, and that the improvisational nature of individual poems is only apparent; often they retain conventional formal structures and effects even though these are subdued.

It is important also to emphasize that *Life Studies* is a sequence. Although not overly schematized it can almost be read as if there were a narrative progression of a set of themes. Thus, 'Beyond the Alps' is about renunciation of a former world view. It is a post-Christian poem involving an imaginative rebirth of the self into a human secular, natural landscape and initiating an endeavour to see humans as figures belonging to that landscape. The poems that follow explore the implications of an embracing of materiality and of no longer possessing an abstracting view of the world. After a series of confrontations with artistic, familial, historical and private crises, the speaker of *Life Studies* comes in 'Skunk Hour' to face the self alone, desperately requiring a point of reconnection to others. It is important to emphasize not only the themes in the sequence of *Life Studies* but the poetic form that this sequence takes. In breaking down the boundary of the individual poem, Lowell requires the reader to see a series of often complex echoes of images from poem to poem, section to section. There is an abundance of connected images in *Life Studies*, so that the later poems embrace a powerful accumulation of meaning. This point can be missed if we study the individual poem in an anthology selection of Lowell's work, and this is partly why the original omission of '91 Revere Street' was so unfortunate. The poems of *Life Studies* need to be experienced in the context that Lowell made for them.

Some good examples of connecting images are in the poem 'Ford Madox Ford' from Part Three of the book, which comprises four poems on twentieth-century writers. There is a fairly broad thematic unity to this section, as Lowell explores artistic displacement and the forms of integrity that the alienated modern artist possesses. Certainly, a reading of 'Ford Madox Ford' in isolation would reveal this theme in a general way. Ford is represented as a maker of fictions (imaginative novelistic fictions as well as tall tales and lies) and on one level is commemorated for this art. But this elegiac recognition is destabilized by the accompanying recognition that Ford's fictions were the means of his disengagement from others. The terrible images of displacement gradually proliferate in the poem. As the clutter of contradictory images depicting Ford increases, the speaker seems to give up and close the poem with a simple statement pointing out Ford's generosity and his decline: 'Ford, you were a kind man and you died in want'. The poem is partly about writing an elegiac poem, of seeking some image or central symbol as summation of the life of the deceased, yet about not being able to muster such a clinching image. The images in this poem become so discrete as to be contradictory (both misanthropic Timon *and* convivial Falstaff), and not readily available to a single controlling discourse.

Although a reasonable enough reading of 'Ford Madox Ford', this does not take into account the complex connections between images from this poem and other parts of *Life Studies*. For instance, the opening of the poem recounts Ford's tall tale about playing golf with Lloyd George and audaciously chipping a shot on the green to make a birdie. The significance of the anecdote does not come only from this poem. The reader needs to perceive a contrast between Ford and the representation of Lowell's own father. In the ironically formal elegy 'Commander Lowell', Lowell's father will be described as a dogged but poor golfer, taking 'four shots with his putter to sink his putt'. The prosaic literalist timidity of Lowell's father contrasts sharply with the imaginative style and bravado of Ford's self-representation, as someone who 'used his niblick on the green'. The father's unassertive self-effacement that so upset the young Robert Lowell is being subtly erased by a hero-worship of Ford's style and self-assurance. The connection makes implicit something crucial to the poem but not made explicit within it: the fact that Ford is an idealized father figure for Lowell. The imagistic connection with Lowell's maternal grandfather, another alternative father, is also apparent, in the association with the car.

But this connection is also qualified, as the similarities rather than differences between Ford and Lowell's father are also implied. For instance, Ford's 'gagging for air' and 'huffing' recall both how the father 'gasped and wheezed', and the description of him as a 'fish out of water'. In '91 Revere Street' the father is described as 'a mumbler'; Ford is a 'master, mammoth mumbler'. The actual 'dress sword and gold braid' of Lowell's father for which his son longs in 'Commander Lowell' is matched by the 'worn uniform, gilt dragons on the revers of the tunic' in Ford's anecdote. The imaginative self-representations (or self-delusions) of both men seem to merge and become ludicrous, filled with pathos and unintentionally self-isolating gestures. Ford is appealing because he appears to have metamorphosed the failures of Lowell's father into success. But the inconsistencies and tall tales only bring him closer to the actual father in terms of failure and displacement. The final lines about Lowell's father's death in 'Terminal Days at Beverly Farms' are on one level reductively bathetic: 'his last words to Mother were: / "I feel awful"'. They are also pointedly in contrast to the heroic dying words of 'Count' Bowditch as reported in '91 Revere Street' ('I'm all right. Get on the job, Bilge'). But they are actually very similar to the last lines of 'Ford Madox Ford' in substituting a simple declared truth in straightforward language for elaborate fictions and distortions of the self. These connections suggest that although in this section of *Life Studies* Lowell seeks a liberating alternative to his family, the terms of that family failure are constantly rehearsed elsewhere.

There are many other connections between 'Ford Madox Ford' and other parts of *Life Studies*. The 'pernod-yellow' sun is linked to the 'spumante-bubbling' sea of 'Sailing Home from Rapallo' and both phrases suggest inappropriate opulence. There are images connecting Ford and Billy 'Battleship Bilge' Harkness as representatives of exaggerated manhood. Ford's elephantine aspect is echoed at the end of 'To Speak of the Woe that is in Marriage' as a coarse image of sexuality (where the husband's climacteric also recalls the antics of Billy Harkness on father's 'rhinoceros hide' arm-chair). The phrase 'sport of kings' describing war in 'Ford Madox Ford' means commanding a destroyer in '91 Revere Street'. Ford's 'pockets turned inside out' anticipate Hart Crane's profit, 'a pocket with a hole'. Ford's story of being 'mustard gassed' is immediately echoed in 'To Delmore Schwartz' with the refrigerator that gurgles mustard gas. Even the name 'Ford' recurs: 'the clashing colours of my Ford' from 'Sailing Home from Rapallo', 'my Tudor Ford' from 'Skunk Hour'.

Such connections between 'Ford Madox Ford' and other parts of *Life Studies* provide only one example of the myriad associations that Lowell creates in *Life Studies*. Symbols are fragmented and unavailable as structuring devices in the individual poem, but images accumulate and proliferate throughout the book, as do names and characters. This aspect is oddly neglected in existing criticism on *Life Studies*, even though it was one which other poets who were immediately influenced by Lowell also utilized. Sylvia Plath's *Ariel*, for example, also makes use of cumulative imagery by which the significance of the individual lyric is superseded by the overall book. The technique of *Life Studies* does place particular demands on the reader and does require a certain kind of creative and imaginative response. Instead of reading and comprehending the individual poem as a discrete unit of knowledge, the reader is required to recognize the blurring of the boundaries between poems. Furthermore, the reader is required to participate to a degree in the thought processes evident in the poems, to realize that their characteristic shifts and ellipses indicate not only an uncertain consciousness behind the poems but are gestures towards readerly participation. Although John Ashbery is no admirer of Lowell, his poetic technique of including the dynamic processes of thought rather than only the object of thought is very similar to that of *Life Studies*.

Thematically, *Life Studies* broadly addresses the topic of disintegration and the individual's attitude towards it. While it is best to be wary of approaching *Life Studies* as if it were deliberately or carefully schematized, Steven Yenser's (1975) book *Circle to Circle* usefully makes the point that the volume touches on disintegration in different ways. The four parts of the book, he submits, correspond to disintegration and decline in four areas; at certain historical moments, in the family, in the role of the writer in society, and in the individual. Certainly these do not exist separately. For example, '91 Revere Street' could be said to focus mainly on a family dynamic that is failing. But equally it touches importantly on all of the other areas of failure. Indeed, it is important to remember that the name 'Lowell' had a public resonance in New England, so that when Lowell wrote about his private life and his family there was inevitably a public and historical dimension. This certainly qualifies any assumptions about the private and personal nature of *Life Studies*; as Elizabeth Bishop shrewdly noted in a 1957 letter to Lowell, 'I could write in as much detail about my Uncle Artie, say – but what would be the significance? . . . Whereas all you have to do is put down the names!' (Bishop, 1994, p. 351).

'91 Revere Street' opens with reference to a Lowell ancestor, Mordecai Myers, whose semitic first name ('he has no Christian name') establishes him as being out of place among the names Lowell, Winslow and Stark, so redolent of New England Protestantism and English heritage. This suggests a historical displacement, and one which connects back to the 'Mad Negro Soldier' of the poem that immediately precedes '91 Revere Street' (Myers is described as 'a dark man, a German Jew'), and forward to Delmore Schwartz. Myers suggests displacement, but, like Schwartz and the black soldier, also implies the possession of an energy which is both menacingly destructive and liberating. Although imagined as passionate, Myers is disappointingly 'tame and honourable'. The black soldier's energy must also be tamed through confinement. Both he and Schwartz are potentially characteristic of Lowell's own self-representation; tamed, tranquillized and holding a 'locked razor'.

In multiple ways, the theme of family breakdown in '91 Revere Street' is refracted so that it does not exist apart from the larger set of themes that the book considers. Again, it is important not to represent *Life Studies* as if it were a conclusive work. Part of its great power derives from Lowell's own wavering in his attitudes towards his themes. For example, it is tempting to depict 'Beyond the Alps' as if it were reasonably straightforward in theme and attitude. Lowell is in transition from 'the city of God', from a religious apprehension of experience, towards a secular one. Leaving Rome also suggests leaving the project of literary Modernism; particularly, focusing on the figure of Mussolini, rejecting its association with fascism. The poem can be acceptably paraphrased in this way, and its importance for the rest of *Life Studies* can readily be established. But the attitude towards what is being left behind is far from simple. There is a deeply inscribed regret, a sense of loss and diminution – even anger

concerning the declared doctrine of the Assumption which alienated so many
Catholics in the 1950s. Lowell envies the consumption and confidence of the Victorians; it is 'Much against my will' that he leaves Rome. 'Beyond the Alps' is on one
level about potential being released, about liberation from the grand narratives that
the individual may occupy, and in which the individual might be paralysed. But it
is also about loss, failure (it opens with an image of failure) and reduction. This deep
ambivalence drives *Life Studies*. Disintegration and decline are the facts behind the
book. They may release new energies that will regenerate society and the individual.
But they also threaten the individual, and the sense of being fallen, or of being imprisoned, of life itself having been reduced, diminished, is very strong: to be 'cured' is to
be 'frizzled, stale and small' Lowell writes in 'Home After Three Months Away'. It is
in this respect that the book can be seen as itself poised between what Modernism
was and what postmodernism would become. Lowell's sense of the past leads to a
moral judgement of fragmentation; he cannot embrace contradiction and displacement in the ways that the later postmodern writer will.

Perhaps this helps to explain one aspect of *Life Studies* which has attracted insuffi-
cient critical attention: the extent to which it is an elegiac book. In part this has to
do with Lowell's age and life experiences during the 1950s. Parental death, effectively
the passing of a generation, naturally stimulates introspection in the bereaved child,
perhaps intensified in the case of an only child. For Lowell, the death of his father
(1950) and his mother (1954) came during his own early middle age, and form crucial
narrative points in *Life Studies*. The book is suffused with imagery related to death
and bereavement. In 'Beyond the Alps' the grotesque imagery related to the death of
Mussolini is interestingly countered by the image of the doctrinal denial of Mary's
physical death, and imagery related to the appalling incompatibility of life and death
recurs, notably in 'My Last Afternoon with Uncle Devereux Winslow'. More specifically, much of the book's sense of disengagement, displacement and potentially
destructive self-analysis has its starting point in the death of the parents, with whom
Lowell had a troubled relationship. That those parents themselves stand almost as
metonyms for a historical past intensifies the individual's sense of historical displacement. If we look at *Life Studies* as a narrative, the deaths of the parents form the book's
emotional climax, after which the survivor must radically assess his own life and the
remaining connections to others. In this respect, Part Four's sequence of five elegiac
poems for the parents, 'Commander Lowell', 'Terminal Days at Beverly Farms',
'Father's Bedroom', 'For Sale' and 'Sailing Home from Rapallo' repays special attention. Strikingly, the sequence offers the material for formal elegy yet simultaneously
indicates a loss of control over that material and, at times, over language itself. These
are poems in which nothing quite coheres, in which jumbles of things or images are
brought together but which seem to lack overall coherence or purpose. 'Father's
Bedroom', for example, reads like an inventory made by an executor, a list of remnants. There is no animating principle to the poem, even though as metonyms the
things in the list are revelatory. The blue kimono and plush Chinese sandals indicate
the slightly effeminate nature of the dead father, his unease with bold masculine

figures, and also suggest a frustrated orientalism to his character. On one level the poem is grimly focused on absence, since each thing indicates a lost connection to the father. But the details themselves are carefully chosen and point also to human isolation and lack of love; this is, markedly, *father's* bedroom not, say, 'My parents' bedroom'. The inscription on the book's flyleaf, 'Robbie from Mother', notably lacks even the conventional gesture of writing 'love'. Ironically, this writing tells not through what it says but through what is left out. In this way it is connected to the 'grandiloquent lettering' on the casket of the dead mother in 'Sailing Home from Rapallo', where 'Lowell' has been misspelt *'Lovel'*. The misnaming ironically suggests 'love', but as in 'Robbie from Mother' testifies, primarily to its absence.

The sequence indicates a larger aspect of *Life Studies*. In it Lowell searches for a coherence or at least for a cohering principle, but is left with its absence. 'Sailing Home from Rapallo' begins with a literal incoherence, the failure of Lowell to communicate with the nurse of the dead mother. The poems in this sequence are profoundly concerned with attempts to find appropriate images of connection, coherence, but loss, grief and frustration mean disconnection, incoherence and fragmentation. It is not until 'Skunk Hour' that the tormented mind can begin to find coherence and start to remake a pattern in life. This is a formal pattern too, in that 'Skunk Hour' is brilliant in its formal achievement. The buried rhymes that Lowell so admired in the poetry of Browning are here made his own, and the poem's stanzaic organization is as powerful as that of Yeats. It is a poem about making a coherent pattern as much as it is about the restorative power of selfless altruistic instinct imaged by the mother skunk. Language that was on the verge of incoherence earlier in the sequence is here reclaimed and reorganized.

By way of conclusion, it is important to emphasize that Lowell is not completely in control of the poems in *Life Studies*. Some of the critical assessments of the book imply that he has a Flaubert-like mastery over his material and the connections, and that the book's structure, organization and themes are systematic and deliberate. While it does provide a directed narrative sequence, *Life Studies* is not written in fulfilment of some prior plan. Part of its greatness is in its heuristic improvisational quality, indicative of an individual seeking coherence and significance in a disordered, troubled life. Some of Lowell's own comments on the book as an 'outpouring' demonstrate this lack of deliberation (Rosenthal, 1967, p. 67). Nor was Lowell ever quite comfortable with the book or convinced that it fitted easily into the shape of his work. Others hailed *Life Studies* as a success far more readily than Lowell himself did; Anne Sexton, for instance, in her poem 'To A Friend Whose Work Has Come to Triumph', figures Lowell as Icarus (both ascending and descending). Lowell's doubts about *Life Studies* were never really dispelled. 'Why not say what happened?' he persistently asks; the question appears in one of his last poems, 'Epilogue' – a question as relevant to *Life Studies* as it is to his last book, *Day by Day*. The defiant tone of the question is more apparent than real, as Lowell acknowledges the potentially paralysing conflict between the imagination and accuracy. But one of the real triumphs of *Life Studies* is exactly in its creative inscription of doubt and uncertainty. 'I cannot make it cohere' lamented Pound in *The Cantos*. It is typical of Lowell's being poised between Modernism and postmodernism that he too laments the loss of such coherence, while simultaneously distrusting the grand narratives that Modernism endorsed as coherence.

BIBLIOGRAPHY

Axelrod, S. G. (1978). *Robert Lowell: Life and Art.* Princeton, NJ: Princeton University Press.

Axelrod S. G. and Deese, H. (eds) (1986). *Robert Lowell: Essays on the Poetry.* Cambridge: Cambridge University Press.

Bell, V. (1983). *Robert Lowell: Nihilist as Hero.* London: Harvard University Press.

Bishop, E. (1994). *One Art: The Selected Letters*, ed. Robert Giroux. London: Chatto and Windus.

Hamilton, I. (1982). *Robert Lowell: A Biography.* London: Faber.

Hobsbaum, P. (1988). *A Reader's Guide to Robert Lowell.* London: Thames and Hudson.

Kalstone, D. (1977). *Five Temperaments.* London: Oxford University Press.

Lowell, R. (1961). 'An Interview with Frederick Seidel', in Lowell, *Collected Prose*, ed. Robert Giroux. London: Faber, pp. 235–66.

Lowell, R. (1969). 'Et in America Ego: The American Poet Robert Lowell talks to the novelist V. S. Naipaul.' *The Listener*, 4 September 1969, pp. 302–4.

Lowell, R. (1971). 'A Conversation with Ian Hamilton', in Lowell, *Collected Prose*, ed. Robert Giroux. London: Faber, pp. 267–90.

Lowell, R. (1987). *Collected Prose*, ed. Robert Giroux. London: Faber.

Matterson, S. (1988). *Berryman and Lowell: The Art of Losing.* Houndmills: Macmillan.

Mazzaro, J. (1965). *The Poetic Themes of Robert Lowell.* Ann Arbor: University of Michigan Press.

Meiners, R. K. (1970). *Everything to be Endured: An Essay on Robert Lowell and Modern Poetry.* Columbia: University of Missouri Press.

Montgomery, J. (1965). *The Fifties.* London: Allen and Unwin.

Parkinson, T. (ed.) (1968). *Robert Lowell: A Collection of Critical Essays.* Englewood Cliffs, NJ: Prentice-Hall.

Perloff, M. (1973). *The Poetic Art of Robert Lowell.* Ithaca, NY: Cornell University Press.

Price, J. (ed.) (1974). *Critics on Robert Lowell.* London: George Allen and Unwin.

Rosenthal, M. L. (1967). *The New Poets.* London: Oxford University Press.

Seidel, F. (1961). 'An Interview with Frederick Seidel', in Robert Lowell, *Collected Prose.* London: Faber, pp. 235–66.

Williamson, A. (1974). *Pity the Monsters: The Political Vision of Robert Lowell.* New Haven, CT: Yale University Press.

Yenser, S. (1975). *Circle to Circle: The Poetry of Robert Lowell.* Berkeley: University of California Press.

39

Louis MacNeice:
The Burning Perch
Peter McDonald

The Burning Perch was published in 1963, a matter of weeks after Louis MacNeice's death at the age of fifty-five. It was an early death, and at the time of writing this volume MacNeice can have had little notion that it would be his last; indeed, the poems were composed during a period when the writer was making a new start in his working and private lives, having moved away from London and on to a part-time contract with the BBC (where his long and prolific career as a radio writer and producer had begun in 1942), and having established a successful relationship following the collapse of his second marriage. For all that, *The Burning Perch* is a dark book, full of the kinds of foreboding and anxiety that seem to belie the biographical new start from which it emerges; MacNeice himself recognized as much in the volume's dedicatory lines, where the contents are summarized as 'nightmare and cinders', and his partner Mary is asked to 'Forgive what I give you'. Ironically, perhaps, it is this last and posthumous collection of poems which has come to be seen as one of MacNeice's strongest volumes, and, in terms of its influence on later poets, his most original and influential book.

At the time of his death MacNeice was a known and respected, but no longer a widely celebrated poet. Like other members of his generation, including W. H. Auden, he was often read as a survivor of the 1930s; his best-known work, the book-length *Autumn Journal* (1939), was interpreted as the most characteristic product of a wide-ranging, but slick and journalistic poet, who had largely failed to develop his talents after the circumstantial impetus of the years of pre-war tension and crisis had lessened. Like Auden too, MacNeice was routinely criticized for no longer being the kind of poet he once was (or, more accurately, for being no longer the kind of poet which in truth he never was in the first place). At all events, *The Burning Perch* is the work of a writer who lives in the shadow of a distorted past, and whose claims on a future have to be fought for; as a result, the poems are written self-consciously against the odds, and this struggle becomes in part their subject. If one of the book's preoccupations is the past (seen in terms both of history and of the personal memory), another is the future – a future under various incalculable threats, notably from the Cold War and its 'Runways in rut, control / Towers out of control, and burns / Whose gift is not to cure' ('The Pale Panther'). To imagine a far future, in the early 1960s, was necessarily an act of faith as well as imagination, and MacNeice's interest in posterity, in *The Burning Perch*, results in poetry which makes an issue out of keeping faith: with memory, with imagination, and with language itself.

The Burning Perch is filled with the personnel, the gadgets and the impedimenta of modern life: dentists and tax-collectors, pet shops, taxis, battery-hens, satellites, computers, traffic-jams, electric fences, sleeping pills, frozen sperm, spacemen and telephone kiosks populate the poems as aspects of a contemporary world seen with particular sharpness. This much, of course, had in one respect always been the case in MacNeice's writing: *Autumn Journal*, too, was similarly exact in its eye for detail. But by 1963 MacNeice sees these things as aspects of a present over which the past and the future cast strange lights and long shadows, and the resultant effects are less documentary than surreal:

> On the podium in lieu of a man
> With fallible hands is ensconced
> A metal lobster with built-in tempi;
> The deep sea fishermen in lieu of
> Battling with tunny and cod
> Are signing their contracts for processing plankton.
>
> On roof after roof the prongs
> Are baited with faces, in saltpan and brainpan
> The savour is lost, in deep
> Freeze after freeze in lieu of a joint
> Are piled the shrunken heads of the past
> And the offals of unborn children.

Lines like these, from the poem 'In Lieu', move from a horror of mechanization to the mechanization of horror, following a nightmare logic of association (the fishermen lead to 'baited' in the next stanza, while faces, brains and heads accumulate to grisly effect). And, as with many of the volume's images, these are recapitulated in other poems: mechanical actions proliferate, as in 'Spring Cleaning', where 'under the water / Black fingers pick at the ocean bed', or 'New Jerusalem', in which 'Bulldozer, dinosaur, pinheaded diplodocus / Champ up forgotten and long-dry water-pipes'; human fingers, too, recur in odd ways, so that 'October in Bloomsbury' has 'amputated delicate fingers tingle', while 'Memoranda to Horace' watches 'one's precious identity / Filtered away through what one had fancied / Till now were one's fingers, shadows to shadows'. The horrific 'offals of unborn children' is part of a recurring concern with children unborn or unconceived, so that 'Memoranda to Horace' insists on how 'the point was to recognize / The unborn face', and 'Off the Peg' imagines 'when the coffinlike cradle pitched on the breaking bough / Reveals once more some fiend or avatar'; 'Spring Cleaning' hears how 'In spruce new wards new mothers shriek' while 'New deaf incapsulated souls / Gaze out at noisy birds of dawn'. The poem 'Perspectives', too, ends with an unborn child:

> And down at the end of the queue some infant
> Of the year Two Thousand straddles the world
> To match the child that was once yourself.
> The further-off people are sometimes the larger.

The image of the child is double: it reflects in terms of personal memory back into the past, and in terms of a chillingly impersonal posterity into the future, while in both aspects it can as easily become an image of horror as of hope. The symbolic economy, so to speak, of *The Burning Perch* relies on such relations, and the book's contemporary surface has these for its depth of sombre background.

One of the most impressive achievements of the collection is its concentration of means, through which recurring images become more unsettling and strange. This is not the only kind of concentration at work, however, for MacNeice is at the height of his powers as a verse technician in *The Burning Perch*, and there are many poems in which the cadences of the speaking voice are heightened and intensified to produce poetry whose formal pulse beats unnervingly, and to disconcertingly original effect. MacNeice wrote of how he wanted to escape 'the "iambic" groove' in English verse rhythm, and in *The Burning Perch* this is achieved without the artificial gimmicks of either free verse or pastiche classicism. In 'Charon', for example, MacNeice is able to play off line division against the speaking voice within a framework that never adopts the 'iambic groove', and at the close he brings things to a dead halt:

> We flicked the flashlight
> And there was the ferryman just as Virgil
> And Dante had seen him.   He looked at us coldly
> And his eyes were dead and his hands on the oar
> Were black with obols and varicose veins
> Marbled his calves and he said to us coldly:
> If you want to die you will have to pay for it.

The laconic, bitten-back final line here sends shudders through a poem in which rhythmic instability (mimicking perhaps the stop–starting of the other-worldly bus journey it describes) has been of the essence; a dactylic impetus never quite produces a completely dactylic line, while the run-ons of sense across line-endings further complicate rhythmic matters, but the overall sound of MacNeice's writing is both compelling and fluid. Earlier work (and particularly the lyric poetry of his previous two volumes *Visitations*, 1957 and *Solstices*, 1961), had seen the maturing of MacNeice's formal originality, but the rhythmic fluency and power of *The Burning Perch* are the products of a lifetime's acuteness of hearing.

'Soap Suds', the poem with which MacNeice opens the collection, provides an excellent example of the formal command which enables poetry to make new shapes and sounds for its subject matter. The poem's principal idea is simple enough – that of personal recollection – but its understanding of that idea becomes a series of complications, twists and turns in sequential time, in which the recollecting self is dizzyingly implicated. 'Soap Suds' uses a long line, of shifting rhythmic identities, without rhyme to build its four-line stanzas, and it deploys its images at the beginning with an open-handed clarity:

> This brand of soap has the same smell as once in the big
> House he visited when he was eight: the walls of the bathroom open
> To reveal a lawn where a great yellow ball rolls back through a hoop
> To rest at the head of a mallet held in the hands of a child.

Even lines as long as these are not quite long enough to contain the poem's voice within them: the prominent enjambment of 'big / House' makes it hard to voice any pronounced rhythmic pattern for the first line, so that already MacNeice is creating a sense of speed in the verse, of a voice running on from one thing to the next. At the same time, the ways in which image opens out from image, as recollection from recollection, become almost subliminally associated with this sense of speed: nothing stands still here, whether croquet ball or bathroom wall, and the sentence (and stanza) ends somewhere a long way in time from the point at which it began – '*This* brand of soap' is being smelled by an adult, while 'the hands of a child' are those of the child this adult once was, now long gone, who can be summoned only by enumeration of the things in the house which he prized:

> And these were the joys of that house: a tower with a telescope;
> Two great faded globes, one of the earth, one of the stars;
> A stuffed black dog in the hall; a walled garden with bees;
> A rabbit warren; a rockery; a vine under glass; the sea.

It is with this list that MacNeice slows down the verse, as though the moment of recollection, where detail develops into detail, could create a kind of stasis in which nothing can happen, and so nothing will change. In fact, the details are not haphazard, and several find their way into poems elsewhere in the volume which is here beginning (there will be a poem near the end of *The Burning Perch*, entitled 'Star-Gazer', for example, while a dog will feature in 'The Taxis' and – with overtones of the dog Cerberus in Hades – in 'Charon'; the sea will be the subject of the poem 'Round the Corner').

However, the stasis of the second stanza of 'Soap Suds' does not last into the poem's second half. Returning to the initial recollection of the croquet game with its mallet and yellow ball, MacNeice speeds up the verse to accommodate recollections that start to run away with themselves as they hurtle towards the present tense:

To which he has now returned.   The day of course is fine
And a grown-up voice cries Play!   The mallet slowly swings,
Then crack, a great gong booms from the dog-dark hall and the ball
Skims forward through the hoop and then through the next and then

Through hoops where no hoops were and each dissolves in turn
And the grass has grown head-high and an angry voice cries Play!
But the ball is lost and the mallet slipped long since from the hands
Under the running tap that are not the hands of a child.

The formal momentum seems unstoppable; but it stops, and stops with a child who is emphatically not here. The lines move to an almost bewildering number of different possible measures, and the lines protract themselves into each other so that, for instance, the repeated triple stresses of 'a great gong booms from the dog-dark hall' are not the end of a line, but a prelude to the rhyming and running on 'and the ball / Skims'. In terms of imagery, visual and otherwise, the poem resolves into an expanding (or contracting) series of circular figures: the soap, the ball, the globes, the gong, the hoops, and finally again the ball and the soap. The circular movement of the poem itself brings the reader back to the adult hands of the beginning, not with recollections clarified and given meaning, but with the remembering self unsettled and threatened by an irruption of images with a life and intent of their own.

The poem's 'grown-up voice', which soon becomes an 'angry voice', is a voice in a garden, and seems to have overtones of God's voice in Eden; it is possible to read 'Soap Suds' as an exercise in memory under the shadow of the Fall. But 'Play!' echoes from this into other poems in the book, such as 'Sports Page' where 'On your Marks! En Garde! Scrum Down! Over!' modulates into a conclusion that 'The lines of print are always sidelines / And all our games funeral games', or 'Children's Games', with its virtuoso amalgamation of playground rhymes and activities. The hoop, which in 'Soap Suds' is both a croquet hoop and a child's hoop, returns in one of the five-line pieces making up 'As in their Time':

He had clowned it through.   Being born
For either the heights or the depths
He had bowled his hoop on the level
Arena; the hoop was a wheel
Of fire but he clowned it through.

The games of children in *The Burning Perch* prefigure, and are also implicit in, the suffering and the deaths of men. 'Soap Suds' begins the book by compressing such knowledge into a kaleidoscopic series of recollections, and allowing these to complicate simple distinctions between past and present, between first things and last things. In miniature, the poem expresses the tendency of MacNeice's book as a whole.

The Burning Perch is haunted by many ghosts, some from the past and others from the future. The result of this is that the poetry's take on the present time is one in which everything, no matter how definite, prosaic or concrete, is subject to the sudden destabilization of uncanny shifts into the future or past. 'October in Blooms-bury' looks at tourists and visitors near the British Museum, where 'Black men and schoolchildren rummage for culture', but warns of how 'the tutelary spirits are hard to please':

> Those epicureans who haunt the lawns, whose amputated delicate fingers tingle,
> Whose delicate eyelids are dropped for ever not to be pained by the great new
>   institutes,
> Who sometimes even when out of mind become what we miss most,
> In the callbox for instance lifting a receiver warm from the ear of a ghost.

While the contemporary world (and, in particular, the contemporary London of poems like 'Charon', 'New Jerusalem' and 'Goodbye to London') is busy chewing up the past, or picking its bones, the past has a way of surging back into these modern perspectives. MacNeice also writes poems which inhabit places where the past has become a modern business-opportunity: 'Constant' visits Istanbul, where there is

> too much history
> Tilting, canting, crawling, rotting away,
> Subsiding strata where ghosts like faults, like mites,
> Reminders of stagnation or collapse,
> Emerge into the mist.

'Rechauffe' and 'This is the Life' take similarly jaded views of Egypt, while 'Ravenna' is itself written explicitly from the visitor's point of view of the mosaics and 'A bad smell mixed with glory'. In all these places, ghosts are both present and disconcertingly without apparent meaning or intent for the present-tense observers, who seem to be merely on the way to becoming ghosts themselves.

Traditional literary ghosts want to communicate; but the ghosts of *The Burning Perch* have no such designs. On the other hand, these ghosts are present in the very means and acts of communication (like the telephone 'receiver warm from the ear of a ghost') between the living. The designer-city of 'New Jerusalem' is one in which people pretend to be separate, but live therefore in a state of illusion:

> As for the citizens, what with their cabinets
> Of faces and voices, their bags of music,
> Their walls of thin ice dividing greynesses,
> With numbers and mirrors they defy mortality.

The state of 'greyness' recurs often in these poems, as the drab background to modernity (elaborated in the poems 'The Grey Ones' and 'Greyness is All'), but the recognition that one cannot, after all, 'defy mortality' need not confirm the drabness. 'Round the Corner' speaks of the sea as 'The only anarchic democracy, where we are all vicarious / Citizens', and insists that we remember this 'as we remember a person / Whose wrists are springs to spring a trap or rock / A cradle'; the images are puzzling at first, but like others in the book they intensify by echoing through different poems, and they represent perhaps the counterbalancing alternatives to the condition of 'greyness', places for good ghosts rather than drab ones.

'The Introduction' is one of MacNeice's most powerful – and most subtly disturbing – love poems, but it is also a way of tuning in to the ghostly, or the uncanny, in the very intimacy which such things might conventionally threaten. Much possessed by death, the poem will not let go of love, even though it is pitched into the disorientating confusion of past with present, future with past, of so many of the *Burning Perch* poems. Beginning with 'They were introduced in a grave glade', the poem works a number of verbal transformations and variations to reach its destination in 'They were introduced in a green grave'; on the way, the pastoral scenery undergoes its own transformations:

> Crawly crawly
> Went the twigs above their heads and beneath
> The grass beneath their feet the larvae
> Split themselves laughing.

The lovers themselves are afraid: 'she frightened him because she was young / And thus too late' is a conventional enough fear, but the poem's hall of mirrors within a few lines turns this into 'he frightened her because he was old / And thus too early'; the attempted conclusion, 'You two should have met / Long since, he said, or else not now' is not the end of the matter. Instead, the poem repeats and changes until it reaches the 'green grave': it is important that the colour is green, and not grey. MacNeice's dedicatory lines end with the promise to 'keep my appointment / In green improbable fields with you', and the love poetry of 'The Introduction' is as good as the poet's word in this respect. Mortality is accepted as well as defied here.

The Burning Perch makes acceptances like these partly by allowing the future, for which it is always already 'too early', to zoom into the poetry's perspectives. In 'Budgie' a pet bird stands on duty to see in whatever the future holds; as the poem concludes, the difference between remote past and remote future is difficult to discern, and while individual destruction is assured, expression itself, resolved into its barest minimum, remains an irreducible fact:

> The radio telescope
> Picks up a quite different signal, the human
> Race recedes and dwindles, the giant
> Reptiles cackle in their graves, the mountain
> Gorillas exchange their final messages,
> But the budgerigar was not born for nothing,
> He stands at his post on the burning perch –

> I twitter am – and peeps like a television
> Actor admiring himself in the monitor.

The irony of the poem's return to its ground bass of contemporary observation at the end is typical of *The Burning Perch*'s refusal to leave behind the present, as is the added irony of MacNeice's domestication of the Yeatsian golden bird in 'Sailing to Byzantium' into a creature from *The Burning Perch*'s own menagerie (thus linking with a poem like 'Pet Shop' – and perhaps prompting the reader to remember that Byzantium itself has turned up already in the seedier report of 'Constant'). But the bird's nobility, and the nobility of its calling, seem if anything the stronger for these layers of irony. Again, a larger poetic strategy is being triumphantly compressed here.

The long, four-part poem 'Memoranda to Horace' appears more relaxed in its meditations on such a strategy, and it is, in many ways, a virtuoso performance in its combination of intricate form with supple conversational scope and command. And yet MacNeice's sustained meditation here on language is far from casual. The initial question of 'why bother?', in the face of 'Dissolving dialects' and the transitory nature of language itself, to write poetry and so raise 'a monument / Weaker and of less note than a mayfly / Or a quick blurb for yesterday's detergent' receives indirect, but important answers as the poem progresses. In crossing from age to age, and from reader to reader, writer to writer, it is poetry itself which becomes the agent of a seemingly impossible communication. It is not, in fact, so much the communication of the dead with the living, as that between the dead and those living readers who will themselves become the dead in time: Horace, like other ghosts in *The Burning Perch*, teaches us how to be what inevitably we will become. MacNeice talks to the past, as it were, for the future to hear:

> It is noisy today as it was when Brutus
> Fell on his sword, yet through wars and rumours
>   Of wars I would pitch on the offchance
> My voice to reach you. Yours had already
>
> Crossed the same gap to the north and future,
> Offering no consolation, simply
>   Telling me how you had gathered
> Your day, a choice it is mine to emulate.

This faces the facts equably: there is 'no consolation', in any easy sense, to be had from the kind of communication poetry offers, and there is at best 'the offchance' of success. Nevertheless the 'choice' on offer is real, and it can be made, in a way that sounds through those 'wars and rumours / Of wars' which it will not drown out.

Certainly, the world of *The Burning Perch* is a grim one. Just as certainly, however, the poems themselves are possessed of a real and compelling vitality. The paradox is one which the poetry seems often to acknowledge, and which MacNeice himself acknowledged when he wrote of how 'Fear and resentment seem here to be serving me in the same way as Yeats in his old age claimed to be served by "lust and rage"'. In the same note (written after the book had been selected as a Choice of the Poetry Book Society), the poet wrote of how 'most of these poems are two-way affairs or at least spiral ones: even in the most evil picture the good things, like the sea in one of these poems, are still there round the corner'. If the vitality of the writing is confirmed by the number of readers who, in the years since MacNeice's death, have found it both memorable and inspiring, so too, perhaps, is the writing's brooding on matters of posterity and communication across time made relevant by the ways in which the collection has been a potent influence on later poets: much of Paul Muldoon's work, for example, is indebted to MacNeice's last poems in direct ways, and many other poets have been similarly enabled by the book's originality and power. For a volume so taken up with death (and so unfortunately and inadvertently prophetic of Mac-Neice's own death), *The Burning Perch* remains extraordinarily vital, and truly a new start rather than a dead end, so much so that poets other than MacNeice himself have been able to follow the start made there. For poetry of this quality, as MacNeice's bewildered victim in 'After the Crash' discovers, 'It was too late to die'.

BIBLIOGRAPHY

Brown, T. (1975). *Louis MacNeice: Sceptical Vision*. Dublin: Gill and Macmillan.

Devine, K. and Peacock, A. J. (eds) (1998). *Louis MacNeice and his Influence*. Gerrards Cross: Colin Smythe.

Longley, E. (1988). *Louis MacNeice: A Study*. London: Faber and Faber.

McDonald, P. (1991). *Louis MacNeice: The Poet in His Contexts*. Oxford: Clarendon Press.

MacNeice, L. (1979). *Collected Poems*, ed. Dodds, E. R. London: Faber and Faber.

MacNeice, L. (1987). *Selected Literary Criticism*, ed. Heuser, A. Oxford: Clarendon Press.

Marsack, R. (1982). *The Cave of Making: The Poetry of Louis MacNeice*. Oxford: Clarendon Press.

Stallworthy, J. (1995). *Louis MacNeice*. London: Faber and Faber.

40
Sylvia Plath: *Ariel*
Sue Vice

Sylvia Plath's *Ariel* (1965) is undoubtedly the volume of poetry for which she is best known. It includes her most famous late poems, such as 'Daddy', 'Lady Lazarus', 'Fever 103°' and 'Tulips'; even Annie Hall, eponymous heroine of Woody Allen's 1977 film, had a copy on her shelves.

There is a multitude of reasons for the popularity of this collection. No one would deny the distinctive, disturbing voice and surreal imagery of the poems; and their publication soon after Plath's death in February 1963 not only made *Ariel* a bestseller, but allowed readers to imagine they could see clear connections between the trajectory of the collection and that of its author's life, as for instance in 'Edge':

> The woman is perfected.
> Her dead
> Body wears the smile of accomplishment,
> The illusion of a Greek necessity.

To see her work in less biographical terms, the moment of Plath's writing offers a particularly stark combination of discourses, both socially – Betty Friedan's 'problem without a name' (Friedan, 1963), the start of the Swinging Sixties – and historically – the rise of the ecology and disarmament movements, the legacy of the Second World War and, in the US, the end of the McCarthy era. These sit alongside poetic influences and references to popular culture, including cinema (see Britzolakis, 1999). Such varied discourses appear strikingly in Plath's work, as does a distinct strand of autobiographical discourse. This is not to say that Plath's poetry is transparently 'confessional'; indeed, Stanley Plumly refers to it more aptly as 'persona poetry' (in Alexander, 1985, p. 16). Nor is it to say that reading *Ariel* gives us any direct insight into Plath's life. Rather, archetypal stages in a female biography inflected by the 1950s and 1960s appear in the poems. These stages include the acquisition of language ('Daddy'); Oedipal – or, as Plath has it, Electral – rivalry ('Daddy'); learning to acquire the veneer of adult femininity ('The Applicant'); married life ('Tulips'); maternity ('Balloons', 'You're') and other kinds of creativity ('Wintering'); disillusionment with a male partner ('The Rabbit Catcher'); speculation about the self's own role within these stages ('Lady Lazarus'); and deathly despair ('Contusion').

Perfection of Life or Art

The published version of *Ariel* also includes poems from earlier eras in Plath's life, and although it may seem, in Robert Lowell's words, that 'these poems are playing Russian roulette with six cartridges in the cylinder' (quoted in Perloff, 1990, p. 176), we are actually reading a rather different volume from the one Plath herself prepared in a black spring-binder during the last months of her life. Ted Hughes's role in posthumously editing Plath's work – only *The Colossus* was published during her life-time – has become notorious. Marjorie Perloff argues that the effect of Hughes's editorial decisions, which included both altering the order of the poems and replacing some Plath had selected with others, is to make *Ariel* tell a tale of mental illness culminating in suicide, rather than that told by Plath's own ordering, of justified fury at marital infidelity.

It is true that the effects of poetic reordering and substitution are significant, although Perloff's interpretation tends to beg the biographical question. *Ariel 1*, as Perloff calls it, is Plath's chosen collection, identified in print only in the notes to the *Collected Poems*; *Ariel 2* is Hughes's, the published version; while there is a third Ariel in the chronological ordering to be found in the *Collected Poems*. In *Ariel 2* Hughes left out eleven of Plath's selection of forty-one poems and added instead nine poems written during the last months of her life, including 'Edge', 'Kindness' and 'Contusion'. Perloff sees a plot afoot in the particular omissions Hughes decided upon, which include 'Purdah' and 'The Rabbit Catcher': 'Hughes presents us with a Sylvia Plath who is victimized by her time and place rather than by a specific personal betrayal' (Perloff, 1990, p. 192). However, so keen is Perloff to find a particular tale in the poetry that, as Neil Roberts argues (1999, p. 22), she falls victim to excessive back-shadowing in conscripting poems, such as 'Elm', written *before* Hughes's adulterous relationship with Assia Wevill began, as evidence for the betrayal narrative. Margaret Uroff, by contrast, sees the period *after* 'Elm' as crucial in the disintegration of Plath's marriage (Uroff, 1979, p. 144). Hughes's own view on the matter of his editorial versus his personal responsibilities is compellingly put in his 1971 article 'Publishing Sylvia Plath': 'there are quite a few things more important than giving the world great poems' (Hughes, 1994, p. 167).

Hughes's omissions in the published *Ariel* also alter the context in which certain poems are read, according to Perloff (1990, p. 187). Hughes has, for instance, placed 'The Applicant' between 'Sheep in Fog' – a poem apparently 'safely' concerned with its persona's interiority (although Hughes's meticulous account of its evolution (Hughes, 1994) suggests he may have had other reasons for wanting to include it)

– and 'Lady Lazarus'; while in Plath's *Ariel 1* it is found between 'Thalidomide' and 'Barren Woman'. It is true that the latter two poems are both starkly anguished in tone, although 'Lady Lazarus', for all its black comedy, is scarcely a reassuring alternative. Perloff's reading is that in its original context it is all too clear that 'The Applicant' relates directly to the end of Plath's marriage and presents an 'awful little allegory', in Plath's own phrase (she is speaking about 'Daddy', quoted in Alvarez, 1971, p. 65), of a triangular relationship, not simply a smart look at contemporary sexual mores. In this view the 'sardonic' (Perloff 1990, p. 187) tone is directed at the male and the two female characters in the poem: the first 'living doll' is Plath's self-parodying vision of herself, while the second, barely distinguishable doll is her rival.

Seeing the poem in this way is revelatory. Without such an awareness of its four entities (the speaker and three addressees: applicant, first 'thing', and 'sweetie' in the closet) it can seem as self-contained and inert as some of Plath's other allegorical work, including 'Mushrooms' and 'Stillborn'. However, 'The Applicant' is as likely to suffer a decontextualized reading from its place in the *Collected Poems* (published in 1981, three years before Perloff's article first appeared in the *American Poetry Review*). Indeed, the appearance of this widely read and strictly chronologically arranged volume, which dissolves the reader's sense of discrete volumes of poetry, reduces the significance of Hughes's editorial interventions. Biographical knowledge is obviously not necessary in order to tease out the variety of subject-positions in 'The Applicant'; nor does it help to analyse another striking feature of the poem, which is a genderlessness curious for a poem apparently about 'woman's entrapment in marriage' (Rosenblatt, 1979, p. 112). Of the four characters in the poem only the 'sweetie in the closet' is clearly identified as a particular gender: 'Naked as paper to start / But in twenty-five years *she*'ll be silver' (my italics). The 'applicant' is asked if s/he has 'rubber breasts', and offered a figure of comfort who remains as much an 'it' as the 'Black and stiff' suit the applicant is also invited to propose marriage to. It seems that this particular vacancy is always already structured according to such strict gender roles that biological sex is irrelevant: it is automatically read into the scenario. To see the poem purely biographically is to lose such subtlety.

Plath's sequence for *Ariel* was designed to begin with the first word of 'Morning Song', which is 'love', and end with a note of hope in 'spring', the last word of 'Wintering'. It is striking that the effect of Hughes's reordering is to remove this hopeful ending, as his stated aim was the rather different one of omitting 'the more *personally* aggressive poems from 1962' (Hughes, 1981, p. 15, my italics). Critics have seen the loss of 'spring' as the loss of a narrative of a specifically feminine rebirth (Sandra Gilbert's (1979) essay is particularly concerned with Plath's representation of rebirth, in poems such as 'Fever 103°' and 'Stings'), further hardening opinion in some quarters against Hughes's patriarchal interventions. It is clear that Hughes's reordering of the collection was, understandably, based on biographical readings and it is important to bear in mind that this is what Perloff is responding to, however much one questions her doggedly biographical reading of the order of *Ariel*.

History

Plath is caught in something of a double bind in the sense that her work is read as both relentlessly autobiographical and private, yet also as appropriating public historical discourses. However, it is the interaction between the two realms which creates the poetry's shock-value and its meaning; indeed, the deployment in the poetry of the elements of her own internal 'drama', in Ted Hughes's term (1994, p. 179), acts as another strand of historical rather than confessional discourse.

Although Plath's poetry draws upon a variety of twentieth-century events, including the Second World War, the bombing of Hiroshima, the medical disaster of thalidomide and general ecological unease, it is the references to the Holocaust – the Nazis' extermination of the Jews – which have caused the fiercest critical controversy. George Steiner, in a polemical essay on *Ariel*, at first appeared to praise the poems 'Lady Lazarus' and 'Daddy', which most obviously encode Holocaust references in *Ariel* (though see also 'Getting There'), by likening them to Picasso's Spanish Civil War painting 'Guernica'. Almost at once, however, he goes on to accuse Plath of a 'subtle larceny' – as she was quite unconnected with the events of the Holocaust – and of importing images already replete with extreme associations into a poetry which is only personal (Steiner, 1979, p. 189).

It may seem that Steiner is correct to query Plath's use of Holocaust imagery. In 'Daddy', for instance, the speaker's urge to appropriate a particular identity and the insistent use of the same word appears crude on first reading:

> An engine, an engine
> Chuffing me off like a Jew.
> A Jew to Dachau, Auschwitz, Belsen.
> I began to talk like a Jew.
> I think I may well be a Jew.

However, these lines are actually *about* the very 'larceny', the putting on of a new identity, that Steiner criticizes – 'I think I may well be a Jew'; as Al Strangeways argues, Plath's poems 'enact' the problem of conventionalizing and metaphorizing the Holocaust (Strangeways, 1996, pp. 384–5). The subject of these lines from 'Daddy' is also quite specific; the 'engine' in the first line quoted above is not just a death-train but the 'obscene' engine of the German language. The repetitive, mechanical noise of the train and the daughter's efforts to name herself in German, the father's language, sound alike:

> Ich, ich, ich, ich,
> I could hardly speak.

The poem is self-consciously concerned with forging its own language, psychoanalytically, nationally and poetically. The final line can be read as the rejection of all kinds of patriarchal systems, including an alien poetic tradition:

Daddy, daddy, you bastard, I'm through.

This line is ambiguous; the idiomatic 'I'm through' can suggest both an end for the speaker (she is through with it all), or a new beginning (she has achieved a break-through). The latter, more positive meaning harks back to the phone line being 'off at the root'; although official means of communication are impossible, a new way can be pointed out. This tension between old (masculine, mechanical, Germanic) and new (feminine) means of communication depends on the opposition between 'Panzer-man' and Jew. Such an opposition appears interestingly to draw on and reverse traditions in nineteenth- and early twentieth-century anti-semitic literature which insisted that one of the unchangeable 'racial' features of Jews was their way of speaking. For instance, in Oskar Panizza's 1893 anti-semitic classic *The Operated Jew* (Zipes, 1991), the supposedly Jewish feature of mindless verbal repetition is the first sign of pro-tagonist Ignaz Faigel Stern's involuntary return to his roots after careful training and surgery have failed to convert him into an Aryan. In 'Daddy' Plath suggests that, by contrast, such mechanical word-use belongs to those in power.

Plath famously observed that she believed her poetry should be 'generally relevant, to such things as Hiroshima and Dachau and so on' (quoted in Alvarez, 1971, p. 64). Stan Smith, in a compelling reading of Plath's Holocaust-related poetry, continues this line of thinking by arguing that human subjectivity is always constituted out of historical reality. Public events and traumas make up the vocabulary of our inner life as much as the details of our private histories (Smith, 1982; see also Rose, 1991, pp. 222–38). In Plath's case, this means that her personal symbols – the dead father, the daughter who tries to die in order to return to him but survives to be reborn – are mingled with the public discourse of genocide and war. In other words, the appearance of Holocaust imagery in Plath's poetry is disturbing not because it is a special case of 'larceny', but because it follows an unremarkable pattern using remarkable details.

The Body

Although the best-known poems in *Ariel* possess a relatively accessible combination of striking local imagery with direct utterance, and, some commentators have argued, a strong sense of narrative as well (Dickie, 1984; Roberts, 1999), other poems in the collection have notoriously defeated sure critical analysis. These include 'Cut' and 'Nick and the Candlestick'. In my view these poems can best be explained in terms of Julia Kristeva's bodily discourse of abjection (Kristeva, 1982; see also Rose, 1991, esp. pp. 52–3). For Kristeva, the term 'abjection' refers to a state in which order is disrupted: the strict distinction between subject and object, life and death, one's own body and the outside world begins to blur. When these symbolic-order binaries are threatened, the human subject reacts with a psychic and bodily distress signalling the frailty of the symbolic realm, which is constantly liable to collapse back into what

Kristeva calls the 'semiotic', the pre-linguistic, pre-Oedipal realm of unity with another body.

In contemporary reviews, 'Cut' was described as a puzzling 'circular string of uncontrolled conceits' (Stilwell, 1984, p. 45), apparently going nowhere. Later critics have noted the disjunction registered in the poem between the persona's body and her subjectivity (Larrissy, 1990, p. 137): the speaker describes this domestic incident with a detachment that unnervingly – for the reader – echoes the injury. The opening lines of the poem suggest that the bleed of analogies for a cut thumb is caused by the accident: 'My thumb instead of an onion'.

However, I would argue that the sequence goes the other way around: it is the onion itself which, by fatally and even thrillingly resembling the body, has caused the accident – if we can assume even on a fictional level that such an injury has taken place. It is telling that no mention is made of how the injury occurred: all we get is the registering of substitution – 'instead'. It is as if the cut represents a breach of a psychic kind. Sigmund Freud (1955) interestingly discusses a hallucination undergone by his patient the Wolf Man of a similar injury – the Wolf Man saw his thumb dangling by a thread of skin but it was actually unharmed – which, not unexpectedly, Freud reads as a transferred castration anxiety. This is also an anxiety not far beneath the surface of 'Cut'.

Onions possess, at least metaphorically, qualities which can seem worryingly anthropomorphic. They have a fine, peelable skin; and they can cause tears with their own sweated juices. Indeed, the potentially abject ambiguity of which properties are human, which vegetable, is preserved in the poem's next lines. The top of the onion-thumb is quite gone,

Except for a sort of hinge

Of skin

Clearly the gap between the stanzas here imitates not only the object being described but also a 'hinge' of sense – the reader's horrified realization that it is not the onion top which is gone but a bit of a human body. Such a realization allows for the images that follow. Once the abject knowledge of similitude, rather than difference, between animate and inanimate has been exposed it cannot be stopped, as the sequence of associations shows. The speaker next invokes a turkey wattle which unrolls like a carpet from the heart. The compression here is grammatical as much as visual. The uneven red of a turkey wattle turns into something else – a red carpet – even as it rolls out to greet the famous, wounded protagonist, disturbingly following the rhythm of the persona's heartbeat. This is conducted with an authenticity that the phrase 'straight from the heart' both suggests and ironizes.

Kristeva observes that 'food loathing is perhaps the most elementary and most archaic form of abjection' (Kristeva, 1982, p. 2). Food can provoke daily domestic encounters with things that may be disgusting yet life-giving. In *Powers of Horror*

Kristeva – or the text's first-person speaker at this point – describes an abject moment with the skin on milk which she is expected to drink (ibid., pp. 2–3). Just like the onion, which is well known for the layers which can be discarded to reveal a central truth, the skin on milk has an uncanny resemblance to human skin and is the substance which most links the subject to his or her mother. Rejecting milk is, in Kristeva's view, akin to rejecting one's parents; in 'Cut' it is the subject's own body which is in danger of being rejected. The 'redcoats' which bleed out of the wound may have seemed safe and life-enhancing when inside the body, but the rupture to the boundary of skin makes their status uncertain. The speaker asks whose side they are on: the answer is that they are on the outside, which is the wrong side.

The focus of the poem changes early on from the first-personal '*my* thumb' to a second-person address: '*Your* turkey wattle', representing the dangerously split subjectivity that is associated with abjection. Again the apparent causal relation between the domestic accident and this split is actually the opposite way round. A papery feeling is not caused by the injury but causes it to seem threatening; the persona is already unwell, and addresses the thumb as something resembling a person, a 'homunculus'.

The 'homunculus', a detachable body-part, is to the speaker radically different from the speaking subject, 'I': to think of one's body as separate from oneself allows for the possibility of suicide, as Esther Greenwood in Plath's novel *The Bell Jar* (1966) realized when only pity for her own veins prevented her slitting her wrist. Marjorie Perloff discusses the 'papery' image in Plath's poetry at some length, observing that in most of its appearances it suggests fragility and dissociation (Perloff, 1984, p. 121). Paper is skin-like and can act as a veil, allowing the subject to see the world and her body at a remove (rather as the caul with which the Wolf Man was born lingered on into adult life as a sensation of distance and unreality; Freud, 1955). It is also, of course, the medium on which poems such as 'Cut' are written; and the metafictional link between one's fingers, a tool and the ability to write poetry has appeared in other writers' work – see, for instance, 'Digging' by Seamus Heaney. It is perhaps not too far-fetched to see 'Cut' as representing ambivalence about 'the blood-jet' of poetry ('Kindness'); the flow of blood and images is indistinguishable, and although the cut provokes a crisis in the subject it also enables the poem to be written. Indeed, the paper appears to metamorphose into a bandage for the wound. The speaker does not say that she has wrapped up the cut, but describes the stain on its

> Gauze Ku Klux Klan
> Babushka.

These lines associate, again in flicker-book form, images that do not go well together. The white Klan robes suddenly 'bloom' with blood ('Poppies in October'), giving a sign of crimes whose racial motivation is a theme the poem has hinted at all along in its uneasy invocation of the scalping Indian – a 'redskin' – and swarming redcoats.

Unnervingly, this violent image flips over into one of violence perpetrated, as the blood turns up on a Russian grandmother's hat. The boundaries of sense, morality and grammar all bleed unnervingly into one another; and the abjection which is the poem's subject cannot be prevented from affecting the reader too.

The final stanza of the poem winds back down to its first cause, as the persona invokes, in order, a trepanned veteran, dirty girl, and thumb stump. The pain and punishment of the trepanned veteran, who may have had holes drilled in his skull to combat something like a papery feeling, turns suddenly into an abject acknowledgement of the speaker's gender in the invocation of the dirty girl. The girl is 'dirty' because this blood is associated with the feminine alone; Kristeva identifies menstrual blood as the most abject of all substances (Kristeva, 1982, p. 96). In her discussion of the biblical taboos surrounding menstruating women Kristeva argues that the very possibility of menstruation means that femininity is itself at all times unacceptable: women are always already dirty, not allowed to touch sacred documents or to enter holy buildings. Unglamorously in 'Cut' the reader and poem are brought back to the beginning – to the thumb stump which allowed for the linguistic haemorrhage – but not in a senseless circle.

My second example of a poem which springs into new meaning if read in the terms offered by Kristevan abjection is 'Nick and the Candlestick', a poem which Margaret Dickie Uroff calls 'cryptic' (Uroff, 1979, p. 149). This poem is about a maternal ambivalence which is enacted by the poem's division into two different halves. Although Margaret Dickie rightly says that 'the time-span and cause–effect sequence' are often hard to discern in Plath's late poetry (Dickie, 1984, p. 173), in this case both are quite clear. In the first half (stanzas 1–7) the speaker is preoccupied with the alien sensation of breastfeeding; in the second (stanzas 8–14), she has finished feeding and is provoked by her baby's objective presence into a more celebratory mode. The poem's title suggests this split: Nick, the child, is balanced against the candlestick.

In the first stanzas, in which the speaker gets up in the middle of the night to nurse her child by candlelight, the candle is unpleasantly mingled with the speaker's sense of her own body. As a miner, she enters internal regions where oxygen is low and the light burns blue. Watching the candle drip 'waxy stalactites' becomes a bodily melting; these are 'tears /The earthen womb / Exudes'. It sounds as if the teary, milky oozings and the 'dead' womb – the child has, after all, already been born – belong to the speaker; the candle cannot be detached in her mind from her own bodily state. Even the 'Old cave of calcium' is not just a geographical but a bodily space: perhaps the mouth, the skull, or the milk-producing breast. Many of the images which follow in the next stanzas are of uncomfortable or painful – homicides, panes of ice, a vice of knives, a piranha religion – mergings or parasitic feedings – 'They weld to me like plums', 'drinking . . . out of my live toes'. The child at the breast is not mentioned, but analogies for him are. Sardonic religious imagery is clear throughout in the references not only to carnivorous religion and holy Joes, but to the fish-sign of Christ, whose body is also consumed at 'communion'.

An influx of oxygen – 'The candle / Gulps and recovers its small altitude' – allows the speaker to separate herself from the candle, which she can refer to again in a straightforward way. (Several critics compare this poem to Coleridge's 'Frost at Midnight', which has a similar structure: the poem's speaker sits by the fire late at night watching a film on the grate and charts his inner state by its alterations.) It is as if she wakes up a little, and is more alert to the decreasingly abject separation of subject and object. The speaker's question to the baby – 'how did you get here?' – is at once existential and quite concrete. After the blurred mental state which accompanied the initial feeding, realization of the baby's separateness is like a second birth (he is addressed as an embryo) – perhaps particularly as the child is now safely inert in sleep. The pain has resolved itself into something that is the mother's alone ('not yours'). Although Plath said of this poem that in it 'A mother nurses her baby son by candlelight and finds in him a beauty which, while it may not ward off the world's ill, does redeem her share of it' (quoted in Hardy, 1985, p. 65), it seems that the speaker's difficulty in distinguishing internal and external states continues. Crippling mercury atoms may still drip into a terrible well of real ecological disaster, but they also return to the uneasy exudations of the candle-body into a deep hollow which we read about at the poem's start. The final stanza suggests that the child is another miraculous baby in the barn, but this reference is also fraught with ambiguity. Earlier on Christianity appeared in a troubling guise of sacrifice and introjection of the body; even here the child's memory of an earlier 'crossed position' is not reassuring. The pain he wakes to may well not be his, but he will be asked to take it on, as Christ did.

'The Rabbit Catcher'

'The Rabbit Catcher' was included in Plath's own 'Ariel' collection but not in the published *Ariel*. It was presumably excluded as one of the 'more openly vicious' poems, as Hughes puts it (Hughes, 1994, p. 166). The poem's 'viciousness' resides in its comparison between traps set for rabbits and the 'constriction' of a sexual relationship. The shape of the 'snares' – zeros, which shut on nothing – mimics the 'hole in the hot day', which is the speaker's refusal to hear the shrieks of death; the same shape appears as the 'tea mug' around which dull, blunt murderous fingers circle – fingers which might equally circle the speaker's throat (Perloff, 1990, p. 186) or wear the kind of ring that both signifies marriage and 'Slid[es] shut on some quick thing, / The constriction killing me also'. This link between traps and marriage is reinforced by the description of the victims – who are not identified in the poem itself as rabbits:

> How they awaited him, those little deaths!
> They waited like sweethearts. They excited him.

Describing the creatures as 'little deaths' instead of naming them suggests that the poem is not really about the rabbits, despite the fact that it is apparently based on an actual incident (see Rose's discussion of its biographical treatment in Rose, 1991, pp. 136–7), but that they represent dark episodes, perhaps sexual ones, in the speaker's relationship with the 'catcher'. Their relationship is described as if its components were as material and as deadly as the construction of the traps:

> Tight wires between us,
> Pegs too deep to uproot, and a mind like a ring.

Ted Hughes published a poem of the same title in his 1998 collection *Birthday Letters*, which is a lyric narrative about his life with and loss of Plath. Reviewers of the collection almost without exception saw it as a reply to the widely held view of his relations with Plath – the 'stone man' and 'the burning woman', as Hughes puts it in 'Fever' – but were undecided as to whether it constituted the imposition of a final word (Viner, 1998) or the opening up of a dialogue (LeStage, 1998, p. 93; Maguire, 1998, p. 11). Once again Hughes takes up what looks like a biographical approach. Janet Malcolm quotes from a letter in which he says, 'The only thing I found hard to understand was her sudden discovery of our bad moments ("Event", "Rabbit Catcher") as subjects for poems' (Malcolm, 1994, p. 143; see also Malcolm's account of Hughes's response to Rose's analysis (Rose, 1991, pp. 136–40), of a sub-merged fantasy of lesbian sex in the opening lines of 'The Rabbit Catcher', Malcolm, 1994, pp. 178ff.). The speaker in his 'The Rabbit Catcher' offers an alternative view of the scene from Plath's poem, but his poem is so different from Plath's in narrative, mode and tone that it does not function as a 'reply'. The poem's speaker has an almost self-consciously bewildered male persona, describing his female partner's inaccessible anger as a moon-directed menstrual and mythical dybbuk fury. The speaker is not only detached but excluded from this female drama:

> I simply
> Trod accompaniment, carried babies.

The reviewer Ruth Padel says pithily of these lines, 'Despite the mental illness, there's enough archetypal confrontation here for all men to identify with that "I simply" stuff, and for all women to recognize that male bafflement which always seems a cop-out' (Padel, 1998, p. 7).

The description in Hughes's poem of the man's discovery of a snare – 'Copper-wire gleam, brown cord, human contrivance' – returns the rabbit-trap to the quotidian from its symbolic weight in Plath's poem. Indeed, the battle for meaning over the snares is represented as simultaneously a battle between poetic styles and one over opposing cultural heritages. His impulse is to read the snares as part of a pagan and proletarian history of the British countryside. He sees desecrated the

> hard-won concessions
> From the hangings and transportations
> To live off the land.

He claims that her view of the snares is ahistorical, visceral and feminine, the culmination of her disgust at England's grubby coastal and psychic edges:

> You saw blunt fingers, blood in the cuticles . . .
> You saw baby-eyed
> Strangled innocents.

Hence her poem; and hence his.

Hughes's 'The Rabbit Catcher' is full of backshadowing; the woman's fury precedes any knowledge of the snares, and the male speaker predicts an end which only seems inevitable from the vantage-point of the present: he remembers thinking that she will do something crazy, and he speculates that the thing the woman saw caught in the snares might have been her doomed self, her tortured, crying and suffocating self. In the concluding lines the speaker turns around the image of the murderous disc or circle from Plath's poem. Instead of the blunt fingers around a white mug the speaker describes how her verse encircled the incident with terrible, hypersensitive fingers and felt it alive. In an even more ironic reversal, it is she who is responsible for the death of a living creature:

> The poems, like smoking entrails,
> Came soft into your hands.

The implication is that the woman was so keen to see some meaning in the countryside snares, like a soothsayer looking into 'smoking entrails' for a sign, that she killed the creature – or the moment, or the relationship itself – to search it out. Hughes's poem cleverly, and vengefully, turns around Plath's meaning and accuses the female figure in the poem of being the true rabbit catcher. In this sense his poem is actually *about* biographical readings of Plath's work, despite the incomprehension at her poetic method expressed in the letter Malcolm quotes. Hughes's 'The Rabbit Catcher' presents the reader with the story of how a nightmarish family outing became the kernel of a poem about something rather different – gender difference, sexual trouble, and, as Jon Rosenblatt puts it, 'the ironic interplay of birth and death' (Rosenblatt, 1979, p. 44). Thus Hughes's poem is not so much a response to or refutation of Plath's 'The Rabbit Catcher', but a poem about the earlier one. It makes Plath's 'The Rabbit Catcher' into both a signifier and a signified.

Plath toyed with various different titles for the collection she finally named *Ariel*, including *Daddy* and *The Rival*. It is clear what a difference such titles would have made to our reading of this work: one emphasizes the shadow of patriarchy, the other the split, sometimes internally warring, feminine subject. *Ariel*'s title poem is about riding a horse, although, as in 'The Rabbit Catcher', the animal is not identified within the poem. The rider invokes deathly, self-transcending motifs: the landscape, like life itself, shoots past in a blur of image and sensation. Yet the 'unpeeling' of the self, its shedding 'Dead hands' and 'child's cry' alike, does not have a negative conclusion. Like the dew, the speaking subject may melt away in the glare of the sun, but is united with something of great power, creativity and rebirth: 'the red / Eye, the cauldron of morning'. The spiky, uncomfortable images of 'Lady Lazarus' reappear in a more accepting form here. Such a view of this poem might be extended to *Ariel* as a whole, particularly if we avoid the lure of a death-oriented biographical reading.

NOTE

Thanks to Helen Blakeman for help with the bibliography.

BIBLIOGRAPHY

Alexander, Paul (ed.) (1985). *Ariel Ascending: Writings about Sylvia Plath*, New York: Harper & Row.

Alvarez, A. (1971) [1963]. 'Sylvia Plath', in Charles Newman, *The Art of Sylvia Plath*, Bloomington and London: Indiana University Press.

Britzolakis, Christina (1999). *Sylvia Plath and the Theatre of Mourning*, Oxford: Oxford University Press.

Dickie, Margaret (1984). 'Sylvia Plath's Narrative Strategies', *Critical Essays on Sylvia Plath*, ed. Linda W. Wagner, New York: G. K. Hall.

Freud, Sigmund (1955) [1914]. 'From the History of an Infantile Neurosis', *Standard Edition of the Complete Psychological Works of Sigmund Freud*, trans. and ed. James Strachey, vol. XVII, London: Hogarth Press.

Friedan, Betty (1963). *The Feminine Mystique*, New York: Norton.

Gilbert, Sandra (1979). 'A Fine, White Flying Myth: The Life/Work of Sylvia Plath', *Shakespeare's Sister: Feminist Essays on Women Poets*, ed. Sandra M. Gilbert and Susan Gubar, Bloomington: Indiana University Press.

Hardy, Barbara (1985). 'Enlargement or Derangement?', in Paul Alexander (ed.) *Ariel Ascending*, New York: Harper & Row.

Hughes, Ted (1981). 'Introduction' to Plath, *Collected Poems*. London: Faber.

Hughes, Ted (1994). *Winter Pollen: Occasional Prose*, ed. William Scammell, London: Faber.

Hughes, Ted (1998). *Birthday Letters*, London: Faber.

Kristeva, Julia (1982). *Powers of Horror: An Essay on Abjection*, trans. Léon S. Roudiez, New York: Columbia University Press.

Kroll, Judith (1976). *Chapters in a Mythology: The Poetry of Sylvia Plath*, New York and London: Harper Colophon Books.

Larrissy, Edward (1990). *Reading Twentieth Century Poetry: The Language of Gender and Objects*, Oxford: Blackwell Publishers.

LeStage, Gregory (1998). 'Keeping Hungry: Al Alvarez in Conversation with Gregory LeStage', *Poetry Review* (88) 1, pp. 88–94.

Maguire, Sarah (1998). 'An Old Fresh Grief', *Guardian* 23 January, p. 11.

Malcolm, Janet (1994). *The Silent Woman: Sylvia Plath and Ted Hughes*, London: Picador.

Newman, Charles (ed.) (1971). *The Art of Sylvia Plath*, Bloomington and London: Indiana University Press.

Padel, Ruth (1998). 'Telling not Showing: Humanely Shattering, Poetically Inert', *Independent*, 31 January, p. 7.

Perloff, Marjorie (1984). 'Angst and Animalism in the Poetry of Sylvia Plath', in Linda W. Wagner, *Critical Essays on Sylvia Plath*, New York: G. K. Hall.

Perloff, Marjorie, 1990 [1984]. 'The Two *Ariel*s: The (Re)Making of the Sylvia Plath Canon', *Poetic License: Essays on Modernist and Postmodernist Lyric*, Evanston, IL: Northwestern University Press.

Plath, Sylvia (1965). *Ariel*, London: Faber.

Plath, Sylvia (1966). *The Bell Jar*, London: Faber.

Plath, Sylvia (1981). *Collected Poems*, ed. Ted Hughes, London: Faber.

Roberts, Neil (1999). *Narrative and Voice in Postwar Poetry*, London: Longman.

Rose, Jacqueline (1991). *The Haunting of Sylvia Plath*, London: Virago.

Rosenblatt, Jon (1979). *Sylvia Plath: The Poetry of Initiation*, Chapel Hill: University of North Carolina Press.

Smith, Stan (1982). 'Waist-Deep in History: Sylvia Plath', *Inviolable Voice: History and Twentieth-Century Poetry*, Dublin: Gill & Macmillan.

Steiner, George (1979) [1965]. 'Dying is an Art', *Language and Silence: Essays 1958–1966*, Harmondsworth: Penguin.

Stilwell, Robert L. (1984) [1968]. Review of *Ariel*, in Linda W. Wagner, *Critical Essays on Sylvia Plath*, New York: G. K. Hall.

Strangeways, Al (1996). ' "The Boot in the Face": The Problem of the Holocaust in the Poetry of Sylvia Plath', *Contemporary Literature* 37 (3), pp. 370–90.

Uroff, Margaret Dickie (1979). *Sylvia Plath and Ted Hughes*, Urbana, Chicago, and London: University of Illinois Press.

Viner, Katherine (1998). 'The Blood of Poetry', *Guardian* 20 January, p. 2.

Wagner, Linda W. (1984). *Critical Essays on Sylvia Plath*, New York: G. K. Hall.

Zipes, Jack (ed.) (1991). *The Operated Jew: Two Tales of Anti-Semitism*, London and New York: Routledge.

41

Ted Hughes: *Crow*

Rand Brandes

If our deepest grief could speak, it would speak *Crow*. *Crow* is Ted Hughes's most bleak and disturbing volume. No one who truly engages *Crow* can forget it; it becomes a terrible touchstone in one's memory field. In retrospect, *Crow* is clearly Hughes's 'dark night of the soul', and it is disturbingly prophetic. Hughes's fourth volume, published in 1970, *Crow* follows the dark world of *Wodwo* (1967), haunted shadows and ghosts, to its source, a black hole where neither light nor language can escape. In *Crow*'s world the heaviness of History, with its perpetual genocides and wrong turns, crushes hope; mass graves litter the landscape. DNA, with its Darwinian determinism, intertwines with the self-fulfilling prophecies of Christianity in an Apocalyptic *danse macabre*. Logic and reason, severed from intuition and emotion, lead to deadly technologies and environmental disasters. The oppressed Id wreaks its revenge as Oedipus dies with Ophelia. In the end, only the singing 'soul' or savage spirit survives the scorched earth of *Crow*.

Death was the midwife that delivered *Crow*. Shortly after Ted Hughes's wife, Sylvia Plath, committed suicide in 1963, the American artist Leonard Baskin, in an attempt to engage the poet, asked Hughes to write poems to accompany a series of sketches. The sketches were of crows. Hughes, however, did not begin writing the poems until the mid-1960s. The first edition of *Crow* appeared in 1970 and contained 59 poems; in 1972 an augmented edition of *Crow* appeared containing 66 poems. In addition to the seven additional poems there are many uncollected *Crow* poems and a plethora of unpublished poems (now held by Emory University in Atlanta, Georgia). The manuscript poems, usually written on the backs of scrap paper, verify Hughes's comments that the poems came quickly and were a shock to write. Sifting through the piles of pages one senses the extent to which *Crow* took possession of Hughes and Hughes of *Crow*. This mass of material also confirms Hughes's comments that *Crow* is part of a much larger narrative project.

Crow, as a character in a narrative poem, is a polyglot of possible meanings. Crow is a life force; the embodiment of raw power, conscienceless, moving through time and space. Crow is what has been written out of the Bible. Crow appears as poetic poltergeist, a supernatural 'character' in a cosmic psycho-drama. Crow is a fusion of shamanistic and mythic figures from around the globe. Crow is a shape-shifting Celtic war goddess. Crow is an epic hero like Beowulf or Cuchulain fighting monsters and his own fate. Crow is Beckett's everyman, living on the edge of articulation in an absurd universe plagued by disembodied smiles, grins and laughs. Crow is a Looney Tunes cartoon character on the loose. Crow is the provisional self in a relative world. Crow is the poet's Yeatsian mask, the anti-self absolutely necessary for poetic creation of the highest order. Crow is a common bird found nearly everywhere on the planet.

Although *Crow* is an experiment in 'style' for Hughes, *Crow* is first and foremost a mytho-religious poem. *Crow*'s poetic mainframe is supported by three mythic operating systems: the global, the national and the personal. At the core of *Crow* is the wound – three victims of suicide (Hughes's wife, Sylvia Plath in 1963, and Hughes's partner, Assia Wevill and their two-year-old daughter, Shura, in 1969); his mother's death in 1969, and his father's First World War 'shell-shock'. These personal tragedies, just under the surface of all the poems and occasionally erupting in a few, such as 'The Lovepet', 'A Bedtime Story' and 'Crow Improvises', compound the volume's sense of hopelessness and confusion. However, like Eliot or Yeats, Hughes avoids the confessional and disparaging by translating individual suffering into a universal experience through myth in *Crow*.

Hughes does not simply ask 'Why me?' in *Crow*; he asks 'Why?' and attempts to follow this question to its source. *Crow* fits Hughes's own view of myth in that it records a 'subjective event of visionary intensity'. He states: 'only when the image opens inwardly towards what we recognize as a first-hand-as-if-religious experience, or mystical revelation, [do] we call it visionary, and when "personalities" or creatures are involved, we call it "mythic"'. Hughes concludes: 'The world of the mythic poem . . . is a self-validating world' (Hughes, 1992, pp. 35–6). This 'subjective event of visionary intensity' is continued with revisions in Hughes's subsequent volume, *Cave Birds* (1975). However, in later volumes, such as *Wolfwatching* (1989) and *Birthday Letters* (1998), Hughes returns directly to the wound without the mythic machinery. While Hughes's personal myth is central to the power of *Crow*, his treatment of it within larger national and international mythic spheres is what demonstrates his genius and distinguishes the book.

In his first book, *The Hawk in the Rain* (1957), Hughes had distinguished himself from the mainstream Movement poets of the time by acknowledging in his poetry the symbiotic relationship between violence and the sacred. Hughes found this relationship pre-existing in nature and first articulated in ritual, myth and sacred song. Continuing the trajectory away from the 'myth kitty', as Philip Larkin called it, of poets such as Eliot, Lawrence and Yeats, the Movement poets adopted a detached and ironic tone (labelled 'suburban' by some) heard in the minor works of W. H. Auden. Ted Hughes returned to myth, not as an amateur, but as an adept. In addition to his exposure to the mythic in Anglo-Saxon literature, Shakespeare, Blake and Yeats, Hughes had studied anthropology and archeology in university. However, unlike Eliot or David Jones, Hughes had access to a broad range of 'new' thinking about myth. In addition to the standard works, such as the collected Jung and Graves's *The White Goddess*, Hughes encountered a wealth of mythic material, in Mircea Eliade's *Shamanism* and Paul Radin's *The Trickster*.

Moving beyond these secondary sources, Hughes immersed himself in the primary works (many only recently available at the time) of traditional cultures from the Balkans to Bali. His work as a reviewer of books of and on the 'literature' of traditional peoples, and his role as an editor of *Modern Poetry in Translation* (in the mid-1960s), provided a more global mythic framework. Hughes was going door-to-door in the Global village, long before many people knew it existed. Unlike the High Moderns who 'applied' myth to their poetry, Hughes internalized not only the materials of myth, but also its essential elements – its language, rhythms and structures. *Crow* does not 'use' myth; it *is* myth. Hughes was mythically multicultural before the concept was coined. From this perspective, Crow – as culturally other – may be seen as an early postcolonial response to the new world order.

Hughes's use of Irish myth in *Crow* is one important instance of his cultural diversity. In the late 1990s the literary exchanges between Britain and Ireland are as regular as Ryan Air, but in the mid-1960s this was not the case. Ireland before the EU and the Celtic Tiger was certifiably a developing nation, and not the hot holiday (literary) property of today. Hughes went beyond Yeats to the mythic core of Irish culture in an act of personal attraction and cultural affirmation. As mentioned, *Crow* is related to the Celtic Goddess of war and destruction Morrigna, a triadic composite that includes Macha, the Crow; Morrigan, battle-goddess; and Badbh, referred to as 'Badbh Catha' – the battle Crow. One of Morrigan's most famous appearances in Irish myth is in *The Táin*, the national epic of Ireland. Like Crow, she is capricious and capable of changing shapes. In a battle with the hero of *The Táin*, Cuchulain, Morrigan's shape-shifting from eel, to she-wolf to heifer is comparable to that of Crow. More directly, Cuchulain is the source of 'Crow's Battle Fury' and as consummate head-hunter, stands behind the 'King of Carrion's' 'palace of skulls'.

In 'Crow's Battle Fury' Crow's distorted body is that of Cuchulain in his 'warp-spasm' as described in Thomas Kinsella's (1969) translation of *The Táin*: "His [Cuchulain's] shanks and joints, every knuckle and organ from head to foot, shook like a tree in the flood. . . . His body made a furious twist inside his skin, so that his feet and shins and knees switched to the rear and his heels and calfs switched to the front. . . . Then, tall and thick, steady and strong, high as the mast of a noble ship, rose up from the dead centre of his skull a straight spout of black blood' (150). In 'Crow's Battle Fury', 'his [Crow's] heels double to the front, . . . Blood blasts from the crown of his head in a column – such as cannot be in this world'. More than mere allusion in his use of Irish myth, Hughes put a Celtic spin on *Crow* that is unique among contemporaries and charged with postcolonial potential.

This internalization of non-Western mythic materials by Hughes, unfiltered from its troubling colonial sources, is not the decorative Orientalism or fetishized exotica of the High Moderns. While the political implications of what 'happens' in

Crow are complex, the appearance of the book at a time of national and global crisis signifies a solidarity with those who foresaw the fall of Babylon. Crow sings along with the street-poets of Brixton and Berkeley in the 1960s. In *Crow* Hughes does not appropriate the mythic materials of other cultures, he translates them. This poetic approach gave Hughes access to the myths, and the mythic energy, he needed to articulate his dark vision. His vision was deepened by the belief that England was still suffering from a national spiritual crisis and that this crisis, only fully engaged in Elizabethan England, was also the 'skeleton key' to all of Shakespeare's work. Not surprisingly, then, this skeleton key also opens many of the doors to *Crow*'s mythic passages.

In addition to those *Crow* poems that move the narrative forward or those that seem to be meditations on the food-chain, there is a significant cluster of *Crow* poems that address the 'big' issues of life and death from Hughes's specific mytho-historical perspective. This angle was originally presented in Hughes's *With Fairest Flowers While Summer Lasts: Poems from Shakespeare* (in Britain *A Choice of Shakespeare's Verse*, 1971) and much elaborated upon in *Shakespeare and the Goddess of Complete Being* (1992). The majority of these poems in *Crow* explore three contending fields of discourse: the Great Goddess, Reformed religion, and the Scientific spirit. Though some early reviewers of *Crow* complained that it lacked an historical core, they failed to read carefully enough because everything in the book is considered from a highly developed mytho-historical perspective. Hughes sees the history of humanity (especially in the Western world) as one of steady decline. This decline began with Plato, whose distrust of passion (and certain poets) produced a sterile logic which worshipped abstraction and was ultimately appropriated by a masculine strain of Christianity that denied the body and demonized Nature and its sovereign Goddess. As Hughes states:

> In both the Greek world and Shakespeare's the archaic reign of the Great Goddess was being put down, finally and decisively, by a pragmatic, sceptical, moralizing spirit: in Greece by the spirit of Socrates, in England by the spirit of the ascendant Puritan God of the individual conscience, the Age of Reason cloaked in the Reformation. (Hughes, 1992, p. 85)

Running parallel to this line but against its grain are those esoteric Hermetic forces that stayed in touch with ancient mystical beliefs and magical practices, as well as those still connected, through seasonal rituals and everyday experiences, to the Goddess and Nature. According to Hughes, Shakespeare's plays record the battle between these forces:

> The Reformation in England, as it defined itself from the 1560s in the general rise of Puritanism, together with its accompanying materialist and democratizing outlook and rational philosophy, had very specific consequences. But the most important of these, as far as Shakespeare's poetry is concerned, was the drastic way the Queen of Heaven, who

was the goddess of Catholicism, who was the goddess of medieval and pre-Christian England, who was the divinity of the throne, who was the goddess of all sensation and organic life – this overwhelmingly powerful, multiple, primeval being was dragged into court by the young Puritan Jehovah. (Hughes, 1971, pp. xii–xiii)

This crisis preoccupied Hughes for over thirty years, and he remained convinced of the verity of his mytho-historical prognosis. Written during the same time as *With Fairest Flowers*, Hughes's *Crow* examines the origins of this decline that brought us to the point where, as Yeats describes it in 'The Second Coming', 'The falcon cannot hear the falconer; / Things fall apart; the centre cannot hold; / Mere anarchy is loosed upon the world'.

Given the convincing case made for hopelessness in *Crow* (some say nihilism), it is surprising and instructive that Nobel Laureate Seamus Heaney looks to *Crow* for a quintessential sign of hope in Hughes's work. When asked to contribute to the volume *The Epic Poise*, which was to celebrate Hughes's seventieth birthday, but which ultimately commemorated his death, Seamus Heaney wrote a short prose piece on 'Littleblood', the final poem of *Crow*. Heaney's singling out of 'Littleblood' from the immense body of Hughes's work is significant. The twelve-line poem begins,

> O littleblood, hiding from the mountains in the mountains
> Wounded by stars and leaking shadow
> Eating the medical earth.

and ends,

> Sit on my finger, sing in my ear, O littleblood.

Heaney argues that 'Littleblood' is related to the pre-historic and archetypal spirits of the shaman's world, while finding closer relatives in Shakespeare's fairies: 'Littleblood. The name could belong to oral tradition, to fairytale, to the world of *A Midsummer Night's Dream*. . . . Like the names of Shakespeare's fairies (and the fact that Littleblood eats "the medical earth" confirms this impression) it could be the name of an ingredient in folk medicine. . . . It feels as if it might belong to a whole system of story or lore . . . preserved more for its anthropological than its literary interest'. Heaney concludes: 'I have always tended to read "Littleblood" as an instance of that kind of transition [from the tragic to the transcendent]. It is as if, at the last moment, grace has entered into the Crow-cursed universe.'

Heaney's comments direct us to W. B. Yeats's great poem 'Meditations in Time of Civil War', in which Heaney argues that Yeats succeeds in balancing the tender and the terrible: 'O honey-bees, / Come build in the empty house of the stare'. Hughes's 'O Littleblood' calls upon the same healing powers as Yeats's 'O honey-bees'. They are emblems of poetry's power to redress the historical and everyday imbalance between what Heaney calls the 'murderous and the marvellous'. *Crow*, published in 1970, with the Cold War's atomic core still engaged, with civil rights marchers being beaten in the streets of Birmingham, Alabama, with the Vietnam War brutalizing the world, with bombs in Belfast blasting the headlines, with the jungles of Africa aflame, and Hughes's own personal catastrophes, 'O littleblood' is anything but an escapist ploy. One can say of 'Littleblood' what Hughes has said of Vasko Popa's poems: 'they precipitate out of a world of malicious negatives a happy positive' (Hughes, 1980, p. 184). 'Littleblood' is a grace note – a note unheard in *Crow*'s opening poem, 'Two Legends', or the sixty-five poems that follow it.

'Two Legends' introduces all that will follow in the volume. There is the stripped-down language, the use of repetition and parallelism of oral poetry, the predominance of body parts as central images, an informing Primitivism, a mythic infrastructure, and the breakdown of metaphor.

> Black was the without eye
> Black the within tongue
> Black was the heart . . .
>
> Black also the soul, the huge stammer
> Of the cry that, swelling, could not
> Pronounce its sun.

The absence of similes collapses the distance between word and thing or concept. The first line does not read: 'Black was *like* the without eye'. This fusion of word and thing essentially turns the word into a thing, thus solidifying the connection and increasing its impact. As with the Druids of Celtic mythology or medicine men of Native American tribes, in *Crow* words themselves possess the power to create and destroy. Hughes comments,

> You see, I throw out the eagles and choose the Crow. The original idea was to write his songs, the songs that a Crow would sing. In other words, songs with no music whatsoever, in a super-simple and a super-ugly language which would in a way shed everything except just what he wanted to say without any other consideration. (Hughes, 1980, p. 208)

In opposition to the ability of words to become the essential thing itself, the ability of a word to signify many things at once and the indeterminacy of language is presented immediately in the play on 'eye' ('I') and later in 'sun' ('Son'). This postmodern word play is reminiscent of Shakespeare or Beckett and reappears throughout the book. (Of course, the potential of words to mean 'nothing' as in modern advertising is another concern of Crow.)

Another important aspect of 'Two Legends', as with many of the poems, is that the songs about Crow or that Crow sings border on the cacophonous. The physicality of the language adds to this discord. Also in the opening poem one is aware of the creation myth mirroring *Genesis*; however, this 'black' myth as worked out in the entire volume offers a more convincing anti-creation myth. In the beginning was not the 'word' but 'the huge stammer' that does not, could not, proclaim the Son. Long before the Deconstructionists, Hughes questions the absolute authority of the Logos and logocentrism. Biology and not belief makes Crow's world go round. Out of this devolving world comes the 'black rainbow', Crow.

The rainbow, God's covenant and a sign of reconciliation, is black. Like an eclipse in *King Lear*, it is an ominous omen. As with 'Two Legends', the poems that follow – 'Lineage', 'Examination at the Womb Door', 'A Kill', 'Crow and Mama' and 'The Door' – are mythic presentations of Crow's origins from a mostly non-Western perspective. These poems place *Crow* clearly within the tradition of pre-historic creation myths as it deconstructs those of *Genesis*.

A subtext for the entire volume, this deconstruction can be traced through a series of significant poems that deal explicitly with Christianity. The series begins with 'A Childish Prank' and 'Crow's First Lesson', moves through 'Crow Communes', 'Crow's Theology', 'A Horrible Religious Error', 'Crow Blacker Than Ever', 'Crow's Song of Himself', 'Apple Tragedy', and ends with 'Snake Hymn'. Hughes has referred to Crow as God's nightmare, and critics have seen this as Hughes's belief in a form of Manicheanism, where good and evil, light and darkness have fought on the earth since the beginning. Even if Hughes constructs a cosmos that was flawed from the start, based upon his mytho-historical perspective, the real trouble appears in the Garden of Eden. In 'A Childish Prank', 'Man's and woman's bodies lay without souls'. While considering this problem, God falls asleep. Crow's answer to the problem is sexual, not spiritual:

> He bit the Worm, God's only son,
> Into two writhing halves.
>
> He stuffed into man the tail half
> With the wounded end hanging out.
>
> He stuffed the head half headfirst into woman.

Crow, as elemental life-force, causes the Fall and not 'the Worm'. Christianity's inability to accommodate the physical, sexual self is clear. In the poem Crow is the pagan 'Trickster'. This figure appears in many traditional cultures around the world, especially Native American mythology. Hughes was familiar with the Trickster from many sources. The Trickster is an amoral, comic, disruptive and dangerous figure, who often enters the scene when life has become stagnant and needs rejuvenating. The Trickster is a wild-card, often behaving in self-contradictory ways. He is a life-force for whom good and evil, right and wrong are meaningless categories. This amoral force often manifests itself sexually by breaking social and religious codes and causing 'trouble', while simultaneously bringing forth new life. Crow as the mischievous 'sexual' source also appears in the subsequent poem, 'Crow's First Lesson', where Crow's inability to 'Say, Love' as God instructs leaves man and woman struggling 'together on the grass. / God struggled to part them, cursed, wept – // Crow flew guiltily off'. In Crow's world Christian love is meaningless. This can be seen again in 'Snake Hymn', where Adam's blood is the 'everlasting' love that ironically engenders death.

> The blood in Eve's body
> That slid from her womb –
> Knotted on the cross
> It had no name.

Many of the poems go to the heart of Christianity and question the significance of the crucifixion. Crow even participates, by 'Nailing heaven and earth together', in 'Crow Blacker Than Ever', with the final result being 'Man could not be man nor God God' – doomed to division. Crow appears demonic in this poem; however, even when attempting to do 'good', the results from Hughes's perspective are counterproductive, as in 'A Horrible Religious Error'. In the poem, 'the serpent' 'earth-bowel brown, / From the hatched atom', overcomes God, Adam and Eve: 'They whispered "Your will is our peace"'. Crow 'Grabbed this creature by the slackskin nape, / Beat the hell out of it, and ate it'. The 'error' is that, like evangelical Christianity, by demonizing the serpent, Crow has denied humanity access to a powerful natural life-force.

Later in the volume, in 'Apple Tragedy', it is Adam that kills this force:

> Now whenever the snake appears she screeches
> 'Here it comes again! Help! O help!'
> Then Adam smashes a chair on its head,
> And God says: 'I am well pleased'
>
> And everything goes to hell.

Again, fearing the biological, natural, sexual world, Christianity's attempts to 'save it', kill it. Ironically or tragically 'everything goes to hell' in the poem because of the demonization of nature and rejection of the instinctual self.

Hughes's reading of Christianity must be considered from a historical perspective. He is not advocating free sex and mindless bestial behaviour; it is the lopsided, irrational self cut-off from the naturally rational being that commits the crimes against the Goddess. He is arguing that Christianity made a huge mistake when it denigrated the physical and natural and elevated the spiritual and dogmatic.

Hughes argues in *Crow* that Christianity's distrust of nature and the natural self found a friend in the new science of seventeenth-century England. The logic and materialism of science when combined with the Puritanism of the Reformation was a brutal blow. Hughes is not alone in his historical view that the Western world took a turn for the worse in Elizabethan England; while Blake lived it, other writers, such as

Lawrence, Yeats and Eliot, held similar beliefs. But as Hughes notes: 'The Shakespearean fable, in other words, is really the account of how, in the religious struggle that lasted from the middle of the sixteenth century to the middle of the seventeenth, England lost her soul. To call that event a "dissociation of sensibility" [as T. S. Eliot did] is an understatement. Our national poems are tragedies for a good reason' (Hughes, 1971, p. xxi). The immense implications of this loss of soul can be seen in one of *Crow*'s most significant poems, 'Crow's Account of St George'.

As the title suggests, 'Crow's Account of St George' immediately focuses our attention on a masculine, military and mythic England. This is not simply the patron saint of England; it is the saint of science who 'sees everything in the Universe / Is a track of numbers racing towards an answer'. As a representative of the Age of Reason, 'He picks the gluey heart out of an inaudibly squeaking cell'. The connection between St George and the modern-day scientist becomes clear when after a few glimpses of a 'demon', 'Something grabs at his arm. He turns. A bird-head, / Bald, lizard-eyed, the size of a football, on two staggering bird-legs / Gapes at him'. Crow-like, the dragon of the myth assumes its traditional role as demon, but in this case it has not appeared to eat a virgin but as a response to the heartless pursuits of the scientist. Science in its rational pursuit of abstract, absolute truths mirrors Reformed religion's apotheosis of abstract love. The demon dragon signifies the illogical and the natural world as seen through the Calvinistic lens of the Reformation and new science.

Smashing two more demonic creatures with a chair (as Adam does in 'A Horrible Religious Error'), St George faces 'An object four times bigger than the others'. The saint 'snatches from its mount on the wall a sword' and 'log-splits' the monster. For those raised on movies like *Friday the Thirteenth* or *Alien*, this is familiar stuff (and not unrelated to Hughes's vision). However, the intensity of the imagery and the savagery of the action, within a mythic framework and not simply trendy designer violence, can only be found in works like *The Táin*. The real horror closes the poem, when St George runs from the house where he has just savaged his family and not the dragon of his dementia. This is a hallucinatory scene straight from the Shakespearean stage, and it reminds one of bloody scenes in Kurosawa's Shakespeare adaptations *Ran* or *Throne of Blood*. Domestic in scope, universal in effect, this is the most intimate and deadly result of the fight between the Goddess and Jehovah.

Almost everything that is life-negating and soul-destroying in *Crow* can be traced to 'Crow's Account of St George'. The detergents, the bulldozers, the 'excreta'-poisoned seas, the nuclear holocausts, all originate in the number-crunching mentality and the sanitized religion of the Reformation. This is clearly presented in 'Crow's Account of the Battle':

> Reality was giving its lesson,
> Its mishmash of scripture and physics
> With here, brains in hands, for example,
> And there, legs in a treetop.

Hughes's vision not only helps to organize and move massive amounts of mythic and historical material; it also gives this material 'meaning'. Based on Hughes's reading of Shakespeare and impending global disasters, at least there is a logical explanation for our self-destructive behaviour and suffering – whether or not we like or agree with the explanation.

While many find this doom and gloom analysis off-putting (especially when presented in a primitive poetic package), what really disturbs them is the extreme to which Hughes took it in *Crow*. People suffering and dying because we have denied the Goddess of our complete being is one thing. People suffering and dying for *no* reason is another. Probably the most disturbing poem in *Crow* from this perspective is 'In Laughter'. Anticipating Oliver Stone's film, *Natural Born Killers*, 'In Laughter' depicts a cruel and violent world where the 'laugh-track' has been left on. The contrast between the horrible events and the laughter is beyond irony, beyond Nietzschean defiance, beyond the only sane response to the absurd:

> Cars collide and erupt luggage and babies
> In laughter
> The steamer upends and goes under saluting like a stuntman
> In laughter
> The nosediving aircraft concludes with a boom . . .
>
>   in laughter
> The meteorite crashes
> With extraordinarily ill-luck on the pram

The poem encapsulates all that seems beyond good and evil in *Crow* – the random, the accidental, the meaningless, the truly tragic. These are life experiences that brutalize belief and logic. Many critics mistakenly took this apparent 'nihilism' as Hughes's final position.

Even if taken on its own terms and in isolation, *Crow*, like all great works, leaves the case open to appeals and even a retrial. As Seamus Heaney argues, something does survive the 'Crow-cursed universe' beyond 'two strange items remaining in the flames / Two survivors . . . / Mutations . . . / Horrors – hairy and slobbery, glossy and raw' of 'Notes for a Little Play'; what survives is a hard-won hope. To acknowledge this hope is not to 'soften' *Crow* and give it a happy-ever-after Disney ending. In *Crow* Hughes looks death in the face and fearlessly follows it into the abyss. All of the 'bad' things that happen in *Crow* are part of 'reality', but so are the possible 'good' things. Given Hughes's personal tragedies and history's compounding miseries, it would have been easier not to write *Crow*. But in *Crow* 'nothing' is 'something' – something to hold on to. Without *Crow*, Hughes could not have gone on to write his most powerful works of rebirth and redemption: *Cave Birds*, *Moortown Elegies*, *River* and *Birthday Letters*. 'Littleblood' comes out of the 'foul rag-and-bone shop' of the cosmic heart and was *Crow*'s lifeline to the future. Ted Hughes's *Crow* is one of the most convincing poetic expressions of the human spirit's ability to keep faith of our time.

BIBLIOGRAPHY

Bentley, Paul (1998). *The Poetry of Ted Hughes: Language, Illusion and Beyond.* New York and London: Longman.

Eliade, Mircea (1964). *Shamanism.* London: Routledge.

Gifford, Terry and Roberts, Neil (1981). *Ted Hughes: A Critical Study.* London: Faber and Faber.

Graves, Robert (1961). *The White Goddess.* London: Faber and Faber.

Heaney, Seamus (1980). 'Englands of the Mind', in *Preoccupations*, pp. 150–69. London: Faber and Faber.

Heaney, Seamus (1999). 'Omen and Amen: On "Littleblood" '. In Nick Gammage (ed.), *The Epic Poise: A Celebration of Ted Hughes*, pp. 59–61. London: Faber and Faber.

Hughes, Ted (1971). *A Choice of Shakespeare's Verse.* London: Faber and Faber.

Hughes, Ted (1980). 'Ted Hughes and *Crow*', in Ekbert Faas, *Ted Hughes: The Unaccommodated Universe*, pp. 197–208. Santa Barbara, CA: Black Sparrow Press.

Hughes, Ted (1992). *Shakespeare and the Goddess of Complete Being.* London: Faber and Faber.

Kinsella, Thomas (1969). *The Táin: From the Irish Epic Táin Bo Cuailnge.* Dublin: Dolmen Press.

Radin, Paul (1956). *The Trickster.* London: Routledge.

Roberts, Neil (1999). '*Crow* in its Time: Trickster Mythology and Black Comedy', in *Narrative and Voice in Postwar Poetry.* London and New York: Longman.

Sagar, Keith (1978). *The Art of Ted Hughes.* Cambridge: Cambridge University Press.

Sagar, Keith and Tabor, Stephen (1998). *Ted Hughes: A Bibliography.* London: Mansell.

Scigaj, Leonard (ed.) (1992). *Critical Essays on Ted Hughes.* New York: G. K. Hall.

42

Seamus Heaney: *North*

Bernard O'Donoghue

On the way to the Nobel Prize many of Seamus Heaney's individual books of poems were singled out for high praise, beginning with the greeting of *Death of a Naturalist* as a first volume of huge promise and extraordinary powers of accurate description in 1966. In his 35-year publishing life, divisions can now be made on thematic grounds into early, middle and later stages of Heaney's career: the early Wordsworthian poems of the country person's tactile awareness ('up to *North*, . . . that was one book', the poet said himself: Haffenden, 1981, p. 64); the middle period of public concern and anguish; and a post-*Seeing Things* (1991) period in which Heaney presents the heart as lightening and ready to 'credit marvels'. Inevitably there has been debate about what the best book was, or the best poems, or the best period; probably *Field Work* (1979) with its great sombre elegies is the commonest nomination now for the book of greatest weight. And there have been other authoritative nominations: for instance, Neil Corcoran has said that *Wintering Out* was 'the seminal single volume of the post-1970 period of English poetry' (Corcoran, 1983, p. 182).

Yet there is little doubt, I think, for those who have lived through the years of Heaney's reception that the book that made the greatest impact was *North* in 1975. Great claims have always been made for it: Helen Vendler described it as 'one of the few unforgettable single volumes published in English since the modernist era' (*The New Yorker*, 23 September 1985). And, though her recent study of Heaney has insistently confined itself to practical–critical rather than 'thematic' readings of the poems – an approach which might sound relatively unsympathetic to the historical strengths of *North* – it is clear that her admiration for it is undimmed. Most responses to the book, whether favourable or hostile (and strong views were expressed on both sides of the question), attributed its high profile – its 'unforgettable' quality – to the same thing: its closeness to the political urgencies of its time and place. (Contemporary reactions to *North*, including Vendler's, are usefully summarized and extracted in Andrews, 1998, ch. 3, pp. 80–119.) Vendler has, if anything, strengthened her positive view of *North*; in her study *Seamus Heaney* (Vendler, 1998) she describes her first encounter with the poems of *North* in Sligo in 1975, 'which I thought then – and still think now – one of the crucial poetic interventions of the twentieth century, ranking with *Prufrock* and *Harmonium* and *North of Boston* in its key role in the history of modern poetry' (Vendler, 1998, p. 3).

Vendler also makes it clear where she saw the importance of Heaney's work (of which she sees *North* as the supreme example) to lie: 'it is . . . an *oeuvre* of strong social engagement, looking steadily and with stunning poetic force at what it means to be a contemporary citizen of Northern Ireland – at the intolerable stresses put on the population by conflict, fear, betrayals, murders' (ibid., p. 2). It was useful to be reminded of this impact of *North* in 1998 when Heaney's celebrity was a common-place and his major public poems almost over-familiar; those poems were being written in the first half of the 1970s, during the very worst period of violence and sectarian murder in the Northern Irish 'Troubles' of the last third of the twentieth century. To understand the impact of such poetry at that time, it must also be borne in mind that in the late 1960s poetry in English which dealt in explicit terms with politics was very unusual. Yeats's revolution of subject matter, which brought poli-tics centre-stage as a subject for poetry in such poems as 'Meditations in Time of Civil War', was well over by the 1950s. The famous appeal 'against the gentility principle' by Al Alvarez in his preface to *The New Poetry* in 1962 hailed a new roughness in reac-tion to the 'gentility' of form and language that characterized the intervening Move-ment poets, but there was little suggestion that this anti-gentility should have much to do with politics. It is significant that the Morrison–Motion anthology twenty years after Alvarez began by declaring that 'the new spirit in British poetry began to make itself felt in Northern Ireland during the late 1960s and early 1970s', going on to identify 'another reason why recent British poetry has taken forms quite other than those promoted by Alvarez: the emergence and example of Seamus Heaney' (Morrison and Motion, 1982, pp. 12–13). It is significant too that the poem Morri-son and Motion go on to quote in full to substantiate this high claim is 'The Grauballe Man' from *North*, ending with an exemplary reading of the poem's analysis of the 'forces of disintegration' (ibid., p. 15) that the book grew out of.

Not all readers received those poems with the same grateful admiration as Vendler and Morrison and Motion. No doubt the return of politics as a subject in the work of Northern Irish poets was inevitable. However, its return was not universally welcome; as several of those poets said at the time, the situation of writers there was difficult, as was emphasized by Frank Ormsby's preface to his crucial anthology *A Rage for Order* (Ormsby, 1992, p. xvii). If poets wrote about the Troubles, they were accused of exploiting suffering for artistic ends, or – at its worst – of taking sides in a horrific sectarian war; if they ignored them, they stood accused of ivory-towerism and heartless indifference to public suffering. Heaney was of course far from alone in the movement towards public themes: James Simmons's magazine *The Honest Ulster-man* was of huge importance in shifting the context of Northern Irish poetry in social and political directions; some writers – for example John Montague in *The Rough Field* (1972) – had published poetry before *North* addressing political circumstances in

Ireland. In a crucial essay some years later, Heaney declared that the tumultuous developments in Derry and Belfast in the summer of 1969 changed everything: 'From that
moment the problems of poetry moved from being simply a matter of achieving the
satisfactory verbal icon to being a search for images and symbols adequate to our
predicament' (Heaney, 1980, p. 56).

Yet, while recognizing the urgency of this predicament and the inevitability of the
politicizing – in some sense and to some degree – of the writing that must engage
with it, some Irish reviewers responded to *North* with fierce hostility. The fiercest was
Ciaran Carson's review in *The Honest Ulsterman*, ' "Escaped from the Massacre"?'
(extracted in Andrews, 1998, pp. 84–7). Carson takes his title from 'Exposure', the
last poem in *North*, suggesting by the question-mark that Heaney's escape carries
the history of the massacre with him (something, of course, which the poem itself
implies). The essence of Carson's case against the book, especially against the 'Bog
poems', is that 'Heaney seems to have moved – unwillingly perhaps – from being a
writer with the gift of precision, to become the laureate of violence – a mythmaker,
an anthropologist of ritual killing, an apologist for "the situation", in the last resort,
a mystifier' (ibid., p. 84). It is surprising that 'archeologist' is missing from this
anaphoric list, since that would describe the Heaney drilling metaphor more precisely;
indeed the most sustained of the charges against *North* has been that the metaphor of
a northern recidivism into violence as a response to something under the ground has
been expressed too deterministically. This charge I think is defused by noting that
it is the same metaphor that Heaney uses to describe the poetry of Kavanagh and
Montague in 'The Sense of Place', delivered in 1977 (Heaney, 1980, pp. 131–49).

Oddly, Carson's vigorously adversarial way of putting it is not that different in
substance from Heaney's declared ideal, quoted above, of advancing from the search
for 'the satisfactory verbal icon' (that is, 'the gift for precision') to finding 'images and
symbols adequate to our predicament'. Still, Carson's unease with Heaney's move
towards a heavier stress on political subjects is not unparalleled. The most noted
review of *North* at the time was Conor Cruise O'Brien's in *The Spectator*. O'Brien's
view that the intersection between poetry and politics is 'unhealthy', and his salutary
wariness about poetry that responded to what he himself epigramatically called 'the
politics of the latest atrocity', were firmly on record before his 1975 review (reprinted
in Allen, 1997, pp. 25–9). He finds Heaney's gift for accuracy to be undiminished;
in a famous sentence O'Brien writes 'I had the uncanny feeling, reading these poems,
of listening to the thing itself, the actual substance of historical agony and dissolution, the tragedy of a people in a place: the Catholics of Northern Ireland' (ibid.,
p. 25).

It is striking here again that the tension is seen as one between accuracy ('the thing
itself') and socio-political representation, as it was in Carson's review and in Heaney's
own opposition between the 'verbal icon' and 'poetry adequate to our predicament'.
I have begun by dwelling on the context of reception of *North*, rather than with the
poetry itself, because we need to be reminded, a generation later, of the exact ways in
which the volume was so controversial, and to recognize this public writing as an

untypical 'intervention' (Vendler's term) in the poetic world of its time. Heaney's
exalted reputation from the first meant that *North* was launched on a poetry public
of a rare breadth and expectancy. As Carson said, 'everyone was anxious that *North*
should be a great book'. Heaney's suggestion that the volumes up to (and presumably
including) *North* amounted to 'one book', confers a further importance on the book
as the culmination of his lauded work up to that point. It is certainly true that there
is no clean break before *North*; in *Wintering Out* (1972), the immediately preceding
volume, Heaney had already moved towards serious engagement with public events.
If we were to make a break in the early volumes, it might indeed be more accurate
to see the ground-breaking point in Heaney's development – his move to being a
major annalist of public events – in the course of the writing of the poems in *Wintering Out*, so that Vendler's 'unforgettable' volume is really an amalgam of *North* with
some of the poems of the previous volume. (Yeats's *The Tower* is a famous reminder
that the publication date of a volume or the order of poems within it are not its only
temporal significance.)

There were two immediately striking features of *North*, both already evident in
Wintering Out. The first is a formal tightening and abbreviating of the poetic line from
the richly indulgent eloquence of the early poetry – 'A thick crust, coarse-grained as
limestone rough-cast' ('Churning-Day') – towards an altogether more austere form:
'the skinny stanza', in Edna Longley's neat phrase. These short lines are much in evidence in *Wintering Out*:

> A stagger in air
> as if a language
> failed, a sleight
> of wing,

is the opening quatrain of the beautiful snipe poem 'A Backward Look'. The spare-
ness and exactness of this lyric form will be used to great effect in the public poetry
of *North*. The second important development associated with *North* is Heaney's use of
the figures in *The Bog People* by the Danish archeologist P. V. Glob as subjects and
images, to provide an analogy to the events in 1970s Northern Ireland. Glob's book,
centring on the bog-preserved bodies of what seemed to be Iron Age victims of ritual
execution, appeared in English translation in 1969, and was distinguished by classi-
cally framed black-and-white photographs (in 'The Grauballe Man' Heaney makes a
point of telling us that he first saw 'his twisted face / in a photograph'). Heaney's
employment of Glob's figures is always associated with *North* for good or ill, though
that too is first manifest in *Wintering Out*.

The organization of *North*, like its most imperative subjects, followed the design
of *Wintering Out*, which was divided into two parts, the first moving towards public
subjects, from the 'we' of the first line of the opening poem 'Fodder', speaking for
Heaney's farming world as a whole. Even before that, the dedicatory poem to David
Hammond and Michael Longley starts with 'the new camp for the internees' and

a bomb-crater. In general it has been felt that those relatively public poems were more successful than the domestic closed world of Part Two, precisely evoked as those were (though the terms in which I am making the contrast are too crude; it is one of the compulsions of *Wintering Out*, as of Heaney's poetry generally, that the dividing-line between the personal and the public is blurred). But it would be generally agreed that, for all the power of the place-name poems such as 'Broagh', the culmination of *Wintering Out* was the poem that signalled the direction Heaney's major poetry was to take, 'The Tollund Man', with its sonorous and ominous conclusion:

> Out there in Jutland
> In the old man-killing parishes
> I will feel lost,
> Unhappy and at home.

Here we see the 'artesian quatrain' (Blake Morrison's term for it: Morrison, 1982, p. 53) in action for the first time: the penetrating structures of short lines – Heaney compared them to augers – drilling below the surface of public events for their cause or essential meaning. It is also the first of the 'Bog poems', the great centre-pieces of Heaney's *oeuvre* inspired by his reading of Glob's disturbing study of ritual killing, in Jutland but paralleled in other parts of Northern Europe. Heaney famous-ly said of his encounter with Glob's *The Bog People*, 'my roots were crossed with my reading', indicating that he found a haunting reminder of sectarian killings and punishments in Northern Ireland in the mannered brutality of the executions itemized in Glob's book with its extraordinary photographs. The other 'Bog poem' in *Wintering Out* is 'Nerthus', following 'The Tollund Man' and in its cryptic four lines hinting at the timeless link between the beauty of the ash-handle of the pitchfork (an image Heaney will return to triumphantly), 'the unsleeved taker of the weather', and the violence of which implements are also capable, represented here by the 'gouged split'. This is an early linking of beauty and violent death that provoked such anguish in Heaney's readers such as O'Brien. Nerthus is the goddess to whom violent tribute was paid in Glob's narrative, a figure that will assume a troubled central place in *North*.

There is no doubt that it was these poems in *Wintering Out*, with their political and moral weight, in combination with Heaney's fast-growing reputation and the increas-ing spiral of violence in Northern Ireland, that led to *North*'s being so eagerly awaited; as Carson said, the anxiety that it should be 'a great book'. The new volume followed the bipartite division, though from the start it is an altogether more considered and self-commentating performance. The division functions differently too: Part 1 uses symbols – especially the Bog images – to represent political events, while Part 2 describes Northern Irish experiences and attitudes more directly. (The best discus-sion of *North* within Heaney's development as a whole is Corcoran, 1998, ch. 3.) *North* starts with a brilliant diptych of dedicatory poems to his aunt Mary Heaney, with the exactness of a Dutch interior and exterior, Vermeer and Brueghel; Heaney's descriptive and sympathetic powers have never been greater. In *North* they work as a warranty both of the book's technical skills, in the elegant precision of the 'Seed Cutters' sonnet:

> The tuck and frill
> Of leaf-sprout is on the seed-potatoes
> Buried under that straw

and of its moral earnestness and humaneness in 'Sunlight', one of Heaney's supreme masterpieces:

> And here is love
> like a tinsmith's scoop,
> sunk past its gleam
> in the meal-bin.

We are to bear these two earnests of Heaney's project – precision and sympathy – in mind throughout the book's travails; we should note too that the easy humanity of 'Sunlight' is expressed through the constrictions of the short-lined artesian quatrains. In support of this view of the prefatory poems, Corcoran quotes Heaney's essay 'Belfast': 'At one minute you are drawn towards the old vortex of racial and religious instinct, at another you seek the mean of humane love and reason' (Corcoran, 1998, p. 55; Heaney, 1980, p. 34).

The focused seriousness of *North* is then unmistakable from the start, as is its fixity of purpose. *North* extends to seventy-three pages, but it is a much shorter book than that might suggest, containing twenty-two poems, two of which are balancing six-part sequences. The prevailing note is sombre, very different from the preceding books, something which is stated directly at several points:

> I grew out of all this
> like a weeping willow
> inclined to
> the appetites of gravity.

Heaney has imposed a very exacting and, in the event, risky demand upon himself: everything is filtered through the poet's own voice. Hence, although 'The Grauballe Man' is a companion-poem to 'The Tollund Man' in *Wintering Out*, the impact is very different in the new book, where it functions as part of an elaborate and personally derived conceit. The poet now is, as Carson said, the present anthropologist observing the Irish political world and taking responsibility for his observations. The critical controversy that the book aroused is directly due to this exacting conceit. The criterion according to which poems are included in the book is their fittingness to this project of placing the modern condition into a larger symbolic context.

Accordingly *North* begins with 'Antaeus', dated 1966 and therefore presumably left out of both *Door Into The Dark* (1969) and *Wintering Out* (1972). The date at the end of 'Antaeus' is a statement, as with the dedicatory diptych, that the poem has been selected for some appositeness. At first reading it looks like a Yeatsian Apollonian–Dionysian opposition: Antaeus as the son of Earth and Sea, in combat with the new hero who has to wrestle 'with me before he pass / Into that realm of fame'. This could be a restatement of the death of the naturalist, as well as an anticipation of the point at which the poet will himself pass into the realm of the 'sky-born and royal' in *Seeing Things* (1991). But in the context of *North* the poem's end will develop a more threatening and defiant sense:

> He may well throw me and renew my birth
> But let him not plan, lifting me off the earth,
>   My elevation, my fall.

This has been heard as the voice of the defiant subjugated. The second poem, 'Belderg', describes the extraordinary neolithic landscape in north Co. Mayo, where 'blanket bog' can be stripped off to reveal 'a landscape fossilized'. This poem too ends with an unprepared-for threatening note in its final line, intruding on an archeological fantasia that up to this point had seemed almost idyllic–domestic:

> in my mind's eye saw
> A world-tree of balanced stones,
> Querns piled like vertebrae,
> The marrow crushed to grounds.

Suddenly it is a world where the marrow (a Yeatsian metaphor for the inherently and vulnerably human) is crushed by these devices from history.

By now the book's prefatory material is complete; with 'Funeral Rites' we are into the world of death and funerals from the start. The melancholy, fascinated evocation of family funerals in the Irish countryside belongs with the early Heaney world of 'Mid-Term Break'; but the hideous modern adult reality in Northern Ireland breaks in with horrific suddenness at the start of the second section, with one of Heaney's most quoted phrases:

> Now as news comes in
> of each neighbourly murder
> we pine for ceremony.

The world of the domestic is destroyed. The 'black glacier' of the funeral cortege in Part 1 is willed towards the megalithic doorway of Newgrange, in an appeal for a burial that will appease and break the sequence of revenge. This end to the cycle of violence, which was often the legal objective of negotiations in the Norse sagas, is represented by Gunnar of *Njalssaga* who, though violently killed, lies beautiful in his tomb, 'chanting / verses about honour' and looking at the moon. But it will emerge in the course of *North* that honour, like reputation, is a dubious inspiration; the two Norse berserks who 'club each other to death' in 'Summer 1969' from the book's closing and culminating sequence 'The Ministry of Fear', do so 'for honour's sake'. The poem's title is dated at the start of the major period of the Troubles, and its warning about the mutually destructive demands of 'honour' is starkly prophetic.

This pattern of cyclic recurrence, ending with an uncertain resolution, characterizes the major series of 'Bog' poems which dominate the rest of the first part of *North*. One of Heaney's most enthusiastic admirers, John Carey, said in his review of *Sweeney Astray* that his 'whole poetic input could be seen as a hymn to doubt' (*Sunday Times*, 12 June 1988), something which is profoundly true of *North*. The Bog series begins with the title-poem which is firmly first-person confessional, and is the first use by Heaney of a prosopopoeia in which the narrator is given directives, mostly about writing, by a voice other than a literal living person. Here it is the longship's tongue-prow, suggested both by the saga context of the preceding poem, and by the northern placing of the whole volume. But what this enjoins is precisely the quality for which Heaney had always been praised, and which Carson and O'Brien will express anxiety at his putting at risk: precision and clarity of description.

> Keep your eye clear
> as the bleb of the icicle,
> trust the feel of what nubbed treasure
> your hands have known.

The implication is that this ideal has to be held in view while the poet's major themes are being worked through; clarity after all is an ideal means of expression, not the end expressed. (I have argued this point at some length – possibly *ad nauseam* – in my book on Heaney's language: O'Donoghue, 1994, p. 68). The condition of the writer of these poems is most clearly put in section IV of 'Viking Dublin: Trial Pieces', where the narrator is revealed fully, as a Hamlet-figure:

> smeller of rot
> in the state, infused
> with its poisons,
> pinioned by ghosts
> and affections,
> murders and pieties.

Nothing could say more plainly that this figure cannot 'escape from the violence'. But it is also a figure of 'dithering, blathering' with Hamlet's desperate, indecisive wordiness. There is another sinister indeterminate ending:

> My words lick around
> cobbled quays, go hunting
> lightly as pampooties
> over the skull-capped ground.

Two other poems or sequences dwell on the question of the adequacy to the predicament of language itself. 'Bone Dreams' seeks a root of language, to correspond to the root of ritual found in Glob's burials. Strikingly, this root is Old English; the Anglo-Saxon poet's 'twang' provides a radically expressive, consonantal language with the French element in English stripped away. Like its myths, the grammatical structure of the language of *North* is invariably Germanic; Gaelic-derived vocabulary has been collected by Morrison and Corcoran, but it occurs within a Germanic syntax and morphology. Significantly, there are no Celtic myths in the book. The history of English might logically have gone further back, to peel off also the Germanic invaders' importations into an indigenous language of British–Celtic experience. But *North* is a Germanic book; the anthropologist it addresses is the Tacitus of *Germania*. It is closely concerned with England: not only its relations with Ireland (though they are prominent too) but in itself. 'Bone Dreams' ends by quartering the country, from Hadrian's wall and the Pennines in the north to Maiden Castle and Devon in the southwest. Eamonn Hughes, in his interesting essay on 'Representation in Modern Irish Poetry', sees Part 2 of *North* as 'a sustained interrogation of Heaney's intimacy with English culture' (Allen, 1997, p. 78). Heaney rationalizes this as an interest in the English lyric which he is obliging to 'eat stuff that it has never eaten before' (quoted in Corcoran, 1998, p. 53), and famously at the end of 'The Ministry of Fear' he will grumble:

> Ulster was British, but with no rights on
> The English lyric.

The mixed language of 'Broagh' in *Wintering Out*, with its beautifully assembled amalgam of Ulster–Scots, English and Irish, has been replaced by a stiffer uniform linguistic structure which cannot hope to reach any resolution of a hybrid situation.

The conclusive language poem 'Kinship' comes after the book's two powerful centrepieces which I will end this discussion with, and it summarizes the bog poems' impact and meaning. Here Heaney uses for the first time a profound linguistic image which will culminate with the recognition of writing as genetics – 'the hieroglyph for life itself' – in *Seeing Things*, despairing perhaps of the capacity of normal language to be 'adequate to the predicament'. 'Kinship' opens with a disturbing image of the imprint of the Nerthus sacrifice on the modern landscape, as on the horrifyingly renewed contemporary consciousness:

> Kinned by hieroglyphic
> peat on a spreadfield
> to the strangled victim,
> the love-nest in the bracken.

This poem is a densely knit web of the imagery not only of *North* but also of Heaney's whole highly consistent *oeuvre*; for example, this opening section's hymn of love to the Irish bog ends by calling it

> a moon-drinker
> not to be sounded
> by the naked eye.

We recall that Gunnar at the end of 'Funeral Rites' turned 'with a joyful face / to look at the moon'. The 'sounding' of the bog recalls 'the wet centre is bottomless' from 'Bogland' in the 1969 *Door Into The Dark* (the idea of the bog as repository of history and meaning was not first implanted in Heaney's mind by Glob); it also links to a moment of great excitement in *Beowulf* (quoted here from Heaney's 1999 translation), when Hrothgar reports that the boggy morass where the Grendels live is of such a depth that

> the mere-bottom
> has never been sounded by the sons of men.
> (lines 1,366–7)

The capacity of language to 'sound' experience or emotion has been one of Heaney's abiding themes, from 'Blackberry Picking' to 'Alphabets'.

It is arguable, I think, that these clusters of sustained imaginative density in the imagery of *North* are what give it its lasting significance. Two of Heaney's best critics express some disquiet about the narrowness of imagistic range in the volume and the impacted language and metrical forms linked to it; Edna Longley notes Heaney's description of the book's genesis from the Haffenden interview, that 'those poems came piecemeal now and again, and then I began to see a shape' (Haffenden, 1981, p. 64). Longley regards this 'system, homogenization' as a disimprovement on 'the fecund variety of *Wintering Out*' (Allen, 1997, p. 53). Neil Corcoran finds the poems 'intensely, even claustrophobically obsessive and intimate' (Corcoran, 1998, p. 62), though he goes on to explain this as the attempt to 'disrupt the smoothness of the English lyric in a way appropriate to the violence of their material, and with a certain political implication' (ibid., p. 63). The Yeatsian distancing in 'a certain' illustrates the way that critics have always wanted to enter a caveat about violence in the poems: indeed about politics in poetry as a whole, though that is too wide-ranging a matter to go into here. Heaney himself will see the return to the longer line in his next collection *Field Work* as a kind of release, back perhaps towards the freedom with which he said he wrote the place-name poems in *Wintering Out*, though no poems could be more taken up with political violence and tragedy than the great elegies of *Field Work*, 'Casualty' and 'The Strand at Lough Beg'. It is interesting, incidentally, that from the first, critics have attempted to co-opt the poet himself into an uncertain view of *North*'s politics, though the evidence in his own pronouncements is hard to find. Blake

Morrison, in his excellent founding critical study of Heaney, proposes that the 'niggardly representation of *North* in his 1980 *Selected Poems*' suggests that the poet came to incline to the disapproving Belfast view of the book (Longley and Carson), rather than the hugely approving London view (Carey).

Yet surely nothing that Heaney has done so incontestably proves his possession of the Coleridgean 'shaping spirit of imagination' than the insistent way in which *North*'s sustained central metaphor symbolizes its subject. The centralizing device in the Bog poems is the exploitative artistic gaze, most troublingly male upon female, as an image of the imposition of political power. Male writing has always assigned responsibility for this exploitation to chosen female symbols: hence Heaney's invocation in 'Aisling' of Diana, the hunted conveniently turned huntress, as well as the notorious Nerthus, the Germanic goddess whose very name grammatically suggests her male construction, and as 'Bog Queen', a hideous figure of voyeurism constructed on a body preserved in a Co. Down bog in the eighteenth century. This exploitative gaze culminates in 'Punishment'.

But first 'The Grauballe Man', the major poem that precedes 'Punishment', raises the poetry–politics crisis and its contradictions in a non-gendered but shocking way: the coinciding of 'beauty and atrocity', and the exploitative way the artist will ensure that the tortured figure's 'twisted face' is 'perfected in my memory'. But the artist's aestheticization does not triumph, despite the force of his rhetorical questions:

> Who will say 'corpse'
> to his vivid cast?
> Who will say 'body'
> to his opaque repose?

The poem ends with the neighbourly murders,

> with the actual weight
> of each hooded victim
> slashed and dumped.

'Punishment', the most controversial poem in *North*, follows a similar pattern. Here the aestheticization is relentlessly presented in sexual terms, with the result that the punishment of the title is meted to the poem's speaker as much as it is to the Windeby Girl, the 'little adulteress' in Glob's book. If the poetry's public concerns and its concentration of symbols are what makes *North* an outstanding book, the refusal of this poem to take refuge from judgement makes this the most important single poem. Accordingly, the poem has itself provided the phrase 'artful voyeur', which its most impassioned critic has taken as half of her title in the criticism of *North* (Edna Longley, in Allen, 1997, pp. 30–63). The artist is always the voyeur Actaeon of Heaney's 'Aisling', and he must expect punishment.

Part 2 of *North* returns from the symbolic to the literal–historical to pass judgement on the larger Part 1. In the last poem, 'Exposure', the 'artful voyeur' is punished by failing to see the comet, the event of greatest moment. But of course the comet is not clearly visible; poetry makes nothing happen and (in Yeats's phrase) there is no 'clear fact to be discerned'. *North* reaches no conclusions. But this is its triumph: in Carey's terms, the human ability to live in doubt. The book began in 'a sunlit absence'; it ends with another absence, one deficient in light and heat. But in its course it has represented public events with a power to disturb unmatched in poetry in English since Yeats's 'Meditations in Time of Civil War'. Since 1975 poetry and politics have become increasingly uncoupled. While this may avoid the dangers articulated by O'Brien, it also risks artistic self-disabling by evading the centre of seriousness in the world of political animals. The distinction of *North* was to face this risk squarely in one of its most fraught contexts.

BIBLIOGRAPHY

Allen, Michael (ed.) (1997). *Seamus Heaney*, London: Macmillan.

Andrews, Elmer (ed.) (1998). *The Poetry of Seamus Heaney*, Cambridge: Icon.

Corcoran, Neil (1993). *English Poetry since 1940*, London and New York: Longman.

Corcoran, Neil (1998). *The Poetry of Seamus Heaney: A Critical Study*, London: Faber and Faber.

Haffenden, John (1981). *Viewpoints: Poets in Conversation with John Haffenden*, London: Faber and Faber.

Heaney, Seamus (1972). *Wintering Out*, London: Faber and Faber.

Heaney, Seamus (1975). *North*, London: Faber and Faber.

Heaney, Seamus (1980). *Preoccupations*, London: Faber and Faber.

Morrison, Blake (1982). *Seamus Heaney*, London: Methuen.

Morrison, Blake and Andrew Motion (eds) (1982). *The Penguin Book of Contemporary British Poetry*, Harmondsworth: Penguin.

O'Donoghue, Bernard (1994). *Seamus Heaney and the Language of Poetry*, Hemel Hempstead and New York: Harvester Wheatsheaf.

Ormsby, Frank (ed.) (1992). *A Rage for Order: Poetry of the Northern Ireland Troubles*, Belfast: Blackstaff.

Vendler Helen (1998). *Seamus Heaney*, Cambridge, MA: Harvard University Press.

43

John Ashbery: *Self-Portrait in a Convex Mirror*

David Herd

John Ashbery's *Self-Portrait in a Convex Mirror* is home to a handful of the most accomplished short lyrics in American poetry. In various ways each of, say, 'Worsening Situation', 'As You Came from the Holy Land', 'Grand Galop', 'Hop o' My Thumb', 'Mixed Feelings' and 'The One Thing That Can Save America' is a superbly adroit articulation of the poet's cultural situation. Each finds Ashbery at the top of his form, and in other circumstances each would have attracted much attention. Appearing as they do, however, alongside Ashbery's most famous poem they have been largely (though not, of course, completely) overlooked. They are not the only ones. For many readers (though not, of course, all), 'John Ashbery' equals 'Self-Portrait in a Convex Mirror', the rest of his often dazzling *oeuvre* being eclipsed by a poem which the poet himself has described as the product of 'three months of not very inspired writing' (Shoptaw, 1994, p. 174). The measure of this eclipse is the sheer number of critical articles on Ashbery which address themselves exclusively to 'Self-Portrait', tying the poet to his hit poem in a way that Eliot was never tied to *The Waste Land*, Stevens was never tied to 'An Ordinary Evening in New Haven' and Auden was never tied to anything. To understand why Ashbery should have become so identified with a single – albeit genuinely impressive – poem (the poet's distancing tactics notwithstanding) one needs clearly to appreciate what makes that poem stand out. And to appreciate what makes 'Self-Portrait in a Convex Mirror' stand out, one has first to know something of its background.

Written in 1973, the poem's immediate background was complicated. Two years previously Ashbery had completed *Three Poems*. A work of prose poetry, *Three Poems* answers Stevens's call for a supreme fiction by continuing a tradition of spiritual inquiry which, as Ashbery's writing reminds us, begins with Pascal and runs through Emerson, James, Auden and De Chirico. A profoundly affecting engagement with a Godless present, the book was little less than an expression of faith for a secular age. It carried Ashbery's writing into new and exhilarating territory, and firmly established him as one of the most remarkable poets of his generation. At the same time, and by no means coincidentally, Ashbery was increasingly finding himself the subject of academic and journalistic curiosity. In itself such critical interest was not new: Ashbery's 1964 poem, 'The Skaters', having won an award from the American National Institute of Arts and Letters, and Harold Bloom having singled him out for attention in essays that would eventually become central to *The Anxiety of Influence*. What was new was both the volume of interest Ashbery's poetry was now attracting, and, more decisively, the form it was increasingly taking.

In the early seventies the means of choice by which critics were increasingly seeking to understand contemporary poetry was the interview. For Ashbery, who has been more interviewed than most, this form of critical interest proved a mixed blessing. On the one hand it promised direct contact with an audience whose existence the very presence of the interviewer appeared to imply. On the other, what became acutely apparent was that, whether by dint of the difficulty of the writing, or of their own failure to give it the attention it deserved, the majority of Ashbery's early interviewers had very little idea what the poetry meant to say and do. Alfred Poulin Jr., who interviewed Ashbery at the Brockport writers convention in 1972, was an unfortunate case in point.

> *Poulin*: Can we get back, then, to that central question of what it is you're communicating? My feeling is that in the middle of the difficulty of your poetry there is a very personal element, disguised by this difficulty.
> *Ashbery*: Is that all? I don't see quite what you mean by a very personal element.
> *Poulin*: . . . When I read the poetry I feel there is a personal core that is attempting to come through the syntax and the juxtapositions.
> *Ashbery*: As I told you before, I don't write very much of my experiences, except in a way of afterthoughts. . . . These are not autobiographical poems, they're not confessional poems. (Poulin, 1981, p. 251)

The whole of Poulin's interview with Ashbery is like this. Time and again the interviewer tries to reduce the poetry to a 'personal element'. Time and again the poet insists that such a reading could hardly be further from the truth. Indeed, not only is Ashbery's poetry not, in the sense that Poulin means it, an act of self-expression; but, in the sense that Poulin means it, Ashbery's poetry doubts the existence of a self to be so expressed. As often, then, as Poulin tries to drag the interview back to the autobiography of the poet, Ashbery denies that this is relevant. That he fails to get this fundamental point across is partly because, the interview form being what it is, the writer's self suggests itself as the natural subject of inquiry. But partly also it is because Poulin is so caught up in the fashionable view (after Lowell) that poetry is properly about the individual poet, that any other kind just doesn't register as poetry.

How was Ashbery to respond to this unhappy state of affairs? Conceivably he could ignore it. (Dumb interviewer gets poetry all wrong. So what?) The trouble is that to ignore the interviewer would be, in effect, to ignore the reader. If Poulin (in common with other interviewers) thinks this way about poetry in general, and about Ashbery's poetry in particular, what reason does one have to suppose that the audience on behalf of whom he is asking questions does not think this way also? If the poetry is to communicate – and as Ashbery has repeatedly insisted in interview, there is nothing his poetry means more than to communicate – some account of the voice of the interviewer had to be taken.

This, then, was the complicated background to 'Self-Portrait in a Convex Mirror': the poet arriving at the height of his powers, only to receive the news that what he was writing was being roundly misunderstood. What to do? In the interviews themselves Ashbery's remedial tactic was to redirect the questioner's gaze. Seeking at every opportunity to deflect the conversation away from himself, what the poet sought repeatedly to bring into view was the background against which the conversation was taking place:

> *Ashbery*: Most of my poems are about the experience of experience.... We're sitting here, presumably having a nice discussion about somebody's poetry, and yet the occasion is something else also. First of all, I'm in a strange place with lots of lights whose meaning I don't quite understand, and I'm talking about a poem I wrote years ago and which no longer means very much to me. I have a feeling that everything is slipping away from me as I'm trying to talk about it – a feeling I have most of the time, in fact – and I think I was probably trying to call attention to this same feeling in 'Leaving the Atocha Station' and in other poems as well. Not because of any intrinsic importance that feeling might have, but because I feel that somebody should call attention to this. Maybe once it's called attention to we can think about something else, which is what I'd like to do. (Poulin, 1981, p. 245)

'Call[ing] attention to this', to the background against which his expression is taking shape, has long been important to Ashbery. Take 'The Picture of Little J.A. in a Prospect of Flowers', the poem from Ashbery's first volume, *Some Trees*, which most readily bears comparison with 'Self-Portrait in a Convex Mirror'. Published in 1956 – Auden having judged it the winner, a year earlier, of the prestigious Yale Younger Poets award – *Some Trees* did not sell well. For those who did read it, however, and were curious about this new young poet, the poem that most promised a clear sight of him was 'The Picture of Little J.A.' And for the reader who looked hard enough, Ashbery was to be found in that poem – albeit not quite in the place one would ordinarily expect. The beginning of the third section of the poem goes to the heart of the matter.

> Yet I cannot escape the picture
> Of my small self in that bank of flowers:
> My head among the blazing phlox
> Seemed a pale and gigantic fungus.
> I had a hard stare, accepting
> Everything, taking nothing
> As though the rolled-up future might stink
> As loud as stood the sick moment
> The shutter clicked.

This image of self might seem familiar. If the speaker (who would seem to be the poet) cannot escape the picture of his younger self, is that not because the child is father to the man, and is the continuity of self the poem proposes not thus unproblematically Romantic? In fact Ashbery's argument is something like the opposite. He cannot escape the image of his younger self, not because he is fundamentally unchanged since his youth, but, on the contrary, because like his younger self he is in a state of constant flux, his identity changing according to his situation.

To make this clear in terms of the poem's own, already carefully evolved terms, it is appropriate, if intriguingly bizarre, for the poet to describe his young head as a fungus, because his young self is in the habit, as he observes, of accepting everything. Thus, just as a fungus is a parasite feeding on, and so taking its shape from, its environment, so the identity of the young Ashbery – his state of acceptance making him open to all that goes on around him – is to be located not in some psychologically framed interior, but in the circumstances in which he finds himself.

That this sense of an absorbent self is important to Ashbery is evident from the way in which, in this poem, he links it to his literary background. Take the poem's complex, but highly instructive opening line: 'Darkness falls like a wet sponge'. 'Darkness falls' is an allusion, or rather, an allusion to an allusion; the phrase coming from Stephen Daedalus's repeated misremembering (in *The Portrait of the Artist as a Young Man*) of the first line of Nashe's poem 'In Time of Pestilence'. What Stephen remembers as 'Darkness falls from the air' should in fact read 'Brightness falls from the air'. The original owner of Ashbery's 'wet sponge' is a little more difficult to trace. But not too difficult, a firm hint to his identity being given by the poem's epigraph. The epigraph, as it turns out, is the last line of Boris Pasternak's memoir *Safe Conduct*. A quite crucial text in the collective history of the New York School poets – the others of whom were Frank O'Hara, Kenneth Koch and James Schuyler – *Safe Conduct* speaks directly to Ashbery's poetry in so far as it both issues and embodies Pasternak's defining aesthetic principle that 'The clearest most memorable feature of a work of art is how it arises, and in telling of the most varied things, the finest works in the world in fact tell us their own birth' (Pasternak, 1959, p. 213).

That this idea was central to Pasternak is evident from the number of times he reformulated it. Thus it is the same thought, if more strikingly formulated, that underpins Pasternak's famous complaint in his 1922 manifesto 'Some Theses'. 'People now', Pasternak grumbled, 'imagine that art is like a fountain, whereas it is a sponge. They think that art has to flow forth, whereas what it has to do is absorb and become saturated.' That Pasternak's thinking about art was, in turn, influential on Ashbery is evident from the American poet's repeated insistence in interview that his poems 'characterize the bunch of circumstances they are growing out of' (Bloom and Losada, 1972, p. 20). And 'A Picture of Little J.A. in a Prospect of Flowers' is a case in point. Thus, not only is the poet's young self absorbent – accepting everything; lost, or rather found, 'among' the 'blazing phlox' which surround it – but so too is the poem's language. Alluding to Marvell in its title, Joyce, Nashe and Pasternak in its opening line, and borrowing from Shakespeare, Coleridge and Wordsworth throughout, 'The

Picture of Little J.A.' is itself a sponge, shaped by, because it has fully absorbed, the reading which is the history of its own birth.

Ashbery's poetic development can be understood as a process of ever greater absorption, his poetic scope expanding throughout the sixties as his sense of the circumstances of the poem's birth grew ever more generous. Perhaps no writer since Rabelais has been a more gargantuan consumer of his environment, and the languages which mediate that environment, than Ashbery. Certainly few, if any, poets since the Second World War have worked harder to keep poetry viable in an age of rapid change, excessive information, and radically specializing discourses. In absorbing and re-presenting the background against which it is written, Ashbery's poetry has continued to present the increasingly complex background against which ordinary human communication now takes place, and of which such communication must be aware if it is not to be rendered obsolete by events. Poetry that undertakes this task in the present age is itself necessarily quite complex. Complex enough, certainly, that by the early seventies, as the interviewers were making clear, many readers of poetry (though not, of course, all) were unsure what to make of Ashbery. Two decades on, then, from the writing of 'The Picture of Little J.A.' and after the very considerable effort of getting his poetry up to speed with his times, Ashbery's interview experience seemed to present him with a stark choice: to retreat into the isolation of the avant-garde, disregarding readers who could not or would not make the time to understand him; or, in so far as he could do so without diminishing his poetry, to explain himself. *Self-Portrait in a Convex Mirror* is the product of this choice. A number of poems, and rather more than is often noticed, entertain the first option: 'The Tomb of Stuart Merrill', 'Mixed Feelings' and 'Tenth Symphony', for instance, articulating a sharp distaste for an American public too conservative in its reading habits to accept what the poet has to offer. Mostly, however, and the poet having got his irritation off his chest, *Self-Portrait in a Convex Mirror* opts to explain. And nowhere more so than in the title poem: 'Self-Portrait in a Convex Mirror' being a brilliantly conceived and superbly executed, if ultimately costly, act of poetic self-explanation.

The poem's title is taken from the painting by the sixteenth-century Italian painter Parmigianino on which it hangs, and whose own conception and execution Vasari describes in detail:

> Francesco one day set himself to take his own portrait, looking at himself in a convex mirror, such as is used by barbers. While doing this he remarked the curious effect produced by the rotundity of the glass, which causes the beams of the ceiling to look bent, while the doors and all other parts of the buildings are in like fashion distorted, and recede in a very peculiar manner. All this, Francesco took it into his head to imitate for his diversion. He accordingly caused a globe or ball of wood to be made by a turner, and having divided it in half and brought it to the size of the mirror, he set himself with great art to copy all that he saw in the glass, more particularly his own likeness. ... But as all the nearer objects thus depicted in the glass were diminished, he painted a hand, which he represented as employed in drawing, making it look a little larger

than true size, as it does in the glass, and so beautifully done that it appears to be the living member itself (Vasari, 1885, pp. 359–60)

The history of the poem, as Ashbery reports in the introduction to the Arion Press edition of the poem, was more protracted.

> I began writing 'Self-Portrait in a Convex Mirror' during a month's residence at the Fine Arts Work Center in Provincetown in February 1973. I always wanted to 'do something' with Parmigianino's self-portrait ever since I saw it reproduced in the New York Times Book Review in 1950, accompanying a review of Sidney Freedberg's monograph on the painter. This half-conscious wish was reinforced when I saw the original in Vienna in 1959. Then one day when I was walking around Provincetown during my stay there I passed a bookshop with an inexpensive portfolio of Parmigianino's work displayed in the window – the self-portrait was illustrated on the cover. I bought the book, took it back to my studio and slowly began to write a poem about it, or off it.

Both Ashbery's initial fascination with Parmigianino's painting in 1950, and his decision, in 1973, finally to realize a long-nurtured poetic desire to 'do something' with it, are understandable. The year 1950 was when Ashbery wrote 'Picture of Little J.A. in a Prospect of Flowers', the poem in which he first directed the reader to Pasternak's *Safe Conduct*, and to which 'Self-Portrait' (as one might expect, given the poems' shared reflective quality) alludes (the painter, like the young J.A., being described as 'accepting everything') (Ashbery, 1977, p. 71). For the young poet with Pasternak's aesthetic on his mind, Parmigianino's 'Self-Portrait' would have seemed intriguing. As a painting of the painter painting himself, it is an immaculate instance of a work of art telling the history of its own making, and so in an important sense it speaks directly to Ashbery's sense of the occasion of the poem. In another respect, however, it is a most un-Ashberyan artefact, in that its apparent sense of its own occasion is radically truncated, the problem having to do with the relation of background to foreground the painting construes.

In so far as Ashbery tends to prefer self-explanation to self-alienation in *Self-Portrait in a Convex Mirror*, it is central to his strategy that he should find ways of shifting the reader's focus of attention: foregrounding background in an effort to signal his concern with their shared situation. Key to this realignment of background and foreground, and in some ways the term on which the volume hinges, is the word 'as'. It is the word with which the book opens, the first poem being 'As One Put Drunk into the Packet-Boat'. It is also the first word of the title poem – 'As Parmigianino did it, the right hand / Bigger than the head' – the trochaic rhythm swinging down heavily on the opening word. It is most to the fore, however, in 'As You Came From The Holy Land', a poem which explicitly calls for a shift of attention:

> as you came from that holy land
> what other signs of earth's dependency were upon you
> what fixed signs at the crossroads

> what lethargy in the avenues
> where all is said in a whisper
> what tone of voice among the hedges
> what tone under the apple trees

The 'as' of Auden's 'Musée des Beaux Arts' rather than the 'as' of 'as if' in Stevens's 'Notes Towards a Supreme Fiction', the term functions here as a subordinating conjunction, Ashbery indicating what is going on while or during an apparently more important event is taking place. 'As You Came From The Holy Land' it was not your coming, but what was going on as you were coming that counts.

The problem with Parmigianino's painting from Ashbery's perspective is that because of the manner in which it is painted it is all foreground: the hand, larger than life, swimming out towards the viewer; the head it seems to protect occupying the middle distance; while the studio window, through which one might catch sight of the world beyond, and so the background to, the action of the painting is reduced by the optical illusion to a most insignificant opening. Or as Freedberg, in the monograph of 1950 from which Ashbery quotes in the poem, puts it:

> The hand, distortedly large as it would in fact appear in such a mirror, looms in the very foremost plane and instantly catches the spectator's eye, but does not hold it: the hand serves as a bridge into the depth of the picture where the head is placed. Details of clothing, background, etc. are reduced to quite summary terms. (Freedberg, 1950, p. 105)

At its grandest, art-historical, level, Ashbery's argument with Parmigianino is an argument about perspective. Using a term Ashbery cites in his poem, Freedberg describes the painting as a 'bizarria' on 'High Renaissance style', which comments on that style by carrying it to its logical conclusion. By his use of the convex mirror, Parmigianino accentuates the laws of perspective to an incredible degree, the background disappearing behind a shockingly over-emphasized individual. From Ashbery's point of view, then, Parmigianino's 'Self-Portrait in a Convex Mirror' is both an immaculate instance of art telling the history of its own coming into being, and a radical manifestation of the self- (not other-) absorbed artist. Ashbery's rediscovery of the painting in Provincetown in 1973 might thus be thought serendipitous. At a time when interviewers were trying to pin his poetry down to a 'personal element', and he was trying to correct this view of his work by indicating what was going on as they were presenting it, Parmigianino's painting provided a prime opportunity for self-explanation.

That Ashbery meant to explain himself in terms the reader would understand is evident from the poem's seemingly conventional manner and structure. For a start it appears to have a continuous subject. This is not precisely the case, in that the painting is less the subject of the poem than the hook on which its meditations hang, but the fact that the poet allows the appearance of such a subject indicates his willingness to accommodate readerly expectations. It also differs from most Ashbery poems in having a clearly identifiable and sustained narrative voice: the speaker, who seems indistinguishable from the poet, engaging in a dialogue with Parmigianino, often addressing the painter directly ('Can you stand it, / Francesco? Are you strong enough for it?'). Ashbery addresses the painter in this way as a means of addressing the needs of the reader, the effect of this new style of address being, as critics have variously remarked, that the poem is 'more realized in terms of the reader'; that 'here Ashbery himself has been reader'; and that in this poem the poet is a 'one-way interviewer of Parmigianino' (Miklitsch, 1980, p. 118; Costello, 1982, p. 587; Heffernan, 1993, p. 184). Aiming to draw the reader, and his surrogate the interviewer, into his poetic, Ashbery accommodates them by incorporating their voice into his poem.

Having thus drawn the reader to his poem, Ashbery proceeds to emphasize its explanatory purpose by what he calls its 'essayistic thrust': the poem making scholarly references (it quotes Vasari and Freedberg); offering etymological digressions (the word 'speculation', we are advised, derives from 'the Latin *speculum*, mirror'); and unpacking allusions that ordinarily the reader might be expected to get for themselves ('As Berg said of a phrase in Mahler's Ninth'). Chiefly, though, the poem accommodates itself to the need to explain by conducting the reader through a carefully staged argument.

The logic of the poem's argument is contained in the ambiguity of its opening clause,

> As Parmigianino did it, the right hand
> Bigger than the head, thrust at the viewer
> And swerving easily away, as though to protect
> What it advertises.

On the one hand, as John Shoptaw has observed, what this indicates is that the poet will write in the manner of the painting (Shoptaw, 1994, p. 182). His poem will be coherent, autonomous (in that it is self-explanatory), and its contents will appear organized because presented from a single point of view. On the other hand the purpose of the poem is to draw the reader away from the self-regarding view of art articulated by the painting, and to encourage them to consider what it appears to exclude. Its object, in other words, is to indicate what was and is happening 'As Parmigianino did it', as the poet contemplates him doing it, and as the reader contemplates both.

The beauty of the argument is the incremental pace at which it draws the reader towards this new way of seeing. Thus, in the first of the poem's six sections the painting is presented in its own terms. Ashbery quotes Vasari on the making of the painting, and offers a more or less faithful verbal reproduction of the image of self the painting contrives. 'What the portrait says', as the poet makes clear, is that one's soul or self is private, sealed off from factors outside it and so, by definition, incommunicable. Viewing the painting from an Emersonian point of view, what the poet would like to believe is that therefore the self in Parmigianino's 'Self-Portrait' is 'restless', 'longing to be free'. In itself, however, the painting does not say this but insists, rather, that one's

> life is englobed.
> One would like to stick one's hand
> Out of the globe, but its dimension,
> What carries it, will not allow it.

So convincing is Parmigianino's Self-Portrait (so persuasive is the illusion he creates) that nothing in the painting itself would seem to allow one to argue, on the contrary, that one's life is not englobed. To make that argument requires one, first, to step beyond the confines of the painting, and so to show what Parmigianino excludes in the achievement of his *trompe-l'oeil*.

Each of the five sections that follow is a digression from the painting. In section two the poet's attention begins to drift – as it does when one is looking at a painting – and he finds himself thinking first of his own circumstances:

> I think of the friends
> Who came to see me, of what yesterday
> Was like.

and then, by association, of the circumstances that might have been passing through the painter's mind:

> How many people came and stayed a certain time,
> Uttered light and dark speech that became part of you
> Like light behind windblown fog and sand,
> Filtered and influenced by it, until no part
> Remains that is surely you.

The self, this passage suggests, like Ashbery's poetry, is a collaboration, so much the product of factors beyond oneself that the individual self, as such, barely exists. Section three follows this consideration of what takes place as one views or produces a painting by considering how much more difficult it is to represent such experiences.

> Tomorrow is easy, but today is uncharted,
> Desolate, reluctant as any landscape
> To yield what are laws of perspective
> After all only to the painter's deep
> Mistrust, a weak instrument though
> Necessary.

Nothing is more difficult to get into perspective than the present, and so art which works according to the laws of perspective necessarily falsifies the circumstances in which it finds itself. Section four develops the point historically, drawing on Freedberg to present the High Renaissance background out of which Parmigianino's painting emerges. While moving from Parmigianino's situation to a contemplation of the poet's own, section five remarks how

> The shadow of the city injects its own
> Urgency: Rome where Francesco
> Was at work during the Sack: his inventions
> Amazed the soldiers who burst in on him;
> They decided to spare his life, but he left soon after;
> Vienna where the painting is today, where
> I saw it with Pierre in the summer of 1959; New York
> Where I am now, which is a logarithm
> Of other cities.

This is a beautiful transition, the history of Parmigianino's painting leading Ashbery to recount the history of his relationship with the painting, and so the history of the writing of his poem; a history which does not, as Parmigianino pretends, begin and end in the studio, but extends outwards to incorporate the city (and all it contains and stands for) in which the poem was written. Step by step, then, the poem indicates what Parmigianino's painting excludes, and what it encourages its viewer to exclude, drawing the reader in the process away from the painter's aesthetic and towards the poet's own. The result is that by the sixth section – the painting by now having all but disappeared from view – both poet and reader experience a release.

The poet is released in that having illustrated the limitations of another's aesthetic, he is now in a position to propose his own:

> Is there anything
> To be serious about beyond this otherness
> That gets included in the most ordinary
> Forms of daily activity, changing everything
> Slightly and profoundly . . . ?

And because Ashbery's poem, unlike Parmigianino's painting, is serious about this 'otherness', about the circumstances that surround us as we produce or consume art, and because his poem, as he hopes, has redirected our attention to that 'otherness', so the reader also should, at this point, feel a release:

> And we must get out of it even as the public
> Is pushing through the museum now so as to
> Be out by closing time. You can't live there.

Ashbery's poetic, like Emerson's 'Divinity School Address', but unlike Parmigianino's painting, leads the reader beyond the confines and conventions of artistic practice and into an encounter with their own experience.

Ashbery's 'Self-Portrait' could hardly have been more subtly done. Instinctively resistant to the idea of self-explanation – suggestive, as it is, of a didactic attitude to the reader – Ashbery reveals himself in the negative: presenting himself to the reader by showing what another artist, apparently unlike him, is not. As such the poem works like Stein's *Autobiography of Alice B. Toklas*, or, more so, like Pasternak's account of Mayakovsky in *Safe Conduct*, the writer, in each case, revealing himself as the other of his subject. Even so, and for all its brilliant ironies, Ashbery has consistently sought to distance both the reader and himself from 'Self-Portrait in a Convex Mirror'. The tactic is understandable. Ashbery wrote the poem by way of a bargain, going over to the reader's way of speaking in the hope that the reader would in turn be drawn to his. While many readers have, undoubtedly, fulfilled the terms of Ashbery's bargain, very many, also, have not, academic readers in particular having become more attracted to the manner of the poem's argument than to its implications. The concrete result of this has been that a poem which was intended to alert readers to the rest of Ashbery's work has instead, all too often, been singled out from it. All of which is by no means to suggest that the new reader should not look at Ashbery's most famous poem. Instead, it is an argument for looking beyond.

BIBLIOGRAPHY

Ashbery, J. (1977). *Self-Portrait in a Convex Mirror*. Manchester: Carcanet Press.

Ashbery, J. (1978). *Some Trees*. New York: Ecco Press.

Bloom, H. (1973). *The Anxiety of Influence: A Theory of Poetry*. New York and Oxford: Oxford University Press.

Bloom, J. and Losada, R. (1972). 'Craft Interview with John Ashbery.' *New York Quarterly* 9, 11–33.

Costello, B. (1982). 'John Ashbery and the Idea of the Reader.' *Contemporary Literature* 23: 4, 493–514.

Freedberg, S. J. (1950). *Parmigianino: His Works in Painting*. Cambridge, MA: Harvard University Press.

Heffernan, J. A. W. (1993). *Museum of Words: The Poetics of Ekphrasis from Homer to Ashbery*. Chicago and London: University of Chicago Press.

Lehman, D. (1998). *The Last Avant-Garde: The Making of the New York School of Poets*. New York: Doubleday.

Miklitsch, R. (1980). 'John Ashbery.' *Contemporary Literature* 21: 1, 118–35.

Pasternak, B. (1959). *Safe Conduct: An Autobiography and Other Works*. London: Elek Books.

Poulin Jnr., A. (1981). 'The Experience of Experience: A Conversation with John Ashbery.' *Michigan Quarterly* 2: 3, 242–55.

Schultz, S. M. (ed.) (1995). *The Tribe of John: Ashbery and Contemporary Poetry*. Tuscaloosa: University of Alabama Press.

Shoptaw, J. (1994). *On the Outside Looking Out: John Ashbery's Poetry*. Cambridge, MA: Harvard University Press.

Vasari, G. (1885). *Lives of the Most Eminent Painters, Sculptors, and Architects*, vol. 3, trans. Mrs. J. Foster. London: Henry G. Bohn.

Derek Walcott: *Omeros*

Bruce Woodcock

Omeros (1990) helped Derek Walcott win the Nobel Prize for Literature in 1992. This achievement gave further international recognition to the creative outpouring from the Caribbean since 1945. Walcott's own part in this is outstanding and his work places him as one of the foremost poets in the second half of the twentieth century.

Omeros, with its appropriations of Homeric epic tradition, is a product of 'translation', not so much in the linguistic sense, but in the wider sense of 'cultural translation' as invoked in postcolonial studies. The idea of the postcolonial subject and writer as 'translated' is one which Salman Rushdie proposed in his essay 'Imaginary Homelands' (1992), where he points out that the word 'translation' is derived from the Latin for 'bearing across': 'Having been borne across the world, we are translated men. It is normally supposed that something always gets lost in translation; I cling, obstinately, to the notion that something can also be gained' (Rushdie, 1992, p. 17). What Stuart Hall calls 'such cultures of hybridity' are 'the product of several interlocking histories' (Hall, 1992, p. 310), and create a postcolonial awareness which translates the world around it. Walcott himself has been shaped by a process of cultural translation which informs his 'translation' of the Homeric epic in *Omeros*. At the end of Book Three, in one of the most moving passages in the poem, he introduces the figure of his mother, suffering memory loss associated with old age, unable to recognize her son who tries desperately to remind her of her past since she has 'a lot to remember'. Her response 'as she fought / her memory' is '[s]ometimes I ask myself who I am'. This resonates throughout *Omeros*, not least for the narrator himself, displaced from his island roots by his life in America and feeling the dislocation as seemingly irrecoverable histories which he nevertheless knows himself to be part of. Invoking the language of slavery he states

> I felt transported,
> past shops smelling of cod to a place I had lost
> in the open book of the street, and could not find.

> It was another country, whose excitable
> gestures I knew but could not connect with my mind,
> like my mother's amnesia; untranslatable . . .
>
> with tongues of a speech I no longer understood,
> but where my flesh did not need to be translated.

Walcott is well aware of the contradictory legacies of such cultural translations. Hence, *Omeros* is a work which, rather than translating Homer, translates Walcott's home island of St Lucia into the epic dimension of the Homeric form; but at the same time, it interrogates the notion of such translations, and asserts the actuality of the lived experience of the island, outside the artificial confines of literature and art. It aims to heal the cultural schizophrenia of a hybrid history and the translations of the colonial process. Walcott was born in St Lucia in 1930. The island was fought over by the British and the French, and is predominantly French Roman Catholic (90 per cent) with a strong French creole element even though English is the official language. Walcott's family, however, was Methodist: he had white grandfathers and black grandmothers, and was brought up in an atmosphere dominated by English culture. This gap between black French Roman Catholic and white English Methodist cultural traditions Walcott has seen as a schizophrenia (Walcott, 1998, p. 4) between which he translates and is translated, 'wrenched by two styles' (Walcott, 1972, p. 61).

This might suggest Walcott suffers from a Naipaul-like sense of the West Indies as a void. For instance, in 'What the Twilight Says' Walcott asks: 'Slaves, the children of slaves, colonials, then pathetic, unpunctual nationalists, what have we to celebrate?' (Walcott, 1998, p. 18), which suggests a sense of hopelessness, exile or loss which might be epitomized by his poem 'The Gulf'. But the question is not merely rhetorical; it is open, and shows Walcott's divergence from Naipaul. In 1972 Naipaul famously damned the West Indies by saying 'nothing has ever been created in the West Indies, and nothing will ever be created'; in 1974, Walcott took this formula and turned it on its head by saying '[n]othing will always be created in the West Indies . . . because what will come out of there is like nothing one has ever seen before' (Hamner, 1993, p. 54). In both poetry and drama Walcott shows what West Indians do have to celebrate: a sense of newness, strength and potential emerging from the distortions of history and poverty. One of the ways in which he celebrates this is by exploiting and translating (almost in an alchemical sense) his cultural schizophrenia, rather than merely suffering from it. He recognizes his capacity for what he calls 'cunning assimilation' (Walcott, 1998, p. 43), for being a 'mulatto of style', a 'mongrel . . . bastard . . . hybrid' who exploits the cultural diversity from which he comes (ibid., p. 9). He visualizes 'the forging of a language that went beyond mimicry . . . by the writer's making creative use of his schizophrenia, an electric fusion of the old and the new' (ibid., pp. 15–16). For Walcott, the 'Muse of History' should enable, not enslave, the writer's imagination (ibid., pp. 36–64). The fundamental drive of *Omeros* is to liberate the island and the writer from the colonial past, translating them so they may be seen anew.

There are a number of narrative strands in *Omeros*, functioning on individual and socio-historical levels. The opening focus is the rivalry between the close friends Achille and Hector for Helen. The story charts the relationships between the three characters as Achille's friendship is riven by jealousy when Helen leaves him for Hector, until Hector's death leads to Helen's return. Broadening from this are the stories of other villagers: Philoctete's wounded shin and eventual healing are used to explore themes of redemption and renewal, both personal and historical; the blind Seven Seas acts as both a character in his own right and as a *griot* surrogate for Homer/Omeros, who takes various forms throughout; Ma Kilman's shop becomes a focus for communal gatherings and she acts as seer and obeah woman; while the fishing community more generally provides a social back-cloth, dramatizing the changing nature of the village in the face of increasing commercialism. In addition, Achille's dream journey to Africa invokes the history of the Caribbean from a black perspective, re-enacting slavery and the Middle Passage, while Helen acts as the emblem of the island of St Lucia itself.

Alongside these stories and involved with them is the story of retired Regimental Sergeant Major Dennis Plunkett and his wife Maud (who, like Hector, dies at the end of the work). Elements of Plunkett's story parallel that of Achille, in particular his past journeying, his sense of loss and displacement and his investigation of history. As with Achille's African dream, this involves the legacies of a personal and historical community, in this case the British Empire and the character of Midshipman Plunkett: sent as a spy for Admiral Rodney to reconnoitre Dutch forces prior to the Battle of the Saints in 1782 which gave control of St Lucia and the West Indies back to the British. He is adopted by Plunkett as the son he never had.

The final strand belongs to a poet–narrator figure whose function is both to tell the stories of the villagers and to disrupt the narrative illusion, calling into question the role of the poet in relation to literary tradition and life. The narrator's story, like Walcott's own, is one of displacement from his home island, exile in Boston, and also of failed love and marriage. He also recounts the story of nineteenth-century Native American supporter Catherine Weldon, and has had an affair with a Greek sculptress named Antigone whose bust of Homer (Omeros) is the seed for his imaginative translation of his island and its people. The narrator is seen as the point of origin of the stories and at the same time becomes involved with the characters: after Maud's death we find him 'attending / the funeral of a character I'd created', meeting Plunkett, and revealing that he had been trained by him as a cadet. Such effects create a metafictional displacement designed to expose the fictionality of the story being told so convincingly while reasserting the fictional illusion. Walcott's narrator undermines the realism of the story, only to reinforce it as part of a drive to make the reader see the characters in a true light, not just as figments of poetic imagining.

The structure of the poem indicates the extent to which this strategic imperative takes over. *Omeros* is in seven books. Book One introduces all the main characters, including the narrator, but is dominated by the stories of Achille's argument with Hector over Helen, and the tensions between Plunkett and his wife. Book Two covers

Plunkett's investigations of the island's history and the story of the young Midshipman, then deals with the Achille, Helen and Hector story through the medium of
the island's election campaign. Book Three covers Achille's dream journey to Africa
to witness the enslavement of his father's people and his eventual return, but it ends
with the re-emergence of the narrator. The narrator's story dominates Books Four and
Five, developing into a virtual tour of European colonialism. Book Six finds the narrator back on the island directly involved with his imagined characters as Hector dies
in a crash and Maud dies of cancer. Book Seven concludes the work with the narrator accompanying his mentor, the ghostly Omeros, on a Dantesque journey to the
island's volcano, releasing the narrator from his own artistic blindness to a fresh vision
of the island and its people.

    This theme of transformation and renewal is at the heart of the work, but equally
so is an investigation of the corruption of St Lucia by past European colonialism and
by current economic imperialism embodied in tourism. Thus *Omeros* is both an exposé
and a celebratory paean. Walcott's involvement with the life of the island has always
been integral to his artistic practice, an autobiographical exploration of which figured
strongly in his Caribbean version of Wordsworth's *The Prelude, Another Life* (1973). In
Omeros he continues this with vivid depictions of the natural environment as well as
the people, but he also inflects it with a wider historical dimension. The island
becomes representative of a significant section of world history, through its role in the
story of European colonialism, and this allows an 'epic' dimension. Walcott's characters are seen within history, and those individual, communal and world-historical
levels run in tandem throughout. At the same time the poem insists on the immediacy and individuality of life on the island, which is threatened by present trends. This
double edge, critique and celebration, is embodied in the recurrent image given to
the narrator by the ghost of his dead father at the end of Book One: 'simplify / your
life to one emblem, a sail leaving harbour / and a sail coming in'. This image recurs
a number of times, reinforcing Walcott's more general sense as a poet of the double-
ness of experience and of art: the sail is both a loss and a return, and could be either
or both. For Walcott's poetic practice, the ambiguity of the image is all and is the
'truth' of poetry.

    When Achille returns from his dream journey to Africa, Seven Seas asks him to
rake up the leaves in his yard and Achille decides to 'clean up this whole place'. His
desire to sweep away the past inevitably leads to its uncovering: the day is 'one of
those Saturdays that contain centuries' with 'the strata of history layered underheel'.
He sees the iguana, after whom the original inhabitants of St Lucia, the Aruacs, named
the island 'Iounalao', and Seven Seas reminds Achille that, before colonialism and
slavery, 'this used to be their place'. 'Achille / found History that morning' as he
uncovers a carved Aruac totem which he throws away in fear. The episode is a reminder
of the contradictory act of desecration and celebration which opens *Omeros* as Philoctete
recites for the tourists the story of how the fishermen cut down the cedars to make
their canoes. This 'decimation' is seen as both a defamation of the Aruac gods of the
forest and as a necessary sacrifice: the fishermen are 'like barbarians' in the aftermath

of the lost culture of the Aruacs, having to create a culture of their own. The narrator suggests as much later in the poem when he reflects on the problematic translations involved in the process of 'diaspora, exodus', recalling this opening episode:

> Men take their colours
>
> as the trees do from the native soil of their birth,
> and once they are moved elsewhere, entire cultures
> lose the art of mimicry, and then, where the trees were,
>
> the fir, the palm, the olive, the cedar, a desert place
> widens in the heart. This is the first wisdom of Caesar,
> to change the ground under the bare soles of a race.

While people are not 'simply chameleons, self-dyeing our skins / to each background',
connections to place and environment help shape identity. Physical translation from
Africa to the Caribbean meant that the ex-slaves had to translate themselves and their
inheritances into a new register. Achille's ancestor, Afolabe, was himself translated
into 'Achilles' by his slave master, 'which, to keep things simple, he let himself be
called'. The 'wisdom of Caesar' is the colonial legacy against whose internal and external imperatives the 'liberated' ex-colonials must still struggle. But equally a creative
acceptance of change is seen as something to be embraced in the forging of a new
culture, a process of re-naming the New World which has always obsessed Walcott.
Weaving language and imagery to intersect different strands and sections, Walcott
connects the lives of the individual characters with the complex web of colonial and
pre-colonial histories working at a personal and more generally social level and shadowing the present.

This dense overlapping of histories is present in all the threads of the narrative structure. When the narrator asks 'Where did it start?' his question refers simultaneously
to the stories of the characters in the poem, including the narrator himself, the history
of the island, of the empire which shaped it, of the Africans who were its displaced
victims and survivors, and those lost Aruac tribes who originally inhabited the island.
As Plunkett realizes, 'All roots have their histories.' The poem reveals just how intertwined those roots are, aiming to release the present and future from the past by confronting it, acknowledging its legacies as both bad and good, and moving on.

Plunkett's past is the contradictory heritage of the British Empire. Physically and
psychologically wounded in the Second World War, Plunkett naively seeks a new life
with Maud in an 'Eden', 'somewhere . . . where what they called history could not
happen.' Ironically, his choice of St Lucia leads him to confront the brutal legacy of
British imperialism and to witness its overthrow. This is miniaturized in the quarrel
between Maud and Helen, who works for the Plunketts as housemaid. Maud sees
Helen as 'our trouble . . . the arrogant servant that ruled their house'; at the same time
'the island was once / named Helen', suggesting an analogy between the power struggle being waged in the Plunkett household and the struggle for independence in the

ex-colonial territories. Plunkett's realization that 'Empire was ebbing' is manifested in Helen's appropriation of Maud's yellow dress and in Plunkett's own obsession with Helen's beauty. His investigations into the island's history transfer his obsession from one to the other, becoming a virtual infidelity to Maud. Plunkett realizes that the history which he wants to preserve and celebrate, the days when 'history was easy', the history of Admiral Rodney, of his ancestral Midshipman and the empire he served, 'will be rewritten / by black pamphleteers, History will be revised, / and we'll be its villians [*sic*], fading from the map'. But equally he re-enacts the imperialistic imperative in his obsessive lust for Helen, which he hides behind his apparently paternalistic concern. Plunkett cannot escape the bitter realization of the Empire's demise, leaving 'deserts whence our power / withdrew'. That Maud dies of the 'empire of cancer' and leaves a quilt which the narrator sees as stitched with 'an empire's guilt' reinforces the sense that the personal is imbricated with the historical and political. Yet given this role as the embodiment of a collapsed Empire, Walcott's portrait of Plunkett as 'an armchair admiral' is notably sympathetic, indicating the level of complexity which the poem achieves in its characterization and thematic treatment. With his understanding of the contradictory legacies of history and empire, Walcott does not dismiss this character as a stereotyped remnant of a past to be simplistically despised.

For the other characters, the legacies of history are equally contradictory and inescapable, shadowing the island's present attempts to remake itself. They are the 'deep evil' of Empire which Achille confronts in his dangerous dive for the tainted imperial money he hopes will win Helen back. They are also epitomized by the wine bottle 'crusted with fool's gold', which sank with Midshipman Plunkett in the Battle of the Saints only to be captured by the Cyclops-like octopus and then put on show in the island's museum. Meanwhile the narrator himself encounters history in its colonial manifestations in two forms, both very personal. While in America in Books Four and Five, he reads the memoir of Catherine Weldon, a nineteenth-century American who was deeply concerned about the plight of the Sioux, witnessing the effects of the white betrayal of the various treaties and the dispossession and massacre of tribes. The sense of white America as an imperialist entity, as 'an empire . . . that had raked the leaves of the tribes into one fire', is reinforced by linking glances at the history of plantation slavery with the narrator sardonically answering the racism of white American culture by wryly addressing Herman Melville in the mock tones of the stage negro. This episode reveals the dangers for art when it has 'surrendered / to History with its whiff of formaldehyde', and sets the scene for the poet–narrator's own odyssey towards redemption. Under the direction of his father, the narrator undertakes a tour of European colonialism at the opening of Book Five: he visits Lisbon, the port where 'Europe / rose with its terrors' after Pope Alexander VI's papal decrees of 1493 to apportion the New World between Spain and Portugal. He visits London to find Omeros transformed into a Charon-like bargeman living as a down-and-out in Thatcher's cardboard city, while 'the tinkling Thames drags by in its ankle-irons'. The narrator delivers a vitriolic series of questions echoing the Demogorgon section of

Shelley's exposé of Empire, *Prometheus Unbound*, designed to indict the aftermath of Empire. He returns to America and Catherine Weldon's witnessing of the Native American 'diaspora' and genocide with the realization that 'all colonies inherit their empire's sin, / and these, who broke free of the net [i.e. white America] enmeshed a race'.

Such imagery of slavery haunts the poem from the outset, along with 'the shame, the self-hate' which is its residue, and the need to confront and transform that past. Emblematic of this is Philoctete's incurable wound, caused by an anchor but which 'he believed . . . came from the chained ankles / of his grandfathers. Or else why was there no cure?' Achille witnesses the enslavement of his own forefather's tribe in his dream journey to Africa and it is partly from Africa that the cure for history's wound comes. Achille's view of the historical enslavement is contradictory, since he wants to save his father and his people and at the same time he knows the future to which it will lead, a future he would not wish to deny. Out of the horrendous suffering and lost identities of slavery, the poem envisages the potential for a translated identity emerging, as the survivors who crossed the Middle Passage 'felt the sea-wind tying them into one nation . . . in the one pain'. It is Ma Kilman, in her role as obeah woman, who cures Philoctete's wound using a plant whose seed came from Africa carried by the sea swift whose presence haunts Achille's journey as an almost anthropomorphic emblem. Ma Kilman bathes the wound using 'one of those cauldrons from the old sugar-mill', an emblem of how the colonial past is being transformed by the present. The 'self-healing island' epitomizes a wider sense of renewal and creativity in the aftermath of empire, which is what motivates Walcott to reveal how the individual stories of St Lucians and of the island embody an 'epical splendour' of survival and re-creation.

The interactions of individual and history are partly what gives *Omeros* its epic dimension, placing the life of the island on the stage of world history. The narrator's view of 'our epic horizon' suggests that the lives of these people matter and that their histories are a significant part of the broader flow of world history. This epic dimension is reinforced through Walcott's deliberate and often ironic invocations of epic parallels with Homer. So the names of the main characters, Achille, Hector, Helen, Philoctete, are analogous with central characters from Homer, Philoctete sharing the fate of his namesake in the form of his seemingly incurable wound. There are many incidental echoes in imagery, with the Cyclops appearing as a lighthouse and as the covetous colonial octopus guarding the treasure which Achille tries to plunder, as well as the hurricane which devastates the island. Hector's van in which he dies is seen as a 'chariot', the satirical portrayal of the island's election is fought as a war between Greeks and Trojans, while the narrator eventually sees Plunkett as a 'khaki Ulysses' to his own Telemachus. There is a similarly flexible re-creation of some aspects of Homeric style, with modified epic similes employed to describe Rodney's ships in battle as pelicans, for example. Often there is a self-knowing quality about these invocations of Homeric analogies. At one point, the narrator thinks of the blind 'Old St Omere', known as Seven Seas from his claim to have sailed the world, possibly nodding in tribute to Walcott's St Lucian friend, painter Dunstan St Omer; only to realize wryly 'Homer and Virg are New England farmers, / and the winged horse guards their gas-station'. The parallels are also consciously displayed within the text, as when Plunkett pursues 'Homeric coincidence' in the analogy of Helen with the island. The Homeric links have direct thematic functions, as with the Circe imagery associated with the experience of slavery and the pig farm which Plunkett runs. Both are seen as products of a 'swinish' Empire manacling slaves and masters equally, a dialectical vision of the imperial legacy which has similarities with George Lamming's view of the colonial process as a 'reciprocal' one in which Prospero is as dehumanized as Caliban, however differently (Lamming, 1960, p. 156). Part of the 'odyssey' in the poem's navigation of history is to disrupt the binaries of colonial power so 'that parallel / is crossed, and cancels the line of master and slave'.

Nevertheless, the poem does not seek too easily to assuage the sufferings of the past. The wry request of the African tribal *griot* to 'remember us to the black waiter bringing the bill' shows how flexibly Walcott moves between the different levels, settings and times of the poem, reminding us that the legacies of the colonial process continue in the neocolonialism of tourism and the corruption of the island's culture. Achille sees 'what was happening to the village' as analogous to Helen: 'She was selling herself like the island', while the village 'was dying in its change, the way it whored / away a simple life' and the young 'took no interest in canoes. / That was longtime shit.' In the desperate drive to make money, the village 'had become a souvenir / of itself' under the reductive gaze of tourism's desire for 'photogenic poverty'.

But the poem makes plain that the narrator himself is also in danger of not seeing what is truly there. The narrator accuses himself of wanting to keep the island picturesque for the purposes of poem-making:

> Didn't I want the poor
> to stay in the same light so that I could transfix
> them in amber, the afterglow of an empire,
>
> preferring a shed of palm-thatch with tilted sticks
> to that blue bus-stop?

From this viewpoint, the narrator realizes, 'Art is History's nostalgia', incapable of making the real contribution to the making of a new culture demanded by the circumstances of actual cultural translation. The narrator's desire to translate the island into the epic forms of Homer is interrogated as the wrong kind of translation. Book One introduced the narrator invoking Omeros, and the incident which might be seen as the origin of the poem, his lost love affair with the Greek sculptress Antigone, who had made a bust of Homer and taught the narrator to pronounce 'Omeros' correctly. It is the narrator's pursuit of this muse figure which leads him into a misrepresentation of his island, as he becomes 'blinded' by the 'elegies' of history. But the narrator gradually realizes that this desire to ennoble his island through Homeric translation embroiders a falsifying pattern onto life, as with Maud's imperialist quilt, trapping the present in a past transposed from elsewhere. Looking at Helen, the narrator acknowledges that, like Plunkett, he has misrepresented her:

> There, in her head of ebony,
> there was no real need for the historian's
> remorse, nor for literature's. Why not see Helen
>
> as the sun saw her with no Homeric shadow.

In his desire to 'enter that light beyond metaphor' the narrator commits himself to an art that can contribute a genuine truth to life by seeing 'the light of St Lucia at last through her own eyes', answering the poem's opening view that he can only 'catch the noise / of the surf lines' through the 'egg-white eyes' of the blind Omeros. His misrepresentation of his island through the lens of Homeric tradition, like Philoctete's wound or the corruption of the island by tourism, must be purged before any renewal can be achieved, personal or communal. It is for this reason that the narrator undertakes his dream journey to the volcano with Seven Seas/Omeros as a purgation from which he wakes healed. This self-interrogation and self-indictment of its own project is one of the most remarkable aspects of the poem, since it questions what contribution art can really make to the process of creating a new culture. All the narrative dislocations of the poem, in which the narrator both tells the story and interacts with his own characters, are designed to create for the reader this sense of encountering actual life not merely as fiction but as reality.

Walcott has said in interview that his aim was not to create a 'reproduction' of Homer, nor a Homeric template in the manner of Joyce's *Ulysses* (Henriques, 1993). Indeed the whole drive of the poem is to expose such a project as delusory, reflecting ironically back on his own continuing obsession with a Caribbean odyssey (see Thieme, 1999, pp. 151–97). This is brilliantly satirized in the last book, when the poet–narrator confronts his mentor, Omeros, and admits that he'd never read his master's work, 'not all the way through', while 'the gods and the demi-gods aren't much use to us'. Instead his use of Homer is, as usual with Walcott's appropriation of literary styles and traditions, extraordinarily flexible. Not content with having his Omeros be Homer, he also has him as Virgil and Dante. In the last book, Omeros/Seven Seas takes the narrator on a visit to the island's volcano, called Malebolge after a region of Hell in Dante's *Inferno* (Canto 18), where the satirical encounters with speculators making money from the island and with a pit full of poets trying to drag the narrator down to their own level are clearly modelled on Dante. The form of the poem, too, in general is a modified version of Dante's *terza rima*, but as with his other creative appropriations, Walcott's use of this form is in no way restricted to the original. He keeps enough of the pattern to maintain shape but is quite willing to playfully depart from it as necessary (Hamner, 1997, pp. 4–5).

As this suggests, Walcott mixes a wide variety of traditions, rather than forcing Homer onto his material. He also deploys African folk-tale methods and gods in the description of the hurricane, exuberantly cross-hatching them with Greek elements.

This flexibility is part of the emerging traditions of the postcolonial long poem, in which diverse elements are creatively re-cast and translated. Examples which spring to mind are Seamus Heaney's 'Station Island', Les Murray's *Fredy Neptune*, Vikram Seth's *The Golden Gate* and Paul Muldoon's 'Madoc – A Mystery'. This last is of particular interest since it also engages with Native American issues. Some critics have seen the scope of *Omeros* with its inclusion of such material and its geographical wanderings as leaving it structurally flawed (see Hamner, 1997, pp. 92–5, 106), but it is more a testament to the versatility of Walcott's imagination and the immense artistry with which he has invented this marvellous self-interrogating translation of the life of his island 'still going on'.

BIBLIOGRAPHY

Baugh, Edward (1978). *Derek Walcott: Memory as Vision: Another Life*. London: Longman.

Brown, Stuart (ed.) (1991). *The Art of Derek Walcott*. Chester Springs, PA: Dufour.

Burnett, Paula (1993). 'Hegemony or Pluralism? The Literary Prize and the Post-colonial Project in the Caribbean.' *Commonwealth Essays and Studies*, 16: 1, 1–20.

Burnett, Paula (1996). 'The Ulyssean Crusoe and the Quest for Redemption in J. M. Coetzee's *Foe* and Derek Walcott's *Omeros*.' In Lieve Spaas and Brian Stimpson (eds), *Robinson Crusoe: Myths and Metamorphoses*. New York: St Martin's.

Hall, Stuart (1992). 'The Question of Cultural Identity.' In Stuart Hall, David Held and Tony McGrew (eds), *Modernity and its Futures*. Cambridge: Polity Press.

Hamner, Robert D. (1993). *Critical Perspectives on Derek Walcott*. Washington: Three Continents Press.

Hamner, Robert D. (1997). *Epic of the Dispossessed: Derek Walcott's Omeros*. Missouri: University of Missouri Press.

Henriques, Julian (1993). 'Derek Walcott: Poet of the Island.' *Arena* BBC 2.

Hoegberg, David E. (1995). 'The Anarchist's Mirror: Walcott's *Omeros* and the Epic Tradition'. *Commonwealth Essays and Studies*, 172, 67–81.

Lamming, George (1960). *The Pleasures of Exile*. London: Michael Joseph.

Lernout, Geert (1992). 'Derek Walcott's *Omeros*: The Isle is Full of Voices.' *Kunapipi*, 14: 2, 90–104.

Morris, Mervyn (1979). 'Derek Walcott.' In Bruce King (ed.), *West Indian Literature*. London: Macmillan.

O'Brien, Sean (1990). 'In Terms of the Ocean.' *Times Literary Supplement*, 4, 563, 977–8.

Ramazani, Jahan (1997). 'The Wound of History: Walcott's *Omeros* and the Postcolonial Poetics of Affliction.' *PMLA* 112: 3, 405–17.

Rushdie, Salman (1992). *Imaginary Homelands: Essays and Criticism 1981–1991*. London: Granta.

Terada, Rei (1992). *Derek Walcott's Poetry: American Mimicry*. Boston, MA: Northeastern University Press.

Thieme, John (1997). 'After Greenwich: Crossing Meridians in Post-colonial Literatures.' In Marc Delrez and Benedicte Ledent (eds), *The Contact and the Culmination: Essays in Honour of Hena Maes-Jelinek*. Liege: University of Liege.

Thieme, John (1999). *Derek Walcott*. Manchester: Manchester University Press.

Walcott, Derek (1972). *The Castaway and Other Poems*. London: Cape.

Walcott, Derek (1991). *Omeros*. London: Faber.

Walcott, Derek (1998). *What the Twilight Says: Essays*. London: Faber.

PART V
The Contemporary Scene

45

Contemporary American Poetry
Roger Gilbert

The story of the first half of the twentieth century in American poetry is largely a story of individual poets: Frost, Stevens, Pound, Williams, H. D., Moore, Eliot, Crane. By comparison the second half of the century looks muddy and crowded. While a few postwar poets have achieved demi-canonical stature, there still seems to be little agreement about which individuals or groups have mattered most in the last fifty years. This means that doing justice to the richness and variety of the period requires something other than the major-poet paradigm that has governed most accounts of the first half of the century. No half-dozen or dozen figures can be taken as 'representative' of the full range of contemporary American poetry. I propose instead to use three complementary frames of reference, each of which provides a slightly different perspective on the period and its achievements. The frames I have in mind are decades, generations and poetic schools. All of these ways of dividing up the period contain an element of the arbitrary, but by looking at contemporary American poetry through each one in turn I hope to construct a more rounded picture than any of them can give by itself.

Decades

The 1950s began under the sway of the New Criticism and its criteria for poetic excellence; the early work of Randall Jarrell, John Berryman, Elizabeth Bishop, Robert Lowell, Richard Wilbur, Karl Shapiro and Howard Nemerov all fell into the New Critical mode. This kind of tightly wrought poem continued to be written well into the fifties, but the dominant tendency of that decade was towards a loosening of the formal and stylistic criteria the New Criticism had established. That loosening took several forms. Poems began to open themselves to a broader, more miscellaneous range of detail; a certain randomness began to replace the controlled coherence of the New Critical style. Syntactically this shift manifested itself as a tendency towards parataxis, loose concatenations of words and clauses rather than the logically subordinated grammar of the New Critical poem. More broadly it showed itself in a preference for structures based on juxtaposition and accumulation like lists and narratives, rather than the more syllogistic organization typical of forties poems. Poems in the fifties no longer centred themselves on a single metaphor that rigorously determined all its details. Instead they often favoured metonymic associations between images and ideas, connections based on accidental features of proximity, contiguity or succession. Tidy containment gave way to unruly sprawl, most prominently in Allen Ginsberg's *Howl* (1956), with its long Whitmanesque lines and wildly associative inventories.

These stylistic changes reflected a more basic shift from a conception of the poem as a self-contained artefact to an idea of the poem as a rendering of experience in all its temporal flux and variety. This experiential aesthetic led to an increasing intimacy of tone and subject matter. Where New Critical poems tended to sound somewhat aloof and impersonal, poems in the fifties spoke in a variety of personal registers from conversational candour to urgent self-revelation. And where New Critical poems often focused on cultural and historical subjects with no direct connection to the speaker's life, poems in the fifties frequently dealt with personal circumstances and occasions in great detail. The fifties were of course when the so-called Confessional mode emerged in the openly autobiographical work of poets like W. D. Snodgrass and Robert Lowell. But many poets in the fifties not directly associated with the Confessional style also wrote poems grounded in the particulars of their own private experience.

Much has been said about the supposed split between academic and avant-garde poets in this period – between the 'raw' and the 'cooked', to use the terms put forward by Lowell. But while it's true that distinct camps and coteries existed, as reflected most famously in the rival anthologies *New Poets of England and America* (1957) and *The New American Poetry* (1960), the dominant fifties style cut across those factional divisions. The most significant and influential works of the period from both academic and avant-garde circles shared a desire to accommodate a larger, more diverse range of fact and experience than had been possible under New Critical norms. Books like Theodore Roethke's *Praise to the End* (1951), Charles Olson's *Maximus Poems / 1–10* (1953), Elizabeth Bishop's *A Cold Spring* (1955), Robert Lowell's *Life Studies* (1959), W. D. Snodgrass's *Heart's Needle* (1959), Gwendolyn Brooks's *The Bean Eaters* (1960), Randall Jarrell's *The Woman at the Washington Zoo* (1960), Kenneth Koch's *Thank You* (1962) and Frank O'Hara's *Lunch Poems* (1964, but written mainly in the fifties), despite their manifest differences of style and subject, all reflect the general widening and loosening of manner that transformed American poetry in the fifties.

The 1960s saw a shift from this densely detailed, experiential style to a starker, more visionary mode that often seemed to leave the realm of experience behind in its push towards the ineffable. The expansive parataxis of the fifties gave way to a hushed and elliptical style; lines, sentences and poems all grew shorter, as though striving for a condition beyond language. The influence of modern European and Latin American poetry showed itself in a preference for isolated, dreamlike images that resisted narrative or thematic articulations. Robert Bly was the most influential spokesman for this new style; his 1963 essay 'A Wrong Turning in American Poetry' attacked the empirical cast of fifties poems and called for a freer, less rational kind of imagery. The work of Bly and his friends James Wright, Galway Kinnell and Louis Simpson exemplified what came to be called the Deep Image style, loosely grounded in Jungian psychology. The style might be characterized as a marriage of Poundian Imagism with European and Latin American Surrealism; the emphasis is at once on the presentation of sharply defined images and on the exploration of unconscious associations and resonances.

Much work in the sixties shared in the general movement away from empirical fact and towards various modes of the unconscious and the ineffable. Sylvia Plath's *Ariel* (1965), perhaps the decade's most famous book of poems, clearly partakes of this visionary tendency despite its superficial link to Confessional poetics. Other volumes that typify the sixties style include Bly's *Silence in the Snowy Fields* (1962), Wright's *The Branch Will Not Break* (1963), Simpson's *At the End of the Open Road* (1963), Denise Levertov's *O Taste and See* (1964), Adrienne Rich's *Necessities of Life* (1966), Kinnell's *Body Rags* (1967), W. S. Merwin's *The Lice* (1967), Gary Snyder's *The Back Country* (1967), Robert Duncan's *Bending the Bow* (1968) and Mark Strand's *Reasons for Moving* (1968). Many of these volumes also share the conjunction of anti-rational poetics and oppositional politics that the critic Paul Breslin has described under the rubric 'the psycho-political muse'. The Vietnam war in particular inspired an apocalyptic strain of vision quite distinct from earlier, more realistic modes of war poetry.

One of the effects of the general shift from empirical representation to ineffable vision was a marked change in the vocabulary of contemporary poetry. The proper names and concrete nouns that swelled the lines of fifties poems gave way to a more restricted set of words evoking dream rather than reality: light, dark, water, stone, field, sky, star, bone, and so on. Generic terms replaced particulars; poets tended to write of animals, birds and trees rather than squirrels, jays and sycamores. A kind of purifying of poetic language seemed to be at work, as though poets wished to cleanse their medium of the contaminating effects of history, culture, even nature. Such purification eventually runs up against hard limits; many critics began to complain of the monotony that resulted from the continual recycling of the same handful of elemental words. By the early seventies the stark, stripped-down style of much sixties poetry, which initially seemed daring and fresh, had come to seem mannered and artificial.

In the 1970s the reaction against the sixties style took the form of a return to what the critic and poet Robert Pinsky called 'prose virtues'. Pinsky's influential book *The Situation of Poetry* (1976) criticized what he took to be the extreme nominalism of sixties poetry, which led in his analysis to a thoroughgoing distrust of language as a medium for thought and representation. Rather than limiting itself to shadowy evocations of the silence beyond speech, Pinsky argued that contemporary poetry should avail itself of all the resources of language, including generalization, description and narrative. Pinsky's umbrella term for the qualities he felt needed to be readmitted to poetry was 'discursiveness', and the term is a useful one for characterizing the larger tendencies of seventies poetry. If poets in the sixties appeared to be pushing poetry as far from prose as possible, establishing a special vocabulary and syntax wholly distinct from ordinary usage, poets in the seventies seemed intent on reclaiming much of the idiom of prose as a legitimate part of poetry's domain.

The discursive style of the seventies had as one of its hallmarks a more elaborate syntax, devoted not to the proliferation of factual detail, as in the fifties, but to the complexities of abstract thought. The short declarative sentences favoured by poets in the sixties were replaced by longer sentences full of qualifications, parentheses, semi-colons and subordinate clauses. Lines became longer as well in order to accommodate this more expository, discursive syntax. Many poems in the seventies openly modelled themselves on prose forms like the letter, the essay and the journal. Perhaps the book that most fully established this new style was John Ashbery's much-honoured *Self-Portrait in a Convex Mirror* (1975), whose title poem drew on the language of art history, philosophy and cultural criticism. Other books in the vein included A. R. Ammons's *Sphere* (1974), James Merrill's *Divine Comedies* (1976), Richard Hugo's *31 Letters and 13 Dreams* (1977), C. K. Williams's *With Ignorance* (1977), Adrienne Rich's *The Dream of a Common Language* (1978), Robert Hass's *Praise* (1979), Pinsky's *An Explanation of America* (1979) and Douglas Case's *The Revisionist* (1981). Even the late work of older poets like Elizabeth Bishop, Robert Lowell and Robert Hayden reflected the influence of the discursive mode; Lowell's *History* (1973), Bishop's *Geography III* (1976) and Hayden's *American Journal* (1978) all contain a higher proportion of prose idiom and discursive elaboration than their previous books.

The 1980s saw a turn from the rational continuity of the discursive style to a more splintered, disjunctive idiom that emphasized the mind's inability to make satisfactory connections and generalizations. Like the fifties, the eighties were characterized by highly visible rifts between different poetic factions: those working in traditional forms, those in the revitalized avant-garde, and those writing in the autobiographical free verse codified by creative-writing workshops. Again, however, the period style cut across these lines. Formalists, experimentalists and workshop poets alike began producing poems heavy with information, fragments of cultural, social, political and physical data without obvious interconnections. While this style shared the paratactic looseness of the fifties style, it lacked the experiential ground that unified most fifties poems, the sense that however random a poem's particulars might seem they all originated in the poet's own experience. Instead this style reflected the precipitous growth of computer and media technologies, which triggered an enormous increase in the availability of raw information without providing ways of sorting and assembling it into coherent wholes. One analogy sometimes invoked for this style was channel-surfing, the restless wandering among unrelated images and narratives made possible by the proliferation of cable TV channels.

Many eighties poems laid special emphasis on the ironic dissonance between political and ethical questions on the one hand and aesthetic and sensual pleasures on the other. Images of suffering and exploitation were often set beside images of consumption and enjoyment with little or no commentary, as though the mere contrast spoke for itself. The result was a poetry of troubled yet vague conscience, passively reflecting the contradictions and disjunctions of its time. Some books in this mode include Albert Goldbarth's *Arts and Sciences* (1986), Alice Fulton's *Palladium* (1986), Jane Miller's *American Odalisque* (1987), Leslie Scalapino's *Way* (1988), Ron Silliman's *What* (1988), Donald Hall's *The One Day* (1988), Bob Perelman's *Face Value* (1988), Robert Hass's *Human Wishes* (1989), Frederick Seidel's *These Days* (1989), Paul Hoover's *The Novel* (1990) and Robert Pinsky's *The Want Bone* (1990). For all their formal differences, these books share a densely informational texture in which clauses, lines and sentences become atomized 'bits' crowded together without apparent logical or narrative design. Vikram Seth's surprisingly successful verse-novel *The Golden Gate* (1986), written in Pushkin's rhymed sonnet stanzas, displays a similarly high density of information and a comparable irony about the clashing values of American culture, albeit with a light patina of plot and character to hold the work together.

In the 1990s the flattened, fragmented, quintessentially 'postmodern' poetics of the eighties modulated towards a new lyricism that brought with it a return to spiritual and even religious themes. Words that had become nearly taboo in the ironic eighties began to reappear in poems and even book titles: soul, God, sky, angel, saint, spirit. The religious beliefs betokened by this vocabulary were hardly orthodox, and while they may have shared something with the various spiritual practices known under the rubric 'the New Age', they tended to be darker and more uncertain in their sense of cosmic authority. In fact a number of nineties poets could be described as Gnostic in their evocation of a hostile universe ruled by an alien God. Others offered glimpses of a more benevolent divinity, but with little faith in its accessibility through human institutions.

Stylistically this turn to religious or transcendental concerns showed itself in a variety of ways. The relentless contemporaneity of reference that marked much eighties poetry did not recede completely, but was balanced by more archaic elements. Poems in the nineties became more allusive, evoking or expounding older texts and voices as though to authorize their own spiritual exploration. Augustine, Dante, Traherne, Dickinson, Emily Brontë and Wittgenstein were only a few of the tutelary figures summoned up by poets in the nineties. Classical myth, once scorned by contemporary poets as a throwback to the dusty erudition of Pound and Eliot, now reappeared, albeit in sleekly updated forms. Syntax became more porous and elliptical than it had been in the eighties, less freighted with information and more open to the ineffable. Yet the disjunctiveness of the eighties mode persisted; few nineties poets wrote with the kind of discursive clarity and coherence prevalent in the seventies. Nor did the nineties witness a return to the elemental, 'pure' diction of sixties poetry; vocabulary in the nineties remained diverse, with heterogeneous words and idioms often placed in sharp counterpoint. Examples of this style include Li-Young Lee's *The City in Which I Love You* (1990), Jorie Graham's *Region of Unlikeness* (1991), Allen Grossman's *The Ether Dome* (1991), Thylias Moss's *Rainbow Remnants in a Rock Bottom*

Ghetto Sky (1991), Sandra McPherson's *The God of Indeterminacy* (1993), Brenda Hillman's *Bright Existence* (1993), Ann Lauterbach's *And For Example* (1994), Carolyn Forche's *The Angel of History* (1994), Rita Dove's *Mother Love* (1995), Anne Carson's *Glass, Irony and God* (1995), Susan Stewart's *The Forest* (1995), Lucie Brock-Broido's *The Master Letters* (1995), Michael Palmer's *At Passages* (1995), Reginald Shepherd's *Angel, Interrupted* (1996), Larissa Szporluk's *Dark Sky Question* (1998) and Kathleen Peirce's *The Oval Hour* (1999). Once again these books differ in many ways, but they share a longing for the sublime, whether conceived as light or dark, that pulls them away from the thick realm of information inhabited by much eighties poetry.

Generations

The generation of poets born between 1905 and 1920 is the first that can legitimately be regarded as 'contemporary', though most of its key figures are long dead, many of them prematurely: Theodore Roethke, Delmore Schwartz, Randall Jarrell, John Berryman, Charles Olson, Robert Lowell, Muriel Rukeyser, Elizabeth Bishop. (The most prominent survivors are Stanley Kunitz, Gwendolyn Brooks and Ruth Stone, all of whom have remained remarkably active well into their seventies and eighties.) These are poets who struggled in the shadow of the senior modernists, most of whom were alive and productive for much of the younger poets' own careers. Their primary innovation was to adapt the techniques of modernism, with its aesthetic of impersonality, to a more directly autobiographical kind of poetry. As the first generation of American poets to grow up in the age of Freud, they returned obsessively in their poetry to familial and especially parental themes and conflicts, often refracted through childhood memory. Indeed their most visible legacy may simply be the claiming of family life in all its ambivalence as a subject for poetry.

With a few exceptions the careers of these poets seemed to share a general trajectory from early success to later disappointment, a movement that was often exacerbated by various forms of self-destructive behaviour. While individual temperament certainly played a part in these tendencies, it must be noted that this generation occupied a difficult transitional phase in the cultural status of the American poet. Older modernists like Frost, Sandburg and Eliot had revived the image of the public poet, a figure lauded in print and lionized at lectures and readings. Like most of their generation they remained largely outside the academy, supporting themselves primarily through extra- or para-literary endeavours. Lowell's generation, by contrast, lived within yet often on the fringes of the university, not holding tenured jobs for the most part but moving nomadically from one post to another. At the same time the spectacle of the modernist titans seems to have bred in many of these younger poets an urgent sense of competitiveness. Olson, Berryman, Roethke and Lowell in particular all apparently felt themselves to be vying for the title of 'top bard', and this aggressive drive for pre-eminence both fuelled and in certain respects disfigured their work. Lacking both the amateur status of the modernists and the professional security of younger poets fully ensconced in the academy, many of these poets found themselves assuming the role of literary celebrities, rewarded not for their expertise in the classroom but for their enactment of various public ideas of poethood. The career of Dylan Thomas, who spent much of his later life in America, established the pattern for this generation, both in its achievements and its disasters.

The next generation of poets, those born between 1920 and 1935, is an extraordinarily rich one. For the most part these poets did not suffer from the personal and professional tribulations that afflicted the previous generation. Perhaps because they came of age when the great modernists were already fading from the scene, they also seem to have felt less burdened by their legacy. Under the influence of New Critical doctrines many of these poets began their careers writing tightly controlled formal verse, but then abruptly shifted to a more 'open' or 'naked' style in the sixties; these included James Wright, W. S. Merwin, Robert Bly, Galway Kinnell, Donald Hall, Anne Sexton, Adrienne Rich, Sylvia Plath, and to a lesser degree John Ashbery and James Merrill. Others, like Allen Ginsberg, A. R. Ammons, Frank O'Hara, Robert Creeley and Amiri Baraka, worked in open form more or less continuously. By and large this was a privileged and well-educated cohort; many of them attended Ivy League schools like Harvard, Princeton and Columbia, and several made their debuts in the pages of the prestigious Yale Younger Poets Series, then judged by W. H. Auden, who along with William Carlos Williams served as the group's unofficial mentor. Today this generation continues to be a dominant presence in American poetry, producing important works, receiving major awards, and occupying the country's most prestigious academic positions.

Perhaps one reason the poets of this generation have exhibited such remarkable staying power is that they did not all emerge at once. A few, like Ginsberg and Snodgrass, made their greatest impressions in the fifties; others, like Plath, Wright, Creeley, Merwin and Bly, received more attention in the sixties; while still others, like Ammons, Ashbery, Merrill and Rich, did not have their full impact until the seventies. This staggering of recognition allowed more members to find an audience for themselves, thus mitigating the kind of competitive jockeying the previous generation had seen. There seems to have been a tacit agreement among these poets to share the shrinking amount of cultural capital granted American poetry in the period, rather than fighting over who would receive the greatest rewards. This freed them to explore a wide variety of styles and modes, from traditional form to radical experiment, from aesthetic meditation to political address, from personal narrative to nebulous myth. As a result many of these poets were able to forge highly original and distinctive voices. Indeed not since the first-generation modernists had a group of American poets sounded so different from one another and so like themselves; one need only read a line or two by Ammons, Ginsberg, Merrill, Rich, Ashbery, Merwin, Plath or Creeley to recognize its authorship.

In some respects the next generation of poets, those born between 1935 and 1950, are in a position analogous to the Lowell generation, working in the shadow of the high modernists. But while the continued prominence of their elders has certainly slowed their own reception, this younger generation has also benefited enormously from the increasing professionalization of American poetry. The first generation of poets largely shaped by graduate creative-writing programmes, almost all of them have moved into teaching positions in such programmes. In addition to paying respectable salaries, these creative-writing programmes also support a vast network of journals, readings, prizes, grants and fellowships, a system sometimes cynically referred to as 'Po Biz'. But while this institutional system has provided them with greater cultural and financial stability than earlier generations had enjoyed, it has also fostered higher degrees of conformity and factionalism. Perhaps inspired by their critical colleagues, poets of this generation have tended to align themselves with particular ideologies or styles and then proselytized on their behalf to their students. The result has been a general decline in originality, and a tendency for popular styles to reproduce themselves with little variation. It may also be, as Donald Hall has suggested, that this generation suffers from a diminishment of poetic ambition, and that a desire for professional advancement has replaced the hunger for immortality that once drove poets, reducing the overall amount of risk-taking, genuine innovation and thematic scope in their work. It's possible, of course, that a few members of this generation will yet emerge as major figures. Certainly many of them are tremendously gifted, but so far there is no Seamus Heaney among them.

It's too early to make any firm assessment of the next and for all practical purposes last generation of twentieth-century American poets, those born between 1950 and 1965. But there are hopeful signs of a new catholicity and adventurousness in many of them. This spirit shows itself partly in a willingness to combine or synthesize styles and techniques that had been considered incompatible by their predecessors. Thus traditional lyricism and avant-garde disjunctiveness have begun to mingle in interesting ways in the work of some younger poets. A desire to address broader political and metaphysical themes has also begun to make itself felt. For the most part these poets are as much products of the workshop system as their immediate predecessors, subject to the same pressures and disincentives. Yet they may well prove more successful at resisting the lure of professionalism. This generation will only be coming into full maturity during the first years of the new millennium, and if history is a guide major literary innovations tend to occur at such times. Whether the American poets now in their thirties and forties will manage, as Yeats did, to remake themselves as poets of a new century or will simply preserve the language of the century they were born in remains to be seen, but there is cause for optimism.

Schools

Finally, it's worth paying some attention to the various 'schools' and other affiliations of poets that have flourished in contemporary American poetry. These need to be treated with a certain scepticism; often they prove to be critical artefacts rather than strongly grounded movements promoted by the poets themselves. Nonetheless they have exerted considerable influence in the presentation and reception of contemporary poetry. I shall only briefly mention those schools most dominant from 1950 to 1970, several of which are treated separately in this volume. The Confessional poets were never particularly receptive to the label bestowed on them by the critic M. L. Rosenthal; their relations with one another were more social than polemical. The Black Mountain school, by contrast, were active correspondents and pedagogues who spent much time and energy articulating and defending their poetic principles. The Beat poets also developed some fairly programmatic ideas about their work, though their statements are generally less weighty and theoretical than those of the Black Mountain group. The New York school, led by Frank O'Hara, John Ashbery and Kenneth Koch, tended to be much more playful in their poetics, often mocking the manifesto-like rhetoric of other schools. These last three groups were largely established and codified by Donald Allen's anthology *The New American Poetry*, which organized its contributors into sections based on aesthetic affiliation and included a thick appendix of poetic statements. In the 1960s the Deep Image group emerged under the leadership of Robert Bly, whose influential journal *The Sixties* provided a vehicle for the dissemination of their poems and poetics. In the same decade a group of politically outspoken African-American poets associated with the Black Arts movement formed, whose members included Amiri Baraka, Sonia Sanchez, Audre Lorde, June Jordan and Don L. Lee. Finally we can identify a *de facto* school that might be dubbed the 'university wits'; this company included Richard Wilbur, Anthony Hecht, Daryl Hine, John Hollander and Richard Howard, all poets of exceptional elegance, erudition and urbanity.

As these older groups have gone into various stages of ossification, new poetic schools and consortiums have continued to spring up in the last thirty years. The most polemically focused and organized of these newer groups are undoubtedly the Language school and the New Formalists, representing extremes of avant-gardism and traditionalism respectively. Despite their radical differences in aesthetic orientation, there are some surprising symmetries between these groups. Both consider themselves marginal in relation to what they regard as the hegemony of mainstream poetry (which the Language poets like to call 'official verse culture'). Both have produced copious treatises on behalf of their poetics, with the Language poets arguing that conventional syntax, traditional verse form, and linear narrative all transmit conservative ideologies, and the New Formalists claiming that the dominance of free verse represents an elitist withdrawal from poetry's potentially vast popular audience. Both movements are led by a small group of vocal propagandists: the Language school by Charles Bernstein, Ron Silliman and Bob Perelman, the New Formalists by Timothy Steele, Frederick Turner and Dana Gioia. Despite their claims to marginality, both these groups are well-represented in magazines and anthologies, and their members hold tenured positions at a number of major universities. Indeed it's clear that the considerable attention their work has received owes a great deal to its group packaging and the polemics that accompany it.

The hegemonic mainstream targeted by both the Language and New Formalist poets is most often identified with graduate creative-writing programmes, which many accuse of breeding dull uniformity and joyless professionalism. In fact American creative-writing programmes are by no means homogeneous; many have distinct characters of their own. But it's also true that their proliferation has helped create a kind of insider culture modelled on other academic fields; this can be seen in the proliferation of acronyms like MFA (Master of Fine Arts), AWP (Associated Writing Programs) and APR (*American Poetry Review*, the most visible outlet for mainstream poetry), which constitute a kind of professional code. The process of 'workshopping' poems can indeed have the effect of eradicating eccentricities and imposing a kind of shared decorum; poems produced in or influenced by writing workshops tend to favour first-person narrative and meditation in a relatively subdued style. But again it should be noted that not all programmes are equivalent. To mention only two, poets trained at the Iowa Writer's Workshop, under the guidance of faculty like Donald Justice, Marvin Bell and Gerald Stern, generally practise varying blends of the Confessional and Deep Image styles (though recently there are signs of change under the influence of the younger and more experimental poet Jorie Graham); while Stanford, thanks to the enduring influence of the poet–critic Yvor Winters, has produced a number of poets working in a more discursive and intellectual vein, like Robert Pinsky, Robert Hass, James McMichael and John Matthias.

When we look beyond academia, the most significant development in American poetry of the last two decades has been the emergence of a vibrant performance culture. The most popular manifestations of this culture are the events known as 'poetry slams', which combine poetry reading and sports contest. Selected audience members typically rate a series of poets on a scale of one to ten, based on the quality of their poems and the skill with which they perform them. Obviously such a procedure tends to reward crowd-pleasers, and a group of poets has grown up who specialize in this kind of work, with a heavy emphasis on humour, rhythm and theatrics. The influence of rap lyrics is plainly audible in much of this poetry, as is that of stand-up comedy. But the true begetters of this mode are the Beats, who gave raucous readings in coffee-houses and bars during the 1950s, often with jazz accompaniment. In the eighties and nineties the atmosphere of those events was recreated in new venues like the Nuyorican Poets' Cafe, the unofficial centre of performance-poetry culture in New York.

This performance culture has tended to be quite ethnically diverse; Latino and African-American poets in particular have been drawn to the performance scene, perhaps because of their rich vernacular traditions. In the mainstream poetry world there has also been a dramatic upsurge in the number of minority poets publishing and teaching. While they are sometimes gathered into ethnically specific anthologies – African American, Asian American, Latino, Native American, etc. – they also form a broader coalition, too diverse to be called a school, that usually goes under the banner of multicultural poetry. Such poetry tends to be autobiographical and often explores personal and family history as it intersects with broader ethnic narratives; Rita Dove's *Thomas and Beulah* (1986) is a particularly celebrated example of this mode. Many gay and lesbian poets also focus on the relation between individual experience and group identity, and they too are sometimes treated as a distinct poetic community, whose significant voices include Frank Bidart, Mark Doty, Marilyn Hacker, Paul Monette and Minnie Bruce Pratt. Region is another category that distinguishes particular groups of poets, most notably those from the South, many of whom retain a distinct vision and style linked to the long tradition of Southern literature; notable members of this group include Robert Penn Warren and James Dickey in the older generations, Dave Smith, Robert Morgan, Andrew Hudgins and Rodney Jones in the younger. Finally we can identify a loose conglomeration of committed or activist poets, mainly on the left, who define their work primarily in terms of its political engagement and efficacy. This is by no means a small or specialized group, embracing as it does the work of mainstream poets like Adrienne Rich, Allen Ginsberg, Carolyn Forche and Philip Levine, as well as important minority poets like Amiri Baraka and Gwendolyn Brooks. The last two decades have seen renewed interest in the openly political poetry of the 1930s and 1960s; many young poets in particular seem eager to revive aspects of that tradition.

Ultimately, of course, our sense of the significant patterns and tendencies of late twentieth-century American poetry will depend on the shape and direction of twenty-first-century American poetry. Whether this period will be known for its plethora of competing schools and styles or as the crucible of a new poetic synthesis must for now remain uncertain. The story of contemporary poetry cannot be fully told while it is contemporary.

BIBLIOGRAPHY

Altieri, Charles (1979). *Enlarging the Temple: New Directions in American Poetry During the 1960s*. Lewisburg: Bucknell University Press.

Altieri, Charles (1984). *Self and Sensibility in Contemporary American Poetry*. Cambridge: Cambridge University Press.

Bloom, Harold (1976). *Figures of Capable Imagination*. New York: Seabury Press.

Bly Robert (1991). *American Poetry: Wildness and Domesticity*. New York: Harper and Row.

Breslin, James (1984). *From Modern to Contemporary: American Poetry, 1945–1965*. Chicago: University of Chicago Press.

Breslin, Paul (1987). *The Psycho-Political Muse: American Poetry Since the Fifties*. Chicago: University of Chicago Press.

Damon, Maria (1993). *The Dark End of the Street: Margins in American Vanguard Poetry*. Minneapolis: University of Minnesota Press.

Feierstein, Frederick (1989). *Expansive Poetry: Essays on the New Narrative and the New Formalism*. Santa Cruz, CA: Story Line Press.

Holden, Jonathan (1986). *Style and Authenticity in Postmodern Poetry*. Columbia: University of Missouri Press.

Kaladjian, Walter (1989). *Languages of Liberation: The Social Text in Contemporary American Poetry*. New York: Columbia University Press.

Longenbach, James (1997). *Modern Poetry After Modernism*. New York: Oxford University Press.

Molesworth, Charles (1979). *The Fierce Embrace: A Study of Contemporary American Poetry*. Columbia: University of Missouri Press.

Nelson, Cary (1981). *Our Last First Poets: Vision and History in Contemporary American Poetry*. Urbana: University of Illinois Press.

Perelman, Bob (1996). *The Marginalization of Poetry: Language Writing and Literary*

History. Princeton, NJ: Princeton University Press.

Perkins, David (1987). *A History of Modern Poetry, Volume Two*. Cambridge, MA: Harvard University Press.

Perloff, Marjorie (1991). *Radical Artifice: Writing Poetry in the Age of Media*. Chicago: University of Chicago Press.

Pinsky, Robert (1976). *The Situation of Poetry: Contemporary Poetry and Its Traditions*. Princeton, NJ: Princeton University Press.

Rasula, Jed (1996). *The American Poetry Wax Museum: Reality Effects, 1940–1990*. Urbana, IL: National Council of Teachers of English.

Shetley, Vernon (1993). *After the Death of Poetry: Poet and Audience in Contemporary America*. Durham, NC: Duke University Press.

Spiegelman, Willard (1989). *The Didactic Muse: Scenes of Instruction in Contemporary American Poetry*. Princeton, NJ: Princeton University Press.

Stein, Kevin (1996). *Private Poets, Public Acts: Public and Private History in Contemporary American Poetry*. Athens: Ohio University Press.

Vendler, Helen (1995). *Soul Says: On Recent Poetry*. Cambridge, MA: Harvard University Press.

Von Hallberg, Robert (1985). *American Poetry and Culture, 1945–1980*. Cambridge, MA: Harvard University Press.

Williamson, Alan (1984). *Introspection and Contemporary Poetry*. Cambridge, MA: Harvard University Press.

46

Contemporary British Poetry

Sean O'Brien

Quite properly in advance of the political developments which have seen a loosening of formal ties between the peoples who constitute the United Kingdom of Great Britain and Northern Ireland, the identity and work of a number of poets have invited questions about what the term 'British' might mean. For a Scot such as Douglas Dunn, the term may seem an anachronistic imposition. And what of poets of Irish extraction, including Carol Ann Duffy and Ian Duhig, living and working in England; or Irish-born poets permanently resident here, including Bernard O'Donoghue, Maurice Riordan and Matthew Sweeney? There are also those long-time UK residents born in the United States such as Michael Donaghy, Anne Rouse and Eva Salzman, all of whom contribute to 'British' poetry and can coherently be read within its frame of reference. It would seem that if the term 'British' is to go on being used, it needs to be seen as a convenience – which is how the term is applied in the following essay – rather than a sign of allegiance.

From the vantage point of 1999, when a Labour prime minister declared the class war to be at an end, it is striking that two of the outstanding poets of the last thirty years, the Yorkshireman Tony Harrison (b. 1937) and the Scot Douglas Dunn (b. 1942) have devoted much of their best imaginative energy to demonstrating otherwise (see Dunn's *Barbarians*, 1979, and *St Kilda's Parliament*, 1981, and Harrison's poems from 'The School of Eloquence' in *Selected Poems*, 1987). Not for the first time, poets have declined to say what politicians would like to hear.

Dunn and Harrison are the leading exponents of what has been called 'the scholarship boy's . . . Revenge' (Dunn, 'Acute Accent', in *Tony Harrison*, 1991), where working-class writers, those 'of the wrong world' (Dunn, 'The Come-On'), take control of the means of artistic production – specifically the elaborate formalities offered by the English verse tradition. In their hands, expertise is a means both of memorious revenge and of triumphant assertion; as Luke Spencer puts it, they fashion 'oppositional meanings out of fundamentally bourgeois establishment poetic forms'

(Spencer, 1994, p. 16). Thus Harrison declares: 'So right, yer buggers, then! We'll occupy / your lousy leasehold Poetry' ('Them and Uz').

In this part of his work Dunn's choice of verse forms is wide and his subjects tend to be historical rather than autobiographical. Harrison's poetry is dominated by the sonnet — specifically the sixteen-line 'Meredithian' variation associated with George Meredith (see *Modern Love*, 1862), and while there is an obvious and important historical dimension to his work, he also dwells repeatedly on his direct experience and that of his family. For Harrison the talents and interests which create his life's opportunities are also the means by which he is separated from his own people. When his friends whistle up at his window to join them for an evening out in the street, he says 'Ah bloody can't ah've gorra Latin prose!' ('Me Tarzan'). Elsewhere, he remarks: 'I'd like to be the poet my father reads' ('The Rhubarbarians'). Dunn, on the other hand, imagines a revolutionary moment in the eighteenth-century English countryside ('Gardeners') or the elaborate fiction of 'An Artist Waiting in a Country House', where the artist who has come to visit his patron is kept waiting until he finds himself as much a commodity as the rest of the house's contents:

> He waits, although that door will never open,
> Unless he opens it, and walks away
> And leaves the pictures hanging in the room
> Focussed on the sofa where he waited.

In Dunn's 'The Student' a member of a Mechanics' Literary Club is studying Tacitus while remembering the failure of a radical uprising in the streets of Paisley. Now, he records, 'Difficult Latin sticks in my throat / And the scarecrow wears my coat'. Class, power and the ownership of language are at the heart of both poets' endeavours.

Dunn is also concerned with an extra dimension, namely nationality, which bulks as large in his work as Classical Greek literature does in Harrison's. Poems such as 'The Apple Tree', 'An Address on the Destitution of Scotland' and 'The Harp of Renfrewshire' are elegies for an idea and, implicitly, dreams of its embodiment in a hitherto unspoken tense. Furthermore, by the time Dunn returned from Hull to live in Scotland in the early 1980s, his work had also fully developed what might be called its internationalist dimension. The underrated *Europa's Lover* (1982) is a blend of elegy and love song to the anima of Europe. Following the early death of his first wife, Lesley Balfour, Dunn wrote the acclaimed *Elegies* (1985), and since then his work has been extremely varied while dwelling intently on Scottish themes.

Harrison has written numerous verse plays (see *Theatre Works*, 1986), almost singlehandedly asserting the vitality of a form widely felt to be unworkable nowadays, in his adaptations of classical Greek texts, as well as Molière. He has also developed — indeed, it could be said that with the producer/director Peter Symes he has invented — the television poem–film. His most controversial work in this field is *v* (1985). Set in a vandalized Leeds graveyard during the 1984–5 miners' strike, it revisits Harrison's basic themes in a debate between the poet and his skinhead alter-ego. The poem combines 'bad language' with a skilful recasting of an English classic, Thomas Gray's 'Elegy Written in a Country Churchyard'. Here and in numerous other works Harrison has carried poetry from the page into the public arena of television. Most recently he has written and directed the ambitious feature film *Prometheus* (1999), revisiting the legend of the rebellious fire-stealing Titan ('the first martyr in the Socialist calendar') in the setting of post-industrial Britain and post-communist Eastern Europe. No one else has worked as boldly as Harrison to place poetry in the public eye without compromising his utter seriousness.

The picture of poetry written 'from below' needs to be complicated by the addition of at least two other names, Jeffrey Wainwright (b. 1944) and Ken Smith (b. 1938). Wainwright's fastidiously musical work includes the major sequences '1815', a series of bold cross-sections through war and industrialism ('the English miracle') and 'Thomas Muntzer', a group of dramatic monologues spoken by the sixteenth-century German Protestant revolutionary. Like Dunn and Harrison, Wainwright is also a gifted lyric poet – as is Ken Smith, though Smith's relationship to tradition is very different from those of the other poets in this grouping. A central theme for Smith is exile, both external and internal: it is no accident that he withholds his assent from much English poetry after Wordsworth, finding examples instead in the USA, in poets such as John Haynes and W. S. Merwin. Among his major works are 'Fox Running', an account of destitution and breakdown, *Terra* (1986), a key text of the Thatcher–Reagan period, and *Wormwood* (1987), derived from work at the prison of Wormwood Scrubs. *The Heart, the Border* (1990) and *Wild Root* (1998) reveal his increasing fascination with the borders and migrations of Eastern Europe. 'The Shadow of God' evokes the renewed resonance of the name of the Muslim conqueror Suleyman the Magnificent: 'In his dream the far world / Is a basket of heads at his saddlebow'.

Different again is the work of the prolific Peter Reading (b. 1945). Described by Tom Paulin as 'the laureate of junk Britain', Reading is an unflinching and at times reactionary pessimist who reads in the violence and ignorance of contemporary Britain the signs of a species in decline. In numerous book-length works he juxtaposes classical metres with found materials, news items, scientific information and the stray opinions of the uneducated. There is scarcely a poetic form or mode he has not employed, but his versatility bears an unmistakable signature, and our sense of the work's unity is enforced by Reading's concern with the production of his books as objects. An admirer of poets as different as Gavin Ewart and Roy Fuller, he cannot be simply placed: rather, he generates his own context.

The situation of contemporary poetry has been described as a 'collision between postmodernism and realism' (Gregson, 1996, p. 238), but this risks an oversimplification of the interpenetration of native realist modes and postmodernist energies emerging from elsewhere. Postmodernism is not so philosophically unanswerable as to be able to insist on functioning as the defining container of contemporary poetry; but neither is it so inimical to native habits as not to interbreed with them. The activity of poetry is a process, not a time-limited event, and part of that process is the way in which native preoccupations ask us to look again at what postmodernism actually consists of. It is, for example, possible to see a postmodernist dimension in the way Dunn and Harrison make subversive use of their studies in tradition, turning skill against its supposed proprietors – though for some this might sound too politically partisan an approach to qualify as 'true' postmodernism, which might be held to place greater emphasis on the playful exploitation of instabilities of meaning and identity than on their further application. As we shall see, it is in women's poetry that the most original attempts to square the circle of verbal ingenuity and political seriousness take place. But the clearest early evidence of postmodernism entering the poetic mainstream in Britain is to be sought among Oxford-linked 'Martian' poets such as Craig Raine (b. 1944) and Christopher Reid (b. 1949). The term 'Martian' was first used by the poet James Fenton to describe their work. Neither in fact is quite original: earlier examples are to be found, in particular in Elizabeth Bishop and Norman MacCaig, but the ingenuity of Raine and Reid is startling none the less. The technique involves what might be called a rhetorical suspension of knowledge: the visible world in particular is read for the possibility of fruitful misinterpretation, as by the alien visitor in Raine's 'A Martian sends a Postcard Home', where the metaphorical ambitions of poetry are insistently laid bare:

> Caxtons are mechanical birds with many wings
> and some are treasured for their markings –
>
> they cause the eyes to melt
> or the body to shriek without pain.

Initially it is the domestic sphere which interests both poets and this, allied to the air of slightly immodest confidence which both reveal, has raised questions about the moral seriousness of their work. In 'Arcadia', Reid, who is more of a dandy than Raine, and more drawn to artistic analogies, invests the domestic with the strangeness of a child's storybook world:

> In this crayoned dream-town,
> the chimneys think smoke
> and every house is lovingly
> Battenburged with windows.

Such spectacular effects obey the law of diminishing returns and both poets have pursued other lines of enquiry in latter years. Raine has worked as a librettist (*The Electrification of the Soviet Union*, 1986) and verse-novelist (*History: the Home Movie*, 1994). Reid's most interesting book has been *Katerina Brac* (1985). Written in the persona of a woman poet from behind the Iron Curtain, it raises tantalizing questions about identity, authenticity and the language of translation.

Reid's contemporary James Fenton is at once the most ambitious and least prolific of significant recent poets to emerge from Oxford. *Terminal Moraine* (1972) introduced a poet of great versatility, at home with satire and light verse, as well as substantial historical narratives and the unsettling blend of exploded narrative and accumulated detail which has produced his most distinctive work. 'The Pitt-Rivers Museum', which cunningly ushers us into the heart of an anthropological museum and leaves us there, leads on to the later country house poems 'Nest of Vampires' and 'A Vacant Possession', with their sense of the poisonous inertia of outmoded but obdurate privilege and waste, as well as 'A Staffordshire Murderer', perhaps Fenton's finest work to date. These are all apparent narratives. They open far more questions than they answer; they interfere with their own narrative frames; they remove the ground from under the reader's feet; they demonstrate, in the words of Ian Gregson, 'the impossibility of a fully comprehending vision' (Gregson, 1996, p. 65). Perhaps the finest of this group (and its logical terminus) is 'A Staffordshire Murderer'. This bizarre narration, with its unsettling address to the second person, evokes the 1970s crimes of the Black Panther against a backdrop of familiar crime-novel impedimenta and seemingly random but resonant bits of local knowledge. Unease becomes horror; as in 'The Pitt-Rivers Museum', there is no exit:

> This is where the murderer works. But it is Sunday.
> Tomorrow's bank holiday will allow the bricks to set.
> You see? he has thought of everything. He shows you
> The snug little cavity he calls 'your future home'.

The overall effect of these poems has been well described by Ian Gregson. In them, he suggests, 'the linguistic representation of "otherness" encounters an experiential otherness so extreme that it subverts representation itself' (Gregson, 1996, p. 69). The political applications of Fenton's work can be most readily seen in 'A German Requiem', which is a litany of deliberate omission and false consciousness, charting the refusal or inability of postwar Germany to engage with *Vergangenheitsbewaltigung*, the coming to terms with its past.

Where Raine and Reid are political agnostics, Fenton begins in a commitment to the Left and persists in the treatment of large public themes. His work as a journalist took him to Vietnam and the Philippines. *Out of Danger* (1993) includes poems about conflict in Iran and Jerusalem. Running counter to Fenton's extreme complexity is a melancholy plainness:

> And each man wears his suffering like a skin.
> My history is proud.
> Mine is not allowed.
> This is the cistern where all wars begin,
> ('Jerusalem', 1993)

Very different routes into postmodernism have been followed by three near-contemporaries, Peter Didsbury (b. 1946), John Ash (b. 1948) and John Hartley

Williams (b. 1944). Based in Hull, Didsbury resembles neither Larkin nor Dunn, producing an eccentrically learned religious poetry, at its most intense in the compelling narratives 'The Drainage' and 'Eikon Basilike'. Ash looks back to French Symbolist poetry in a form seemingly unmediated by Modernism, inventing a route not taken and then following it, to conspicuously decadent and lavishly detailed effect (*The Goodbyes*, 1982; *The Burnt Pages*, 1992). Hartley Williams, who has lived for many years in Berlin, has equally little in common with mainstream poetry in Britain. His anarchic humour, eroticism and torrential energy take in the Western (*Bright River Yonder*, 1987) and the 'automatic' poems of *Canada* (1997).

Fenton, along with the Northern Irish poet Paul Muldoon, has set out the geography of much contemporary poetry in Britain, whether postmodernist or not. One of the fullest explorations of the renewed possibilities of narrative has been made by the prolific Andrew Motion (b. 1952), though the very different approaches of the influential poet–teacher John Fuller (b. 1937; *Collected Poems*, 1996) Alan Jenkins (b. 1955; *Greenheart*, 1990), Mick Imlah (b. 1956; *Birthmarks*, 1988) and Don Paterson (see below) are also deserving of attention. Motion's debut, *The Pleasure Steamers* (1978), was notable for its haunted lyrical plangency, but 'The Letter', a 'secret' narrative of love and death during the Second World War, indicated how his work would develop. Years afterwards, a woman remembers finding the body of a German pilot, 'His legs / splayed in a candid unshamable V', an image which has multiple but unresolved resonances for her. Motion's friend Philip Larkin professed himself baffled by the poem. The poems of Larkin, the leading poet of the Movement, are full (as Motion's are) of the sense of the impossibility of squaring wishes with facts, but his poems also depend on a sense of meaningful shape which it is their task to disclose. In Motion's work the refusal of (we are led to suppose) life to 'add up' and offer the reader the assurance of closure becomes an important feature of what Motion calls his 'Secret Narratives', including poems with historical settings, such as 'Bathing at Glymenopoulo' and the end-of-Raj poem 'Independence'. These read like cross-sections from larger works, but as the speaker in 'Firing Practice' comments: 'You realized nothing connected / with anything, ever'. Motion combines the sense that religious or social or aesthetic structures of meaning have vanished from the world with an intense Englishness in regard to landscape. If this seems paradoxical, it makes it the more interesting that Motion has accepted the most public and flak-catching role in English poetry, that of the Laureate, in succession to the late Ted Hughes.

The emergence of poets such as Raine, Fenton and Motion coincided with the temporary occlusion of some significant writers of the immediately prior generation, notably David Harsent and Hugo Williams (both born in 1942). Any account of narrative will have to include Harsent. His early work (*A Violent Country*, 1969, and *After Dark*, 1973) showed affinities with the minimalist dramatic lyricism of the loose grouping of poets associated with the influential 'little magazine', *The Review* (Hugo Williams, Colin Falck, Michael Fried, and more occasional affiliates including Douglas Dunn and John Fuller). The editor, Ian Hamilton (b. 1938), advocated and wrote a rigorous poetry whose emotional truth sought to grow in proportion to its brevity (*Fifty Poems*, 1998). Influences on this school (though that is not a term with much currency in England) included imagist features of modernism, the American Confessional poets including Robert Lowell and John Berryman, and American neo-symbolist writers such as James Wright and Robert Bly. In Harsent's work the personal life is certainly present: a line from 'Haircut' – 'We have learned to pretend that we live like this' – is a classic of controlled *Review* despondency. However, he goes on to allow himself a fictive latitude, a use of character and persona, which Neil Corcoran has called 'a way of diverting the lyric impulse into the obliquity of dramatic presentation' (Corcoran, 1993, p. 148). Where Motion's poems tend to withhold resolution, Harsent's withhold the explanatory context for their concern with sex, violence and psychic extremity. Readers are faced with brilliant and haunting lines and images in a setting whose obscurity sometimes suggests that it might be a pretext for the poet's local gifts. But *A Bird's Idea of Flight* (1998), a set of twenty-five monologues whose speaker is trying to broach the mysteries of death, is a triumphant vindication of Harsent's approach.

If Harsent and Motion remain at heart lyric poets, Michael Hofmann (b. 1957) might appear to have abandoned virtually every item of poetic equipment except, perhaps, words. *Nights in the Iron Hotel* (1983) and *Acrimony* (1986) work with an acoustic which is both literally and figuratively dead. Alan Robinson has commented on 'From Kensal Rise to Heaven' that 'With studied impassivity [Hofmann's] omnivorous gaze unreflectingly assimilates objects and people into a common dehumanization' (Robinson, 1988, p. 49). Although *Corona, Corona* (1993) and *Approximately Nowhere* (1999) are not exactly unbuttoned, 'all that regular guy / homme du peuple stuff that so dismayed me' ('de passage') seems at least possible, and Hofmann's best work to date is a series of elegies for his father.

What Hofmann and Hugo Williams have in common is exclusion. Among Williams's exclusions are vast tracts of political and historical subject matter: nearly all his work comes, with withering honesty, from direct experience, insisting on the authority and value of the personal life – love and sex, rhythm and blues, schooldays and his father (the actor Hugh Williams). Much of the equipment of image-making and argument is also eventually ditched (though a strong early influence was Thom Gunn). He exploits sentence structures which seem to stand halfway between the spoken and the written in order to generate an air of melancholy, inevitability and the collision of pain and bathos. *Billy's Rain* (1999), which charts the course of a love affair, marks a high point in the evolution of Williams's style, for example in the mordant regret of 'Mirror History':

> Re-reading what I have written up till now
> I am conscious only of what is not being said,
> the mirror history running underneath all this
> self-pitying nonsense. To hear me talk
> you'd think I was the aggrieved party,
> whereas we both know it was my own decision
> to do nothing that made nothing happen.

It might be argued that Williams's concerns – love, sex, betrayal, embarrassment – equip him very well for the role of Poet Laureate, given the recent situation of the royal family.

With the exception of Michael Hofmann, all the poets discussed so far either did fall, or could have fallen, within the remit of the influential 1982 anthology *The Penguin Book of Contemporary British Poetry*. Its editors, Blake Morrison and Andrew Motion, saw in their chosen poets 'an extension of the imaginative franchise' in the works of the Martian poets, in Fenton, Dunn, Harrison and those influential poets from the North of Ireland who fall outside this discussion. The work which has come to attention in the intervening years bears out this sense of expanded possibility without following in direct line of descent.

If narrative has been significant in recent poetry in Britain (and Ireland), so too has form. This sounds tautological, but there has been a tendency among younger poets to re-examine the possibilities of given (as distinct from organic) form, as though to replace the example of Ted Hughes, a powerful improviser, with those of, among others, Derek Mahon and Paul Muldoon, both of whom affirm the importance of rhyme – and in some cases to go further. For some readers, concern with verse-form, and with formality, suggests anti-modernist attitudes; but an interest in form, in the how as well as the what of poetry, is characteristic of modernism, and it is possible to see in contemporary practice both an understanding of modernist principles and a sense that tradition has been 'repaired' following the necessary disruptions caused by pioneering modernists such as Pound and Eliot. But this is not an area which lends itself to clear-cut generalizations; there are many attitudes to form among contemporary poets – compare George Szirtes (b. 1948), Carol Ann Duffy and Glyn Maxwell, for example – and most of them lie outside the scope of this brief survey.

In recent years a similar concern has made itself heard in American poetry under the heading of New Formalism. Leading Formalist poets such as Dana Gioia and Brad Leithauser have worked against the prevailing free-verse orthodoxy and sought examples in the work of, among others, the influential poet–critic Yvor Winters. Michael Donaghy (b. 1954) is hardly a Wintersian, but his work is driven by love of shape and form. 'The Tuning' tells of an encounter between artist and Muse ('the angel of death') in which exposure to her voice – 'the sound of trees growing, / The noise of a pond thrown into a stone' (*Shibboleth*, 1988) – makes the ordinary world intolerable. A sense of vocation, and its cost, stands behind the elegance, the scholarly wit and the bawdiness of Donaghy's work, where a residually Catholic sensibility ponders questions of meaning raised by contemporary experience. The London–Irish Ian Duhig (b. 1954) is also a learned poet, at home on the backstairs of history and literature, whether in comic monologues such as 'Fundamentals', which imagines a Victorian missionary (David Livingstone, perhaps) addressing African converts across the vast cultural gulf, or the grimmer 'Baphomet', spoken by a Cathar heretic under torture. Exile or a simpler homelessness are perennial themes in Duhig's work, which is now inclining strongly towards ballad form. The wry, sombre inventiveness of both poets is shared by Jamie McKendrick (b. 1955).

English versions of the renewed interest in form are exemplified by Simon Armitage (b. 1963) and Glyn Maxwell (b. 1962), from Yorkshire and the Home Counties respectively. Frequently paired in discussion, they have collaborated on *Moon Country* (1996), in which they retrace the footsteps of W. H. Auden and Louis MacNeice's 1936 Icelandic journey. Armitage in particular has attained the kind of prominence once granted to the young Auden. His poems blend formality and improvisation and incorporate a classless, youthful, Northern vernacular; their literary inspirations are wide-ranging – the New York poet Frank O'Hara, alongside Ted Hughes and Paul Muldoon. Underpinning them is an unquenchable Northern directness, for example on the subject of class:

> . . . on the day they dig us out
> they'll know that you were *really something* fucking fine
> and I was nowt.
> Keep that in mind,
>
> because the worm won't know your make of bone from mine.
> ('The Two of Us', *The Dead Sea Poems*, 1993)

Glyn Maxwell is more elaborately formal. His intricate stanzas and oblique, periphrastic manner are immediately recognizable. He is a narrative poet who resists telling the story straight. His air of gravity and mystery, the riddling movement of his verse and his use of strongly 'English' settings, mean that he is also the more Audenesque poet of the two:

> We did not care muchly who, in the murder,
> we turned out to be, providing whoever
> used to inhabit the white chalk figure
> frozenly pawing the blood-stained sofa
> was not one of us but a different dier.
> ('The Uninvited', *Out of the Rain*, 1992)

Alongside male political poets and postmodernism in its various forms, poetry written by women has made an increasing impact in the last twenty years. In the complex and sometimes obscured genealogy of women's poetry, the significance of such different writers as Stevie Smith, Elizabeth Bishop, U. A. Fanthorpe and Fleur Adcock, and perhaps above all Sylvia Plath, is becoming apparent. It seems that now more than ever the woman poet can get on with her work without being hobbled or distracted by the sense (among male critics) that she is a special or even peculiar case.

The work of Carol Rumens (b. 1944) is perhaps the most direct example of the impact of feminism (in its socialist incarnation) on the poetic mainstream. Her poems enact in various ways the conviction that 'the personal is political', moving naturally between love and domestic life ('Rules for Beginners') and larger historical contexts – often of repression or atrocity ('Outside Oswiecim', 'The Hebrew Class'). It can seem that, like older poets such as Elizabeth Jennings and Ann Stevenson, Rumens's work is not marked by any great departures in form or manner, but her readings of postwar England have their own sombre originality. The novelistic 'Our Early Days in Graveldene' ambitiously traces national decline and accompanying amnesia through a highly detailed reading of working-class women's lives in language whose ground-level restraint achieves its own eloquence:

> There was Stell the single mother, Rose the widow
> – Women who worked and were always dashing out
> For cod and chips. There was the Rasta, Cyril,
> Who slashed his throat that time the bailiffs came.
> When they came to us we hid behind the door.

Rumens's near contemporaries Vicki Feaver (b. 1943) and Ruth Padel (b. 1947) illustrate the range of practice within the mainstream: they are mythopoeic and intensely sensuous writers. Helen Dunmore (b. 1952) reveals, like Rumens, a powerful strand of humane protest in her often exultantly lyrical work. Carol Ann Duffy (b. 1955), the most popular woman poet of the time, is in some ways a more immediately accessible writer than any of her peers, combining emotional directness with powerful construction in poems with a strong narrative element and a frequent sense of the collapse of social and political consensus, backlit by memories of childhood in the 1950s and 1960s. Among her most popular work are dramatic monologues written from below or outside the centres of power, such as 'Warming Her Pearls', where a lady's maid confides to us her secret love for her mistress:

> Next to my own skin, her pearls. My mistress
> bids me wear them, warm then, until evening,
> when I'll brush her hair. At six, I place them
> round her cool, white throat. All day I think of her . . .

In *The World's Wife* (1999) wives and partners from Mrs Midas to Mrs Darwin rewrite myth and history from a female perspective, to satirical and broadly comic effect. 'Circe', for example, is a revenger's recipe:

> Look at that simmering lug, at that ear,
> did it listen, ever, to you, to your prayers and rhymes,
> to the chimes of your voice, singing and clear? Mash
> the potatoes, nymph, open the beer. Now to the brains . . .

For signs of an *écriture féminine* prepared to discard the conventions of realism we should turn first to Selima Hill (b. 1945). Carol Rumens has aptly described Hill's world as 'hermetic but inviting' (Hamilton, 1994, p. 228). It is Hill's childlike decisiveness which convinces the reader of the authenticity of her strange pronouncements, the stranger properties of her farmyard magic realism, and of the intimacy (alarming to some male readers) of a poem such as 'Coition':

> You'll have to lie perfectly still
> like a nude with a rat;
>
> and when I have finished,
> you'll have not a hair on your head . . .

This brief poem exemplifies Hill's effort to cut out the literary middleman, to think – and to carry the reader – back beyond familiar interpretative categories to the quick of perception, where desire and anxiety live in unmediated forms. Breakdown – of the individual in *The Accumulation of Small Acts of Kindness* (1989), and of marriage in *Violet* (1997) – gives a piercing seriousness to what has sometimes been mistaken for whimsy.

The effort to discard given social identity, and to explore a female self which is not 'officially' fixed according to the maps of male understanding, but instead capable of flexibility and transformation, is also the concern of Jo Shapcott (b. 1953). 'Thetis', her version of a story from Ovid's *Metamorphoses*, opens: 'No man can frighten me. Watch as I stretch / my limbs for the transformation'. Significantly, Shapcott shifts the narration into the first person and the tense into the present: Thetis makes her story her own, rather than Ovid's. Just as, according to Ovid, Thetis knew the fate that would befall her son, the warrior Achilles, so in Shapcott's version she knows that she will be raped in order to produce him. This sombre contrast between the freely creative female self and the habits of male oppression shows how high the stakes are in the comic fantasies which Shapcott more often writes, which include the deft social observations of the 'Robert and Elizabeth' series (Robert suggesting both Browning and Lowell, Elizabeth both Barrett Browning and Hardwick), as well as the numerous 'beast' poems like 'Goat' or the ongoing Mad Cow series. Shapcott writes as much about the body as the mind: her animals insist on the acknowledgement of their full physical reality; and there is a corresponding interest in the erotic: in 'The Roses', a version from Rilke, the bud of the rose speaks as the object of desire.

Identity is also a powerful theme for Jackie Kay (b. 1961). *The Adoption Papers* (1991) interweaves the voices of three women – birth mother, black child and adoptive mother – the last of whom remarks: 'I always believed in the telling anyhow', a statement of faith within the story and one which applies in Kay's work as a whole. She confronts racial and sexual prejudice in language which demonstrates the resonance of ordinary speech:

> You tell your little girl to stop calling
> my little girl names and I'll tell my little girl
> to stop giving your little girl a doing.

The ideals of the political Left are honoured in Kay's work, for example in 'The Shoes of Dead Comrades'. At the same time, she arms herself against utopianism of a kind risked by subsequent identity politics in the matter-of-fact 'Somebody Else':

> If I was not myself, I would be something else.
> But actually I am somebody else.
> I have been somebody else all my life.
>
> It's no laughing matter going about the place
> all the time being somebody else:
> people mistake you; you mistake yourself.

Older black poets might wonder what has changed in the half-century since the arrival of the *Empire Windrush*. James Berry (b. 1924), who came to London in 1948, wrote in 1989 that 'The consciousness-expansion process that black people's presence has set up in Britain is just about beginning to help the learners to feel that when they have calmed down they are bigger, deeper and more expansive human beings', but in the light of the Lawrence Enquiry and other recent cases even this qualified affirmation may seem over-optimistic. The highly politicized Linton Kwesi Johnson (b. 1952) utilized reggae accompaniment to offer a harsher view:

> Inglan is a bitch
> dere's no escapin' it
> Inglan is a bitch fi true
> is whey wi a goh dhu 'bout it?
> (*Tings an Times*, 1991)

The 1981 riots in cities such as Bristol and Liverpool were a partial answer to a question which has not gone away. While white poets at work in Britain can claim to eschew (or contrive to evade) political issues, for black poets they are inescapable. As Fred D'Aguiar puts it, Kwesi Johnson's 'dub' poetry became, like reggae itself, 'a form of protest as opposed to simply an expression of protest' (Hampson and Barry, 1993). Elsewhere there is the decision to write in Nation Language – a term proposed by Kamau Brathwaite (b. 1930) – or Jamaican or Standard English, or another variant. There is the contemplation of ethnic and sexual identity, as in Grace Nichols (b. 1950) or Jackie Kay, or the restless and witty Lambchop and Sally Goodman poems of E. A. Markham (b. 1939). There is the study of imperial and colonial history and of slavery, as in the work of David Dabydeen (b. 1956) and Fred D'Agiuar (b. 1960). Dabydeen's *Turner* (1994) speaks through the figure of a drowned negro slave in J. M. W. Turner's painting *The Slave Ship*, to create a complex meditation on history and subjection:

> The sea has mocked and beggared me for centuries,
> Except for scrolls in different letterings
> Which, before they dissolve, I decipher
> As best I can.

The echo of T. S. Eliot's fragments of civilization 'shored' against 'ruin' is bitter indeed. D'Agiuar, meanwhile, takes on some of the precepts of modernism, as filtered through the work of a leading novelist, the Guyanan Wilson Harris (b. 1921), in complex, disrupted narratives such as 'The Kitchen Bitch' (*Airy Hall*, 1989).

The postwar Caribbean Diaspora, then, has been accompanied by a spectacular aesthetic flowering. The result is a range of poetry which can, for example, accommodate the 'European' romanticism and formalism of the St Lucian Derek Walcott (b. 1930) and the combination of modernist and African approaches developed by the Barbadian Kamau Brathwaite, as well as maintaining a sense of poetry's nearness to spoken language and to music. A number of black poets are much admired as performers; some, including John Agard (b. 1949), Jean 'Binta' Breeze (b. 1956) and Benjamin Zephaniah (b. 1958) are acclaimed 'Performance Poets', whose work is best appreciated at live readings. While poetry readings have had some popular currency in Britain since the 1950s, black writers have done much to disseminate the idea of poetry as a public event.

Jackie Kay's fellow Scot, Kathleen Jamie (b. 1962), is concerned less with racial prejudice than with the internal barriers which might lead Scots from her working-class background to 'mistake' themselves by colluding in historical amnesia. 'Forget It' tackles the need for 'the telling', faced with the shamed resistance of an older generation:

> . . . this is a past
> not yet done, else how come
> our parents slam shut, deny
> like criminals: *I can't remember, cannae*
> *mind*, then turn at bay: *Why?*
>
> *Who wants to know?'*

In her 'Condition of Scotland' book, *The Queen of Sheba* (1994), Jamie examined other versions of Scottishness, including mild provincialism in 'Mr and Mrs Scotland are Dead' and the pawky narrow-mindedness that forbids people (women in particular) to get 'above' themselves in the title poem. Jamie's work has steadily run more clear and pure, until the lyric and political impulses are inseparable. Among several younger poets of great talent, she seems the closest to becoming a major figure.

Believers in the Muse might argue that she has recently transferred her operations from Ireland to Scotland, so impressive (not to mention prolific) is the work of the leading handful of poets born between the mid 1950s and early 1960s. The oldest of these, the prolific John Burnside (b. 1955), dwells on the threshold between the everyday and the mystical. His is an obsessive poetry of near-revelation, domestic yet solitary, 'alone, at the edge of the world / with your face to the light' ('Faith', *The Myth of the Twin*, 1994). A comparable but more strenuously argumentative concern with what escapes the definitions of reason has emerged in the poems of Don Paterson (b. 1963). A witty, dandaical poet with a taste for the erotic and for elaborate Borgesian narratives ('Nil Nil', 'The Alexandrian Library', _Nil Nil_, 1993), Paterson has produced a book of versions from Antonio Machado, _The Eyes_ (1999), charting the discovery of 'something we were yesterday / that we discover still alive, / like a river's pulse / just below the ancient streets'. Though less pronounced, something of the same concern can be felt in Paterson's fellow Dundonian W. N. Herbert (b. 1961), who along with Robert Crawford (b. 1959) has made the case for poetry in Scots. Herbert in particular composes his books bilingually (for example, _Forked Tongue_, 1994) and has been seen as the poetic descendant of Hugh McDiarmid. Herbert is a versatile poet, adept in love lyrics, ballads, comic fantasies and elaborate near-epics such as the title poem of _The Laurelude_ (1998), which celebrates the comedian Stan Laurel, born in the Lake District. Robert Crawford, who is also a leading critic of modern Scottish literature, produces a series of richly allusive and imaginative maps of possible Scotland, in language marked by a bizarre serenity. While the task of prediction does not fall to this cramped essay, it is clear that 'British Poetry' possesses the energy and the imagination to enter the new century with confidence. We are not at the end but rather _in medias res_.

BIBLIOGRAPHY

Astley, Neil (ed.) (1991). _Tony Harrison: Bloodaxe Critical Anthologies, 1_. Newcastle upon Tyne: Bloodaxe.

Corcoran, Neil (1993). _English Poetry since 1940_. London: Longman.

Crawford, Robert (1993). _Identifying Poets: Self and Territory in Twentieth Century Poetry_. Edinburgh: Edinburgh University Press.

Dunn, Douglas (ed.) (1992). _The Faber Book of Twentieth Century Scottish Poetry_. London: Faber and Faber.

Gregson, Ian (1996). _Contemporary Poetry and Postmodernism: Dialogue and Estrangement_. London: Macmillan.

Hamilton, Ian (ed.) (1994). _The Oxford Companion to Twentieth Century Poetry_. Oxford: Oxford University Press.

Hampson, Robert and Barry, Peter (1993). _New British Poetries: The Scope of the Possible_. Manchester: Manchester University Press.

Hulse, Michael, Kennedy, David and Morley, David (eds) (1993). _The New Poetry_. Newcastle upon Tyne: Bloodaxe.

Kennedy, David (1996). _New Relations: The Refashioning of British Poetry 1980–1994_. Bridgend: Seren.

Morrison, Blake and Motion, Andrew (1982). _The Penguin Book of Contemporary British Poetry_. London: Penguin.

O'Brien, Sean (1998). _The Deregulated Muse: Essays on Contemporary British and Irish Poetry_. Newcastle upon Tyne: Bloodaxe.

O'Brien, Sean (ed.) (1998). _The Firebox: Poetry in Britain and Ireland after 1945_. London: Picador.

Roberts, Neil (1999). _Narrative and Voice in Postwar Poetry_. London: Longman.

Robinson, Alan (1988). _Instabilities in Contemporary British Poetry_. London: Macmillan.

Spencer, Luke (1994). _The Poetry of Tony Harrison_. Hemel Hempstead: Harvester Wheatsheaf.

Thwaite, Anthony (1996). _Poetry Today: A Critical Guide to British Poetry 1960–1995_. London: Longman.

47

Contemporary Irish Poetry

Lucy Collins

The development of the Irish poetry scene since the 1960s has been remarkable in its scope and intensity. Its dynamic nature at once sustains and is sustained by a series of aesthetic and political tensions which are mediated, to a large degree, through the changing relationship between the text and its readership. It is clear that while new poetry from Irish presses is plentiful and receives the attention of reviewers, it is not widely read, nor is it submitted to rigorous investigation by critics. While this is in many ways unsurprising, it suggests that the desire to hear a multiplicity of voices has already had far-reaching effects on the cultural climate in Ireland and in particular on the perceived relationship between centre and margin. This shifting relationship can be explored in terms of language, of form, of gender, politics or geography, and exposes the changing shape of power in contemporary Irish writing. The arrangement of this essay around a series of tensions within Irish poetry today is not intended to highlight (or produce) antagonisms, but rather to explore the ways in which such tensions have influenced both the criticism of poetry and the production of the work itself. If the focus on issues of national identity is beginning to shift at last, there remains a continuing interrogation of cultural influences which are now explored in more flexible and searching ways than ever before.

The issue of tradition lies at the heart of this essay and it is one which is fraught with difficulty, since it suggests a kind of cohesion which is contrary to literary production. As the vexed question of the poetry anthology proves beyond doubt, there are as many readings of collective identity as there are editors to provide them. If tradition may be judged to be a manipulated pattern serving cultural or political ends, then its failure to offer some of its members adequate room to explore their private identity necessitates the formation of a separate space from which to write. Some contemporary Irish poets perceive the mainstream as an inherently limited place and their construction of an alternative position is both determined by their work and exerts an important shaping force upon it. One experimental poet, Catherine Walsh, explained: 'You need to be incorporated into the tradition to be an Irish writer, and you exist as an Irish writer on those terms or you might as well not exist' (Goodby, 1998, p. 46). The burden of tradition implies the continuing importance of the past for contemporary writers, and the poets I have chosen to examine here deal with the crucial nexus of personal and public in ways which often involve a complex rendering of history. This mediation between past and present highlights the extraordinary pace of change in Ireland since the mid-1960s. Though two of the older poets were in print before this time, their most significant and considered work dates from subsequent decades. All of those who feature have registered the difficult choices between tradition and innovation, between centre and margin, in challenging and imaginative ways.

Two poets who bear a particularly interesting relation to the perceived centre of Irish poetic tradition are Thomas Kinsella (b. 1928) and John Montague (b. 1929). Kinsella's career cannot be touched upon without reference to its stark and difficult changes. His transition from lyric poet to opaque modernist was followed by the decision in 1972 to begin publishing his work in pamphlets from his own Peppercanister Press, which contributed to his increasing obscurity and signalled a changed attitude towards the position of his work in Irish culture. Together with his contemporaries John Montague and Richard Murphy, Kinsella sought to create a poetic that was at once Irish and modern, but he has arguably displayed the most complex approach of the three to these issues. Kinsella questions the concept of a singular tradition: 'every writer in the modern world . . . is the inheritor of a gapped, discontinuous, polyglot tradition' (Kinsella, 1970, p. 66). The idea of a mutilated past is one which clearly shapes much of Kinsella's own poetry, making his treatment of history ambiguous in its depth and complexity. This perhaps accounts for what Eavan Boland sees as the poetry's simultaneous desire for and suspicion of order. Certainly the search for order is not a straightforward one for Kinsella, whose poetry is often suspended between the desire for organic unity and the acceptance of inevitable fragmentation, as this image of the newly laid egg falling through the 1973 poem 'Hen Woman' aptly demonstrates:

> Through what seemed a whole year it fell
> – as it still falls, for me,
> solid and light, the red gold beating
> in its silvery womb,
> alive as the yolk and white
> of my eye; as it will continue
> to fall, probably, until I die,
> through the vast indifferent spaces
> with which I am empty.

Kinsella's work dwells on the relationship between the individual and the universe, which is often expressed in the image of a solitary figure and in the motif of the journey with a doubtful starting point and destination. The family also provides an important connection to the past, but the level of intimacy which this scheme suggests is rarely realized in Kinsella's poetry. That intimate relationships should prove illusory may be typical of a poet who gravitates towards difficult philosophical questions. Yet Kinsella remains deeply engaged with the realities of a changing Ireland and uses the medium of poetry to interrogate the political in a manner which has proved disconcerting to some critics.

Montague's progress has been of an altogether different order. His poetry lacks Kinsella's challenging obscurity and his linking of modernism and romanticism clearly has implications for his own writing. Like Kinsella he cites a range of American and European poets as key influences and in doing so breaks the insular notion of identity which was a recurring feature of Irish poetry earlier this century. Yet his work also makes ample use of such personifications as the *cailleach* and of the spéirbhean of the *aisling* tradition and does so in a way which suggests acceptance of these culturally marked forms. In this sense, then, the need to deconstruct certain traditional elements has clearly proved less pressing for Montague than for Kinsella. His poems vary from those which assume orthodox styles and those which use a conversational register, an alliance of the speech act with that of writing which Montague sees as vital to the creative process. He is attracted to the lyric and his use of the poetic sequence (*The Great Cloak*, 1978, is an example) owes much to the desire to combine lengthier exploration with a lyric precision.

The relationship between private and public in his work is highlighted in the proliferation of love poetry and while the influential *The Rough Field* (1972) drew explicitly on historical and political material – and *The Dead Kingdom* (1984) by Montague's own acknowledgement takes many of these political assessments a stage further – there is a tendency for the enduring life of the individual to remain prominent in his work. From early in his career Montague has been aware of the need to forge an original poetry and has commented on the lack of useful precursors for him as a young writer. Keen to position himself as a poet striking out in new directions, he has called himself 'the missing link of Ulster poetry' (O'Driscoll, 1989, p. 60). His relationship to the growing body of so-called 'Northern' poets is ambiguous, however. He shares with Heaney a concern for the specificity of place and the Garvaghey of his youth is vividly evoked in his work. The kinds of change which Montague registers make the reclamation of childhood places more than simple reconstruction of the past and he is deeply unhappy about the destruction of the natural environment. Landscape also has a role to play in the erotic poems, where the land becomes a lover's body or shapes a journey which is also an exploration of desire. The recurrence of journeys in his work is a feature which he shares with Thomas Kinsella, though Kinsella's topography is resolutely urban, while for Montague the route is often between regions and draws attention to the North–South divide and its implications.

Northern Ireland is the site of the most striking achievements in recent Irish poetry. Seamus Heaney's (b. 1939) Nobel Prize confirms the international recognition not only of his own work but also that of his peers. Heaney's pre-eminence can scarcely be denied – or ignored – and his keen ear and extraordinary technical skill as a young poet have developed into an assured exploration of sophisticated and intellectually challenging areas. In this way, it seems, Heaney is a poet who embodies the modern need to explore national mythologies in an international poetic context. His preoccupation with his origins remains strong and his use of rural tradition at once evokes the sensual immediacy of childhood and probes the implications of literary tradition itself. The combination of consummate craftsmanship and intuitive handling of subtle emotional territories links Heaney's poetic process with his key themes; this suggestive interweaving is accompanied by a range of poetic influences from Dante to Robert Lowell. Heaney's attention to the Gaelic heritage also suggests the necessity of mediating between traditions. While at times a poet such as Tom Paulin shares with Heaney a tendency towards densely physical language and a sharp critical intelligence, there is an entirely different sensibility – and not one easily submitted to the clichés of cultural division – at work in his writings.

The question of politics looms large for all writers who have grown up in – or spoken from – Ulster, and as Eiléan Ní Chuilleanáin has remarked, readers often approach these poets as though they already know what they will say. Heaney has been variously castigated for saying too much and for not saying enough about the Northern conflict; certainly his treatment of it has resisted the kind of highly charged response which might be repented at leisure. The kind of individualism which another northerner, James Simmons, both demonstrates in his poetry and comments upon in his criticism suggests that personal vision may be an important way of re-examining traditional sectarian allegiances. Derek Mahon (b. 1941) and Michael Longley (b. 1939) are two of the most noteworthy of Heaney's contemporaries and they too have felt the pressures of writing out of the northern situation. Mahon claims Louis MacNeice as an important precursor and in doing so asserts his own ambiguous position in relation to his native Belfast. The limitations of a commitment which poetry may inevitably invite are felt by both Heaney and Mahon but handled differently by each. Mahon's poetry began with, and continues to assert, a strong sense of modernism's intellectual territories; indeed the notion of territory itself is both personalized and politicized in his work. Mahon's speakers are constantly on the move, seeking to explore new spaces and continually questioning their relationship to the centre, whether geographical or poetic.

The hidden life is important to Mahon and secrecy is both thematic and formal in his poetry. If Longley's work is attentive to such diverse matters as botany and the classical world, it is with a view to illuminating them through minute observation and a finely tuned lyrical gift. Mahon, by contrast, tends towards the intellectually oblique. The absent self complicates the perspective of a number of his poems and of course suggests that the self is somehow present elsewhere. Unlike Longley, who remained resident in Belfast for the duration of the troubles, Mahon left the province while still a young man and has questioned this decision, though typically in a manner which does not truly invite an answer, as in the poem 'Afterlives': 'Perhaps if I'd stayed behind / And lived it bomb by bomb / I might have grown up at last / And learnt what is meant by home'. This evasiveness is in keeping with the difficulty the reader faces in interpreting the poems. Mahon's tight linguistic control, his intellectual vigour and latterly his sophisticated intertextuality present a taut and accomplished style, but one which is at odds with his often apocalyptic vision. At the borders of his poetry the ungovernable violence of Irish history everywhere threatens the aesthetic order. While Longley seeks to restore links with the past in his work and to use a detailed natural world to evoke potential wholeness, Mahon questions the possibility of such meaningful connections and resists the easy appropriation of history. Although he has said at least twice that he is 'through with history' he is attuned to the different levels at which the story of the past may be told.

The next generation of northern writers reflects the trends of postmodern variety and play. The texture of this work is radically different to that of the older poets and takes an entirely new stance in relation to the intersection of poetic practice and context. The two most interesting of this generation are Paul Muldoon (b. 1951) and Ciaran Carson (b. 1948). Both of these poets revel in the unexpected and use traditional form reflexively, to question its own purposes and meanings. Both also incorporate a diverse range of cultural influences into their work. Muldoon has chosen widely different forms to express his talent: short lyrics, long narrative poems, a libretto. Within the poems themselves, perspective shifts suddenly and in disconcerting ways, suggesting endless alternatives for interpretation. Muldoon's ludic sensibility draws attention to the multiple definitions within language and to the rich possibilities of the act of writing itself, as the poem 'Lunch with Pancho Villa' suggests:

> I rang the bell, and knocked hard
> On what I remembered as his front door,
> That opened then, as such doors do,
> Directly on to a back yard.
> Not any back yard, I'm bound to say,
> And not a thousand miles away
> From here. No one's taken in, I'm sure,
> By such a mild invention.

Yet the need to make such play suggests that the reader *may* indeed be taken in. Though the voice remains a strong feature of Muldoon's work, little sense of the personal is to be found there and autobiographical detail appears in such profusion that it actually obscures rather than clarifies the contexts of the poems. Helen Vendler finds in his poetry 'a hole in the middle where the feeling should be' (Wills, 1998, p. 15) and though Muldoon has achieved considerable international recognition, his sophistication has drawn fire from other critics such as John Carey, who has described the poems as standing around 'smugly, knowing that academic annotators will come running' (O'Driscoll, 1995, p. 98).

Ciaran Carson's attention to language is somewhat different. Shaped by the urban environment of his native Belfast and equally by the rhythms and patterns of Irish traditional music, Carson makes repeated use of two particular forms: the long narrative poem and the sonnet. His mastery of the long line owes much to the work of the American C. K. Williams, but is strongly influenced too by his musical background. Perhaps more than any Irish poet now writing he concerns himself with the poetic possibilities of story, especially of the labyrinthine nature of narrative form, of tales glimpsed and inconclusively told. In this sense the oral tradition marks Carson's work in memorable ways, making him a truly modern practitioner of an ancient and traditional art.

Carson's use of the sonnet is even more remarkable. His recent versions of the French testify to an attentiveness to the spaces between languages, already familiar in his return to Irish poetic history. Such a reworking of this tight and crafted form had precursors in the Belfast sonnets prominent in two collections from Carson's most formative period – *The Irish for No* (1988) and *Belfast Confetti* (1989). In order to render the destructive yet enduring nature of that city's violence, Carson produced mutilated versions of this most musical of poetic forms. Language is a casualty of the political situation, implicitly in the entire dynamic of North and South as it is shaped and acknowledged by poets and critics alike, and explicitly here in the breaking of form and the intertwining of verbal and political mechanics: 'Suddenly as the riot squad moved in, it was raining exclamation marks, / Nuts, bolts, nails, car-keys. A fount of broken type' ('Belfast Confetti'). The poem becomes an object to be manipulated and reshaped according to its context; thus Carson finds a way of establishing witty and meaningful links between form and theme.

Another northern poet, Medbh McGuckian (b. 1950), exhibits the postmodern play of intertextuality especially characteristic of Muldoon. McGuckian's abstract and challenging work has drawn a range of devotees and detractors, all anxious to locate what is most liberating – or most damaging – about contemporary poetry in English. She has been variously described as 'fluid' and 'mannered', as 'forward-looking' and 'non-visionary'. McGuckian's language describes and dwells in an inner world, and in doing so becomes arguably more important than public speech, more articulate in its exploration of a multiplicity of identities, more flexible in its connections between real and imaginative worlds. Her poetry has been described as womanly but the poet's own views on the shaping power of gender are ambiguous; she exhibits a desire to subvert the linear in poetry, yet she does so in order to push language to the limits of its potential.

This kind of movement continues to cause readers problems, however, and there is a sense of wilful obscurity in much of her work which raises issues about the kind of meaning she wishes to uncover. She has said that she never writes 'blindly' but instead sits down with a collection of words, referring here to an actual accumulation of noted phrases often gleaned from her current reading and assembled and reshaped to form a poem. Such an overt use of intertextuality is apparently at odds with the drifting rhythms and dissociated images of the poetry and there is a problem of significance too, since it is difficult for us to keep up with this literary recycling unless we are explicitly alerted to it. This is a rich process, though, and gives the work a textured and handled quality.

Such unreliability of language may denote a willingness, indeed a determination, by some of the most exciting women poets working in Ireland today to overturn expectations – not only those imposed by the largely male establishment but by women themselves. As Eiléan Ní Chuilleanáin (b. 1942) said in a recent discussion, 'there has to be a way in which you can disappoint the expectations of your audience' and this desire to disappoint means an assertion of an *individual* identity and creative trajectory, not one which follows an explicitly political agenda. Her own poems exhibit a tantalizing ability to withhold knowledge from us; they are full of inexplicable gaps, spaces where meaning is lost or slips away. In *The Brazen Serpent* the keeping of secrets constitutes both subject and form. By disrupting our expectations of what a poem will yield, Ní Chuilleanáin eases us towards the kind of attentive reading which poetry so badly needs. It is of special concern to critics of contemporary Irish women writers that the establishment of a voice, rather than attention to what that voice is saying, remains a damaging focus for many readers and consequently for writers themselves. The sheer range and originality of poetry written by Irish women – from the observant Mary O'Malley to the humorous Rita Ann Higgins, from Paula Meehan's subversive voice to Biddy Jenkinson's resistant one – promises an enduring body of poems. It is surely a feature of a movement from margin to centre that a more stringent criticism can and must be applied to this work.

Eavan Boland (b. 1944) has outlined the key transition from object to subject made by women. Her response to the Irish tradition in both its linguistic forms is a guarded one, since she sees women's role there as iconic or metaphorical and argues that this may remove the obligation to interrogate the real conditions of women's lives. As the title of her 1990 collection *Outside History* suggests, Boland is preoccupied with the need to write women back into a national history from which she feels they have been excluded: 'as far as history goes / we were never / on the scene of the crime' ('It's a Woman's World'). She also registers the lack of woman's literary history acutely, though there are other critics who contest this view. Anne Stevenson objects to Boland's claim to be disadvantaged by her national past, citing a medieval Irish tradition of women poets which could provide vibrant and educative models for the modern writer. In spite of the truth of this suggestion the marked lack of continuity evident when considering Irish poetic foremothers has proved disruptive for the contemporary writer.

Boland is the most vocal of Irish women poets on the issue of tradition and her own poetic career testifies to these continuing preoccupations. Beginning with orthodox forms, her most sudden technical manoeuvre occurred around 1980 with the publication of *In Her Own Image*. This collection witnessed a dramatic shift towards an outspoken and subversive position and inaugurated a radical remaking of the female, both through new forms of poetic representation and the evocation of an interior world which had hitherto remained hidden in the poetry. A number of Boland's poems deal with a kind of history which is autobiographical yet manages to retain a broader significance: she herself demonstrates Ireland's duality in her own person – raised in England, the sense of being divorced from her own place, her geography and history, is strong:

> let the world I knew become the space
> between the words that I had by heart
> and all the other speech that always was
> becoming the language of the country that
> I came to in nineteen-fifty-one:
> barely-gelled, a freckled six-year-old,
> overdressed and sick on the plane
> when all of England to an Irish child
>
> was nothing more than what you'd lost and how
> ('An Irish Childhood in England: 1951')

Tensions between margin and centre assert themselves even more vigorously in the debate on the role of the Irish language in contemporary Irish letters. Ireland's dual tradition, which involves a subtle mediation between English and Gaelic literary forms, not only reflects the complex diversity of these two cultural positions but often explicitly examines the movement between them, making this transition itself the focus of language. Nuala Ní Dhomhnaill's (b. 1952) energetic work not only places her poems among the most important in the Irish language this century but spills over into her comments on writing in that tradition. She recognizes that the decision to write in Irish is often a difficult and emotive one for poets. Michael Hartnett (b. 1941), raised in his grandmother's Irish-speaking household, at first found this his natural language for poetry. His work combines a fresh originality with an attentiveness to the great poets of the Gaelic tradition, while younger poets such as Cathal Ó Searcaigh use the language to expose themes of individualism and isolation. Irish is not always an exclusive medium for these poets, however; both Hartnett and the versatile Mícheál Ó Siadhail have returned to the English language to explore its creative potential further.

Ní Dhomhnaill's 1990 collection *Pharaoh's Daughter* features translations by many of the most distinguished of contemporary Irish poets, including Medbh McGuckian, Derek Mahon and Paul Muldoon. The stylistic shifts which this kind of project records provide a fascinating insight into the process of translation itself, yet it can also have disturbing consequences for the objectification of the female, as Ní Dhomhnaill herself recounts:

> A few years ago a number of poets, mostly as it happens male, collaborated in a book of translation of my work. . . . Immediately the critics hailed me in terms of being a kind of Muse. Now let us get one thing quite clear. I was not their Muse: they were my translators. (Dorgan, 1996, p. 115)

While the difficulties in creating and maintaining a subject position in poetry are exposed clearly here, there is a strong sense in this collection of the way in which a translator is involved in re-creating the work, rather than simply transposing it from one language to another. The final poem from *Pharaoh's Daughter*, 'Ceist na Teangan' / 'The Language Issue' is translated by Paul Muldoon and in keeping with the concerns of both writer and translator, language as a means of communication, as itself the vehicle for personal and cultural hopes, is highlighted from the opening line: 'I place my hope on the water / in this little boat / of the language'. Ironically, the reception of the poem, which in fact constitutes its meaning, is absent from the text entirely.

There are other poets too for whom a readership has a vital role; those who have achieved a considerable popular following both through the immediacy of their themes and the power of their public performance. Such popularity keeps poetry squarely in the public arena yet limits the subtlety of its linguistic play. Here cultural context plays a heightened role in both the reception and creation of the poem; if the subject matter addresses contemporary issues in the raw, the form combines the traditional and the experimental in at times surprising ways. Brendan Kennelly (b. 1936) has always had a sharp eye for social ills and the lyrical voice of his early work has given way since the 1980s to the exuberant and near-uncontrollable perspective of the long sequence. The most successful of these to date has been *Cromwell* (1983), which centres on the notorious figure whose political power had such bloody consequences for Ireland. This poem uses jokes, profanities and grotesque depictions to subvert not only the familiar structures but the accepted expression of history.

Kennelly's play with language has its limitations, however, and Edna Longley's approving assessment that his words 'are means to an end: the instruments of fact, fiction and fantasy' (Longley, 1994, p. 198) is really an admission of an ultimately unadventurous approach to the possibilities of language. He chooses the sonnet as the structural unit of the sequence, but the containment this particular form seems to represent is quickly rebuked by Kennelly: 'Trouble is', as Ed Spenser says in 'Master', 'sonnets are genetic epics. / Something in them wants to grow out of bounds', which is exactly what they do in this poem. It is a problem which has also dogged Kennelly's later projects, the lengthier sequences *The Book of Judas* (1991) and *Poetry My Arse* (1995). Lack of discipline is now a core poetic statement for Kennelly and it proves increasingly unwieldy for the reader. This has not lessened the tremendous popularity of his work, though, which is seen as debunking the self-regarding cleverness of more sophisticated poets.

Paul Durcan (b. 1944) shares with Kennelly an ability to mesmerize audiences with his public performances and a similarly acute social awareness. His observant verse partakes of its particular context in different ways, however, in that it addresses its shaping forces more directly and it uses the language and forms – in particular those associated with Catholic ritual – of the very institutions which Durcan seeks to expose. The titles of his poems alone are often revealing: 'Archbishop of Kerry to have

Abortion'; 'The Haulier's Wife Meets Jesus on the Road Near Moone'; 'Wife Who Smashed Television Gets Jail' and there is an amusing sharpness in Durcan's observations, as the latter poem demonstrates:

> Justice O'Bradaigh said wives who preferred bar-billiards to family television
> Were a threat to the family which was the basic unit of society
> As indeed the television itself could be said to be the basic unit of the family
> And when as in this case wives expressed their preference in forms of violence
> Jail was the only place for them. Leave to appeal was refused.

The broader cultural context is vital for the appreciation of this kind of work, not merely to explicate some of the references to contemporary events but because for such a poem to rise above the banal, it must display yet transcend the limitations of its society. Poets like Durcan and Kennelly are important because they often succeed in doing just that.

From poets at the centre of Ireland's cultural development we move to those at its periphery, to several poets no longer resident in Ireland who mix a sensibility attuned to Irish culture with influences and images from elsewhere. There are many reasons why this apparently marginal position crucially informs the centre, not least because of the persistent importance of the figure of the emigrant (both forced and voluntary) in Irish culture. Eamon Grennan (b. 1941) has mediated between America, where he now lives, and Ireland, which he considers his real home, by using the natural world. His attention to detail captures the sensory realism of this world and affirms his debt to Kavanagh which is acknowledged and considerable. It also suspends the reader between the particular and the universal in an uncanny way. Matthew Sweeney (b. 1952) displays a similar attention to detail but with a tendency towards a sinister and often inexplicable world. Morbidity is combined with humour and the ways in which the familiar can become strange seem central here, though this in itself does not account for the destabilizing force of Sweeney's best work.

The contemporary can by definition never be static and thus the shape of the Irish poetry scene is constantly changing and constantly requiring redefinition. A number of the younger poets have already achieved considerable attention, both at home and abroad, and bring these levels of confidence and of cultural diversity directly into their poetry. Gallery Press, as well as publishing many established poets, supports the work of newer talents such as Vona Groarke, Conor O'Callaghan and David Wheatley, whose finely crafted and whimsical poems have already earned him a Rooney Prize. Justin Quinn, now living in Prague, has recently published a second collection with Carcanet, confirming the considerable promise of his earliest work. While a vibrant poetry scene will not always foster real achievement, it may encourage productive debate. The future of Irish poetry depends upon this kind of dialectic, upon rigour as well as inclusiveness and upon a receptive reading of cultures other than our own.

BIBLIOGRAPHY

Andrews, E. (1992). *Contemporary Irish Poetry: A Collection of Critical Essays*. London: Macmillan.

Boland, E. (1996). *Object Lessons: The Life of the Woman and the Poet in Our Time*. London: Vintage.

Corcoran, N. (ed.) (1992). *The Chosen Ground: Essays on the Contemporary Poetry of Northern Ireland*. Bridgend: Seren Books.

Corcoran, N. (1999). *Poets of Modern Ireland: Text, Context, Intertext*. Cardiff: University of Wales Press.

Dawe, G. (1991). *How's the Poetry Going?: Literary Politics and Ireland Today*. Belfast: Lagan Press.

Dawe, G. (1995). *Against Piety: Essays in Irish Poetry*. Belfast: Lagan Press.

Dorgan, T. (ed.) (1996). *Irish Poetry Since Kavanagh*. Dublin: Four Courts Press.

Garratt, R. F. (1989). *Modern Irish Poetry: Tradition and Continuity from Yeats to Heaney*. Berkeley: University of California Press.

Goodby, J. (1998). 'Who's Afraid of Experimental Poetry?' *Meter* 5, 41–8.

Irish University Review. 24, 1. Special edition on Derek Mahon.

John, B. (1988). 'Contemporary Irish Poetry and the Matter of Ireland – Thomas Kinsella, John Montague and Seamus Heaney.' In R. Wall (ed.), *Medieval and Modern Ireland*. Gerrard's Cross: Colin Smythe.

John, B. (1996). *Reading the Ground: The Poetry of Thomas Kinsella*. Washington, DC: Catholic University of America Press.

Kinsella, T. (1970). *Davis, Mangan, Ferguson? Tradition and the Irish Writer*, writings by W. B. Yeats and Thomas Kinsella. Dublin: Dolmen Press.

Kinsella, T. (1995). *The Dual Tradition: An Essay on Poetry and Politics in Ireland*. Manchester: Carcanet.

Longley, E. (1994). *The Living Stream: Literature and Revisionism in Ireland*. Newcastle upon Tyne: Bloodaxe Books.

Mahon, D. (1996). *Journalism*. Meath: Gallery Press.

Matthews, S. (1997). *Irish Poetry: Politics, History, Negotiation*. London: Macmillan.

Murphy, S. (1998). ' "Roaming Root of Multiple Meanings": Intertextual Relations in Medbh McGuckian's Poetry.' *Meter* 5, 99–109.

O'Brien, S. (1998). *The Deregulated Muse: Essays on Contemporary British and Irish Poetry*. Newcastle upon Tyne: Bloodaxe Books.

O'Driscoll, D. (1989). 'An Interview with John Montague', *Irish University Review* 19, 1, 58–72. Special edition on John Montague.

O'Driscoll, D. (1995). 'A Map of Contemporary Irish Poetry.' *Poetry*, 167, 1–2, 94–106.

Wills, C. (1993). *Improprieties: Politics and Sexuality in Northern Irish Poetry*. Oxford: Oxford University Press.

Wills, C. (1998). *Reading Paul Muldoon*. Newcastle upon Tyne: Bloodaxe Books.

48

Contemporary Postcolonial Poetry

Jahan Ramazani

In recent decades much of the most vital writing in English has come from Britain's former colonies in the so-called Third World. For readers of fiction the geographic explosion of Anglophone literature is by now self-evident: postcolonial novelists like Chinua Achebe, V. S. Naipaul, Salman Rushdie and Arundhati Roy have clearly redrawn the map of English-language fiction in our time. By comparison, 'contemporary poetry' remains strikingly provincial in the Anglophone West. With the exception of Derek Walcott's work, 'contemporary poetry' is typically limited to the United States, Britain and Ireland, perhaps with some inclusion of former white settler colonies like Canada. Whether favouring poetry that is 'postmodern' or 'postconfessional', 'neoformalist' or 'mainstream', 'ethnic' or 'white', most anthologies, critical essays and conferences reassert these boundaries. In recent years American poetry has expanded to include minority writers of African, Asian and Latino descent, and British poetry has also begun to include 'black British' writers. But the story of the globalization of English-language poetry remains largely untold.

Yet a rich and vibrant poetry has issued from the hybridization of the English muse with the long-resident muses of Africa, India, the Caribbean, and other decolonized territories of the British Empire. Postcolonial poets have dramatically expanded the contours of English-language poetry by infusing it with indigenous metaphors and rhythms, creoles and genres. The Indian poet A. K. Ramanujan imports the metaphoric compression and accentual evenness of literary Tamil into English, the Jamaican poet Louise Bennett the phonemic wit and play of Jamaican creole words like 'boonoonoonoos' for 'pretty' or 'boogooyagga' for 'worthless'. The Ugandan poet Okot p'Bitek adapts vivid images, idioms and rhetorical strategies from Acholi songs: his spurned character Lawino complains – in language unprecedented in English poetry – that her husband's tongue is 'hot like the penis of the bee' and 'fierce like the arrow of the scorpion, / Deadly like the spear of the buffalo-hornet'. At the same time, postcolonial poets have brilliantly remade the literary language and forms of the colonizer. Wole Soyinka engrafts resonant Elizabethan English onto Yoruba syntax and myth, Derek Walcott turns the Greek Philoctetes into an allegorical figure for postcolonial affliction, and Lorna Goodison adapts Western figures of femininity, such as Penelope and the Mermaid, to a Caribbean geography and history. Belonging to multiple worlds that are transformed by convergence, postcolonial poets indigenize the Western and Anglicize the native to create exciting new possibilities for English-language poetry.

In light of these achievements, why is postcolonial poetry so much less visible than fiction and drama? T. S. Eliot's remark in 'The Social Function of Poetry' (1945) remains suggestive more than half a century later: 'no art', he said, 'is more stubbornly national than poetry'. Yet Eliot's transcultural practices were already stretching the European Romantic concepts of a national poetry or *Sprachgeist*. More recently, in the Anglophone West the field of contemporary poetry has become polarized between supporters of mainstream 'postconfessional' verse and avant-garde 'language' poetry. But neither poetry conceived as the lyric expression of personal feeling nor as the postmodern negation of commodified language is sufficient to help us understand and value poets beyond the First World – poets like Louise Bennett, Okot p'Bitek or A. K. Ramanujan, who use poetry to mediate between oral traditions and imported literary forms; to reclaim indigenous histories, landscapes and traditions; and to constitute imagined communities in the wake of their threatened colonial destruction.

Like poetry studies, postcolonial studies has also been surprisingly unreceptive to postcolonial poetry, for two primary reasons. On the one hand, the field is largely grounded in mimetic presuppositions about literature. But since poetry mediates experience through a language of exceptional figural and formal density, it is a less transparent medium by which to recuperate the history, politics and sociology of post-colonial societies. On the other hand, postcolonial studies has been preoccupied with continually interrogating itself, questioning its complicity in European discourses, the (non-)representability of 'other' cultures, and the definition of its primary terms. While such theoretical inquiry is not necessarily inimical to poetry (informing, indeed, my analysis), the genre also demands specifically literary modes of response and recognition – of figurative devices, generic codes, stanzaic patterns, prosodic twists and allusive turns.

Postcolonial studies and poetics nevertheless offer a potentially valuable blend of strategies for exploring postcolonial poetry. Poetics helps to highlight the literary energies of these texts, which aesthetically embody the postcolonial condition in particular linguistic and formal structures. The best postcolonial poems are resonant and compelling in no small part because of their figurative reach, verbal dexterity, tonal complexity, and their imaginative transformation of inherited genres, forms and dramatic characters. In turn, the concept of postcoloniality – indigenous cultures once subjugated under colonial rule and responding to its continuing aftermath – provides a useful comparative and historical framework. (I set aside as historically distinct such white settler colonies as Australia and Canada, as well as the more ambiguous case of Ireland – now of the First World but once kin to the Third.) Although the terms 'postcolonial', 'Third World' and 'non-Western' have often been criticized for erasing cultural and historical differences (McClintock), these terms can be useful in high-lighting similarities and differences across various cultures still grappling with their colonial histories. They can help to illuminate the robust variety of indigenous cultures living in the shadow of empire, whereas more local perspectives (e.g. West Indian poetry, African poetry, Indian poetry) often make it difficult to recognize such cross-cultural relationships. By using national and regional contexts in concert with the postcolonial horizon, we can better appreciate how Louise Bennett, for example, participates in both a West Indian performance tradition and a broader postcolonial poetics of irony. Similarly, A. K. Ramanujan compares artificial 'Waterfalls in a Bank' in Chicago to 'wavering snakeskins' and thus borrows an ancient Tamil metaphor, but we miss something unless we also notice that his double vision is rooted in the postcolonial condition. Okot p'Bitek was trained at Oxford as an anthropologist specializing in East African oral literature, yet his poetry instances a postcolonial ambivalence towards the discipline, both appropriating ethnographic modes of representation and fiercely rejecting British anthropology's Eurocentric values and Christian bias in the 1960s.

Among the pre-eminent Anglophone poets of such decolonizing nations as India, Uganda, Nigeria, Barbados, St Lucia, Jamaica, Gambia and Ghana, we find a wide range of literary practices and proclivities, from the literary internationalism of Derek Walcott and Wole Soyinka to the 'folk' orality of Okot p'Bitek, Louise Bennett and Kofi Awoonor; from Walcott's and Kamau Brathwaite's epics and Okot's long poems to A. K. Ramanujan's lyric ruminations, Bennett's pithy ballads and Lenrie Peter's skeletal lineation. What do these widely diverse poets have in common? To begin with, they were all born to colonial populations under British rule and continued to write in the aftermath of political decolonization. They all had a British colonial education, which Walcott has called 'the greatest bequest the Empire made': 'precisely because of their limitations our early education must have ranked with the finest in the world' (Walcott, 1993, p. 50). The gift of education may also have been the greatest curse of empire, purveyed initially by missionaries and then by imperial governments as a tool for altering native minds and even turning them against themselves. Educated as imperial subjects yet immersed in indigenous traditions and customs, these postcolonial poets grew up in the potentially productive tension between an imposed and an inherited culture – productive, that is, for the powerful literary mind that can create imaginative forms to articulate the dualities, ironies and ambiguities of this cultural in-betweenness. Poetry – a genre rich in paradox and multivalent symbols, irony and metaphor – is well-suited to mediating and registering the con-tradictions of split cultural experience. These poets respond with emotional ambiva-lence and linguistic versatility to the experience of living after colonialism, between non-Western traditions and modernity, at a moment of explosive change in the rela-tion between Western and native cultures.

Postcolonial studies offers the metaphor of 'hybridity' as a potent lens through which to explore interculturation in the postcolonial world. Since the term can be misleading if it muffles the power differences between cultures or oversimplifies the multi-layered deposits within any single culture, I use it to describe the intensified hybridization of already mixed and politically unequal cultures, where 'native' represents a prior knotting together of diverse strands, as does the amalgamation 'British'. Edward Said, Homi Bhabha, Stuart Hall, James Clifford, Paul Gilroy and others have theorized a postcoloniality that is interstitial, beyond identitarian boundaries. Other writers have revealed the hybridity of specific postcolonial regions. 'Cultural traditions in India are indissolubly plural and often conflicting', remarks Ramanujan (1989, pp. 188–9). Anthony Appiah (1992, p. 24) highlights the 'extraordinary diversity of Africa's peoples and its cultures'. And Edouard Glissant has theorized the 'cross-culturality', Kamau Brathwaite the 'creolization' of the Caribbean. Members of a small educated elite, Anglophone poets of the Third World are perhaps especially hybridized by their intensive exposure to Western ideas and values through higher education, travel, even expatriation. Further complicating the matrices of identity, many postcolonial poets have an oblique relation to the 'native' culture that they are assumed to 'represent': Walcott grew up a Methodist in a predominantly Catholic country; Ramanujan spoke Tamil at home, along with English, in an area where Kannada was the dominant language. These intercultural and intracultural dynamics – whether experienced as a condition of tragic mixture and alienation, or as the comic integration of multiple energies and sources – have fuelled some of the most powerful poetry of our time.

Before examining the hybrid language and form of postcolonial poetry, we need to remind ourselves of the primary historical cause of this confluence between Third World and Western cultures. Anglophone poetry in the Third World, like many other culturally hybrid forms, was an indirect consequence of the violent intersection between the British Empire and various native cultures – not a mysterious species that spontaneously generated itself in random parts of the world. Postcolonial poetry, as the term itself suggests, is largely unintelligible without some sense of its historical origins. The vast scope of postcolonial poetry in English is directly related to the size of the empire that initially wrapped much of the globe in its language and, more recently, to the expanding technological and economic might of the United States. The British Empire – the largest, most powerful, best organized of its peers – colonized enormous chunks of the non-Western world, expropriating land, raw materials and labour from its overseas territories. By the beginning of the First World War, more than three quarters of the earth's surface was under direct European dominion, with most of this colonization having occurred during the preceding hundred years. The deep and lasting effects of this colonial expansion still reverberate around the world today, long after the postwar political breakup of most of the British and other European empires. The First World and not just the Third would be unrecognizable without its colonial history. Underscoring Europe's dependence on Third World labour for economic advancement, Frantz Fanon (1963, p. 102) remarks starkly: 'Europe is literally the creation of the Third World'.

Fanon's *The Wretched of the Earth* still stands as the single most vivid reminder of the historical violence of modern European colonialism. According to Fanon this violence is military (the force by which the settler takes land from the native), cultural ('the violence with which the supremacy of white values is affirmed') and existential ('a systematic negation of the other person') (ibid., pp. 43, 250). Fanon famously describes the colonial world as 'a Manichaean world', 'a world cut in two', with the native continually debased and dehumanized (ibid., pp. 41, 38). Systematic, efficient and all-encompassing, modern colonialism forces 'the people it dominates to ask themselves the question constantly: "In reality, who am I?"' (ibid., p. 250). Modern colonial history was not identical, of course, in different European empires, and even British imperialism took on vastly different forms in different regions of the Third World. Crudely put, its most consequential ingredient in the Caribbean was the massive enslavement and deracination of Africans; in Africa its history was shorter than in the Caribbean and its implementation more brutally dualistic than in India; and its historical evolution was more incremental in India, its political structure less rigidly Manichaean. These broad differences are reflected in the less overtly political tenor of much Anglophone Indian writing, the binary structure of much postcolonial African literature, and the agonized quest for an ancestral home in many Caribbean texts.

But none of these propensities is exclusive to a single region. The retrospective quest in Caribbean literature, for example, has its equivalent in other postcolonial literatures. Fanon's analysis suggests why historical recovery should be such an urgent and pervasive imperative of postcolonial poetry: 'By a kind of perverted logic, [colonialism] turns to the past of the oppressed people, and distorts, disfigures, and destroys it. This work of devaluing pre-colonial history takes on a dialectical significance today': namely, 'native intellectuals . . . decided to back further and to delve deeper down; and, let us make no mistake, it was with the greatest delight that they discovered that there was nothing to be ashamed of in the past, but rather dignity, glory, and solemnity' (ibid., p. 210). Searching through oral inheritances, written histories and personal memories, postcolonial poets seek to give voice to a past that colonialism has degraded, garbled, even gagged. The Nigerian Christopher Okigbo builds poems around the precolonial Igbo river goddess Idoto, as does Soyinka around the Yoruba god Ogun; Okot p'Bitek animates the pages of *Song of Lawino* with the preliterate wisdom and traditions of the Acholi. In the Caribbean, the lesser availability of the ancestral past often spurs a still more intensive quest for its recovery. Bennett emphasizes the African provenance of Jamaican words like 'nana' (Twi for grandparent) and 'gungoo' (Kongo for pea), and even Walcott, though suspicious of the longing for ancestral return, makes it a centrepiece of *Omeros*: the sunstruck hero Achille believes he travels back to his forebears in Africa, and Ma Kilman listens intently for natural signs of African gods that may have survived the Middle Passage. One way of approaching the question 'Who am I?', these poets suggest, is to ask 'Who were we?'

The recuperative quest in postcolonial poetry is nevertheless qualified by a countervailing scepticism. Even the most 'nativist' poets, such as Bennett and Okot, acknowledge that this past has been transformed irrevocably by colonialism and modernity. Here again Fanon provides insight, when he warns against efforts to fetishize and embalm the precolonial past: artists who 'turn their backs on foreign culture, deny it, and set out to look for a true national culture, . . . forget that the forms of thought and what it feeds on, together with modern techniques of information, language, and dress have dialectically reorganized the people's intelligences and that the constant principles which acted as safeguards during the colonial period are now undergoing extremely radical changes' (Fanon, 1963, p. 225). In postcolonial poetry this scepticism is often intertwined with the recuperative dynamic it checks. Upon Achille's imaginative arrival in Africa, Walcott's hero – like the poet himself – cannot help but see his ancestral land through the prism of Hollywood rivers, hippopotami and warriors in 'African movies / he had yelped at in childhood' (Walcott, 1990, p. 133). In the West Indian epic *The Arrivants*, when Edward Kamau Brathwaite likewise 'come[s] / back a stranger / after three hundred years' to the mother continent, he feels he has a 'hacked / face, hollowed eyes, / undrumming heart' (Brathwaite, 1973, pp. 124, 132): he learns that centuries of creolized life in the New World have made it impossible to merge with his African heritage. Brathwaite's and Walcott's scepticism should not be confused with the postmodernist renunciation of all nostalgias, since it is inextricable from the continuing postcolonial drive to rediscover the past.

Postcolonial poets often figure the desire to recuperate the precolonial past as the troubled search for an ancestral home, irreparably damaged by colonialism, as in 'The Weaver Bird' by the Ghanaian Kofi Awoonor:

> The weaver bird built in our house
> And laid its eggs on our only tree
>
> . . . .
> We look for new homes every day,
> For new altars we strive to re-build
> The old shrines defiled by the weaver's excrement.

With the departure of the colonizers, this defilement has in many cases continued, now unleashed by the native regimes that replaced the visiting weaver bird. Like the district commissioners and security forces of an earlier era, African dictators, thugs and thieves have ravaged the native home in many sub-Saharan states. Having 'longed for returning', the Gambian Lenrie Peter writes of bitter disillusionment in his poem 'Home Coming':

> There at the edge of town
> Just by the burial ground
> Stands the house without a shadow
> Lived in by new skeletons.

To return home is in many cases to re-enter mere ruins haunted by the murdered and massacred dead. Often the African poet has returned after a period of solitary confinement or exile. Handcuffed, the Malawian Jack Mapanje watches his mother furiously challenge the police, 'How dare you scatter this peaceful house?' ('Your Tears Still Burn at My Handcuffs', 1991). Imprisoned for three and a half years without charge or trial, Mapanje is released too late to learn from his now-dead mother 'the rites / Of homing in'. Fearing for their lives, African poets have often had to leave home: another Malawian, Frank Chipasula, has lived abroad during the long dictatorship of Hastings Banda, Okot spent the years of Idi Amin's brutal rule in exile, and Soyinka secretly left Nigeria when General Sani Abacha's regime confiscated his passport. Other poets have stayed at home and died. Christopher Okigbo was killed in his mid-thirties while fighting on the Biafran side in the Nigerian civil war – the first of many civil wars to tear apart post-independence Africa. His prophetic 'Come Thunder' compounds frightful details with terrifying abstractions:

> The smell of blood already floats in the lavender-mist of the afternoon.
> The death sentence lies in ambush along the corridors of power;
> And a great fearful thing already tugs at the cables of the open air,
> A nebula immense and immeasurable, a night of deep waters –
> An iron dream unnamed and unprintable, a path of stone.

The political homelessness lamented with mounting despair in African poetry has, for obvious reasons, no equivalent in Anglophone Indian or Caribbean poetry, yet poets from these parts of the world have also accused postcolonial regimes of defacing the native dwelling. Appalled by the damage inflicted by the tourist industry on the landscape of St Lucia, Walcott, for example, places in the volcanic hell of *Omeros* 'the traitors // who, in elected office, saw the land as views / for hotels'.

Seeking to reclaim the native home despoiled by both European colonialism and the internalized colonialism of more recent governments, postcolonial poets nevertheless worry that their quest for the precolonial home paradoxically shunts it beyond their grasp. In 'Postcard from Kashmir' Agha Shahid Ali suggests that memory and artifice transform the very past he pursues:

> Kashmir shrinks into my mailbox;
> my home a neat four by six inches.
>
> I always loved neatness. Now I hold
> the half-inch Himalayas in my hand.
>
> This is home. And this the closest
> I'll ever be to home. When I return,
> the colours won't be so brilliant,
> the Jhelum's waters so clean,
> so ultramarine. My love
> so overexposed.

The postcolonial poem, like a postcard, risks miniaturizing, idealizing and ultimately displacing the remembered native landscape. The Kashmiri Ali dramatizes the post-colonial and diasporic condition that Homi Bhabha, adapting Freud's *das Unheimliche*, terms 'unhomeliness – that is the condition of extra-territorial and cross-cultural initiations' (Bhabha, 1994, p. 9). When Okot p'Bitek returned to Africa to collect 'folk' songs of the Acoli and Lango, his Oxford training in anthropology had irrevocably transformed his relation to his native home.

Whether going abroad or staying home, postcolonial poets have been unhoused by modernity and colonialism, by war and politics, by education and travel, even perhaps by their own artifice, and are thus unable to rest securely in what Bhabha calls the idea of culture 'as a homogenizing, unifying force, authenticated by the originary Past' (ibid., p. 37). An expatriate speaker affirms 'home' in 'Wherever I Hang' by the Guyanese writer Grace Nichols, but only as a self-conscious fiction of belonging wherever she finds herself. Playing on Walcott's famous tortured lines about being 'divided to the vein' in 'A Far Cry from Africa', possibly answering Brathwaite's agonized question, 'Where then is the nigger's / home?' in *The Arrivants*, she writes:

> To tell you de truth
> I don't know really where I belaang
>
> Yes, divided to de ocean
> Divided to de bone
> Wherever I hang me knickers – that's my home.

The Britishness of 'knickers' doesn't deter the poet from transvaluing it as an ironic marker of 'home', any more than the imperial origins of her language hinder her from recolonizing it. Housed only in houselessness, unified only in such ironic self-division, the postcolonial poet knows that cultural identity, as Stuart Hall puts it, 'is not a fixed essence. . . . It is not a fixed origin to which we can make some final and absolute Return. Of course, it is not a mere phantasm either. It is *something* – not a mere trick of the imagination' (Hall, 1990, p. 226). At once sceptical and recuperative, ironic and nostalgic, postcolonial poets recathect the precolonial past as a powerful locus for identity, yet self-consciously probe the multiplicity and constructedness of the home they dislocate in the moment of reinhabiting it.

The richly conflictual relation between postcolonial poets and the English language is another important source of their 'unhomeliness'. Martin Heidegger famously describes language as the home of being, but what if we experience the language we live in as primary home to another? What if that home has been imposed on us by missionaries and governments that consider us racially and culturally inferior? What if we remain attached to another home even as we try to live in and help to refashion the new one? The result is what Gilles Deleuze and Félix Guattari have labelled a 'minor literature' – the literature of minorities, immigrants and others who live in, write in, and are 'forced to serve' a 'deterritorialized' European 'language that is not

Jahan Ramazani

their own' (Deleuze and Guattari, 1986, p. 19). In this literature, 'everything takes on a collective value', in contrast to the 'individual concerns' of 'major literatures' (ibid., p. 17). Reflecting on the mixed European provenance of her name and her poetic language, Eunice de Souza, a poet of Goa, India, comments ruefully on the postcolonial condition of linguistic estrangement in 'De Souza Prabhu':

> No matter that
> my name is Greek
> my surname Portuguese
> my language alien
>
> There are ways
> of belonging.
>
> I belong with the lame ducks.

Sometimes seen as an 'alien' and unassimilable intrusion, the English language is experienced, at its worst, as a tool of oppression: 'My tongue in English chains', laments the Indian poet R. Parthasarathy (Mehrotra, 1992, p. 5). More often the imposed language is seen as both a liability and a treasure – a 'radiant affliction' in Walcott's splendid oxymoron (Walcott, 1990, p. 323). In 'Missing Person' by the Bombay poet Adil Jussawalla, the colonial letter 'A' is said to be – in contrast to the native alphabet that has been displaced – 'here to stay. / On it St Pancras station, / the Indian and African railways'. As a schoolboy, the South Asian child sees the letter 'A' – inextricable from British colonial expansion in India and Africa – as potentially dangerous ('aimed at your throat') and potentially beautiful ('a butterfly's wing'). Travelling to the seat of empire, Jussawalla's speaker is made to feel, like many former colonial subjects, as if he is stealing and corrupting someone else's language: ' "You're polluting our sounds. You're so rude. // Get back to your language," they say'. Having been forced into an 'unhomely' language and then trying to assimilate it as their own, postcolonial poets ironically risk being seen – by both Western and indigenous detractors – as occupying a language to which they have no rightful claim.

One postcolonial response to this dilemma is to abandon English and return to a native language, a strategy that the Kenyan novelist Ngugi wa Thiong'o famously urged for 'decolonizing the mind'. But many postcolonial writers reject the assumption – traceable in some forms to European Romanticism – that the English language has an inherent relationship to only one kind of national or ethnic experience. Instead, like Caliban in the famous postcolonial allegory, they appropriate Prospero's language and remake it to serve their own ends. Brathwaite comments that 'it was in language that the slave was perhaps most successfully imprisoned by his master, and it was in his (mis-)use of it that he perhaps most effectively rebelled' (Brathwaite, 1971, p. 237). In 'Listen Mr Oxford don', the Guyanese poet John Agard speaks of 'mugging de Queen's English' and 'inciting rhyme to riot'. He playfully represents his use of West Indian creole as political rebellion by poetic means. However defiant he may be, the speaker recognizes that his relation to standard English is complex:

I slashing suffix in self-defence
I bashing future wit present tense
and if necessary

I making de Queen's English accessory
to my offence

As it turns out, the Queen's English is not only the object of the poet's revolt but also, potentially, an instrument and ally. Sometimes critics reduce postcolonial litera-tures to a comic-book simplicity, in which the colonized wage a heroic textual war on the colonizers. But the resistance is seldom unambivalent. In 'A Far Cry from Africa', Walcott can refer to 'this English tongue I love' even as he recalls having 'cursed / The drunken officer of British rule', much as the Irish poet Yeats conceded, 'everything I love has come to me through English; my hatred tortures me with love, my love with hate' (Yeats, 1961, p. 519). Because their relation to the English lan-guage is mediated by a vexed political history, by other languages, and by non-Standard forms, postcolonial poets transform literary English – both angrily and affectionately – in an astonishing variety of ways.

Anglophone poets write in response to different linguistic contexts in different parts of the Third World. In postcolonial Africa, they grow up speaking not only English but one or more indigenous languages. In India, a minority of the popula-tion (perhaps 3 per cent) speaks English fluently, and English-language poetry is only a small subset of the many bodies of poetry in different Indian languages. By contrast to India and Africa, almost everyone in the West Indies is from elsewhere ancestrally, so that an Ngugi would find it hard to return to a 'native' language, in the wake of the colonial destruction of most Arawaks, Caribs and other indigenous populations. In the Anglophone West Indies many poets can avail themselves of an English creole formed centuries ago out of the confluence of English with African and European lan-guages and now heard every day on the street. In the wake of attempts by Claude McKay and others, Louise Bennett was the first poet to master West Indian English as a language for poetry, and many West Indian 'dub' or performance poets, such as Michael Smith and Linton Kwesi Johnson, have followed her example. To the charge that Jamaican English is a 'corruption of the English language', she makes this spir-ited response: 'if dat be de case, den dem shoulda call English language corruption of Norman French an Latin and all dem tarra [other] language what dem seh [say] dat English is derived from' (Bennett, 1993, p. 1). Sharing this suspicion of linguistic hierarchy, many West Indian poets splice together their Standard English with local creoles – even a poet as different from Bennett as Walcott, whose 'code-switching' *Omeros* and 'Sainte Lucie', for example, leap from Standard English to English and French creoles. In a related strategy, an African poet like Okot p'Bitek leaves untrans-lated and unglossed many Acholi words for native plants, animals and religious beliefs, forcing the English-language reader to puzzle them out by context. By their maca-ronic language, postcolonial poets thus challenge the Standard as the exclusive norm for poetry.

Even when they write in neither an overt English creole nor a native language, postcolonial poets can still subtly creolize Standard English. Schooled in the colonizer's landscape, they pepper Standard English with local place names like Jejuri or Ibadan and intently name flora like the mango and Red Champak tree, fauna like the Paradise Flycatcher and colobus-monkey. Sometimes all the words are the same as those of a Standard English dictionary, but the postcolonial poet may still successfully indigenize English and English poetic forms. Agha Shahid Ali comments on his attempt at the 'biryanization . . . of English', specifically his desire to bring 'the music of Urdu' into English-language poetry (Mehrotra, 1992, p. 4). Before Brathwaite adapted the rhythms of Carnival, the propulsive force of this and many other Afro-Caribbean traditions had not been felt in English poetry: 'And / Ban / Ban / Cal- / iban / like to play / pan / at the Car- / nival' (Brathwaite, 1973, p. 192). Straddling languages, Okot p'Bitek inserts literally rendered Acholi idioms and tropes into English (e.g. the earlier cited metaphor, a tongue is 'hot like the penis of the bee'). The astonishingly elastic syntax of Soyinka's poetry, particularly in his earliest volumes, yorubizes English-language poetry. The difficulty of the poem 'Dawn' instances the effect of this hybridization of two syntactic systems:

> Breaking earth upon
> A spring-haired elbow, lone
> A palm beyond head-grains, spikes
> A guard of prim fronds, piercing
> High hairs of the wind

What is the subject? Is the word 'spikes' a noun in apposition to the palm or is it a verb? Delaying the introduction of finite verb and subject for another four and five lines ('steals / The lone intruder' or sun), Soyinka is forcing English syntax to stretch well beyond its normal breaking point. In this and other ways, postcolonial writers open up the possibilities of contemporary poetry by yoking English to their local syntax, vocabulary, rhythms and idioms.

Postcolonial poetry is thus hybrid not only in language but also in form. We might think of Lorna Goodison's poem 'On Becoming a Mermaid' as a dramatization of this process: fish and flesh combine to become what she wonderfully calls – in a line appropriately rife with compounds – 'a green-tinged fish / fleshed woman / thing'. Because of its stylization, poetry formally embeds a long memory of its diverse cultural inheritances. Brathwaite concludes *The Arrivants* with the hope that Afro-Caribbean peoples, weaving together the disparate sounds and myths deposited in their history, will make, much as he has in his polyphonic poem,

> with their
>
> rhythms some-
> thing torn
>
> and new

But this new composite form, made of a union of disparate fragments of postcolonial inheritance, is seldom a matter of seamless intercultural fusion. Perhaps 'hybridity' suggests too neat and complete a union of disparate parts. As what he calls a 'mulatto of style', Walcott encodes in his Greco-African characters and intercontinental genres his 'schizophrenic' experience (Walcott, 1970, pp. 9, 4), as either 'nobody' or 'a nation' (Walcott, 1986, p. 346). At the level of the image, Ramanujan suggests the dizzying gap that separates, even while visual similarities connect, the Indian and the Western parts of his life:

> The traffic light turns orange
> on 57th and Dorchester, and you stumble,
>
> you fall into a vision of forest fires,
> enter a frothing Himalayan river,
>
> rapid, silent.
> On the 14th floor,
> Lake Michigan crawls and crawls
>
> in the window.
> ('Chicago Zen')

In a hallucinatory switch, orange traffic lights flare into forest fires, and a memory of a Himalayan river – leaping across hemispheres – drops into Lake Michigan. The postcolonial poem often mediates between Western and non-Western forms of perception, experience and language to reveal not only their integration but ultimately the chasm that divides them.

Perhaps the clearest example of formal interculturation in postcolonial poetry is the hybridization of Western literary models and non-Western oral traditions. Because Caribbean poets grow up hearing vibrant English creoles on the street and in the yard, they draw more heavily on oral traditions than do most Indian poets, whose English tends to be more literary, recalling an ancient written inheritance in indigenous languages. A poet like Kofi Awoonor Anglicizes the Ewe dirge tradition in a poem like the earlier quoted 'The Weaver Bird'. For him, as for many African poets, the most powerful indigenous models are typically oral poems in native languages, so that we can trace images, rhetorical strategies and whole lines from his 'Songs of Sorrow' to traditional Ewe songs. When Okot p'Bitek assumes the agitated voice of a village woman who excoriates her Westernized husband as a slave to 'white men's ways', he hybridizes Acholi songs of abuse with Western dramatic monologue (p'Bitek, 1966, p. 49). Boldly satirizing Jamaican racism, emigration and even independence, Louise Bennett welds together and thus transfigures both the English ballad and the witty creole strategies of Anancy tales (trickster stories), 'labrish' (gossip) and 'broad talk' (performative oratory).

To do justice to the formal hybridity of postcolonial poetry, we need to track closely the dazzling interplay between indigenous and the Western forms. The postcolonial poem sometimes melds, at other times sets these resources against each other. It may ironize one, both or neither of its intertexts. In the most successful examples, the result of this intercultural dynamic is transformative – a poem that would have been unimaginable within the confines of one or another culture. As many of us seek to understand our relation to an increasingly intercultural and interlocking globe, post-colonial poets have a great deal to teach us about the aesthetics, language and experience of the contemporary world.

BIBLIOGRAPHY

Agard, J. (1985). *Mangoes and Bullets: Selected and New Poems 1972–84*. London: Pluto Press.

Ali, A. S. (1987). *The Half-Inch Himalayas*. Middletown, CT: Wesleyan University Press.

Appiah, K. A. (1992). *In My Father's House: Africa in the Philosophy of Culture*. Oxford: Oxford University Press.

Ashcroft, B., G. Griffiths and H. Tiffin (1989). *The Empire Writes Back: Theory and Practice in Post-Colonial Literatures*. New York: Routledge.

Awoonor, K. (1964). *Rediscovery and Other Poems*. Ibadan: Mbari Publications.

Bennett, L. (1983). *Selected Poems*, ed. Mervyn Morris. Kingston: Sangster's.

Bennett, L. (1993). *Aunty Roachy Seh*, ed. Mervyn Morris. Kingston: Sangster's.

Bhabha, H. K. (1994). *The Location of Culture*. New York: Routledge.

Brathwaite, E. K. (1971). *The Development of Creole Society in Jamaica, 1770–1820*. Oxford: Oxford University Press.

Brathwaite, E. K. (1973). *The Arrivants: A New World Trilogy*. Oxford: Oxford University Press.

Breiner, Laurence A. (1998). *An Introduction to West Indian Poetry*. Cambridge: Cambridge University Press.

Brown, L. W. (1978). *West Indian Poetry*. Boston: Twayne.

Chamberlin, J. E. (1993). *Come Back to Me My Language: Poetry and the West Indies*. Urbana: University of Illinois Press.

Deleuze, G. and F. Guattari (1986). *Kafka: Towards a Minor Literature*, trans. D. Polan. Minneapolis: University of Minnesota Press.

De Souza, E. (1990). *Ways of Belonging: Selected Poems*. Edinburgh: Polygon.

Eliot, T. S. (1957). *On Poetry and Poets*. New York: Farrar, Straus and Giroux.

Fanon, F. (1963). *The Wretched of the Earth*, trans. C. Farrington. New York: Grove.

Glissant, E. (1989). *Caribbean Discourse: Selected Essays*, trans. J. M. Dash. Charlottesville: University Press of Virginia.

Goodison, L. (1992). *Selected Poems*. Ann Arbor: University of Michigan Press.

Goodwin, K. L. (1982). *Understanding African Poetry*. London: Heinemann.

Gowda, H. H. A. (1983). '"Refin'd with the accents that are ours": Some reflections on modern English poetry in India, Africa and the West Indies.' In H. H. A. Gowda (ed.), *The Colonial and the Neo-Colonial: Encounters in Commonwealth Literature*. Mysore: University of Mysore.

Hall, S. (1990). 'Cultural Identity and Diaspora.' In J. Rutherford (ed.), *Identity: Community, Culture, Difference*. London: Lawrence and Wishart.

Jussawalla, A. J. (1976). *Missing Person*. Bombay: Clearing House.

King, B. (1987). *Modern Indian Poetry in English*. Delhi: Oxford University Press.

Mapanje, J. (1993). *The Chattering Wagtails of Mikuyu Prison*. Oxford: Heinemann.

Mehrotra, A. K. (ed.) (1992). *The Oxford India Anthology of Twelve Modern Indian Poets*. Calcutta: Oxford University Press.

Nichols, G. (1989). *Lazy Thoughts of a Lazy Woman*. London: Virago.

Okigbo, C. (1971). *Labyrinths, with Path of Thunder*. London: Heinemann.

p'Bitek, O. (1966). *'Song of Lawino' and 'Song of Ocol.'* London: Heinemann.

Peters, L. (1981). *Selected Poetry*. London: Heinemann.

Ramanujan, A. K. (1989). 'Where Mirrors are Windows: Toward an Anthology of Reflections.' *History of Religions*, 28, 187–216.

Ramanujan, A. K. (1995). *The Collected Poems*. Delhi: Oxford University Press.

Said, E. (1993). *Culture and Imperialism*. New York: Knopf.

Soyinka, W. (1967). *Idanre and Other Poems*. New York: Hill and Wang.

Thiong'o, N. W. (1986). *Decolonising the Mind: The Politics of Language in African Literature*. London: James Currey.

Walcott, D. (1970). 'What the Twilight Says: An Overture.' *Dream on Monkey Mountain and Other Plays*. New York: Farrar, Straus and Giroux.

Walcott, D. (1986). *Collected Poems, 1948–1984*. New York: Farrar, Straus and Giroux.

Walcott, D. (1990). *Omeros*. New York: Farrar, Straus and Giroux.

Walcott, D. (1993). 'Meanings.' In R. D. Hamner (ed.), *Critical Perspectives on Derek Walcott*. Washington, DC: Three Continents Press.

Willis, S. (1982). 'Caliban as Poet: Reversing the Maps of Domination.' *The Massachusetts Review*, 23, 615–30.

Yeats, W. B. (1961). *Essays and Introductions*. London: Macmillan.

Index